The Hitler Filmography

ALSO BY CHARLES P. MITCHELL

*The Devil on Screen: Feature Films Worldwide,
1913 through 2000* (McFarland, 2002)

BY PAUL PARLA AND CHARLES P. MITCHELL

*Screen Sirens Scream! Interviews with 20 Actresses
from Science Fiction, Horror, Film Noir
and Mystery Movies, 1930s to 1960s*
(McFarland, 2000)

The Hitler Filmography

Worldwide Feature Film and Television Miniseries Portrayals, 1940 through 2000

by CHARLES P. MITCHELL

McFarland & Company, Inc., Publishers
Jefferson, North Carolina, and London

Library of Congress Cataloguing-in-Publication Data

Mitchell, Charles P., 1949–
The Hitler filmography : worldwide feature films and television
miniseries portrayals, 1940 through 2000 / by Charles P. Mitchell.
p.   cm.
Includes index.

ISBN 0-7864-1295-X (illustrated case binding : 50# alkaline paper)

1. Hitler, Adolf, 1889–1945—In motion pictures.   2. Motion
pictures—Catalogs.   3. Television mini-series—Catalogs.   I. Title.
PN1995.9.H514M58   2002   791.43'651—dc21   2002006496

British Library cataloguing data are available

On the front cover: Heinz Schubert as Hitler in the 1978 film *Our Hitler*

Manufactured in the United States of America

McFarland & Company, Inc., Publishers
Box 611, Jefferson, North Carolina 28640
www.mcfarlandpub.com

To the memory of my father-in-law,
Colonel Warren P. Downing,
who during World War II was in charge of United States
coastal defenses along the Northern Atlantic seaboard

ACKNOWLEDGMENTS

The author wants to thank the following individuals and organizations for their assistance and encouragement in the preparation of this volume: Jane Agee, Bangor Public Library, John Berrien, Alastair Bird, Eddie Brandt's Saturday Matinee, Robert Brosch, Paul Burton, William Chadwick, Duke University's Lilly Library, Jeremy Dyson, Lee Eckhardt, L. M. Garnett, Richard Gordon, Joe "Phantom of the Movies" Kane, Brendan Keown, Simon Krysl, Francis Lederer, Curt Lowens, Dewayn Marzigalli, Marty McGee, Jean & Dick Norris, Paul & Donna Parla, Bill & Cheryl Pitz, Alexander Prokhorov, Frank Reichert, Brian Russo, Dr. Ronald & Amelia Schwartz, Paul R. Sclafani, Aizu Shingo, the University of Maine's Fogler Library. In particular, three individuals deserve special mention. The first is H. Robert Rotter of Vienna, Austria, for his assistance in researching German language sources for me, as well as his advice and help in translating German dialogue in various films. Robert W. Schmidt of Avenel, New Jersey, was helpful in tracking down and identifying character actors who had unbilled parts in various films. Finally, my wife Roberta deserves special thanks for her patience in viewing with me a huge number of films for this book, many of which were eventually not selected for inclusion because they did not meet the criteria, such as *Canaris Master Spy* (1954), *Verboten* (1959), *Battle of the Bulge* (1965), *Breakthrough* (1978), *The Tin Drum* (1979) and *Hanussen* (1988). She reviewed the first draft, providing suggestions as to grammar, content and style. She also helped in translations for the French language films. Without her help, this book never would have been completed.

TABLE OF CONTENTS

Preface 1

Overview: Hitler Portrayals 5

THE HITLER FILMOGRAPHY 11

Appendix One: MGM's Aborted Hitler Western 257

Appendix Two: Hitler on Series Television 259

Appendix Three: Possible Hitler Film Projects 263

Index 267

PREFACE

The search for Hitler has apprehended not one coherent, consensus image of
Hitler but rather many different Hitlers, competing Hitlers, conflicting
embodiments of competing visions, Hitlers who might not recognize each
other well enough to say "Heil" if they came face to face in Hell.
                                        Ron Rosenbaum, *Explaining Hitler*

At the close of the 20th century, noted historians, enumerating the most influential figures of the past hundred years, invariably include Adolf Hitler near the top of their short lists. Indeed, the dark presence of Hitler seems hard to avoid, especially since he is the individual who most closely embodies the essence of evil. True, there may be other individuals who might have exceeded his total number of victims, such as Josef Stalin or possibly Pol Pot if we consider the proportionate number of casualties under their rule. Yet Hitler remains unique and unforgettable, almost mythic, an archetype of mankind's infamy. Even youngsters with no interest in history know the image of Hitler, while they might never have heard of Stalin. This book will examine Hitler as he has been portrayed by actors in feature films and television miniseries. It will reveal a multitude of Hitlers in various guises, some frightening, some fascinating, some absurd, some funny, but none attractive or sympathetic. He might be presented as a precocious child, a mother-obsessed lunatic,

a living disembodied head, a hippie thespian, a doddering old man or a denizen of the netherworld.

The main body of this book is comprised of 100 entries, a fortuitously round number. Although American productions dominate, the entries are international in scope, with German, French, Russian, Czech, Polish, Japanese, Swedish, British and others including a number of multinational projects. The criteria used to determine these selections can be expressed simply: the work must be a filmed narrative, either a feature or a miniseries, in which the figure of Adolf Hitler appears and is portrayed by an actor. Broadly interpreted, the character of Hitler may be a clone or even an impostor, as long as he is intended to represent the Führer. (Incidentally, the term "Führer," German for "leader," is used throughout the book as a synonym for Hitler, a reference popularized by films, in which it is often used in a satirical sense.)

The inclusion criteria might best be illustrated by examining the type of pro-

1

ductions excluded. A major example is the documentary genre, which relies principally on authentic footage intercut with real life interviews and occasional dramatic recreations. *The Hitler Filmography* is concerned solely with cinematic interpretations of the Führer, not with historical documentary footage of Hitler himself. Likewise, motion pictures in which the real Hitler appears through archival or newsreel clips are outside the realm of consideration. Many films include these authentic snippets of the Führer, from *Charlie Chan in City in Darkness* (1939) and *Sink the Bismarck!* (1960) to *A Bridge Too Far* (1977) and *The Ogre* (1996). Similarly, films are also excluded that have audio extracts of the real Hitler, including *Theater of Blood* (1973), *Le Silence de la Mer* (1947) and *Tarzan Triumphs* (1943), in which Cheetah the chimpanzee mocks the Führer while hearing his voice on the short-wave radio. Of course, a number of films in which an actor plays Hitler might also contain archival footage of the real Führer, and these picture are among the entries.

Short subjects are not covered, including two-reelers by the Three Stooges like *I'll Never Heil Again* (1941), or the knockabout wartime cartoons such as *Russian Rhapsody* (1944) in which Mel Blanc (the voice of Porky Pig and countless other characters) ridicules the Führer.

"Near miss" films are also avoided, such as *Night of the Generals* (1965) which shows a bomb being placed under a map table at a Hitler briefing, but the Führer himself is completely hidden behind several other figures. In *The Man I Married* (1940), a massive Hitler rally in Berlin is attended by stars Francis Lederer and Joan Bennett, but the Führer is never glimpsed on screen.

Films with characters that are simply meant to suggest Hitler are also not considered. Examples of these shadow half–Hitlers can be found in *Jonathan* (1970),

the German horror film in which Paul Albert Krumm plays a vampire count who seems to suggest the Nazi dictator; *Escapement* (1958), a science fiction film featuring a power mad industrialist named Paul Zakon who turns celebrities into his followers, brainwashing them with a dream machine; and *Hitler* (1997), an Indian film by Muthyala Subbaiah, in which the main character is nicknamed Hitler because of his nasty temperament.

Hitler's mention in the title of a film does not necessarily mean that he appears, so films such as *Hitler—Beast of Berlin* (1939); *Hitler's Children* (1943), *Adolf Hitler—My Part in His Downfall* (1972) and *Hitler's Daughter* (1990) fail to qualify.

Finally, the figure of Hitler has often been used in adult film entertainment, both hardcore and soft, such as the Spanish *Historia de "S"* (1978), a study in sadism, or *Dracula Sucks* (1979). The present filmography has bypassed this field.

Amateur efforts are not included.

The entries are intended to be definitive within the stated criteria but with so many unbilled appearances, it has no doubt been impossible to find all relevant films.

All entries are numbered and presented in alphabetical order. In most cases, the title is the one used in the print viewed, but commonly known alternate titles are also represented. The actor playing Hitler is then highlighted, with notation if the role is a cameo. For purposes of this study, a cameo is an appearance lasting under a minute in length. The category of the film follows. Over a quarter of the films are comedies. The major production credits are listed, including the screenwriter, the cinematographer, the editor, the composer, the producer and the director. This section ends by noting whether the print is color or B & W (or both in some cases) and the film's length rounded off to the nearest minute.

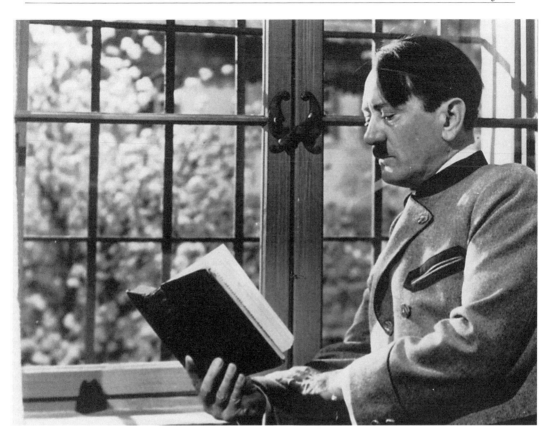

The actor who most frequently portrayed Hitler on film was Robert "Bobby" Watson, shown here in *The Hitler Gang*.

The ANNOTATED CAST LIST features the names of the performers followed in parentheses by the names of the characters they play, in italics, and with a concise annotation. In *Ace of Aces*, for example, you will find: "Jean-Paul Belmondo (*Georges 'Jo' Cavalier*, French flying ace & later boxing coach at the 1936 Berlin Olympics)." If the character is identified by a generic term, such as Reporter or Butler, then it is not italicized.

The next section is the combined AP-PRAISAL AND SYNOPSIS, detailing the action of the picture as well as a thorough critical analysis. Whenever possible, the historical accuracy of the production details is among the items discussed. For example, in *The Magic Face*, the plot mentions that Adolf Hitler attended a variety stage revue in Vienna on March 17, 1938. In actual fact, Hitler had returned to Berlin by this date.

Attention turns next to the HITLER PERFORMANCE, concentrating on the quality and effectiveness of the actor's interpretation. Such aspects as historical accuracy and appropriateness of the portrayal are also examined. Whether the performance matches the genre is also important, as the film may be an historical drama, a horror film, a comedy, a fantasy, a thriller or an example of alternate history.

The final section is a series of REP-RESENTATIVE QUOTES or bits of dialogue which help convey the flavor, viewpoint or atmosphere of each picture.

Major entries receive the full treatment outlined above. There are in addition a number of minor entries, consisting of films that are inaccessible because they are out of circulation or films in which Hitler's appearance is a sight gag unrelated to the plot. In *How to Seduce a Woman*, for example, Hitler appears as a doorman in a luxury apartment building simply to allow the main character to do a double take. In the case of minor entries, the cast lists are not annotated and the other sections are replaced by a COMMENTARY.

The Hitler Filmography has three appendices. The first covers an unrealized Hitler Western that was in production at MGM. The second provides a sampling of Hitler portrayals from various television series. The third covers a number of novels featuring Hitler that could serve as the basis for future screen productions.

The index includes names, titles and subjects, and also historical individuals portrayed in the films. References in the index are to entry numbers. All performers who played Hitler are indicated in the index by an asterisk.

A brief explanation about diacritics might be appropriate. In my research, I discovered that the use of umlauts and accents, particularly with German names, can vary significantly. Göring and Röhm, for example, always appear with umlauts (except in Shirer's *Rise and Fall of the Third Reich*, which avoids all accents), but this is not true with other individuals. In an attempt to be consistent, I have decided to adopt the diacritical marks used by Joachim C. Fest in his biography *Hitler* as my primary model, with *The Dictionary of the Third Reich* by James Taylor and Warren Shaw as my backup.

A short overview of Hitler portrayals follows this preface, providing a few guideposts to the researcher.

In conclusion, let me paraphrase and expand upon the last line of Ernst "Putzi" Hanfstaengl's book *Hitler: The Missing Years*. My one desire is to live long enough to see a world where Hitlers are no longer possible, except on film.

OVERVIEW:
HITLER PORTRAYALS

Adolf Hitler loved movies. Up until the war years, his primary recreation was watching films. He screened them over and over again, including sappy musicals, cartoons, Westerns, comedies, adventure films and thrillers. Unlike fellow dictator Josef Stalin, Hitler did not care to see himself portrayed on screen. The Soviet dictator insisted that he be depicted over and over again, as the wise, calm and virtuous father of his nation. The German film industry, under Nazi control, forbad that Hitler be cast as a character in any film, nor did it want any episodes of the Führer's life to be used as the subject matter of any film. Perhaps he felt no actor could do him justice. Indeed, the genuine Hitler, as demonstrated in Leni Riefenstahl's vivid documentary of the 1934 Nuremberg party rally, *Triumph of the Will*, was a powerful and charismatic screen presence. The real Stalin, on the other hand, came across as stiff and deficient. Other Riefenstahl documentaries which feature Hitler include *The Triumph of Faith* (1933), *The Day of Freedom* (1935) and *Olympia* (1936/38). He also appeared in numerous other German documentaries such as *Hitler Over Germany* (1932), *Good Morning Mr. Hitler* (1939), *March to the Führer* (1940) and *Victory in the West* (1941).

Hitler wanted no artificial Hitlers to rival himself, and so he figured his own appearances in newsreels and documentaries would suffice. Even so, Propaganda Minister Joseph Goebbels complained that the Führer placed a number of limitations on the use of his voice and image in newsreels. Hitler did make one exception in terms of feature films. He permitted footage of himself to be used for a cameo appearance in *Wunschkonzert* (*Request Concert*), a popular 1940 motion picture inspired by Germany's favorite Sunday night radio program. Nonetheless, Hitler's control over his cinematic image was something short-lived. By 1940, as the war waged, a new front was opened in the realm of motion pictures, and over sixty years later, this front is still active.

It is relatively easy to pinpoint the very first Hitler portrayal. It occurred on December 25, 1923, at the Blüte Cafe in Munich. It was a low period for the Nazis. The party was outlawed and Hitler was in jail, awaiting trial for the failed Beer Hall Putsch of six weeks earlier. Hitler's photographer, Heinrich Hoffmann, assisted in organizing a dramatic vignette in the Führer's honor entitled *Adolf Hitler in Prison*. Hoffmann was responsible for cast-

Derek Jacobi as Adolf Hitler in *Inside the Third Reich* **conveys the Führer's fascination with his own screen image.**

ing the piece, and he searched until he located an individual, not a professional actor, who bore an uncanny resemblance to Hitler. The vignette, actually a *tableau vivant,* lasted only a few minutes. The setting was a dimly lit jail cell. A man in semi-darkness is seated at a table with his back to the audience. Snow can be seen falling outside the barred window of the cell. "Silent Night" is softly sung by an offstage male chorus. When the carol is finished, an angel enters the cell, carrying an illuminated Christmas tree. The angel places the tree on the table next to the man, who finally turns to face the audience, and then the scene goes black. The crowd reportedly gasped in amazement, since the Hitler performer looked so much like the Führer that most of the audience was astounded, some convinced it was actually Hitler. As they left the cafe, many of them were in tears. When this event was later relayed to Hitler, he reportedly had no reaction.

The name of this first Hitler performer remains unknown, but this entire episode is mentioned whenever the theory that Hitler used doubles is discussed. Indeed, it has even been suggested that this unknown performer was later recruited as Hitler's double, although there is no evidence to support this hypothesis.

The earliest Hitler performer on screen was Larry J. Blake (1914-1982), a Brooklyn-born actor who made over seventy-five films, usually in supporting roles as a detective, a reporter or a drunk. He was also a frequent second string actor on television with an extensive list of credits. One of his more notable appearances was as Eckhardt, a Nazi in the episode "The Legend" of *Mission: Impossible,* in which Martin Landau impersonated Martin Bormann. Blake's first role in films was in 1937, when he was cast as Adolf Hitler in *The Road Back,* an adaptation of Erich Maria Remarque's sequel to his famous novel *All*

Moe Howard of the Three Stooges was the earliest performer to parody Hitler.

Quiet on the Western Front. James Whale, director of *Frankenstein* (1931) and *The Invisible Man* (1933) helmed the production which included such notable actors as John King, Richard Cromwell, Andy Devine, Barbara Read, Louise Fazenda, John Emery, Noah Berry Jr., Lionel Atwill, Dwight Frye, Greta Gynt, Robert Warwick, E. E. Clive, Samuel S. Hinds, Edward van Sloan, Spring Byington and Slim Summerville. The film told the story of the conditions faced by the defeated German soldiers of World War I when they returned to their home lives. The screenplay was strongly anti–Nazi in sentiment. The Nazis, who sabotaged German showing of the film version of *All Quiet on the Western Front* (1930), launched an all-out

campaign against Universal Studios to abandon the production. As Francis Lederer explained to me in an interview shortly before his death, the Nazis had a strong but clandestine influence in Hollywood in the 1930s as he discovered when he played the lead in *Confessions of a Nazi Spy* (1939). Studio head Carl Laemmle Jr. resisted the pressure, but after he lost control of the management of Universal, the new regime under Charles R. Rogers yielded to many of the Nazi demands. In essence, *The Road Back* was gutted. James Whale was removed from the project and extensive cuts were made that all but eliminated the anti–Nazi tone of the picture. All of the Hitler scenes were removed and destroyed, so Larry J. Blake's performance as the first screen

A behind the scenes view of the staging of the Hitler rally in *Fatherland*.

Hitler was never seen outside of a limited number of the personnel at Universal Studios.

In late 1938, Charlie Chaplin decided to openly defy the Nazis when he decided to make his anti–Hitler comedy, *The Great Dictator*. As with all Chaplin projects, *The Great Dictator* had a long gestation period and did not begin shooting until September 1939, just as World War II started in Europe. The film wasn't released until October 1940. It fell to another famous comedian, Moe Howard of the Three Stooges, to reach the screen with the first Hitler lampoon as Moe Hailstone in a two-reel short, *You Nazty Spy*, made in late 1939 but not released until January 19, 1940. Another Three Stooges Hitler parody followed in 1941, *I'll Never Heil Again*. During the war years, Moe frequently did brief send ups of Hitler in a handful of other shorts, such as *Back from the Front*

(1943), *Higher Than a Kite* (1943) and *No Dough, Boys* (1944), appearing as a Japanese version of Hitler in the last title. Meanwhile, in England, Bill Russell became the first European actor to play Hitler in the 1940 production *Night Train to Munich*, the sequel to Alfred Hitchcock's *The Lady Vanishes* (1938).

The war years brought about a flurry of Hitler screen portrayals, but none of them were really serious or focused on Hitler as the main character until 1944, when Führer parodist supreme Bobby Watson undertook the lead in *The Hitler Gang*. That film remained the benchmark as the dominant film depiction of Hitler for the next thirty years. With Hitler's death and the end of the war, interest declined in the West, but cinematic portrayals of Hitler grew behind the Iron Curtain, largely propaganda films in which Hitler is more or less equated with the great democracies.

On the other hand, America reacted to the Cold War with a series of "Red Scare" films. In fact, in 1951 millionaire filmmaker Howard Hughes took a completed RKO film, *The Man He Found*, in which Hitler was depicted as hiding out in Wisconsin and plotting his comeback. Wanting to issue an anti–Communist thriller, Hughes took over the film, removed the Hitler scenes and recut the film. Then he ordered new scenes filmed to complete the transformation into *The Whip Hand*. Interest in "Red Scare" films passed quickly, particularly with the decline of the fortunes of Senator Joseph McCarthy. Similarly, Soviet films became less rancorous after the death of Stalin.

As for Hitler films, observers could detect three major types of productions that began to emerge: the historical, the fanciful and the humorous. The first were dramas that attempted to stick reasonably close to historical fact, such as *The Desert Fox* (1951) and *The Last Ten Days* (1955). This approach eventually evolved most impressively as serious telefilms, such as *The Bunker* (1980) and *The Plot to Kill Hitler* (1990) as well as miniseries of extraordinary depth and scope such as *The Winds of War* (1983) and *Inside the Third Reich* (1982). The second category of films is more diverse and fanciful, ranging from alternate history like *The Magic Face* (1951) and *Fatherland* (1994), to horror and science fiction as in *They Saved Hitler's Brain*

(1963/68) and *The Boys from Brazil* (1978). Philosophical and existential productions, including *Our Hitler* (1978) and *The Empty Mirror* (1996) could also be considered as offshoots of this category. Although Hitler comedies seemed most appropriate during the war years, they also continued on, with numerous peaks such as *On the Double* (1961), *Zelig* (1983) and *Stalag Luft* (1994). Many believe the ultimate Hitler comedy is undoubtedly *The Producers* (1968), which also became a Broadway stage sensation thirty-three years later.

Interest in Adolf Hitler as a cinematic subject has flourished toward the end of the 20th century, producing such varied and clever works as *Conversation with the Beast* (1996), *Snide and Prejudice* (1997) and *Hitler Meets Christ* (2000), imaginative and perceptive pieces that have yet to receive proper distribution to the public at large. There is a great irony in the fact that Hitler, a loathsome ideologue of the worst kind, is able to inspire such a brilliant array of works in literature as well as film. It is almost as if humankind is not content to let their most evil representative go, but must probe and question how such an individual could manage to secure power and succeed, even if only for a short period of time, in causing unparalleled human suffering. Hitler still poses a nearly insoluble puzzle, but by obsessively focusing on him, filmmakers apparently hope to insure that his like will never rise again.

THE HITLER FILMOGRAPHY

1.   *The Ace of Aces*
(AKA *L'As des As*) (1982)

Gunter Meisner as Adolf Hitler
Adventure/Comedy

Gaumont/Cerito Films. Written by Gérard Oury & Daniele Thompson; Photographed by Xaver Schwarzenberger; Edited by Albert Jurgenson; Music by Vladimir Cosma; Produced by Thomas Schühly; Directed by Gérard Oury. Color 105 minutes

ANNOTATED CAST LIST: Jean-Paul Belmondo (*Georges "Jo" Cavalier*, French flying ace & later boxing coach at the 1936 Berlin Olympics); Gunter Meisner (*Angela Raubal*, Hitler's twin sister); Marie-France Pisier (*Gaby Delcourt*, Sports reporter); Frank Hoffmann (*Günther von Beckman*, German flying ace & later a Luftwaffe general); Benno Sterzenbach (*Hermann Rosenblum*, Jewish book dealer who was Hitler's commanding officer during World War I); Rachid Ferrache (*Simon*, Rosenblum's grandson); Yves Pignot (*Emile*); Jean-Roger Milo (*Lucien*, Assistant boxing coach); Stepane Ferrara (*Michaud*, Leading French boxer); Florent Pagne (French boxer); Hans Wyprachtiger, Gerd Frösch, Hubert Munster, Christopf Linder, Agnia Bogoslavia, Jacqueline Noëlle, Ernest von Rintelen, Dominique Nato, Peter Semler, Hans Strecke.

APPRAISAL AND SYNOPSIS: *The Ace of Aces* was one of the biggest successes of Jean-Paul Belmondo's career, but for some unknown reason it received very little play outside of Europe, although the humor would certainly appeal to American audiences, even if the film is in French with a smattering of German. The last half of the story seems based in part on an observation that some critics made about *The Sound of Music* (1965), that when the von Trapp family crossed over the mountain at the end of the film, they would have wound up in Berchtesgaden. *The Ace of Aces* depicts a family of Jewish émigrés, believing they have escaped from Nazi Germany but ending up instead taking refuge in the Führer's own home. This sets up one of the funniest and most absurd comic sequences

in any Hitler film. To top it off, the patriarch of the family turns out to be Hitler's former commander from the Western front during World War I. The plot also mixes in a feud between Hitler and his sister, an amorous bear, a satire of Leni Riefenstahl's *Olympia* (1938) and bumbling Gestapo agents. At the center of the tale is Georges "Jo" Cavalier, France's top wartime aviator, the "Ace of Aces," and his exploits when he attends the 1936 Olympics as coach of the French boxing team.

This French-German co-production sets the scene with a magnificent aerial dogfight between Cavalier and Günther von Beckman, the enemy's top flier. As they battle, the French aircraft is fired upon from the ground by an awkward foot soldier, Adolf Hitler, who is chewed out for his incompetence by a frustrated officer, Hermann Rosenblum. The two aviators crash, and continue their battle in a fistfight until shelling forces them to dive together into the nearest foxhole. Twenty years later, Jo is France's top boxing trainer. En route to the Olympic games, Jo crosses reporter Gaby Delcourt, who gets her revenge by writing a story quoting his intemperate comments to his comrades. They make up and become allies after they encounter Simon, a Jewish boy who is traveling to Germany to locate his grandparents. Concerned, Jo takes Simon under his wing and brings him to his grandfather's bookstore. Gestapo agents are ransacking the shop, and Jo battles them when they try to take him on. Jo escapes when he disguises himself as the torchbearer for the Olympic games. The coach then hides Simon and his family at his hotel with his boxing team. The boy's grandfather turns out to be Hitler's old commanding officer.

The next day, Jo encounters von Beckman, his old rival, now a Luftwaffe general, who protects him when the Gestapo comes to arrest him. Von Beckman, disapproving of the Nazis, agrees to help smuggle the Rosenblum family out of the country. The Olympic Games begin, and the Führer attends the opening ceremony. Footage from

Olympia is adapted to humorous effect. For example, when a flock of doves is released, feathers and droppings are shown splattering down on the Führer and his entourage. Later, the Gestapo enter the gym where the French boxers are in training, but Jo has vanished. They intercept a call from the coach to Lucien, his assistant, and learn that he is near Munich, driving south. Traveling with Simon in von Beckman's sports car, they camp out in the woods, where they encounter a bear cub and its mother during the night. The next day they break through a roadblock, and are chased by Nazi bikers, but Jo causes his pursuers to crash along the road. Finally, they are captured, but they manage to escape with the entire Rosenblum family with von Beckman's cooperation. Soon, they are on a mountain path that recalls the finale of *The Sound of Music*. A farmer leading a herd of cows, brushes past a road sign, accidentally reversing the directions to Berchtesgaden and the Austrian border. Soon, Jo and the Rosenblums arrive and take the wrong road. When they come to a wire fence, they assume it is the border, but in fact it is the perimeter of the Berghof, Hitler's home. Meanwhile, Gaby travels to Berchtesgaden to interview the Führer. As she questions Hitler, he reacts broadly, guffawing quite loudly to his own dry quips. He introduces Gaby to Angela, his twin sister, who manages the Berghof for him. Once in private, Hitler and Angela argue over her brother's invitation to Eva Braun to visit the Berghof. She threatens to quit for good.

A storm breaks out, and Jo and the Rosenblums are drenched. They seek refuge in the Berghof, thinking it is a resort. Angela mistakes them for musicians for that evening's festivities. Jo asks Angela if there is a radio he could use, and she takes him to her brother's study. The coach tunes in the Olympics broadcast as Michaud, the leading French boxer, begins his bout. Hitler enters the room behind Jo, who shadow boxes exuberantly along with the blow-by-blow account. Michaud wins, and Jo spins around, coming face to face with the Führer. The coach is startled beyond any reaction. A cuckoo clock sounds, and Jo turns to see an eagle pop out of the door and give a Nazi salute to mark each hour. Jo excuses himself and Hitler waves him a limp wrist salute as he leaves the room.

Many guests show up for the evening party, including General von Beckman. Jo knocks out a Nazi guard and takes his uniform. He then mingles with the other uniformed guests and makes contact with the general. Meanwhile, Hitler enters the room with the Rosenblums and asks them to start playing. Mrs. Rosenblum passes out at the sight of Hitler, but the guests believe that it was due to the honor of being close to the Führer. Villagers dressed in rustic costumes arrive at the patio and Hitler greets them. The Rosenblums are provided with instruments, and start to play, but they only seem to know Jewish tunes. Hitler is intrigued, but slightly confused by the music. A German oom-pah band joins in playing with the Rosenblums, leading to a strange musical amalgam and a wild folk dance performed by the villagers.

Jo cooks up a plan of escape. He sends Simon to slip a love letter under Angela's door, purportedly from von Beckman, asking her to elope. The general plays along, and whisks her away in his car. Meanwhile, the real musicians arrive, and the Rosenblums escape in Hitler's own car with Jo disguised as the Führer. When Hitler sees his car drive off, he is told that Angela is eloping. He hops in a car and chases after her. When the pursuing car pulls alongside, Hitler yells, "Angela!" but is shocked instead to see Lieutenant Rosenblum, his old commander, seated in the back seat. The Führer does a double take, then a triple take when he sees Jo wearing a copycat moustache. Jo bumps the other car off the road, and Hitler goes tumbling down the ravine splashing into a duck pond, where he shrieks at the ducks and geese. Jo speeds the car to crash through the border, bringing his Jewish friends to freedom (at least for the time being). He stops and hugs Simon, and sees that the bear has also followed them into Austria. The last half hour of *The Ace of Aces* is a complete laugh riot, combining slapstick, the wildest musical parody outside of *The Producers* and pure satire. There are a few loose plot threads. One wonders whatever happens to General von Beckman and Angela, not to mention Gaby, who get lost in the shuffle. The historical details in the story vary in their accuracy. It is true, for instance, that Angela Raubal used Eva Braun as the reason for leaving as housekeeper of the Berghof. Having Hitler serve under a Jewish officer during the war is also based on fact. His name was Lieutenant Hugo Gutmann, and he was largely responsible for Hitler being awarded the iron cross, first class. The controversy over the French athletes giving the Nazi salute to Hitler during the Olympic parade is another accurate point. On the other hand, Hitler stayed for the entire Olympics and did not run off to Berchtesgaden. Jewish persecution was kept under wraps during the Olympics, so a Gestapo raid on Rosenblum's bookstore would have been unlikely. Most of the other elements of the picture, cinematography, music, editing and acting are superb. The aerial photography is stunning, from the opening dogfight to the scene where Jo parachutes out of von Brinkman's plane after they pass the Neuschwanstein castle of King Ludwig II. Only the bear scenes seem too hokey and out of place. The use of the historic footage from *The Olympia* is expertly intercut with the new footage, including that of Hitler huffing and puffing as he roots for the German runner to catch Jesse Owens, or when the released flock of doves splatter him, one of the all-time best Hitler sight gags.

HITLER PORTRAYAL: Gunter Meisner is brilliant in an extraordinary double role as Adolf Hitler and his twin sister, Angela. In real life, Angela Raubal didn't resemble her half brother, but the effect is quite hilarious in this production. Meisner is a truly outrageous female impersonator and knockabout comedian with remarkable timing, yet he does retain enough composure so that his straight

Hitler scenes are convincing as well. This was not always true with some of his later serious Hitler renditions such as *The Winds of War*. Without doubt, most of the humor of *The Aces of Aces* can be traced to Meisner, who is always on target in this performance. His opening appearance, in the German trenches, reveals him as a bungler, as he manages to drop the pants of his superior officer while feeding the ammunition into his machine gun. His most hilarious moment may be during the folk music sequence, in which Meisner's facial expressions, sometimes beaming or quizzical or suspicious, are unparalleled. The give and take with Angela is a double triumph, with the soft spoken sister more than holding her own with her barking, growling brother. Hitler's interview with Gaby, where the Führer tries too hard to make his point, is also well played. The final scene, splashing around with the quacking geese, is unforgettable. Without doubt, Meisner joins the ranks of Charlie Chaplin, Robert Vaughn and Bobby Watson for creating the funniest Hitler lampoon. It is a genuine art to transform this notorious figure of hatred and evil into one of ridicule.

REPRESENTATIVE QUOTES

• For three years with the 16th Bavarian regiment, I have been through hunger, mud and the cold, all in support of the Fatherland, but it is hard, Corporal Hitler. *(Rosenblum to Hitler in the trenches)* Very hard, Lieutenant Rosenblum. *(Hitler)* But you, Corporal Hitler, make it even harder! *(Rosenblum)*

• Adolf, I am a prisoner here. If that Braun woman sets her foot inside the door, I'll leave. It is her or me! *(Angela to Hitler)* No ultimatums! That doesn't work with me. *(Hitler)*

• Very pretty music! What is it? *(Hitler, as the Rosenblums play a Yiddish tune)*

2. *The Adventures of Picasso* (1978)

Magnus Harenstam as Adolf Hitler (cameo)
Comedy

Svenska Ord. Written by Hans Alfredson, Tage Danielsson & Gosta Ekman; Photographed by Tony Forsberg & Roland Sterner; Edited by Jan Persson; Music by Gunnar Svenson, Erik Satie, Modeste Mussorgsky & Giacomo Puccini; Produced by Staffan Hedqvist; Directed by Tage Danielsson. Color 88 minutes

CAST LIST: Gosta Ekman (*Pablo Picasso*); Hans Alfredson (*Don José Picasso*); Margaretha Krook (*Dona Maria*); Lena Olin (*Dolores*); Bernard Cribbins (*Gertrude Stein*); Wilfrid Brambell (*Alice B. Toklas*); Lennart Nyman (*Henri Rousseau*); Per Oscarson (*Guillaume Apollinaire*); Olle Ljungberg (*Ernest Hemingway*); Birgitta Anderson (*Ingrid Svenson-Guggenheim*); Elisabeth Soderström (*Mimi*); Sune Mangs (*Winston Churchill*); Yngve Gamlin (*Sergei Diaghilev*); Lars-Ake van Vutee (*Erik Satie*); Lisbeth Zachrisson (*Olga*); Lena Nyman (*Sirkka*); Sven Lindberg (*Dr. Albert Schweitzer*); Ulf von Zeigbergh (*Salvador Dali*).

COMMENTARY: *The Adventures of Picasso* is a broad Swedish farce in a similar vein to *Young Einstein* (1988). Gosta Ekman plays a goofy rendition of Pablo Picasso as if he were a cross between Jacques Tati and Adam Sandler. The film was intended for marketing across Europe, so the dialogue is a smattering of English, French, Spanish, German as well as Swedish. A voice-over narration then clarifies the storyline for each language. In the English version, the narration is delivered by Bernard Cribbins in drag, as Gertrude Stein. The plot ranges from outrageous slapstick to gentle whimsy. At one point, it turns into an operatic satire of *La Bohème*. Later, there is a madcap takeoff of a Diaghilev ballet. The Hitler cameo is a quick sight gag after the World War I sequence. Gertrude Stein proclaims, "Never will there be another war. A new generation of artists came to Paris to build a better world." The camera pans to reveal two street artists painting on easels side by side. Hitler gives a Nazi salute to Picasso, and Churchill flashes his "V for Victory" gesture. Both men then transform these motions into brush strokes on their canvases. Magnus Harenstam is somewhat too tall as Hitler, but he is not bad as part of a throwaway sight gag. There is a second Hitler reference later in the film. Picasso has an affair with a Finnish cabaret singer who only knows one song. As time goes by, Picasso comes to hate the tune. He uses her as a model, painting her as a grotesque harpy, as Gertrude Stein proclaims that this was the origin of Picasso's new style, monsterism. The film then switches to an extended animated sequence, satirizing Walt Disney's *Fantasia* (1940). Misshapened creatures, resembling Picasso's sketches, battle it out to music from Mussorgsky's *Pictures at an Exhibition*. Hitler's voice is heard over the music, rising to a fever pitch as the cartoon ends. This section is one of the cleverest portions of the entire film.

3. *Après Mein Kampf Mes Crimes* (AKA *Mein Kampf—My Crimes*) (1940)

Georges Fronval as Adolf Hitler
Drama

Les Films Cristal. Written by José Lacaze; Photographed by Georges Blanc; Music by Jacques Eiger; Produced by Jacques Haik; Directed by Alexandre Ryder. B & W 72 minutes

CAST LIST: Roger Karl (The Colonel); Nicholas Amato (The Lieutenant); Jean Heuzé (The Austrian Captain); Lino Noro (*Frieda*); Pierre Labry (*Ernst Röhm*); Alexandre Mihalesco (Tailor); Dalmais (*Engelbert Dollfuss*); Jacques Henley (*Kurt von Schleicher);* Sandra Milovanoff (*Madame Schleicher*); André Valmy (*Karl Ernst*); Alain Cuny; Jacqueline Noëlle; Kelly Pierson; Jainine Vienot; Albert Monys.

COMMENTARY: Independent filmmaker Jacques Haik rushed to get this anti–Nazi production to the French screens by mid–March 1940. The film, although low budget, effectively portrayed a number of Hitler's crimes committed since the publication of *Mein Kampf*. Within two months, however, the

French forces were defeated by the Nazi Blitzkrieg and *Après Mein Kampf Mes Crimes* was banned, with most prints confiscated and destroyed. Producer Haik, because of both his Jewish background and his involvement with this anti–Nazi film, went into hiding. However, the British film industry took a print and used it to prepare an English language version, with additional scenes shot at Berlwyn Studios. Called *Mein Kampf—My Crimes* and *After Mein Kampf*, the film had a different structure which made it seem more like a documentary than the French original, and its running time is only 50 minutes long. Interestingly, two future stars were involved in the English version. It was the screen debut for Herbert Lom, who went on to play Napoleon, Beethoven and the Phantom of the Opera. Peter Ustinov appeared as Marius van der Lubbe, the man accused to be the arsonist responsible for the Reichstag fire. The Hitler scenes are reportedly identical in both films.

4. *Battle of Britain* (1969)

Rolf Stiekel as Adolf Hitler (cameo)
Historical drama

United Artists. Written by Wilford Greatorex & James Kennaway; Photographed by Freddie Young; Edited by Bert Bates; Music by Ron Goodwin & William Walton; Produced by Harry Saltzman & S. Benjamin Fisz; Directed by Guy Hamilton. Color 133 minutes

ANNOTATED CAST LIST: Laurence Olivier (*Sir Hugh C. Dowding*, Air Chief Marshal); Trevor Howard (*Keith Park*, Air Vice Marshal); Michael Redgrave (*Evill*, Air Vice Marshal); Patrick Wymark (*Trafford Leigh-Mallory*, Air Vice Marshal); Ralph Richardson (*Sir David Kelly*, British Minister in Switzerland); Michael Caine (*Canfield*, RAF Squadron leader); Christopher Plummer (*Colin Harvey*, RAF Squadron leader); Susannah York (*Maggie Harvey*, His wife, a section officer); Robert Shaw (*Skipper*, RAF Squadron leader); Sarah Lawson (His wife); Kenneth More (*Baker*, RAF Group Cap-

tain); Nigel Patrick (*Hope*, RAF Group Captain); Harry Andrews (British civil servant); Anthony Nichols (British Cabinet Minister); Curt Jürgens (*Baron von Richter*, Hitler's peace envoy); Hein Reiss (*Hermann Göring*, Reich Marshal); Peter Hager (*Albert Kesselring*, German Field Marshal); Wilfred von Aacken (*Osterkamp*, Luftwaffe General); Karl Otto Alberty (*Hans Jeschonnek*, Luftwaffe Chief of Staff); Dietrich Frauboes (*Erhard Milch*, Inspector General of the Luftwaffe); Malte Petzel (*Beppo Schmidt*, Luftwaffe Colonel); Manfred Reddemann (*Falke*, German Major); Alexander Allerson (*Brandt*, German Major); Alf Jungermann (Brandt's navigator); Paul Neuhaus (*Föhn*, German Major); Wolf Harnish (*Fink*, Luftwaffe General); Reinhard Horras (*Bruno*); Helmet Kircher (*Böhm*); Ian McShane (*Andy*, RAF pilot); Isla Blair (His wife); Edward Fox (*Archie*, RAF pilot); David Griffin (*Chris*, RAF pilot); Michael Bates (*Warrick*, RAF Warrant officer); Robert Flemyng (*Willoughby*, Wing Commander); Tom Chatto (Willoughby's assistant); Barry Foster (*Edwards*, RAF Squadron leader); W.G. Foxley (*Evans*, RAF Squadron leader); Jack Gwillim (Senior Air Staff Officer); Duncan Lamount (*Arthur*, RAF Flight Sergeant); Nicholas Pennell (*Simon*); Andrzej Scibor (*Ox*); Jean Wladon (*Jean Jacques*); John Baskomb (Farmer).

APPRAISAL AND SYNOPSIS: There are numerous big budget international films built around major events of the Second World War—epics such as *The Sands of Iwo Jima* (1949), *Longest Day* (1962), *Battle of the Bulge* (1965), *Tora! Tora! Tora!* (1970), *Stalingrad* (1993), *Hiroshima* (1995) and *Pearl Harbor* (2001) to name but a few. These productions have a similar approach: the actual events are largely portrayed through the eyes of fictional characters, often intermingling with historical characters such as the major military and political leaders. This is blended with a human interest subplot, usually totally fictitious, sometimes bordering on soap opera. The origin of these lengthy films can even be traced to mammoth 19th century novels, such as Tolstoy's *War and Peace* and Stendahl's *The Red and the Black*. These pictures are also heavily sprinkled with cameos by famous stars in bit parts. At their best, these picture are entertaining and enlighten their audiences about interesting tidbits of history. At their worst, they are muddled or confusing bores. Unfortunately, *Battle of Britain* falls largely into the second category. The script does a poor job of clarifying or explaining the events it portrays. In fact, simply following the film requires one to know the story, tactics and turning points of the struggle. Similar films make judicious use of explanatory headings, but *Battle of Britain* largely wastes the few headings it employs. Instead, it provides endless sequences of planes firing upon each other intercut with close ups of the eyes of pilots wearing leather flight masks. It is almost impossible to distinguish which planes, Allied or Axis, are being shot down. *Midway* (1976), for example, brilliantly kept the audience informed through onscreen graphics, which also helped to intensify and clarify the action. The confusion of *Battle of Britain* likewise could have been alleviated by the inclusion of a brief scene of pilots in training learning how to quickly distinguish different aircraft. The editing is another disappointment, seeming clumsy, repetitive and monotonous. Since these dogfights are the essence of this picture, this failure is crucial. Even when viewed in its wide screen version, the air battles are ineffectual. The film also misuses its interpolation of scene with the historical figures, with the exception of Laurence Olivier as Sir Hugh Dowding. Even so, his pretitle scene, urging that England conserve its remaining planes as France falls, is played opposite a nameless official performed by Harry Andrews. Later, Dowding has another meeting, this time with an unnamed Cabinet Minister. Prime Minister Churchill is entirely absent, his words represented second hand by a radio commentator before the opening credits appear. Göring, an essential figure, appears far too late in the story to have an impact, and even then he is underused. The use of Hitler is mishandled as well. For example, early in

the picture, Baron von Richter is summoned to a critical meeting with the Führer, but the camera remains in the foyer. The substance of the interview only trickles through to the audience later in piecemeal fashion. This technique of concentrating on the periphery rather on the central action further handicaps the production.

Battle of Britain is divided into four sections. The first covers the downfall of France, as the RAF prepares for the upcoming air battle over England. The second part concentrates on the opening phase of the German raids in July 1940, when they concentrated their efforts on destroying British airbases. The initial German mistake in failing to knock out British radar stations is merely glossed over. Nevertheless, this course of action was gradually leading to German success. The third section covers the events leading to the crucial Nazi mistake of abandoning military targets and switching to the terror bombing of London. This came about by accident. A German bomber becomes lost, and finding himself over London, decides to drop his lethal payload rather than return to base fully armed. Thinking it a new policy, the British bombed civilian targets in Berlin. Hitler was outraged, and ordered Göring to break the will of the English people by initiating the Blitz in early September 1940, an attempt to destroy London by mass bombing raids. Of course, the German bombers became easy targets for the RAF, who start to pick them off with ease. Some RAF fighters are lost in combat with German fighters, but they still are successful in inflicting high casualties. In the last installment, the attrition of German planes proves decisive, and the Nazis pull back on their efforts by October 1940. Like the actual air campaign, the action peters out, ending not with a bang but a whimper. The picture ends with the gallant commentary of Winston Churchill, "Never in the field of human conflict was so much owed by so many to so few." However, these words are not enacted or even heard. The text merely appears onscreen before the credits.

Despite the film's shortcomings, it has a number of positive features. The ambiance of wartime England is portrayed very effectively. The performances are uniformly good. The German characters are well portrayed and speak their lines in German. The cinematography where the aircraft are depicted as seen from the ground is very impressive, particularly the scene in which Göring and his entourage watch their numerous squadrons crossing the English Channel. The devastating impact of the Blitz is vividly captured as well. The sound effects of the film are magnificent, particularly the impressive drone of the aircraft. The aerial stuntwork itself, blending together with actual historical footage, is top notch, despite the fact that the film dilutes the quality of their work. It is a shame these excellent elements fail to gel in the final product.

HITLER PORTRAYAL: Adolf Hitler is depicted in only one scene, his speech at the Berlin Sports Palace on September 4, 1940. The film fails to note the location, the date or the purpose of the speech. It was a charitable event organized by the Nazis called Winterhilfe or "Assistance for the Winter." Millions of food parcels were distributed to the poor and needy each year. Families were encouraged to have "one pot meal" days and contribute the cost of their usual meal instead to the cause. On the other hand, many workers were forced to contribute ten per cent of their salaries during the winter toward the fund. This was an afternoon speech, and the film reflects this only by the large number of youth attending the speech. Journalist William L. Shirer attended the event, and noted that the audience was largely female, consisting of nurses and social workers. He described Hitler's speech as one of the most humorous and sarcastic of his career. The section of the speech included in the picture contained the most serious section of the Führer's address, his pledge to match by tenfold every bomb dropped on German cities. The speech also contained one of the most famous wartime quotes: "The English are wondering, they are asking, 'Why doesn't he come?' Be patient! Be patient! We are coming. We are coming." This statement unleashes an ecstatic response from the crowd. Rolf Stiekel is masterful in this scene, mimicking Hitler's speaking voice and gestures perfectly. However, Stiekel is only viewed from a distance, or from behind with an over the shoulder shot. Perhaps a close up was avoided because his resemblance to Hitler was minimal. This was Stiekel's only screen appearance.

REPRESENTATIVE QUOTES

• The Führer is being very reasonable. He offers guarantees. *(Baron von Richter to Sir David Kelly in Switzerland)* Experience shows that the Führer's guarantees guarantee nothing. *(His response)*

• Our latest intelligence is that Herr Hitler is sightseeing in France. *(Cabinet Minister to Dowding)* It is rather pleasant weather *(Dowding's wry comment)* I mean it. He is on holiday. *(Cabinet Minister)* I'm not complaining. *(Dowding)*

• Last night, the English dropped bombs on Berlin. So be it. Two can play at that game.... If they mount a large scale attack on our cities, then we will wipe out their cities. The hour will come when one of us must crack and it will never be National Socialist Germany. *(Hitler during his speech of September 4, 1940)*

• If we lose the war now, we deserve to have our arses kicked. *(Göring to himself as he observes a huge armada of German planes flying across the English Channel)*

5. *Blazing Saddles* (1974)

Ralph Manza as Adolf Hitler actor (cameo)
Comedy

Paramount. Written by Andrew Bergman, Mel Brooks, Richard Pryor, Norman Steinberg & Alan Uger; Photographed by Joseph Biroc; Edited by Danford Greene & John C. Howard; Music by Mel Brooks & John Morris; Produced by Michael Hertzberg; Directed by Mel Brooks. Color 93 minutes

CAST LIST: Cleavon Little (*Bart*); Gene Wilder (*Waco Kid*); Harvey Korman (*Hedley Lamarr*); Madeline Kahn (*Lili von Schtupp*); Slim Pickens (*Taggart*); Mel Brooks (Governor, Indian, Aviator); Alex Karras (*Mongo*); Burton Gilliam (*Lyle*); David Huddleston (*Olson Johnson*); Liam Dunn (*Rev. Johnson*); John Hillerman (*Howard Johnson*); George Furth (*Van Johnson*); Carol Arthur (*Harriet Van Johnson*); Claude Ennis Starrett, Jr. (*Gabby Johnson*); Robert Ridgely (Hangman); Gilda Radner (Churchwoman); Dom DeLuise (Director of French dance routine); Count Basie (Band leader).

COMMENTARY: *Blazing Saddles* was the first in a hilarious series of spoof films by Mel Brooks, many of which included quick sight gags with Adolf Hitler. For the first 75 minutes, the satire focused on the genre of Westerns, but in a wild diversion, Brooks pulls back the camera to reveal that the action is actually set in a movie studio. On a neighboring set, male dancers in tuxedos are performing a ludicrous dance entitled "The French Mistake." Suddenly, a melee of battling cowboys bursts onto their set, and everyone joins in the free-for-all. Then the action switches to the studio commissary, where an actor dressed as Adolf Hitler sits down at a table with his lunch tray. His companion addresses him as "Joey" and asks how many days he has left to work. He replies, "They lose me after the bunker scene." The fighting cowboys and dancers crash into the canteen, and Hitler cries out, "What the hell is that?" A food fight breaks out. Hitler jumps onto the counter in the back of the room and raises and lowers his arm in a Nazi salute. Harvey Korman appears out of the rest room, observes the fracas, disguises his face with whipped cream and sneaks off. In the last cafeteria shot, Hitler is still seen in the back of the room placing his left arm on his hip while raising and lowering his right arm, and pivoting back and forth. This vignette is quite hilarious, and Manza performs the Hitler cameo with the perfect light touch. The addition of the Führer adds a surreal element to the scene, adding to the belly laughs.

6. *The Boys from Brazil* (1978)

Jeremy Black as clones of Adolf Hitler
Horror

20th Century–Fox. Written by Heywood Gould based on the novel *The Boys from Brazil* by Ira Levin; Photographed by Henri Dacae; Edited by Robert E. Swink; Music by Jerry Goldsmith; Produced by Martin Richards & Stanley O'Toole; Directed by Franklin J. Schaffner. Color 123 minutes

ANNOTATED CAST LIST: Gregory Peck (*Dr. Josef Mengele*, War criminal & mad scientist who breeds 94 clones of Hitler); Laurence Olivier (*Ezra Lieberman*, Hunter of Nazi war criminals); James Mason (*Colonel Eduard Seibert*, Secret Nazi organization official); Lilli Palmer (*Esther Lieberman*, Ezra's sister); Uta Hagen (*Frieda Maloney*, Jailed Nazi war criminal); Steve Guttenberg (*Barry Kohler*, Student tracking Nazis in Paraguay); Denholm Elliott (*Sidney Beynon*, Viennese police official); Richard Marner (*Doring*, Murdered German father of clone); Rosemary Harris (His wife); Anne Meara (*Mrs. Curry*, American mother of Hitler clone); Michael Gough (*Harrington*, Murdered British father of clone); Prunella Scales (His wife); Linda Hayden (*Nancy*, Harrington's border); John Dehner (*Henry Wheelock*, Pennsylvania farmer & dog breeder killed by Mengele); John Rubinstein (*David Bennett*, Hardline Nazi hunter); Bruno Ganz (*Professor Brückner*, Geneticist); Walter Gotell (*Captain Gerhardt Mundt*, Nazi agent); Monica Gearson (*Gertrude*, His wife); David Hurst (*Strasser*, Lieberman's landlord); Wolfgang Preiss (*Lofquist*, Murdered Nazi posing as a Swede); Joachim Hansen (*Fassler*, Maloney's lawyer); Gunter Meisner (*Captain Farnbach*, Old comrade of Mengele); Carl Duering (*Major Ludwig Trausteiner*, Nazi agent); Georg Marischka (*Rolf Günther*, Wealthy South American Nazi); Raul Faustino Saldanha (*Ismael*, Youngster in Paraguay who aids Kohler); Guy Dumont (*Dietrich Hessen*, Young Nazi agent); Jurgen Anderson (*Wolfgang Kleist*, Young Nazi agent); Wolf Kahler (*Rollo Schwimmer*, Young

Jeremy Black as the young Hitler clone chooses sides in the standoff between Dr. Mengele (Gregory Peck) and Lieberman (Laurence Olivier) in *Boys from Brazil.*

Nazi agent); David Brandon (*Schmidt*, Nazi at ball); Mervyn Nelson (*Stroop*); Gerti Gordon (*Berthe*, Doring's mistress).

APPRAISAL AND SYNOPSIS: *The Boys from Brazil* is undoubtedly one of the oddest entries in *The Hitler Filmography*. Many viewers may not recognize it as a horror film until its finale. It is also disturbing that a real life war criminal, Dr. Josef Mengele, is transformed from an undistinguished quack who tortured and experimented upon human beings to no real purpose, into a mad doctor bordering on genius. His rival is Nazi hunter Ezra Lieberman, a thinly disguised version of Simon Weisenthal, although the fictional character is far more of a lone wolf, aided primarily by his sister. The other Nazi characters in the story are fictional, with the exception of Adolf Hitler. In fact, there are 94 Hitlers in the film, identical clones bred by Mengele from a blood sample and skin scrapings he took from Hitler in 1943, but only

four of these clones appear onscreen. The resulting film is a grand guignol of the absurd, quite entertaining at times, but one that requires total suspension of disbelief due to the enormous plot loopholes.

The film opens with stark credits against a black screen, accompanied by Jerry Goldsmith's music, a manic, bloated distortion of a Viennese waltz. A young American student, David Kohler, inspired by the work of Nazi hunter Ezra Lieberman, is tracking the movements of former Nazis in Paraguay. He telephones Lieberman in Vienna, who is not impressed and advises the young man to return home. Later, Kohler offers a young boy a radio in exchange for planting a listening device at the mansion of Rolf Günther, a rich German industrialist. That evening, he tapes a secret meeting between Dr. Josef Mengele, the former Auschwitz doctor in charge of human experimentation, and six operatives of a clandestine Nazi organization.

Mengele instructs them to kill 94 men in their mid-sixties, minor officials living across Northern Europe, the United States and Canada. If possible, the deaths should resemble accidents, but in no case should the other family members of the victims be involved or harmed. When the listening device is discovered, Mengele and his thugs track Kohler down to his hotel room, where the student is playing his recording over the phone to Lieberman. Kohler is killed, and Mengele listens to Lieberman's voice as he calls out for the young man to answer. Mengele hangs up the phone, convinced the Nazi hunter will not be able to stop him.

Lieberman feels honor-bound to follow up on Kohler's work, and he requests the Austrian authorities to furnish him with notices of all sixty-five-year-old bureaucrats in the United States and Europe who come to suspicious ends. The Nazi agents murder the first group of victims based on Mengele's list, killing them according to his timetable. At his retreat in the Brazilian jungle, Mengele is delighted as he receives reports of the deaths from Colonel Seibert, his liaison with the Nazi movement. Seibert also tells him that the officials are concerned that Ezra Lieberman has been active in investigating the project. In fact, the Nazi hunter traveled to Gladbeck in Germany to interview Mrs, Doring, the widow of the first victim. Mengele dismisses Lieberman as insignificant.

In America, Lieberman questions Mrs. Curry, the widow of another victim, and is surprised to see that her thirteen-year-old son Jack is the exact double of Erich Doring, the son of the first victim. Later, Mrs. Curry confesses that her son was adopted, and that the person who arranged the adoption was Frieda Maloney, a woman who was recently arrested on charges of being a war criminal. Questioning the former concentration camp guard in prison, Lieberman learns that she worked at an adoption agency in the 1960s with rather unusual criteria. She worked only with couples in which the father was a minor government official who was approximately twenty years older than his wife. All

of the babies were boys who had been born in Brazil.

David Bennett, a militant Nazi hunter, volunteers to help Lieberman, and in England he encounters a third identical boy who is the son of a victim. Lieberman consults with Professor Bruckner, a renowned geneticist, to help him puzzle out the mystery of Mengele's plans. Bruckner proposes that Mengele had been experimenting with human embryos, and that the children of the murdered men might be clones. He also theorizes that the men are being murdered in order to replicate the environment of the original clone donor. Bruckner and Lieberman study the pattern and conclude that Mengele had managed to create a series of identical clones of Adolf Hitler.

While attending a Nazi ball in Paraguay, Mengele is upset when he sees one of his assassins on the dance floor. He attacks the man, accusing him of treason, since he was scheduled to be in Europe that night to eliminate another victim. Siebert shows up at the ball and tells Mengele that further assassinations have been canceled due to Lieberman's investigations. Defiant, Mengele decides to continue the assassinations by himself. He travels to Pennsylvania to kill Henry Wheelock, a well-to-do farmer and dog breeder. When he arrives at the farm, Wheelock mistakes him for Lieberman who had phoned for an appointment that very afternoon. Shooting the farmer, Mengele decides to wait for Lieberman, and amuses himself by looking through a photo album with pictures of young Bobby Wheelock, the Hitler clone. When Lieberman arrives, Mengele shoots him but the Nazi hunter proves to be more resilient than he thought, and then Wheelock's pack of Dobermans, trained attack dogs, appear and keep the adversaries at bay. They talk, and Mengele boasts that Hitler had provided him with blood and skin scrapings in 1943 in order for him to experiment on cloning. It took him years, but he finally managed to produce 94 clones in a secret jungle laboratory. He manage to place them in homes that duplicated the formative

years of Hitler. The final step was to eliminate the father as the Hitler clones entered
their teenage years. Mengele predicts that at
least one of the clones will be able to reshape
the world in his own fascist image. When
Bobby returns home, he grabs his camera and
starts to photograph the strange men held in
check by the dogs. When Mengele tells
Bobby that he is the duplicate of Adolf Hitler, the boy doubts the man's sanity. When
Lieberman tells the boy that Mengele had
just murdered his father, Bobby orders the
dogs to kill the Nazi. He then makes a bargain with the wounded Lieberman, calling
an ambulance in exchange for his silence regarding the murder of Mengele. Lieberman
manages to retrieve the list of the names and
addresses of the clones from the dead man's
body before he passes out. He later awakens
in the hospital. Bennett is at his bedside, determined to ruin Mengele's plans and demanding the list of names so that the Hitler
clones can be exterminated. Lieberman suggests they are merely children, and that if
they are killed, then their murderers would
be the same as the Nazis. He burns the list,
saving the children, but leaving the future
world in peril.

The Boys from Brazil is a fascinating and
entertaining movie despite the many outlandish twists and turns of the plot. The cinematography, music, editing and set design
are of the highest quality. The acting, however, is over the top as both Gregory Peck
and Laurence Olivier chew the scenery with
complete abandon. Some critics even praised
Olivier's eccentric interpretation of Lieberman, which in many ways is the wilder of the
two performances. His bizarre accent seems
to have been derived from *The Great Gabbo*
(1929), an Erich von Strohiem film about a
mad ventriloquist. Olivier duplicates both
the voice and expression of Otto, the dummy
alter ego of Gabbo. To top it off, Olivier
reprised the same accent seven years later in
Wild Geese II (1985), in which he played
Rudolf Hess. The other cast members are
also fairly well played, including Bruno Ganz
as Professor Bruckner, Uta Hagen as Freida

Maloney, Walter Gotell as Captain Mundt,
one of the old line Nazi assassins and Gunter
Meisner as Captain Farnbach, a friend of
Mengele's from his days at Auschwitz. Meisner himself played Hitler in several films.

It is in the plot intricacies, however, that
the film's real weakness lies. Professor Bruckner should have pointed out that there are
far more environmental factors than could
ever possibly be duplicated. What compo-
nents made Hitler Hitler? Could it have
been his failure to be accepted at the Academy of Fine Arts in Vienna? Or his experiences in World War I? Or his mother's slow,
agonizing death, tended by a Jewish physician? Or was it all of these factors together
plus others that are indefinable? This is the
underlying weakness of the premise. Is there
any reason to believe that any of the cloned
Hitlers would ever amount to anything more
than an insignificant backwater agitator or a
two bit artist? Perhaps Lieberman found
comfort in this possibility. However, the filmmakers wanted to dangle the possibility that
each of these clones had been imbued with
a special, almost supernatural evil, making
each of them a unpredictable and violent
threat. Perhaps the film's weakness is not
that great a weakness after all, since it can
stimulate a great deal of thought in the
viewer.

In real life, Dr. Josef Mengele lacked the
charisma and brilliance with which Gregory
Peck endows him. In fact, the genuine Mengele hid out on a cattle ranch in Nova Europa, Brazil, and later in a shack in one of
the poorer suburbs of Sao Paulo, where he
was living at the time of this film's release.
Mengele used the name Peter Hochbuchler, having no other plans than trying to remain anonymous. He died of a stroke while
swimming in the Atlantic Ocean on February 7, 1979, a very mundane death, and he
was buried as Wolfgang Gerhardt, the name
of a former Nazi friend who allowed him to
use his own identity papers at times. Mengele was a man undistinguished by any talents except for a capacity to ignore the
human misery for which he was responsible.

Although there is no evidence to suggest that Mengele ever read *The Boys from Brazil* or saw the film, it would be interesting to speculate what he would think of the image of himself as depicted in the story.

HITLER PORTRAYAL: Young Jeremy Black does an exceedingly credible job in the role of four thirteen-year-old clones of Adolf Hitler. These four boys are Jack Curry, a New Englander, Simon Harrington, a British boy, Erich Doring, a German and Bobby Wheelock, another American living in Pennsylvania. Each of these boys has the exact same temperament, spoiled, arrogant and artistic. Each of them specialized in a different talent. Erich, for example, plays the clarinet, Simon is a puppeteer and Bobby is a camera buff. One unlikely characteristic is that the four boys would have identical haircuts. Even if the Hitler forelock is a natural tendency, it is unlikely that each of them would maintain the same length and style of hair. Black does excellent work, however, with the national accents which distinguish the four boys. It would have been fascinating if the screenplay had featured more of the 94 clones, and no doubt Black could have been just as convincing as the others. The clone with the most screen time is Bobby Wheelock, who arrives home from school at his large, Pennsylvania Dutch farmhouse, to find the feuding Mengele and Lieberman at a standoff due to the presence of his father's Dobermans. Black's characterization is a chilling one, revealing Bobby as a cold, amoral sociopath at age thirteen. Mengele tries to win him over, but Bobby is more interested in photographing the two strange intruders covered in blood. When Mengele tells Bobby the truth about himself, the teenager rejects Mengele as a crackpot, finally ordering the dogs to tear him to pieces. The close-up of Bobby's face as he watches the bloody carnage is malevolent, yet gratifying since Mengele is the victim of the carnage. The clone then makes a deal with the badly wounded Lieberman, saving his life in exchange for his silence. Reluctantly, Lieberman agrees, and this "bargain" bears an iron-

ical parallel not only with Chamberlain at Munich, but with the German people who in essence made a Faustian pact with the Führer, yielding him power in exchange for order. In the final scene, Lieberman justifies his protection of Bobby and the 93 other Hitler clones with the excuse that they are just children. Yet knowing the future, would Lieberman have made the same choice if he had encountered the first Adolf Hitler in 1903? One also wonders about the future of Bobby Wheelock, the only one of the clones who knows the truth. How long after his initial rejection of Mengele's information will he have second thoughts, as he visually confirms his resemblance to Hitler in the mirror and in his own mind. It is a disturbing conclusion to this horror film that none of these clones will turn out well, and most of them will render harm to mankind to one degree or another. The possibility exists in this horror film that Mengele will be victorious after all.

REPRESENTATIVE QUOTES

• Do you kill Nazis when you catch them? *(Erich Doring, a German Hitler clone to Lieberman)*

• Do you know what I saw on the television in my hotel room at one o'clock this morning? Films of Hitler! They are showing films about the war, the movement. People are fascinated, the time is right. Adolf Hitler is alive! ... When he heard what was theoretically possible, that I could create one day not his son, not even a carbon copy, but another original, he was thrilled by the idea, the right Hitler for the right future, a Hitler tailor made for the 1980s, 90s, 2000! *(Mengele to Lieberman, as he holds him at gunpoint)*

• You are the duplicate of the greatest man in history, Adolf Hitler! *(Mengele to Bobby Wheelock, an American Hitler clone)* Oh man, you're weird. *(The boy's reply)*

• I think you will die if I don't call an ambulance for you. I could just go out right now. My mom won't be home until late. You will be dead by then. If I call the police, will you tell them what I did? OK, shake.

Come on, shake. You've got a deal. *(American Hitler clone to the injured Lieberman, who reluctantly agrees)*

7. *The Bunker* (1980)

Anthony Hopkins as Adolf Hitler
Historical drama

Time-Life. Written by John Gay based on the book *The Bunker* by James O'Donnell; Photographed by Jean-Louis Picavet; Edited by Greyfox; Music by Brad Fiedel; Produced by Aida Young, George Schaefer & David Susskind (Executive); Directed by George Schaefer. Color 145 minutes

ANNOTATED CAST LIST: James Naughton (*James O'Donnell*, British officer researching the last days of Hitler); Richard Jordan (*Albert Speer*, Munitions Minister); Susan Blakely (*Eva Braun*, Hitler's mistress); Cliff Gorman (*Dr. Joseph Goebbels*, Propaganda Minister); Piper Laurie (*Magda Goebbels*, His wife); Michael Lonsdale (*Martin Bormann*, Hitler's private secretary); David King (*Hermann Göring*, Reich Marshal); Michael Sheard (*Heinrich Himmler*, Interior Minister & Head of SS); Edward Hardwicke (*Dieter Stahl*, Munitions procurer & Speer's friend); Andrew Ray (*Colonel Otto Günsche*, Hitler's personal adjutant); Tony Steedman (*Alfred Jodl*, General & Chief of Operations); John Paul (*Wilhelm Keitel*, Field Marshal & Chief of the High Command); Yves Brainville (*Heinz Guderian*, General placed on sick leave due to defeatism); Michael Culver (*Wilhelm Mohnke*, SS general); Jullian Fellows (*Colonel Nicolaus von Below*, Hitler's Luftwaffe adjutant); Terence Hardiman (*Hermann Fegelein*, SS General, Eva Braun's brother-in-law); Michael Kitchen (*Sgt. Rochus Misch*, Bunker guard); Martin Jarvis (*Johannes Hentschel*, Bunker mechanic); Karl Held (*Hans Baur*, Hitler's personal pilot); John Sharp (*Dr. Theodor Morell*, Hitler's personal physician); Morris Perry (*Prof. Werner Haase*, Doctor who tends the wounded in the Chancellery); Frank Gatliff (*Dr. Schenck*); Sarah Marshall (*Traudl Junge*, Hitler's dictation secretary); Robert Austin (*Walter Wagner*, City official who marries Hitler & Eva Braun); David Swift (*Hans Rattenhuber*, SS Chief of Hitler's bodyguards); Pamela St. Clement (*Constanze Manzialy*, Bunker cook).

APPRAISAL AND SYNOPSIS: *The Bunker* is a stately, somber and unflinching portrait of Hitler's last few months, spent in the cramped and smelly bunker underneath the Berlin Reich Chancellery. James O'Donnell strove for authenticity in his original book, basing almost every page on his interviews with the survivors. Most of the scenes directly dealing with Hitler, however, came from one major source, Albert Speer, who reportedly also served as an unofficial consultant for the production. Therefore, the film basically presents Adolf Hitler as experienced by Speer. While there is nothing inappropriate in this, since Speer was a very perceptive observer, still this formulation remains basically the viewpoint of a single observer. *The Bunker* was a co-production of SFP France and the television division of Time-Life, and it was originally broadcast on CBS television on January 27, 1981.

The scenario opens in occupied Berlin in June 1945. James P. O'Donnell, on assignment for *Newsweek*, tours the last refuge of Hitler, the Führer Bunker beneath the grounds of the Chancellery building. He is struck by the cramped confines, now partially flooded. His voiceover narration begins to relate the story of the 105 days in which Hitler lived in this tomb-like structure. Flashing back to January 16, 1945, German army personnel are rushing to prepare the bunker for occupancy. Bormann and the top officers are depressed after touring the facilities, knowing there is a bunker seven times larger with full communications facilities only a few miles outside the capital, but the Führer refuses to leave Berlin. One of them complains that they have seen better switchboards in cheap hotels. The place also smells, being only twenty feet below the sewer.

Albert Speer, Hitler's architect who now serves as the Armaments Minister, arrives at the bunker, where he tries in vain to dissuade Hitler from implementing his plan of

Susan Blakely as Eva Braun and Anthony Hopkins as the Führer in *The Bunker*.

why he refuses to execute the scorched earth policy. Hitler reads it and dismisses it, presenting Speer with a birthday present instead, an autographed photograph. He again asks Speer to carry out his plans for total destruction, and the architect meekly nods but says nothing. Speer later tells Stahl, however, that he will go through the motions, but he will not carry out the orders.

Hitler conducts a series of desperate, almost surreal meetings with his General Staff. When one of his leading officers, General Guderian, tries to talk plainly about the hopelessness of the struggle, the Führer places him on a forced medical leave. At another meeting, Hitler questions Speer about the effect on arms production after the American forces take the Ruhr Valley, and he replies that the Third Reich is on the verge of total collapse. After the meeting, Speer is led to a small side room by a guard. The architect fears he is about to be shot, but instead he finds Hitler in the room cuddling newborn puppies, the offspring of Blondi, his pet German Shepherd. The Führer gives him a pep talk, saying that Germany should be prepared to accept defeat after defeat knowing that they will be victorious in the end. For an instant, Hitler roars his convictions, "I will destroy Bolshevism! I will wipe out the scourge and pestilence of Jewish Marxism! I will defeat them all! I will defy the entire world!" If his Munitions Minister is no longer able to believe in that final victory, Hitler insists that he still must be able to hope for it. He gives Speer 24 hours to decide if he can still hope for victory. Another flashback is inserted (flashbacks within flashbacks), as Speer recalls Hitler's enthu-

total destruction of all German towns in the path of the oncoming enemy. Hitler's mind is firmly set, however, and the architect considers how he can avoid carrying out the monstrous proposal. He considers killing the Führer by placing poison gas in the air vent of the bunker. Speer asks his friend, Dieter Stahl, the Chief of Munitions, to procure a lethal quantity of mustard gas. By the time he receives the canister, Speer discovers that the air vent is now protected by a cement chimney, rendering his plan useless, and Speer abandons his assassination attempt. Instead, he writes a long, heartfelt memorandum to the Führer outlining the reasons siasm for his architectural plans years earlier, and how he beamingly referred to him as "my genius architect." He also recalls Hitler frolicking like a schoolboy with Eva Braun, as she photographs him with her movie camera. When Speer appears before Stahl, his friend is surprised that Speer is still alive. The architect can only conclude that Hitler is actually fond of him. The next day, when Speer affirms his ability to hope, Hitler grasps him and mutters, "Thank you, Speer, thank you."

The war news continues its catastrophic turn on all fronts for the German forces. On April 12th, Goebbels brings the Führer news of the death of Franklin Roosevelt. The Propaganda Minister radiates enthusiasm, claiming this to be the turning point. He compares Hitler to Frederick the Great, who was almost defeated but managed to emerge victorious. Goebbels next produces an astrological chart which predicts an unexpected turn in fortune for the German cause in the latter half of April. The Führer's new confidence comes crashing down moments later, as Bormann arrives with news of the fall of Vienna to the Russians, and he quietly walks out of the room leaving Bormann and Goebbels staring at each other.

Eva Braun arrives at the bunker shortly after, quietly determined to share Hitler's fate, now that the war is entering its final phase. On April 20th, Hitler celebrates his 56th birthday, and for the last time most of his old comrades, including Göring and Himmler, gather to pay him homage. Dr. Morell, Hitler's physician, gives him an additional injection to prime him for the reception. A small party with food and music is set up in the vestibule of the Chancellery, and Hitler makes an appearance and a brief speech, ending in a mutter, "We will not be defeated. We will not be defeated."

As Russian troops begin to surround Berlin, Hitler conceives a plan involving a counterattack by troops under the command of General Steiner. The leaders of the German military realize that Steiner's forces are too weak to mount any offensive, but they also know Hitler will not accept that basic fact.

A reenactment follows of the last newsreel footage of Hitler, as he greets members of the Hitler Youth in the garden of the Chancellery. Hitler then descends into the bunker, never again to emerge alive.

Goebbels, his wife and six children move into the bunker at Hitler's request. Bormann urges Hitler to leave Berlin and move his headquarters to Berchtesgaden, but Hitler is adamant about staying in the capital. At his next General Staff meeting, the Führer has his final outburst when he learns that Steiner's attack has not occurred. "I'll die in Berlin. I've been betrayed!" he screams at the generals. Then, in a soft voice, he finally accepts the obvious truth. "The war is lost." The generals are stunned by his admission of defeat.

Bormann continues in his attempts to manipulate Hitler into leaving Berlin. Failing that, he manages to orchestrate the downfall of both Himmler and Göring. The SS leader had been tendering peace offers through the Swedish Ambassador. Göring had sent a telegram inquiring at what point he should assume authority as Hitler's successor if communications with the bunker are lost. Bormann interprets the message to be treasonous instead, and this infuriates Hitler. Meanwhile, Speer returns to the bunker to say farewell to Hitler. He finds the Führer in a nostalgic mood, reflecting on his lost plans and dreams. Speer openly admits to Hitler that he deceived him about the scorched earth policy, but the Führer no longer cares, and talks only of Eva Braun and their plans for suicide. Before Speer leaves, he visits with Eva, who tells him that Magda Goebbels plans to kill herself and her children as well. The architect tries to dissuade Magda, who seems radiant, considering the grisly task to be an act of honor.

Hitler retreats into a dreamworld, spending his time entertaining the Goebbels children, having tea and crumpets with his secretaries or playing with the puppies. Goebbels reads a children's book to him about Frederick the Great. Hitler agrees to marry Eva. At the ceremony, he is withdrawn and quiet.

He starts to tremble as he signs the marriage document, and Eva gently helps him steady his hand. A small reception is held, and Goebbels toasts the newlyweds. The Führer withdraws early to dictate his will, delivered in a detached and mechanical fashion. He decides upon naming the head of the navy, Admiral Karl Dönitz, as his successor.

Goebbels organizes a formal dinner for his friends in the Chancellery. Professor Haase, who is running a makeshift hospital in the ruins of the building, is asked to provide six wounded soldiers as guests for the party. The Propaganda Minister makes a final speech, blaming the Jews for the loss of the war. The guests are then serenaded by a chorus of war songs performed by the Hitler Youth.

Hitler is deeply distressed when he hears reports of Mussolini's death and how his body was defiled by the partisans. The Führer examines the cyanide capsules provided to him and orders that they be tested on his dog, Blondi. The puppies are killed as well. Hitler asks that the remaining occupants of the bunker gather in a reception line, and he and Eva bid them farewell, shaking hands in a cold and almost remote manner. They finally withdraw to their sitting room. There are no words of farewell between them. Hitler merely instructs Eva to "bite down hard" as he hands her a cyanide capsule. He shoots himself in the temple as he bites into his own capsule. A few seconds later, Bormann and the others enter the room, and the bodies are carried to the Chancellery garden where they are soaked in gasoline and set ablaze. Russians shells rain down on the scene, as Goebbels and the others give a final Nazi salute to the corpses as the men cower just outside the entrance to the bunker.

Magda Goebbels puts her children to bed, explaining to them that they will all fly to Berchtesgaden in the morning with the Führer. She gives them each a cyanide capsule, explaining that it will prevent air sickness. As she carries out this task, Goebbels lights a cigarette (with the Führer's death, the ban on smoking in the bunker is disre-

garded) and launches into a rambling monologue to the remaining officers about his recollections of the heyday of the Nazi party and their legacy to the world. The officers continue to drink and pay little attention to him. He finally gets up and accompanies Magda to the Chancellery garden, commenting to the others, "At least you good people won't have to carry our bodies up this long flight of stairs." Their suicide occurs off screen. Bormann and the remaining men plan a breakout, hoping to escape from the war torn city. The last man in the bunker, the mechanic Hentschel, sits by himself after inspecting the bedroom with the bodies of the Goebbels children. He turns on the radio and tunes in some music, which is interrupted by a bulletin announcing that Hitler died fighting in Berlin. He hurls a stack of papers at the radio, as a closing narration reveals the fate of each of the survivors of the bunker.

HITLER PORTRAYAL: Anthony Hopkins' performance as Adolf Hitler won the Emmy for the best dramatic leading actor, nonseries. His interpretation is thoughtful, deliberate and understated, which renders his tantrums all the more effective when they appear. On the whole, he endows his reading with more depth and less bombast, often depicting the Führer as a mere shell of his former self, devoid and incapable of any genuine human emotion other than rage and regret. He often seems robotic, detached and in a stupor. Hopkins generally speaks in hoarse, low tones, often punctuating his comments with a slow bass laugh, "Haaaa!" He has brief, volcanic tantrums, when his voice sinks to a throaty growl, but these rages quickly pass, as he lapses back into his groggy languor in the blink of an eye. This transformation is both ghastly and fascinating, but Hopkins manages to make it seem convincing. His relationship with Eva Braun in the bunker is strangely empty and nonexistent. There are no words of affection or kindness between them, only a shadowy vacuum. Oddly enough, the weakest moments of Hopkins' portrayal are in the flashbacks, particularly the one at the conclusion of the film in which he is shown delivering a harangue to an adoring crowd. It is the only moment in the entire production where he is unconvincing. The real measure of Hopkins' craft is that he is able to convey a weak and defeated Hitler as a human being but one who is unworthy of any sympathy or pity. That is a remarkable accomplishment, one that makes his performance fully worthy of the Emmy award. The other Nazi hierarchy are played in a range of fair to excellent. Cliff Gorman makes Goebbels an empty-headed gasbag, a dreary person who continually drones on in an endless monologue. His voice really begins to grate as the film wears on until the viewer cannot stand his presence. David King is disappointing as Göring, giving a rather shallow portrayal. On the other hand, Michael Lonsdale is superb as Bormann, even if his large frame is physically the opposite of Hitler's rather diminutive right hand man. Lonsdale shades his reading to show the unctuous Bormann as continually calculating and plotting to the bitter end. Richard Jordan is also good as the troubled yet somewhat ineffectual Albert Speer, the only Nazi who appears to have a conscience. The finest portrayal of the inner circle, however, is that of Michael Sheard as Himmler. Sheard later played Hitler himself in several films.

REPRESENTATIVE QUOTES

• I can't guarantee what you are about to see is historical truth. Memory always distorts, of course. But I do believe their stories present a psychological truth, and are, perhaps, as close as we can come. *(Opening narration by O'Donnell, concerning his research and interviews with the survivors of the Bunker)*
• The German people that are left would not deserve to live. The good ones would have died already fighting for their Fatherland. *(Hitler to Speer, discussing the fate of the German people if the war is lost)*
• There have been questions, I know, about my health. Well, you see me now. It is true there is a certain, er, I have a certain trembling in my arm and in my legs, but I can assure you, good friends, the trembling has not reached my head nor my heart. No, my heart will never tremble. Never! *(Hitler to the guests at his birthday reception)*
• I've never acquired anything of value in my life. I have nothing. I have nothing. *(Hitler to Speer upon his leave-taking)*
• My life is in your hands. I wish to live until the fifth of May. *(Hitler to General Mohnke)* There is some significance to that date? *(Mohnke, somewhat perplexed)* The fifth of May is the anniversary of Napoleon's death. We are both men born before our time, so much the worse for Europe. History will be my judge, as it was for him. *(Hitler)*.

8. *Chaplin* (1992)

Robert Downey, Jr., as a caricature of Adolf Hitler
Biographical drama

Carolco. Written by William Boyd, Bryan Forbes & William Goldman, based upon a story treatment by Diana Hawkins of *My Autobiography* by Charles Chaplin; Photographed by Sven Nykvist; Edited by Anne V. Coates; Music by John Barry; Produced by Richard Attenborough & Mario Kassar; Directed by Richard Attenborough. Color and B & W 144 minutes

CAST LIST: Robert Downey, Jr. (*Charlie Chaplin*); Geraldine Chaplin (*Hannah Chaplin*); Moira Kelly (*Hattie & Oona O'Neill Chaplin*); Paul Rhys (*Sydney Chaplin*); John Thaw (*Fred Karno*); Anthony Hopkins (*Chaplin's book editor*); Dan Aykroyd (*Mack Sennett*); Marisa Tomei (*Mabel Normand);* Penelope Ann Miller (*Edna Purviance*); Kevin Kline (*Douglas Fairbanks*); Maria Petillo (*Mary Pickford*); Milla Jovovich (*Mildred Harris*); Kevin Dunn (*J. Edgar Hoover*); Deborah Maria Moore (*Lita Grey*); Diane Lane (*Paulette Goddard*); Nancy Travis (*Joan Barry*); James Woods (*Joseph Scott*); David Duchovny (*Rollie Totheroh*); Matthew Cottle (*Stan Laurel*); Jack Ritschel (*William Randolph Hearst*); Robert Stephens (*Ted*).

COMMENTARY: *Chaplin* is a thoughtful "official" screen biography, occasionally uneven in quality, but worthwhile nevertheless, particularly for the amazing performance by Robert Downey, Jr., in the lead role. Wisely, director Richard Attenborough chose not to recreate many of Chaplin's screen highlights in the course of the film, using instead genuine Chaplin film clips at the conclusion. One exception, however, is *The Great Dictator*, which receives considerable attention during the last quarter of the film. First, we observe Downey as Chaplin running newsreel film clips of Adolf Hitler. As Hitler speaks, Charlie imitates him, substituting double talk and words like "hair dryer" and "pizza pie" for the German phrases. Charlie's half-brother Syd comes on to the sound stage, and lashes into Charlie, saying nobody wants to see a film about Adolf Hitler. Charlie responds, "I know this man, born the same year, four days apart. He is like me, capable of anything." They argue, and Charlie insists he has got to give it a try. The action then cuts to the making of the film. Downey is now dressed as Adenoid Hynkel, a caricature of Hitler. His impersonation of Chaplin's delivery of the final speech of *The Great Dictator* is virtually letter perfect. The films segues from the scene being shot, to a small screen projection in the office of J. Edgar Hoover, who is upset by what he believes to be the Marxist implications of the speech. He dispenses an agent to California to cause trouble for Charlie. Finally, the speech is played on the large screen of a movie palace. Someone in the audience, presumably one of Hoover's men, tosses a tomato at the Chaplin/Hitler image on the screen. The end of this sequence is a major distortion, because it was actually Chaplin's *Monsieur Verdoux* (1947) which encountered organized hostility, not *The Great Dictator*, but the script seems to confuse this. In any case, the Hitler caricature reappears at the end of the picture, when the genuine Chaplin is shown as Adenoid Hynkel, dancing with the giant balloon of the globe, from *The Great Dictator*, at the 1972 Academy Award tribute sequence that closes the film.

9. *Citizen Kane* (1941)

Bert Young (?) as Adolf Hitler (cameo)
Drama

RKO. Written by Hermann J. Mankiewicz & Orson Welles; Photographed by Gregg Toland; Edited by Robert Wise; Music by Bernard Herrmann; Produced & directed by Orson Welles. B & W 119 minutes

ANNOTATED CAST LIST: Orson Welles (*Charles Foster Kane*, Wealthy publisher); Buddy Swan (*Charles Foster Kane*, Age 8); Agnes Morehead (*Mary Kane*, His mother); Harry Shannon (*Jim Kane*, His father); Joseph Cotton (*Jedediah Leland*, Newsman & Kane's friend); Ruth Warwick (*Emily Norton Kane*, First wife); Sonny Bupp (Their son); Dorothy Comingore (*Susan Alexander Kane*, Singer & second wife); Everett Sloane (*Bernstein*, Kane's general manager); Erskine Sanford (*Herbert Carter*, Editor of *Inquirer*); Ray Collins (*Jim W. Gettys*, Corrupt political boss); George Coulouris (*Walter Parks Thatcher*, Banker & Kane's ex-guardian); Paul Stewart (*Raymond*, Head butler of *Xanadu*); Fortunio Bonanova (*Matisti*, Singing teacher); Gus Schilling (Head waiter of *El Rancho*); Georgia Backus (*Bertha Anderson*, Librarian of Thatcher Library); Joe Manz (*Jennings*, Thatcher Library guard); Philip Van Zandt (*Rawlston*, Newsreel executive); William Alland (*Jerry Thompson*, Reporter assigned to research Kane's last words & Narrator); Irving Mitchell (*Corey*, Doctor who attends Susan); Tom Curran (*Theodore Roosevelt*, President supported by Kane); Alan Ladd, Arthur O'Connell, Milton Kibbe, Eddie Coke, Louise Currie (Reporters).

APPRAISAL AND SYNOPSIS: In most circles, *Citizen Kane* is generally regarded as the finest motion picture ever made, with ample justification. Like the greatest artistic works, Tolstoy's *War and Peace*, Dante's *Divine Comedy* and Shakespeare's *Hamlet*, it is a work that continually amazes us each time we approach it. Numerous books and countless essays have examined the film, yet they haven't come close to exhausting the subject.

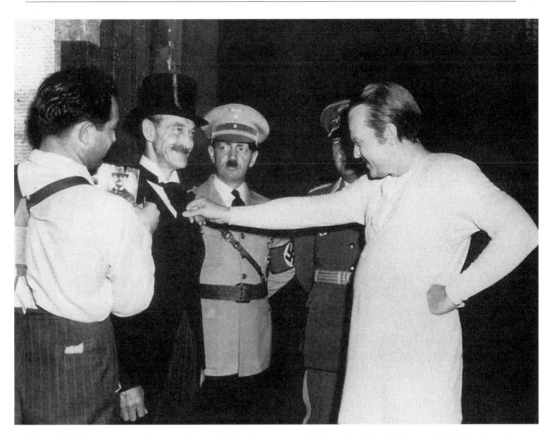

Orson Welles inspects the wardrobe of the characters of Chamberlain, Hitler and Göring for the newsreel section of *Citizen Kane*.

The innovations in terms of story construction, cinematography, sound, editing and acting are still spellbinding. A recent book by Ronald Schwartz, *Noir: Now and Then*, makes a strong case that the film can even be regarded as the stylistic genesis of film noir. Originally titled *American*, the basic plot follows the efforts of an investigative reporter, Thompson, to examine the life of wealthy newspaper mogul Charles Foster Kane and discover the meaning of his last spoken word, "Rosebud." After seeing Kane through the eyes of various individuals with different interpretations, a technique later refined in *Rashomon* (1950), Thompson concludes that "Rosebud" is just a missing piece in the jigsaw puzzle that made up the life of Kane. The secret is revealed to the audience, however, as his boyhood sled is burned along with other items from Kane's estate. The

sled is named "Rosebud," signifying, among other things, the lost simple pleasures of youth and innocence. However, critics will no doubt be arguing this point, along with the William Randolph Hearst allusions and the layers and symbols of this masterpiece for decades to come.

Years later, Welles sardonically suggested the idea of applying the technique of *Citizen Kane* to a life of Hitler, with "Schmorpfanne" (Casserole) being his dying word. This notion was probably only an Wellesean joke, but he never revealed the secret meaning of Hitler's supposed last word.

HITLER PORTRAYAL: Orson Welles was given the pick of central casting to select the numerous extras in *Citizen Kane*, especially for the scenes of parties both at the *Inquirer* offices and the Xanadu picnic, political rallies, the sequence with the opera *Salammbô* and figures in the *News on the March* sequence. The names of many of these performers are no longer known, except for Tom Curran who played Theodore Roosevelt, campaigning with Kane from the rear platform of a train. Initially, many historical figures were planned to appear in the newsreel with Kane, including William Jennings Bryan, Al Smith, Alf Landon, Josef Stalin, Franklin D. Roosevelt and Winston Churchill. In the filmed version, the historical characters who appear are Theodore Roosevelt, Neville Chamberlain and Adolf Hitler. The Führer and Charles Foster Kane appear together on a balcony, apparently overlooking a crowd. Hitler is on the left, next to Kane, shifting feet and turning. A little further off to the left are two other Nazi leaders in uniform. One has his back to the camera, and the other, apparently Hermann Göring, is practically out of camera range. The words of the narrator as the Hitler scene appears, are "...often support, then denounce," indicating that Kane newspapers turned against Hitler in the late 1930s. In the brief sequence, the Hitler scene looks very authentic, and no doubt many viewers thought this scene was constructed by splicing in Orson Welles with actual newsreel footage of Hitler. In fact, the actor appearing in this scene is one of the earliest Hitler depictions on film. The name of the actor in this scene, based on production photographs, is most likely Bert Young, a bit player who was active in films between 1935 and 1942. Film lovers can spot Young in occasional films, such as the taxi driver in *Here Comes Mr. Jordan* (1941) with Robert Montgomery and Claude Rains. He appeared most often in shorts with the Three Stooges, including their two Nazi shorts in which Moe Howard satirized Hitler. He plays one of the four storm troopers with raincoats and umbrellas in *You Nazty Spy* (1939) and a guard in *I'll Never Heil Again* (1941). Ironically enough, another cast member of *Citizen Kane* also appeared in shorts with The Three Stooges, Dorothy Comingore, who played Susan, Kane's second wife.

REPRESENTATIVE QUOTES

• For forty years appeared in Kane newsprint no public issue on which Kane papers took no stand. No public man whom Kane himself did not support or denounce. Often support, then denounce. *(Newsreel narration during the scene in which Kane appears with Hitler)*

• I talked with the responsible leaders of the great powers—England, France, Germany and Italy. They are too intelligent to embark upon a project which would mean the end of civilization as we now know it. You can take my word for it, there will be no war. *(Charles Foster Kane to a reporter upon returning from a European trip)*

10. *Conversation with the Beast* (1996)

Armin Mueller-Stahl as Adolf Hitler
Comedy

Steiner Films. Written by Armin Mueller-Stahl; Photographed by Gerard Vandenberg; Edited by Ingo Erlich; Music by Klaus-Peter Beyer; Produced by Rudolf Steiner; Directed by Armin Mueller-Stahl. B & W/Color 96 minutes

CAST LIST: Bob Balaban (*Arnold Webster*); Katharina Böhm (*Hortense*); Mark Böhm (*Dr. Hassler*); Peter Fitz (*Dr. Segebrech*); Kai Rautenberg (*Horst Sievers*); Dieter Laser (*Peter Hollsten*); Joachim Dietmar Mues (*Heinrich Pfarmann*); Harald Juhnke, Otto Sander (Hitler doubles).

COMMENTARY: *Conversation with the Beast* is an atypical comedy set in 1992 in which an American historian, Arnold Webster encounters a very elderly man who claims to be Adolf Hitler. Although he believes the man to be pulling a hoax, Webster becomes fascinated by the man's story as he interviews him over several days in his run down and claustrophobic Berlin apartment. The 103-year-old explains that Goebbels had hired six doubles to play Hitler during his years in power. The story drifts off into an examination of what is illusion and what is reality.

Hitler explains that during many historical key moments, it was actually a double rather than himself who appeared as Hitler. At the end of the war, one of the doubles, Andreas Kronstadt, volunteers to die in his place, and he and Hitler trade identities. After the war, Hitler continues to live as Kronstadt. He meets and marries Hortense, who gradually starts to dominate him until he is reduced to a henpecked and forgotten man in a wheelchair. Nobody believes him when he claims to be Hitler. Finally, he decides to reveal his entire story to Webster. After their conversation, Webster relentlessly examines ever aspect of the old man's narrative, hoping to prove it false. In the end, however, he uncovers proof in Paris that the elderly figure is indeed the genuine Adolf Hitler.

Conversation with the Beast was made in Germany, filmed in English and later dubbed into German. The picture has received very few bookings outside of Germany, and reviewers are fairly evenly divided as to the quality of the film. Two sequences in particular are liked. The first involves the Führer's difficulties in his bathroom. Because of the way the room is laid out, he has to simulate a Nazi salute in order to reach his hair dryer. The other is one of the flashback scenes in which a double recites Hamlet's famous "To be or not to be" soliloquy in the Führer's style. This scene is also a tribute to Jack Benny and Ernst Lubitsch. The flashback scenes are all shot in black and white. This film was the first to be directed by actor Armin Mueller-Stahl, who is best remembered for his performance in *Shine* (1996). He was cited for the irony and subtlety that he brought to his performance as Hitler. Bob Balaban is best known for his performance as François Truffaut's assistant in *Close Encounters of the Third Kind* (1977). *Conversation With the Beast* would certainly be worth a viewing if the picture were brought into wider distribution, either through video or cable broadcast.

11.   *Countdown to War* (1989)

Ian McKellan as Adolf Hitler
Historical drama

Granada. Written by Ronald Harwood; Edited by Roger Brown; Music by Richard Harvey; Produced by Norma Percy; Directed by Patrick Lay. Color and B & W 78 minutes

ANNOTATED CAST LIST: Michael Aldridge (*Neville Chamberlain*, British Prime Minister); Tony Briton (*Sir Nevile Henderson*, British Ambassador to Germany); John Woodvine (*Joachim von Ribbentrop*, German Foreign Minister); Peter Vaughan (*Hermann Göring*, Riech Marshal); Hilary Minster (*Birger Dahlerus*, Swedish businessman & friend of Göring); John Stratton (*Dr. Emil Hácha*, President of Czechoslovakia); Alex Norton (*Josef Stalin*, Soviet dictator); Michael Cronin (*Vyacheslav Molotov*, Soviet Foreign Minister); Barrie Rutter (*Benito Mussolini*, Italian dictator); James Laurenson (*Count Galeazzo Ciano*, Italian Foreign Minister); Stephen Moore (*Jozef Beck*, Polish Foreign Minister); Bill Stewart (*Josef Lipski*, Polish Ambassador to Germany); David Swift (*Édouard Daladier*, French Prime Minister); Robert Ashby (*Georges Bonnet*, French Foreign Minister); Michael Mellinger (*General Maurice Gamelin*, Chief of French General Staff); Bob Sherman (*William C. Bullit*, American Ambassador to France); Ronnie Stevens (*Sir Eric Phipps*, British Ambassador to France); Bernard Brown (*Charles Corbin*, French Ambassador to Great Britain); Michael Culver (*Lord Halifax*, British Foreign Minister); Anthony Bate (*Sir John Simon*, British Foreign Secretary); Lee Montague (*Leslie Hore-Belisha*, Secretary of State for War); Jack Galloway (*Malcolm MacDonald*, Secretary of State for Dominion Affairs); Jonathan Coy (*R. A. Butler*, Foreign office official); Bernard Gallagher (*Arthur Greenwood*, Opposition leader in Parliament); John Elmes (*Ian Colvin*, British journalist).

APPRAISAL AND SYNOPSIS: This British telefilm makes an extraordinary effort to maintain historical accuracy, basing almost all of the dialogue upon primary sources and using it in proper context. Subtitles carefully identify the locale of the major scenes as well as the identity of the participants. Seven noted historians served as official advisors, including Jonathan Haslam, Anthony Reed and David Irving, author of *Hitler's War*, one of the most detailed and documented volumes dealing with the German side of World War II. Interesting to note, Irving later became a controversial figure when his views began to veer toward fringe groups who deny the Nazi's program of genocide.

The action covers the period from March 15, 1938, when Hitler's forces marched into Moravia and Bohemia, the remaining areas of Czechoslovakia, through September 3, 1939, when England and France declared war on Germany. The focus of attention is fairly equally divided between Neville Chamberlain and the British cabinet and Adolf Hitler and his advisors, principally Reich Marshal Göring and Foreign Minister von Ribbentrop. There are also side trips to the offices of Stalin, Mussolini and Daladier, the French Prime Minister. The meticulous account is largely seventy minutes of talking heads, with occasional newsreel footage of the events being discussed. The events unfold like a intricate chess match over the future of Europe, with both Chamberlain and Hitler continually misreading each other. In the long run, Hitler anticipated an eventual war against the Allies, perhaps in 1942, but his limited goal was the recovery of Danzig, a city with a German majority. Hitler was willing to trade Czech territory to Poland in exchange for the recovery of the former Prussian lands. It is only when he is rebuffed by the Poles that he grows obstinate and greedy, planning to devour the bulk of Poland. The film's point is fascinating, particularly when they compete for an alliance with the Soviet Union, as Stalin chuckles to himself that he has competing suitors.

Countdown to War is compelling as it shows the European governments blunder and bluster into the most destructive war of all times. Some notable events that are usually overlooked, such as the Nazi occupation of the Lithuanian port city of Memel on March 23, 1939, are included and placed in proper context in the scenario. Oddly enough, the script omits several major figures from the film. Winston Churchill is excluded, for example, and his name is mentioned only once, when the British implication that excluding Churchill from the cabinet was a gesture to the Nazis showing that they are willing to negotiate. Other notables not on the scene include Franklin Roosevelt, Joseph Goebbels and Francisco Franco.

The film is filled with many intriguing scenes, all the more impressive because they are based on documented fact. The scenes between Ribbentrop and Stalin are spellbinding. Ribbentrop tries to act like a diplomat, whereas Stalin acts like a blunt peasant, cutting to the chase by demanding what price Hitler is willing to pay in terms of territory in exchange for an alliance. Other memorable bits include Hitler munching on popcorn while watching newsreels, Count Ciano's distress at Berchtesgaden after being served a salad dressed with flour and vinegar, Mussolini's absurd request to Hitler for a huge donation of natural resources and the revolt of Chamberlain's cabinet when he vacillates over issuing an ultimatum for German withdrawal from Poland. At the conclusion, Hitler turns to Ribbentrop after receiving the British ultimatum and exclaims, "Now what?" The end credits rolls as wailing air raid sirens provide the answer to Hitler's rhetorical question. For anyone who prefers straight historical drama, *Countdown to War* certainly fills the bill. Michael Aldrige's reading of Chamberlain is quite unique, and the other supporting players are admirable, although the British accents sported by the entire cast is occasionally disconcerting.

HITLER PORTRAYAL: Ian McKellan portrays Hitler in a more dry and business-like fashion than most other performers, with a minimum of tantrums and histrionics. Although argumentative, he is more often pensive, calculating and unemotional as he attempts to bluff and outmaneuver his opponents. On occasion, since the actor makes no attempt to disguise his British accent, his reading as Hitler even seems droll. Up until the end of the picture, the Führer is convinced the Allies will back down over his scheme to annex Danzig and the Polish corridor. His brinkmanship finally backfires, due to his arrogant assessment of the appeasement policy and his reliance on the dubious judgment of Joachim von Ribbentrop. Although McKellan presents Hitler with a more human personality, his actions lead to the same abhorrent results, which renders his matter of fact tone rather chilling. McKellan must have relished his interpretation as Hitler, because he applied it almost whole cloth to his version of *Richard III* (1995). In fact, Shakespeare's entire play is reset from the 15th century to the 1930s, and McKellan plays Richard as if he were a fascist dictator, an innovative and stimulating concept.

REPRESENTATIVE QUOTES

• I hope nothing happens to him. We don't want a dead Czech in the Chancellery. *(Ribbentrop to Göring when Dr. Hácha passes out while talking with Hitler)*

• I was terribly ill for the whole trip. I have to admit it, I am not a good sailor. I had to stay up half the night on that dreadful ship waiting for the Lithuanians to make up their minds. Oh God, was I seasick. (*Hitler to himself while watching a newsreel on the takeover of Memel*)

• We have repeatedly told you that Italy will not be ready for war until 1942 at the earliest.... Does the Führer have a date in mind? (*Count Ciano to Hitler*) Yes, within fifteen days, at the latest by the end of this month. The advance must be completed before the rains turn Poland into an impossible swamp. It could happen at any moment. (*Hitler*)

• The British and the French want us to agree to the Russian army entering Polish territory? ... It's outrageous! If we let them in, they will never leave... With the Germans, we may risk losing our freedom. With the Russians, we lose our souls. (*Josef Beck by telephone to the Polish Ambassador to France*)

• There are no outstanding personalities in Britain and France. I saw them at Munich. Our enemies are small fries, no masters, no men of action. (*Hitler to Göring during a war council*)

12. *The Death of Adolf Hitler* (1972)

Frank Findlay as Adolf Hitler
Historical drama

London Weekend Productions. Written by Vincent Tilsey; Photographed by Jeremy Godwin; Edited by Rex Firkin; Music by Jerome Kern; Produced & directed by Rex Firkin. Color 107 minutes

ANNOTATED CAST LIST: Caroline Mortimer (*Eva Braun*, Hitler's mistress); Oscar Quitak (*Dr. Joseph Goebbels*, Propaganda Minister); Marion Mathie (*Magda Goebbels*, His wife); Mark Praid (*Helmut Goebbels*, Their eldest son who is brought by Hitler into the military briefing); Ed Devereaux (*Martin Bormann*, Hitler's private secretary); Michael Lees (*Albert Speer*, Munitions Minister); Robert Cawdron (*Hermann Göring*, Reich Marshal); Michael Sheard (*Heinrich Himmler*, Interior Minister & Head of SS); Ray McNally (*Dr. Karl Gebhardt*, Himmler's doctor who asks for Red Cross position); Dan Meaden (*Colonel Otto Günsche*, Hitler's personal adjutant); Tony Steedman (*Alfred Jodl*, General & Chief of Operations); Raymond Adamson (*Wilhelm Keitel*, Field Marshal & Chief of the High Command); Julian Fox (*Colonel Nicolaus von Below*, Hitler's Luftwaffe adjutant); Inigo Jackson (*Hermann Fegelein*, SS General executed for desertion); Clare Jenkins (*Gretl Fegelein*, His wife & Eva Braun's sister); Derek Francis (*Dr. Theodor Morell*, medical quack who serves as Hitler's personal physician); Peter Blythe (*Dr. Ludwig Stumpfegger*, Hitler's surgeon who cares for him after Morell's departure); Harry Brooks, Jr. (*Artur*

Axmann, Head of the Hitler Youth); Michael Turner (*Hans Krebs*, Chief of Army General Staff); Clifford Rose (*Karl Koller*, Chief of Luftwaffe General Staff); Willy Bowman (*Robert Ritter von Greim*, Officer who flies to the bunker to be appointed new head of Luftwaffe); Myvanwy Jenn (*Hanna Reitsch*, Greim's female pilot who idolizes Hitler); Wanda Moore (*Traudl Junge*, Hitler's dictation secretary); Mitzi Rogers (*Gerda Christian*, Hitler's filing secretary); John Ringham (*Walter Wagner*, City official who marries Hitler & Eva Braun); John Carlin (*Wilhelm Zander*, SS Officer dispatched with Hitler's will and marriage license); Richard Hampton (*Heinz Lorenz*, Official also entrusted with a copy of Hitler's will); Carole Boyd (*Constanze Manzialy*, Bunker cook); Jonathan Elsom (*Heinz Linge*, Hitler's valet); Alan Brown (Telephone adjutant in the bunker); Richard Bebb (*Admiral Karl Dönitz*, Head of the Navy & Hitler's appointed successor); Norman Ettlinger (*Vice Admiral Erich Voss*, Dönitz's liaison officer in the bunker); Geoffrey Toone (*Joachim von Ribbentrop*, Foreign Minister); Hector Ross (*Wilhelm Burgdorf*, Chief of Military Personnel); Michael Richmond (Jewish baker in Hitler's nightmare); Sally Sanders, Christine Ozanne (Women brought into the bunker by the staff); Mary Henry (Sewer prostitute in Hitler's nightmare); Peter Elliott (Male sewer prostitute in Hitler's nightmare); Lindsay Narker, Marion Thanich, Mandy Perryment, Martine Chapman, Lisa Moss (Goebbels' children); David de Keyser (Narrator); Sabre (*Blondi*, Hitler's dog).

APPRAISAL AND SYNOPSIS: *The Death of Adolf Hitler* is an eccentric English telefilm initially broadcast on videotape, but later released on film in the Far East, Australia and South Africa. The historical drama is basically constructed like a domestic soap opera crossed with Edward Albee's *Who's Afraid of Virginia Woolf?* It is presented more or less as a stage play, with all of the characters having hidden psychological agendas. There are numerous weeping fits by the secretaries,

Göring, Goebbels, Eva Braun and Hitler himself. Magda Goebbels, for example, actually hates her husband and essentially intends to murder her children as her subliminal revenge on him. Eva Braun is depicted as pushy and arrogant, moreover she is somewhat mad, a condition that becomes most apparent in her farewell scene with Albert Speer, when she depicts the afterlife as an endless series of picnics with the Führer. As for Hitler, he is completely daft, as he blathers on non-stop for most of the production, continually shouting, with only a few quiet moments, the inverse of the approach of Anthony Hopkins and Alec Guinness in similar productions. In fact, Findley's performance can give many viewers a headache, since it is very difficult to understand his bellowing which even becomes distorted on the soundtrack. The drama concentrates on the last ten days of Hitler's life, from his birthday on April 20, 1945, until his suicide in the middle of the afternoon of April 30th. After his birthday reception, however, the plot immediately begins to ramble. Dr. Gebhardt has an audience with the Führer, seeking confirmation of his appointment as head of the German Red Cross. He makes Hitler sick when he informs him that the shade of his desk lamp is made out of human skin from concentration camp victims. The Führer rushes to the bathroom where he vomits. Incidentally, the decor of the bunker set is far too elaborate. The bathroom, for example, is stylishly tiled, and the Führer's sitting room includes a marble fireplace. Eva begins a campaign to persuade her lover to stop sleeping with his military uniform on. Instead, her persuasions only inspire the Führer to have a nightmare set in the sewers of Vienna where a Jewish baker refuses to sell him bread because he is penniless. Next, several prostitutes, both male and female, try to lure him into their clutches. Finally, he is harassed by rats, which sets him screaming. The rat/sewer illusion haunts Hitler for the rest of the film, and it seems rather flimsy to blame Hitler's anti–Semitism upon a Jewish baker who refused to spare him a stale crust of bread when he was destitute in his youth.

The story proceeds to depict the principal events in the bunker, namely the endless military conferences during which the Führer explodes when the counterattacks that he orders to relieve the siege of Berlin all fail to materialize. When Göring's radiogram regarding his succession as Führer is interpreted by Goebbels as an ultimatum, Hitler launches into another towering rage against "the drug addict." Then, when news of Himmler's feelers for negotiations is discovered, the pattern of the Führer's outrage is again repeated. The Russian army continues their stranglehold on Berlin, coming closer and closer to the bunker. Meanwhile, Eva's campaign begins to succeed, since the Führer wears fewer and fewer clothes to bed each evening. One night, when Eva happens to mention marriage, Hitler consents. Eva becomes delirious with joy, but the next day he refuses to allow her to wear white at the ceremony, since she hasn't been entitled to wear white for years (clearly alluding to their history of carnal relations).

Suddenly, a new obsession begins to consume Hitler. After he has cyanide capsules tested on Blondi, the dog appears to suffer inordinately. Hitler then asks to see a copy of his original order to purge Europe of Jews and other inferior races, to make sure he didn't mention dogs in the document. His two secretaries, Traudl Junge and Gerda Christian explain that this had never been an official order. The Führer rants and bullies them into searching their files again and again to find the order, finally tossing their files around in a furious tirade.

Hitler and Eva marry, but the sullen Führer fails to answer any questions, such as those relating to his freedom from any heretical disease, but merely gives a slight nod in each case. That night, Hitler finally goes to bed with Eva wearing only a nightshirt. He complains to her about his secretaries. She suggests that they merely retype the order with the original date from 1941, and then he could resign it. Hitler pops out of bed,

throws on an overcoat, and dictates a new order for his secretaries: "Kill the Jews!" When they point out that he never would have issued such a curt document, he rattles off an elaborately worded command that basically says the same thing. Later, when Traudl brings him the document, he criticizes her because the date listed is 1941 (which is what he had ordered). He then tears up a cardboard model of proposed government buildings for the city of Linz, asking the confused secretary if she wishes him to autograph the fragments for her.

By the time Hitler is ready to commit suicide, Traudl brings him the retyped document bearing the current day's date. When he and Eva seclude themselves to end their lives, the Führer takes the paper with him to sign as his last official act. Eva asks him why the document is important, and Hitler launches into a long, incoherent explanation and winds up ripping up the document as he speaks. He finally sits on his couch and asks Eva to help him steady the gun as he aims it against his temple. Outside the room, the other Nazis wait nervously until they hear a shot ring out. In the room, Hitler's position is unchanged on the couch, with a small wound on the side of his head with only a small trickle of blood. Eva plays her favorite song, "Smoke Gets in Your Eyes," on the phonograph. She then bites down on the cyanide capsule as she embraces Hitler's corpse, finally collapsing in his lap. The scene blacks out with the sounds of a crackling fire, presumably their makeshift funeral pyre in the Chancellery garden just outside the bunker entrance.

It is difficult to determine the intended point of Vincent Tilsey's script. The story seems to shuffle here and there to no real purpose. Perhaps he might have intended it as a black comedy, but if so it misfires because of the uneven script. It is also difficult to catalog the number of idiosyncrasies of this production. For example, the Goebbels children bring a boardgame into the bunker called "Catch the Jews!" Eva even boasts that with this game Holde Goebbels has already

Frank Findlay, before and after the suicide, from *The Death of Adolf Hitler*. **Caroline Mortimer is Eva Braun.**

killed 45, 000 Jews and she is only seven. Of course, this board game is merely a figment of the writer's bizarre imagination. The prop game illustrates how everything is overdone in the production. To embarrass his military advisers, Hitler prompts young Helmut Goebbels to lecture them with his theory about how to defeat the Allies. (Incidentally, Goebbels in fact called each of his six children with names beginning with H to honor Hitler.) When Field Marshal von Greim's pilot, Hanna Reitsch sees the Führer, she throws herself at his feet, kissing the hem of his trousers until he starts to scream for her to get out. Speer, in his farewell meeting with Hitler, dramatically pours out his scorn upon him, leaving the Führer weeping. While Speer did reveal that he ignored the scorched earth orders, he certainly didn't throw a fit as Michael Lees does in the scene. When Hitler and Goebbels plan to execute General Fegelein for attempting to desert, they both pound the table screaming, "Blood! Blood! Blood!" until they collapse in laughter. Since General Fegelein was married to Eva's sister, Hitler later tells Eva that her brother-in-law's death is intended as a wedding gift. Like much of this film, the comment is a pointless gesture which neither Eva, nor the audience, can understand.

HITLER PORTRAYAL: Frank Findlay is a distinguished actor with an extraordinary career, earning an Academy Award nomination for his performance as Iago in *Othello* (1965). His interpretation of Hitler is undoubtedly one of the most unconvincing of all, not merely because his resemblance to the historical Hitler is very weak. The real problem is that his reading totally lacks any insight, fervor or notoriety. It is simply an empty, hollow rant, and even traditional gestures associated with Hitler are seldom used. It is all "sound and fury signifying nothing." Moreover, several of Findlay's unending monologues are largely incoherent because many of his words cannot even be understood even though he speaks pure English throughout. In fact, all of the characters speak straight English without any trace of a German accent. Even the word "Führer" is never used, sticking with the plain word "leader" instead, which lacks the distinctive edge the German word has, but then they are inconsistent, saying "Heil Hitler" instead of "Hail Hitler." Since most of the cast also speak with a rather stuffy upper crust British dialect, it gives the production a rather awkward air. At one point, it seems that Findlay might have intended his performance to be molded around the numerous injections given to Hitler by Theodor Morell, the unconventional doctor who served as his personal physician. Dr. Stumpfegger, the SS surgeon who took over the Führer's medication after Dr. Morell left the bunker, considered that these shots actually made Hitler a drug addict, but this aspect was simply dropped as the rest of the story unfolded. The only conclusion that can be drawn from Findlay's performance is that Hitler was simply and unquestionably a madman, and there is no need for any additional explanation.

REPRESENTATIVE QUOTES

• Wanted me to take my clothes off. She doesn't know. She doesn't understand. She doesn't understand. I slept in my clothes for years. Had to, had to, in the sewers with rats. *(Hitler while petting his dog Blondi, having just left Eva in his bed)*

• You can't even laugh either, can you, eh? By my one and only God, I would like to kill you, but you are necessary. *(Hitler to Bormann as an aside while he jokes with Goebbels)*

• Do you want me to go down in history as a coward? Millions of dead Jews … if I didn't have the courage to put it in writing, it will make me seem little and evil and frightened. … Am I frightened? Am I little? Am I evil? See what you are doing to me? *(Hitler shrieking to his secretaries as he tosses around the papers in their office)*

• Power needs energy and energy needs fuel. Hate is the only fuel of the breadless…. We must hate. How can we hope to survive if we don't hate? It doesn't matter who we hate so long as we hate. *(Hitler to Eva just before their suicide)*

13.   *The Desert Fox* (1951)

Luther Adler as Adolf Hitler
Historical drama

20th Century–Fox. Written by Nunnally Johnson based on the biography by Desmond Young; Photographed by Norbert Brodine; Edited by James B. Clark; Music by Daniele Amfitheatrof; Produced by Nunnally Johnson; Directed by Henry Hathaway. B & W 88 minutes

ANNOTATED CAST LIST: James Mason (*Erwin Rommel*, Field Marshal known as "The Desert Fox"); Jessica Tandy (*Lucie Rommel*, His wife); William Reynolds (*Manfred Rommel*, Their son); Cedric Hardwicke (*Dr. Karl Strolin*, Mayor of Stuttgart); Leo G. Carroll (*Gerd von Rundstedt*, Field Marshal & commander of Western forces); George Macready (*General Fritz Bayerlein*, Officer at El Alamein who urges Rommel to ignore his order from Hitler); Richard Boone (*Captain Hermann Aldinger*, Adjutant to Rommel); Eduard Franz (*Colonel Claus von Stauffenberg*, Officer who plants bomb in Hitler's briefing room); John Hoyt (*Wilhelm Keitel*, Field Marshal & Chief of the High Command); Everett Sloane (*Wilhelm Burgdorf*, General who informs Rommel of the treason charge); Robert Coote (British officer); Dan O'Herlihy (British Commando Captain); Paul Cavanagh, John Goldsworthy, Walter Kingsford, Peter van Eyck, Carlton Young (German military officers); Desmond Young (Himself, author of a biography about Rommel); Michael Rennie (Narrator).

APPRAISAL AND SYNOPSIS: Six years after the end of World War II, 20th Century–Fox released this sympathetic film about the leading military figure of the Third Reich. Called *The Desert Fox*, the picture is subtitled *The Story of Rommel*. It is certainly a far cry from the wartime portrayal of Erwin Rommel by Erich von Stroheim in *Five Graves to Cairo* (1943). Here James Mason crafts a sensitive portrait of an honorable man who is forced to confront the madness of the Nazi regime, which even treats its own soldiers with indifference and inhumanity. The crux of the film shows how Rommel abandons his military code of conduct to apply a higher ethical standard, even if it is treason. This film is based on the definitive biography about Rommel by Lieutenant Colonel Desmond Young, a British officer who crossed paths with the Field Marshal briefly after being taken prisoner by the Germans during the campaign in North Africa. That this film could be made so close to the end of the war is a tribute to Rommel, who was regarded with respect even before word of his participation in the conspiracy against Hitler became public knowledge.

The picture begins with a long pre-credit sequence of a raid by British commandos on Rommel's headquarters early in the North African campaign. After the credits, the film focuses on Desmond Young, his wartime encounter with Rommel and his post-war research on the man, including interviews with his widow, son and associates. Young plays himself in these scenes, but his voice as the narrator is provided by Michael Rennie. The film then flashbacks to a number of key moments in Rommel's career during the last half of the war. He is outraged when he receives absurd or suicidal orders from the Führer not to regroup or yield an inch of ground or to fight on until victory or death. At the battle of El Alamein, he asks for a repeat of an order from Hitler, crumples it and pulls back his troops to a new formation. He still defends Hitler to his subordinates, but his words sound hollow and without conviction. Later, Rommel is in a hospital in Germany when his army in North Africa is abandoned by Hitler, who makes no effort to evacuate them, and they are forced to surrender *en masse* to the Allies at Tunis. Rommel himself has lost faith in Hitler, whom he feels has betrayed his men.

Rommel is visited in the hospital by his wife Lucie, his son Manfred and Dr. Karl Strolin, the Mayor of Stuttgart, who sounds out the Field Marshal about his opinion of the war and of Hitler's leadership. Rommel believes that Germany should sue for peace, but that would be impossible as long as Hitler is in command. When he is released from the hospital, he tours the coastal defenses of France, which he finds deplorable. He reports to General von Rundstedt, commander of the Western forces, that an army of children could come ashore at most of the beaches. von Rundstedt confesses that Hitler himself now makes all tactical decisions, making a proper defense impossible.

Dr. Strolin visits Rommel again at his home, explaining that a large group of conspirators are planning to overthrow Hitler, and asks him to join the cause. Rommel, surprised by the number of prominent people in this movement, agrees to think it over. When D-Day arrives, von Rundstedt is outraged by the idiotic strategy forced on him by Hitler. When his request for reinforcements to repel the invasion of Normandy is denied, von Rundstedt foolishly tells General Keitel, supreme commander of the army, that they had better sue for peace.

Rommel goes to visit Hitler to make an effort to reason with him. Instead, the Führer is abusive, petulant and arrogant, claiming he is on the verge of unleashing weapons that will bring the Allies to their knees within weeks. At that instant, Rommel becomes fully convinced that Hitler must be removed from power by any means possible, including assassination. Unfortunately, Rommel's car is strafed by an Allied plane three days before the target date, and he is seriously wounded. On July 20th, an attempt is made to blow up Hitler and his staff while they are attending a briefing at his headquarters at Rastenburg in East Prussia. Colonel Claus von Stauffenberg brings a bomb concealed in his briefcase to this meeting, placing it under the conference table. After making excuse to leave the room, von Stauffenberg waits for the explosive to detonate. He flees after the blast, convinced that Hitler was killed, but the Führer emerges from the building only slightly injured.

Over the next few months, Rommel slowly recuperates from his injuries. Back at home, he receives a call from General Keitel, asking him to come to Berlin at once. When Rommel insists he is still not well enough to travel, Keitel sends General Bergdorf to meet with him. Manfred is convinced he will be offered a new command. Instead, Burgdorf informs Rommel that charges of treason have been drawn up against him. At first Rommel vows to fight these charges in open court, but when Burgdorf threatens his family, Rommel agrees to take poison instead. He leaves with Burgdorf after informing Lucie that his death is imminent. After their last embrace, she sees him off as if he were merely leaving on a new assignment.

The narrator reports that the Nazis gave Rommel a hero's funeral, claiming he died of the injuries received in the Allied air attack. The picture concludes with a tribute to Rommel spoken by Sir Winston Churchill, who claims he deserves respect for his hatred of Hitler and all his works, as well as for his efforts to save Germany by joining the movement to overthrow the Nazi regime. Although an interesting and enjoyable film, *The Desert Fox* has a number of weak points, including the over-use of stock footage. Unlike *Is Paris Burning?* (1966), this wartime footage doesn't always fit smoothly into the film, especially since these scenes go on far too long. Finally, the long and tedious pre-credit sequence suggests that this film was padded to bring it up to feature length. It would have been better had they used flashbacks instead to highlight events of Rommel's earlier life. As it is, the film has four or five major set pieces surrounded by tons of overused stock shots. Some of the dialogue between Rommel and von Rundstedt leaves the mistaken impression that the allied invasion of Normandy was a cakewalk accomplished with minimal difficulty and low casualties. Another weakness is the inconsistency of the accents in the picture. James Mason and Leo G. Carroll, for example, speak with their normal British accents. Richard Boone and Jessica Tandy speak like ordinary Americans, but Luther Adler speaks with thick Germanic enunciation in his scenes. Nevertheless, the plot conveys a sense of basic historical accuracy, so *The Desert Fox* seems quite authentic and believable, and the picture is an impressive tour de force for the acting talents of James Mason who makes the role of Rommel his own. The incorporation of historian and Rommel biographer Desmond Young into the film also helps to lend it a very convincing air.

HITLER PORTRAYAL: The distinguished stage and screen veteran Luther Adler is cast as Adolf Hitler in this picture. He doesn't appear on camera until the last third of the picture. When he does, it is in two highly charged and very forceful sequences. The first is his confrontation with Rommel where the Field Marshal tries in vain to make him understand the desperate military situation. Adler does not resemble Hitler very much, and he also seems too squat and jolly to be convincing. When he speaks, however, he has Hitler's vocal tones and gestures down pat, and on the whole he seems rather effective. Part of his secret is that he varies the

Lobby card for *The Desert Fox*.

pitch of his voice persuasively, avoiding the purely guttural monotone that too many Hitler performers adopt. Adler cunningly makes it clear that the Führer has taken leave of his senses, both in his denial of reality and in his almost mystical conviction that a miracle weapon will soon save him. In the second scene at Rastenburg, Adler shows brief flashes of personal charisma and humor, which also serves to broaden his overall conception of the part. He is extraordinarily convincing after the bomb blast, portraying a stunned Führer with understatement as he stumbles out of the ruins of the conference room with blackened face. When a general reaches his side to check on his condition, he calmly tells him that he is all right. One wishes there was a third scene added showing Hitler's outrage when he learns that

Rommel, the nation's most illustrious military figure, had joined the plot against him. Adler also played Adolf Hitler in *The Magic Face*, made the same year. Years later, in *The Twilight Zone* episode "The Man in the Bottle," Adler plays a man who is granted four wishes by a genie. In one wish, he asks to become the all-powerful dictator of a country who can't be voted out of office. The genie turns him into Hitler on his last day in the bunker as the Russians close in. This portion of the show is the highlight of the episode, and Adler is magnificent as he realizes how cleverly he was tricked by the genie into wasting a wish.

James Mason is regarded as the definitive screen Rommel with his performance in this picture, even though he seldom shows Rommel as the legendary warrior on the front.

Mason delves more into Rommel's internal conflict as he comes to the decision that true patriotism in the current situation technically means becoming a traitor. The entire film, in fact, is based almost exclusively on this issue. The actor conveys this internal struggle in a very skillful manner. Two years later, Mason reprised his role as Rommel in *The Desert Rats* (1953). Many other actors besides Mason and von Stroheim tackled the role over the years, including Robert Culp in *Key to Rebecca* (1985), Werner Hinz in *The Longest Day* (1962), Christopher Plummer in *Night of the Generals* (1967), Wolfgang Preiss in *Raid on Rommel* (1971), Karl Michael Vogler in *Patton* (1970) and Michael York in *Night of the Fox* (1990).

REPRESENTATIVE QUOTES

• It will be a long time before I forget what he did to the *Afrika Korps*. *(Rommel to Strolin, referring to Hitler)*

• Give me a free hand for a few months, and I'd make them pay for it … I might not be able to stop them all, but they'll know they fought an army, not a series of stationary targets. He would never let us, of course. You know how firm corporals are. *(Von Rundstedt to Rommel in regard to Hitler the tactician)*

• While you've been deciding that all is lost, we've been working, working miracles, determining the course of history for centuries to come! In the workshops and the laboratories, we've been turning out machines of destruction such as the enemy has never dreamed of! I have one in mind! I have a weapon in mind! *(Hitler to Rommel)*

• Where's Göring? *(Hitler to his staff at his military briefing in Rastenburg)* On his way now, sir. *(An adjutant's reply)* Well, when you are fat, you don't move so fast. *(Hitler's wry observation)*

14. *The Devil with Hitler* (1942/43)

Bobby Watson as Adolf Hitler
Comedy

Hal Roach Productions. Written by Cortland Fitzsimmons & Al Martin; Photographed by Robert Pittack; Edited by Bert Jordan; Special Effects by Roy Seawright; Music by Edward Ward; Produced by Glenn Tryon & Hal Roach (Executive); Directed by Gordon Douglas. B & W 87 minutes

ANNOTATED CAST LIST: Joe Devlin (*Benito Mussolini*, Il Duce, Dictator of Italy); Rex Evans (*Hermann Göring*, Reich Marshal); Charles Rogers (*Joseph Goebbels*, Minister of Propaganda); Wedgwood Nowell (*Heinrich Himmler*, Gestapo chief); **Island Plot:** Johnny Arthur (*Sukiyaki*, Japanese general); Henry Victor (*Von Popoff*, Nazi foreign minister); Ian Keith (Island Chief); Jean Porter (*Kula*, Island beauty); Frank Faylen (*Benson*, American seaman); Emory Parnell (*Spencer*, Seaman); **Devil Plot:** Alan Mowbray (The devil); George E. Stone (*Sukiyaki*, Japanese diplomat); Sig Arno (*Julius*, Hitler's valet); Herman Bing (*Louis*, Hitler's astrologer); Douglas Fowley (*Walter Hill*, Insurance salesman); Marjorie Woodworth (*Linda Krauss*, Failed spy).

APPRAISAL AND SYNOPSIS: The Three Stooges made two hilarious Hitler parodies called *You Nazty Spy* (1939) and *I'll Never Heil Again* (1941). In these twenty minute shorts, Moe Howard brilliantly lampooned the Führer, even though his impersonation was largely limited to a change in hairstyle and use of the Chaplinesque moustache. Noting the popularity of these releases, Hal Roach released two Hitler shorts of his own, *The Devil with Hitler* (1942) and *That Nazty Nuisance* (1943). At the time, Roach was experimenting with extended shorts called Streamliners which ran about 42 minutes in length. When the Streamliners proved awkward to distribute, Roach recut *The Devil with Hitler* to feature length by combining both pictures, and this is the best known version, released through United Artists.

The spoof opens with a ranting Hitler speech which no doubt startled audiences due to the remarkable physical resemblance between Watson and Hitler. The scene switches to Hades, which operates like a corporation. The board of directors is dissatisfied with the statistical reports about sin, and they consider replacing the devil with Adolf Hitler as the new Chairman of the Board. Hearing of the Board's concerns, the devil recounts a recent escapade of The Führer in which he performed poorly. At this point, *The Devil with Hitler* splices in the plot of *That Nazty Nuisance*. Hitler concludes that he needs a treaty with the mythical island nation of Nuram, and he goes on a secret mission to confer with the island chieftain who will only sign an alliance with the head man of the Axis. Mussolini and Japanese General Sukiyaki get wind of Hitler's mission and accompany him on his submarine. When they arrive, their plans are foiled by a group of American merchant marine sailors whose ship was torpedoed and who are stranded on the island. They capture Hitler and make him look foolish, finally shooting him out of the torpedo tube of his own sub.

Returning to the original *The Devil with Hitler* footage, Satan claims he can maneuver Hitler into doing a good deed within forty-eight hours, and the committee of hell agrees if he can do this, he can remain as Chairman. The Devil travels to Hitler's bedroom, where the Führer is giving a speech from his tub. Making himself invisible, the Devil trips up valet Julius, which ruins the speech and gets Julius fired. The devil then steps into the valet job, handing Hitler his robe. Using the name Gesatan, the devil worms his way into Hitler's confidence by showing up Louis, his astrologer. Try as he may, however, the devil finds it impossible to trick the Führer into doing a good deed. Hitler confers with Mussolini and Japanese diplomat Sukiyaki. When an insurance salesman approaches Hitler, the Führer decides to take a policy out on Mussolini with himself as beneficiary. Mussolini and Sukiyaki get the same idea, however, and all three men plant bombs that evening in an extended routine, but they all manage to escape the blast, and Hitler orders the arrest of the insurance salesman. Growing desperate, the devil decides to impersonate Hitler and do the good deed himself. He orders the release of the salesman as well as Linda Krauss, a failed spy. The Führer himself is arrested as an impostor, and when he straightens matters out, he commands that the two prisoners be immediately executed. In his Hitler guise, the devil lures the Führer, Mussolini and Sukiyaki into chasing him into a munitions warehouse, where he locks them in. Threatening to blow him sky high, he forces Hitler to set free the prisoners. He gives Hitler the key to the door, but the Führer fumbles with the lock and is blown up. The Board of Directors in hell give the devil a standing ovation as he returns with Hitler as his prisoner. Members of the Board grab their pitchforks and start jabbing at the Führer, as the devil orders them to "give him the works."

As a whole, *The Devil with Hitler* is a mixed bag, but the idea of ridiculing the leaders of the Axis during the traumatic early days of the war permits one to overlook a multitude of weaknesses. The threading of the two plots is awkward, and no explanation is given how Hitler, Mussolini and Sukiyaki got back from the island of Nuram. Who is Sukiyaki anyway? He goes from being a general to a diplomat, but the real puzzle is why they didn't use the figure of Tojo, the wartime leader of Japan, instead of this fictitious substitute. Both Johnny Arthur and George E. Stone are terrible in the role. Arthur played a similar role more effectively as the spy Sakima in the serial *The Masked Marvel*. Both Mowbray and Watson are diverting in their satirical roles, and as a curiosity item the film is amusing. Of course, this type of humor dates quickly, and the jokes about concentration camps would never have been made if the full extent of that horror had been known. Likewise the racist remarks about the Japanese is another element that is regrettable, but understandable as a symptom of the hysteria following the attack on Pearl Harbor. Some of the slapstick is hilarious, but most of it is down-

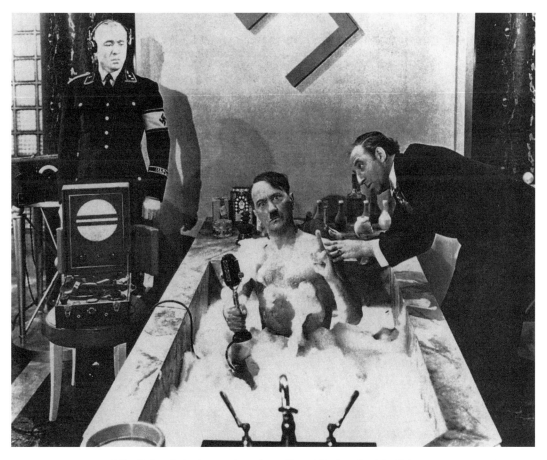

The Führer's bathroom broadcast from *The Devil with Hitler.*

right idiotic. The humor in the island sub-plot is far less funny than in the devil se-quences. The highlight of the slapstick com-edy is the moment when Hitler's hand gets stuck on the handle of a pull down wall map. The invisible devil cuts the cord, and Hitler falls through several floors where people stop and "Heil" him as he crashes through. An-other high point is a silly song warbled by Hitler as he paints a wall mural for relax-ation. The devil's scenes with Hitler are fairly good, although here too there are in-consistencies. At some points, the devil has to rely on a pill to make himself invisible, but at other times, he fades in and out of view at will. Members of the Board of Directors also appear to warn Satan that doing a good deed while posing as Hitler does not count, yet they accept his equally phony solution

by forcing the Führer to release the prison-ers due to a threat on his life. It is ironic to note that hell is managed like a business cor-poration, where the head can be ousted by the rest of the board. It seems Satan is far less authoritarian in hell than Hitler on Earth.

HITLER PORTRAYAL: Robert "Bobby" Watson played the role of Adolf Hitler more than any other performer in a total of eight films (or nine if you include *The Heavenly Body* [1943] in which a photo insert of Wat-son as Hitler is used in the film). In fact, he is the only individual completely successful in playing the role either straightforward or for laughs. Born Robert Watson Kuecher in Springfield, Illinois, one year before the birth of Adolf Hitler in 1889, the actor started his show business career as a vaude-

The Duce (Joe Devlin) and the Führer (Bobby Watson).

ville dancer, appearing in such silent films as *The Song and Dance Man* (1926). He was also the lead in Republic's first musical, *Syncopation* (1930). He also wrote several films which were produced in the 1930s. The highlight of his career in his later years was his memorable routine with Donald O'Connor and Gene Kelly as their elocution teacher in *Singin' in the Rain* (1952), and featured in the song "Moses Supposes." Invariably, most listings of Watson's screen credits confuse him with a child actor with the same name who appeared in the *Boys Town* films and alternatively used the billing "Bobs" Watson. In *The Devil with Hitler*, Watson has many highlights, particularly his hilarious song and dance routine on the scaffolding, showing his unexpected prowess as a physical comedian. His high-pitched screams when he is trapped in the exploding munitions warehouse are also cleverly done and quite funny. Joe Devlin does a good job as Mussolini, Watson's counterpart, which is only a few pegs weaker than Jack Oakie's

masterful rendition of the Duce in *The Great Dictator*. Alan Mowbray does a fine job as the devil, and he delivers his lines with a particular zest. His last line in the film, "This is only the beginning, folks, only the beginning," has a truly malicious ring to it, as he promises the audience that Hitler's torments will indeed last forever in hell.

REPRESENTATIVE QUOTES

• If there is anything on Earth we need, it is Adolf Hitler right here in hell *(Member of Hell's Board of Directors)*

• The new order will change all that. There will be one time, one people, one Reich. *(Hitler to Von Popoff, who is late due to a time zone mix-up)* That's right! *(Mussolini)*

• Look, Gesatan, I can change hands without missing a stroke. *(Hitler while displaying his talents with a paintbrush)*

• You are you and I am me and never we shall meet! *(Hitler to the devil)*

15. *The Dirty Dozen: Next Mission* (1985)

Michael Sheard as Adolf Hitler (cameo)
War drama

MGM/United Artists. Written by Michael Kane; Photographed by John Stanier; Edited by Alan Strachan; Music by Richard Harvey; Produced by Harry R. Sherman; Directed by Andrew V. McLaglen. Color 97 minutes

ANNOTATED CAST LIST: Lee Marvin (*Major Reisman*, Maverick American officer); Ernest Borgnine (*General Worden*, Reisman's superior); Richard Jaeckel (*Sergeant Bowren*, Reisman's aide); Wolf Kahler (*General Sepp Dietrich*, SS district commander of Southern France); Ken Wahl (*Louis Valentine*, Commando); Sonny Landham (*Sam Sixkiller*, Commando); Stephen Hattersley (*Otto Deutsch*, Commando); Ricco Ross (*Arlen Driggers*, Black sharpshooter commando); Jay Benedict (*Didier Leclair*, French commando); Dan O'Herlihy (*Conrad Perkins*, Commando); Rolf Saxon (*Robert Wright*, Commando); Larry Wilcox (*Tommy Wells*, Commando); Michael John Paliotti (*Baxley*, Commando); Paul Herzberg (*Reynolds*, Commando); Jeff Harding (*Sanders*, Commando); Sam Douglas (Anderson, Commando); Russell Somers (*Gary Rosen*, Commando dismissed by Reisman); John Malcolm (*Field Marshal Meisterlein*); Morgan Shepherd (German general); Bruce Boa (German colonel); Crispin DiNys (*Schmidt*, chess playing officer shot by Dietrich); Denis Holmes (*General Pierre Fontaine*, Allied officer playing golf); Alan Barry (*General Bulldog Bardsley*, Allied officer playing golf); Don Fellows (*General Trent Tucker*, Allied officer playing golf).

APPRAISAL AND SYNOPSIS: The original *Dirty Dozen* (1967) was one of the cleverest, most entertaining movies with a World War II setting, a cross between *The Seven Samurai* (1954) and the TV show *Combat*. Audacious, outrageous and boasting one of the strongest cast of character actors ever assembled, the plot of the film involves twelve army prisoners, misfits all facing execution or long stretches at hard labor, who are recruited for a near suicide mission behind enemy lines with a full pardon awaiting the survivors. Eighteen years later, MGM decided to make a telefilm as a sequel. Since eleven of the Dirty Dozen were killed in the original, the production recruited three of the other characters, squad leader Reisman (Lee Marvin), his drill sergeant Bowren (Richard Jaeckel) and shifty American General Worden (Ernest Borgnine), and they concocted a retread plot in the same fashion as Yul Brynner did for *Return of the Magnificent Seven* (1966), with equally anemic results. There are two main flaws in the film. First, the characters and personalities of the new dozen are drab, bland and forgettable. Whereas the original had the colorful talents of John Cassavetes, Telly Savalas, Donald Sutherland, Charles Bronson, Clint Walker and others, each with a unique, bizarre personality, the retreads are indistinguishable and interchangeable, with only Stephen Hattersley as Deutch and Ricco Ross as Driggers providing the slightest spark of individuality. Then, the mission devised is one of the most foolish and asinine imaginable. As the lynchpin of the plot, it is so irrational that it is nearly insults the audience. A small group of golf playing Allied generals at a British course get wind, in autumn 1944, that another plot is afoot against Hitler. One of them, General Worden, gets the idea that if Hitler is replaced by a more competent leader, the war might last longer. No one even questions this absurd conclusion. In fact, had the Rastenburg assassination of Hitler succeeded in July 1944, the new government would undoubtedly have sought an immediate end to the conflict. If one considers for a moment the lives that could have been saved, civilian and military, if the war had ended in autumn 1944, the numbers are staggering. For example, the deaths in the concentration camps accelerated during the last eight months of the war, including millions of Jews, gypsies, clergy and other opponents of the Nazi regime. Yet to see these out-of-touch Allied generals, hunting for a lost golf ball, develop the policy to send a commando mission to destroy General Sepp Dietrich, Hitler's potential assassin, is almost infuriating. Therefore, the next mission of the new Dirty Dozen is simply to save Hitler, the inverse of the equally bizarre wartime poverty row effort, *Hitler— Dead or Alive*.

As the plot unfolds, Major Reisman is facing a court martial for pilfering a truckload of steaks intended for the brass as a treat for the soldiers of his unit. General Worden rescues him before he is sentenced, and in exchange he must organize another Dirty Dozen unit recruited from army prisoners facing either the death sentence or long prison terms. His drill sergeant actually locates thirteen volunteers for the suicide mission, but the superstitious Reisman dismisses the first recruit who cracks wise as an object lesson to the rest, bringing the number back to the traditional dozen. The training scenes which follow are bland and lifeless. The only good moments are bits of dialogue lifted and recycled from the original. Very little thought appears to have been spent on analyzing their mission. For example, the marksman of the group, Driggers, is black. Yet, their game plan calls for him to pose as a Nazi soldier at a German airport. Everyone is so slow on the uptake, that it is only moments before their arrival that Driggers speaks up and says that it is unlikely he could pass for a German soldier, so Reisman bandages him like a mummy. Of course, his hands are not covered, and a Gestapo agent spots him. The dozen, who recruit a bus, have to fight it out with the motorcycle patrol, whom they wipe out, but the bus crashes in the process. Having lost their bus, the gang begin a haphazard campaign to rendezvous with the train on which General Dietrich is traveling. Meanwhile, the general is playing chess on the train with another officer. This match is supposed to demonstrate that Dietrich is Germany's leading tactician, but instead he seems like a bungler, and he kills his opponent when he

questions his loyalty to Hitler. The efforts of the Dirty Dozen are likewise unimpressive, as they run into one obstacle after another, including another shoot out with German troops who question the presence of a black German soldier in the squad. A number of the dozen are killed, but since they never stood out as individuals, their elimination is not missed. Somehow, they make contact with the French Underground and parachute to the spot where Dietrich's train has stopped. They watch as several items, including Beethoven's piano, are loaded onto Dietrich's treasure train. Then an airplane arrives and lands on the field next to the train. Hitler emerges to inspect the treasure. This visit is never explained in the plot. Hitler undoubtedly has many pianos once used by Beethoven (not to mention those of Wagner, Mozart, etc.) What lures him to fly to the south of France in a small plane? Was this part of Dietrich's plan to kill Hitler? The audience is never told.

Driggers, the sniper, is preparing to kill General Dietrich, but gets a better idea when he sees Hitler. He believes that a well placed bullet could end the war. The survivors of the dozen all think that is a great idea, except Major Reisman, who insists their target is Dietrich. not Hitler. Reisman bullies Driggers into doing it his way, and Dietrich is slain, but Hitler escapes unscathed. (Can you imagine the audience cheering, "Wow! Hitler is safe! Our guys have succeeded! The mission is a success! Yippee!") Anyway, the dozen, their ranks thinned to four men and Reisman, fight off the German troops and steal Hitler's plane, flying back to Allied territory. (How fortunate one of the surviving men is a pilot). They find a briefcase filled with jewels under one of the seats, and Reisman tells the survivors to split the booty. Driggers, wounded in the last gunbattle, finally expires. They crash their plane on a farm after crossing the English Channel, and as the film ends, the men try to convince the gun toting local militia that they are Yanks. It is a good thing they didn't tell the farmers that they just saved Hitler's life, or they probably would have been shot. Here the picture mercifully ends. Yet, the Dirty Dozen managed to return for two more telefilms, *The Dirty Dozen: The Deadly Mission* (1987) and *The Dirty Dozen: The Fatal Mission* (1988). Lee Marvin and Richard Jaeckel wisely avoided these efforts, but Ernest Borgnine hung around as General Worden, finding another sap to head the ragtag squad, Major Wright, played by none other than Telly Savalas (who played Maggot, one of the original Dirty Dozen). Reportedly, these two telefilm were a genuine improvement over *Next Mission*, so the Fox network tried a TV series in 1988, filmed in Yugoslavia. This series crash and burned relatively quickly.

HITLER PORTRAYAL: Michael Sheard, a character actor of Scottish descent, is no stranger to the role of Adolf Hitler, having first assumed the part in 1973 episode of *The Tomorrow People*. His other Hitler screen performances are chronicled in this book, as well as his portrayal of Himmler in *The Bunker*. Sheard played Göring's double in an episode of '*Allo, 'Allo*, a comedy set in a Parisian café during the occupation. His most significant role, however, was as Admiral Ozzle, the Imperial fleet commander in *The Empire Strikes Back* (1980), who is executed by Darth Vader for being "as clumsy as he is stupid." The scene of Sheard gasping for air as Darth Vader makes use of the "force" is one of the most memorable in the Star Wars saga. Most of Sheard's scenes in *The Dirty Dozen: Next Mission* are distant shots, as seen through binoculars or the sight of Digger's rifle. Sheard wears a gray military uniform with a trenchcoat draped over his shoulders in cape-like fashion. When General Dietrich is shot, his blood splatters all over the Führer, who is momentarily stunned and stands still, amazed. Then he spins around and quickly takes cover. Sheard handles this scene very well, making it the highlight of this film with his credible reaction shot. Unfortunately, it is about the only worthwhile scene in the dismal production. Incidentally, using the figure of Sepp Diet-

rich as the potential Hitler assassin is an unusual choice, for the historical Sepp Dietrich was a die-hard Nazi ruffian dating back to the mid-'20s. He also served as the Führer's personal bodyguard and was a loyal squad leader in the purge of 1934. Far from being the idealized Aryan portrayed by Wolf Kahler, the real Dietrich was coarse-looking, vulgar and distinguished by his prominent broken nose. He was also not a military genius as suggested by the script, Dietrich was merely an adequate officer. Neither was he killed during the war but survived, serving two separate prison terms for his brutal conduct during the Nazi regime. Dietrich died a free man in 1966.

REPRESENTATIVE QUOTES

• Our intelligence reports there is going to be another assassination attempt on Hitler. *(General Fontaine)* Again? They can't do that, kill their own Führer, that's cheating… Hitler is our best ally. We need him alive. He is valuable to us. *(General Worden)*

• Army mentality never ceases to amaze me. *(Reisman upon learning his mission is to save Hitler)*

• He can't kill Hitler if he is dead himself. *(Worden to Reisman)* No sir, not even in the army. *(The major's reply)*

• Do you realize who that is? I shoot him, the war is over. Now. Right here. *(Driggers to Reisman, who continues to insist that the marksman kill Dietrich and not Hitler)*

16.   *The Empty Mirror* (1996)

Norman Rodway as Adolf Hitler
Fantasy

Universal/Lion's Gate. Written by Barry J. Hershey & R. Buckingham, based upon a story by Barry J. Hershey incorporating selections from the writings & speeches of Adolf Hitler; Photographed by Frederick Elmes; Edited by Marc Grossman; Music by John Frizzell and Richard Wagner; Produced by David D. Johnson, M. Jay Roach & William Dance; Directed by Barry J. Hershey. Color 119 minutes

ANNOTATED CAST LIST: Camilla Soe-berg (*Eva Braun*, Hitler's mistress); Joel Grey (*Dr. Joseph Goebbels*, Propaganda Min-ister); Glenn Shadix (*Hermann Göring*, Reich Marshal); Peter Michael Goetz (*Sigmund Freud*, Renowned psychiatrist); Doug McKeon (Hitler's typist); Hope Allen (Woman in black); Lori Scott (Floating fe-male spirit); Raul Kobrinsky (Jailer with nightstick); Sara Benoit (Nurse); John Paul Jones (Large man); Alan Richards (Strange looking man); Randy Zielinski, Shannon Yowell, Courtney Dale, Elizabeth Hershey, Christopher Levitus, Chip Marks, Enzo Pace, Heather Rogers (Hitler Youth); Ce-line Clements, Elaine Collins, Isabelle Dahlin, Kathryn Dwyer, Gudrun Giddings, Valerie Hemmerich, Bridget Holloman, Krista Kendall, Kristen Kloster, Debora Ann Krey, Emily Love, Heather Leigh Morgan (Blond women); Eric Balsim, Kolby Dav-enport, Aquarelle Emery, Brock Hutchins, Callie Marks, Virginia Mutton, Taylor Pearson, Jake Schnablegger, Alexandra Still-well, Kiley White (Blond children).

APPRAISAL AND SYNOPSIS: *The Empty Mirror* is an extraordinary film, as if Luigi Pirandello's *Six Characters in Search of an Author* had been crossed with *The Rise and Fall of the Third Reich*. It provides greater screen time for Adolf Hitler than any other motion picture, a two hour phantasmagoria in which Norman Rodway is front and center almost continually, and when he is not, the image of the real Hitler is, taken from newsreels, *The Triumph of the Will*, Eva Braun's home movies or photographic stills. This film is a psychodrama, almost a one-man show in which Hitler attempts to justify himself to himself and fails. There can be differing in-terpretations of the setting of the film. To some, this is an internal conflict as Hitler recollects his legacy during his final days in the bunker. Or it could be his last night-mare, in which he feels he has to explain himself to the youth of Germany, elucidat-ing his philosophy. To others, Hitler is al-ready dead, and this is his prison in hell, where he is eternally damned to rationalize

his countless crimes. In either case, Hitler is in a surreal prison, in which he has the abil-ity to conjure up individuals to facilitate his self-assessment, including the eminent ana-lyst, Siegmund Freud. Hitler spends most of his time in this limbo watching old films, dictating a new set of memoirs and chatting over old times with Goebbels, Göring or Eva Braun. Significantly, it seems only one of these people can be present at any one time. Sometimes he lectures groups of chil-dren, or members of the Hitler Youth or himself in the mirror. Toward the end, his prison starts to overflow with blood, as he seems overwhelmed with images of the holocaust. Hitler deteriorates into an aged shell of a man. He tries to escape through the projection screen showing images of his heyday, but while his arms penetrate into this mysterious dimension, he himself is un-able to pass through. The last shot of the film is a close up of the elderly Hitler, all his defenses peeled away as he has no answer to placate the evil he has unleashed upon the world.

The Empty Mirror is primarily an art house film, since general audiences might lack the patience to sit through two hours of unadulterated Hitler. Some viewers might object to the somewhat positive view of Hitler that emerges at times, failing to no-tice the dark undercurrents and mockery that accompany these moments. On the other hand, certain aspects of Hitler's past are not explored or even mentioned, such as his obsession with his niece, Geli Raubal, who was either murdered or driven to sui-cide because of her uncle. Benito Mussolini is also totally absent from the proceedings. On the whole, Barry Hershey has crafted his first feature film with extraordinary care, leaving a number of deliberate ambiguities for the audience to resolve. His cast selec-tions are fine, particularly Joel Grey as the sardonic Goebbels. At certain moments, Grey seems to relish the parallel to his cin-ema triumph as the master of ceremonies in *Cabaret* (1972). Glen Shadix renders Göring as a figure of comic relief in the drama, the

target of the Führer's secret loathing. Camilla Soeberg portrays Eva Braun as cool
and simple, totally devoted to Hitler, yet
somehow unreal and insubstantial. Peter
Michael Goetz plays Freud as a stock figure,
a dramatic device who is able to probe and
question Hitler. His presence reminds one
of Steve Allen's show *Meeting of Minds*, in
which four historical characters are brought
together to engage in conversation and de-
bate. In their relationship, of course, Hitler
has no interest whatsoever in Freud other
than as a sounding board.

The strength of *The Empty Mirror* lies in
its script, largely drawn from Hitler's own
words and writings, in addition to a few observations borrowed from other works of literature, and the clever cinematic magic show
that Hershey weaves around his drama. The
cinematography is exceptional, as is the use
of music which relies heavily on Wagner.
On the downside, the exposition is rather
static and rambling, and the motion picture
definitely could have used a stronger conclusion. Perhaps Hitler should have come
into direct contact with some of his victims,
face to face, just as he did earlier with his
young followers. The indecisive finish ends
the film on a weak note.

HITLER PORTRAYAL: Norman Rodway, a
veteran performer with the Royal Shakespeare Company, delivers a meticulous, finely
nuanced performance as Hitler, one of great
variety and depth. His features bear only a
superficial resemblance to Hitler, but the
film accepts the challenge of this by having
him confront and stand beside the image of
the real Hitler on the projection screen, so
that within a short time Rodway is himself
readily accepted as the genuine Hitler in the
minds of the viewers. At no point does Rodway attempt to speak with an accent, using
pure and cultured English throughout, indistinguishable from your average educated
Englishman. At times, he sounds remarkably like Derek Jacobi, another memorable
Hitler. On the whole, Rodway is dazzling
and complex, reproducing Hitler in many
guises, including orator, actor, philosopher,

Norman Rodway in *The Empty Mirror*.

braggart, hatemonger, liar, artist, lover and
monster. It is a *tour de force* unlikely to be
equaled, yet, oddly enough, his impact
weakens in the closing moments of the film,
where his Hitler ages dramatically, becoming totally gray and the actor starts to lose
his visual approximation of the Führer. Up
until the end, his mastery of gesture and
vocal range plus his sheer bravura makes his
interpretation of Hitler one of the most unforgettable on film.

Rodway's performance is also enhanced
by the exceptional cinematography, the brilliant employment of countless historic photographic images and the exceptional use of
wardrobe and props, including Albert Speer's
scale models for the rebuilding of Berlin,
dominated by the massive domed hall at one
end and a giant column with an eagle on the
other. At one point, Joel Grey, as Goebbels,
places the column next to a model of the
Eiffel Tower, demonstrating that the Berlin
column is the larger of the two. Rodway's interaction with his co-stars is quite good, particularly with Joel Grey and Camilla Soe-
berg as Eva Braun. His relationship is more
testy with Glen Shadox as Göring, whom
he actually seems to loathe, and confronta-
tional with Sigmund Freud, with whom he
engages more openly as the film progresses.
Each viewer will likely be impressed by
different highlights, such as Hitler's mocking ridicule of the Aryan Heinrich Himmler, or the dictator's various crusades, against
tobacco and food additives, and in favor of

Norman Rodway as the Führer and Joel Grey as Goebbels study Albert Speer's architectural models in *The Empty Mirror*. Note Hitler holds the top of the dome behind his back.

organic gardening and animal rights. His boastful mention of being *Time* magazine's "Man of the Year" is cleverly done, interspersed with his observation that FDR received the same honor three times. At another point, Hitler is openly vexed and puzzled why the English translation of his book, *Mein Kampf*, uses the German title instead of its English equivalent, *My Struggle*. Perhaps the film's finest visual sequence occurs when Hitler plays "Unto Us a Son is Given" from Handel's *Messiah* on his phonograph, and he starts to conduct along with the music. The lighting is stunning as it silhouettes the arm-waving Führer against a stream of a bright beacon. The fascinating thing is that as he continues to direct the music, characteristic gestures from his speeches begin to appear in his conducting, including the Nazi salute accompanying the words "Wonderful!" and "Councillor!" from the chorus. Eventually, a series of dissonant sounds and brutal images of explosions and goose stepping ends this extraordinary interlude.

The power of Rodway's reading, however, is the multi-layered depth of his characterization. His vision of Hitler is a man of some remarkable talents, yet an individual fatally flawed by his basic lack of humanity. Rodway's Hitler would proclaim that the music of Richard Wagner is the central component of his personality, but in truth his actual essence is his virulent anti–Semitism, a hatred so deep that it pollutes every fiber of his being. This fact is the key to Hitler's depiction in *The Empty Mirror*.

REPRESENTATIVE QUOTES

• Write this: Fire fascinates Hitler. It consumes without accepting or rejecting. *(Hitler to Freud, spoken after Wagner's* Magic Fire Music *is heard on the soundtrack)*

• You are the one thing that brought me peace. *(Hitler to Eva)*

• I would not allow smoking in my presence. We discouraged tobacco consumption. We insisted on the humane treatment of pets and farm animals. I even issued a decree regulating the cooking of lobsters to minimize their suffering. I reduced chemicals in fruits and vegetables. The SS planted organic gardens. I am not a brutal man by nature. *(Hitler lecturing young children)*

• Historians will study your childhood, examine your relationships.... They will exaggerate your slightest scribbles into irrefutable clues. You will be the source of endless fascination. *(Goebbels to Hitler)* Perhaps ... there is my thousand year Reich. We gave them all much to brood over, didn't we? *(Hitler's reply)*

• Envy Stalin? Pah! A footnote, a footnote if he is fortunate. Stalin killed millions of his own people, but he killed without grace. He ruled by fear. I ruled by passion and ecstasy! *(Hitler, ranting at images of Stalin on the projection screen)*

• The grander your grandiosity, the more brutal and grotesque the propaganda had to be to hide the truth! *(Goebbels to Hitler)*

• I, too, was trapped in the whirlwind we created, an empty mirror filled with hate. I expected God to reach down and stop me, but He never did. *(Hitler to himself at the film's conclusion)*

17. *Ernst Thälmann—Führer Seiner Klasse* (1955)

Fritz Diez as Adolf Hitler
Historical drama/propaganda

DEFA. Written by Willi Brendl & Michael Tschesno-Hell; Photographed by Karl Plintzner & Horst Brandt; Edited by Lena Neumann; Music by Wilhelm Neef; Produced by Adolf Fischer; Directed by Kurt Maetzig. Color 131 minutes

ANNOTATED CAST LIST: Günther Simon (*Ernst Thälmann*, Communist party leader); Carla Hoffmann (*Rosa Thälmann*, His wife); Hans-Peter Ninetti (*Fiete Jansen*, Dedicated young Communist soldier); Karla Runkehl (*Anne*, His wife & dedicated Communist);

Paul Henker (*Robert Durhagen*, Comrade shot by the Nazis as Anne watches); Karl Brenk (*Walter Ulbricht*, Communist leader & Thälmann's friend); Hans Wehrl (*Wilhelm Picek*); Gerd Wehr (*Wilhelm Floren*); Nikolai Krjutschkow (Soviet Major & tank commander); Michel Piccoli (*Fleuger*); Wilhelm Koch-Hodge (*Captain Schroeder*); Harry Riebauer (*Lieutenant Meyer*); Erich Franz (*Arthur Wierbreiter*); Ericka Dunkelmann (*Erika Wierbreiter*); Raimund Schelcher (*Kriseham Daik*); Hans Schäffer (*Krüger*); Walter Jupé (*Diebold*); Fred Kötteritzsch (*Franz von Papen*, Leader of Catholic Center Party & Hitler's Deputy Chancellor); Werner Peters (*Quaddle*, SS prison official); Kurt Wetzel (*Hermann Göring*, Reich Marshal); Hans Stuhrmann (*Joseph Goebbels*, Minister of Propaganda).

APPRAISAL AND SYNOPSIS: East Germany produced an epic two-part film in the mid–1950s based upon the figure of Ernst Thälmann (1886–1944), the chairman of the German Communist Party during the last days of the Weimar Republic. Most historians consider him partially responsible for the rise of Adolf Hitler because he seldom combated the Nazis, whom he dismissed as irrelevant, concentrating his efforts to undermine the Social Democrats parties, thwarting their attempts to maintain a stable government. Even after Hitler assumed the chancellorship, Thälmann regarded the Social Democrats as his primary foes, and offered little significant resistance to Hitler whom he underestimated. The Communists of East Germany, however, accorded him hero status and glorified him in these films. Part One, released in 1954, ran 124 minutes in length and was entitled *Ernst Thälmann—Sohn Seiner Klasse* (Ernst Thälmann—Son of his Class). It covered his career through the 1920s. The second part was *Ernst Thälmann—Führer Seiner Klasse* (Ernst Thälmann—Leader of His Class). These films are epic in scope and grandiose in presentation, including huge crowd scenes, carefully reproduced sets (like the Reichstag), bombastic music and blatant propaganda. The picture devotes, for example, much footage to doddering old capitalists in their plush offices deciding to defeat Thälmann by throwing their support to Hitler. Undoubtedly if Thälmann had come to power, the result would have been a radical leftist totalitarian regime as repressive as that of the Nazis. Hitler and the Nazi leaders, however, take center stage for the last half of the second film while Thälmann languishes in a prison cell.

The film opens in Germany in 1930. Ernst Thälmann spends his time recruiting members for the German Communist party, assisting miners who are on strike and planning for the next election. One of his most devoted followers, Fiete Jansen, is released from prison and reunites with his beloved, Anna. They maintain a room at their apartment for use by Thälmann, and they dedicate themselves to promoting the Communist cause. In the Reichstag, Thälmann leads the Communist delegates, and he defies the Nazi brownshirts and their leaders Goebbels, Göring and Hess. At this point, the film alters history. In 1932, Thälmann refuses to join an antifascist alliance with the Social Democrats to support Theodor Düsterberg, their candidate for President of Germany and runs himself. In the script, however, it is the Social Democrats who refuse to cooperate instead of vice versa. In his speeches, Thälmann gains an enthusiastic following, but Adolf Hitler and the Nazi party make a greater impression. Paul von Hindenburg, the war hero, receives eighteen million votes, Hitler eleven million, Thälmann five million and Düsterberg two and a half. Hindenburg wins the runoff, but the Communists totals drop by over a million votes. In October 1932, Thälmann is acclaimed at the Communist Internationale conference in Paris. He delivers the keynote speech in which he calls for solidarity among the workers of different nations. Thälmann visits the cemeteries of the war dead, and lays flowers on the graves of both the French and German soldiers. In January 1933, Hitler is appointed chancellor after making a

deal with Franz von Papen. In a bold grab for power, the Nazis burn down the Reichstag and blame the Communists. Hitler is granted emergency powers, and he imprisons Thälmann and the other Communist leaders. The film depicts him as being held in the same fortress-style prison, but in reality, Thälmann was shifted through various places such as Berlin-Moabit until 1937 and Hanover until 1943. He eventually wound up in Buchenwald. Thälmann's Communist friends attempt to break him out of prison shortly after his arrest, but their plan is exposed and fails. Meanwhile, Fiete goes to Spain to fight for the Loyalist cause.

When Hitler tours a tank factory, he is outraged when he sees a huge chalk graffiti message: "Freedom for Ernst Thälmann!" He orders Göring to handle the matter. The Reich Marshal goes to visit Thälmann in his prison cell, but the Communist leader rebuffs him, refusing to shake his extended hand. When the war breaks out, the Nazis have a series of spectacular triumphs, culminating in the invasion of Russia. (The film avoids any mention of the pact between the Nazis and the Soviets). When Fiete leaves to join the Soviet cause, Anne gives him a large red banner bearing the image of Thälmann. Fiete is given command of a tank unit known as the Thälmann Brigade. Anne keeps busy making and distributing anti-Nazi fliers until she is arrested and thrown into prison. She refuses to reveal the names of any of her comrades. She later causes a riot when she hears news that the Nazis have been defeated at Stalingrad and she yells out news of the Red victory. In his cell, Thälmann hears and is overjoyed. Later, when the prison is on alert due to an air raid, Anne spots Thälmann at the window of his cell and shouts out his name. He responds, but Anne is killed when a bomb strikes the prison. This event, however, is purely fictitious.

The Russian army is on the offensive, and Fiete flies the Thälmann banner from his tank. Hitler begins to panic as the war news turns bad. Many Germans betray their country and collaborate with the advancing Red Army. At this point, the film again distorts history, showing Hitler retreating to his bunker and making it seem that Thälmann was executed only a day or two before his prison was about to be liberated. In fact, Thälmann was executed in Buchenwald in August 1944, in the sweep of the Führer's enemies after the failure of the Rastenburg assassination plot. Curiously, the conclusion of the film rips off the ending of *The Robe* (1953), assuming that few East Germans had seen the religious epic. As Jean Simmons and Richard Burton are ordered to their deaths by Caligula (Jay Robinson), they walk out of the Senate chamber and the background dissolves into a bright blue sky as triumphant music plays, an intricate and impressive process shot. The Thälmann film ends identically, as the Communist leader is taken from his cell and marches down the prison corridor, which dissolves and is replaced by a flapping red banner as triumphant music is heard.

Ernst Thälmann—Führer Seiner Klasse has numerous strengths and many hilarious flaws, similar to the Soviet propaganda epics such as *The Fall of Berlin*. The choreography of the big scenes, the strikers march against the police, the Reichstag session, the public rallies, the Internationale convention and the battle scenes are all impressively staged. The cinematography, the use of color and the editing are outstanding. The performances range from acceptable to pure bathos. The Hitler scenes are so exaggerated as to seem like farce. The music is pompous and awful, with clumsy paraphrases mostly of the third movement from Tchaikovsky's *Symphony No. 6 "Pathétique."* The distortions with true history are too obvious, although probably they matched up with history as it was taught in East Germany at the time. Unfortunately for the scriptwriters, the exploits of the hero of the film are meager since he is trapped behind bars for the last half, making it difficult for the picture to build any excitement. The exploits of Fiete, first in Spain and then on the Russian front, are

simply too remote to be successful. Several of the battle scenes go on for too long, padding the last hour of the picture. Finally, Günther Simon, as Thälmann, is extraordinarily bland and dull, totally lacking in charisma. He is definitely not "a man for all seasons."

HITLER PORTRAYAL: Fritz Diez provides for a somewhat unconventional Hitler, having a bit of a lantern jaw and craggy features that are uncharacteristic of the Führer. He plays Hitler as if he were on uppers, moving and speaking erratically and in great haste. His gestures are too broad. He barks, spits and growls his way through his public speeches. In one early scene, he throws a tirade while conferring with Goebbels, and the scene blacks out, but Hitler's voice continues to be heard over the black screen, his outburst gradually trailing off as the volume is lowered. He is best in his one scene at a formal dinner party with a group of capitalists, dressed in a tuxedo and toasting von Papen with a glass of champagne. It is perhaps the only scene in which he is restrained. It is the only scene in which he is even partially convincing He is at his worst during a long conference scene toward the end, in which he pounds the map table repeatedly and starts tossing the pieces around on the table as if they were houses and hotels from a Monopoly game. In the same scene, he wears a tiny sling for his left hand which looks positively silly. Twelve years after *Ernst Thälmann—Führer Seiner Klasse*, Diez appeared again as Hitler in a number of film projects behind the iron curtain.

REPRESENTATIVE QUOTES

• There will be something new this time, nothing like it since Nero. *(Hitler to Göring and Goebbels, anticipating the Reichstag fire)*

• You'll decay alive, but we'll rule Europe. *(Göring to Thälmann while visiting him in prison)*

• The word "surrender" I deleted from the German vocabulary in 1933 *(Hitler to his General Staff)*

18. *Europa, Europa*
(AKA *Hitlerjunge Solomon*)
(1991)

Stanislaw Zatloka (?) as Adolf Hitler
Historical drama

Paramount. Written by Agnieszka Holland based on the memoirs of Solomon Perel; Photographed by Jacek Petrycki & Jacek Zaleski; Edited by Isabelle Lorente & Ewa Smal; Music by Zbigniew Preisner; Produced by Janusz Morgenstern & Lew Rywin; Directed by Agnieszka Holland. Color 115 minutes

ANNOTATED CAST LIST: Marco Hofschneider (*Solomon "Solly" Perel*, Jewish boy who hides out in the Hitler Youth); Solomon Perel (*Solomon Perel*, Appearing as an old man); Rene Hofschneider (*Isaak Perel*, Solly's brother); Piotr Kozlowski (*David Perel*, Solly's brother, a soldier); Klaus Abramowski (*Azriel Perel*, Solly's father); Michele Gleizer (*Rebecca Perel*, Solly's mother); Marta Sandrowiicz (*Bertha Perel*, Solly's sister, murdered in a riot); Nathalie Schmidt (*Basia*, Hunchbacked girl); Delphine Forest (*Inna Moyseyevna*, Orphanage teacher); Andrzej Mastalerz (*Zenek*, Polish student hostile to Jews); Wlodzimierz Press (*Yakov Dzhugashvili*, Stalin's son); Martin Maria Blau (*Ulmayer*, German soldier) Klaus Kowatsch (*Schulz*, Soldier); Holger Hunkel (*Kramer*, Soldier*)*; Bernhard Howe (*Feidwebel*, Soldier); André Wilms (*Robert*, Soldier & former actor*)*; Hanns Zischler (*Captain von Lerenau*, German officer who sends Solly to school in Germany); Anna Seniuk (*Rosemarie*, Nazi party official who escorts Solly to school); Jorg Schnass (Hitler Youth leader); Norbert Schwarz (*Hermann Schwabe*, Hitler Youth cadet); Erich Schwarz (*Goethke*, Hitler Youth teacher); Julie Delpy (*Leni*, Solly's German girlfriend); Ashley Wanninger (*Eric Gerd*, Cadet who mates with Leni); Halina Labonarska (Leni's mother); Wolfgang Bathke (Nazi policeman); Aleksy Awdiejew (Soviet major); Holger Kunkle (*Wagner*).

APPRAISAL AND SYNOPSIS: *Europa, Europa* is based on the true life story of Solomon Perel, a Jewish youth who survived the war years in Nazi Germany by posing as Josef Peters, an Aryan refugee and member of the Hitler Youth. Polish writer and director Agnieszka Holland adapted Perel's memoirs, altering a few incidents for dramatic effect but not altering the basic events, and this remarkable film won the prestigious Golden Globe Award as the Best Foreign Film of 1992. The original European title of the film is *Hitlerjunge Salomon* or *Hitler Youth Solomon*. This title serves as an allusion to *Hitlerjunge Quex* (1933), a famous Nazi film. The subtitled English language version, however, was retitled *Europa Europa*, which sometimes leads to confusion with another excellent film from 1992 entitled *Zentropa* (but originally called *Europa*), which was set in Germany immediately after the war. *Europa, Europa* is a magnificent film on all levels, sometimes compelling, sometimes ironic and often fresh and brilliant. The screenplay, cinematography and editing are of the highest caliber. The music by Zbigniew Preisner is quite poignant. The various languages shift from German to Polish and Russian, but the English subtitles are exceptional clear, unlike many foreign films. The entire cast of the film is exceptional, particularly Marco Hofschneider, the young protagonist around whom the entire film is constructed. It is through his eyes that the remarkable plot unfolds, as he is forced by circumstance to hide his true identity and assume a role in order to survive. Naturally, his own identity is often confused in his mind as he has to praise Hitler, the man whose actions has lead to the destruction of his family. The film contains brief flashes of frontal male nudity, as well as brutality of the victims of warfare, including children.

The story begins as the audience is introduced to Solly Perel and his family, shoe store owners in Peine, Germany. With the rise of the Nazis to power, the Perel family decide to emigrate to Poland after Bertha, their young daughter, is killed in an anti–Semitic riot spearheaded by Nazi thugs. Trouble returns when war breaks out in September 1939. The father sends two of his sons, Isaak and Solly, to travel to the eastern border of Poland. When the Soviet Union invades from the East, refugees crossing a river are perplexed whether to return or continue on. The brothers become separated, as Jewish refugees jump from the boat to flee the Germans while other Poles turn the boats back to German-held territory. Solly is fished out of the river by a Russian soldier, who brings him to an orphanage run along Soviet lines. Solly feigns becoming a loyal Communist in order to fit in. The teachers attempt to brainwash the students. When one of them insists that God exists, the teacher instructs him to pray to God for candy. When she later suggests asking Comrade Stalin for candy, sweets are tossed down from a grate in the ceiling.

When Germany invades Russia in June 1941, the students from the orphanage attempt to flee, but Solly becomes separated from the others. He gets captured by German soldiers and is warned by other prisoners not to reveal he is Jewish or he will be shot. Solly speaks to his captors in fluent German, calling himself Josef Peters, a native German. Knowing both Russian and Polish, Solly serves as translator for the German squad. They interview a noteworthy prisoner, who turns out to be Stalin's son, a prize catch. Later, another prisoner, Zenek, who had been at the orphanage, tries to tell the soldiers that Solly is really a Jew. They fight, Zenek runs off and is hit by a truck. Solly passes out and has a vision of both Hitler and Stalin.

The German troops befriend Solly and start to grow fond of him, regarding the sixteen-year-old boy as their lucky mascot. One of them, a former actor named Robert, discovers that Solly is Jewish because he has been circumcised. Robert promises not to tell the others, since he himself is a homosexual, a persecuted group under the Nazis. Later, Robert and a pocket of German troops are killed in an engagement with the Russians. Solly tries to defect, but as he approaches the Soviet line, they surrender when a wave of fresh German troops appear behind Solly. The boy is now hailed as a hero for leading the charge on the Russian position. Captain von Lerenau, proud of Solly, desires to adopt him and arranges for him to be sent to the finest Hitler Youth school in Germany. The young men welcome him as a hero who has been tested in battle.

Solly, still using the alias Josef Peters, feels less secure at the school, since the slightest slip up could reveal he is a Jew. He tries to disguise his genitals, to hide the fact that he has been circumcised. He makes friends with a beautiful German girl named Leni, a rabid Nazi who hates Jews. She suggests that they become intimate, and after Solly turns her down, she turns instead to Gerd, one of the other Hitler Youth members. Solly avoids having a physical with the school doctor by feigning a toothache. He has a nightmare in which he visits his family and winds up hiding in a closet with Hitler. During his vacation, Solly goes to visit the Jewish ghetto in Lodz, where he believes his family is imprisoned. He is only allowed to ride through the ghetto by bus, however, and watches the residents intently through a crack in the painted-over bus window.

Back at school, Solly tries to visit Leni, but her mother tells him that Leni has left home. Solly confesses to the kindly woman that he is really Jewish, and she embraces and comforts him as he starts to weep. Later, Solly is summoned by the police, who insist that he produce a certificate of racial purity. Fearful that his masquerade is about to fail, Solly is saved when Allied bombs fall on the police station, destroying it moments after the boy leaves the premises. As the German lines collapse at the front, the Hitler Youth are called upon to take up arms, but Solly refuses to fire his rifle. He defects to the Russians, but they are disbelieving when he claims he is Jewish. He is about to be executed by them, when he is recognized by his brother, Isaak, who has just been rescued from a concentration camp. After his brother hears Solly's exploits, he urges him to keep it secret, for no one would believe it. Solly and his brother eventually emigrate to Palestine. The scene shifts 65 years later, and the real Solomon Perel plays himself in the film's brief coda. On repeated viewings, different aspects of this remarkable film become apparent, even humor, such as the scene in which a Hitler Youth instructor uses Solly as the racial example of Aryan superiority. The irony remains that in almost all aspects of the school, Solly, the incognito Jewish boy, is lauded as the ideal Nazi youth.

HITLER PORTRAYAL: The actor who plays Hitler is not identified in the credits of the film, however a European internet source credits Stanislaw Zatloka for appearing in the role. The first glimpse of Hitler in the film is the real Führer as he is shown during a newsreel at the Polish movie theater. This is authentic footage, featuring the authentic Hitler. The next scene is Solly's bizarre vision when he faints after witnessing the bloody death of Zenek. Hitler and Stalin appear in the main hall of the orphanage, where they are waltzing with young girls dressed as ballerinas. The music is an odd arrangement of *Deutschland Über Alles* played on piano and glockenspiel. Showers of candies fall down again from the grate in the ceiling as Hitler and Stalin now dance together, no doubt representing the German-Soviet pact. Hitler looks very close to the image of the genuine Hitler that appeared in the newsreel, whereas Stalin looks much younger than the real Stalin. This is no doubt due to the fact that only younger, more idealized images of Stalin were on display at the Bolshevik orphanage, and Solly is not aware of the Soviet dictator's actual age. The waltz ends and Stalin vanishes. Hitler turns and stares at a bust of Stalin which explodes in half, revealing the Soviet leader lurking behind the statue. At this point, Solly's vision ends. The second appearance of Hitler occurs when Solly is at the Hitler Youth school. He envisions a visit

to his family, as they sit at the table eating a ritual meal of hard boiled eggs. Bertha is there also, back from the dead. Solly speaks to them, but they do not respond. They all rise from the table, except for Isaac, and when Solly approaches him, he sees that his brother's face is wrapped in bandages. Bertha reappears and pushes Solly into a closet, telling him to hide. Hitler is also hiding in the closet, dressed in his usual Nazi uniform, but with his hands clasped over his genitals. Bertha comments, "He's Jewish too. That's why he covers it with his hands." In the shadows of the closet, the Führer holds his finger up to his lips and whispers to Solly not to give him away. In the darkness, Hitler becomes transformed into Captain von Lerenau, who looks at him kindly until he appears to be shot in the head, his blood splattering over Solly, who wakes up screaming. Other images of Hitler appear throughout the scenes set in Germany, including photographs, paintings and a mammoth-sized bust in the courtyard of the school, to which Solly swears allegiance at the ceremony when he joins the Hitler Youth.

REPRESENTATIVE QUOTES

• I remember that my birthday fell on the same day as that of the future chancellor of the Third Reich, Adolf Hitler. *(Solly's opening narration)*
• Beloved Comrade Stalin, send us candies. *(Inna's instructions to students in the orphanage)*
• Captain von Lerenau said that Hitler said that we needn't kill them [the Jews]. We'll just send them to Madagascar. *(Solly to Leni)* Lice must be crushed! *(Leni's reply)* The Führer knows best! *(Solly)*
• Don't give me away! *(Hitler hiding in the closet to Solly during his nightmare)*

19. *Fall of Berlin*
(AKA *Padeniye Berlina*) (1949)

V. Savelyev as Adolf Hitler
Historical drama/Propaganda

Mosfilm. Written by Mikhail Chiaureli & Pyotr Pavlenko; Photographed by Leonid Kosmatov; Edited by Tatyana Likhachyova; Music by Dimitri Shostakovich; Produced & directed by Mikhail Chiaureli. Color Original version 167 minutes; revised version 148 minutes

ANNOTATED CAST LIST: Mikhail Gelovani (*Josef Stalin*, Soviet dictator); Boris Andreyev (*Alexei Ivanov*, Heroic Russian steelworker turned soldier); M. Kovalyova (*Natasha Vasilnyeva*, Alexei's beloved, a teacher captured by the Nazis); S. Giatsyntuva (Alexei's mother); G. Timoshenko (*Kostya*, Alexei's friend); A. Urasalyev (*Yusupov*, Alexei's friend); Nikolai Bogolyubov (*Kumchinsky*, Steel mill superintendent); Jan Werich (*Hermann Göring*, Reich Marshal); M. Novakova (*Eva Braun*, Hitler's mistress); M. Petrunkin (*Dr. Joseph Goebbels*, Propaganda Minister); Vladimir Pokrovsky (*Alfred Jodl*, General & Chief of Operations); Nikolai Plotnikov (*Walter von Brauchitsch*, Head of German army dismissed by Hitler); V. Renin (*Gerd von Rundstedt*, Field Marshal) Viktor Lyubimov (*Wilhelm Keitel*, Field Marshal & Chief of the High Command); K. Roden (*Charles Bedston*, Representative who negotiates with Göring to provide secret British aid for the German forces invading Russia); Viktor Stanitsyn (*Winston Churchill*, British Prime Minister who meets Stalin at Yalta); Oleg Frelich (*Franklin D. Roosevelt*, U.S. President who meets Stalin at Yalta); P. Gurov (*Archbishop Cesare Orsenigo*, Papal nuncio in Berlin); Fyodor Blazhevich (*Marshal Georgi Zhukov*, Supreme Russian Army Commander); Anatoly Poyarkov (*General Vasili Kuznetsov*, Commander of Russian Third Army); Vladimir Kenigson (*General Hans Krebs*, German officer sent by Goebbels to report Hitler's death); Boris Tenin (*Colonel General Vasili Chuikov*, Russian officer who receives Krebs).

APPRAISAL AND SYNOPSIS: Josef Stalin controlled the Soviet film industry with an iron fist, literally overseeing productions such as the war epic, *The Fall of Berlin*, which presented its story as if it were straight history instead of revisionism of the most blatant sort. In essence, the film is an unabashed Stalinist fantasy celebrating the Soviet dictator. Originally shown in two parts, it was intended to be viewed by the audience on successive nights. Later in the mid–1950s, the picture was edited down to a standard length of 148 minutes, intended to be seen in a single sitting. During this revision, a scene with Lavrenti Beria, head of Stalin's secret police who had been executed in 1954, was among those excised. Unlike Hitler, who refused to allow himself to be portrayed by any screen actor during his years in power, Josef Stalin loved to see himself depicted larger than life in movies, and Mikhail Gelovani was his favorite cinematic double. Starting in the late 1930s, Gelovani played Stalin no fewer than nine times in films, including *The Great Glow* (1938), *Wings of Victory* (1941) and *Fortress on the Volga* (1942), leading up to *The Fall of Berlin*, the ultimate screen glorification. As a propaganda piece, it lacks the artistry of Leni Riefenstahl's *The Triumph of the Will* (1934), although at times it tries to emulate it. At the climax of *The Fall of Berlin*, the victorious soldiers start to call out their home towns, "I'm from Kiev!," "I'm from Stalingrad!" and "I'm from Moscow!," recalling how the soldiers at the Nuremburg rally called out their home regions. The message is the same as well. Just as Hitler is the personal savior of Germany, resurrecting the country from the ashes in *The Triumph of the Will*, Stalin is the individual solely responsible for the management of the military campaign and its triumphant outcome. Of course, whereas *The Triumph of the Will* is a documentary, recording an actual event, *The Fall of Berlin* is a distortion of reality. Also, while the German film manages to capture some of the actual charisma of Hitler, but Gelovani, like Stalin himself, is actually a flat and colorless individual.

As the epic opens, the workers in a factory town are presented as prosperous and ecstatically happy to be living in the worker's paradise administered by Comrade Stalin.

Alexei Ivanov is a model steel worker who amazes everyone with his remarkable productivity. He is summoned to meet with Stalin, who is planting trees and observing the birds in his garden. Alexei tells Comrade Stalin about his attraction to Natasha, the beautiful schoolteacher in his home town, and Comrade Stalin approves. When he returns home, Alexei and Natasha go for a walk in the fields as he shares with her the wisdom of Stalin. Meanwhile, they fail to notice an armada of airplanes that crowd the sky behind them. Explosions start to go off as tanks begin to rip through the countryside. Rushing back to the village, Alexei collapses when a shell goes off in front of him.

Alexei awakens from a coma three months later. He learns that the Germans have invaded, and their troops are at the gates of Moscow. He also learns that all the schoolchildren in town were hanged by the Nazis, and Natasha was captured and taken to a detention camp in the Third Reich. Alexei vows to avenge his country, join the army and liberate Natasha. Meanwhile, calm and cool, Stalin plans the defense of Moscow with his generals. He plans a parade on November 7, 1941, celebrating the anniversary of the Bolshevik seizure of power in order to goad Hitler into launching an attack with his overextended forces. The scene switches to Berlin, where Hitler and his devotees are prematurely celebrating their victory over Russia. When Hitler hears about the Soviet parade in Moscow's Red Square, he orders an all-out assault, including a thousand plane raid, but the Germans suffer a great defeat and not a single plane reaches Moscow. In actual fact, the November 7th parade did take place, but there was no German air raid that day due to heavy overcast skies. The Germans continued to advance until December 2nd, and were finally driven back by a massive counterattack launched by Marshal Zhukov on December 6th.

Göring negotiates with a secret representative of the British government, Charles Bedston, who arranges to insure delivery of the raw materials necessary to fuel the Ger-

man offensive against Russia. The British supporter assures the Reich Marshal that there will be no second front, and that any air raids by the Allies on Germany will be mere publicity stunts. While lunching with his mistress Eva Braun (who is portrayed as an elegant and haughty fashion model), Hitler gets the inspiration to make Stalingrad the main objective of his future plans against Russia. He summons his generals to carry out his idea. This leads to military disaster and a series of reversals, as Alexei, now a sergeant, seems to be forcing the Germans to retreat almost single-handedly. All the war action is concentrated on the Russian front, with no mention of the Allied invasions of Italy and France.

Part One of the film ends at the February 1945 Conference at Yalta, where Comrade Stalin is able to outwit the devious Winston Churchill, who keeps reneging on his pledges to the Soviet Union. Franklin D. Roosevelt is portrayed as remote, but more cooperative with Stalin. Churchill wants Stalin to drink a toast to the King of England, but FDR alters it to Mikhail Kalinin, the Russian official who serves as the figurehead President of the Soviet Union. This incident is actually a distortion of an actual exchange during the Teheran conference in November 1943, not Yalta.

Part Two concentrates on the battle for Berlin, masterly conceived by Comrade Stalin. Marshal Zhukov, the actual head of the Soviet military is reduced to the part of a lackey who carries out Stalin's plans. Hitler, on the other hand, is in a state of panic. He orders his troops to ignore the Allies on the Western front, and concentrates his forces against the Soviet Army. He hopes that the American forces will arrive in Berlin and take up the battle against the Russians. A steady stream of couriers report Russian advances, and Hitler decides to move down to the cavernous bomb shelter beneath the Chancellery.

Russian troops liberate a concentration camp, from which Natasha emerges looking rather hale and hearty. She also heads to

Berlin with the army. Hitler decides to kill himself, but Eva persuades him to marry her as a final gesture. He orders the subway tunnels flooded, despite the fact that many Berlin citizens are down there seeking shelter. Two German soldiers rush into the bunker to report further Russian advances, and are stunned to learn a wedding reception for the Führer is in progress. They leave the bunker convulsed with laughter and are killed by an exploding shell. Throughout the city, Berliners shake their fists at the sky, cursing Hitler. Eva Braun arranges to test her cyanide capsules on Blondi, the Führer's pet German Shepherd. The dog topples over, and the scene fades out as Hitler and his wife decide to take their poison with their desert at their wedding reception.

The Soviet troops storm the Reichstag, and Alexei's two friends, Yusupov and Kostya die in the last moments of the struggle. As the Soviet flag is hoisted over the Reichstag, a single plane descends from overhead after buzzing the city bringing Comrade Stalin to Berlin to celebrate May Day. (The fighting in Berlin did not actually end until May 2nd.) While cheering the dictator, Natasha spots Alexei in the crowd and they are reunited. But Natasha suddenly leaves his side to plant a kiss on Comrade Stalin, who proclaims a new era of peace. Suddenly, a handful of American and French troops begin to show up and shout praises to Stalin in English and French. Triumphant music blares as Stalin looks on magnanimously, and the film finally ends.

The Fall of Berlin is best regarded as a burlesque of the war's end rather than a serious attempt at portraying history. It is filled with many misinterpretations and outright doctored facts, such as Hitler's supposed massive flooding of the subway on his wedding day and the imaginary collaboration between Hitler and the Western allies. At the same time, the film manages to avoid any reference to Stalin's own pact with Hitler which led to the initial outbreak of the war, as well as the Soviet invasion of Poland and Finland in 1939. No mention is made of the

wholesale looting authorized by the Red Army, nor the large scale incidents of rape of many German woman by the Russians. Instead, the film concentrates on mythical events such as Stalin's gallant May Day visit to Berlin before the actual end of the war. The real Josef Stalin, instead of accepting a kiss from Natasha, would have sent her to a slave labor camp in Siberia, since his General Order No. 270 proclaimed that all soldiers and workers taken prisoner by the Nazis were to be considered traitors and deserters. As Alexsander Solzhenitsyn so eloquently detailed in *The Gulag Archipelago*, Stalin's own rejection and imprisonment of his own liberated soldiers was among his many crimes that raised his total number of victims into the millions, possibly surpassing Hitler. The non-stop apotheosis of Stalin renders this film one of the biggest ego trips in the history of cinema.

This is not to say that *The Fall of Berlin* doesn't have its share of impressive moments too. The massive tank operations, the formidable battle scenes coordinating plane and troop movements are stunning. Besides the cinematography, the music is exciting, written by Dimitri Shostakovich, one of the greatest composers of the twentieth century. Even here there are some ironies. Shostakovich disliked having to write patriotic music in praise of Stalin. For this film, he borrowed heavily from some of his other compositions, notably from the opening movement of his *Seventh Symphony ("Leningrad")*. In his memoir, *Testimony*, Shostakovich revealed that the snide march representing the enemy was originally conceived by him to depict Stalin and his purges. In fact, *The Fall of Berlin* is best remembered today due to the stirring music of Shostakovich, represented by multiple recordings on compact disk (such as Capriccio 10 405).

HITLER PORTRAYAL: V. Savelyev delivers one of the most bizarre interpretations of Hitler on screen, as if he were a some sort of evil gnome from a Grimm fairy tale. In Part One of the film, he barks, guffaws, sniggers and swaggers his way through his meetings with generals and sycophants alike. Savelyev bears an uncanny resemblance to the Führer, perhaps the best on film after Bobby Watson. He has most of the Hitler's characteristic gestures down pat in Part One. However, every time he speaks, he bares his teeth in a most eccentric fashion, that it seems the actor is wearing oversized dentures. In Part Two, moreover, Hitler seems to revert to a semi-human state. He shuffles about slouched over in simian fashion, like a misshapened gargoyle or Quasimodo. This is most pronounced in the surreal wedding sequence in which Eva Braun is made up to resemble Elsa Lanchester in *The Bride of Frankenstein* (1935). Shostakovich accentuates the uncanny couple with a bloated, exaggerated rendition of Felix Mendelssohn's "Wedding March" from *A Midsummer Night's Dream*. Their wedding procession seems to last forever as they tramp around the huge dining hall in the bunker, with most of Hitler's general staff in attendance. The entire sequence seems like a madcap Lewis Carroll nightmare than anything else. Furthermore, the editor intercuts scenes of people drowning in the flooded Berlin subway, to accentuate the grotesque nature of this feast. After their vows, the married couple settle down before an enormous wedding cake, and they bury their cyanide capsules in the layers of frosting in their own cake slices. For sheer demented bravura, Savelyev's absurdist depiction of Adolf Hitler stands in a class by itself.

REPRESENTATIVE QUOTES

• Orsenigo, what I need is a Papal encyclical against the Bolsheviks, and I would like to see you on the throne of St. Peter. You are a real Nazi, Orsenigo. You shouldn't be wearing a cassock but a uniform, haw, haw haw! *(Hitler to Archbishop Orsenigo, the Papal representative to the German government)*

• We are in the vanguard. England and

America need us. Do you think that Churchill is sincerely on Stalin's side? *(Laughs)* I'll lead the crusade! They should understand in London and in Washington that I'm doing their job. Do you hear me? Their job! *(Hitler to his generals, ordering an attack on Moscow)*

• You should wash your hair every day with my elixir. Show me your nails. Mussolini's nails are always perfect. *(Eva Braun to Hitler, snacking on pastries)* I'll finish the war in Stalingrad. It will be a good plan, to finish Stalin at Stalingrad. *(Hitler)*

• Where are the damn Americans? Krebs, help them get to Berlin faster. I'll pit them all against each other. They'll tangle before my very eyes. *(Hitler to General Krebs, planning the defense of Berlin in his bunker)*

• It's too late. They'll soon show me in the Museum of Curiosities. I'm doomed. *(Hitler to his secretary, dictating his will)*

• Like a gangster, like a gambler who lost, he hid from the people. *(Stalin to himself, after hearing of Hitler's suicide)*

20.   *Fatherland* (1994)

Rudolph Fleischer as Adolf Hitler
Alternate history

HBO. Written by Stanley Weisner & Ron Hutchinson based on the novel *Fatherland* by Robert Harris; Photographed by Peter Sova; Edited by Tariq Anwar; Music by Gary Chang; Produced by Gideon Amir, Ilene Kahn & Frederick Muller; Directed by Christopher Menaul. Color 106 minutes

ANNOTATED CAST LIST: Rutger Hauer (*Major Xavier March*, SS homicide detective); Miranda Richardson (*Charlotte Maguire*, American newswoman); Peter Vaughan (*General Artur Nebe,* Head of the criminal police); Michael Kitchen (*Max Jaeger*, SS detective); John Woodvine (*Franz Luther*, Foreign Ministry official planning to defect); John Shrapnel (*Odilio Globocnik*, General in command of the Gestapo, known simply as

Opposite: **The image of the seventy-five-year-old Hitler dominates many scenes in *Fatherland*. Ruger Hauer (left) as Major Xavier March continues his investigation.**

Globus); Clive Russell (*Karl Krebs*, Gestapo officer); Clare Higgins (*Klara Eckhart*, Ex-wife of March); Rory Jennings (*Pili*, March's young son); Zdena Seifertova (Max's wife); Petronella Barker (*Helga*, Foreign press guide); Garrick Hagon (*Walter Elliott*, Correspondent for CBS); Jan Kahout (*Joseph P. Kennedy*, American President); Michael Shannon (U.S. Ambassador); Sarah Berger (*Leni Kalder*, Nazi party archivist); Jan Bidlas (Bellboy); Stuart Bunce (Blind soldier); David Ryal (*Franz Kruger*, Administrator of Blind Soldier's Home at Wansee); Rupert Penry-Jones (*Hermann Jost*, SS cadet who discovers the body of Buhler); Marek Vasut (SS cadet instructor); Bob Mason (*Dr. Eisler*, Coroner); Pavel Andell (Man in dark coat); Charles De'Ath (Porter); Neil Dudgeon (*Gunter*, Sexual crimes officer); David McAllister (Party official anchor); Petr Meissel (Young policeman); Patrick Opaterry (*Heinz*); Milan Simacek (SS man at press compound); Jean Marsh (*Anna von Hagen*, Actress & Luther's mistress); Rupert Degas (Narrator).

APPRAISAL AND SYNOPSIS: *Fatherland* is an excellent example of alternate history. In the last forty years, the genre of alternate history (combining historical research with imaginative speculation) has come to its own as a literary staple. Alternate history novels first appeared as early as 1836 with Geoffroy-Chateau's *Napoleon and the Conquest of the World*, and in anthologies such as *The Ifs of History*, printed in 1907. Two novels from the early 1960s helped spark interest in this field, namely *If the South Won the Civil War* by MacKinley Kantor and *The Man in the High Castle* by Philip K. Dick. Needless to say, the American Civil War and World War Two remain the two most popular background subjects for these books. Harry Turtledove, the most successful and prolific of recent writers specializing in novels of alternate history, has covered both of these topics in depth. His fascinating series *Worldwar* is pure science fiction, as Earth is invaded by aliens from outer space in the middle of the Second World War, and the feuding leaders, Hitler, Churchill, Roosevelt and Stalin, have to form an alliance to combat the menace and save mankind. This story is vividly presented in epic terms, based upon a compelling premise. Other noted alternate histories involving the Nazis include: *SS-GB* by Len Deighton; *Hitler Victorious*, an anthology edited by Gregory Benford and Martin H. Greenberg; *Disaster at D-Day*, an anthology edited by Peter Tsouras; *The Hitler Options*, an anthology edited by Kenneth Macksey, as well as numerous others.

The premise of *Fatherland* is intriguing. The story depicts the fictional world of 1964, resulting from a decisive defeat for the Allies when the Normandy invasion is crushed in June 1944. The United States withdraws from the war with Germany, turning its full attention to its battle with Japan. Churchill is forced to flee, and Great Britain reaches an accommodation with Hitler. The war with Russia drags on, however, into a twenty-year stalemate characterized by endless guerrilla warfare. The Nazis, weary of the struggle, consider an accord with the United States as the only way to conclude their endless war of attrition on the eastern front. Hitler reaches out to the President of the United States, the elderly Joseph P. Kennedy, asking him to come to Berlin for a summit to begin an era of detente. Kennedy, facing a stiff presidential battle in the fall against the hardline Republican candidate, Senator Barry Goldwater, sees an alliance with Hitler as a way of securing his reelection.

Against this backdrop, the Nazi government is courting American reporters, who are invited to Berlin to cover the festivities for Adolf Hitler's 75th birthday celebration. One of these journalists, Charlotte "Charlie" Maguire, is approached by an old Nazi, Franz Luther, who wants to defect. He offers Charlie a package of detailed documents revealing the greatest secret of the war, one the Nazis are desperately trying to cover up now that an alliance with the United States seems possible.

The main character of the film is Major Xavier March, who works as a homicide

Rudolph Fleisher receives a last minute makeup adjustment as the aged Hitler.

detective in Berlin. A former U-boat Captain, March joined the SS when it assumed the duties of the regular police force. He is divorced from his wife, and is lukewarm about Nazi ideology, preferring traditional values instead. He tries to instill these virtues in Pili, his young son who is steeped in Nazi dogma. When March is assigned to investigate the mysterious death of Josef Buhler, a retired party bigwig, he finds a credible witness, an SS recruit, who identifies General Globus, head of the Gestapo, in the vicinity of the dumped body. Later, March is removed from the case when the Gestapo assumes jurisdiction. He is assigned a second murder case, that of another party official, Wilhelm Stuckart, whose body had been discovered by Charlie Maguire, the American reporter. When March finds the Gestapo moving in on this case as well, he joins forces with the reporter to discover the reason for these crimes. Seeking a link between the murders, March discovers that Buhler and Stuckart both had attended a secret con-

ference at Wannsee, a Berlin suburb, on January 20, 1942. Moreover, all of the attendees of this conference are now dead, with the exception of Franz Luther.

Meanwhile, Charlie has a clandestine meeting on a train with Luther. He tells the reporter that his mistress has the document files which contains evidence so explosive that it could bring down the government. After the train arrives at the station, the Gestapo agents move in and kill Luther. March drives Charlie to the home of Anna von Hagen, the noted actress who was Luther's lover. Charlie bluffs her into turning over the documents and learns the dark secret of the Third Reich. They did not transplant the Jews of Europe to the Ukraine and other former Russian provinces, as they have been asserting for the past twenty years. Instead, they murdered them in extermination camps. Now the Gestapo is eliminating all traces of this crime, killing those who carried out the deed as well as those who planned it at the Wannsee conference.

Stunned, March plans to help Charlie smuggle the documents back to the United States. He wants to take his son Pili with him, but the youngster calls the Gestapo instead, informing them that his father is intending to defect. They shoot March as he flees, but he manages to telephone his son before he dies, forgiving him and telling him that the Nazis are liars. Meanwhile, the Kennedy-Hitler peace conference is about to commence. Joseph and Rose Kennedy fly to Berlin on Air Force One. Hitler plans a gala outdoor reception. Charlie manages to give the documents to Walter Elliott, a CBS correspondent. As the President's motorcade passes, Elliott stops the vehicle, passing on the evidence. After Kennedy scans the photographs of the Nazi atrocities, he orders his motorcade to return to the airport, leaving the aged Hitler waiting to receive him at a lectern before a huge crowd. Charlie no longer tries to escape, but sits down on a park bench to await capture by the Gestapo. A closing narration by Pili, spoken years later, tells of the collapse of the Nazi regime and how his father and Charlie Maguire gave their lives so the world would know the truth. *Fatherland* is an exceptional effort in almost every way. One of the most compelling aspects of this film is the exacting detail in portraying the latter day Third Reich. With exceptional use of matte drawing, we see Berlin as conceived by Albert Speer, including the Great Domed Hall, a thousand feet tall and the Arch of Triumph that would tower over its Napoleonic counterpart in Paris. The art direction of the film is magnificent as it brings the vision of the novel to life, not only in terms of the architecture, fashion, technology and overall style, but in the mood and details of the era. For instance, one sees posters in Berlin advertising the newest singing sensation, the Beatles. Snippets of radio and television broadcasts contribute additional fascinating details to the story, commenting, on Kennedy's opponent in the fall election, Barry Goldwater. Charlie Maguire's hairstyle and clothes also perfectly reflect the era of the mid–1960s.

The screenplay actually improves upon the novel by Robert Harris in numerous ways. For example, the last half of the book becomes bogged down with endless Nazi documents concerning the holocaust. The film instead relies upon a few photographs and an elegantly evil depiction of the extermination process by Jean Marsh as Anna von Hagen. The novel sets the Kennedy-Hitler summit in the fall, beyond the scope of the story, whereas the film sets it to coincide with Hitler's birthday, showing the Führer's conference and future plans collapsing in front of his eyes. The poignant postscript of the film, related by the grown Pili, is visionary and moving compared to the rather prosaic conclusion of the novel, as Charlie fails in her escape. Other changes in the screenplay either tighten the story or render it more effective. In the novel, Reinhard Heydrich is still head of the Gestapo, but the film identifies Globus as the Gestapo chief. Since the historic Heydrich was assassinated in 1942, this change seems logical. Other changes seem more random. The novel explains that Göring died in 1951 and Himmler perished in a plane crash in 1962. Neither leaders are mentioned in the film. The book portrays Churchill as living in Canada in 1964, but the movie claims he died in the 1950s. The film also states that Stalin is still living and running the Soviet resistance, but the book has no mention of this. The prologue in the movie attributes Hitler's success in the war to the failure of D-Day, whereas the novel credits it to a victory at Stalingrad.

It is fascinating to note which characters in the novel and film are genuine and which are fictional. Almost all the major Nazi characters are real, all having attended the infamous Wannsee conference. The first murder victim, Josef Buhler, in real life was executed for war crimes in 1948. Wilhelm Stuckart, the second murder victim, in reality perished in a car accident in 1953. Franz Luther was named Martin Luther in real life, but the film changed his name so as not to confuse him with his namesake, the leader of the

Protestant Reformation. He died in May 1945, as did General Odilio Globocnik, commonly known as Globus, who committed suicide upon his capture. Artur Nebe, Xavier's considerate boss in the film, was executed by the Nazis in real life for involvement in the conspiracy to assassinate Hitler in July 1944. Joseph P. Kennedy, the American President in the story, had been the U.S. Ambassador to Great Britain, but was pressured out of office for his supposed sympathies with the Nazi regime. In real life, he is noted as the founder of the Kennedy dynasty, but neither the film nor the novel make any reference to Kennedy's sons John, Robert or Ted. The character of Walter Elliott is highlighted in the film only, and he is likely based upon William L. Shirer, the CBS representative in Nazi Germany at the start of the war and author of *The Rise and Fall of the Third Reich.*

The only drawback to the scenario of *Fatherland*, book and film, is the likelihood, twenty years after the fact, of the Gestapo being able to track down and kill anyone who knew of the activities of the death camps, including the special squads, the guards, the camp personnel, etc. Could any dictatorship, no matter how well organized, keep tabs on so many people, particularly when the time frame to carry out their cover up is relatively short. It also seems implausible that the myth of Jewish resettlement zones in occupied Russia would have been accepted so easily since it would be relatively easy to show that these places did not exist. However, the premise that a later Nazi government would suppress evidence of their wartime crimes is plausible, so to make the story work, we have to have suspension of disbelief that six million (or more) Jews would not be missed.

HITLER PORTRAYAL: The cast does magnificent work in *Fatherland*, particularly Rutger Hauer in one of the finest performances of his career, filled with a deep sense of humanity and a brooding rejection of the society of which he is a part. Hauer makes Xavier March a genuine flesh and blood in-dividual, a tragic hero of stature. Miranda Richardson, Peter Vaughan and Sarah Berger are also exceptional. Jean March is brilliant as the brutal, anti–Semitic actress Anna von Hagen. Her vivid exchange with Richardson, when she discusses people being turned into "smoke," is utterly chilling and unforgettable.

The figure of Adolf Hitler looms throughout *Fatherland*. The genuine Hitler first appears in newsreel footage during the opening narration, making speeches, haranguing the crowds and playing with his dog Blondi at Berchtesgaden. In 1964, Berlin is plastered with images of Hitler on billboards, on souvenir mugs, in massive statues and decorative busts, in photographs on office walls and in newspaper graphics. All this builds expertly until the Führer's actual appearance at the podium during the rally where he intends to welcome and woo American President Joseph P. Kennedy. Fleischer is absolutely convincing as the seventy-five-year-old Hitler. He has limited dialogue, mainly leading the crowd in the traditional Nazi chant, "Sieg Heil!" The stunned look when he realizes that his grand scheme has fallen through is also memorable, particularly when Pili March snaps off his television image, reflecting his repudiation of the dictator and his ideology. *Fatherland* marked the only screen appearance of Rudolph Fleischer.

REPRESENTATIVE QUOTES

• In the years after the war, country after country of the Old Europe had become part of the vast Nazi empire of Germania. The Führer's architect, Albert Speer, built a monument to the thousand year Reich. Germania's capital, Berlin, became a Nazi showplace.... As the Fifites came to a close, Hitler was able to put a more civilized face on the greater Reich. *(Opening narration)*

• Führer, my Führer, bequeathed to me by the Lord, protect and preserve me as long as I live. *(Pili's invocation before eating)*

• Times are changing, Globus, This is the age of detente. *(General Nebe to Globus, defying the Gestapo chief)*

• How do I tell my son that I served murderers? How do I explain this was not a glorious war for national survival, just extermination. *(The stunned March to Charlie after reviewing the holocaust documents)*

• Because of the Bolshevik unrest, these celebrations are hereby canceled. President Kennedy is returning to America immediately and takes with him the good wishes of the German people. *(Loudspeaker announcement at the rally, attempting to explain Kennedy's abrupt departure)*

21. *Fighting Film Album # 1* (AKA *Boyevoj Kinosbornik 1*) (1941)

Pyotr Repnin as Adolf Hitler
Anthology

Mosfilm. Written by Leonid Landi, Boris Laskin & Leonid Leonov; Photographed by Yuli Fogelman & Naum Naumov-Straza; Music by Nikolai Kryukov; Produced by Sergei Gerasimov & Alexei Olenin; Directed by Sergei Gerasimov, I. Mutinov & Y. Nekrasov B & W 76 minutes

CAST LIST: Vladimir Kantsel, Natalya Petropaviovskaya, Boris Chirkov, A. Gehr, M. Yandultsky.

COMMENTARY: With the German invasion of Russia in June 1941, the Soviet film industry was commissioned to fully participate in morale boosting to help the war effort. Documentaries and newsreels were given top priority, followed by motion pictures specifically designed to entertain the troops. An anthology picture series entitled *Fighting Film Album*, was developed for this purpose. Three separate featurettes usually composed each release, with no interconnecting theme to the pictures except to provide an uplift for the viewers. This first film in the series, however, had a special introduction and bridge segments to the three dramas, and this is reportedly where the Hitler sequence is contained. *Meeting with Maxim*, based on the character from the enormously popular *Maxim* trilogy, is the first segment of the anthology. It was di-

rected by Sergei Gerasimov, soon to become the key figure in the Soviet industry when he was appointed to oversee the documentary film division. The second featurette was entitled *Three in a Shell Hole*, the first war drama of the new conflict. The finale was called *Dream in the Hand*, a lighter effort.

22. *Fighting Film Album # 7* (AKA *Boyevoj Kinosbornik 7*) (1942)

Sergei Martinsen as Adolf Hitler
Anthology

Mosfilm. Written by Nikolai Erdman, Iosif Manevich, Klimenti Mints, Lev Nikulin, Yevgeni Pomeshchikov, Nikolai Rozhikov, Aleksei Sazonev, Mikhail Vitukhnovsky & Mikhail Volpin; Photographed by Grigori Ganibyan & Iosif Martov; Produced by Klimenti Mints, Sergei Yutkevich, Alexei Olenin & Sergei Yutkevich; Directed by Klimenti Mints, L. Altsev, Albert Gendelshtein, Rafail Perelshtejn, Alexander Rau, Sergei Yutkevich & A. Bendelstein B & W 116 minutes

CAST LIST: Vladimir Kantsel, Ernst Garin, Mikolai Okhlopkev, A. Gehr, Ivan Lyueznov.

COMMENTARY: Considered the finest of the series ground out for the entertainment of the Soviet troops, this anthology contained six episodes, and demonstrated a new sophistication and sense of irony as well as genuine confidence. The six episodes are: *Depot for Catastrophes*, *Exactly at Seven*, *Elixir of Courage*, *The Most Valiant*, *A Real Patriot* and *The Good Soldier Schwenck in the Concentration Camp*. *The Most Valiant* contains the Hitler story, featuring one of the leading Soviet actors, Sergei Martinsen, in the part. Martinsen remained active in the Soviet film industry until the mid–1980s, but he considered his work in *The Most Valiant* to be among his best, particularly since this release was cited as an exceptional morale booster.

23. *Flesh Feast*
(AKA *Time Is Terror*) (1967)

Otto Schlesinger as Adolf Hitler
Horror

Viking International. Written by Thomas B. Casey & Brad F. Ginter; Photographed by Thomas B. Casey; Edited by Al Doucette, Richard Pierce & Brad F. Ginter; Produced by Veronica Lake & Brad F. Ginter; Directed by Brad F. Ginter. Color 71 minutes

ANNOTATED CAST LIST: Veronica Lake (*Dr. Elaine Frederick*, Research scientist); Phil Philbin (*Karl Schumann*, Supporter of underground Nazi movement); Heather Hughes (*Kristine*, Nurse & undercover reporter); Brad F. Ginter (*Dan Carter*, Reporter killed at airport); Thomas B. Casey (*Ed Casey*, Newspaper editor); Yanka Mann (*Virginia*, Casey's secretary); Chris Martell (*Max Bauer*, Guinea pig patient); Dian Wilhoute (*Gail*, Frightened nurse); Eleanor Vale (*Sharon*, Nurse); Doug Foster (Airport assassin); Harry Kerwin (*Benito Perez*, Nazi operative); Brad Townes (*Jose*, Bearded guard); Dete Parsons (Guard with dark glasses); Craig McConnell (Nazi agent); Bill Rogers (Armed man who attacks the lab); Kat Tremblay (Hospital nurse); Monica Dagovitz (Hospital receptionist); Debbie Kuhn (Stolen corpse); Bill Kuhn (*Hans*, Frederick chauffeur).

APPRAISAL AND SYNOPSIS: *Flesh Feast* is a borderline professional film shot on a shoestring in Miami Florida. The picture was made only because Veronica Lake agreed to appear it, and in fact she helped to produce it. After the film was completed in 1967, it sat on the shelf for a number of years before it had a limited release, largely on the drive-in film circuit. The cast list must be taken with a grain of salt because most of the names are pseudonyms. Director Ginter also appears unbilled as the reporter who gets killed in the airport phone booth by a maintenance man with a spear concealed in his broom handle. The level of the performances is amateurish, the camerawork is shoddy and the plot is threadbare. Veronica Lake, looking a very old fifty, is adequate, largely because she keeps her tongue planted firmly in cheek, and she tries to have fun with the part. None of her other cohorts, however, shares her approach, so it

Lobby card for *Flesh Feast*.

always seems that she is in a different picture than the rest of the cast. Viewers might enjoy watching *Flesh Feast* if they see it with some witty friends who are quick with amusing one-liners, because on its own the picture has very little to offer the audience.

The picture opens in a cinema verite style at the Miami airport. Reporter Dan Carter (later referred to as "Tyler" by reporter/nurse Kristine) telephones newspaper editor Ed Casey and tells him that bigwig Karl Schumann, a known Nazi collaborator, has just arrived on a flight from South America. As he reports to his boss, a cleaning man disposes of Carter, and the credits roll as Dr. Elaine Frederick drives Schumann to her secret laboratory, concealed in the garage of her modest Miami abode. At the newspaper, Casey decides to take over Carter's case himself. He learns that the paper already has a reporter on the scene, working undercover as one of Frederick's three nurses. (What foresight!) But the good doctor does not have enough work for three nurses, so they moonlight at the local hospital where they occasionally pick up spare body parts for their employer. Schumann and Dr. Frederick appear to be lovers, and they share other secrets as well. It turns out that Frederick had previously been committed to an asylum in Northern Florida, and Schumann managed to win her release. Frederick is working on a treatment to reverse human aging. The key ingredients in her plastic surgery treatment are specially bred maggots, which feed off the body parts her staff picks up for her. When a number of these unique maggots are placed in the right proportions on a human face, they are able to restore their host's entire body to youthful vitality. Schumann arranges for a test subject for Frederick, an aged Nazi named Max Bauer. Dr. Frederick smears her maggots on Bauer, and then wraps him in bandages.

Meanwhile, Ed keeps in contact with Kristine, urging her to cooperate fully with Dr. Frederick. So the nurse decides to swipe an entire body from the hospital, arranging the dead woman in a wheelchair and pre-

tending to take her for a walk. This entire sequence is played deadpan, without a hint of humor. Later, Hans, the doctor's chauffeur, helps saw up the corpse to feed to the maggots. Benito Perez, a Nazi operative with two armed guards, shows up at Frederick's home and places everyone under guard. Perez tells Schumann that "the leader" is anxious to begin treatment as soon as the experiment on Max Bauer is concluded. Nurse Gail, frightened by this turn of events, decides to explore the secret lab and is horrified when she sees the body parts suspended on hooks over trays supposedly filled with maggots. She cracks up and runs out of the lab screaming. Kristine makes friends with one of the guards, a beatnik who resembles Bob Denver from his days as Maynard G. Krebs on *The Doby Gillis Show*. Kristine pumps him for information, but gets very little.

The bandages are removed from Bauer and—*Voila*—he is a young man again. Perez sends word to the leader. Max has his youthful impulses again, and he goes to Kristine's room and tries to rape her. Jose comes to her aid, killing Bauer. Schumann, hearing the commotion, agrees to hide Max's body in the garden. He then urges Jose to run off when Benito drives up in a car with the leader. Kristine gets word to Casey, who prepares an armed assault on the Frederick home. Meanwhile, the leader is ushered into the garage lab and is strapped down on a table. Dr. Frederick urges the leader to raise his head so she can place a pillow under him. For the first time, the leader's face comes into camera range, and he is Adolf Hitler. He and Dr. Frederick engage in some small talk, after which the doctor points out a painting of her mother hanging on the wall of her lab. Then the doctor reveals that her mother died during a Nazi medical experiment at a concentration camp. Hitler panics as the doctor starts to apply her maggots, but these are not the same ones that were applied to Bauer. Instead, these are maggots bred to entirely strip the flesh from their victim. Hitler starts to scream.

Casey leads an armed assault, and Karl Schumann is shot, guarding the entrance to the garage. He explains what is really going on to Kristine and Ed as he dies. Hitler is being tortured to death in revenge for his countless atrocities. Back in the lab, Dr. Frederick begins to go insane, laughing maniacally as Hitler yells in agony, and "The End" appears in a freeze frame of his contorted features.

The conclusion of the film is extraordinarily abrupt. No explanations are given as to how Hitler managed to escape at the end of World War II or what his plans are for the future. Instead, the film attempts an O. Henry twist by revealing that Schumann and Frederick are in league to execute the Führer, not to aid him. Many loose ends are dangling as the film ends. Veronica Lake's scenery chewing makes the conclusion both tolerable and funny. The rest of the picture is so dreary, however, that the brief, ludicrous bravura fails to generate enough stimulation to make the picture a bad movie cult favorite. Instead, it is simply a grotesque entry, both for Veronica Lake who died six years later after moving to England, and for films featuring depictions of Adolf Hitler.

HITLER PORTRAYAL: Little is known about Otto Schlesinger except that he served as a grip for *Flesh Feast*. In fact, most of the cast doubled as members of the crew. Schlesinger was able to produce a rather amusing and comedic German accent. Some critics stated the belief that the actor merely wore a Hitler mask, but close observation dispels this notion. The actor is wearing makeup. When Schlesinger first appears in the film, he is shot from the waist down. He walks firmly, although he uses a cane. He is then photographed from behind, and he is wearing dark glasses and a rustic alpine hat. He is led off to the laboratory, and when next we see him, he is lying down on an operating table. He objects when Dr. Frederick starts to strap him down, saying, "It was supposed to be the face." The doctor calmly replies that it is necessary. After tying him down,

she pats his chest as if he were a baby, saying she will return in a moment. The camera cuts away to the start of the assault by Casey and his men, and when the scene returns to the lab, Dr. Frederick is bringing in a large while bowl filled with maggots. It is only when the doctor asks him to raise his head, that his face is revealed to the audience, accompanied by a dramatic fanfare on the soundtrack. The only problem is that Hitler looks no older than he did in 1945. He would be seventy-seven years old, but he still seems in his mid-fifties. (With his relatively youthful demeanor, what is the point of the treatment?). Frederick points out a portrait of her mother, and the Führer beams that she seems to be a good German woman. His attitude changes when the doctor reveals that she was a medical guinea pig at Ravensbrück, a prison camp for women located south of Berlin. "It was for medical science," he starts to protest. Realizing that he is caught in a trap, he starts to blame others for any mistreatment in the camps. "No, it was you, only you!" the doctor proclaims, as she starts to toss the maggots at him. In the close up of Schlesinger, there are indeed live maggots placed on his face, but in the shots with Veronica Lake, she seems to be handling oatmeal or rice instead. She tells the Führer to remember, 'This is all in the interest of medical science." Dr. Frederick screeches as she becomes more and more irrational, receiving a charge from Hitler's suffering. The final shot of the film is a close up still of the Führer as his screams are altered electronically on the soundtrack. While not really a convincing Hitler, Schlesinger performs the role in camp fashion, mugging as best he can for the screen, and his enthusiasm is one of the few positive aspects of this dismal film.

REPRESENTATIVE QUOTES

• You know, the treatment isn't simple. I want to be sure before I use it on the leader. In order to do that, I must have enough time for experimentation. *(Dr. Frederick to Schumann)*

• Every moment is precious. Let's get on with it! *(Hitler to Schumann)*

• Are you insane… I had nothing to do with it. It was Eichman und Goebbels! *(Hitler to Dr. Frederick, when she reveals her mother died in a concentration camp in a medical experiment)*

• No, don't go in! Let her finish! It's the best thing I ever did! *(Schumann to Kristine, after he is shot)* Did you plan it this way? *(Her comment)* Everything but this. *(Schumann as he dies)*

• What's the matter? Don't you like my little maggots? Ah, well, I understand. Mother didn't like them very much either. Ha, Ha, Ha, Ha, Ha. Heil Hitler! *(Dr. Frederick to Hitler, strapped to a table, as she tortures him)*

24. *For Freedom* (1940)

Bill Russell as Adolf Hitler (cameo)
Comedy/Drama

Gainsborough Pictures. Written by Leslie Arliss & Miles Malleson; Photographed by Arthur Crabtree; Edited by R. E. Dearing; Music by Walter Goehr & Louis Levy; Produced by Edward Black; Directed by Maurice Elvey & Castleton Knight. B & W 87 minutes

CAST LIST: Will Fyffe (Newsreel office chief); Terry-Thomas (News reader); Millicent Wolf (Secretary); Jack Raine, Pat Williams (Newsreel cutters); Anthony Hulme (*Steve*); Arthur Goullet (*Ivan*); E.V.H. Emmett (*Ted*); Guy Middleton (*Pierre*); Hugh McDermott (*Sam*); Albert Leben (*Fritz*).

COMMENTARY: Bill Russell, who first appeared as Hitler in *Night Train to Munich*, follows with a second brief cameo in *For Freedom.* The setting of the story is a British newsreel company that is populated with eccentric employees, as they follow the events leading up to the war and culminating in the hunt for the German pocket battleship *Graf Spee* in December 1939. Most of the picture is lightweight, only turning serious toward the end with an outright propaganda message. Several actual British naval officers played themselves in the film's conclusion.

Since the early war news for the British was generally downbeat, the showdown with the *Graf Spee*, which was scuttled by the Germans themselves on December 17, 1939, was a rare triumph. A definitive version of this naval engagement was provided in *The Pursuit of the Graf Spee* (1956). *For Freedom* was once considered a lost film, but a print was located several years ago in the film library of an Australian television station.

25. *A Foreign Affair* (1948)

Bobby Watson as Adolf Hitler (cameo)
Romantic comedy

Paramount. Written by Charles Brackett, Billy Wilder & Richard Breen; Photographed by Charles B. Lang, Jr.; Edited by Doane Harrison; Music by Frederick Hollander; Produced by Charles Brackett; Directed by Billy Wilder. B & W 116 minutes

ANNOTATED CAST LIST: Jean Arthur (*Phoebe Frost,* Fussy Iowa Congresswoman); Marlene Dietrich (*Erika von Schlütow,* Cabaret singer in Berlin); John Lund (*Captain John Pringle,* Officer who romances Erika); Milliard Mitchell (*Colonel Rufus J. Plummer,* Officer who serves as Congressional liaison); Peter von Zernick (*Hans Otto Birgel,* Nazi war criminal in love with Erika); Stanley Prager (*Mike,* GI trying to pick up German girls); Bill Murphy (*Joe,* His buddy); Raymond Bond (*Pennecot,* Congressional committee chairman from New Hampshire); Boyd Davis (*Griffin,* Delegation member from Texas); Robert Malcolm (*Krauss,* Delegation member from Illinois); Charles Meredith (*Yandell,* Delegation member from Virginia); Michael Raffetto (*Salvatore,* Delegation member from New York); Gordon Jones (MP who pesters Erika); Freddie Steele (His partner); Frank Fenton (*Major Matthews*); James Larmore (*Lieutenant Hornby*); William Neff (*Lieutenant Lee Thompson*); Harland Tucker (*General McAndrew,* Reception committee officer who meets the delegation); George Carlton (*General Finney,* Reception committee officer); Damion O'Flynn (Lieutenant General); Joseph Goebbels (*Dr. Joseph Goebbels*, Propaganda minister in newsreel).

APPRAISAL AND SYNOPSIS: *A Foreign Affair* is a fascinating comedy by Billy Wilder with numerous satirical references. The entire opening, for example, is a take off on the opening scene of Leni Riefenstahl's *Triumph of the Will* (1934), which begins as Hitler's plane emerges from the clouds over Nuremberg, and the shadow of the aircraft streaks across the city. In *A Foreign Affair*, the airplane with the Congressional delegation similarly emerges from the clouds, and its shadow is portrayed against the bombed out and devastated rubble of Berlin. The parallel to the famous documentary is remarkable and probably overlooked by the majority of the audience. Jean Arthur plays Phoebe Frost, a straight-laced and no-nonsense Congresswoman from Iowa. To a certain extent, she is a counterpart to Greta Garbo in *Ninotchka* (1939), who is transformed from a cold-hearted ideologue into a loving woman. Phoebe Frost seems to be the only member of her delegation to take the mission seriously, to investigate the morale of the American troops stationed in Berlin in 1946. Colonel Plummer, the army's liaison, provides a tour and overview for the group, but Phoebe sets off on her own, upset by the degree of fraternization between the American soldiers and the young German women. She is picked up by two GIs, Mike and Joe, who mistake her for a local and bring her to a sleazy cabaret called the Lorelei, where she is dismayed by the antics of sultry singer Erika von Schlütow. Erika sings a song "Black Market," which outrages the Congresswoman. She enlists the aid of Captain Johnnie Pringle, a fellow Iowan, to investigate Erika and her Nazi past, not knowing that Johnnie is actually Erika's protector.

Phoebe uncovers an old newsreel which shows that Erika was an intimate of a major Gestapo figure, Hans Otto Birgel, believed to be dead. Not only that, the newsreel shows she was quite friendly with Adolf Hitler, a revelation which surprises Johnny. He tries to save Erika by diverting Phoebe's attention. He makes a pass at her, and the Congresswoman responds, falling in love with Johnnie. Erika becomes resentful when she finds out, and tries to break them up. Meanwhile, Colonel Plummer orders Johnnie to maintain his relations with Erika. He explains that Birgel is alive and in hiding. However, Birgel is obsessed with Erika, and news that she is romantically involved with Johnny will force him out of the shadows. Erika takes Phoebe to her partially demolished apartment building to prove that Johnnie is her lover. Phoebe is stunned when Johnny shows up and confirms this. Brokenhearted, she plans to leave with the delegation and refuses to listen to Plummer when he tries to explain that Johnnie is on an undercover assignment. Plummer lies, telling the group that their flight is grounded. On the drive back to their hotel, he tells them the case of Erika von Schlütow and how she is bait for a notorious war criminal. News comes of a shooting at the Lorelei. Phoebe rushes in with Plummer, believing Johnny has been killed. The dead man, however, is Birgel, killed while trying to murder Johnny. Erika is turned over to the denazification court, and Phoebe is reunited with Johnny, who admits that he loves her.

A curious mixture of German rubble film, social satire and light and frothy comedy, *A Foreign Affair* works on various levels. It is a social portrait of a defeated people and the American efforts to both rehabilitate them and get them back on their feet to build a democratic society. The script also reveals a troubling dark underside to a number of Germans. Then there are the Russians, still portrayed as allies, but with increasing suspicion as to their methods and aims. The stories of Russian plunder are clearly evident in the plot. On another level, the film clearly shows the individual American soldiers as generous and big-hearted, but often willing to exploit the occupation. The issue is clearly open whether they are taking advantage of the German women or being used by them.

Finally, there are the two faces of Captain Johnny Pringle, a domineering Lothario who in one early scene threatens to knock Erika's teeth if she doesn't follow his wishes. Yet the same Johnnie falls for the naive American Congresswoman with a passion for investigation. The sparks really fly in their romantic entanglement. Behind it all, the shadow of Hitler still looms in 1946 Berlin, from the youngster who scrawls swastikas in chalk wherever he can to the endless ruins of Berlin, dramatically revealed during Colonel Plummer's tour. The screenplay, cinematography, music and acting brilliantly mix these elements in magnificent style, a great tribute to Billy Wilder, an Austrian of Jewish descent who made his start in German films before fleeing the Nazi regime in 1933, first to France and then to America, where he was eventually hailed as a cinematic genius. Wilder served as a Colonel in the US army and was stationed in Germany in 1945, which no doubt inspired his work on this picture.

HITLER PORTRAYAL: This is probably the finest Hitler cameo ever done by Bobby Watson, since he interacts with a major star, Marlene Dietrich, who was admired oddly enough by the genuine Adolf Hitler. The cameo occurs in a newsreel screened by Phoebe Frost and Johnnie Pringle in her investigation of Erika. The title of the newsreel is *Die Wache im Walde* (The Week in Pictures), but no actual date is included. The newsreel is either silent or the German narration is turned off on the projector. It begins with a speech by Joseph Goebbels in Breslau. "That's Goebbels telling them how they are winning the war," Johnnie explains. The next scene covers the premier of a new production of the opera *Lohengrin* by Richard Wagner. A box seat is shown, and Phoebe instantly picks out Erika seated next to Hans Otto Birgel, a bigwig from the Gestapo. The scene later switches to the lobby during intermission, where the Führer starts to mingle with the patrons. He gives the Nazi salute and makes a beeline to Birgel and his companion, kissing Erika's hand. The news-

reel frame zeros in on Hitler and Erika, as they amiably chat, chuckling and whispering in each other's ear. Hitler is beaming with delight when Phoebe says, "That's enough" and the projector is turned off. "No small fry she," Phoebe comments. The impact of this scene is electric. Johnnie had been trying to hoodwink Phoebe by claiming that Erika's association with the Nazis had been at the lowest level. Johnny himself is flabbergasted by the footage, showing Erika flirting with the Führer in such an intimate fashion. Watson's remarkable resemblance to Hitler was never so cunningly exploited as it is by Billy Wilder in this sequence. Of course, Watson had other opportunities to perform with major stars, such as Donald O'Connor and Gene Kelly in the "Moses Supposes" production number in *Singin' in the Rain* (1952).

REPRESENTATIVE QUOTES

• What you Germans need is a better conscience. *(Johnny, playfully, to Erika)* I have no good conscience. I have a new Führer now. Heil Johnny! *(Erika's reply, giving a Nazi salute)*

• Here is the Reich Chancellery where the Führer fixed himself up a little duplex. As it turned out, one part got to be a great big padded cell and the other a mortuary, Underneath there's a concrete basement. That's where he married Eva Braun and that's where they killed themselves. A lot of people say it was the perfect honeymoon. *(Plummer during his guided tour of Berlin to the Congressional delegation)*

• Why didn't you tell me you were in that deep ... having your hand kissed by Hitler. Hope you had it sterilized afterwards. Always looked to me that he had a little rat poison in that moustache. *(Johnny to Erika after he views the newsreel with Hitler and Erika)*

26. *Le Führer en Folie* (1973)

Henri Tissot as Adolf Hitler
Comedy

Les Films de la Seine. Written by Philippe Clair; Photographed by Alain Levent; Produced & directed by Philippe Clair. Color 95 minutes

CAST LIST: Luis Rigo (*Harry*); Maurice Risch (*Johnny*); Patrick Topaloff (*Toto*); Michel Galabru (*Monsieur Achtung*); Pierre Doris (The Colonel); Philippe Clair (The Curé); Alice Saprich (*Eva Braun*); Georges de Caunes (Storyteller*)*.

COMMENTARY: *Le Führer en Folie* is a knockabout comedy in which Hitler is envisioned to be a soccer fanatic. He decides to handle German foreign policy based on the results of soccer matches. If a country defeats Germany, they are left in peace. But if the German team defeats them, then they face a Nazi Blitzkrieg. France has the world's foremost soccer team, and Hitler vows that they must be defeated. France sends three zany spies on a mission to kidnap Hitler before the coming match, but they fail. In an alternate plan, they wind up as members of the German soccer team, and plan to sabotage it from within. *Le Führer en Folie* was only a lukewarm success, and the film was never exported. It also received very few plays on French television in recent years.

27. *The Gathering Storm* (1974)

Ian Bannen as Adolf Hitler
Historical drama

BBC. Written by Colin Morris based on the book *The Gathering Storm* by Winston Churchill; Photographed by Dennis Channon; Edited by Andrew Morgan; Music by Camille Saint-Saëns; Produced by Jack LeVien; Directed by Herbert Wise. Color 76 minutes

ANNOTATED CAST LIST: Richard Burton (*Winston Churchill*, Anti-fascist spokesman in British Parliament); Virginia McKenna (*Clementine Churchill*, His wife); Angharad Rees (*Sarah Churchill*, His daughter); Leslie Dunlop (*Mary Churchill*, His daughter); Clive Francis (*Randolph Churchill*, His son); Thorley Walters (*Stanley Baldwin*, Prime Minister who retires May 1937); Robin Bailey (*Neville Chamberlain*, Prime Minister, May 1937—May 1940); Robert Beatty (*Lord Maxwell Beaverbrook*, Newspaper magnate); Michael Elwyn (*Anthony Eden*, Conservative MP); Robert Hardy (*Joachim von Ribbentrop*, German Ambassador); John Phillips (*Von Brendorff*, German general who consults with Churchill); Geoffrey Bayldon (*Dr. Kurt von Schuschnigg*, Austrian Chancellor); Steve Plytas (*Maisky*, Soviet Ambassador); Ian Ogilvy (*Edward VIII*, British king forced to abdicate); Dennis Lill (*George VI*, His successor); Patrick Stewart (*Clement Atlee*, Labor Party leader); Edward Evans (*David Lloyd George*, Liberal Party statesman); Lawrence Hardy (Speaker of Parliament); John Rutland (*Leo Amery*, MP who urges Chamberlain to resign); Richard Leech (*Admiral Pound*); Terence Longdon (*Admiral Browning*); Brook Williams (*Lt. Commander Thompson*); Fiona Walker (*Miss Hamblin*, Churchill's secretary); John Kane (*Brendan Bracken*, Conservative MP); Patsy Byrne (*Mrs. Brown*, Churchill's cook).

APPRAISAL AND SYNOPSIS: This BBC telefilm is a plain, straightforward and largely unvarnished production based upon *The Gathering Storm*, the first volume of Winston Churchill's memoirs of World War II, covering the five years leading up to his appointment as Prime Minister. Most of the film is presented on three or four sets, primarily Chartwell, the actual home of Winston Churchill, and a precise recreation of the House of Commons. There is no music in the film except for occasional passages from Camille Saint-Saëns' *Third Symphony* also known as the *Organ Symphony*. The acting is somber and low-key. Richard Burton, for example, does not resemble Winston Churchill, but he concentrates his efforts on Churchill's actual words, and his resemblance to Churchill's actual voice is uncanny and impressive. There is very little action in the film, and some viewers may be bored by its dry tone, regarding its presentation as a mere talkfest. This is particularly true if one is unfamiliar with the personalities or policies of such people as Stanley Baldwin or David Lloyd George. Many of the issues can pass right over one's head. This production does not underline its key points, and if your attention wanders, you might miss an important event. Chamberlain's three visits to see Hitler are summed up, for example, in one very brief exchange. Yet this scene does distill the essence of the Munich conference quite nicely indeed. The editing and the flow of *The Gathering Storm* are uneven and rather jerky. It is best described as a series of vignettes, not always chosen with the best of care but each one memorable in its own way. For example, when Edward VIII reads his abdication speech over the radio, Randolph Churchill dismisses it as sentimental and worthless. He then learns from his mother that the speech was largely written by his father, who earlier had pleaded with the king not to take this step. The special relationship between Clementine and Winston is also highlighted, from her comments on his spendthrift nature to her suggestions as he practices his speeches in front of her. Instead of a full color portrait of Churchill at this stage in his career, *The Gathering Storm* seems more like a vibrant sketch, and within its own narrow terms, it does its job quite well.

Events in the picture begin in 1936. During this period, Churchill was like an Old Testament prophet, crying out warning after warning about the threat posed by Adolf Hitler and the Nazi regime, but he was largely ignored, particularly by the members of his own party such as Prime Minister Stanley Baldwin. When Hitler marches into the demilitarized zone in the Rhineland in 1936, Baldwin notes that the Führer is only taking a walk in his own backyard. Instead of foreign affairs, the British government is preoccupied with their monarch, Edward VIII, and his love affair with an American divorcee, Wallis Simpson. Churchill urges the king not to abdicate, but Baldwin and his ministers help to engineer his decision to vacate the throne.

Churchill is downcast after Baldwin re-

tires and is replaced by Neville Chamberlain. Instead of ignoring foreign policy like his predecessor, Chamberlain actively seeks an accord with Hitler. Joachim von Ribbentrop, the new German ambassador, visits Churchill and tries to soften his criticism, saying the real enemy of Britain is Communism. Churchill remains unconvinced. Meanwhile, Hitler tries to pressure von Schuschnigg, the Austrian Chancellor, into yielding to his demands which will pave the way for a German takeover. Eventually, Austria is forced to yield. Hitler then turns his attention to the Sudetenland, the German-speaking province of Czechoslovakia. Chamberlain's policy of appeasement leads to a round of meetings with Hitler, after which the Führer manages to absorb the entire Czech nation in a few months. Chamberlain finally takes a stand when Hitler attempts a similar takeover in Poland. By this time, however, Hitler has made a pact with Russia that partitions Poland between them, leaving France and England alone in their declaration of war. Churchill's analysis of each of these events in Parliament demonstrates the validity and clarity of his anti-fascist policy.

With the coming of war, Chamberlain calls upon Churchill to rejoin the government as First Lord of the Admiralty. He undertakes the position with his usual vigor, but he finds his efforts hampered by the cautiousness and timidity of both the war and foreign offices. After Hitler's seizure of Norway in spring 1940, a storm of protest sweeps through Parliament forcing the resignation of Chamberlain. King George VI asks Churchill to form a new unity government. He delivers a passionate, defiant and resolute speech before Parliament to prosecute the war with every fiber of his being. All the Members of Parliament (MPs) rise to their feet and enthusiastically applaud Churchill's oration as the end credits appear.

HITLER PORTRAYAL: The Scottish actor Ian Bannen seems on the surface to be an unusual choice to play Hitler. In his two scenes, he comes across as a high strung schoolmaster rather than the Nazi dictator.

Bannen's appearance is not bad, although the haircut seems a bit too closely cropped. His voice is good when he is shouting, such as in his refrain, "I shall march! March!" But when his voice is used in softer tones, it sounds sing song with the slightest hint of an upper crust British accent. Unlike Derek Jacobi or Norman Rodway who succeeded as Hitler with a straight English accent, Bannen is totally unconvincing and recalls the actor's role as St. John Rivers in *Jane Eyre* (1971) rather than the Führer. His first appearance as Hitler occurs almost halfway through the film, as Hitler attempts to pressure the Austrian Chancellor von Schuschnigg into yielding to his demands. Instead of seeming threatening, Bannen seems more like an exasperated teacher who is unable to get his point across. His second scene, the meeting with Chamberlain, is an improvement, because Bannen is more successful as Hitler the unctuous charmer than as Hitler the bully and gambler. Even here, he lacks credibility, and his performance is one of the weakest in the film. Comparatively, the performances of Virginia McKenna as Clementine Churchill, Ian Ogilvy as Edward VIII, Patrick Stewart as Clement Atlee and Edward Evans as Lloyd George are brilliant. Nevertheless, the film stands or falls with Richard Burton, who undoubtedly resolved to give a Churchill reading for the ages. In this, he largely succeeds. Burton earlier performed the vocal part of Churchill in the exceptional documentary series from 1960 called *Winston Churchill—The Valiant Years.* Most viewers of the program believed that Churchill himself had recorded the voice-over selections.

REPRESENTATIVE QUOTES

• My words sink into the sand in which they bury their heads. We muddle along, hoping for peace, and moving irrevocably toward war. *(Churchill's somber assessment to General von Brendorff, a German general who opposes Hitler)*

• I don't believe anyone will hinder me. Italy? With Mussolini I have complete understanding. England would not lift a finger for Austria. And France, two years ago when I marched into the Rhineland with a handful of battalions, I risked a great deal. But now, it is too late *(Hitler, bullying the Austrian Chancellor)*

• Your visit alone has saved an invasion. *(Hitler to Chamberlain)* I can see in your face that you are a man I can trust. *(Chamberlain's reply)*

• We have before us an ordeal of the most grievous kind. I will say to the House I have nothing to offer but blood, toil, tears and sweat. *(Churchill's call to arms in his first speech as Prime Minister)*

28. *Die Gefrorenen Blitze* (1967)

Fritz Diez as Adolf Hitler (cameo)
Thriller

DEFA. Written by Juhus Mader, Harry Tüick & Janos Veiczi; Photographed by Gunter Haubold; Edited by Ruth Ebel & Karen Kusche; Music by Gunter Hauck; Produced by Erich Kühne; Directed by Janos Veiczi. B & W 165 minutes

CAST LIST: Alfred Müller (*Dr. Grunwald*); Reimar J. Baur (*Dr. Kummerov*); Helga Labudda (Kummerov's wife); Leon Niemczck (*Stefan*); Emil Karewicz (*Jerzy*); Dietrich Körner (The Baron); Ewa Wisniewska (*Hanka*); Mikhail Ulyanin (*Alexei Gorbatov*); Renate Blume (*Ingrid*); Werner Lierck (*Dräger*); Georges Aubert (*Peter Mollard);* Victor Beaumont (Head of British Secret Service); John Peet (Head of British Intelligence); Victor Grossman (Churchill's secretary); Walter Kaufmann (*Colonel Briggs*); Mark Dignam (*Sir John*); Clara Gansard (*Micheline*); Adam Perzyk (Cemetery guard); Rolf Ripperger (Hitler's adjutant); Jindrich Narenta (*Heinrich Himmler*); Klaus-Dieter Ihlow (Himmler's driver); Gerd Michael Henneberg (*Albert Speer*); Achim Schmidtchen (*Altenburg*); Hans-Joachim Hegewald (Labor camp Kommandant); Horst Schön (Luftwaffe Colonel); Christopher Bayerett (SS troop leader); Ivan Darvas (Atomic scientist); Jiri Vrstala (*Professor Rahn*); Harald Hauser (*Professor Delattre*); Lena Delanne (*Jeanine*); Bernard Papineau (*Bravine*); Jean-Marie Lancelot (Brasson); Hans Lucke (*Albert Kuntz*); Hans Pitra (*Zenner*); Elliott Sullivan (U.S. General).

COMMENTARY: *Die Gefrorenen Blitze* is an East German thriller based upon the development of the V-1 missile, and how forced laborers working on the project were able to pass word to the Allies of the project's location at Peenemunde so it could be targeted. It more or less follows the identical plot as Hammer Films' *Missiles from Hell* (1958) with Michael Rennie and Christopher Lee, except filmed on a grander scale and in a more sophisticated manner. Hitler is not portrayed in the British film, and his appearance in the German film is brief.

29. *The Great Dictator* (1940)

Charlie Chaplin as a caricature of
   Adolf Hitler
Comedy

United Artists. Written by Charlie Chaplin; Photographed by Karl Strauss & Rollie Totheroh; Edited by Willard Nico; Music by Charlie Chaplin, Meredith Wilson, Richard Wagner & Johannes Brahms; Produced & directed by Charlie Chaplin. B & W 128 minutes

ANNOTATED CAST LIST: Charlie Chaplin (*Adenoid Hynkel*, Dictator of Ptomania called *Der Phooey* & Jewish barber who resembles Hynkel); Paulette Goddard (*Hannah*, Laundress friend of the barber); Reginald Gardiner (*Schultz*, Officer whose life is saved by the barber); Henry Daniell (*Garbitsch*, Hynkel's Minister of Propaganda); Billy Gilbert (*Herring*, Hynkel's Reich Marshal); Jack Oakie (*Benzino Napoloni*, Dictator of Bacteria called *Il Digaditche*); Grace Hayle (*Madame Napoloni*, His wife); Carter De Haven (Bacterian Ambassador); Maurice Moskovich (*Jaeckel*, Ghetto elder); Emma Dunn (*Mrs. Jaeckel*, His wife); Bernard Gorcey (*Mann*, Ghetto resident); Paul Weigel (*Agar*, Ghetto resident);

Chester Conklin (Ghetto resident shaved by barber); Hank Mann, Richard Alexander, Eddie Gribbon (Storm troopers); Leo White (Hynkel's barber); Rudolf Anders (Official who greets the barber, mistaking him for Hynkel).

APPRAISAL AND SYNOPSIS: *The Great Dictator* is Chaplin's most popular talking film, frequently appearing on lists of the hundred best films ever made. Due to its familiarity, an in-depth synopsis is unnecessary. The film is set in Ptomania (Germany), under the thumb of dictator Adenoid Hynkel (Hitler). The dictator bears a striking resemblance to a Jewish World War I veteran suffering from amnesia. When the former soldier escapes from the hospital, he returns to his barbershop in the ghetto, which he believes he left just a few weeks earlier. The barber, partially based on Chaplin's traditional tramp character, is never called by name in the film. Some viewers have suggested that his name could be Maru Tondadoz, which appears on the sign of his barber shop. In any case, the picture flips back and forth between the activities of Hynkel and the barber. One man, Commander Schultz, knows both Hynkel and the barber, whom he regards as a friend since he saved his life during the war. When Hynkel plans to unleash a pogrom in the ghetto, Schultz revolts and hides out with the barber until both are captured and sent to a concentration camp. Hynkel plans to invade Osterlich (Austria), the neighboring country, but is hindered by Napoloni, the dictator of Bacteria (Italy). When Napoloni calls from Aroma (Rome), his capital, Hynkel invites him to a summit, which proves to be the comic highlight of the film. Securing a treaty, Hynkel feels free to launch an invasion. He goes duck hunting while he makes up his mind. Schultz and the barber break out of the concentration camp, which is in the same area. Camp guards capture Hynkel and knock him out. The barber, dressed in a military uniform, is mistaken for the dictator. He and Schultz wind up leading the invasion of Osterlich. Taken to the capital,

Charlie Chaplin as Adenoid Hynkel, *The Great Dictator*.

Schultz prompts the barber to address the crowd. The speech is to be broadcast around the world. At this point, the character of the meek and absent-minded barber becomes unexpectedly transformed into a literate, inspirational speaker who delivers a spellbinding discourse on liberty and justice. The film ends as Hannah, a persecuted friend of the barber, stares up at the sky as strains of Wagner's *Lohengrin* are played on the soundtrack.

There are a number of startling coincidences associated with Charlie Chaplin's first full talking picture, *The Great Dictator*. For instance, the picture began shooting on September 3, 1939, the date England and France declared war on Hitler. Chaplin and Hitler were born a mere four days apart, and when Hitler adopted his famous moustache, it was the identical one used by Chaplin since his second screen appearance in 1914. The script of *The Great Dictator* makes passing references to using gas to kill people and when Schultz, the disgruntled military officer wants to kill the tyrant, he conceives of doing it with a bomb, exactly as Stauffenberg would do in July 1944.

Chaplin initially faced resistance to his Hitler satire when he began to work on it in 1938. Other films, such as *Confessions of a Nazi Spy* (1939), also ran into the same roadblocks, including veiled threats to the director, Anatole Litvak and stars such as Francis Lederer. Looking back, it is difficult to comprehend the strength of pro-Nazi interests in the United States, but they were considerable. So Chaplin's decision to push ahead was courageous, even when many friends and associates advised against the controversial project. The course of events certainly validated Chaplin's endeavor, but it also might have led to Chaplin's unfortunate decision to step out of character in the last five minutes of the film to deliver a propaganda speech. The film would have been far greater if he could have found some way to make his points without abandoning the storyline when the barber is mistaken for Hynkel. There is also a serious mistake in his opening title cards. They state the story takes place in the period between two world wars. However, the ending of *The Great Dictator* suggests that the Second World War was avoided due to the dramatic closing speech. In fact, Chaplin filmed a montage of Axis soldiers abandoning the fascist cause. It is also fascinating to consider that Chaplin considered satirizing Stalin as well as Hitler and Mussolini in his film particularly after the Soviet Union invaded Poland.

Chaplin cast his estranged wife, Paulette Goddard, as Hannah, the barber's sweetheart. Other key roles were filled by Reginald Gardiner, Billy Gilbert, Henry Daniell and Bernard Gorcey. Keystone veterans Chester Conklin and Hank Mann also filled important supporting roles. A plum role was handed to Jack Oakie as Napoloni, and Chaplin encouraged him to play the part as broadly as he could, and to try to steal as many scenes as possible. Today, these scenes are regarded as classics. Oddly enough, Chaplin filmed all his sequences as the barber first, and then those as Hynkel. While doing the Hynkel scenes, Chaplin reportedly stayed in character and was aloof and overbearing on the set. The last scene filmed was the closing speech, about which Chaplin apparently was of two minds. After making the decision to step out of character, the comedian was continually forced to defend it. President Roosevelt liked the speech, and asked that Chaplin repeat it over the radio as a personal request. Chaplin opponents insinuated the speech had Marxist overtones. Today, it seems an idealized, sincere and hopeful plea, but of interest principally because this appeal for kindness and decency is spoken by a mirror image of Hitler.

HITLER PORTRAYAL: Even after sixty years, Charlie Chaplin's lampoon of Hitler remains one of the most brilliant and spellbinding of all portrayals, and also one of considerable substance. It is interesting to note the parameters of Chaplin's approach. First, he purposefully does not copy Hitler's trademark hairstyle with straight hair and drooping forelock. Instead, he maintains his own traditional curly locks, as if to point out that it is Hitler who resembles Chaplin, not vice versa. He copies Hitler's somewhat baggy and rumpled appearance by dressing in a slightly oversize uniform. While speaking as the barber, Chaplin uses a straightforward, conversational tone in English, without any trace of an accent. But when Der Phooey delivers a speech, or becomes upset, he lapses into Teutonic doubletalk filled with humorous sounding phrases (and sprinkled with words such as "katzenjam-mer," "sauerkraut" and "schnitzel") that hilariously mimic Hitler's speech pattern. Most of these tirades were frequently improvised by Chaplin, as they were not in his script, but he redubbed many of his lines whenever a better idea came to mind. For instance, when he calls Napoloni "a cheesy ravioli," it is obvious that this line was dubbed in later. It is also remarkable, at one point, that Chaplin actually sneaks in the first use of the "F word" in a major feature film. This occurs in the food fight scene, when Carter De Haven, the Bacterian ambassador says, "Your excellency, to quote an old Latin phrase…" but Chaplin interrupts him, barking out the forbidden word in his face, perhaps with an odd inflection but still quite clear. Similarly, Chaplin was the first performer to get away with the raised middle finger in *City Lights* (1931), when he removes the loose finger of a glove early in the film. It was part of his pattern of always pushing the envelope. The Breen censors, however, only requested he excise the use of the word "lousy" in *The Great Dictator*, missing the obvious.

Chaplin is particularly brilliant in his parody of Hitler's gestures. He exaggerates and skewers the Führer's most exceptional skill, his ability as a public speaker. At one point, for example, after a volatile tirade, he pauses for a sip and water and also deliberately pours some down his trousers, a subtle visual statement on his overheated rhetoric. On the other hand, he adds bits of business that seem unrelated to Hitler, such as his comic piano playing or his ludicrous dance with Madame Napoloni. Many critics have cited his ballet with the giant globe, set to the music of Wagner's *Lohengrin*. It is a remarkable moment and a phenomenal metaphor of Hitler's grab for world power. It may be the most striking cinematic scene involving Hitler. Yet in terms of pure filmmaking, it balances off the barber's shaving pantomime with the *Hungarian Dance No. 5* by Brahms. Finally, there is some evidence that Hitler actually saw *The Great Dictator*, smuggling a

viewing copy to Berlin through Spain. Supposedly, he watched it two nights in a row, once with his entourage and the following night all by himself. There is no report, however, as to the Führer's reaction. When Chaplin heard this story, it fascinated and intrigued him for years to come, wondering what Hitler actually thought of his caricature.

REPRESENTATIVE QUOTES

• Democratzie schtonk! *(Hynkel's address to the nation)* Democratcy is flagrant. *(Translator)* Liberty schtonk! *(Hynkel)* Liberty is odious. *(Translator)* Free spreken schtonk*! (Hynkel)* Freedom of speech is objectionable. *(Translator)*

• Brunettes are troublemakers. They're worse than the Jews. *(Garbitsch to Hynkel)* Then wipe them out. *(Hynkel's immediate reply)* Too small. Not so fast. We'll get rid of the Jews first, then concentrate on the brunettes. *(Garbitsch)* We shall never have peace until we have a pure Aryan race. *(Hynkel)*

• Schultz, you need a vacation, fresh air, a little outdoor exercise. I'll send you to a concentration camp. *(Hynkel to Schultz, after he speaks against anti–Semitism)*

• There is an old Ptomanian proverb, "Un schtruken faben untazaden sekunflute, unterspeine adooten phnute." *(Hynkel to Napoloni)* Ha Ha Ha Ha Ha! Thatsa' very funny! I awish I understand it. *(Napoloni, laughing uproariously)*

30.   *Hamsun* (1996)

Ernst Jacobi as Adolf Hitler
Historical drama

Nordisk Film. Written by Per Olav Enquist based on *Processen mod Hamsun* by Thorkill Hansen; Photographed by Mischa Gavrjusjov & Jan Troell; Edited by Ghita Beckendorff & Jan Troell; Music by Arno Part, Bela Bartok, Richard Wagner & Johann Strauss, Jr.; Produced by Erik Crone; Directed by Jan Troell. Color 152 minutes

ANNOTATED CAST LIST: Max von Sydow (*Knut Hamsun*, Norwegian writer & Nobel

Prize winner); Ghita Norby (*Marie Hamsun*, His wife, a former actress); Annette Hoff (*Ellinor Hamsun*, His daughter); Asa Soderling (*Cecilia Hamsun*, His daughter); Eindvide Eidsvold (*Tore Hamsun*, His son); Gard Eidsvold (*Arild Hamsun*, His son who volunteers to fight for the Germans); Sverre Anker Ousdal (*Vidkun Quisling*, Party leader & Nazi collaborator); Liv Steen (Quisling's wife); Edgar Selge (*Josef Terboven*, Reich Commissioner for Norway); Per Jansen (*Harald Grieg*, Opponent of Quisling government); Erik Kranstal (German minister); Sven Erik Brodal (*Holmboe*, Hamsun's friend & translator); Jesper Christensen (*Otto Dietrich*); Johannes Joner (*Finn Christensen*); Erik Hiuju (*Dr. Gabriel Langfeldt*, Hamsun's state-appointed analyst); Jorgen Langhelle (*Eide*, Judge at Hamsun's trial); Rut Tellefsen (*Mrs. Stray*, Hamsun's lawyer); Hakon Rosseland (*Odd Vinje*, Prosecutor); Per Christensen (Hamsun's publisher); Eva von Hanno (Nurse at rest home); Rasmus Lanje (Projectionist of Holocaust films).

APPRAISAL AND SYNOPSIS: *Hamsun* is an unusual collective effort of eleven different film studios in Norway, Sweden, Denmark and Germany, with Nordisk Films assuming the operational lead. The version released in American is the Swedish version, however the Danish cut runs almost seven minutes longer. *Hamsun* had only limited distribution outside Scandinavia, and American viewers in particular might find the film rather talkative, slow moving and difficult to follow. The title should not be confused that of another film, *Hanussen* (1988), a German-Hungarian co-production that details the career of a famous psychic who was opposed by the Nazis. Although Hitler and his persona is at the core of *Hanussen*, the Führer himself never appears on screen. The central character of *Hamsun* is one of the towering figures of Norwegian literature, Knut Hamsun (1859–1952), winner of the 1920 Pulitzer Prize in literature for his monumental novel *The Growth of the Soil*. The picture dwells on the aged, partially deaf Hamsun, who wrote newspaper articles in support of the German side during World War II. He was later arrested with other collaborators, judged by a psychiatrist to be mentally impaired, and finally brought to trial, after which he was fined and released. The impact of Max von Sydow's performance only gains stature in the second half, during his detention and medical evaluation, in which the dignity and humanity of this iconoclast is brought fully to light. The scene in which the author is shown films of Nazi atrocities is of exceptional power, as Hamsun becomes ill when he is presented with the evidence of the horrors of the death camps.

The story of Marie, Hamsun's wife, is given almost equal weight in the film. She and her husband have a brief separation in the mid–1930s, during which time she becomes an active member of the quasi-fascist National Union party, founded by Vidkun Quisling, the former defense minister. Both Hamsun and his wife become supporters of the Nazi intervention in 1940, but the writer is later disturbed by the appointment of a German official, Josef Terboven, as Reich Chancellor to oversee Quisling's government. Hamsun tries to intercede on behalf of some members of the Norwegian Resistance, but Terboven ignores his pleas for leniency. The Nazi has the Norwegians executed, and also conducts a pogrom against the Jews, sending them to concentration camps. Finally, Hamsun agrees to go to Vienna in 1942 to make a statement denouncing the British war effort and voice support for the Nazis. He is invited to visit the Führer at his summer house at Berchtesgaden. The meeting is a disaster, as the deaf Hamsun ignores Hitler's artistic chitchat and demands the removal of Terboven, insisting on the independence of Norway after the war. The Führer storms out of the room, ordering that the famous author be sent on his way.

After the collapse of the German war effort, Hamsun publishes a sympathetic obituary for the Führer. Terboven commits suicide, Quisling is arrested and executed, and Marie Hamsun is arrested and given a three year prison sentence as a Nazi collaborator. The elderly author, however, is treated with kid gloves since he is still regarded as a national treasure. He is arrested and sent to a rest home, and the government officials actually hopes that he will die before they have to bring his case to trial. Hamsun, however, continues to insist that his case be heard. The court orders a mental evaluation, and the author is sent to an asylum where he is treated as if he were insane. Dr. Gabriel Langfeldt, in charge of the evaluation, probes Marie for all the intimate details of their marriage. Hamsun is outraged when he learns about this, and vows never to see Marie again. The doctor finally issues a report that Hamsun should be regarded as senile, suffering from permanent mental impairment. Nevertheless, Hamsun is finally brought to trail where he speaks eloquently on his own behalf. He is found guilty of collaboration, but is only issued a token fine and released.

Several years pass, and Hamsun writes another book, *On Untrodden Paths*, as if to demonstrate that he is not mentally impaired. He finally relents, and asks Marie to return home. They spend their final years together, until the 93-year-old writer passes away peacefully, having restored his dignity and reputation.

HITLER PORTRAYAL: The meeting between Hitler and Hamsun is the highlight of the film, set at the Berghof, the Führer's retreat in the Bavarian Alps. As Hamsun is driven up the mountainous roads, he keeps rehearsing his greeting to the Führer and asking him to recall, replace or issue new instructions to Chancellor Terboven. As he emerges from his limousine, Hitler greets him on the stairway of the Berghof. Actor Ernst Jacobi, a veteran of German cinema, makes an excellent first impression in the role, dressed in a simple military uniform. After he removes his hat, Jacobi's moon-like face dispels the resemblance. In fact, he actually resembles Sidney Miller, the comedian who essayed the role of Hitler in the Jerry Lewis film *Which Way to the Front?* The Führer points out the mountain peaks to Hamsun from the large picture window, before they sit down for a snack of tea and pastry. A little girl wanders into their midst, and Hitler gently talks to her, mentioning that she is Albert Speer's daughter. He then tells the child to find her mother who must be looking for her. As Hitler speaks only in German, and as he and Hamsun try to converse through a translator, they immediately begin to talk at cross purposes. The translator also alters Hamsun's comments, attempting to sweeten them for the Führer. Being partially deaf, Hamsun starts to speak louder and louder. The Führer starts to become upset over the criticism of Terboven, and shifts in his seat, becoming increasingly restless and impatient. Jacobi makes deft use of his facial expressions, body language and vocal tones as he transforms from the cordial Hitler to the petulant one. The actor is very effective in this metamorphosis. Jacobi's Hitler does not erupt in anger, he is simply annoyed that his guest wants to meddle in statecraft, and he considers him an irritant to be banished at once. He merely gets up and walks off, proclaiming that Hamsun knows nothing and should be sent away at once. Hamsun, sputtering on in Norwegian, is stunned at the abrupt end of their meeting. Oddly enough, the failure of his encounter with Hitler did not diminish Hamsun's support of him. This did not occur until he viewed the atrocity footage of the Nazi regime years later.

REPRESENTATIVE QUOTES

• I have always taken a great interest in artists, in how you turn your experiences into art.... Tell me, how did you go about writing *The Growth of the Soil?* Do you write at dawn or at night? The daily rhythm of a poet and a politician is similar. *(Hitler to Hamsun, through an interpreter)*

• Send him away. I never want to see a man like him again. *(Hitler to his aide, as he stomps out of his meeting)* Is he throwing me out? *(Hamsun to himself as he is hustled off)*

• He was a warrior, a warrior for mankind. He preached the gospel that all countries had rights. He was a reformer of the first water. It was his historic destiny to work in a time of extreme brutality which eventually destroyed him. That is how Western Europe should look upon Adolf Hitler. *(Hamsun's obituary for Hitler)*

31. *Hard Rock Zombies* (1984)

Jack Bliesener as Adolf Hitler
Horror

Paramount. Written by David Ball & Krishna Shah; Photographed by Tom Richmond; Edited by Amit Bose; Music by Paul Sabu; Produced & directed by Krishna Shah. Color 90 minutes

ANNOTATED CAST LIST: Ted Wells (*Ron*, Rock band manager); E.J. Curcio (*Jesse*, Lead singer of band); Geno Andrews (*Chuck*, Band member); Sam Mann (*Sam*, Band member); Mick Manz (*Mick*, Band member); Lisa Toothman (*Elsa*, Hitler's beautiful blonde daughter); Jennifer Coe (*Cassie*, Shy town girl who falls in love with Jesse); Richard Vidan (Sheriff of Grand Guignol); Emmanuel Shipoff (*Grandfather*, Hitler in disguise); Nadia (*Grandmother Eva*, Hitler's wife); Vincent DeStefano (*Olaf*, Hitler's son with an ax); Christopher Perkins (*Christian*, Hitler's son with a camera); H.G. Golas (*Mickey*, Hitler's grandson, a dwarf); Gary Friedkin (*Buckey*, His semi-human dwarf brother); Crystal Shaw (*Mrs. Buff*); Susan Prevatte (Female werewolf); Michael David Simms (*Don Matson*, Rock talent agent); David Schroeder (Cassie's father); Jack Albee (Town elder who explains about Hitler); David O'Hara (*Ed*, Town redneck); Jonathan King (*Red*, Town redneck); Donald Moran (*Ted*, Town redneck); John Fleck (*Arnold*, Town Councillor).

APPRAISAL AND SYNOPSIS: *Hard Rock Zombies* is an amateurish film that seems more like a series of stitched together music videos linked by comedy shticks. The filmmakers clearly are unable to tell a coherent story, and by the last third of the film, any

pretense of plot has totally disintegrated. A bottom rung rock group is touring the remote desert towns of California. The first quarter of the film features a number of mediocre songs, followed by some partying with nubile young groupies. Ron, their manager, has to urge the band to move on, and they hit the road in their van. Jesse, the leader of the band, makes a tape of a song he found in a book that supposedly can raise the dead. The group stops to pick up a shapely blonde hitchhiker, Elsa. In an earlier clip, this girl had been revealed as a killer, wiping out two lusty young guys who gave her a lift. Elsa invites the group to spend the night at her family's mansion at Grand Guignol, the site of their next scheduled concert. The strange household consists of Elsa's grandparents, her brothers Christian, a camera buff, and Olaf, who always carries an ax. There are also two dwarfs, Mickey and Buckey, her nephews. The sheriff of Grand Guignol tries to stop the concert by arresting the band, but Elsa bails them out. Jesse becomes enamored of Cassie, a beautiful but shy girl. Cassie's father gets upset when he sees her with Jesse. The Grand Guignol town council holds a meeting and passes an ordinance outlawing rock and roll.

That evening, the members of the band are all murdered by their strange hosts. Elsa kills one who tries to watch her shower. The grandmother turns into a werewolf and kills another. Jesse manages to pass his recording of his "Raise the dead" song to Cassie before he is slain. Ron is stunned by the mysterious deaths. He dines with the family, and the grandfather offers him a job. A buzzer goes off, and the grandfather stands up, triumphant, saying that the time has come to remove his disguise. He rips off his mask and is revealed to be Adolf Hitler. The grandmother is Eva Braun Hitler, but she has no need to wear a disguise. He tapes a speech proclaiming the Fourth Reich. Meanwhile, Cassie plays Jesse's tape at his graveside. As the music plays, all four members of the band rise from their graves as zombies, and they begin a wave of destruction.

Hitler brings Ron to his underground lab, showing off his new crematorium and his improved formulas of poison gas. When he asks Ron again to work for him, the manager refuses. Olaf seizes him and drags him off, tying him to a table. The zombie of Jesse shows up and sets him free. One by one, the zombies attack the family members, killing them. Hitler comes across the body of Olaf, and starts to flail his arms and shout in lamentation. As the four zombies surround him, the Führer accuses them of being Communists and Jews. He shoots at them, but they close in on him and kill him.

The villagers of Grand Guignol gather at the town office. An ancient man with a long beard speaks to them, revealing that the grandfather who had been revered as the town patriarch is actually Adolf Hitler. He explains that the activities of Hitler and his evil family have provoked the wrath of the Almighty in the form of the walking dead. Each victim killed by these ghouls will turn into a zombie, and they will completely obliterate the town. Exhausted by his lengthy speech, the old man collapses and dies.

One of the town rednecks heads toward the mansion and fondles the dead body of Eva. Hitler revives and rips off the head of the offender. All of the dead bodies start to return to life as zombies. Ron hides out with Cassie to wait out the attack. Meanwhile, the dead band members head off to their next gig. Don Matson, a record company talent scout, shows up to hear them. He is impressed by their act, unaware that they are really dead. When Matson follows them to offer the band a contract, he is attacked and eaten by a pack of zombies. The townspeople come up with a plan to end the attack, following an ancient ritual to lure them with a virgin to the top of the highest hill at midnight, which will render them dormant for a hundred years. They capture Cassie to use as bait, tying her to a tree near the summit of the hill. The zombies are now led by Hitler, who keeps giving a Nazi salute. The

rock band zombies start to sing, however, attracting the horde of the dead like the Pied Piper, and they follow the band to Hitler's lab, where his poison gas causes them to disintegrate. Ron rescues Cassie, and the film comes to an end.

Part of the problem with *Hard Rock Zombies* is the lack of any coherent meaning. For example, what is the mysterious signal that informs Hitler to rip off his disguise? What is the purpose of the family's killing spree? How many of them are werewolves? Why are they werewolves? Toward the end of the war, the Nazis had a guerrilla force called werewolves, meant to operate behind enemy lines. Is this just a gag reference to them? These and most other plot points just pass by unexplained. It is a difficult task to attempt to satirize George Romero's *Living Dead* films because they are satirical in their own right. The musical excerpts were third rate, the cinematography and editing poor and jumbled, and most of the acting is simply nonexistent. Characters appear and disappear in the storyline at random and without purpose. A few of the jokes are mildly amusing. For example, Elsa sings Leonard Bernstein's "One Hand, One Heart" from *West Side Story* while she fondles the disembodied hand of one of her victims. But much of the humor fails to work, and watching the film becomes an exercise in pure tedium.

HITLER PORTRAYAL: The major bright spot of this grade Z film production is Jack Bliesener's ludicrous take off of Hitler. The Führer's survival from the bunker and relatively youthful appearance is never explained, except for some vague insinuation that it is connected with the supernatural. Bliesener, in his only screen appearance, delivers a vigorous and wacky spoof filled with many interesting touches. For instance, his eyes sparkle with delight when he discusses his special blends of "blue gas" and "yellow gas" and their deadly effects. When he walks from building to building, Hitler sings a barely audible rendition of "Der Führer's Face," the satirical number made famous by Spike Jones and used in a memorable wartime Donald Duck cartoon. Bliesener's manic recreation of Hitler's speaking style is outrageous. Bliesener's impersonation is fairly decent, capturing the tone and cadence quite well, but he speeds up the tempo to a frantic pace. He then turns on and off his oratorical flourishes like a switch. He adds a number of *sotto voce* remarks that are also amusing. After Hitler is killed by the dead rockers, he reappears himself as a zombie, staggering around in the later monster attacks, with his recollection and use of the Nazi salute as his only vestigial memory.

Actually, there are two Hitlers in the film since one must also include the 95-year-old "Grandfather Hitler" played by Emmanuel Shipov. Shipov's German accent is more pronounced than that of Bliesener. The editing of the film becomes very erratic toward the end of the picture, inserting flashback images, so that in one scene, Shipov and Bliesener seem to appear together. This makes no sense, but at this point in the film, common sense has been thrown to the winds, and the story line collapses. One expects the rock band to reawaken in their dressing room to discover that their trip to Grand Guignol was simply a bad acid trip. Such a contrived ending would have been the only logical one.

REPRESENTATIVE QUOTES

• Can it really be you? *(Ron to Hitler after he removes his disguise)* You think I shot myself down in some bunker someplace? You think that I am stupid? *(Hitler)*

• No more Mr. Nice Guy. No more waiting. Today's the day that counts. The Third Reich is dead. The Fourth Reich lives. Juden, kill machen toast! Schwarze, kill machen toast! Alles Schwarze toast! Intellectuals, toast! Amerikaner Schweiner, toast! Toast toast alles toast! We make pure. We make right. Today California, tomorrow the world! Sieg Heil! *(Hitler's videotaped speech)*

• Now, admit that you were excited. Now won't you accept my job offer? *(Hitler to Ron)* No. No. Let me go! *(Ron)* American youth, it's all the same, no ambition. Pol-

luted blood. You will be the first we will eliminate. It's a shame. He is a nice boy. *(Hitler muttering to himself as Ron is dragged off)*

32. *He Lives* (AKA *The Search for the Evil One*) (1967)

Peet Herbert as Adolf Hitler
Thriller

Majestic Films. Written by Don Fearheighly; Photographed by Gary Galbraith; Edited by Verna Fields; Music by John Caper, Jr.; Produced by E. Stanley Williamson; Directed by Joseph Kane. B & W 70 minutes

ANNOTATED CAST LIST: Lee Patterson (*Anton Becker*, Undercover spy who tracks down Hitler); Henry Brandon (*Martin Bormann*, Leader of Nazi Resurgence); Lisa Pera (*Ellen Meyer*, Becker's Nazi girlfriend); H. M. Wynant (*Karl Meyer*, Her father, a Nazi leader); Jennifer Lea (*Julie Ranson*, Physician in Darocar & Anton's former girlfriend); Peet Herbert (*Hasso*, Hitler's double who dies in his place); James Dobson, Allen Joseph, Paul Crabtree, Steve Abbott, Max Klevin, Jim Stanford, Maurice Demsky, Jim Organ, Ed Livingston, Chuck Doughty, Tom Cash, Bob Smith, Bob Bransford, George Brazil, Henry Arnold.

APPRAISAL AND SYNOPSIS: *He Lives* is an unusual minor effort, characterized by a curious, lackadaisical air. The film is not bad enough to be campy and too low-budget and threadbare to be taken seriously. The director, Joseph Kane, was a veteran of numerous Westerns, but he leads this film in a rather haphazard fashion. The basic plot involves Israeli intelligence in their attempts to capture Hitler in South America, only to find him a pathetic, burnt-out remnant of his former self, a senile puppet under control of Martin Bormann, the actual villain of the piece. But the script does not know how to resolve the plot, and instead the film ends in a series of weak action scenes combining *The*

Most Dangerous Game (1932) with *Mission: Impossible*. This picture could be easily dismissed, except for a few, brief, isolated moments which are not only memorable, but absolutely haunting.

The film opens in the bunker in Berlin during the last days of the war. Hitler is quietly planning his future course of action. When the camera cuts away to show the man to whom the Führer is speaking, it turns out to be his double, a mirror image of the dictator himself. Having been poisoned, the man crumples over and dies, while Hitler reflects on how much time and effort had been spent on his double's teeth so that they would perfectly match his own. Then the Führer's new bride collapses as well from poison, and Hitler steps over to the couch where she lies and gingerly pats her cheek, saying that she had been a good companion although really not worthy of him. "I belong to something far greater than a mere woman." When Bormann enters the room, Hitler orders him to shoot his double through the mouth (thereby ruining the effort spent on his dental work). Hitler, Bormann and his driver slip out of the bunker to begin their escape. The next title card places them in Madrid, where the three men cower in darkness while awaiting their next contact. Hitler, with altered appearance, seems to be looking forward to arriving at his retreat in South America.

The time then jumps forward to Buenos Aries twenty-two years later. Businessman and food importer Anton Becker is planning to break up with Ellen, his arrogant blonde girlfriend who proclaims the racial superiority of the German people. Ellen is unaware that Anton's actual last name is Levy and his background is Jewish. Becker is approached by the OSI, the Israeli Security forces, who wish to recruit him due to his involvement with Ellen. They believe her father is an intimate of Martin Bormann, who has an armed stronghold at a castle in the foothills of the Andes Mountains along the western border of Argentina. Anton's uncle, who helped him escape from a German con-

centration camp when he was a child, is in a hospital in Tel Aviv. From his deathbed, he implores his nephew to cooperate. Anton is briefed on Bormann's activities, which include launching a worldwide neo-Nazi movement. Ellen, his girlfriend, often invited Anton to visit the castle in Darocar, the location of Bormann's headquarters. Anton's actual mission is to determine whether Adolf Hitler is alive and present at this site. A team of Israeli agents will keep the compound under constant observation to pick up any infrared light signals flashed by Anton from a special device that resembles an ordinary camera. He will also be accompanied by Emilio, an Israeli spy who will pose as his assistant.

Anton resumes his relationship with Ellen and accepts her invitation to visit the castle. When they arrive in Darocar, Karl Meyer, Ellen's father greets them. Ellen feels ill, and Anton escorts her to see the local doctor, who turns out to be Julie, his old girlfriend. He pretends not to know her, and she reciprocates until they are alone when he explains his delicate undercover mission. Meanwhile, Karl kills Emilio, claiming his arrow accidentally slipped while testing his new hunting longbow. Later, Anton learns Ellen's illness was a ruse so that Emilio could be killed. The rule of the castle only permits one newcomer to be present at any time, so Emilio was expendable.

Martin Bormann greets Ellen and Anton when they arrive at the castle, but he declines to tell Anton his name. The compound is run like a military base with watchdogs and armed guards wearing Nazi uniforms. The next day, Bormann leads them in a hunting expedition. When the Nazi leader falls off a small cliff, Anton rushes to his aid. This action relieves Bormann of his suspicions about Anton. That evening, Anton is invited to a special gathering in the bunker beneath the castle. An old speech by Hitler is played on a loudspeaker. At a dramatic moment, the lights are turned off, and a spotlight shines on the elderly Adolf Hitler, who begins to speak about establishing a Fourth Reich. After a few sentences, his thoughts ramble and he lapses into silence. Bormann goes to his side and offers to help, as Hitler's eyes assume a wild and vacant stare. He tries to resume speaking, but he quickly becomes incoherent, as he proclaims his advocacy of terror. Bormann takes the old man aside, and a guard escorts him out of the room, as the members of the group shout, "Heil Hitler!" Bormann quietly dismisses the group, except for Anton, with whom he openly discusses the plans for world conquest, and Anton pledges himself to the Nazi movement.

Later, Ellen catches Anton in the act of signaling to the Israeli agents. She denounces him, and Bormann is outraged by the news. He berates Ellen for her poor judgment when she invited Anton to the castle. "All mistakes must be punished," he announces as he shoots Ellen. He tells Anton that he has known about him all along, and he is taken away to be tortured. Ellen's father is told that Anton killed his daughter, and he wants to execute him immediately, but Bormann has other plans. He decides to make sport of Anton by using him as a target in a human hunt. He escapes to Darocar and seeks out Julie for help, but both are captured by Bormann and his troops. After they are returned to the castle, the Israelis start to shell the compound in a mortar attack. Hitler believes that he is back in Berlin during the Soviet siege and he starts to wander aimlessly around the grounds. Bormann tries to lead the Führer back to the safety of the bunker, but he is killed by a mortar shell. Hitler continues to ramble about until another shell explodes near him. Anton and Julie mount a horse and escape, and there is no resolution to the battle between the small Nazi army and three Israeli agents with a mortar launcher. Instead, the film ends as Anton and Julie, now safely away, plan their future together and embrace.

HITLER PORTRAYAL: Peet Herbert was a nondescript character actor best known for playing the Los Angeles coroner for a number of seasons in the *Perry Mason* television series. It seems the coroner's role suited him, since he later appeared in *Kolchak: The Night Stalker* in the same capacity. He also was a frequent bit player in TV Westerns. His role in *He Lives* seems to have been the most significant one of his career, but since so few people ever saw *He Lives*, it largely went unnoticed. His performance is not without merit, particularly in his later scenes as the elderly, senile Hitler. In the opening scene of the film, he plays a dual role as both Hitler and Hasso, the double who dies in Hitler's place. The rest of the bunker scene is very drab and matter-of-fact, despite the dramatic circumstances, including the dramatic suicide of Eva Braun. The only idiosyncrasy of Herbert's performance is his pronunciation of Goebbels' name, which sounds like "Gables" instead, as in *House of the Seven Gables*. The brief scene in a cafe in Madrid is a bit more interesting. Hitler has shaved his mustache, altered his hairstyle and wears shaded glasses. His finest moment, however, comes in his address to his followers in his replicate Berlin bunker in South America. His memory falters half way through his diatribe, and as Bormann attempts to come to his aid, Herbert's wide-eyed, vacant stare reveals that this Hitler is only a doddering shell of a man, completely incoherent. In fact, he is merely programmed by Bormann. It is the finest moment in the film, a superb highlight for Herbert who otherwise is lackluster throughout the film. As the elderly Hitler, his hair is entirely gray, but he has regrown his mustache, but since it too is gray, it is almost invisible. To a certain extent, Herbert walks a fine line, because he needs to avoid making Hitler appear sympathetic in his pathetic, mindless haze. In his last scene when his compound is shelled, Herbert rambles on mechanically, making little impression as he portrays the mindless Hitler thinking he is back in Berlin and trying to make his escape. He appears to be hurt by a mortar shell, but the scene is so poorly staged that it is unclear if he is actually killed or not.

As Bormann, Henry Brandon acts as the main villain of the film, with his arrogant dreams of glory and his ruthless exploitation of Hitler, his former master. Brandon's career had been an extraordinary one since his debut as the scoundrel Barnaby in the Laurel and Hardy version of *Babes in Toyland* (1934). He also played Fu Manchu in the classic serial *The Drums of Fu Manchu* (1940). Walt Disney used him to model Captain Hook in the animated version of *Peter Pan* (1953), and toward the end of his career he had an astonishing success in *Where the North Wind Blows* (1975). Brandon lends an air of professionalism to this low budget effort. His Germanic accent is also the only one which sounds authentic. Of course, Brandon is quite tall, whereas the historical Bormann was shorter than Hitler.

REPRESENTATIVE QUOTES

• A few men will be sacrificed: Göring, Goebbels, Himmler. The world must believe the total leadership has collapsed. *(Hitler to Hasso)*

• My dear Hasso, you no longer have to listen to the explosions. I envy you. *(Hitler to the body of his double)*

• My dear Bormann, what would I do without you? Göring is a drunk. Goebbels is a mindless puppet and Himmler has proven himself faithless. Only you have remained constant and true. *(Hitler, embracing Bormann in the bunker. These exact lines are repeated by the senile Hitler at the end of the film)*

• Yes, Anton, the Führer is old, but he is still our guiding force! In his moments of lucidity, he still has the vision that tells us how to succeed, but he is old. Sometimes he talks too much. Sometimes he forgets where he is. He never leaves his bunker because he feels safer here. It is the exact duplicate of the one in Berlin. *(Bormann to Becker)*

33.   *Highway to Hell* (1990)

Gilbert Gottfried as Adolf Hitler (cameo)
Fantasy/Horror

Hemdale Films. Written by Brian Helgeland; Photographed by Robin Vidgeon; Edited by Todd Ramsay & Randy Thornton; Music by Hidden Faces; Produced by Mary Anne Page & John Byers; Directed by Ate de Jong. Color 93 minutes

ANNOTATED CAST LIST: Chad Lowe (*Charlie Sykes*, Youth who storms hell to find Rachel); Kristy Swanson (*Rachel Clark*, Charlie's fiancée); Patrick Bergin (*Beezle*, The Devil); Adam Stroke (*Royce*, Leader of the bikers in hell); Richard Farnsworth (*Sam*, Owner of a gas station who guards the highway to hell); Pamela Gidley (*Clara*, Sam's love, taken to hell); C. J. Graham (*Bedlam*, Hell Cop); Jarrett Lennon (*Adam*, Child apprenticed to Beezle); Kevin Peter Hall (*Charon*, Ferryman across River Styx); Lita Ford (Hitchhiker); Amy Stiller (*Cleopatra*); Ben Stiller (*Attila the Hun);* Jerry Stiller (Desk cop in hell); Anne Meara (*Medea*, Waitress); Be Deckard (Dentist); Julian Charles Wright (Doctor); Darren Mark Edwards (Clown); Troy Tempest (Exterminator); Buddy Douglas (Page); Doug Harriman (Bartender); Michael Dellafemina (Woodsman); Gregory Mars Martin (State policeman); Michael Reid McKay (Demon posing as Rachel); Michael Waxman (Beer commercial spokesman); Paul MacKey (Palace guard); Helen Bradley, Kenneth Bridges, Marina Palmer (Victims of "Good Intentions" pavers); Das Psycho Rangers (Royce's gang).

APPRAISAL AND SYNOPSIS: This is a mercurial and rather clever fantasy that was largely ignored by critics. It is filled with delightful surprises, including an imaginative reworking of the myth of Orpheus in the Underworld. Unfortunately, a number of ideas flop in this presentation, one of them being the comic portrayal of Adolf Hitler by humorist Gilbert Gottfried, a genuine missed opportunity for first class satire. The film starts as a young couple, Charlie Sykes and Rachel Clark, are eloping. Afraid that Rachel's mother may have called the police, they take a back road to head to Las Vegas where they plan to marry. They stop at a remote gas station whose owner warns them to double back and take the main highway, because the route they are on is very hazardous at night. His dark warning proves true when they encounter Hell Cop, a demonic policeman who kidnaps Rachel and takes her to hell itself. Charlie returns to the gas station for help and learns from Sam, the proprietor, that his own fiancée was abducted by Hell Cop many years previously. He tells Charlie that Rachel can still be saved if he can overtake and free her before Hell Cop brings her to Hell City. Sam provides Charlie with a specially equipped car and instructs him how to make the dimensional jump to hell. Meanwhile, Hell Cop stops at Pluto's, a roadside greasy spoon frequented by the animated corpses of cops in various states of decay, most of them gnawing on stale doughnuts. Charlie almost catches Hell Cop's patrol car, but his vehicle breaks down and is salvaged by Beezle, a helpful repair man. Charlie learns he has twenty-four hours to accomplish his mission or he will be forever trapped in hell.

Charlie tracks Hell Cop and Rachel to Hoffas, a truck stop founded by the Teamster's leader, Jimmy Hoffa. Attila the Hun, Cleopatra and Adolf Hitler are among the clientele. Hitler is dressed in full military uniform and speaks in a thick accent. He insists he is not really Hitler, and Attila keeps telling him to shut up. As the short scene ends, Hitler barks that he always winds up sitting at the same table as the Flintstones. Meanwhile, Charlie gets into a shootout with Hell Cop, who blasts him in the chest. Beezle shows up and revives him, explaining that it was possible only because his soul is still uncorrupted. Charlie sets off again after Beezle shows him a shortcut to Hell City. Bribing Charon, the ferryman, Charlie is transported into Hell City where he tracks down Rachel and begs Satan to let them go. Surprisingly, he agrees, on condition they don't look back as they leave. After they depart, the Devil looks in the mirror and transforms into Beezle, his alter ego, who chortles, "Now we'll have some fun."

The young couple have a series of hair-raising adventures, and finally Charlie figures out his pal Beezle is actually the devil. Charlie suggests a wager, offering their souls in a race with Hell Cop. Sportingly, Beezle agrees. "I don't always get what I want," he says, but he would enjoy having children with Rachel.

The Devil brings them to a desert strip, pointing out an exit point. If they can reach it before they are caught by the Hell Cop, then they will be free, and they can also free Adam, a youngster who is serving as Beezle's apprentice. Unknown to the Devil, Sam equipped the car with a rocket booster, giving them a sudden burst of speed to burst through the exit. Hell Cop follows them to the real world, where Charlie kills him by shattering the demon' dark glasses. Back in hell, Beezle watches these events impassively. The closing scrawl describes the happy life in store for Charlie, Rachel and Adam.

Highway to Hell is filled with many inventive and amusing touches. Hell Cop's handcuffs, for example, are real hands that grips the wrist of his prisoners. The gateway to hell is proclaimed by a neon sign. There is a bumper to bumper traffic jam in hell with nothing but Volkswagen Beetles (which were, in fact, designed by Hitler). Figures from Dante, such as Charon the ferryman and Cerberus, the guard dog to hell, are depicted in brilliant fashion. Almost every scene has a ingenious little kicker. With all these positive qualities, it is a shame that the same resourcefulness wasn't applied to the scene with Hitler.

HITLER PORTRAYAL: Gilbert Gottfried is a comedian best known for hosting the USA Network's bad film fest *Up All Night*, which he uses as a springboard to satirize and mimic a series of third and fourth rate films. He has appeared in a dozen films of his own, such efforts as *Hot to Trot* (1983) and *Beverly Hills Cop II* (1987). Gottfried specializes in playing obnoxious characters, so it is surprising that his bit as Adolf Hitler in *Highway to Hell* falls so flat. It seems just like a weak improvisation where draws a complete blank. All Gottfried manages to do as Hitler is to insist that he really isn't Hitler, while his companions Cleopatra and Attila the Hun remind him that indeed he is Hitler. Most of Gottfried's ranting becomes lost in the background as the camera concentrates on the exchange between Charlie and Beezle on the other side of the room. There is unfortunately not even a single, mild chuckle resulting from Gottfried's farce, and it serves as the weakest point in a rather witty and entertaining effort.

REPRESENTATIVE QUOTES

• Idi Amin, Idi Amin, to the white courtesy telephone please! *(Busboy at Hoffas)* He's not here, go away, *(Attila the Hun)* Get away from here, you lil' disgusting monkey! *(Hitler)*

• Once it's explained, the devil will look at me, and I say, "Goodbye, Devil," and he would (say), "Goodbye, Dolph." *(Hitler, explaining to his companions that Satan will eventually release him)*

• In fact, I am nineteen years old. I like to listen to heavy metal. I like to sit in my room and play air guitar. I like to dance around the room in my underwear. *(Hitler)* Will you just get over it and get therapy, like I did? *(Cleopatra)*

34. *History of the World—Part One* (1981)

Scott Henderson as Adolf Hitler (cameo)
Comedy

Brooksfilms/. Written by Mel Brooks; Photographed by Woody Omens & Paul Wilson; Edited by John C. Howard; Music by John Morris & Mel Brooks; Produced & directed by Mel Brooks. Color 92 minutes

CAST LIST: Orson Welles (Narrator); Mel Brooks (*Moses, Comicus, Torquemada, Jacques, Louis XVI*); **Prehistoric Man:** Sid Caesar, Rudy DeLuca, Leigh French, Richard Karron, Susette Carroll, Sammy Shore, J.J. Barry, Earl Finn, Suzanne Kent, Michael Champion; **Roman Empire:** Dom DeLuise, Madeline Kahn, Ron Carey, Gregory Hines,

Shecky Greene, Margaret Humes, Howard Morris, Charlie Callas, Dena Dietrich, Henny Youngman, Ron Clark, Jack Riley, Paul Mazursky, Diane Day, Hunter von Leer, Fritz Feld, Pat McCormick, Barry Levinson, Sid Gould, Bea Arthur, Robert Zappy, Jim Steck, Ira Miller, Johnny Silver, Rod Hasse, Eileen Saki, Jay Burton, Art Metrano, Lee Delano, John Myhers, Alan U. Schwartz, Hugh Hefner, John Hurt; **Spanish Inquisition:** Jackie Mason, Ronny Graham, Phil Leeds; **French Revolution:** Harvey Korman, Cloris Leachman, Pamela Stephenson, Jack Carter, Jan Murray, Andreas Voutsinas, Spike Milligan, John Hillerman, Sidney Lassick, Jonathan Cecil, Andrew Sachs, Fiona Richmond, Nigel Hawthorne, Bella Emberg, Geoffrey Larder, George Lane Cooper, Royce Mills, Mike Cotrell, Stephanie Marrian, Gerald Stadden, John Gavin, Rusty Goff; **Coming Attractions:** Nathaniel Scott, Michael Miller, Royce D. Applegate.

COMMENTARY: *History of the World—Part One* is Mel Brooks' parody of the historical film genre. It is divided into four main sequences: the caveman era, ancient Rome, the Spanish Inquisition and the downfall of the French monarchy. Although somewhat uneven, the parody has a handful of priceless moments, particularly the Inquisition which is depicted like a Busby Berkeley musical number. Other highlights include Sid Caesar as the caveman elder, Dom DeLuise as Nero, John Hurt as Jesus and Cloris Leachman as Madame DeFarge. The Hitler sight gag is reserved for the very close of the picture, in which Brooks teases the audience with three coming attraction clips from the nonexistent *Part Two* of the film. "See Hitler on Ice!" Brooks intones, and in a long shot Adolf Hitler skates into view, dressed in a neatly pressed Nazi uniform. A bright spotlight shines on him as he spins and twirls through a series of maneuvers, accompanied by the strains of a Johann Strauss waltz. The last of the preview clips is called *Jews in Space*, a send-up of *Star Wars*, and it is probably the funniest scene in the entire film. In a way, it seems the perfect balance to the ice skating Hitler.

35. *Hitler*
(AKA *The Private Life of Adolf Hitler* and *The Women of Nazi Germany*) (1962)

Richard Basehart as Adolf Hitler
Historical drama

Allied Artists. Written by Sam Neuman & E. Charles Straus; Photographed by Joseph F. Biroc; Edited by Walter Hannemann; Music by Hans J. Salter; Produced by E. Charles Straus; Directed by Stuart Heisler. B & W 107 minutes

ANNOTATED CAST LIST: Cordula Trantow (*Geli Raubal*, Hitler's niece & the object of his fixation); Celia Lovsky (*Angela Raubal*, Hitler's half-sister & Geli's mother); Maria Emo (*Eva Braun*, Hitler's mistress); Narda Onyx (*Gretl Braun*, Eva's sister); Martin Kosleck (*Dr. Joseph Goebbels*, Propaganda Minister); John Mitchum (*Hermann Göring*, Reich Marshal); Rick Traeger (*Heinrich Himmler*, Interior Minister & Head of SS); Berry Kroeger (*Ernst Röhm*, Volatile leader of SA); Albert Szabo (*Emil Maurice*, Hitler's bodyguard); John Banner (*Gregor Strasser*, Nazi party leader regarded as Hitler's rival); J. Stanley Jones (*Martin Bormann*, Hitler's private secretary); Theodore Marcuse (*Julius Streicher*, Hatemongerer & editor of Nazi party newspaper); Carl Esmond (*Wilhelm Keitel*, Field Marshal & Chief of the High Command); Walter Kohler (*Alfred Jodl*, General & Chief of Operations); Martin Brandt (*Heinz Guderian*, Top Panzer general); Gregory Gay (*Erwin Rommel*, Field Marshal & leader of *Afrika Korps*); William Sargent (*Count Claus von Stauffenberg*, Colonel who plants a bomb to assassinate Hitler); John Wengraf (*Dr. Theodor Morell*, Hitler's personal physician); Sirry Steffen (*Anna*, Morell's nurse); Lester Fletcher (*Edmond Heines*, Röhm's adjutant); John Siegfried (Officer who dances with Geli); Ted Knight (*Major Buch*); Otto Rei-

chow (SS officer); Norbert Schiller (*Josef Schönberg*, Anti-Nazi prisoner who overhears Hitler's dictation).

APPRAISAL AND SYNOPSIS: *Hitler* was conceived as a serious attempt to provide a psychological interpretation of Hitler, namely that he suffered from a mother fixation. The film traces Hitler's career from his dictation of *Mein Kampf* in Landsberg prison to his last moment in the bunker before his suicide. Much of the film concentrates on his romantic involvement with his niece, Geli Raubal. When she tries to seduce him, Hitler is unable to respond despite her great attraction. When she ridicules him, he slaps her. After she vows to leave, Hitler has Himmler kill her. Later Hitler becomes attracted by Eva Braun, a model working for his photographer. The Führer invites her to Berchtesgaden, but seemingly rejects her advances. Eva slits her wrists, but is saved. She learns about Hitler's obsession, and is successful in helping him to overcome it. Meanwhile, the plot also skims through the public events of Hitler's career, including his consolidation of power after the Reichstag fire, the SA purge and the death of President Hindenburg. He ruthlessly pursues a path of aggression leading to war, with initial victories and finally defeat. His own military plots against him, but he survives a bomb attempt during a briefing. He becomes unyielding in his demands that the military follow a scorched earth policy. Eva follows him when Hitler retreats to his bunker in Berlin. She convinces him to marry her when defeat appears certain. When they withdraw to commit suicide, Hitler's old mother fixation returns when Eva refers to herself as Frau Hitler. The Führer explodes, saying only one woman had the right to that name. Eva takes cyanide rather than listen to the end of Hitler's tirade.

The inspiration for this psychological approach was probably a 1959 interview with Mimi Reitner in *Stern*, the famous German weekly magazine. Mimi Reitner, the daughter of a Berchtesgaden shopkeeper, was one of Hitler's earliest loves, only sixteen when Hitler met her in 1925. Early in their relationship, Hitler kept repeating to her how much she reminded him of his mother. She also reports that he seemed oddly torn, even fearful, about initiating a relationship. Although the screenplay does not include Mimi Reitner, her account clearly seems to be the basis for the impotent, mother-obsessed Hitler in *Hitler*. However, the theory that Hitler was sexually unnatural is undermined by the later portions of Mimi's account. She relates that Hitler's courtship eventually proceeded and was consummated in normal fashion. This part of her story was ignored by the screenplay. Later, Mimi married an Austrian hotel owner. After they divorced, Hitler attempted to entice her into becoming his live-in lover, but she declined, breaking off their association in 1934.

The key relationship in *Hitler* is his romance with his niece, Geli Raubal. His infatuation with her is an historical fact, but much of their liaison is shrouded in mystery. Her death in September 1931, ruled as a suicide, is extraordinarily suspicious, with many historians believing that it was murder. All things considered, the theory is not farfetched. Hitler was certainly capable of ordering it if he felt she was going to abandon him. In the film, Himmler and Emil Maurice, Hitler's bodyguard, are shown murdering Geli and placing the gun in her hand.

The second half of the film centers on his attachment to Eva Braun. Initially drawn to Eva because she resembles Geli, Hitler has the same hang up when she tries to approach him. She breaks through Hitler's psychological barrier after she strips for him, a rather unconvincing development. Oddly enough, the script suggests that Hitler's relationship with Eva succeeds because he really doesn't love her, but is merely comfortable with her and doesn't feel threatened by her. After all, she was just plain "Eva Braun."

This film is a curious mixture of many good and bad elements. One of the drawbacks is the exaggerated hyperbole of the

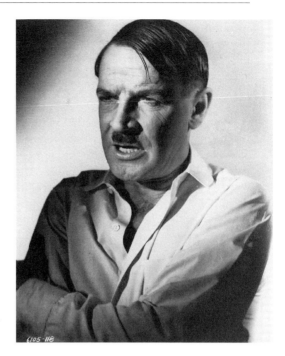

Richard Basehart in *Hitler*.

Martin Kosleck as Joseph Goebbels in *Hitler*. Kosleck first appeared on screen as Goebbels in 1939.

narration, often over the top. The historical fragments of the film are often stilted and full of error. For example, Count von Stauffenberg plans to kill Hitler immediately after the fall of Stalingrad (January 31, 1943). The next scene is the Rastenburg assassination attempt, implying that it directly followed. In fact, 16 months separates these events, and Stauffenberg is portrayed with an eyepatch in January 1943, when the injury in which his eye was wounded occurred in April 1943. Hitler's inner circle is also presented in a rather stilted fashion. For instance, Hermann Göring (John Mitchum) has no dialogue whatsoever, and Rudolf Hess is missing completely. Martin Kosleck, at least, does an excellent supporting job as Goebbels, a role he played in five different films. The military leaders are all indistinguishable from each other. In fact, the picture suggests that they all were part of the Rastenburg plot, even those who were present during the bombing. Stauffenberg is presented with the traditional eyepatch, but he seems to have use of both arms, another gaffe. The sets are very impressive, particularly that of the Berghof, although it resembles the mountain laboratory set from *The Crawling Eye* (1958). The cinematography is excellent, and Hans Salter's musical score is superb, laced with references and snatches from the works of Richard Wagner. The opening credits, with the sound of marching feet as the design of the swastika fills the screen, are done in gothic script and are very compelling and effective. The editing and use of historical footage from *Triumph of the Will* and other sources, is first rate. The costumes are fairly good, but the hairstyles of the women do not reflect the 1930s but rather the 1960s. The anachronism extends to having Hitler mention that his mother wore the hairstyle known as "the flip," such as that worn by Mary Tyler Moore on *The Dick Van Dyke Show*. The script is organized in a strange way and never includes a flashback of Hitler as a child with his doting, possessing mother. It might have clarified what the screenplay was trying to convey by

suggestion. Instead, the entire storyline becomes oblique and rather confusing, which also undermines the production.

HITLER PORTRAYAL: Richard Basehart was renowned for playing unbalanced characters, from the madmen in *Cry Wolf* (1947), *He Walked by Night* (1948) and *House on Telegraph Hill* (1951) to the psychotic hillbilly in *Roseanna McCoy* (1949). He even played a power-crazed leader, depicting the frequently maligned Maximilien Robespierre as a fiend in *The Black Book* (1949). So it is a disappointment that his interpretation of Adolf Hitler, although intense, is terribly erratic and unconvincing. The fault, however, is not really due to Basehart, who read dozens of books and watched hours of Hitler newsreels in preparation for the part. During the initial filming, which he described as an ordeal, he actually lost twelve pounds. However, when the film was first assembled for the studio, they felt that Basehart's reading was too cerebral and too sympathetic. They called him back to reshoot a number of scenes in ranting, raving, scenery-chewing fashion, so now the entire performance seems distorted. Of course, Basehart was hampered as well by the mawkish script that would be impossible for any actor to carry off with verisimilitude. The image of Hitler, eyes filling with tears and tearing his hair in frustration, because he is unable to satiate his lust upon his willing niece, is simply too much to take seriously. It can only seem farcical. Another scene which provokes laughter is when Eva turns up in the bunker and sees Hitler stomping around, dragging his leg behind him in a stiff fashion. She turns to Goebbels to ask, "What's happened to the Führer?" The Propaganda Minister pauses, and one can imagine him replying, "He's trying to walk like me." Basehart's German accent seems far too pronounced, but again this is the way director Heisler wanted him to speak. Given all these handicaps, Basehart manages the part as well as possible in a rather fervent effort. He even excels in one or two instances. His confrontation scene with Röhm during the "Night

Newspaper advertising for *Hitler*.

of the Long Knives" is excellent, and his speech to the Reichstag justifying his action is superb. At this point, he employs the actual words spoken by Hitler, delivering them with great effectiveness. The initial scenes with his sister and her daughters Geli and Friedl also play very well. The middle of the night scene in the bunker in which he wears glasses and sits at the map table when Goebbels and the generals (in their underwear) rush in to observe the Führer, is magnificent, and clearly displays what Basehart was capable of doing with the role. On the whole, the exchanges with Maria Emo as Eva are far more effective than those with Cordula Trantow as Geli. Basehart also works well with Martin Kosleck as Goebbels and John Banner as Strasser. Unfortunately, viewers are so familiar with Banner as Sergeant Schultz in *Hogan's Heroes*, that it makes the scene appear less effective. The lingering question remains, however, exactly how much better Basehart's original concept of the role would have been. Later in his career, Basehart frequently served as a narrator for many documentaries, many of which dealt with Nazi Germany such as *The Rise and Fall of the Third Reich*.

REPRESENTATIVE QUOTES

• You don't have to be a Jew to hold your nose at the sewage pouring out of this imitation Messiah. The German people still believe in law and in order. *(Schönberg to Maurice in Landsberg Prison as Hitler dictates* Mein Kampf*)* He is a perfect example of what I just told you. The world will not accept my warning. Even when they hear it, they won't believe it. *(Hitler to Maurice)*

• For his disciples, Hitler selected those who were, like himself, among the uprooted and the disinherited. Cripples in mind and body, their lives could only have meaning in the unbalanced world of totalitarianism. Among them were Hermann Göring, a morphine-addicted voluptuary; Ernst Röhm, a sadistic pervert; Heinrich Himmler, sinister, inhuman executioner; Joseph Goebbels, club-footed vicious propagandist; Julius Streicher, whip-carrying rabid anti–Semite. Swearing absolute allegiance, each of them had dedicated his life to Hitler and the banner with the black swastika. *(Example of the narrator's rhetoric)*

• The party has nothing whatsoever to do with my personal life. *(Hitler to Strasser, envoking a popular refrain echoed by politicians involved in scandalous matters)*

• Sieg Heil, the Führer has struck a blow for freedom! *(Geli to Hitler after he slaps her)*

• Can you understand this compulsion which fills me with disgust, that turns me away from every woman? I am not like other men. Desire turns to revulsion…. There can be no happiness for me as long as she exists. *(Hitler to Eva, discussing his Oedipus complex)* But she is dead. No matter how real she may seem for you, she only existed in your mind. Adolf, look at me. The proof that she is no longer there is in your eyes. *(Eva after stripping for Hitler)*

36. *Hitler—Dead or Alive* (1942)

Bobby Watson as Adolf Hitler
Adventure/Comedy

Charter House. Written by Karl Brown & Sam Neuman based on a story by Sam Neuman; Photographed by Paul Ivano; Edited by Jack Dennis; Music by Leo Erdody; Produced by Ben Judell & Herman Webber (executive); Directed by Nick Grinde. B & W 70 minutes

ANNOTATED CAST LIST: Ward Bond (*Steve Maschick*, Crime boss & bounty hunter); Dorothy Tree (*Countess Elsa von Brandt*, German actress & double agent known as "Rosebud"); Warren Hymer (*Hans Havermann*, Maschick's triggerman nicknamed "Dutch"); Paul Fix (*Joey Conway*, Maschick's bookkeeper nicknamed "The Book"); Russell Hicks (*Samuel Thornton*, Millionaire who places a bounty on Hitler); Bruce Edwards (*Johnny Stevens*, Canadian pilot whose plane gets hijacked); Felix Basch (*Colonel Hecht*, Concentration camp commandant); Frederick Giermeyer (*Dr. Meyer*, Anti–Nazi who once saved Hitler's life); Kenneth Harlan (*Cutler*, Thornton's lawyer); Faye Wall (*Greta*, Associate to the countess); George Sorel (*Captain Kuhn*, Hecht's adjutant); Joe Forte (*Captain Tanner*, pilot on hijacked plane); Myra Marsh (*Miss Grange*, Thornton's secretary); Eddie Coke (*Jimmy*, Reporter); Jack Gardner (*Lou*, Reporter).

APPRAISAL AND SYNOPSIS: *Hitler—Dead or Alive* is a preposterous, wacky. low-budget effort that succeeds largely due to its very audaciousness. A trio of bootleggers, just released from the penitentiary, notice a news story about an eccentric millionaire who has posted a million dollar bounty on Adolf Hitler, and they volunteer to undertake the hit. This plot formula mixes elements of the genre of gangster comedy, popularized by Edward G. Robinson in *A Slight Case of Murder* (1938) and *Brother Orchid* (1940) and grafting it to Nazi Germany. The concept was no doubt conceived before America's entry into the war and rushed to the screen when American entered the conflict. Charlie Chaplin's *The Great Dictator* (1940) also influenced this effort, but in plot terms Chaplin's earlier short *Shoulder Arms* (1918) was even more influential, particularly when Charlie the soldier goes behind enemy lines to capture the Kaiser and end the war. The same loony atmosphere is reflected in *Hitler—Dead or Alive*. As in the Chaplin short, the film's events are presented with the focus on a single character, in this case crime boss Steve Maschick. If we accept unquestioning his viewpoint and game plan, ignoring all basic reality, then the premise of the film has a consistent logic. Whenever the viewer strays from Maschick's perspective, then the whole edifice comes crashing down. To enjoy this goofy film, the suspension of disbelief has to be absolute. One would not have been surprised if *Hitler—Dead or Alive* ended like *Shoulder Arms*, with the main character awakening in bed at the end with the entire episode having been only a dream. However, this would have under-

mined the propaganda message Maschick spouts at the climax, that not only Hitler but the entire German military complex is evil and must be completely destroyed. This was a message later repeated in many films, such as *Hotel Berlin* (1945), but it was first fully expressed in *Hitler—Dead or Alive*. The formula for this film is a most unusual one, a balancing act combining action, satire, drama, comedy and wartime propaganda, a mixture which barely manages to hold together during the 70 minutes of screen time. The result is very entertaining, an awkward but colorful concoction that was one of the most memorable wartime efforts developed in Hollywood.

The picture opens with a patriotic medley on the soundtrack behind the credits. Two newsmen are interviewing industrialist Samuel Thornton, who is sponsoring a line of bombers for the American war effort. The reporters recall that many months earlier, Thornton offered a million dollar bounty on Hitler, and they ask for the complete story. Thornton then narrates the story of gangster Steve Maschick and his sidekicks, Dutch Havermann and Joey "The Book" Conway who responded to his offer. Just released from prison, the trio make a farcical presentation to Thornton, one just a step above the level of the Three Stooges. Yet the millionaire, whose brother was murdered by the Nazis, immediately offers them a contract. Incidentally, the contract is only for Hitler's death, negating the "*or Alive*" phrase of the title. After closing their deal and getting an advance, Maschick asks if Thornton would like them to take care of Mussolini as well.

Making their way to Canada, Maschick and his cohorts join the RAF as parachute troopers. During practice maneuvers in England, Maschick hijacks a plane and forces pilot Johnny Stevens to fly them to Germany. At first, Stevens thinks the trio are Nazi spies, but their bumbling naiveté makes this seem unlikely. The aircraft runs out of fuel, and they parachute about two hundred miles short of Berlin. (The countryside, of course, looks exactly like the rural backroads of Southern California!) The group shanghai a German military truck, and Dutch Havermann is delighted when he learns that the cargo is beer, reminding him of his bootlegging days. Steven finally figures out that his companions are merely gangsters, and he decides to tag along to learn their plans. The truck is finally chased by Nazi troops on motorcycles. When captured, Maschick claims he is on a secret mission for Hitler. They are taken to the concentration camp at Dachau under the command of Colonel Hecht. He doubts Maschick's story and puts the group in custody. Stevens asks to be treated as a POW, claiming not to be part of Maschick's team, but he is thrown into a cell with them. An extended comic sequence follows as Maschick and his companions play "cat and mouse' with the Nazi guards who have bugged their cell.

Hecht discusses his prisoners with his friend, actress and dancer Countess Else von Brandt. He plans to torture them to learn if they really have a secret message for Hitler, but Else advises he better not interfere in case the group are indeed secret agents working for Hitler. She tells Hecht that the Führer has asked her to dance for him on Saturday night at his special retreat near Dachau. After Hecht leaves, Else plots with Grete, her assistant, to learn the true intent of Maschick and his gang.

At meal time, Stevens finds a playing card in his food, which contains a message from Rosebud, a member of the German underground warning them about Hecht's intent. Prefiguring *Hogan's Heroes*, the group makes fools out of their guards and attempt an immediate escape. They hijack Else's car and burst out of camp, but Dutch is killed as they drive away with Else. She explains that she is Rosebud and directs them to a safe hiding area. After driving off, Else misleads Hecht about the escape. That evening, she sends another member of the underground, Dr. Meyer, to bring Maschick and the others to a secret cellar hideout on the von Brandt estate. Questioning the gangster, else learns that he plans to bump off Hitler in

order to collect a huge reward. The next day, Meyer tells the gang that he actually saved Hitler's life many years earlier when the Führer was attacked by a group of drunken students. His upper lip was disfigured by a broken beer stein during the incident, and the real reason he wears his moustache is to hide the scar. Colonel Hecht visits the countess and reveals that a contract on Hitler's life was discovered on Dutch's body. Hitler has ordered the capture and execution of Maschick and his companions. The Führer also plans to purge the town in which the Americans are eventually found. Hearing this news, Maschick is shocked that Hitler's intended purge would include women and children. Else is issued passes for herself and four musicians to enter Hitler's compound and perform for him that evening.

Else is skeptical about Maschick's scheme and warns him that Hitler frequently uses a double, so when Maschick strikes, he may wind up only killing an impostor. After she leaves, Dr. Meyer decides to join the conspiracy and, together with Maschick, Conway and Stephens, they tie up Else's musicians, dress up in their tuxedos and head off to Hitler's compound. At first Else is startled to see them, but offers to help them. She instructs them to pretend to tune their instruments. The guests at the reception are military officers. Two of them question Maschick about Beethoven, but before he can bluff a reply, Hitler's plane lands at his private runway, and everyone prepares to greet him. Storming into the room full of bluster and bravura, Hitler boasts of his plans for world conquest. The Führer then approaches Else and criticizes her for being overdressed for dancing. Colonel Hecht suddenly spots Maschick, draws his weapon and fires. Maschick grabs Hitler and uses him as a human shield. A gunfight breaks out, and Conway is killed. Hitler panics and orders his guards to stop firing and drop their guns. The dictator offers Maschick five hundred million dollars to release him, but the gunman ignores the offer. Instead, he orders Stevens to take the countess and fly to England in Hitler's plane. He tells them with Hitler as his hostage, he may be able to negotiate an end to the war.

Maschick and Dr. Meyer take their hostage and return to the hideout beneath the von Brandt estate. When they get there, Greta explains that the real musicians have escaped. Maschick takes out a razor and shaves off Hitler's moustache, revealing a jagged scar on his upper lip. Dr. Meyer confirms that their prisoner is indeed the genuine Führer. Hitler begs Meyer to save him a second time, but his pleadings fall on dead ears. Maschick then decides to cut off Hitler's famous forelock as a souvenir. Nazi soldiers storm the hideout. Amazingly, they fail to recognize Hitler with his altered appearance. Maschick tells Hecht that the genuine Hitler outwitted them and escaped. When Hitler yells, "I am your Führer," Hecht slaps him and orders that he be taken outside and immediately shot. "Meyer, tell them about my lip, please," Hitler entreats, but the doctor ignores him. Hitler breaks free and is shot down in the street. Hecht walks up to the wounded dictator and shoots him in the head, saying, "To think that Germany could produce a piece of filth like you." Maschick mutters, "My sentiments exactly." A firing squad is set up. As local women and children are shot before his eyes, Maschick vows that soon all Nazis will be exterminated.

Thornton concludes his story to the reporters, saying that Maschick and Dr. Meyer died bravely, and that the ransom money they earned is being used to build additional bombers for the war effort. Johnny Stevens served as test pilot for the first plane. The reporters are confused, because no announcement was ever made about the death of Hitler. Thornton replies that the Nazis are covering it up, using an impostor. The millionaire admits he was wrong thinking he could end the war by killing Hitler. The warlords of Germany are the real enemy, not any one individual, and they must all be wiped out. As the film concludes, the re-porters and Thornton eulogize Steve Maschick as a great American. The musical fade out paraphrases "My Country 'Tis of Thee."

The pace of *Hitler—Dead or Alive* is pretty breakneck towards the finish, seemingly in an attempt to allow the viewer no time to reflect as the film's implausibilities pile up. For example, why didn't Maschick escape with his hostage on the airplane with Stevens? Certainly it would have been easier to end the war with Hitler a prisoner in England. How did Thornton know Maschick's last words when the only one who could hear him were his Nazi executioners? There are even a number of visual absurdities. When Maschick unpacks his violin case, it is loaded with guns, which he passes out to his group. Then he manages to remove a full-sized violin from the same case. The final absurdity is the sincere blather with which Thornton and the reporters praise Steve Maschick, an irresponsible thug and criminal, as an ideal American. The conclusion manages to tie up the entire film in a neat, surreal package.

HITLER PORTRAYAL: Bobby Watson's performance as Hitler is basically at parody level, cocky and full of wild exaggerations. His German accent is even more elaborate and corny than his previous effort in the short version of *The Devil with Hitler*, using "dere" for there and "vorld" for world. Further distortions include the word "schprang" for sprang and "schpeak" for speak. Watson's vocal exaggerations are usually the weakest point in his Hitler renditions, and his entry scene in the picture are among his poorest vocal effort. His physical resemblance to Hitler, however, remains astonishing. His finest moments come after he is taken hostage. His braggadocio falls away and is replaced by a terrified hysteria that is genuinely funny. His panic-filled cry to his bodyguards, "Stop shootin'! Stop shootin'!" is the comic highlight of the film. Later, Watson even uses his voice in a clever way after Ward Bond shaves off his moustache and forelock, raising it to a higher level so the Nazi thugs are unable to recognize him and slap him around. Even today, seeing

Hitler abused in this scene proves deeply satisfying. When he runs away and is shot, however, his death scene produces no reaction, even when a gun is aimed on his head as he lies in the gutter. his stylized collapsed seems similar to a cartoon character who falls off a cliff. Not only is Hitler's death insignificant, but it makes no change whatsoever to the war effort, as the Nazi leaders employ a double to carry on the illusion that Hitler is still in power. The moral responsibility for the war and its consequences has shifted from Hitler to the German government (and perhaps the people as well) by this point in the film. Hitler is only a meaningless figurehead. Yet this outcome doesn't seem to correlate with the reverential attitude expressed about Hitler by all the other German characters in the film, except for members of the underground. This strange dichotomy (Hitler is everything vs. Hitler is nothing) arises without any resolution or explanation.

Ward Bond's performance as the comic gang leader is the glue which holds the entire production together, and he endows the part with an easy-going vitality. His other cohorts, Warren Hymer and Paul Fix, are enjoyable in small doses, and their deaths in the middle of the story are truly unexpected, since comic sidekicks are seldom disposed of in such a fashion. Russell Hicks is convincing as the eccentric millionaire, a typical stock role he played many times in various films. The other performers are adequate and unexceptional. Dorothy Tree comes off best, even though her role is rather shallow. Bruce Edwards is likable and is perhaps the most normal character in the story, the only member of the cast with whom the audience could identify. Felix Basch as Hecht is an utter failure, and he illustrates how fine a job Werner Klemperer did as Colonel Klink in *Hogan's Heroes* in a rather similar role. Of course, it is impossible to watch the antics of Basch in Dachau without the painful reminder of the actual tragic events that occurred there.

REPRESENTATIVE QUOTES

• Ah, the guy is nothin' but a mobster. He can be had, same as any other big shot. *(Maschick to Thornton, discussing his contract on Hitler)*

• Right now the only thing I want to do is put a stop to the killing of dames and kids by knocking over the only guy in the world that's rotten enough to do such a trick. *(Maschick plotting in von Brandt's hideout)*

• Today Europe, tomorrow the world! Ir resistibly the German might will conquer all foes: Russia, England, America, Japan ... With Russia for a base, with the English navy at my command, with the Americans groveling at my feet, I will take Japan by telephone. *(Hitler boasting to his guests at his country house)*

• Napoleon? It is no honor to surpass his silly little pranks. What I have done is nothing. When you hear of my plans with the conquest of America, then you will have the measure of world greatness. *(Hitler mocking any historical comparisons to himself)*

37. *The Hitler Gang* (1944)

Bobby Watson as Adolf Hitler
Historical drama

Paramount. Written by Frances Goodrich & Albert Hackett; Photographed by Ernest Laszlo; Edited by Eda Warren; Music by David Buttolph; Produced by B. G. De-Sylvia; Directed by John Farrow. B & W 101 minutes

ANNOTATED CAST LIST: Roman Bohnen (*Captain Ernst Röhm*, Officer who hires Hitler to infiltrate a political party, later SA leader); Martin Kosleck (*Dr. Joseph Goebbels*, Chief Nazi party propagandist); Victor Varconi (*Rudolf Hess*, Deputy leader of the Nazi party); Fritz Kortner (*Gregor Strasser*, Nazi party leader who rivaled Hitler); Luis Van Rooten (*Heinrich Himmler*, Strasser's chauffeur, later SS leader); Alexander Pope (*Hermann Göring*, Noted aviator & war hero recruited by the Nazi party); Poldi Dur (*Geli Raubal*, Hitler's niece & object of his affection); Helene Thimig (*Angela Raubal*, Hit-

An early scene from *The Hitler Gang*. Hess and Röhm comfort Hitler after he was shouted down by hecklers who tried to break up his rally.

ler's half-sister & Geli's mother); Ernst Verebes (*Anton Drexler*, Founder of Nazi party); Sig Ruman (*Field Marshal Paul von Hindenburg*, President of Germany who appointed Hitler as Chancellor); Walter Kingsford (*Franz von Papen*, Leader of Catholic Center party & Hitler's Vice Chancellor); Reinhold Schunzel (*General Erich Ludendorff*, War hero & participant in the Beer Hall Putsch); Ludwig Donath (*Gustav von Kahr*, State commissioner in Munich who turned against Hitler during the Beer Hall Putsch); Frank Reicher (*Franz Gürtner*, Bavarian Justice Minister); Rudolf Anders (*Ludwig Stenglein*, Bavarian State Prosecutor); Egon Brecher (*Franz Hemmrich*, Landsberg prison warden); Alexander Granach (*Julius Streicher*, Editor of party newspaper); Tonio Selwart (*Alfred Rosenberg*, Radical Nazi philosopher); Richard Ryen (*Adolf Wagner*, Nazi associate of Hitler, later Bavarian Interior Minister);

Fred Nurney (*General Franz Xaver von Epp*, Röhm's superior who financed the Nazi newspaper); Arthur Loft (*Colonel Walther von Reichenau*, Army official who gives Hitler the ultimatum to depose Röhm); Lionel Royce (*Fritz Thyssen*, Industrialist who supports Hitler); John Mylong (Military doctor at Pasewalk Hospital who treats Hitler when he is blind); Leni Koch (*Helene Hanfstaengl*, Woman who hides Hitler after collapse of the Putsch); Milton Parsons (Nazi grammar school teacher); Ray Collins (*Cardinal Michael von Faulhaber*, Catholic leader in Munich who preaches against Hitler); Ivan Triesault (*Martin Niemöller*, Pastor who visits Hitler to protest his policies); Walter Abel, Albert Dekker (Narrators).

APPRAISAL AND SYNOPSIS: *The Hitler Gang* was the first serious attempt to portray Adolf Hitler in a film, concentrating on his rise to power from an insignificant corporal recuperating in a military hospital in November 1918 to his full assumption of power after the Röhm purge and the death of Hindenburg in the summer of 1934. It is a fifteen year story told as accurately as possible given the sketchy history available to researchers in 1944. Considering the understandable level of anti-Nazi rhetoric, the general overview is reasonably accurate, even considering the highly speculative death/murder of Geli Raubal, Hitler niece. Even today, historians have many unanswered questions concerning this case, but the possibility of Hitler's involvement still cannot be dismissed. Suffice it to say the screenwriters made a reasonable effort to stick fairly close to the facts. Serious effort was also given to casting the parts of Hitler and his entourage with actors who closely resembled these individuals. One has to remember that the Nazi leaders were contemporaries at this point, not historical figures, and events such as the Rastenberg assassination attempt, the Battle of the Bulge and the bunker finale had not yet occurred. So in terms of script, performance, cinematography, music and other technical aspects, *The Hitler Gang* is a substantial achievement.

The film opens at Pasewalk military hospital in Pomerania where a doctor diagnoses one of his patients, Corporal Adolf Hitler, suffering from blindness. The doctor claims his condition is hysterical in origin (although this theory is largely disputed today, since chlorine gas can indeed produce temporary blindness.) An armistice is signed ending the First World War, and when he is dismissed from the hospital, Hitler moves to the barracks of the List Regiment in Munich. After the abdication of Kaiser Wilhelm, Hitler trims the waxed tips of his mustache, adopting one of Chaplinesque proportions. He overhears some soldiers planning an insurrection, and reports the news to Captain Röhm, who hires him as a paid informer. He is assigned to investigate the German Workers Party. Hitler joins the group, and soon becomes their leading spokesman, The army funds the party so it can purchase a newspaper. Hitler assumes control of the

group, which becomes the National Socialist Workers Party or the Nazi party.

Hitler's speaking prowess attracts more and more members, including Rudolf Hess, Gregor Strasser and his chauffeur Heinrich Himmler. The party grows in influence and includes the support of General Erich Ludendorff, one of the most respected German military leaders. When hecklers break up a party meeting, Hermann Göring is persuaded to join the Nazi party and organize troops to keep order. Hitler manipulates various people, including Gustav von Kahr, the Bavarian State Commissioner, when a political crisis develops in November 1923. Taking control of Kahr's political meeting in a beer hall, Hitler proclaims a new government. Kahr consents, but renounces his agreement after he leaves the meeting. Ludendorff suggests that they march, but police fire on them and the Putsch collapses. Hitler is arrested, but receives only a light sentence. He is treated like an honored guest at Landsberg prison, where he dictates a book, *Mein Kampf*, to Hess. An astrologer advises the Führer to take several years to crystallize his ideas before making another grab for power. Goebbels becomes a close associate after the Führer is released from prison. Hitler buys a retreat, the Berghof, at Berchtesgaden, and hires his half-sister Angela Raubal to act as housekeeper. Hitler becomes infatuated with his niece, Geli, who is increasingly alarmed by his attention. The Nazi leaders fear scandal resulting from this relationship, and they endeavor to turn Hitler against her, manufacturing an imaginary romance. Geli is shot, and the case is ruled a suicide. An editor tries to expose the real cause of Geli's death, but the Nazis kill him before he is able to make trouble.

Hitler is appointed Chancellor by the aged German President, Field Marshal Paul von Hindenburg on January 30, 1933. Hitler arranges for the Reichstag to be set on fire, blaming the Communists for the deed. Hindenburg grants Hitler emergency powers which allows the Chancellor to destroy all rival parties and establish the dominance of

Goebbels (Martin Kosleck) and Hitler (Bobby Watson).

the Nazis. The army leadership tells Hitler that they will seize control of the government unless the SA, led by Karl Röhm, is suppressed. On the other hand, if Hitler complies, they will swear allegiance to him and assure him total power after the death of President Hindenburg. On June 30, 1934, Hitler takes action against the SA, claiming they were planning to revolt. Röhm is arrested, and many of the SA leadership are killed. At the same time, the Nazis use the date, known as the "Night of the Long Knives" to wipe out old rivals such as Gregor Strasser and Gustav von Kahr. Pastor Martin Niemöller, a respected minister, visits Hitler to protest Nazi policies, particularly the indoctrination of children. Hitler replies that he intends to restructure religion in his own image, and Niemöller predicts

that people will eventually rise up and bring down the Nazis. Hitler orders Röhm to be shot. The army swears total obedience to Hitler after Hindenburg dies in August 1934. Hitler looks forward to his future plans, but as he does so, he feels haunted by Niemöller's prediction. A brief montage concludes the film, showing the flags of 55 nations that have risen in opposition to Hitler and Nazi Germany.

The primary flaw of *The Hitler Gang* is its structure. Since the story began with the end of World War I, it should have finished with the start of World War II. By ending in 1934, the "Night of the Long Knives" becomes the climax of the film. Although this event had a handful of innocent victims, most of those killed were just other Nazis, members of the vicious SA. The carnage portrayed is Nazis killing Nazis, and despite the butchery, it is hard to feel any sympathy for these brutish men. It is a little puzzling why the film spends so much footage on the "Night of the Long Knives," showing execution after execution. Except for this rather curious sequence, *The Hitler Gang* is an admirable historical drama on almost all counts.

HITLER PORTRAYAL: For one of the few times in his career, Bobby Watson was billed more formally as Robert Watson in the closing credits for *The Hitler Gang* (there are no opening credits). In fact, Paramount had a few initial doubts about using Watson, since he was primarily known as a comedian. He made a screen test, however, concentrating on lowering his voice slightly, and the result instantly removed any doubts as to his casting. Watson's performance was the most convincing screen portrayal until the 1970s. Of course, Watson's physical resemblance to Hitler is a huge plus. The actor jokingly remarked that Hitler resembled him rather than vice-versa since he was one year older than the Nazi dictator. The most significant area of similarity is the eyes. Watson's stare has the same penetrating intensity as Hitler. Watson needed little makeup after duplicating the Führer's hairstyle and mustache. As demonstrated in many photographs, Hitler experimented somewhat with the shape of his mustache, but the basic style is the one Watson adopts in the film. It looks correct, unlike the one he used in *Miracle of Morgan's Creek* or the awkward array of mustaches that many other Hitler impersonators use. The only other change applied to Watson is that his body was slightly padded to make him stockier. The weakest point of Watson's performance is usually his voice, but except for one or two instances, his vocal interpretation ranges from good to excellent. He strictly avoids the comic German accent he used in his other Hitler films. His speechmaking is confined to early public meetings leading up to the Beer Hall Putsch. These moments are convincing, although not the best moments. Watson's strongest highlight

is his office meeting with Fritz Thyssen and other notables in which he outlines his plans for restoring the strength of the German military. In that spellbinding scene, Watson captures Hitler's gestures, speech pattern, powers of persuasion and charisma to a tee. Watson's weakest moments are in his advances toward Geli. Of course the concept of Hitler in love is practically impossible to consider, but as a figure of hatred, of manipulation, of guile and of deceit, Watson is perfect. He also is impressive in the concluding scene as he passes by the Nazi globe on the oversized set, while his mind considers the prophecy of Martin Niemöller. Watson also manages to interact very well with the other actors, performing perfectly in an ensemble. Although Watson is the lead, this film is purposely called *The Hitler Gang*, to stress that it is a collective portrait of evil. The script is well balanced to show the detestable characters of Göring (Alexander Pope), Himmler (Luis van Rooten), Goebbels (Martin Kosleck), as the trio play cards while they gossip about their enemies, or compare lists of victims for the "Night of the Long Knives." Only Hess (Victor Varconi) is presented in a neutral fashion as a lightweight, while Hitler's possible competitor, Gregor Strasser (Fritz Kortner) is portrayed as mysterious and complex. All of these supporting players are magnificent, particularly Kosleck who played the role of Goebbels numerous times, beginning with *Confessions of a Nazi Spy* (1939). At the same time, Watson's Hitler remains the spider at the center of the web, the only one capable of drawing them all together. In this environment, the Nazi government would likely have collapsed from internal squabbling and rivalry if the Führer had been eliminated in 1935 or 1936. Historians might argue about that interpretation, but it is a possibility worth some consideration. The only disappointment with *The Hitler Gang* is that it ends in the mid–1930s. Somehow, the audience feels cheated that the screenplay doesn't depict the Munich Conference. It would have been captivating to see how Watson would have played the behind-the-scenes machinations of Hitler, particularly since this key moment in history has never been fully explored in terms of cinema.

REPRESENTATIVE QUOTES

• People respect power and violence. They thrive under it. Terror is a very wholesome thing. *(Göring to Hitler at their first meeting)*

• Our meetings have been forbidden. It seems that they feel fourteen meetings in one night are a little too much. *(Hess to Hitler)* So, these gentlemen are alarmed at the thought of fourteen meetings. What will they say when we hang the first fourteen hundred, no—the first fourteen thousand from the lamp posts? *(Hitler's response)*

• You mustn't leave me. You are the only friend I have. I am surrounded by people who are just trying to use me, people who are plotting against me behind my back. I've got to have someone near me I can trust. Don't leave, Geli. *(Hitler to Geli)*

• My quarrel is not with the churches. I am against the whole Jewish Communist idea of Christianity! *(Hitler to Rosenberg)*

• National Socialism is more than a political program. It comprises everything of importance to mankind, including religion. *(Hitler to Martin Niemöller)*

38.   *Hitler Meets Christ* (2000)

Michael Moriarty as Adolf Hitler
Tragicomedy

Third Tribe Productions. Written by Michael Moriarty; Photographed by A. Jonathan Benny; Edited by A. Jonathan Benny; Music by Michael Moriarty; Produced by Jeremy Dyson & Brendan Keown; Directed by Brendan Keown. B & W 76 minutes

ANNOTATED CAST LIST: Michael Moriarty (Vagrant who believes he is Adolf Hitler); Wyatt Page (Vagrant who believes he is Jesus Christ).

APPRAISAL AND SYNOPSIS: *Hitler Meets Christ* is a low budget art film shot entirely in black and white on the East side skid row district of Vancouver, Canada. It is based on a play by actor Michael Moriarty, best remembered for his films *Bang the Drum Slowly* (1973), *Q* (1982) and *The Hanoi Hilton* (1987), as well as four seasons as prosecuting attorney Ben Stone on the celebrated television series *Law and Order*. He wrote *Hitler Meets Christ* in the late 1980s, performing it in a dramatic reading on Broadway. Famed Nobel prize winner Elie Weisel was particularly moved by the drama and urged Moriarty to consider making a film based on it. The project lay fallow until two innovative graduate film students from the University of British Columbia became interested in the project. The storyline involves two vagrants who are convinced they are indeed Jesus Christ and Adolf Hitler. Moriarty characterizes the film as both a comedy, since the audience laughs at Hitler, and a tragedy because this poor individual is trapped with the soul of Hitler which approaches the level of genuine possession. These two men meet at a train station in Vancouver and wander through the downtrodden area as they discuss the depth of Hitler's sins and his confusion and fury about the attitude of Christ, whose love and willingness to forgive appears to be limitless. To a certain extent, the film is influenced by *Waiting for Godot*, an existential drama in which a number of philosophical issues are raised, dusted off, examined and sometimes discarded. The basic question is whether Hitler is beyond the possibility of redemption. He tries to convince Christ that this is the case, that his sins are too great, but his companion, filled with the spirit of Christ, tries to convince him that no one is beyond the love of God. The film has been described as philosophical, unconventional and intellectually challenging.

HITLER PORTRAYAL: Michael Moriarty plays his character with total conviction that he is indeed Hitler. His appearance is run down and disheveled, and the audience is

In contemporary Vancouver, two vagrants believe themselves to be Jesus Christ (Wyatt Page), left, and Adolf Hitler (Michael Moriarty). Photograph by Alastair Bird.

reminded that Hitler himself lived a down and out existence as a vagrant in Vienna before World War I. He wears a dark shirt and a windbreaker. He has the traditional dark Hitler moustache, surrounded by the gray stubble of an unshaven beard. His hair is thinning, but frequently he pushes the front strands of his hair forward to resemble the Hitler forelock. His eyes, in particular, assume the hypnotic stare associated with Hitler. His character is a cigarette smoker, however, in his new surroundings. He is waiting and hoping for the release of death, but fearful that he will spend eternity in one body or another knowing he is

Hitler (Michael Moriarty) in prayer, an unusual moment from *Hitler Meets Christ*.

Hitler and bearing the full torment of that knowledge. Wyatt Page forms a perfect counterpoint to Moriarty's Hitler, serene, blissful yet stubborn in his insistence on the power of forgiveness and redemption. Moriarty wants the audience to assume these characters are Hitler and Christ, that casting them as homeless men in Vancouver is merely a device to have a realistic, contemporary setting. He feels the drama would not work if these mythic figures, the personification of good and evil, were projected instead into a shadowy netherworld or a cloudy limbo.

REPRESENTATIVE QUOTES

• I have never been so evil that I willingly became a Christian. I was tortured into my doubts by the unbearable agony of having to live to eternity as Adolf Hitler. But at least I am honest and truthful. I said what I was going to do and I did it. Christians? Love thy neighbor as thyself? They turned their backs on their neighbors so fast, with such speed, that Himmler had no place to put the Jews, they were being identified and informed on in such numbers. *(Hitler to Christ)*

• I can't sleep. As soon as I'm just about to slip off, some anniversary comes, the end of World War II, the beginning of World War II and Auschwitz! If I hear another word about Auschwitz, I think I will go mad. *(Hitler to Christ)*

• There we are, entering Paris, and I'm strutting around like a great clown! And all the while, God was waiting for me, grinning at me like the devil himself, leading me slowly, deeply and ruthlessly to my greatest humiliation—Russia! Russia! Russia! Russia! *(Hitler to Christ)*

39. *Hitler: The Last Ten Days*
(1975)

Alec Guinness as Adolf Hitler
Historical drama

Paramount. Written by Ennio De Concini, Maria Pia Fusco & Wolfgang Rein-

hardt; Photographed by Ennio Guarnieri; Edited by Kevin Connor; Music by Mischa Spoliansky, Richard Wagner & Johann Strauss, Jr.; Produced by Wolfgang Reinhardt; Directed by Ennio De Concini. B & W and Color 108 minutes

ANNOTATED CAST LIST: Simon Ward (*Major Hoffman*, German officer who witnesses the events in the bunker); Doris Kunstmann (*Eva Braun*, Hitler's mistress); John Bennett (*Dr. Joseph Goebbels*, Propaganda Minister); Barbara Jefford (*Magda Goebbels*, His wife); Mark Kingston (*Martin Bormann*, Hitler's private secretary); Timothy West (*Dr. Karl Gebhardt*, Himmler's doctor nominated to head the German Red Cross); John Hallam (*Colonel Otto Günsche*, Hitler's personal adjutant); Philip Stone (*Alfred Jodl*, General & Chief of Operations); Gabriele Ferzetti (*Wilhelm Keitel*, Field Marshal & Chief of the High Command); Julian Glover (*Hermann Fegelein*, SS General executed for desertion); Michael Goodliffe (*Helmut Weidling*, General appointed as commander of Fortress Berlin); John Barron (*Dr. Ludwig Stumpfegger*, Hitler's surgeon); Adolfo Celi (*Hans Krebs*, Chief of Army General Staff); Kenneth Colley (*Gerhardt Boldt*, Aide to General Krebs); Eric Porter (*Robert Ritter von Greim*, Officer who flies to the bunker to be appointed new head of Luftwaffe); Diane Cilento (*Hanna Reitsch*, Greim's female pilot who idolizes Hitler); Richard Pescud (*Colonel Nicolaus von Below*, Hitler's Luftwaffe adjutant); Ann Lynn (*Traudl Junge*, Hitler's dictation secretary); Sheila Gish (*Gerda Christian*, Hitler's filing secretary); Andrew Sachs (*Walter Wagner*, City official who marries Hitler & Eva Braun); Phyllida Law (*Constanze Manzialy*, Bunker cook); William Abney (*Vice Admiral Erich Voss*, Navy adjutant); Joss Ackland (*Wilhelm Burgdorf*, Chief of Military Personnel); Philip Locke (*Karl Hanke*, Himmler's replacement as Gestapo Chief); John Savident (*Walter Hewell*, Ribbentrop's representative); Angela Pleasence (*Trudie*, Courier for the Hitler Youth); James Cossins (Army officer).

APPRAISAL AND SYNOPSIS: This is a thoughtful, well-intentioned film that falls short of its intended goal of accurately recreating the last ten days of Hitler. After the opening credits, there are signed testimonials of accuracy by Hugh Trevor-Roper, author of *The Last Days of Hitler*, and Gerhardt Boldt, an orderly of General Krebs who was present in the bunker for three days during the last week of Hitler's life. But these endorsements are immediately followed by the introduction of a fictitious character, Major Hoffman, through whose eyes we witness most of the events. If historical accuracy is an important factor in the minds of the filmmakers, why do they immediately contaminate their concept with a bogus central figure? It is interesting to parse the endorsements, in which the writers leave themselves loopholes for the fabrications that slip into the story, such as the subway flooding (see *The Last Ten Days* for full details of this exaggerated event). Other problems with the film result from the hybrid nature of the production, in which the international cast and crew do not always seem to blend well together. Finally, the editing and pacing of the story is very stodgy, resulting in many slow gaps that disturbed the flow of the film. The director seemingly chose to rely on the magic of Alec Guinness to hold the entire film together, but whenever the audience becomes aware of Guinness the performer, it undermines the effectiveness of his Hitler portrayal. The film begins with an iris on Alec Guinness as Hitler, which gradually opens as the Führer meets with Dr. Karl Gebhardt, Himmler's physician, who is seeking confirmation of his appointment as head of the German Red Cross. As he speaks of his experiments on concentration camp inmates, news clips of actual victims are flashed on the screen. Gebhardt becomes nervous as Hitler stares at him impassively, but is greatly relieved when he finally replies "I confirm it, you have done excellent work for the Third Reich." The iris closes in on the Führer, and a narrator begins an overview of Hitler's rise and fall. The credits unfold as the soundtrack blares out the *Prelude* to Act III of *Lohengrin* by Wagner and the map of Europe shows the wartime conquests and the eventual reverses of Nazi Germany. The camera draws in to the area of Berlin as the date "20 April 1945" appears in gothic lettering. After another false start with Hitler raging during a military briefing, the film proper begins as a Goebbels radio broadcast is heard proclaiming the Führer's 56th birthday and the figure of Major Hoffman is followed as he approaches the bunker entrance in the Chan-

Alec Guiness as the Führer demands that the Hitler Youth defend the bridges of Berlin in *Hitler: The Last Ten Days*.

cellery garden. As he descends the stairway into the darkness, the accuracy endorsements by Trevor-Roper and Boldt are displayed on the screen. Hitler is impressed with Hoffman as he gives his report on the 3rd Panzer Army, and he orders him to remain at the bunker for further assignments. The General Staff is troubled because Hitler's instructions have become outlandish, ordering his small and reduced forces to attack the well-equipped Red Army, which numbers over two million men. Field Marshal Keitel and General Jodl, his most loyal officers, try to explain these facts to him, which only provokes an angry outburst from Hitler. He then dispatches them personally to oversee the deployment of these forces, particularly the hastily reorganized Twelfth army under General Wenck, whom Hitler expected to counterattack and break the Russian assault on Berlin.

When the attacks he ordered still fail to materialize. Hitler is furious. A series of other disastrous events follow. Göring dispatches a radiogram which Hitler interprets, with the prompting of Goebbels, as a treasonous ultimatum and a grab for power. He then orders the Reich Marshal to be dismissed from office. The Russian stranglehold on Berlin tightens. The Führer orders a Luftwaffe officer, Robert Ritter von Greim, to fly to Berlin for a personal conference. The officer crash lands the following day with Hanna Reitsch, his personal pilot. Hanna is a genuine female warrior and enthusiastic Nazi, deeply enamored of Hitler, and she is stunned when she discovers that Eva Braun, an empty-headed butterfly, has been the Führer's mistress for over ten years. Hitler appoints von Greim as Göring's successor, despite the wounds from his recent landing which made the officer a partial cripple. The Führer instructs him to fly to Munich and order the Luftwaffe to help Wenck's army advance on Berlin. Hitler orders the members of the Hitler Youth, his only reserve, to defend the bridgeheads which would be the access point for Wenck's forces to enter Berlin. The slapdash defense

by these teenagers results in a pointless bloodbath, since no relief forces ever arrived. When news comes of Himmler's attempt to begin peace negotiations, no one in the bunker is willing to pass the information to the Führer. The Nazi leaders finally decide to let Hitler's valet bring him the news. The Führer's rage is kept off camera in this case, instead following a tearful Eva who rushes to Magda Goebbels' side to proclaim Himmler's actions as the ultimate betrayal. Hitler takes his frustration out on General Fegelein, Himmler's representative at the bunker. Since the general is married to her sister, Eva pleads for his life, but in vain.

Goebbels brings to Hitler a member of the Hitler Youth who destroyed a Russian tank single handedly. The Hitler decorates him and pats his cheek, saying "Good boy, now go back and fight." But it seems Hitler himself has given up all hope. He takes a final walk in the Chancellery garden with his dog Blondi, amidst exploding bombshells, as *Siegfried's Funeral March* from *Götterdämmerung* is played on the soundtrack. When he returns down the stairway to the bunker, he has made up his mind to commit suicide, and he calmly discusses his plans with his entourage. He questions the others, including Magda Goebbels, about their plans, and grimly notes her decision to kill her own children.

Eva and Hitler marry in the early morning hour of April 29th. After a brief reception, during which the Führer hands out cyanide capsules as if they were party favors, Hitler secludes himself with his dictation secretary, Traudl Junge, to write his last will and political testament. After four copies are typed and signed, Hitler dispatches couriers to bring the final political statement to his newly appointed successor, Admiral Karl Dönitz, and to other officials. Major Hoffman volunteers to carry one of the documents, and Hitler assigns him to the most hazardous of the delivery routes, to Field Marshal Schörner and his forces, surrounded by the Russian forces sixty miles south of Berlin. (In real life, this assignment was given to Major Willi Johannmeier, an army adjutant.) As soon as Hoffman leaves the bunker, he tears up Hitler's will in disgust and flees. Meanwhile, Hitler orders General Krebs to open the river locks and flood the subway system. Krebs protests that the subways are currently being used as field hospitals and public shelters, and thousands will be drowned. Hitler insists, and a series of still photos appear, giving the mistaken impression that this mass drowning was immediately carried out.

Hitler and Eva withdraw, and Hitler's mood turns bitter. Eva is stunned when her husband admits that he knew the war was lost in February 1943, when the German Sixth Army surrendered at the battle of Stalingrad. Eva is finally disillusioned, and kills herself behind Hitler's back while he starts to rant about the stupidity of women. When he turns and sees her dead body, he considers it yet another betrayal. He shoots himself off camera. As the sound of the gun shot reverberates through the bunker, almost everyone responds with neither joy nor sorrow, but instead by lighting up cigarettes, a privilege refused them in the bunker as long as Hitler lived. The last few minutes of *Die Fledermaus Overture* by Johann Strauss, Jr., is heard as background music for the end credits.

Hitler: The Last Ten Days is weakest at its most serious moments, awkwardly employing historic footage at key points which seems clichéd instead of profound. For instance, when Hitler is informed that Russian and American troops have come in contact with each other, he predicts they will soon be fighting. Then the historic footage is incorporated showing the soldiers embracing and toasting one other. The whole effect is ham-handed rather than ironic. The film is at its best when it employs black humor instead. These moments actually become the highlights, particularly since the humor is low key and almost subtle. One of the first bits occurs after Goebbels gives Hitler Wagner's manuscript score to *Götterdämmerung*, which deeply moves the Führer. But then Magda lets it slip that it is only a reproduc-

tion and Goebbels starts to jostle her with his elbow, all occurring in the background. Then there is the moment when Hanna Reitsch, to her astonishment and jealousy, learns that the type of woman Hitler prefers is Eva Braun, frolicking around in peasant garb. Then there is the anxious byplay between Bormann, Goebbels and General Krebs to determine which of them will bring Hitler the news of Himmler's treachery. The wedding ceremony is also a gem, as Hitler's eyes bulge when he is asked if he is of pure Aryan stock. There is Eva's singing "When You're Smiling" at her wedding party, finally breaking down Bormann's reserve and getting him to sing along with her. Even the final scene, after Hitler's death, has a satirical edge, as one of Hitler's secretaries opens her purse and appears to reach for a cyanide capsule, but grabs a cigarette instead. All of these moments compare favorably to the bland staging of the military conferences, which run on far too long and manage to bring the film to a standstill. The layout of the bunker is much too roomy, avoiding the claustrophobic air that should be part of the production. Hitler also has room in the bunker for Speer's models for the rebuilding of Berlin, which fill an entire chamber. The scenes of Hitler and these models have become something of a cliché in the bunker films. In actuality, Hitler had a tabletop model for Linz; it was not in the bunker but a room in the Chancellery.

HITLER PORTRAYAL: There are numerous advantages as well as liabilities in having an actor of the caliber of Guinness portray Hitler. His makeup is surprisingly good, particularly in far and mid-shots. But then his familiar voice breaks the illusion whenever he speaks with his usual, cultured tones. There is one rather remarkable parallel to *Star Wars* (1977). After reading Göring's telegram, Hitler comments, "I've thought it for a long time, a long time." The actor's tone of voice, phrasing, and even the pause between the repeated words are exactly the same as in *Star Wars* when he says, "Obi-Wan, that's a name I haven't heard for a long time, a long time." This certainly conjures up another interpretation for the "Dark Side of the Force." Incidentally, Guinness speaks in his natural voice, except when he begins to shout, when he mysteriously picks up a German accent. He has most of Hitler's gestures down pat. His uniforms appear rather bulky, giving his Hitler a rather stout appearance. At times, the other actors appear to be standing on platforms, so they can appear to be taller than Guinness. The lighting of the film is seldom dark, without any of the gloomy shadows of Pabst's *Last Ten Days*, for instance. In fact, Guinness seems always to be brightly lit, and it gives his face an other-worldly glow, making him seem ghastly pale and somehow unreal.

Guinness plays Hitler as quiet for the most part, preoccupied and self-absorbed. His screaming outbursts are relatively short and kept to a minimum. In his hands, the Führer only comes to life when he is serving as a genial host, a storyteller or philosopher. He loves to preside at parties where he can ramble on with his favorite topics. He plays with the Goebbels children, although his smile on these occasions is rather chilly. Overall, Guinness' conception of Hitler is quite bourgeois, and out of his depth in other settings, such as the military conferences where he is either comatose or ranting. The Hitler who was an outstanding orator is completely absent. His overall reading is rather simple instead of complex, an egomaniac who is running on mere fumes and wishes to escape to a Teutonic dreamworld where his genius could be appreciated and understood.

The supporting cast is a mixed bag. Simon Ward seems wasted and out of place. He merely disappears into the background for much of the film. John Bennett and Mark Kingston are more than adequate in faithful depictions of Goebbels and Bormann. Doris Kunstmann is brilliant as the childlike Eva, surpassed only by Diane Cilento as the frustrated Walküre, Hanna Reitsch. On the other hand, Adolfo Celi, Barbara Jefford and Gabriele Ferzetti are disappointing and colorless in their parts. The best cameo is by Angela Pleasence, daughter of Donald Pleasence, as a young female messenger sent to the bunker to retrieve an armful of autographed photos of the Führer for the Hitler Youth. The expression on her face as she sets off to return to her unit is astonishing, a blend of fear, wonder and confusion.

REPRESENTATIVE QUOTES

• Some of our most talented singers have allowed themselves to become absurdly fat. It takes away half the joy of going to the opera. The German people will only reach the point of absolute racial superiority when

Hitler (Alec Guiness) finally accepts that the war is lost.

Wagner's operas are performed by all our singers completely naked. *(Hitler to his guests at his birthday supper)*

• I cannot be wrong. Everything I do and everything I say is history. *(Hitler to his General Staff)*

• Keitel, there are people who are so inspired by their enthusiasm for the resurrection of Germany that they look upon me as a second Messiah. I must point out to all good people, with the utmost humility, that I am not the Messiah, a genius, but not the Messiah. Do you see me, Fraulein Braun, as Jesus Christ? *(Hitler to Keitel during a snack before the Field Marshal leaves on a mission)*

• What of your children? *(Hitler to Magda Goebbels)* We can't abandon them at a time like this. Leaving them in a world without you, mein Führer, would be like forcing them to live in hell or an earth without sunshine. *(Her reply)*

• The English have no art at all. In no country in the world, is Shakespeare performed so badly as in England. *(Hitler to the officers toasting his marriage)*

• The lives of millions of mediocre, ordinary people are of no account, Eva. *(Hitler to his wife as they prepare for their suicide)*

40. *Hitler's SS: Portrait in Evil* (1985)

Colin Jeavons as Adolf Hitler
Historical drama

Metromedia. Written by Lukas Heller; Photographed by Ernest Vincze; Edited by John Shirley; Music by Richard Harley; Produced by Aida Young; Directed by Jim Goddard. Color 141 minutes

ANNOTATED CAST LIST: Bill Nighy (*Helmut Hoffman*, Idealistic German student who joins the SS); David Warner (*Reinhard Heydrich*, SS leader who befriends Helmut); John Shea (*Karl Hoffman*, Helmut's brother & a member of the SA); Michael Elphick (*Ernst Röhm*, Volatile leader of SA); John Normington (*Heinrich Himmler*, Interior Minister & Head of SS); Lucy Gutteridge (*Mitzi Templer*, Cabaret singer); Tony Ran-

dall (*Putzi*, Cabaret comic); Robert Demerger (Cabaret manager); Robert Urquart (*Albrecht Hoffman*, Helmut's father, a railroad employee); Carroll Baker (*Gerda Hoffman*, Helmut's mother); Peter Marquis (*Hans*, Age 2, Helmut's youngest brother); Jodie Andrews (*Hans*, Age 7); Caspain Batoris (*Hans*, Age 12, Hitler Youth member); Warren Clarke (*Becker*, Helmut's SS associate); Stratford Johns (*Uncle Walter*, Bar owner); José Ferrer (*Ludwig Rosenberg*, German literature professor fired because he is Jewish); Derek Newark (*Theodor Eicke*, Kommandant of Dachau); James Coyle (*General Heinrich Müller*, Gestapo official); Paul Brooke (*Joseph Blegler*, SA officer driven by Karl); Ivor Roberts (*Rudolf Langner*, Union leader injured in a fall); Ruth Goring (*Mrs. Langner*, His wife); John Dicks (*Viktor Lutze*, SA officer who spies for the SS); Prentis Hancock (*Karl Tessler*); Alec Linsted (*Dr. Werner Best*, Foreign office official investigating Heydrich's assassination); Roland MacLeod (*Meissner*, Stuttgart restaurateur); John Woodnutt (*Pastor Sommers*, Stuttgart minister); Bernard Lloyd (*Sepp Dietrich*, Squad leader during the Röhm purge); Nick Brimble (*Gildisch*, Shop foreman); Peter Craze (*Keilbach*); John Benfield (*Griesch*); Walter Sparrow (*Klaus*); Philip Croskin, Maurice Colbourne, Christopher Gray, Charles Lawson (SS officers).

APPRAISAL AND SYNOPSIS: *Hitler's SS: Portrait of Evil* is an interesting project, perhaps somewhat overly ambitious since its reach seems to have exceed its grasp. It was originally intended to be a three episode mini-series, but was cut back to a lengthy telefilm that was broadcast in a three hour time slot on NBC on February 17, 1985. A limited budget can be detected from several hurried scenes and a number of plot gaps, yet on the whole, the film manages to be fairly effective. The production was no doubt inspired by two earlier miniseries, *Holocaust* (1978) and *The Winds of War* (1983). Although it falls below the standards of these two remarkable series, it is still a worthy effort with a handful of memorable scenes.

The story focuses on two brothers, Helmut and Karl Hoffman, from a middle class family in Stuttgart. As the story commences in 1932, the two brothers attend the baptism of Hans, their youngest siblings. Helmut is an apolitical university student intent on becoming a literature teacher, and Karl is a mechanic who is intrigued by the Nazis. He takes Helmut to an SA rally led by Ernst Röhm, but his brother remains unimpressed. Later, Helmut meets Reinhard Heydrich, a leader of the SS, who provides him with fencing lessons. He eventually persuades Helmut to abandon his studies and join the SS elite as his personal assistant. Karl, on the other hand, joins the SA, where his main duty is as a driver for leading officials. Both Karl and Helmut love Mitzi, a cabaret singer, but as Helmut's duties draw him away from Stuttgart, her relationship with Karl starts to blossom. After Hitler comes to power in 1933, Helmut finds himself drawn into the inner circle of the SS, crossing paths with Heinrich Himmler. He receives advance word that the leadership of the SA is going to be arrested and shot, and he tries to warn Karl to report sick on July 30th, 1934, the scheduled date of the Röhm purge. Karl never receives the message, and he is arrested after driving Blegler, one of the SA leaders. Röhm and his cohorts are executed, and Karl is imprisoned in a concentration camp. Helmut asks Heydrich to help obtain his brother's release. He refuses to become indebted to Eicke, the Kommandant of Dachau, but suggests that Helmut meet with Eicke himself. Karl is released, but he is now completely disillusioned with the Nazis. He becomes reckless in his opinions and is again arrested. Helmut manages to rescue him again, through the intervention of Becker, a calculating SS ally. Karl, however, has to join the army to avoid imprisonment. Helmut also attempts to help his old literature professor, Ludwig Rosenberg, who has been fired because of his Jewish background. He tries to convince him to emigrate, but the old scholar declines. Helmut's visits to his parents become increasingly strained, as they begin to blame him for the misdeeds of the SS.

In August 1939, Heydrich gives Helmut an unsavory mission. He is to go to Dachau and select a number of inmates who are to be dressed as Polish soldiers and then shot. Their bodies are to serve as evidence of a Polish raid across the German border. This incident is then used as an excuse by Hitler to launch the invasion of Poland. Helmut's conscience is troubled by this assignment, but it marks his absorption into the culture of evil represented by the SS.

Karl is wounded on the Russian front, and he deserts after his recovery, no longer willing to help the Nazi regime in any way. Helmut tracks him down at Mitzi's apartment, and warns him about a manhunt to arrest all suspected traitors after the attempt is made on Hitler's life in July 1944. Karl heads back to Stuttgart, where he learns that his parents have been killed during an air raid. He learns that his younger brother, Hans, has been recruited by the Hitler Youth. He returns to Berlin in April 1945, to try and save Hans. He asks Helmut to help, but the SS officer learns that Hans has been completely brainwashed and wants to fight to the death to defend Berlin against the Russian forces. Helmut is killed as he tries to desert, and Hans is killed in action. Karl and Mitzi discover his body as it is being carried away. They walk off arm in arm as the battle of Berlin comes to an end and the Germans surrender.

Although John Shea as Karl and Bill Nighy as Helmut deliver sound performances, it is the supporting players who provide the real interest in this production. Tony Randall shines as Putzi (German for "little fellow"), a grotesque, self-described degenerate who works as a comedian. His politically risqué humor finally arouses the ire of the Nazis, and he is arrested in the wake of the Rastenburg assassination attempt. José Ferrer is remarkable as the cultured Jewish professor who stoically embraces his fate as a victim of the Holocaust. Carroll Baker delivers a quiet, subtle performance that is actually one of the strongest of her career. Finally, David Warner is mesmerizing as Rinehart Heydrich, and his assassination in Czechoslovakia is one of the most exciting scenes in the film. Warner had also played Heydrich previously in the miniseries *Holocaust*.

HITLER PORTRAYAL: Colin Jeavons is a barely adequate Hitler, giving only a superficial reading of the part. His appearances are limited to the opening third of the film. He is first pointed out to Helmut in a Munich hotel, where Hitler is having an unpublicized meeting in the fall of 1932 with a number of influential bankers and industrialists. Reinhard Heydrich tells his apprentice that these people are planning to support Hitler as the next chancellor. "They think they are getting a lap dog for their money, a mongrel that can be housetrained," Heydrich observes. Hitler is seen wearing a dark business suit, warmly greeting these powerbrokers. The second, longer Hitler sequence occurs almost two years later, when Hitler plans to consolidate his power by eliminating the SA, a price demanded by the army in exchange for their support. On Saturday, June 30, 1934, Hitler personally led the early morning raid on the Hanslbauer Hotel in Wiessee, where the SA leaders were gathered for a conference. The actual sequence begins as Hitler and a handful of men load their weapons outside the hotel and prepare to strike. Gun in hand, Hitler leads the way bounding up the stairs to Röhm's suite. He knocks at the door, saying, "I have a message for you." The groggy SA leader opens the door, stunned to see the Führer. Hitler looks over his shoulder, staring at the naked young man sharing Röhm's bed. A look of disgust registers on Hitler face, as he pretends to be he unaware that Röhm is a homosexual. A montage follows showing other SA leaders being similarly awakened and arrested in their bedrooms. Finally, Karl Hoffman pulls up to the hotel while driving SA bigwig Joseph Blegler in a convertible. An SS man pulls Blegler out of the car, and he turns to Lutze, another SA

officer and demands an explanation. Suddenly, an enraged Hitler appears behind Lutze, shrieking that the SA leaders are all traitors who will be executed. At this point, the screen fades to black, and the character of Hitler fails to reappear during the last ninety minutes of the film. This is somewhat strange, even considering the production's cutbacks, since the film's title stresses Hitler's presence and the Rastenburg assassination attempt is a major factor toward the end of the film. It is a bit of a mystery why Hitler was dropped so early. Perhaps Jeavons withdrew for some reason. He had a continuing part as Inspector Lestrade in the Jeremy Brett series of Sherlock Holmes' adventures that was in production at the same time. Perhaps he had a scheduling conflict, and later Hitler scenes were trimmed from the production.

REPRESENTATIVE QUOTES

• I haven't done anything. What have I done? *(Blegler upon his arrest)* What have you done? What have you done? You're a traitor, all traitors! You're going to be shot, all of you shot! *(Hitler, appearing without warning)*

• So, Reinhard Tristan Eugen Heydrich sends his regards, eh? Funny, I always thought he didn't like me. Do you think I've been too sensitive, do you? *(Eicke to Helmut after releasing Karl from Dachau)*

• Did he offer you a job? *(Mitzi to Putzi, after he saw a member of the Army Entertainment Department)* No, what would he want me for? They have enough clowns of their own. Heil Hitler. *(Putzi)*

• The Colonel was about to request a minute of silence for all of our comrades that have fallen in battle this last year. That's a good idea, very good. But as you know, our Führer, the greatest general of all time, is kind enough to take over the conduct of this war himself, and if his performance at Stalingrad is anything to go by, perhaps we should add a couple of minutes for the poor idiots to be slaughtered next year as well. *(Karl's derisive comments to the troops at the New Year's Eve party on the Russian front)*

41. *How to Seduce a Woman* (1974)

Billy Frick as Adolf Hitler (cameo)
Comedy

Cinerama. Written by Charles Martin; Photographed by William Cronjager; Edited by William Sawyer; Music by Stu Phillips; Produced & directed by Charles Martin. Color 108 minutes

CAST LIST: Angus Duncan (*Luther Lucas*); Angel Tompkins (*Pamela Balsam*); Alexandra Hay (*Nell Brinkman*); Jo Anne Meredith (*Melissa*); Judith McConnell (*Ramona*); Heidi Bruhl (*Dr. Winifred Sisters*); Eve Brent (Dr. Sisters' sister); Marty Ingalls (*Jim*); Vito Scotti (*Bill*); Lillian Randolph (*Matilda*); Janice Carroll (*Estelle*); Hope Holiday (*Mary*); Kay Peters (*Jane*); Billy Curtis (*Toulouse*); Joe Alfasa (*Guido*); Maurice Dallimore (Butler); Jack Bailey (*Toklas*); Fran Ryan (*Mrs. Toklas*); Joe E. Ross (Bartender); Marvin Miller (Racetrack announcer).

COMMENTARY: *How to Seduce a Woman* is a lightweight comedy brimming with sexual innuendo along similar lines to *Sunday in New York* (1963), *Sex and the Single Girl* (1964) and *Boeing Boeing* (1965). Playboy writer Luther Lucas has written a book on the gentle art of seduction, and tests his theories by pursuing five beautiful women, using a different technique with each one. For example, with the beautiful psychiatrist Dr. Winifred Sisters (think Joyce Brothers), Luther goes for treatments with her after faking a suicide attempt to win her sympathy. Hitler's appearance in this comedy is unexpected and totally unrelated to the rest of the story. About ten minutes into the picture, Luther drives up in his convertible to his luxury apartment building. The uniformed doorman rushes out to assist him out of the car and park it for him. As the soundtrack intones *Deutschland Über Alles*, Luther observes the doorman closely, suspecting that he could be Adolf Hitler. He asks Bill, his friend and neighbor, "Who's the new doorman?" "I dunno," Bill replies. "They

hired him this morning, just came in from Argentina." Luther pivots to look at the man, who responds by giving him a Nazi salute as he turns. End of gag. There are no further references or comments about the doorman for the rest of the film.

42. *Indiana Jones and the Last Crusade* (1989)

Michael Sheard as Adolf Hitler (cameo)
Fantasy/Adventure

Paramount. Written by Jeffrey Boam based on a story by George Lucas & Menno Meyjes; Photographed by Douglas Slocombe; Edited by Michael Kahn; Music by John Williams; Produced by George Lucas & Frank Marshall; Directed by Steven Spielberg. Color 127 minutes

ANNOTATED CAST LIST: Harrison Ford (*Dr. Indiana Jones*, Archaeologist and professor in 1938); Sean Connery (*Dr. Henry Jones*, His father, a professor of medieval literature); Denholm Elliott (*Marcus Brody*, Museum curator); Alison Doody (*Dr. Elsa Schneider*, Austrian archaeologist); John Rhys-Davies (*Sallah*, Expedition guide); Julian Glover (*Walter Donovan*, Wealthy expedition sponsor); Isla Blair Glover (Donovon's wife); River Phoenix (*Young Indy* in 1912); Richard Young (Rogue explorer in 1912 who gives Young Indy his fedora hat); J. J. Hardy (*Herman*, Young Indy's friend); Bradley Greg (*Roscoe*, plunderer); Jeff O'Haco (Half-breed plunderer); Vince Deadrick, Jr. (Rough rider plunderer); Larry Sanders (*Havlock*, Scoutmaster); Mark Miles (Sheriff); Tim Hisler (Artifact collector with Panama hat in 1912); Paul Maxwell (Same character in 1938); Robert Eddison (Medieval knight who guards the Grail); Kevork Malikyan (*Kazim*, Leader of Grail defenders); Alexei Sayle (Sultan of Hatay); Michael Byrne (*Colonel Vogel*, Head of Nazis in pursuit of Grail); Vernon Dobtcheff (Butler at Castle of Brunwald); Luke Hanson (Principal SS officer at castle); Chris Jenkinson (SS officer at castle); Nicola Scott (Female Nazi officer at castle); Louis Sheldon

(Younger Nazi officer); Paul Humpoletz (Officer at Hitler rally); Martin Gordon (Man at Hitler rally); Ronald Lacey (*Heinrich Himmler*, Gestapo Head, attending rally); Pat Roach (Gestapo agent); Graeme Crowther (Zeppelin crewman); George Malpas (Man on Zeppelin); Stefan Kalipha (Tank gunner); Peter Paley (Tank driver); Tom Branch (Hatay soldier beheaded by Temple booby trap); Eugene Lipinski (Man who approaches Indy at Princeton); Julie Eccles (*Irene*, Indy's secretary at Princeton); Nina Almond (Flower girl in Venice).

APPRAISAL AND SYNOPSIS: The third Indiana Jones film maintains the same mixture of fantasy and high adventure, blended with the authentic historic details that made the first two films notable successes. Most of all, these films revive the spirit of the great serials, particularly those by Republic Studios, in the era of the late 1930s and early 1940s. In fact, the series masterfully recreates many of the great cliffhanger endings that typify the chapterplays. All the major aspects of the film are of the highest order, including the acting, the cinematography, the editing, the script and the music. Tremendous care had been taken with almost each scene. For example, when first discussing the Grail, a clock tolls chiming a motif from *Parsifal*, Richard Wagner's poignant Grail opera. There are a few continuity errors (such as the plane tail rudder that is shot off by Henry Jones, but which reappears intact in the next shot), but they are only minor flaws. On the other hand, the Indiana Jones films are filled with elements that stimulate thought. They serve to inspire younger viewers to read on their own, and explore the history of the Ark of the Covenant, for example, or Arthurian Grail lore. As for historic detail, much of the film is grounded in fact. Take for example the setting of Hatay. Most viewers, no doubt, considered this a fictional country invented for the script. In truth, there was a nation called Hatay that existed for only a short period of time in the 1930s, in the coastal border region between Turkey and Syria. Likewise, the city of Iskenderan

was the site of Alexandretta in ancient times. Hatay is also the location of Antioch, now known as Antakya. Antioch is also associated with Grail lore, being the site where a famous chalice, believed by some to be the Grail, was uncovered. This artifact, now housed at the Cloisters, the medieval branch of New York's Metropolitan Museum, bears a clear resemblance to the Grail as depicted in the movie (although the Cloisters Cup has added embellishments.) Hitler's interest in historical religious relics and artifacts is another accurate detail, although Heinrich Himmler was far more obsessed with mysticism and reviving ancient rituals. The zeppelin originally intended for portrayal in the film was the *Hindenburg*, but the 1938 timing prevented it, since the famous airship blew up (probably by sabotage) in 1937 in Lindenhurst, New Jersey, so an unnamed zeppelin was used instead. Another famous fictional screen hero, Charlie Chan, was depicted as traveling on the *Hindenburg* in *Charlie Chan at the Olympics* (1937).

The basic plot of *Indiana Jones and the Last Crusade* is rather complex for an adventure movie, since much of the action works on different levels, particularly due to the father/son rivalry that permeates the entire film. The story opens in Utah in 1912, where the teenage Indy is on a scouting expedition. While exploring a cave, he and his buddy Herman come across a group of plunderers who have dug up a priceless relic, the Cross of Coronado, originally given to the explorer by Cortez. Indy sends Herman to fetch the sheriff, and he snatches the cross. The plunderers follow him in a wild chase, an episode that explains a number of the trademarks associated with Indy, such as his fedora hat, his talent with a whip, the scar on his chin and his fear of snakes. When Indy arrives home with the relic, his father, Dr. Henry Jones, pays no attention to him, since he is translating a passage of Grail lore. The sheriff arrives, obviously bribed by the plunderers, and he turns the cross over to their sponsor, a greedy collector wearing a Panama hat. The scene shifts to 1938, and

Indy is still trying to retrieve the Cross of Coronado from the same thieving collector, surviving a shipwreck to capture his prize. Indy returns to his teaching post at Princeton University, but he is approached by the millionaire art patron Walter Donovan, who is the sponsor of a Grail expedition led by Dr. Henry Jones. Donovan reports that Indy's father had disappeared while doing research in Venice. Indy agrees to take his father's place, and is surprised to discover that his father had mailed him his most prized possession, his Grail diary filled with his private notes of his research, a lifetime of work.

The rest of the story concerns Indy's search for his father, kidnapped by the Nazis, who are desperately trying to locate the Holy Grail for themselves. Indy winds up exploring a lost crypt underneath the city of Venice and storming a Nazi headquarters in a medieval castle. He discovers that his father's beautiful assistant, Elsa Schneider and Walter Donovan are actually Nazi collaborators. The key scene comes after he rescues Dr. Henry Jones, his father, who insists that they travel to Berlin to retrieve his Grail diary from Elsa. They trace her movements to an evening Nazi rally. After Indy regains the book, he literally bumps into Adolf Hitler, who mistakes the diary for an autograph book which he signs and returns to Indy.

The action switches to Hatay, a small country near Turkey. The Nazis and Walter Donovan have a head start in tracking down the location of the Grail, a mysterious temple carved into the side of a mountain. They are stopped, however, by three deadly booby traps. After Indy and his father are captured, Donovan shoots Henry. Indy realizes that there is only one way to save him, by solving the three traps, finding the Grail and using its healing power. When he reaches the inner chamber, he finds it protected by a medieval knight who has stood guard over the relic for a thousand years. The knight explains that the true Grail is hidden among many impostors. When Donovan drinks

from one of the grails, it is one of the fakes and his body completely disintegrates. Indy chooses the most ordinary cup, one that would be used by a carpenter. It is the true Grail, and Henry's wound is cured as he drinks from it. The Knight warns that the Grail cannot be taken from the temple, and when Elsa tries to take it away, the ground opens up and she falls through to her death, as do the other Nazis. When Indy attempts to retrieve the Grail, at risk of his own life, his father tells him to "let it go." For the only time in the film, he calls him "Indiana" instead of "Junior" since his real name is Henry Jones, Jr. Then they abandon the crumbling temple, and the medieval knight raises his arm to acknowledge them as they depart.

The abrupt conclusion is the weakest moment of the film, as if the scriptwriter simply gave up. The temple is collapsing, with the ancient knight still living but with the Holy Grail irretrievably lost in a deep fissure of the earth. What must this perplexed knight think? He guarded and protected the Holy Grail for centuries, only to have a strange, rowdy group of people barge in, manage to lose the most precious relic in minutes, and whisk away leaving everything in ruins. The only positive element is that the Nazis failed to obtain the cup, but it is a rather pathetic conclusion to a superb and entertaining feature.

HITLER PORTRAYAL: Michael Sheard, the Hitler of *Indiana Jones and the Last Crusade*, is best remembered for his role as Admiral Ozzle in *The Empire Strikes Back* (1980). Displeasing Darth Vader, he is choked to death when the Dark Lord uses the force to dispose of him. Although Sheard did not encounter Harrison Ford in *Empire*, he commanded Julian Glover, who played General Veers in that film. Sheard's scene may be brief in *Indiana Jones and the Last Crusade*, but unforgettable. When Indy and his father have traveled to Berlin to retrieve the Grail diary, in possession of Elsa Schneider, she is attending a book burning rally, presided over by the Führer himself. Dressed as a Nazi officer, Indy confronts her and recovers the book. As the rally breaks up, Hitler pauses to sign autographs for his enthusiastic followers. Indy and his father are jostled by the surging crowd. Indy, backing up, collides with the Führer. Startled, the archaeologist snaps to attention. Seeing the book in his hands, Hitler assumes it is another autograph book. The Führer takes it and opens it, casually signing his name, and handing the Grail diary back to Indy. He walks on, leaving behind a shaken Indy, who is stunned by this unexpected encounter.

There are many unusual elements in this cameo. In historic terms, the Nazi book burnings occurred principally in 1933, five years before the setting of this film. The event depicted is based on the bonfires organized by Dr. Goebbels in 1933, specifically on May 10th outside the Berlin Opera and on May 20th near Berlin University. Hitler did not attend these rallies, which were presided over by Goebbels. Among the authors whose works were targeted for destruction included Thomas Mann, Erich Maria Remarque, Emile Zola, H.G. Wells, Sigmund Freud and Karl Marx. A later plan to burn decadent art, however, was canceled when Hitler and Göring raised objections, since the works by Picasso, Kokoschka, Matisse and Braque could fetch very high revenues in the open market or as bargaining chips in museum trades for artworks desired by the Führer. It is also true that Hitler frequently signed autographs for well wishers, however this practice was more infrequent after 1936. Spielberg considered duplicating the authentic Hitler signature for this sequence, but finally decided to use a clear, legible "Adolf Hitler" autograph instead, so there would be no doubt in the audience's mind as to what Hitler was doing. Of course, it is a great irony that Dr. Henry Jones' reverent notes on the sacred story of the Holy Grail will be forever marked with Hitler's inscription as well. The staging of this encounter between Indy and Hitler is extraordinarily clever and effective, serving as a real highlight of the production.

Sheard's resemblance to Hitler is only passable in the close-up, but more than adequate to make the scene work.

Other Nazi officials can be spotted on the rostrum with Hitler in the scene, including Goebbels, Göring and Himmler, although only the identity of Ronald Lacey as Himmler is confirmed. When Hitler signs the book, the man standing behind him resembles Rudolf Hess, at least he bears the distinct eyebrows that characterize the features of the Reich Deputy. The music used at the rally, incidentally, is not by John Williams but a selection favored by the Nazis of the 19th century Finnish composer Gottfried Piefke, entitled the *Königgrätzer March*. This same piece is played at a train reception in the French Hitler farce *Ace of Aces*. Finally, an additional throwback to the serials can be detected in the scene at Brunwald castle. The painting of Hitler used in this sequence is the identical portrait featured in *The Secret Service in Darkest Africa* (1943), which Rod Cameron jabbed through with his sword in the memorable final chapter.

REPRESENTATIVE QUOTES

• Nazis! I hate these guys. *(Indy to himself when he learns that the castle harbors a secret Nazi headquarters)*
• I told you, [*pausing to grab a machine gun and start shooting at the Nazis*] don't call me Junior! *(Indy to his father during his attempt to rescue him from the castle)* Look what you did! I can't believe what you did! *(Henry Jones in amazement)*
• By the personal command of the Führer, secrecy essential to success, eliminate the American conspirators. *(Hitler to Donovan by telegram)* Germany has declared war on the Jones boys. *(Donovon's comment to Vogel after reading the message)*
• My boy, we are pilgrims in an unholy land. *(Henry Jones to Indy as they near the Hitler rally)*

43. *Inside Out*
(AKA *Hitler's Gold*) (1975)

Gunter Meisner as Adolf Hitler
Adventure/Caper film

Warner Brothers. Written by Judd Bernard & Stephen Schneck; Photographed by John Coquillon; Edited by Thom Noble; Music by Konrad Elfers; Produced by Judd Bernard; Directed by Peter Duffell. Color 97 minutes

ANNOTATED CAST LIST: Telly Savalas (*Major Harry Morgan*, British officer who becomes involved in the Nazi gold caper); Robert Culp (*Sly Wells*, Criminal strategist); James Mason (*Colonel Ernst Furben*, Former Nazi POW camp Kommandant); Aldo Ray (*William Prior*, Master sergeant at Siegfried Prison); Gunter Meisner (*Hans Schmidt*, Actor who portrays Hitler); Wolfgang Lukschy (*Reinhardt Holtz*, Nazi prisoner based on Rudolf Hess); Charles Korvin (*Peter Dohlberg*, Berlin antique dealer); Constantin de Goguel (*Colonel Kosnikov*, Corrupt East German officer); Richard Warner (*Wilhelm Schlager*, Official who summons Kosnikov); Don Fellows (American Colonel in charge of Siegfried Prison); Doris Kunstmann (*Erika*, Berlin nurse who falls in love with Sly); Stephen Curtis (Sly's young chess opponent); Adrian Hoven (*Dr. Ludwig Maar*, Prison doctor who impersonates Holtz); Bernhard Bauer (*Pauli*, Male stripper used to blackmail Maar); Lorna Dallas (*Meredith Morgan*, Harry's wife); Sigrid Hanack (*Siggi*, Dohlberg's assistant); Peter Schlesinger (*Udo Blimpermann*, Overweight owner of theatrical costume firm); Thornton Gerrhus (*Walti*, Youngster who spies on the team's demolition efforts); Marlis Petersen (Walti's mother); Manfred Tummler (*William Reder*, Prior's assistant); Rainer Peets (Truck driver).

APPRAISAL AND SYNOPSIS: *Inside Out* is a very clever caper film that at moments spills over into black comedy. It combines elements of *The Rogues* with *Hogan's Heroes* and James Bond, featuring a literate script, taut direction and a brilliant sense of irony. The

cast, especially Telly Savalas as the capricious rascal Morgan, Robert Culp as the brains of the group and James Mason as the dour former Kommandant, is ideal and their acting more than compensates for the occasional slow moment in the story. The central gimmick centers around Rudolf Hess, who is called Reinhardt Holtz due to some legal technicality in the screenplay. In 1941, Holtz took charge of a valuable shipment of gold bars which he hid before his mysterious peace mission to England. In 1975, Ernst Furben, a retired German colonel gets wind of this missing fortune and seeks to plunder this treasure. He pulls together a team of mercenaries led by Major Harry Morgan, an ingenious con man who had been imprisoned in a POW camp run by Furben during the war. He hires Sly Wells to figure out a plan to pry the information out of Holtz, currently the sole occupant of Siegfried Prison (based on Spandau). Wells concocts a wild scheme to smuggle Holtz out of jail overnight, drugging him to believe he has gone back in time where the Führer confronts him, demanding to know the location of the gold bars.

One of the mercenaries, Hans Schmidt, is an actor who specializes in playing Hitler. The Führer's Chancellery office is reconstructed in an abandoned Berlin courthouse. Dr. Maar, the prison physician, is blackmailed into cooperating with the gang, and he agrees to substitute as Holtz in his cell. Prior, the Master Sergeant at the prison, an old friend of Morgan, also joins the scheme and agrees to facilitate the switch.

The Hitler impersonation sequence is the highlight of the film. While semi-conscious, Holtz is made up to resemble himself when young. When the groggy Nazi leader awakens, he is told that he has been sick in the hospital, but that the Führer demands to see him as soon as he recovers. Disoriented, Holtz accepts Schmidt as the genuine Hitler, and tells him the gold is buried in the air raid shelter at the summer villa owned by Holtz. Unfortunately, the location is in East Germany. The gang dresses up as

American officers and crosses the border, claiming to be on a goodwill mission. When they arrive at the villa, Furben is surprised to note that the location of Holtz's air raid shelter is now underneath a large garage. The old shelter can only be reached by blasting through the concrete floor. Furben contacts Schlager, an East German official who is an old acquaintance. They explain the situation and the East German pretends to cooperate, but instead calls Colonel Kosnikov, an intelligence officer. The greedy colonel shoots Schlager, and offers Morgan his services for a sixth share of the gold.

The gang then poses as a demolition team. Kosnikov evacuates the residents in the neighborhood of Holtz's old estate, and the team blasts through the floor and removes the gold, undisturbed since 1941. Later, when he arrives to claim his share, Kosnikov betrays the others. Schmidt is shot dead in a gun battle, but Wells manages to kill Kosnikov, and the others escape with the gold. Back in Berlin, they endeavor to return the redrugged Holtz to prison before the colonel in charge arrives, but they are delayed due to a street accident. Morgan, disguised as an officer from the medical corps, has to bluff the colonel by claiming Holtz is in need of dental surgery. The American officer grumbles about irregularities, but accepts the story, and the men are able to switch Holtz back before his sedative wears off. When he awakens, the Nazi leader insists that he had seen the Führer, but since he is regarded as crazy, no one pays any attention to his story. Furben, Morgan and Wells celebrate their successful escapade as the film ends.

Almost all caper films, from *Ocean's Eleven* (1960) to *Reindeer Games* (2000) end with the unraveling of the clever scheme. *Inside Out* is unique in that the culprits are totally successful, except for Schmidt who is killed by the treacherous East German colonel. Of course, there are no real victims of their escapade, except maybe for Holtz, who has no use for the buried gold anyway. The film recalls a 1967 entry of *Mission: Im-*

possible entitled "Echo of Yesterday," in which elderly Nazi supporter Wilfred Hyde-White is deceived by a vision of Hitler from the early 1930s. Martin Landau was the Hitler impersonator in that episode. *Inside Out* is also similar to a later film, *Wild Geese II* (1985), in which Hess is again sprung from Spandau. That film abandoned the use of a pseudonym for Hess, who was played by Laurence Olivier, but it is a far less successful effort than *Inside Out*, having a leaden pace and rather pointless story line. The only drawback to *Inside Out* is that they were unable to use the name of Hess (and Spandau as well). On the whole, it is a most entertaining, and often amusing, effort that deserves to be better known.

HITLER PORTRAYAL: Gunter Meisner is excellent as the vain but timid actor Hans Schmidt, who sets the plot in motion after he is relieved of his cargo in a convoy assignment by order of Reinhardt Holtz. Sneaking a smoke, Schmidt learns that the heavy boxes he was to deliver contain gold bars. Sitting on his secret for over 34 years, Schmidt finally reveals the details to James Mason, who then organizes the team to uncover the treasure. Meisner, as Schmidt, an unabashed coward, provides comic relief in the group. Yet, when asked to impersonate Hitler, he suits the role to perfection. Oddly enough, Meisner is far more convincing as the Führer than when he played the actual Hitler in the miniseries *The Winds of War*. He brilliantly embellishes the part like a schoolboy when Holtz is out of sight, dancing while proclaiming, "The Führer loved to dance" and lighting up a cigarette under the watchful gaze of a bronze bust of Hitler. It is ironic when James Mason criticizes his moustache, since it seems far more authentic than the thin oddly-shaped moustache in *The Winds of War*. Meisner's only affectation as Hitler is his rolling of his r's and t's, which resembles a theatrical ham's trick. After his successful impersonation, Schmidt's character becomes letdown, since he is again reduced to a meek subservient. It is also regrettable that his character is killed by

Kosnikov, although his death sets up a brilliant sight gag in which Schmidt's dead body is propped up in the car so that the visitor count tallies when the group crosses the border back into West Berlin. Meisner had an opportunity to expand on his concept of a comic Hitler in *Ace of Aces* made seven years later.

REPRESENTATIVE QUOTES

• Holtz, you have betrayed me ... betrayed the Fatherland! *(Hitler/Schmidt to Holtz)* How? *(Holtz, confused)* Don't shout at the Führer! *(Furben, disguised as a Nazi general)*

• Schmidt, baby, you are beautiful! You're a sensational Adolf! *(Wells to the impersonator)* Sensational! Now why don't we do a double act and I'll play Mussolini. *(Morgan, adding his congratulations)*

• Take off that ridiculous mustache.... The Führer's mustache was nothing like that. Off! *(Furben to Schmidt, unimpressed by his performance)*

• Hey, Sarge, the prisoner has flipped out. He thinks he saw Hitler. *(Reder to Prior)*

44. *Inside the Third Reich* (1982)

Derek Jacobi as Adolf Hitler
Historical drama

ABC Circle. Written by E. Jack Neuman based on the book *Inside the Third Reich* by Albert Speer; Photographed by Tony Imi; Edited by James Heckert, William Belding & Les Green; Music by Fred Karlin; Produced by E. Jack Neuman; Directed by Marvin Chomsky. Color 257 minutes

ANNOTATED CAST LIST: Rutger Hauer *(Albert Speer,* Architect who becomes Hitler's friend); Graham McGarth *(Albert Speer,* Age 11); John Gielgud (Speer's father); Maria Schell (Speer's mother); Blythe Danner *(Margarete,* Speer's wife); Natasha Knight *(Hilde Speer,* Their daughter); Trevor Howard *(Professor Heinrich Tessenow,* Architect & teacher, Speer's mentor); Viveca Lindfors (Gypsy who tells Speer's fortune);

Renee Soutendijk *(Eva Braun,* Hitler's mistress); Randy Quaid *(Ernst "Putzi" Hanfstaengl,* Hitler's Foreign Press chief); Ian Holm *(Dr. Joseph Goebbels,* Minister of Propaganda); Elke Sommer *(Magda Goebbels,* His wife); Stephen Collins *(Karl Hanke,* Chief Assistant to Goebbels); Maurice Roeves *(Rudolf Hess,* Deputy Führer); George Murcell *(Hermann Göring,* Reich Marshal); David Shawyer *(Heinrich Himmler,* Interior Minister & Head of SS); Sky Dumont *(Dr. Karl Gebhardt,* Himmler's doctor who treats Speer); Hans Meyer *(Ernst Kaltenbrunner,* Head of Gestapo); Derek Newark *(Martin Bormann,* Hitler's private secretary); Robert Vaughn *(Erhard Milch,* Field Marshal & Luftwaffe Director of Armaments); Michael Gough *(Dr. Bernhard Rust,* Education Minister); Bernard Horsfall *(Fritz Todt,* Munitions Minister who died in an airplane crash); Geoffrey Whitehead *(Xaver Dorsch,* Munitions department head under Speer); Zoë Wanamaker *(Annemarie Kempf,* Speer's Chief Assistant); Mort Sahl *(Werner Fink,* Jewish comedian); Marian Collier (Lady bartender in Berlin); Leon Lissek *(Wallenstein,* Speer's companion at Hitler's speech at the University); Rowena Cooper (Margarete's doctor); Pat Keen (Maternity nurse); Boris Isarov (Russian forced laborer); Bernard Archard *(Hans Flachner,* Speer's Defense attorney); Don Fellows (American major who interrogates Speer).

APPRAISAL AND SYNOPSIS: The miniseries *Inside the Third Reich* is one of the most remarkable and interesting historical portraits of Hitler and his inner cycle, drawn from the memoirs of architect Albert Speer, who became one of Hitler's closest friends. At times, the script follows Speer's book scrupulously with scene after scene portrayed without deviation. There are, however, some changes of emphasis. For example, the production expands the role of several individuals in the story, namely Speer's father (John Gielgud), his wife (Blythe Danner), Professor Tessenow (Trevor Howard), the architect who guides his early career and Ernst

Derek Jacobi strikes a characteristic Hitler pose in *Inside the Third Reich*.

"Putzi" Hanfstaengl (Randy Quaid), the intellectual friend of Hitler who introduces Speer to the workings of the inner circle. In the book, Putzi is only mentioned once, describing his 1937 flight from Germany after he was the victim of a Goebbels' prank that backfired. This incident, oddly enough, is not depicted in the filmed version of *Inside the Third Reich*, although it was later covered in another excellent miniseries, *The Nightmare Years*. In any case, the expanding of the three characters allow them to serve as a sounding board for Speer in the script, highlighting his career decisions which bring him to the center of the Nazi regime. Field Marshal Milch (Robert Vaughn) plays a similar role toward the end of the production, but unlike the others he figures prominently in the original text.

Inside the Third Reich was broadcast in May 1982, with the first episode premiering on May 9th. The first image depicted is the distinctive red cover of Speer's book, an unusual way to begin, perhaps highlighting the authenticity of the production. A series of clips are shown from *Triumph of the Will*, shifting to wartime newsreel footage and finally ending with the faces of victims from the concentration camps. The story proper opens at the Nuremberg war crimes trials, as Speer meets with his lawyer to discuss his conviction and possible sentence. His lawyer is hopeful, but Speer himself expects to be executed. In his cell, Speer's thoughts wander back, first to his childhood, and then to his university days. He falls in love with Margarete Weber, and when his parents refuse to bless their union, he becomes estranged from them. Speer becomes a teacher at the Berlin Institute of Technology, working as an assistant to Professor Tessenow whom he greatly admires. The professor is outspoken in his criticism of Adolf Hitler, but when the politician is scheduled to speak at the university in January 1931, Speer is curious enough to attend. He is mesmerized by the charismatic Hitler, who delivers a masterful speech which Speer feels is directed at him personally. He believes Hitler can indeed save Germany, and he decides to join the Nazi party.

At first, Speer's usefulness to the party consists of his ownership of a car. He makes friends with Karl Hanke, a young party official, and who, after Hitler came to power in 1933, recommends the architect to his boss, Joseph Goebbels. He receives a commission to design the Ministry of Propaganda. He is then asked to provide some decorative ideas for the first party rally at Nuremberg. Speer shows his sketches to Rudolf Hess, who is uncertain and sends the architect off to Hitler's apartment. The Führer is cleaning his gun and pays little attention to Speer. Hitler instructs him to flip though his sketches slowly, finally dismissing him with a single word, "Agreed." Speer has no idea if he made any impression on the Führer, but Martin Bormann, Hitler's secretary, is outraged when he learned that the young architect had been given a private audience. "You slipped through," Bormann later snarls at Speer. When plans are drawn by Paul Troost, Hitler's architect, for re-

Overall, Derek Jacobi's performance as Hitler is one of the most impressive.

designing the Chancellery, Speer is assigned to serve as a consultant. On a tour of the building, the Führer asks Speer to design a small balcony from which he could greet the crowds in the street. Speer learns that the Führer is fascinated by architecture. Later, Hitler invites Speer to dine with him, and their friendship begins, much to the annoyance of the other members of Hitler's inner circle, except for Putzi Hanfstaengl. The architect is invited to Hitler's mountain retreat at Berchtesgaden, where he joins the Führer on long walks and watches numerous films that are screened for his entourage. Speer also strikes up a friendship with Eva Braun, Hitler's mistress.

Speer uses his new prestige to force the University to rehire Professor Tessenow, who was fired for his controversial political

views. When Paul Troost dies, Speer becomes Hitler's official architect. Margarete Speer, however, is not won over by Hitler's charms, and she shows little reaction when the Führer tells her that her husband will soon be erecting buildings unlike any that have been attempted in four thousand years. Hitler commissions the architect to plan for a grandiose rebuilding of Berlin.

The years pass, and Speer designs and builds a new Reich Chancellery, a massive structure whose design and dimensions deeply impress Hitler. When the war starts in 1939, the Führer is furious when he hears that Speer has offered his services to the military. He insists that his building projects come first. However, as the war drags on, Hitler's attitude changes, and when Dr. Todt, the Munitions Minister, is killed in a plane crash in 1942, Hitler recruits Speer as his replacement, even though the architect is inexperienced in the armaments industry. From this new vantage point, Speer begins to see the brutal results of Hitler's policies, as well as his complete lack of humanity. Speer is only able to produce the quota of arms through the use of forced labor. He is moved, but turns a blind eye to their harsh treatment. He comes to understand the attitude of his wife and father who criticized the Nazis. He also finds considerable opposition to Hitler among the military, even from Field Marshal Milch, who works with him on issues of military supplies.

When an assassination attempt on Hitler fails, Speer is investigated by the Gestapo because the conspirators listed him as a possible minister in their post-Nazi government. After he is cleared, he considers resigning, but Milch persuades him to stay on for the good of the nation, as a check in case Hitler is serious about initiating a policy of total destruction as the German forces retreat. In 1945, Hitler orders Speer to implement this policy. Speer even considers killing Hitler by releasing poison gas into the bunker, but is never able to carry out his scheme. He instructs the military leaders to ignore the scorched earth orders, and most of them are visibly relieved when Speer intervenes. As the Russian armies close in on Berlin, Speer visits the bunker and confesses to Hitler that he deliberately undermined his orders. Expecting to be denounced as a traitor, Speer is stunned when Hitler merely passes over his revelation without any reaction.

The flashback comes to an end. At Nuremberg, Speer is questioned in his cell by an American officer about what he knew of the annihilation of the Jews. Speer denies any knowledge of the event. He receives his sentence from the war crimes tribunal, a term of twenty years. A scrawl at the conclusion reveals that he served his entire prison sentence. After his release, he lived on until September 1, 1981, dying at the age of seventy-six. Finally, a voice-over suggests a list of books that could be consulted for additional information, such as William L. Shirer's *Rise and Fall of the Third Reich*.

Inside the Third Reich is a high quality production on all levels, including the screenplay, cinematography, editing, music and production design. Note, for example, the scene at the Berghof when Hitler screens *Footlight Parade* (1933), concentrating on the aquatic ballet sequence when Dick Powell sings "By a Waterfall." This short sequence demonstrates the technical expertise of the production, cutting from closeups of the Warner Brothers' feature, to the various people watching the film (Hitler leans back, his eyes narrowed to slits, in total bliss). Meanwhile, Eva Braun and Speer slip out of the room to casually chat, with the Busby Berkeley musical continuing in the background behind their conversation. In terms of editing, sound, camerawork, pacing and acting, this almost trivial scene becomes unforgettable. Most of the exceptional cast deliver outstanding performances, with only a few exceptions. George Murcell, for example, is rather weak as Göring, and his overdone makeup doesn't help, and David Shawyer plays Himmler as if he were a friendly grocer, lacking any sinister touch. Fortunately, the other members of the inner circle, such as Ian Holm (Goebbels), Maurice Roeves (Hess) and Derek Newark (Bormann) are brilliant. Marvin Chomsky, who won the Emmy as best director for his work on this production, crafts each scene with particular flair and dedication. If one were limited to viewing only one historical film about the Nazi hierarchy, *Inside the Third Reich* would be at the head of the list.

HITLER PORTRAYAL: Derek Jacobi, the quiet, low key British actor, undoubtedly delivers one of the finest of all performances as Adolf Hitler. It is probably the second best role of his career, surpassed only by his magnificent and highly praised leading role in the miniseries *I Claudius*. Physically, Jacobi's resemblance is only fair. At first glance, his makeup has the effect of making the Führer look like a chipmunk, but after a few moments, the quality and intensity of Jacobi's acting brings his rendition fully to life, including a strong sense of authenticity. The actor is completely successful in making his Hitler seem both charming and charismatic. Jacobi manages to capture the dynamic impact of Hitler as an orator, a quality most other performers, even one as fine as Anthony Hopkins, find elusive. Jacobi is able to make Hitler's effect on an audience seem tangible. Hitler was able to reach each individual of the audience and allow them to feel that he is communiting with them on a personal level, speaking with ordinary common sense rather than with podium flourishes. Bit by bit he raises the enthusiasm until he manages to sweep all his listeners away in a frenzy. In his first scene, Jacobi come closest to approximating this aspect of Hitler, the master public speaker, into his reading. On the whole, his performance is the most well-rounded of all screen Hitlers, from the boisterous robber baron to the broken, nervous wreck in the bunker. Moreover, Jacobi is able to keep his Hitler from being even slightly sympathetic. He is basically a hollow man, filled with nothing more than his own self-importance, yet lacking in any shred of genuine humanity.

Of course, the Adolf Hitler on display in this film is the Führer as seen and experienced by Albert Speer, and the relationship is cast in Faustian terms, with Hitler playing the beguiling and diabolical Mephistopheles to Speer's scholastic Faust. Hitler lures Speer on with dreams of becoming the architect of his era, designing buildings and even cities that are meant to set a new standard for civilization. To do so, Speer has to accept unequivocally the abhorrent political philosophy of Hitler. Both Derek Jacobi and Rutger Hauer craft their performances to reflect this central concept. One even gets the idea that Jacobi's Hitler tries to camouflage his brutal and distasteful side so as not to risk alienating his most special friend. So Jacobi's interpretation stresses his aesthetic side, the portion of his personality that is drawn out by Speer. The Führer was never

happier than when he was studying plans or models of pompous sterile buildings that reflected his tastes. There are other elements of the relaxed Hitler that Jacobi captures to a tee, such as when he cavorts around Berchtesgaden in his lederhosen, or screens syrupy Hollywood musicals for his entourage or entertains them with spirited impersonations of world leaders such as Chamberlain. In his book *Spandau*, Speer published a photo of a somewhat ridiculous Hitler dressed in a loud plaid jacket, rocking in a wicker chair in front of a Christmas tree loaded with decorations of miniature toys. Jacobi, better than almost any other performer, integrates these elements into his reading. Jacobi also makes it clear that Hitler's relationship with Eva Braun is part and parcel of the bourgeois side of his character, which some historians characterize as "Hitler in slippers."

In the war years, however, particularly after Hitler recruits Speer to serve as Munitions Minister, his gentle mask drops and his true loathsomeness becomes apparent. Jacobi's ability to conjure up a fierce Hitler tirade is breathtaking, such as when he learns about the Hess mission to England. His complete lack of humanity is brought home to Speer with his diatribe calling for a total scorched earth policy. Yet even in the end, when Speer openly confesses to Hitler in the bunker that he has defied his orders, Speer is still shielded from the outrage and wrath that Hitler would have poured on any other individual. Hitler the destroyer, the monster, could not turn against this one man who represented his artistic and creative impulses. Jacobi and Hauer show that their relationship was also symbiotic. Jacobi's reading makes it clear that the Führer needed Speer to continue to function. Rutger Hauer, whose own performance equals Jacobi in the depth of his complex role, portrays Speer as blinded by his own ambition until the very end. He wins admiration for his courageous stand against the orders for the scorched earth policy. Yet even at the end, his Speer is irretrievably entwined with Hitler. Even though he considered killing Hitler in the last days of the war, the architect is amazed that he is unable to cry for any of Hitler's victims. Yet when he heard that Hitler is dead, he breaks down sobbing. This scene is also important because it prevents the audience from feeling any empathy with Speer. It must be remembered that Speer himself had a few critics who questioned the sincerity of his stand at Nuremberg, as well as his celebrity after his release from Spandau Prison. This one scene manages to allay any viewers who might feel the viewpoint of the picture is too forbearing of Speer, who chose to be a whole-hearted Nazi, even if he was the least repellent of the leading officials of the Third Reich.

REPRESENTATIVE QUOTES

• I'm afraid we are in for a blowy evening. They tell me he overuses the word "unshakeable." *(Wallenstein to Speer at the start of Hitler's speech)* It is my belief, my absolute unshakeable belief that we... *(Hitler suddenly stopping and looking directly at Speer)* True, oh so true. It is my belief that I use that word much much too often. *(Hitler, quite softly, provoking laughter and applause from the crowd)*

• If I had my way, I would outlaw skiing in this country. Dangerous, freezing, crippling business, hate it, hate it, hate it! The snow makes me so depressed. *(Hitler to Speer while they tramp through the snow outside the Berghof)*

• You eat with him. You go to the movies with him. You talk to him, he talks to you. If he drank, you would drink with him. You are the nearest thing he has got to a friend. I know, I've been there myself, a pretty powerful position being his pal. *(Putzi Hanfstaengl to Speer)*

• I am suggesting that we have all been taken in by that guttersnipe of an amateur general who has never even asked for a count of the dead. *(Milch to Speer)* Field Marshal Milch, do you realize who you are talking to? *(Speer)* Herr Reich Minister Speer, do you realize who you are working for? *(Milch)*

• You know what you are, Speer? Hitler's

unrequited love, and you simply wouldn't know what to do in a world that didn't include Adolf Hitler. *(Milch to Speer, after hearing his friend's scheme to kill Hitler)*

• Believe me, Speer, it is easy for me to end my life. A brief moment, and I am free of everything, liberated from this painful existence. *(Hitler to Speer in the bunker)*

45. *Is Paris Burning?* (AKA *Paris Brûle-t-il?*) (1966)

Billy Frick as Adolf Hitler (cameo)
Historical drama

Paramount. Written by Gore Vidal & Francis Ford Coppola based on the book *Is Paris Burning?* by Larry Collins & Dominique LaPierre; Photographed by Marcel Grignon; Edited by Robert Lawrence; Music by Maurice Jarré; Produced by Paul Graetz; Directed by René Clement. B & W 173 minutes

ANNOTATED CAST LIST: Gert Fröbe (*General Dietrich von Choltitz*, German commander of Paris); Orson Welles (*Raoul Nordling*, Swedish Consul who arranges a truce); Pierre Vanedi (*Roger Gallois*, Resistance leader who slips through the lines to contact the Allies); Charles Boyer (*Dr. Monod*, Physician who accompanies Gallois); Jean-Pierre Cassel (*Lieutenant Henri Karcher*, French soldier who captures Choltitz); Bruno Cremer (*Colonel Rol*, Communist leader of Parisian Resistance); Pierre Dux (*Alexandre Parodi*, Gaullist Resistance leader); Jean-Paul Belmondo (*Yves Morandat*, Gaullist who serves as Prime Minister in occupied Paris); Marie Yersini (*Claire*, Morandat's secretary & fiancée); Alain Delon (*Jacques Chaban-Delmas*, Gaullist representative in occupied Paris); Claude Dauphin (*Colonel Albert Lebel*, French liaison to U.S. Army); Claude Rich (*General Jacques Philippe Leclerc*, French commander who liberates Paris); Kirk Douglas (*General George S. Patton*, Commander of U.S. Third Army); Glenn Ford (*General Omar Bradley*, Head of U.S. 12th Army Group); Robert Stack (*General Edwin Sibert*, 12th Army's

Intelligence Chief); Roger Lamont (*Jade Amicol*, Head of British Intelligence in occupied Paris); Tony Taffin (*Bernard Labé*, French prisoner killed by Nazis); Leslie Caron (*Francoise*, Labé's wife, assisted by Nordling); Hannes Messemer (*Alfred Jodl*, General & Chief of Operations); Peter Jacob (*General Wilhelm Burgdorf*, Hitler's Chief of Military Personnel); Simone Signoret (Cafe owner who welcomes American troops); Anthony Perkins, George Chakiris, Skip Ward (American soldiers); Yves Montand, E.G. Marshall, Michael Lonsdale.

APPRAISAL AND SYNOPSIS: Larry Collins, who served as head of *Newseek*'s Paris bureau and Dominique Lapierre, editor of *Match*, spent years meticulously researching the dramatic story of the liberation of Paris in 1944. Their book, *Is Paris Burning?: Adolf Hitler, August 25, 1944*, became a classic, one of the most respected books about World War II. The film version is also a landmark, perhaps the most masterful blending of actual historic footage within the framework of a dramatization. Unfortunately, the motion picture is also rambling and confusing, and it can only be fully appreciated when viewed after a reading of the original book. The screenplay was an unlikely collaboration between Gore Vidal and Francis Ford Coppola. A major flaw of the film was the rather confusing way it depicted the Paris Resistance movement. As the book made clear, the leftist elements of the Paris resistance intended to set up a Communist government as soon as the Germans left. Other members of the Resistance, as well as De Gaulle and his followers, had to constantly position themselves against this threat almost equally to that of the Nazis. The film never makes clear this subtext, something that could have been done very easily using subtitles. Therefore, the critical importance of not permitting the Communist faction to become well-armed is never clearly spelled out. This weakens the film considerably, and makes it bewildering at times for someone unaware of this conflict within the Resistance movement. On the other hand, the

film portrays the story of the German side and the dilemma faced by General von Choltitz with extreme clarity. The viewpoint of the Allied forces, under command of such notable figures as George Patton and Omar Bradley, are also well portrayed. Oddly enough, the figures of Dwight Eisenhower and Charles De Gaulle are not depicted in the movie, although historic footage of de Gaulle's actual entry into Paris, is included at the end of the film.

The picture begins after a dramatic overture featuring a Nazi-style march played by a large orchestra including a battery of pianos that reproduce the sound of marching feet. An introductory scrawl that explains that the city is facing a moment of critical peril. The opening shot shows a military vehicle driving down a lonely road dwarfed by huge pine trees on either side. A subtitle reveals the time and location. It is August 7, 1944, and Major General Dietrich von Choltitz has been summoned to a personal meeting with Adolf Hitler at his headquarters at Rastenburg in East Prussia. General Burgdorf escorts Choltitz pass the ruins of the structure damaged in an assassination attempt three weeks earlier. Nearing Hitler's office, Choltitz is warned by the Chief of Staff, General Jodl, to be gentle while shaking hands with the Führer. "So he was wounded," Choltitz remarks. "Not badly, merely a scratch, nothing serious," Jodl replies. Choltitz coughs nervously as he is led into the office. Hitler informs Choltitz that he is promoted to a full general, assigning him to be fortress commander of Paris. Growing more agitated, Hitler insists that Paris must not be allowed to fall into the hands of the Allies. If he cannot hold the city, it must be completely destroyed. As the stunned Choltitz replies, "Jawohl, mein Führer," the scene switches to Paris, and a montage of the city's landmarks and people are intercut with scenes of German soldiers who occupy the city. The title of the film fills the screen, but there are no additional credits at this point.

The main body of the film is divided, more or less, into three lengthy sections. The first part follows Choltitz as he assumes command in Paris, and the Resistance plots its strategy. The Swedish Consul, Raoul Nordling, secures from General Choltitz a document allowing prisoners to be transferred to the authority of the Red Cross. When the Resistance begins an insurrection, Nordling convinces Choltitz to permit him to negotiate a ceasefire and truce. After a short time, however, this arrangement breaks down. Choltitz, ordered to destroy the city, recruits Nordling to appeal to the Allied command to advance their armies on Paris as quickly as possible so he won't be forced to execute Hitler's order.

The middle portion of the film concentrates on Roger Gallois, a Resistance leader who slips through the lines to implore the Americans to order an immediate advance on Paris. He eventually is brought before General Patton, who sends him to meet with a military council. Gallois pleads with them to save Paris. General Leclerc, leader of the 2nd French Armored Division, is given order to move on Paris at once. Meanwhile, German demolition forces are shown as they plant explosives at key locations and buildings throughout the city.

The final third portrays events surrounding the liberation. This section is the most varied, filled with many interesting vignettes of actual events as the Free French forces, backed by the American 4th Division, entered and freed the city, as the Germans under von Choltitz put up token opposition. Three colorful incidents in particular are well portrayed in the film. The first concerns the assumption by Yves Morandat of the position of Prime Minister of the Provisional French government. Yves and his secretary, Claire, take over the Prime Minister's residence single-handedly. The second involves a squad of soldiers who take over the apartment of an elderly woman so they can eliminate a German machine gun nest. The elderly woman calmly drinks her tea as her rooms are shot up, and when the squad leaves, their lieutenant kisses her hands and orders his men to "tidy up" the apartment by

picking up their expended cartridge shells. The third involves a wedding ceremony being conducted by the Vichy mayor of Paris. Mid-way through the ceremony is interrupted by members of the Provisional Government who arrest the mayor and then continue with the ceremony.

When Choltitz's headquarters is finally captured, the general calmly surrenders and issues orders for all German soldiers in the city to lay down their arms. As he is escorted away, Choltitz is heckled by a crowd of Parisians. The camera then focuses on a telephone lying open on a desk. Hitler's voice is heard over it screaming, "Is Paris burning?" The picture ends with historical footage of wildly enthusiastic French crowds around the Arc de Triomphe the Place de la Concorde and the Champs-Élysées, intercut with images of the bells of Notre Dame pealing in celebration. The sense of revelry and jubilation is infectious. The picture, black and white until now, switches to color as the end credits appear. A triumphant rendition of a French waltz plays as aerial montage shows Paris and its many historical sites.

Few films provide such an uplifting conclusion, and it makes one forget the occasional awkwardness, lack of clarity and missed opportunities of the entire film. No other picture every employed historical footage so skillfully, and quite often it is difficult to detect the actual footage from the footage shot for the film. Toward the end, there is a scene where a Nazi flag is torn down and shredded by the crowd. This realistic scene, however, was one recreated for the film. At another moment, there are scenes involving a wrecked German vehicle in the street. Approximately half this scene was composed of historic footage, intercut with dramatized footage of the same incident. Only an experienced eye could detect where the actual shot ended and the recreated shot began. Besides the masterful editing and cinematography, the music score by Maurice Jarré is also exceptional. *Is Paris Burning?* was filmed twenty-two years after the events it portrayed. Now forty-four years later, the film still hold up very well, packing an emotional punch that other World War II epics lack.

HITLER PORTRAYAL: Billy Frick is only seen in the film's opening three minute sequence. He is first seen from behind, playing a game of tug with Blondi, his German Shepherd. As Choltitz enters, the Führer releases the stick to his dogs and waves his pet off. Up until this point, Gert Fröbe and Hannes Messemer were conversing in English. As they enter Hitler's presence, the language switches to German. Frick's lip movements don't quite link up with his voice, indicating that there were likely experiments in post-dubbing having Hitler speak in English as well. The guttural German seems to work far better, an excellent approximation of the genuine Hitler as he works himself up into a fury. Frick rises and paces back and forth before a map. His appearance is chillingly exact, no doubt meticulously copied from photographs of Hitler as he appeared in the summer of 1944. His haircut, for example, is reproduced perfectly. The camera positioning concentrates on a three-quarters profile, where Frick's resemblance to Hitler seems strongest. As a cameo, Frick's vignette is powerful and very impressive. Unfortunately, the script fails to bring back Frick in the end, as Hitler repeatedly shouts, "Brennt Paris?" ("Is Paris burning?"). Instead, the camera merely focuses on a telephone receiver lying on a desk as Hitler's madly bellows his query. Hitler's face should have been superimposed at this point. It would have served as a perfect counterpoint to the film's opening. The shot of the phone receiver alone seems a letdown, since Hitler's question serves as the title. Incidentally, Frick appeared in only two other films: Percival in Russ Meyer's *Fanny Hill* (1964) and Hitler in a sight gag skit in *How to Seduce a Woman* (1974).

Many others shine in their performances in *Is Paris Burning?* Jean-Paul Belmondo, Alain Delon and Claude Rich are particularly memorable. Orson Welles is superb in the first half of the film as the Swedish diplomat Nordling who served as a middle man with a near-impossible mission. Unfortunately, the picture omits what happened after Choltitz sends him to the Allies to encourage them to immediately march on Paris. In reality, Raoul Nordling suffered a heart attack as he prepared to leave on his mission. Instead, Nordling sent his brother, Rolf, as his surrogate (since the pass Choltitz gave to him was for "R. Nordling"). Nordling successfully delivered Choltitz's message to General Omar Bradley. The delivery of this message was the key factor in motivating the Allies to advance. Pierre Vanedi is noteworthy in the key role of Roger Gallois, the French Resistance leader who also crossed the lines to reach the Allies. His original mission was to beg for arms for the Resistance, but instead he changed his emphasis to encourage immediate military action. Together with Nordling, Gallois played a pivotal role in the liberation of Paris. Finally, Gert Fröbe is simply magnificent as Choltitz, a brilliant portrait of a military man who decides not to execute Hitler's orders. Fröbe endows the role with extraordinary depth, and it is filled with many subtle and ironic touches, particularly in the dinner scene when the bells of the city start to toll. In truth, he is the unconventional hero of the film, a general who embarks on a dangerous game of clandestine treason in order to save Paris. The scene between Welles and Fröbe where the general asks the diplomat to contact the Allies is one of the finest moments in any war film. (This scene is even more poignant if you realize that Nordling is experiencing the early stages of a heart attack). Fröbe is best remembered for the title role in *Goldfinger* (1964), although an English actor redubbed his dialogue in the James Bond thriller. In German films, Fröbe played Inspector Kras in Fritz Lang's last directorial effort, *The Thousand Eyes of Dr. Mabuse* (1960). *Is Paris Burning?*, however, is without doubt Fröbe's finest effort.

REPRESENTATIVE QUOTES
- You are one of the few officers I can trust. You have always executed my orders. *(Hitler to Choltitz)*
- We're soldiers, not tourists. *(Choltitz to his aide as they look out their window at Paris)*
- History will be grateful to you for having saved a very beautiful city. *(Nordling to Choltitz)*
- Why has Hitler ordered the destruction of Paris? *(Nordling)* Because he is insane. I know it. I saw him in Rastenburg. *(Choltitz in reply)*

46. *Ja, Spravedlnost* (1967)

Fritz Diez as Adolf Hitler (cameo)
Drama

Filmove Studio Barrandov. Written by Milos Macourek & Zbynek Brynych; Photographed by Josef Vanis; Edited by Miroslav Hajel; Music by Jiri Sternwald; Produced by Eliska Nejedla; Directed by Zbynek Brynych. B & W 88 minutes

CAST LIST: Karel Höger (*Dr. Herman*); Angelika Domröse (*Inga*); Jiri Vrstala (*Harting*); Karel Charvat (*Herbert*); Otto Sevcik (*Henry*); Jindrich Narenta (Man with glasses); Jindrich Blazicek (Fat man); Karel Peyer (Garage foreman).

COMMENTARY: *Ja, Spravedlnost* or *I, Justice*, is a Czech psychological drama about a group of individuals who wish to personally see that justice is administered to Adolf Hitler. As with most Czech films, this picture received very limited foreign distribution. Fritz Diez reportedly makes a only brief appearance as Hitler in the film.

47. *Jackboot Mutiny* (AKA *Es Geschah am 20. Juli.*) (1955)

Rolf Neuber (?) as Adolf Hitler (cameo)
Historical drama

Arca-Filmproduktion/Ariston. Written by Werner P. Zibaso & Gustav Machaty; Photographed by Kurt Hasse; Edited by Herbert Taschner; Music by Johannes Weissenbach; Produced by Rudolf Weischert; Directed by G. W. Pabst. B & W 78 minutes

ANNOTATED CAST LIST: Bernhard Wicki (*Count Claus von Stauffenberg*, Colonel who plants a bomb to kill Hitler); Karl Ludwig Diehl (*Ludwig von Beck*, Retired general & leader of anti–Hitler group); Carl Wery (*General Friedrich Fromm*, Home Army commander); Erik Frey (*General Friedrich Olbricht*, Chief of the General Army in Berlin & anti–Hitler conspirator); Willy Krause (*Dr. Joseph Goebbels*, Propaganda Minister); Albert Hehn (*Otto Remar*, Officer who arrests Goebbels and receives a counterorder by Hitler on the telephone); Jochen Hauer (*Wilhelm Keitel*, Field Marshal & Chief of the High Command); Til Kiwe (*Werner von Haeften*, Stauffenberg's aide); Jasper von Oertzen (*General Erich Fellgiebel*, Officer in charge of disrupting communications from Rastenburg); Oliver Hassencamp (*Bertholt*, Stauffenberg's brother); Kurt Meisel (SS general); Ann Maria Sauerwein (Olbricht's wife); Hans Bauer, Gerd Briese, Rolf Castell, Hans Cossy, Heli Finkenzeller, Waldemar Frahm, Harry Hardt, Hans Friedrich, Werner Hessenland, Malte Jaeger, Fred Kraus, Walter Hotten, Eduard Linkers, Siegfried Lowitz, Robert Meyn, Fred Nötter, Ado Riegler, August Reihl, Karl Schaidler, Felix Schreiner.

APPRAISAL AND SYNOPSIS: After G.W. Pabst completed his bunker film, *The Last Ten Days*, he tackled another Hitler project based on the Rastenburg assassination attempt of July 20, 1944. Unlike *The Last Ten Days*, which featured a number of fictional characters and situations, *Jackboot Mutiny* attempted a meticulous recreation of the actual facts. Oddly enough, a second German film was in production at the same time, and both eventually premiered within days of each other in mid–June 1955. The rival film was *Der Zwanzigste Juli*, made under the direction of Falk Harnack, himself a member of the German resistance movement who had been arrested by the Gestapo but eventually released. Harnack's approach to *Der*

Zwanzigste Juli , ironically, was similar to Pabst's approach in *The Last Ten Days*, blending fictional characters and events into the mix. Other films based upon the Rastenburg assassination attempt include *The Plot to Kill Hitler*, which is covered in detail in a later entry and *Operation Walküre*, a 1971 German television documentary series conceived by Franz Peter Wirth. The latter featured interviews with survivors of the conspiracy and historians, such as Joachim Fest, author of *Plotting Hitler's Death*, which are interwoven with reenactments of some of the events.

Jackboot Mutiny remains the most definitive film rendition of the bomb plot, focusing entirely on the 24 hour time period of July 20, 1944, beginning with the early hour bombing raid by Allied planes on Berlin. At the same time, a group of conspirators are meeting to finalize their plans for the assassination of Hitler and the overthrow of the Nazi government. The leader of the group is General Beck, who resigned as head of the German Army in 1938 to protest the policies of Hitler. The man chosen to eliminate Hitler is Colonel Claus von Stauffenberg, the only member of the group who can get close to Hitler without being searched. Stauffenberg is a wounded war hero, having lost an eye, two fingers of his left hand and most his right arm in wartime service. As morning arrives, Count von Stauffenberg talks with his brother, Bertholt, discussing his strategy for planting the bomb in underground bunker at Wolf's Lair, Hitler's headquarters in Rastenburg, East Prussia. He plans to activate the bomb just before entering the meeting, then stepping out on the pretext of making a phone call. On his way to the airport, the count stops at a Catholic Church to pray. The caretaker observes him, commenting to his wife that the officer seems to be bearing a terrible burden. During the air flight to Rastenburg, Stauffenberg and Werner von Haeften, his loyal adjutant, ride in silence. The last leg of their journey is again by auto, as they are driven through three checkpoints to Hitler's well

guarded, but somewhat rustic, headquarters. When they arrive, Stauffenberg consults with General Fellgiebel, who is to call army headquarters in Berlin as soon as the bomb explodes and then disable the communications system at Wolf's Lair.

Field Marshal Keitel briefs Stauffenberg, warning him not to present a downbeat report to the Führer in light of his afternoon meeting with Mussolini. As they leave for the conference, the count leaves his briefcase behind, then returns to break the bomb's detonating trigger with pliers, starting a ten minute countdown to the explosion. The first setback comes when he learns the meeting has been switched from the concrete bunker to the map room in a wooden hut. An explosion in the bunker would have insured the death of everyone present. The open windows in the map room, however, would lessen the impact of the blast. The count places his briefcase under the table a few feet away from the Führer. He leaves the meeting shortly thereafter. One of the officers beside the table, Colonel Brandt, knocks over the briefcase, and moves it to the other side of the table support away from Hitler. Meanwhile, Stauffenberg and Haeften proceed toward their car, ordering the driver to head off the moment they hear the explosion. The count bluffs his way through the three checkpoints, and his car races to the airstrip to fly back to Berlin. Fellgiebel rings General Olbricht to deliver his report that the mission has succeeded. Unfortunately, an aide to Olbricht answers the phone. but fails to hear the message because of a bad connection. Olbricht enters the room a moment later, and tries to phone Fellgiebel back, but finds the line to Rastenburg is no longer in service. Hesitant, Olbricht decides to wait and fails to issue the Walküre alert, which would signal the resistance to seize control of the government, arrest key Nazi officials and arrest the officers of the SS.

Hours pass in confusion and delay until Stauffenberg reaches Berlin. By the time the Walküre effort is launched, it is too late since reports of Hitler's survival have started to filter through the official circles. General Fromm of the Home Guard Army is placed under arrest when he fails to cooperate. Major Remar is dispatched to the Chancellery to arrest Goebbels. When he and his troops confront the Propaganda Minister, they are stymied when Goebbels telephones Hitler. The Führer countermands Remar's previous orders and puts him in charge of stamping out the putsch and rounding up the officers in charge of the mutiny. Hitler later empowers the SS to arrest army officers.

The mutineers realize very quickly that their efforts have fizzled when the units under their control fail to follow their commands. By late evening, the army headquarters is under siege, and Fromm again assumes command. Beck asks for a gun to commit suicide. Fromm orders that General Staff Colonel Mertz von Quirnheim, General Olbricht, Stauffenberg and Haeften be taken to the courtyard of army headquarters for immediate execution. It is nearly midnight of July 20th. As he stands before the firing squad, Stauffenberg says, "Long live holy Germany!" The shots ring out and the camera focuses on the wall behind the mutineers, which is now riddled with bullets. A narrator states thousands more would be arrested and killed by the vengeful Führer in the wake of the events of July 20th.

Pabst's film is sober, austere and unembellished, maintaining a purity of thematic focus. In historical terms, it attempts to stick closely to the facts. Several critics have claimed the film attempts to overglorify the conspirators, but this is certainly a feeble objection, given that these individuals paid the ultimate price for their actions. The weakness of their plans may be open to criticism, but their motives were sound. If the extermination of the Jews was not their uppermost incentive, as General von Beck proclaims, it was nevertheless a tangible factor. Historians have their own disputes about details of the events. For example, the film shows Stauffenberg planting his briefcase under the table, only to be moved by Brandt. Others have suggested that Major Ernst von Freyend, Keitel's aide, took the briefcase from the count when they entered the map room, and it was he who placed the briefcase under the table against the outer table support, where it remained unmoved. There is also some question concerning Stauffenberg's eyepatch. While he was recovering from his original injuries, the count wore an eyepatch, but he appears to be no longer wearing one according to a photograph at Wolf's Lair of Stauffenberg and Hitler on July 15, 1944, five days before the assassination attempt. Had he simply dispensed with the patch, or did he use a glass eye instead? All film portrayals depict Stauffenberg with the eyepatch, perhaps because it looks more dramatic. But was the eyepatch a cinematic convention? *Jackboot Mutiny* also shows Stauffenberg using a prosthetic hand on his right arm. Again, the July 15th photo shows this may not be the case either, as the lower part of the count's right arm shows only an empty sleeve. There is also some dispute over the number of victims executed by the order of Hitler after the failure of the plot. Instead of thousands, the actual figure may have been as low as 500. It is true, however, that Hitler ordered many of the victims strung up by piano wire, and he had their deaths photographed for his personal amusement. Oddly enough, there were a number of conspirators who escaped Hitler's vengeance. Baron Axel von dem Büssche-Streithorst, who had himself attempted to plant a bomb near Hitler earlier in 1944, managed to escape the Nazi dragnet, later working at the Germany Embassy in Washington, D.C. during the 1950s, and surviving until 1993.

HITLER PORTRAYAL: It had been reported that G. W. Pabst was hoping to cast Albin Skota to reprise his role as Adolf Hitler from *The Last Ten Days*, just as he persuaded Willy Krause to reappear as Goebbels. For whatever reason, Skota was unable to come to Munich, where *Jackboot Mutiny* was shot, at the appropriate time, and Pabst was

Historic photograph of the actual Count von Stauffenberg (extreme left) with Hitler on July 15, 1944, five days before the assassination attempt. Please note Stauffenberg does not appear to be wearing an eye patch as depicted in all films.

forced to fall back to his second choice. Sources differ as to the identity of this player, but Rolf Neuber is the name most often cited. He is sometimes referred to as Wolf Nieber. The presence of Hitler is kept to a minimum in the story, appearing only briefly during the conference scene. When Stauffenberg enters the room, Field Marshal Keitel informs the Führer that the count will give a report on the readiness of the new military divisions. Hitler replies, "You're next, Stauffenberg." Then he turns to General Heusinger, who is providing a report on the Eastern front. "Continue, " the Führer says, and the general resumes his report. Hitler is only shown in longshot and midshot, and he appears on screen for just a few seconds. There is no depiction at all of Hitler after the explosion. The second scene to include Hitler is the confrontation in Goebbels' office between Major Remar and the Propaganda Minister. Hitler's voice is heard speaking over the telephone to Remar, but his presence on the other end of the line is never shown.

REPRESENTATIVE QUOTES

• What matters is that mass murder is being committed in the name of the German people. It is our duty to stop this by all means. Neither God nor conscience can absolve us of this duty. *(Beck to the other conspirators, articulating the primary reason for the overthrow of the Nazis)*

• I beg one thing of you, Stauffenberg. Don't paint things too pessimistically to the Führer. The Duce's coming. It's critical that we humor the Führer. *(Keitel to the count just prior to his meeting with Hitler)*

• Do you hear my voice? *(Hitler to Remar on the telephone)* Jawohl, mein Führer! *(Remar)* Convinced it is me? *(Hitler)* Jawohl, mein Führer! *(Remar)* You will crush the revolt with all means. Don't lose time. Be brutal if needed. *(Hitler)*

48. *Jugend Unter Hitler: Blut und Ehre* (AKA *Blood and Honor: Youth Under Hitler*) (1982)

Gunter Meisner as Adolf Hitler (cameo)
Drama

Taurus Films/SWF. Written by Robert Muller & Helmut Kissel; Photographed by Johannes Hollmann; Edited by Kenneth Wagner & Jessica Bendiner; Music by Ernst Bradner; Produced by Linda Marmelstein & Daniel Wilson; Directed by Bernd Fischerauer. Color German version, 296 minutes; English version, 268 minutes

CAST LIST: Bernd Fischerauer (*Dr. Sisler*); Franz Rudnick (*Dr. Bodenheim*); Jeffrey Frank (*Hartmut Keller*); Gedeon Burkhard (*Hartmut Keller* as a child); Stephen Rubling (*Hans Monkmann*); Stephen Higgs (*Hans Monkmann* as a child); Jakob Fruchtmann (*Fritz Kuhn*); David Weidner (*Fritz Kuhn* as a child); Matthew Bader (*Theo Gruber*); Craig Reid (*Theo Gruber* as a child); Leslie Malton (*Renate Keller*); Rolf Becker (*Ernst Keller*); Marlies Engel (*Susanne Keller*); Karlheinz Lemken (*Dr. Erskin Monkmann*); Gila von Weitershausen (*Ruth Monkmann*); Sven-Eric Bertholf (*Gunter Monkmann*); Annegret Schmidt (*Heller Monkmann*); Siegfried Kernan (*Papa Kuhn*); Elisabeth Endriss (*Mrs. Kuhn*); Gunther Malzacher (*Rudolph Gruber*); John Jeffries (Robert Schienz); Aljoscha Walser (*Friewi*); Ulrich von Dobschutz (Hitler Youth leader); Taina Eig (Narrator).

COMMENTARY: *Jugend Unter Hitler: Blut und Ehre* is a two part German television miniseries. The production was shot simultaneously in German and English, but the program received poor distribution in the United States, only shown in syndication on a handful of stations on November 29 and December 6, 1982, under the title *Blood and Honor*. However, the German title was also switched around, so *Blut und Ehre* came first. "Blut und Ehre" was the motto of the Hitler Youth. The screenplay focused on four different Germany families between 1933 and 1939, demonstrating the influence of Nazi propaganda on the youth of German through their manipulation of education and groups such as the Hitler Youth. Jeffrey Frank, who played Michael Caine's son in *The Island* (1980) was the only American performer in the cast. One source reports that Gunter Meisner's scenes were largely dropped during the editing process, particularly for the slightly shorter English language version.

49. *Karl May* (1974)

Rainer von Artenfels as Adolf Hitler
Historical drama

Goethe House. Written by Hans-Jürgen Syberberg; Photographed by Dietrich Lohmann; Edited by Nino Borghi; Music by Eugen Thomass, Johann Sebastian Bach, Frederic Chopin, Charles Gounod, Franz Liszt & Gustav Mahler; Produced & directed by Hans-Jürgen Syberberg. Color 187 minutes

CAST LIST: Helmut Kauter (*Karl May*); Kristina Söderbaum (*Emma May*); Käthe Gold (*Klara May*); Attila Hörbiger (*Max Dittrich*); William Trenk (*Rodolf Lebius*); Mady Rahl (*Pauline Münchmeyer*); Lil Dagover (*Bertha von Suttner*); Rudolf Prack (Justice minister); Leon Askin (*Klotz-Sello*); Marquand Böhm (*Überhorst*); Wolfgang Büttner (*Ehrecke von Morbit*); Peter Chatel (*Horace Herzfelder*); Erwin Faber (*Napoleon Krügel*); Rudolf Fernau (*Bredereck*); Fritz von Friedl (*Larrass*); Peter Jost (*Seyffert*); Penelope Georgiou (*Penelope*); Andre Heller (*Robert Müller*); Guido Wieland (*Bernstein*); Peter Kern (George Grosz); Peter Moland (*Sascha Schneider*).

COMMENTARY: Karl May (1842–1912) was a German writer known for his romantic adventure novels set in the Orient and in the American West. In his youth, Hitler was a devoted reader of May's works. Syberberg's lengthy film about the writer is alternately sentimental, ironical and dreamlike. Syberberg described it as a portrait of the last German mystic in the age of the decline of the fairy tale. Hitler appears briefly in the film, a member of the audience attending May's last public reading in 1912. He is portrayed as an asocial young man of twenty-two, already a fanatic, and fascinated by the exotic heroism of the characters in May's novels.

50. *Kureji No Daiboken* (AKA *That Crazy Adventure*) (1965)

Andrew Hughes as Adolf Hitler
Comedy

Toho. Written by Ryozo Kasahara & Yasuo Tanami; Photographed by Tadashi Imura & Fukuzo Koizumi; Edited by Yoshitami Kuroiwa; Music by Kenjuro Hirose & Tetsuaki Hagiwara; Produced by Akira Watanabe; Directed by Kengo Furusawa. Color 106 minutes

CAST LIST: Hajime Hana (Detective); Hitoshi Ueki (Reporter); Kei Tani (Inventor); Senri Sakurai; Hiroshi Inuzuka; Shin Yasuda; Eitaro Ishibashi; Reiko Dan; Fubuki Koshiji; Sin Otomo; Yutaka Oka; Wataru Omae; Emi Ito; Hisaya Ito; Sholchi Hirose; Somesho Matsumoto; Minoru Takada; Tetsu Nakamura; Masanari Nihei; Keiko Sawai; Fuyuki Murakami; Hisaya Morishige (Prime Minister).

COMMENTARY: The Crazy Cats is a popular Japanese comedy troupe and band formed in 1955. This film was intended as a tenth anniversary extravaganza to celebrate the event. Hana, Ueki, Tani, Sakurai, Inuzuka and Yasuda are all members of the group, and they are the central characters of this comedy. The basic plot involves a puzzling counterfeiting case confronting policeman Hana. Magazine reporter Ueki suspects madcap inventor Tani, who invented a matter transference device, to be the culprit. As he pursues his investigation, he stumbles across a secret organization who kidnaps both Ueki and Tani, taking them to a secret island missile base in the Pacific.

The organization turns out to be a neo–Nazi group led by Adolf Hitler, still brimming with plans of world conquest. Hitler plans to fire nuclear missiles to destroy his principal enemies, but Ueki and Tani manage to launch them to destroy the base itself, saving the world. Hitler is played by Andrew Hughes, an American actor who appeared in a number of Japanese films, including his role as the Australian Prime Minister in _Tidal Wave_ AKA _The Submersion of Japan_ (1975) and as Dr. Stevenson in _Destroy All Monsters_ (1968), a Godzilla free-for-all with Rodan, King Ghidorah, Baragon and Gorosaurus all under the control of aliens from outer space. Hughes also appeared as a Western reporter in _King Kong Escapes_ (1967). He played the ship's wireless operator in the early disaster flick _The Last Voyage_ with Robert Stack, Dorothy Malone, George Sanders and Edmond O'Brien. Hughes reportedly made a convincing Hitler, playing his role as a straightforward heavy, contrasting with the wild antics of the Crazy Cats.

51.   _The Last Ten Days_ (AKA _Der Letzte Akt (The Last Act)_) (1955)

Albin Skota as Adolf Hitler
Historical drama

Cosmopol/Columbia. Written by Erich Maria Remarque & Fritz Habeck based upon the book _Ten Days to Die_ by Michael A. Musmanno; Photographed by Gunther Anders; Edited by Herbert Taschner; Music by Erwin Halletz; Produced by Ludwig Polsterer; Directed by G. W. Pabst. B & W 113 minutes

ANNOTATED CAST LIST: Oskar Werner (_Richard Wüst_, 9th Army Captain sent to Hitler with reinforcement request); Lotte Tobisch (_Eva Braun_, Hitler's mistress); Erik Frey (_Wilhelm Burgdorf_, Chief of Military Personnel); Herbert Herbe (_General Hans Krebs_, Army Chief of Staff); Kurt Eilers (_Martin Bormann_, Hitler's private secretary); Willy Krause (_Dr. Joseph Goebbels_, Propaganda Minister); Helga Kennedy-Dohrn (_Magda Goebbels_, His wife); Hermann Erhardt (_Hermann Göring_, Reich Marshal); Erik Suckmann (_Heinrich Himmler_, Interior Minister & Head of SS); Erland Erlandsen (_Albert Speer_, Munitions Minister); Hannes Schiel (_Colonel Otto Günsche_, Hitler's personal adjutant); Otto Schmole (_Alfred Jodl_, General & Chief of Operations); Leopold Hainisch (_Wilhelm Keitel_, Field Marshal & Chief of the High Command); Otto Wögerer (_Robert Ritter von Greim_, Officer who flies to the bunker to be appointed new head of Luftwaffe); Julius Jonak (_Hermann Fegelein_, SS General & Eva Braun's brother-in-law); Ernst Prockl (_Walter Wagner_, City official who marries Hitler & Eva Braun); Inga Kurzbauer (_Traudl Junge_, Hitler's dictation secretary); Walter Regelsberger (_Major Venner_, Wüst's half-brother stationed in the bunker); John van Dreellen (_Major Brinkmann_); Lilly Stepanek (Brinkmann's wife); Herta Agnst (_Jutta_, Their young daughter); Gerd Zohling (_Richard_, Member of Hitler Youth); Elisabeth Epp (Richard's mother); Otto Guschy (_Franz_, Wüst's driver); Michael Janisch (SS officer); Raoul Retzer (SS officer nicknamed "Giant"); Ernst Walbrun (Astrologer); Guido Wieland (Bunker doctor); Otto Kerry (His assistant); Franz Messner (_Otto_, Canteen worker); Martha Wallner (_Frieda_, Canteen workers).

APPRAISAL AND SYNOPSIS: G. W. Pabst, the famous director of such legendary films as _Pandora's Box_ (1929) and _The Threepenny Opera_ (1931), had planned to do a film about the last days of Hitler for over seven years, since it was suggested to him by the American writer Michael Musmanno, who participated as a judge at the Nuremberg trials. After securing the rights to Musmanno's book about the demise of Hitler, _Ten Days to Die_, Pabst was unable to secure financing for his project in Germany, perhaps due to doubts about the success of a commercial German project centering on Hitler, so Pabst secured Austrian backing through Cosmopol. Pabst asked famed novelist Erich

Albin Skota as Hitler and Willy Krause as Goebbels in the shadowy netherworld of the bunker in
The Last Ten Days **or** *Der Letzke Akt*.

Maria Remarque to work on the screenplay. It is well known that the Nazis despised Remarque's most famous book, *All Quiet on the Western Front*, banning it and even using it as a prop for their book burning campaign in 1933. Pabst had mixed feelings, reportedly, about this script and there is some controversy about how much of it was actually used in the final film despite the writing credit. Instead of a straight historical film, the picture mingled fact with fantasy, using fictional characters and events that made the film somewhat of an allegory. In this fashion, *The Last Ten Days* helped to create or promote a number of myths. This was unfortunate, especially since this was the first film solely devoted to the Führer bunker. It promoted the illusion that this underground

shelter was vast, spacious and well equipped, when in actuality it was claustrophobic, cramped and largely inadequate. Furthermore, the screenplay expanded on a concept from the Soviet picture *Fall of Berlin* in which Hitler flooded the Berlin subway system where people hid out during the Battle of Berlin, both to punish the citizens of Berlin who were unworthy of him and to prevent the Russian troops from traveling through the tunnels. Hitler's deluge became the central event of *The Last Ten Days*, and a metaphor for Hitler's contempt for Germany as a whole. However, the climatic event is largely fallacious. To understand this, the actual facts need to be reviewed. There is a point where the Berlin subway (U-Bahntunnel) travels under the Landwehr

Canal just off the River Spree. On April 27, 1945, Hitler decided that the subway roof should be dynamited at once to prevent Russian forces from infiltrate the heart of the city through this passage. The order, however, was not executed. Sources differ as to whether the command was ever issued or was simply ignored. A week later, on May 2nd, three days after Hitler's death, the tunnel was blasted by some members of the SS as they battled Russian troops, and a portion of the subway was then flooded. Months later, when the tunnel was drained, a number of bodies, possibly as few as fourteen, were removed. In any case, the mass drowning of hundreds of people portrayed in the film is false, particularly since the picture intercuts scenes of the desperate plight of victims with that of Hitler dictating his last will and testament to his secretary. With millions of genuine victims of Hitler's brutal reign, it seems pointless to create an imaginary atrocity to serve as a metaphor. It weakens the overall film, and perhaps Pabst came to this conclusion himself, because in his next Hitler film, *Jackboot Mutiny*, he strove to be as historically accurate as possible.

Much of *The Last Ten Days* has mythological implications. When Captain Wüst first approaches the entrance to the bunker, the cinematography suggests he is entering another realm, the underworld of Dante or, more appropriately, the subterranean kingdom of the Nibelungs from Wagner's *Das Rheingold*. The photography and lighting creates an eerie effect, with gloomy and mysterious shadows. Pabst recalls the heyday of German expressionism with his portrayal of Hitler's final lair. Wüst has been sent by General Busse to request reinforcements for his decimated troops. Instead, Wüst's audience with the Führer is postponed, and the captain bunks with his half-brother, Vanner, who is stationed in the bunker. The scene shifts to Hitler as he is briefed by his generals. When the Führer storms out of the meeting, he sees Wüst smoking and he slaps the cigarette out of his hand. Himmler and Göring leave the bunker after giving birth-

day greetings to the Führer, who then meets and decorates members of the Hitler Youth. The camera follows Richard, one of the preteen fighters, whose mother and siblings live in the rubble of a bombed out apartment building. They move to the subway for safety.

At the bunker, Hitler is outraged that his orders for a counterattack to relieve the siege of Berlin has not occurred. He secludes himself in his study where he addresses the portrait of Frederick the Great and imagines that he is having a conversation with him. He curses the Jews and decides to commit suicide. He orders that the Berlin subway be flooded at once. There is a large rathskeller in the bunker that functions as a beer hall where soldiers gather, sing ballads and songs, and perform skits such as dancing with a lifesize female ragdoll. The men are recruited to carry out Hitler's order to blow up the subway tunnel. Richard, the Hitler Youth, learns about the plan and challenges Captain Wüst to help save his family. Wüst has an audience with Hitler who has an hysterical fit. A soldier rushes into the room and sees Wüst standing over the Führer and shoots the captain. Wounded, Wüst is brought back to his brother's room where he dies cursing the Nazi regime and speaking of the need for peace. The subway tunnel is blown up and hundreds of people are killed. Meanwhile, Hitler prepares to end his life. He marries Eva Braun, his mistress and dictates his final testament. The soldiers in the rathskeller start to party, trying to drown out all thoughts of the world collapsing around them. The Führer finally shoots himself, and his body, together with that of Eva, is brought out of the bunker and cremated. As the flames rise up, the image of Wüst appears again on screen, and his dying words are repeated, followed by the end credits.

In the final mix, about half the screen time is filled with Hitler and his entourage and the other half with the fictional characters of Captain Wüst and Richard, the Hitler Youth. The Hitler scenes concentrate on his futile attempts to bring about a German counterattack, the supposed betrayals of Göring and Himmler, the attempt of Fegelein to flee and his summoning of General von Greim to replace Göring as head of the Luftwaffe. These more or less follow the historical record, but there are also fanciful scenes where Hitler's thoughts are overheard by the audience. These moments are well handled, but diluted somewhat by the countless shifts to the goings-on in the rathskeller. On their own, the fictional subplots are not bad or uninteresting. Skillful editing makes these diverse elements play very well together. But at the same time, the weight of the film is off balance The cast is excellent, particularly Oscar Werner as Captain Wüst, Otto Wögerer as General von Greim and Willy Krause in an exceptional performance as Joseph Goebbels. The creepy, demented atmosphere of the bunker is well captured even if the trappings are less than authentic. By using large and roomy sets, the sense of claustrophobia is missing, but the imaginative and moody camerawork more than compensates for it. Beneath the surface, Pabst manages to touch on many elements disturbing to a German audience, the question of collective guilt, for example, or the harm done to German culture by the influence of the Nazis. In any case, *The Last Ten Days* remains the most successful and important film of Pabst in the postwar years, a lasting achievement.

HITLER PORTRAYAL: Pabst originally considered casting Werner Krauss, the original Dr. Caligari, as Adolf Hitler, in order to stress the expressionistic slant of his concept. He finally yielded his impulse because Krauss, at seventy, was too old to play a viable Hitler, so he turned instead to Albin Skota, a distinguished Viennese stage actor, to undertake the part. Skota had made very few films, so he was a fresh screen presence. His physical resemblance is fairly close to Hitler to be effective, but it is his mastery of voice and gesture that make him such an excellent choice. For most of the film, Skota moves in and out of the shadows of the cavernous bunker, reflecting his thorough fa-

miliarity of the effectiveness of low key lighting. The only problem with Skota's performance is that his Hitler is far too healthy, showing little of the war strain or physical deterioration that affected Hitler toward the end of his life. His clothes seem well pressed and perfectly tailored, his movements energetic and decisive, with no slurring of his speech, no stooped shoulders, trembling hands or other infirmities except toward the very end. His mental imbalance, however, is unquestionably obvious. Pabst chose to have the actor play Hitler as vigorous and evil, certainly under duress but still the master of his fate. There is absolutely no trace of humanity in him, and that includes human frailties, even when Dr. Morell gives him his regular injections to keep up his demonic energy level. His relationship with Eva Braun, for instance, is nonexistent and kept totally offscreen. Skota's most impressive scene is his mental conversation with the painting of Frederick the Great, which seems very close to the actual oval portrait by Anton Graff rather than the traditional but mistaken rectangular painting depicted in almost every other bunker film. It is a chilling scene in which the action takes place inside Hitler's head and we hear his thoughts as he stares diabolically at the image of Frederick, and we half expect to hear Frederick answer like Norman Bates talking with his mother in the last scene of *Psycho* (1959). Skota's concept of the Führer is certainly a figure out of a horror film, particularly those of the era of German expressionism. Besides the influence of the silent screen villains, Skota's interpretation also seems influenced by Wagner, so that he seems like the evil Niebelung Albrich in *Das Rheingold*, the absolute master of a dark, underground realm. Skota's Hitler has become a figure out of legend, not one of flesh and blood.

REPRESENTATIVE QUOTES

• He always loves children so much. *(Goebbels to Himmler, while the Führer decorates members of the Hitler youth)* Especially in uniform. *(Himmler's comment)*

• My Führer, place yourself at the head of your troops and escape to freedom in an historic way. *(Jodl to Hitler)* And if I am wounded, if I fall alive to the violence of my enemies? People would lead me around the whole world in a cage. *(Hitler's reply)*

• And the Jews, that pestilence, that vermin covering the earth with a slimy layer, I let too many of them flee. I should have wiped them out completely, wiped them out to the last infant. *(Hitler addressing the portrait of Frederick the Great)*

• Nothing from me should be left over, not even ashes. *(Hitler to Bormann)*

• If you ever know peace, don't let them take it away. Never let them take it. Don't say *Jawohl*. Don't ever say *Jawohl*. The world can get along without *Jawohl*. Always keep faith. *(Wüst's dying words, repeated on the soundtrack as the film ends)*

52. *Die Letzte Stunde im Führerbunker* (AKA *100 Jahre Adolf Hitler—Die Letzte Stunde*) (1989)

Udo Kier as Adolf Hitler
Drama

DEM Film. Written by Christoph Schlingensief; Photographed by Foxi Bärenklau; Edited by Christoph Schlingensief & Ariane Traub; Music by Tom Dokoupil; Produced by Ruth Bambers, Christian Fürst & Christoph Schlingensief; Directed by Christoph Schlingensief. B & W 60 minutes

CAST LIST: Margit Carstensen; Brigitte Kausch; Dietrich Kuhibrodt; Alfred Edel; Andreas Kunze; Marie-Lou Sellem; Volker Spengler; Asia Verdi.

COMMENTARY: This experimental film attempts to chronicle the last hour of Hitler's life in the bunker from 2:30 P.M. to 3:30 P.M. April 30, 1945. The picture was shot in black and white in an actual World War II era bunker, with much of the action captured by a shaky, hand-held camera, showing how the various denizens of the bunker attempted to forget the lost war in a final

party. The director attempts to draw some parallel in this scenario to the meaning of the Hitler phenomenon. Since the film was released 100 years after Hitler's birth, it was initially entitled *100 Years Adolf Hitler*. Then a subtitle was added, *The Last Hour in the Führerbunker*, by which the film commonly became known. Critical reaction was largely unfavorable, with many critics complaining that the picture made little sense, particularly since Hitler was largely offscreen during much of the action. It has seldom been seen or revived since its debut.

53. *Lisztomania* (1975)

Paul Nicholas as Hitler monster
Fantasy/Musical

Warner Brothers. Written by Ken Russell; Photographed by Peter Suschitzky; Edited by Stuart Baird; Music by Franz Liszt, Richard Wagner, Roger Daltry & Rick Wakeman; Produced by Roy Baird & David Putnam; Directed by Ken Russell. Color 106 minutes

CAST LIST: Roger Daltry (*Franz Liszt*); Paul Nicholas (*Richard Wagner*); Ringo Starr (Pope); Rick Wakeman (*Thor*, the Aryan superman); Sara Kestelman (*Princess Carolyn*); John Justin (*Count d'Agoult*); Fiona Lewis (*Marie D'Agoult*); Veronica Quilligan (*Cosima Wagner*); Andrew Reilly (*Hans von Bülow*); Kenneth Colley (*Frederic Chopin*); Nell Campbell (*Olga*); Imogen Claire (*George Sand*); Rikki Howard (The Countess); David English (Captain*);* Anulka Dziubinska (*Lola Montes*); Murray Melvin (*Hector Berlioz*); Ken Parry (*Gioacchino Rossini*); Otto Diamant (*Felix Mendelssohn*).

COMMENTARY: *Lisztomania* is a totally surreal fantasy based very loosely on the life and career of the great 19th century composer Franz Liszt crossed with leftover fragments of the rock opera *Tommy*. It is directed by Ken Russell who also did similar extravagant biopics of Gustav Mahler, Peter Ilyitch Tchaikovsky, Oscar Wilde and the Pre-Raphaelite artist and poet Dante Gabriel Rossetti. The Liszt picture, however, is the wildest and most absurd of these biographical flicks. The relevant sequence occurs in the last quarter of *Lisztomania*, which is set in the style of a gothic horror film as Franz Liszt sets out to destroy the evil vampire Richard Wagner. He infiltrates Wagner's castle and discovers that Richard is trying to create an artificial creature, the Aryan superman, who turns out to be a musclebound idiot. Using his music, principally *Totentanz*, Liszt decimates Wagner and his work. But later Cosima resurrects her husband through the force of his music and a new ideology, Nazisim. Wagner emerges from his tomb transformed into a grotesque creature who is a cross between Hitler and the Frankenstein monster. Liszt is now destroyed. From heaven, however, Liszt and his female friends look down at the chaos on Earth and decide to put Richard out of his misery, and they send down a missile to destroy him. Although a borderline case, Paul Nicholas's Frankenhitler is one of the most bizarre screen references to the Führer.

54. *Little Nicky* (2000)

Christopher Carroll as Adolf Hitler
Fantasy/Comedy

New Line Cinema. Written by Tim Herlihy, Adam Sandler & Stephen Brill; Photographed by Theodore Van De Sande; Edited by Jeff Gourson; Music by Teddy Castellucci; Produced by Robert Simons, Jack Giarraputo, Adam Sandler (executive), Michael De Luca (executive) & Brian Witten (executive); Directed by Stephen Brill. Color 90 minutes.

ANNOTATED CAST LIST: Adam Sandler (*Nicky*, Third son of the Devil); Harvey Keitel (The Devil); Rodney Dangerfield (*Lucifer*, The retired original Devil & father of the current Devil); Rhys Ifans (*Adrian*, First son of the Devil); Tom "Tiny" Lister, Jr. (*Cassius*, Second son of the Devil); Patricia Arquette (*Valerie*, Artist who becomes Nicky's girlfriend); Allan Covert (*Todd*, Nicky's roommate); Peter Dante (*Peter*, hippie fan of Nicky); Jonathan Loughran (*John*, hippie fan of Nicky); Reese Witherspoon (*Holly*, Angel & mother of Nicky); Blake Clark (*Jimmy*, Devil's chief assistant); Salvatore Cavaliere (*Sal*, Demon); Kevin Nealon (Gatekeeper to hell); Jon Lovitz (Peeping Tom who falls out of a tree and goes to hell); Dana Carvey (Basketball referee possessed by Cassius); Lewis Arquette (Cardinal possessed by Adrian); George Wallace (New York mayor possessed by Cassius); Michael McKean (New York police chief possessed by Adrian); Quentin Tarantino (Blind holy man); John Witherspoon (Street vendor who steals Nicky's flask); Clint Howard (Transvestite); Brandon Rosenberg (*Zachariah*, Nicky's son in epilogue); Sylvia Lopez (TV Newscaster); Henry Winkler (Himself); Regis Philbin (Himself); Bill Walton (Himself); Ozzy Osbourne (Himself); Dan Marino (Himself); Carl Weathers (*Chubbs Peterson*, Helpful man in heaven); Robert Smigel (Voice of Mr. Beefy the bulldog); Jana Sandler, Kalie Stewart-Conner, Tracey Ostrand, Kimberly Velez, Stephanie Chao (Angels); and the Harlem Globetrotters.

APPRAISAL AND SYNOPSIS: Adam Sandler's flamboyant but crude comedic fantasy provided the most recent big screen presentation of Adolf Hitler, in which he serves as an elaborate prop. Yet his very presence shows the endurance of the Hitler image, since this film is largely geared toward teenagers whose cultural range stretches from Ozzy Osbourne to the Harlem Globetrotters. *Little Nicky* heavily relies upon scatological jokes, topical humor and carefully arranged product placement such as Popeye's chicken. If the viewer can get beyond these weak points, the film is a rather effective comedy, a hip upgrading of Olsen and Johnson's madcap *Hellzapoppin'* (1941). The scenes in hell are rather impressive, with dazzling art direction and a spellbinding infernal vista. The overall pace of the film is brisk and fast paced and the jokes and puns come at a breakneck clip, some good, many bad (or gross) and a few downright hilarious. The production has an imaginative cast relying on many witty cameos of such people as Regis Philbin, Henry "The Fonz" Winkler and director Quentin Tarantino. It is undoubtedly Adam Sandler's finest film, although financially the film tanked compared to less expensive efforts such as *The Waterboy* (1999).

We are brought to hell in the film when a peeping tom falls out of a tree and is killed, plummeting at once to the netherworld. He eavesdrops on the Devil, and discovers that the infernal kingdom is itself in turmoil. The Devil is due to retire after ruling hell for 10,000 years, just as his father, Lucifer, had done before him. He must choose his successor from his three children: the conniving and mean-spirited Adrian, the power-hungry Cassius and the sweet and gentle Little Nicky whose features were deformed when his brother hit him in the face with a shovel. The Devil, fearing that Adrian is not ready to rule since he does not understand the balance of power between good and evil, elects to serve another 10,000 year term himself. This delights Little Nicky, but outrages the others. The devil returns to his chores, including his daily torture at 4 o'clock of Adolf Hitler, hell's most evil resident. Meanwhile Adrian and Cassius freeze the gateway to hell as they head off to Earth to launch their own reign of terror. Without the flow of new souls into hell, the Devil starts to disintegrate. His only hope lies with Little Nicky, the only remaining being in hell with the power to travel to Earth. He has forty-eight hours to capture his brothers (in a magic flask) and bring them back to Hades and unblocking the gates.

Nicky travels to New York and has a series of misadventures in his efforts to find his brothers, who have assumed different identities. He is assisted by Little Beefy, a demon in the shape of a bulldog who is the devil's agent in the Big Apple. Little Beefy breaks Nicky in on the dos and don'ts of earthly life, such as eating and not standing in the way of a moving bus. The bulldog sets him up with Todd, an actor in need of a roommate. The devil's son also meets Satanic groupies Peter and John, and an attractive girl named Valerie, with whom he falls head over heels in love. His first break comes while watching a basketball game on television and he observes that the referee uses the same gestures as his brother Cassius. Nicky heads to the arena, where he challenges the referee to a one on one contest during the halftime show. He tells Cassius that he has gained special super powers from the liquid in his flask. When Cassius snatches and drinks from it, his spirit is sucked into the flask.

Adrian, disguised as New York's police commissioner, gets his revenge by alerting the city that Nicky is a mad serial killer. A mob tracks down Nicky in the streets, and he has to transform himself into a swarm of spiders. He lays an elaborate trap in the subway to trick Adrian into drinking from the flask, but at the last moment his brother sees through his trap, and they battle, eventually falling in front of a train. Nicky is stunned to find himself in heaven. He learns that he is half-divine, and his mother, Holly, is an angel. In hell, however, Adrian tries to take over, and his grandfather, Lucifer, is unable to stop him. Adrian arranges to have a segment of hell to rise in the middle of Central Park in a plan to take over Earth. Holly gives him a glowing small globe, a special weapon that God has permitted Holly to give to Nicky.

Adrian is waiting for midnight, at which time his father will totally vanish, and he will take over. A hellish rally is organized in Central Park. For entertainment, Adrian tortures Peter, John and Valerie. Eventually, Nicky unleashes his glowing globe, out of which Black Sabbath rocker Ozzy Osbourne emerges and forces Adrian into the flask. Nicky brings the flask back to hell, and his father, the Devil, is instantly restored. Satan takes the magic flask with Adrian and Cassius, and shoves it up the rectum of Adolf Hitler. The Devil gives his blessing for Nicky to return to Earth and marry Valerie. In a brief epilogue, Nicky and Valerie are shown with Zacharias, their newborn baby, in a perambulator. The film ends as subtitles tells the eventual fate of the various people who appeared in the story. The DVD version of *Little Nicky* contains cuts scenes, extended scenes and an alternate ending, but no additional material with Hitler.

HITLER PORTRAYAL: Christopher Carroll is an active character actor who has appeared in over twenty films and dozens of television shows such as *Friends*, *Cheers*, *The Love Boat* and *Baywatch*, usually in the role of a bank officer, a lawyer or a teacher. One different role that stands out was as Gul Benil, a Cardassian leader in *Deep Space Nine*. As Adolf Hitler, Carroll appears in two scenes in hell near the start and at the conclusion of the film. Hitler is dressed in the outfit of a French chambermaid, with a skimpy black and white uniform and a tiny white cap. He attempts to carry himself with a modicum of dignity, but it is impossible. He is escorted to a cabinet in Lucifer's throne room where he is instructed to pick out a pineapple. Hawaiian music fills the soundtrack as the Führer bends over to pick up a small one. As he does so, his ruffled underwear is clearly visible. As he extends it toward Lucifer, the devil shakes his head and tells him to pick again. Hitler then fishes out a large one, and as the devil takes hold of it, Hitler incredulously mutters, "You're scherious?" Satan instructs him to bend over, and the devil proceeds to shove it up his backside, leafy end first, as Hitler mugs for the camera. At the end of the picture, Hitler has the last line in the film. This time, the devil, restored to his former vigor after his near disintegration, shoves up the magic flask with the spirits of Adrian and Cassius instead of a pineapple. He yells at them to enjoy their new hope, as Hitler exclaims, "Holy shit!" Carroll brings no special flair to the role, which probably could have been played by any of a dozen different actors. On the whole, he is adequate, but does capture the air of resignation in the face of continual degradation very well. Yet, it is torture on a tame scale, if one were to seriously consider the depths of the punishment he would properly deserve if the torments of hell were fully applied. Instead, his fate is a toss off joke, in no worse taste than much of the other vulgar humor that appears in this production.

REPRESENTATIVE QUOTES

• Don't forget, you are shoving a pineapple up Hitler's ass at seven! *(Jimmy to the Devil)*

• You're scherious? *(Hitler to the Devil as he inspects the largest pineapple for his torture)*

• Even in hell I get no respect. *(Lucifer to himself)*

55. *Loose Cannons* (1989)
Ira Lewis as Adolf Hitler (cameo)
Comedy

Tri Star. Written by Bob Clark, Richard Matheson & Richard Christian Matheson; Photographed by Reginald H. Morris; Edited by Stan Cole; Music by Paul Zaza; Produced by Aaron Spelling & Alan Greisman; Directed by Bob Clark. Color/B & W 94 minutes

ANNOTATED CAST LIST: Gene Hackman (*Mac Stern*, Washington D.C. detective); Dan Aykroyd (*Ellis Fielding*, His new partner who suffers from multiple personality disorder); Dom DeLusie (*Harry Gutterman*, Smut dealer who purchased Hitler film); Ronny Cox (*Bob*, Arrogant FBI agent); Nancy Travis (*Riva Lohengrin*, Israeli secret agent); Robert Prosky (*Kurt von Metz*, Leading candidate in West German elections); John Bogler (*Kurt von Metz*, as he appears in the Hitler film); Paul Koslo (*Joseph Grimmer*, Leader of German hit squad); Dick O'Neill (*Captain Del Doggett*, Police chief); Jan Triska (*Steckler*, Man who steals Hitler film from von Metz); Robert Elliott (Monsignor & psychiatrist who helps Ellis); Leon Rippy (*Westkit*, Detective who needles Mac); S. Epatha Merkerson (*Rachel*, Cop who babysits Mac's cat); David Alan Grier (*Delaney*, Vice squad detective); Alex Hyde-White (*Vaslinsky*, television interviewer); Tobin Bell (*Gerber*); Reg E. Cathey (*Willie*): Nancy Parsons (Hospital nurse);

Brad Greenquist (German Embassy official); Margaret Klenck (*Eva Braun*, Hitler's mistress).

APPRAISAL AND SYNOPSIS: *Loose Cannons* is a rather forced comedy built around two eccentric cops in Washington D.C. Although featuring an excellent cast and a decent script by Richard Matheson and his son, the film simply fails to click and becomes rather contrived. Bob Clark, who directed fine efforts as *Christmas Story* (1983) with a deft touch, here seems bereft of ideas. Dan Ackroyd turns in one of his poorest performances, and Gene Hackman is simply off stride.

The entire plot centers on a secret home movie with Adolf Hitler, possessed by Kurt von Metz, leading candidate in the upcoming West German elections. Steckler, one of his associates, steals the film and offers it to the highest bidder, who turns out to be a DC porn dealer named Harry "the Hippo" Gutterman. Von Metz hires a gangster, Joseph Grimmer, to retrieve the film, and he goes on a killing spree in D.C., murdering everyone who saw a screening of it. Detective Mac Stern is assigned to the case, and he is given the captain's nephew, Ellis Fielding as a partner. But Mac is not told that Ellis had been kidnapped and tortured on his last case, and spent a year recovering from multiple personality disorder, brought on by the traumatic experience. When the detectives track down Gutterman, Ellis changes personalities whenever he encounters violence, sometimes acting like the Cowardly Lion from *The Wizard of Oz* (1939), other times like Captain Kirk or Dr. McCoy from *Star Trek*.

Mac and Ellis take Gutterman into protective custody, and he explains about the Hitler film which he has hidden. The detectives run into difficulty with a disdainful FBI agent, who wants to take charge of Gutterman himself. After evading Grimmer's hit squad, the detectives join forces with an Israeli agent who is also on the trail of Grimmer. Gutterman agrees to give the Hitler film to the Israelis if they agree to use it to discredit von Metz, who actually appears in the film as one of the Führer's favorites.

Gutterman and the detectives head to New York, where Gutterman had arranged to meet Steckler to close the deal for the film. Grimmer's men track them to Gutterman's bath house, and launch an armed attack. Steckler is killed, but before he dies he tells Ellis that the film is hidden in Grand Central Station. Grimmer kidnaps Ellis, and takes him to the train depot to get the film. After a slapstick battle, the Israeli agents finally escape with the film. They show it in Germany during a political speech by von Metz, revealing that in fact he helped Hitler to commit suicide in the bunker. The showing of this footage dooms the former Nazi's chances in the election. Meanwhile, Ellis, Mac and Gutterman recover from their injuries in the hospital, where they spend their recovery time entertaining kids in the children's ward.

HITLER PORTRAYAL: The appearance by Ira Lewis as Hitler is among the briefest on film. A clip from the notorious Hitler film only appears in the last moments of the feature, as Israeli agents interrupt von Metz's political rally by showing the black and white footage of a young von Metz together with Hitler in the bunker in April 1945. In fact, Hitler selects von Metz to fire the gun that kills both him and Eva, his wife of one day. The Führer hands the gun to the officer, as he and Eva kneel down and bow their heads, awaiting the fatal shot. Both Hitler and Eva are shown from behind, but the image is somewhat distorted because the Israelis are projecting it on the backdrop curtain behind von Metz. Since the Hitler film was the motivating factor of the entire plot, the brevity of the clip is disappointing, particularly since the film was supposed to be filled with unique historical scenes, and the footage filled an entire reel. Ira Lewis has appeared in only a handful of films, most notably as Tyrell, the murderer hired by King Richard III to murder his nephews in Al Pacino's brilliant Shakespearean film essay, *Looking for Richard* (1996).

REPRESENTATIVE QUOTES

• The gaudier the cop, the snappier the patter. *(Mac to Westkit)*

• This one starred, guess who, Hitler and a couple of Nazi guys. *(Gutterman to Mac)* You saw this with your own eyes? … What's a film like this worth? *(Mac)* Major bucks, a collector would pay anything for a copy of it. *(Gutterman)* Yeah? A bunch of dead Nazis screwing? *(Mac)* No, it's not just a skin flick, its got historical stuff in it too. *(Gutterman)*

• I never had the displeasure of meeting Adolf Hitler… Next they will have me in a bungalow with Marilyn Monroe or in daily communication with your Elvis Presley. *(Kurt von Metz, upon being asked in a TV interview if he had ever been associated with Hitler)*

56. *The Lucifer Complex*
(AKA *Hitler's Wild Women*)
(1975/78)

Keenan Wynn as Adolf Hitler (?)
Gustaf/Beril Unger as Hitler clones (?)
Science Fiction

Vista Films. Written by David L. Hewitt & Dale Skillicorn; Photographed by David E. Jackson; Edited by Val Kuklowsky; Music by William Loose; Produced by David L. Hewitt & David E. Jackson; Directed by David L. Hewitt & Kenneth Hartford. Color 91 minutes

ANNOTATED CAST LIST: William Lanning (Unnamed survivor, living on an isolated island in the Pacific); Robert Vaughn (*Glen Manning*, American secret agent); Merrie Lynn Ross (*April Adams*, Captive who breaks into Manning's hospital room); Keenan Wynn (U.S. Secretary of Defense); Glenn Ramson (*Bernard Vogel*, Nazi scientist); Leo Gordon (*Al Norris*, CIA chief); Victoria Carroll (*Julie Simmons*, Al's secretary); Kieu Chinh (*Major Chinn Lee*, Chinese courier); Aldo Ray (*Karl Krauss*, Nazi compound security chief); Ross Durfee (*Gerhardt Frobel*, Nazi compound administrator); Lynn Cartwright (*Brunner*, His as-

sistant); Corinne Cole (*Greta*, Ringleader of captives); Carol Terry, Ginger Green, Pamela Smart (Captives); Colin Eliot Brown (Nazi guard); Chellio Campbell (*Ann*, Girl in nightclub).

APPRAISAL AND SYNOPSIS: *The Lucifer Complex* is a wacky concoction, with most of its footage and all of its performers (except William Lanning) deriving from an unfinished film by David L. Hewitt entitled *Hitler's Wild Women*, made several years earlier. After this production was abandoned, the jumbled footage was stitched together in a most unusual fashion. A framework was developed using only one actor, a survivor of a nuclear war, who lives by himself on an isolated Pacific atoll. A cave on his island is equipped with a sophisticated computer that contains a visual record of human history. After checking out scenes from rock concerts and some ground action in Vietnam, the survivor spends one afternoon watching the origin of "the great war of 1986" which occurred ten years earlier. The sequence of events, which the survivor actually calls "logical," centers on the exploits of a bumbling American secret agent, Glen Manning, who uncovered a Nazi plot to replace world leaders with fascist clones. The gaps in the Manning story are bridged as the survivor fast forwards his computer tape to watch a later section. To a certain degree, it is a clever gimmick to salvage the sporadic scenes of an unfinished project, however, the quality of the original film is so poor that it hardly seems worth the effort. The real disappointment is that the worthwhile cast, with solid actors such as Robert Vaughn, Keenan Wynn, Leo Gordon and Aldo Ray, is largely wasted. The framing footage may be tedious, but at least it is clever, particularly in depicting the principal footage as past history. Little, however, can be done to salvage the incoherent main plot.

The first relevant episode tuned in by the survivor shows a busload of dignitaries who are mysteriously gassed by the driver while stopping on an isolated road in the desert. The scene then shifts to one of the weakest in the picture. Glen Manning is at a night-club watching a belly dancer perform while simultaneously flirting with another girl seated at the next table. This bit goes on in-terminably until the survivor finally gets bored and pushes the story onward to Man-ning's investigation when he comes across the abandoned bus. Glen suspects foul play. The next jump finds the agent in hot water, as the Secretary of Defense chews out CIA Director Al Norris for relying on Manning. It seems the dignitaries turned up safe and sound, and his report of the empty bus is re-garded as erroneous when Major Chinn Lee, a diplomatic courier who was on the bus, re-ports that the ride was uneventful except for a short delay caused by a flat tire. Neverthe-less, Norris gives Glen another assignment, one recommended by his secretary, Julie Simmons. Three military aircraft have dis-appeared off the coast of South America, and Manning is ordered to fly a reconnais-sance mission and photograph the island area known as "Code Name Lucifer." He undertakes the routine assignment, but when his aircraft reaches the coordinates of the disappearances, his jet is fired upon from the ground and shot down. After parachut-ing to the ground, Manning discovers a mys-terious jungle complex flying a flag with a swastika and guarded by storm troopers. (It actually looks like the set of Stalag 13 from *Hogan's Heroes*.) They track him down and knock him out.

When he awakens, Glen is told that he is recovering from trauma at the Pensacola Naval hospital in Florida. When Julie visits him, Glen starts to recount his sighting of the Nazi compound, but his physician, Dr. Vogel, convinces him that it was only a hal-lucination. Later, an escaped woman pa-tient, April Adams, breaks into Glen's room and insists that they are prisoners at the se-cret Nazi base. Glen later sneaks out of his hospital room and discovers that April's story is true. He tries to rescue the girl, but is captured himself. Now Dr. Vogel reveals the scope of the project, to use Nazi clones to gain world control for the Fourth Reich,

to be led by none other than Adolf Hitler himself, or at least his clone. Gerhardt Fro-bel, the commander of the compound, tries to question Glen about the information that Chinn Lee had been carrying. Apparently, the real Major Lee had been killed before he was replaced by a clone. Glen tells him nothing, and he is scheduled to become a guinea pig for Nazi experiments. The other prisoners in the compound are all women, and April informs them of Glen's presence. She is later tortured by Brunner, the female overseer of the prisoners, with the help of Krauss, a brutal guard. The women revolt and run amok. Freed, Glen joins them and starts to tear the camp apart using Frobel's tank. This sequence, however, ends without any resolution.

When the scene shifts forward again, Glen and April are taken by Frobel to the underground depths of the camp where they confront Hitler. The Führer kills Frobel with a laser beam after proclaiming him to be a total failure. Glen shoots at Hitler, but he is only a projected image. A clone of Glen shows up, and Manning battles with his double. April is uncertain if the victor is the real Glen or the clone. When a laser blast is aimed at Glen, she saves him, deciding he is the real agent. Glen blasts into the next chamber where he shoots Hitler. However, he encounters the Secretary of Defense, spouting off about his plans in a thick Ger-man accent. "So it is you!" Glen exclaims. The plot begins to unravel as the Secretary of Defense proclaims his clones will take over the world, as he opens the sea gates. A huge flood arises and sweeps through the camp, totally destroying it. The Secretary of Defense ducks into an air lock. Glen and April chase after him, and apparently knock him out, but at this point the sequence ends. The survivor forges ahead to later images in which the Secretary of Defense is depicted as chairing a meeting of cloned American officials and announces the island has been destroyed, but they are still able to move ahead with their plans for world conquest. The survivor comments about the terrible war that followed and how mankind was destroyed by it. He shuts off the computer, remarking it that contains the complete record of man. He then sets off to explore other caves on his island as the end credits roll.

The Lucifer Complex is reminiscent of another unfinished film, *The Doomsday Machine* (1967) that was later "salvaged" for release in 1972 with an absurd finale that seemed unrelated to the rest of the picture. There is no real attempt in *The Lucifer Complex* to make any real sense of the confused plot or to tie up any of the loose ends. What happened to Glen and April? How did the unconscious Secretary of Defense escape the island? What was his actual identity and at what point did he take over from the real Secretary? Who were the opponents in the nuclear war if the Nazis had replaced all the key world leaders? The film offers no suggestions, just like the 1949 British version of *The Fall of the House of Usher* in which the onscreen storyteller is asked to explain what happened in the film, and he replies, "I don't know. Your guess is as good as mine." Similarly *The Lucifer Complex* ends in such a muddle that any guess would suffice in decoding the plot.

HITLER PORTRAYAL: The actual presence of Hitler in *The Lucifer Complex* is shrouded in confusion and double talk. It is uncertain whether Hitler is supposed to exist in the flesh, as an illusion or as a clone. One logical interpretation would be that Dr. Vogel obtained a sample from Hitler's body and resurrected him as a clone. The Führer then instructs Vogel to recreate him again, giving him the appearance of a key world leader, such as the American Secretary of Defense, whom he would kill and replace to undertake his world conquest. Manning then became a pawn in his plans, but why he wanted him brought to the island is a puzzlement, since he intended to replace him with a clone. The confrontation of Manning and Hitler is a bizarre choppy sequence, poorly staged and rather bewildering. Manning first confronts the projected image of Hitler (apparently played by Gustaf Unger) before encountering the corporeal Hitler (played by Beril Unger). The Ungers were twins who appeared together in one other film, *The Devil and Max Devlin* (1981), in which they played members of the Satanic Council. Gustav was also occasionally active as a producer, working on the Swedish-made Lon Chaney TV series *13 Demon Street*. Exactly why one twin appeared as the talking image of Hitler while the other appeared as Hitler in the flesh is a mystery, particularly when it appears that Keenan Wynn is playing the genuine Hitler in his guise as the American Secretary of Defense. In any case, this interpretation seems to be the only one with any hint of reason. The projected image of Hitler is a rather ludicrous performance, not looking anything like Hitler and sounding even worse, with an almost indecipherable accent. At least Wynn's German accent had a rugged flair. No matter which actor played Hitler, the projected image of the Führer is without doubt the lamest attempt of any portrayal in cinema history.

REPRESENTATIVE QUOTES

• So you see, the Fourth Reich is a reality, and through cloning we are building a new Master Race. *(Frobel to Manning)*

• There is nothing to stop us now. Very soon, our Führer's dream will become a reality. *(Vogel to Manning)* Too bad the old boy isn't around to see it. *(Manning)* You underestimate the indestructible superiority of the true Aryan. *(Vogel)*

• The Fourth Reich continues to move forward! As for you, Frobel, you are a disgrace to your uniform. Your bungling is unforgivable. You are no longer of any use to the Reich. *(Hitler to Frobel, before he executes him with a laser beam)*

• We were first with the V-2, first with our superior weapons of war. We are the master race. I suggest you save your strength for someone more your equal. *(Hitler to Manning, who vainly shoots at him)*

• Well, it is all here, the rise and fall of mankind. Some day, maybe a hundred years from now, a thousand, ten thousand years from now, some explorers from another planet will discover this time capsule. *(The survivor to himself as he shuts down the cave computer)*

57. *The Magic Face* (1951)

Luther Adler as Adolf Hitler
Alternate history

Columbia. Written by Mort Briskin & Robert Smith; Photographed by Tony Braun; Edited by Henrietta Brunisch; Music by Hershel Burke Gilbert; Produced by Mort Briskin & Robert Smith; Directed by Frank Tuttle. B & W 89 minutes

ANNOTATED CAST LIST: Luther Adler (*Rudy Janus*, Quick change artist & impersonator); Patricia Knight (*Vera Janus*, His wife who becomes Hitler's mistress); Jasper von Oertzen (*Major Fritz Weinrich*, Officer who discovers that Hitler is an impostor); Toni Mitterwurzer (*Hans*, Janus' dresser who trains him to act like a valet); Peter Preses (*Karl Harbacker*, Prison warden); Charles Koenig (*Franz*, Prison clerk); Annie Meier (*Mariana*, Warden's party guest); Heinz Moog (*Hans Harbach*, Prisoner); Ilka Windish (*Carla Harbach*, His wife, tortured by the warden); Manfred Inger (*Heinrich Wagner*, Hitler's personal valet); Michael Tellerring (*Lt. Colonel Heitmeyer*, Hitler's security chief); Erik Frey (*Colonel Raffenstein*); Rolf Wanka (*General Rodenbusch*); Willner (*General von Schlossen*); Hans Shiel (*General Steig*); Bell (*General Franz Halder*, Chief of General Staff); Sukman (*Heinrich Himmler*, Interior Minister & Head of SS); Hermann Erhardt (*Hermann Göring*, Reich Marshal); William L. Shirer (*Himself*).

APPRAISAL AND SYNOPSIS: The only possible way to classify *The Magic Face* is as an example of alternate history, since the events of World War II are markedly distorted and shuffled about in the script. This is apart from the premise of the film, which is that Hitler was assassinated and replaced by an impostor in the period between the fall of France and the planned invasion of England. In this alternate universe, many events of the

war are changed, such as the Rastenburg assassination plot (July 20, 1944) which here occurs before D Day (June 6, 1944). The timing of the fall of Stalingrad (January 31, 1943) seems to have been shifted to a much later date in this reshuffle of history, so that the loss of the German Sixth army at Stalingrad happened just before the Rastenburg plot. A number of key individuals, such as Eva Braun, Martin Bormann, Hans Rattenhuber (Hitler's personal security chief) and Heinz Linge (Hitler's valet), do not exist. In some cases, they are replaced by others, such as Vera Janus as Hitler's mistress. The most dramatic change is in the abilities of Hitler as a military leader. Instead of a talented but flawed and erratic dilettante, he is presented as an unparalleled genius, who builds up a military war machine so strong that it is practically indestructible. The only way it can be wrecked is by replacing Hitler with a duplicate dedicated to the destruction of the Third Reich. Of course, the loopholes in this screenplay are so enormous that the story can only function as a nightmarish fantasy. What might deceive some viewers is the presence of William L. Shirer, the passionate journalist who is one of the foremost scholars about the Nazi regime, as the film's narrator and a character as well. Shirer provides a sense of verisimilitude at the opening, but his tongue is undoubtedly planted firmly in his cheek when he says, "It is a story very difficult not to believe." In the introduction of the film, Shirer is depicted meeting with Vera Janus, and listening as she tells her story about her husband, Rudy Janus and her clandestine affair with Adolf Hitler. Eventually, Shirer protects his reputation by adding, "I don't say it's true or that it isn't. I simply tell it to you and let you judge for yourself." Of course, most viewers can immediately detect with these words that the film is just an elaborate sham.

The story flashes back to Vienna at the time of the Anchluss on the evening of March 17, 1938, when Hitler attends a stage show. (In actual fact, Hitler returned to Berlin on March 16th to a hero's welcome.)

SEE SCANDAL SLAYING OF HITLER IN SIN-RIDDEN BERLIN

...after shameless champagne party!

COLUMBIA PICTURES PRESENTS

THE MAGIC FACE

SEE killer rule Reich from Hitler's love nest!

SEE strange pastimes bring smiles to the thin lips of the Elite Guard!

SEE secret meetings where a faker sits in Hitler's seat—and plots the wreck of the Reich!

HITLER'S WOMAN SWEARS STORY TRUE —and COLUMBIA PICTURES will pay $10,000 to the first person who can authentically disprove this amazing impersonation.

starring LUTHER ADLER · PATRICIA KNIGHT

Written and Produced by MORT BRISKIN and ROBERT SMITH   Directed by FRANK TUTTLE · As told to WILLIAM L. SHIRER

Columbia ran a publicity campaign offering $10,000 to anyone who could prove that a double did not take Hitler's place.

The Führer interrupts the act of Rudy Janus, a noted actor and impersonator. While Janus performs a quick-change act as Benito Mussolini, Haile Selassie and others, Hitler makes goo goo eyes at Vera, Janus' scantily-clad wife who is part of his act. Vera almost spoils Rudy's performance as she continually gazes back at the Führer. After the show, Hitler sends a personal invitation for her to dine with him. Her husband, Rudy, is not invited. Rudy objects, but Vera goes anyway. When Rudy brashly follows her to Hitler's hotel, he is arrested and thrown into jail. Meanwhile, Vera becomes Hitler's mistress.

The Second World War breaks out after Hitler launches the invasion of Poland. When Warsaw falls, the Germans celebrate, including at the jail where Rudy is imprisoned. Karl Harbacker, the prison warden, is entertaining four beautiful women in at a private victory party with his clerk. They decide to ask Rudy to entertain them with some of his impersonations. Janus agrees, borrowing makeup from the women and using the warden's private quarters as his dressing room. He first transforms himself into Neville Chamberlain, and then a startling impersonation of the warden himself. He then asks for some extra time to undertake a third role. Instead, he simply leaves the prison disguised as Harbacker, easily fooling the guards. A half hour later, the warden looks for Rudy and discovers that he has vanished. He orders a search, but then Rudy telephones him with an offer. News of his escape would ruin the warden's career. If he pretends that Rudy Janus has been killed in his escape, then the actor vows to remain in hiding and never reveal how he fooled the warden. Harbacker agrees, and goes so far as killing his clerk and burying his body as that of the escapee.

Rudy hides out in Berlin with Hans, his old dresser. He conceives a plan of revenge and asks Hans to train him to act as a valet. Rudy then assumes a new identity, Karl Vogel, and in that guise befriends Heinrich Wagner, Hitler's valet. Wagner hires Vogel as his assistant, and when Wagner goes on a trip to America, Vogel assumes his duties. Rudy poisons Hitler's milk, disguises himself as the Führer and transforms the body of Hitler into that of Vogel. He then shoots the corpse. As bodyguards pour into the room, Hitler/Janus throws a fit, blaming them all for the outrageous attempt on his life. He orders the body of the attacker, whom he identifies as the actor Rudy Janus,

to be burned. He instructs Heitmeyer, his head of security, to relieve everyone on duty at the time of the attack, including himself. Watching the corpse burning from the window, Rudy says, "Heil Hitler!"

The phony Hitler launches an investigation into how Janus escaped from prison, ordering the death of the warden when his clerk is found in the grave in which he claimed Janus had been buried. Now the actor is free to undertake his real revenge, the complete destruction of the Third Reich by deliberately making bad military decisions. He cancels the invasion of England, orders the invasion of Russia and dismisses the most capable German generals. He allows the Sixth Army to be senselessly destroyed at Stalingrad. Members of the military, led by Count von Stauffenberg, attempt to kill him with a bomb. Surviving the attempt, Hitler/Janus orders the death of his most capable men remaining, such as Field Marshal Rommel. When the Allies invade Normandy, he deliberately delays responding to the invasion, holding back his strongest divisions. One clever officer, Major Weinrich, uncovers evidence that the Führer has been sneaking cigarettes. He attempts to expose Hitler as an impostor, but he is killed by a bodyguard who finds him holding the Führer at gunpoint. Rudy delights in hoodwinking his foes with his deception. Most of all, Rudy enjoys fooling Vera with his disguise and retaining her as the Führer's mistress. Finally cornered in the Chancellery bunker, the General Staff explain to Hitler that they are totally defeated. Instead of a tirade, the Führer says, "Good" and walks off. The generals decide to escape from the bunker. The actor finally removes his makeup and reveals himself to the startled Vera, who screams hysterically and runs off. Rudy then calmly walks out of the abandoned bunker into the flaming ruins of Berlin.

The production values of *The Magic Face* are inconsistent. Some scenes are genuinely impressive, but others seem ground out like a low budget quickie. The musical score is

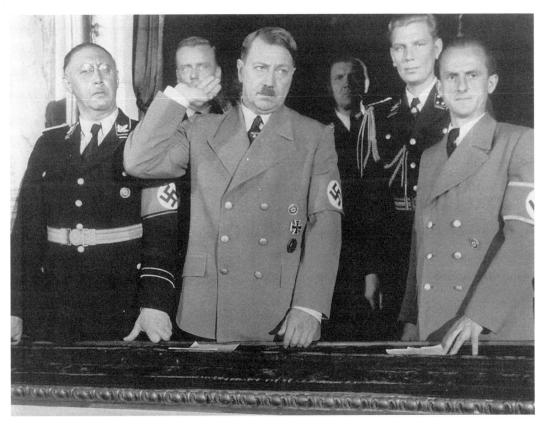

Luther Adler as Hitler, appears with his entourage to watch Janus perform in *The Magic Face*.

memorable, with many references to the German national anthem and Nazi party songs. The acting is fairly good, but the cast contains three unusual performers billed with only a single name: Bell, Willner and Sukman. Not one of these names were ever billed in another motion picture, so the appearance of these three names is a bit of a mystery. The sets are fairly decent, although the cinematography is rather murky. More weaknesses are apparent in the screenplay. Among the major drawbacks is why Rudy took so long and slowly to work his revenge. Couldn't he have found a way to bring about a quicker end to the war, saving the lives of countless innocent people? This alternate history also suggests that Hitler was unaware of the Final Solution, since surely Rudy would not have ordered the extermination of the Jewish people. One could surmise that Rudy himself has gone mad by this point,

and savors the slow, methodical deterioration of the Nazi empire as much as he enjoys fooling his wife. Some of the character names are confusing. Harbacker, for example, is the prison warden, but one of his prisoners is Harbach. The name Janus comes from the two-faced mythological Roman deity who was the god of beginnings and endings. He was also the god of portals, and it is interesting how the film opens and closes with the portal of the bunker. In any case, the film is enjoyable to audiences who like seeing history standing on its head as the impostor carries out this crazy, impossible scheme. If you accept the story with a huge grain of salt, it can be quite entertaining.

HITLER PORTRAYAL: Luther Adler's strengths and weaknesses as Hitler are covered in the entry for *The Desert Fox*. *The Magic Face* does allow some range, since

Adler is the only actor who played both Hitler and Mussolini, not to mention Chamberlain and Haile Selassie. His lampoon of the Duce is particularly entertaining. As an actor, however, he is best in the role of Karl Vogel. He is even more impressive when you consider the use of clever editing and split-screen work to permit the interaction between Hitler and Vogel. It is also very imaginative to watch Rudy slip in and out of his Hitler mode depending on whether he is alone or in the presence of others. Adler is very subtle at these moments, making his overall performance one of the most unusual of the ones covered in this book. On the other hand, there seems little distinction between Adler as the real Hitler and Rudy playing Hitler in front of others. Perhaps a difference would have undermined the basic plot. In any case, Adler must be commended for handling the complicated scenario with genuine style and wit.

REPRESENTATIVE QUOTES

• Most of the rumors begin here, for this is one of the great historical landmarks of the world war. The steps that you see lead down to no ordinary air raid shelter, for this is the cellar where the rat was trapped. Down there is the bunker where Hitler died, if he did die and if he was Hitler. *(William L. Shirer's opening narration)*

• Since the important factor is time, the time is now. *(Hitler to his General Staff, planning the invasion of England)*

• Replace everyone who was on duty when this happened, Everyone.... When you have done that, replace yourself. *(Phony Hitler to Heitmeyer, while watching the burning of the intruder's body, actually the real Hitler)*

• I feel I was persuaded against my better judgment in the matter of an English campaign. It's a mistake. It is exactly what the Soviets are waiting for. So, we postpone the English attack and deal with the Bolsheviks first. *(Phony Hitler to his General Staff, canceling the invasion of England)*

• The Americans have reached the Rhine.

The Russians are in Poland. Tell me the truth, how does the war go? *(Vera to the Führer)* Well. It goes exactly as I planned it. *(Phony Hitler)*

58. *Man Hunt* (1941)

Carl Ekberg as Adolf Hitler (cameo)
Thriller

20th Century–Fox. Written by Dudley Nichols based on the novel *Rogue Male* by Geoffrey Household; Photographed by Arthur C. Miller; Edited by Allen McNeil; Music by Alfred Newman; Produced by Kenneth Macgowan; Directed by Fritz Lang. B & W 105 minutes

ANNOTATED CAST LIST: Walter Pidgeon (*Captain Alan Thorndike*, British sportsman who stalks Hitler); Joan Bennett (*Jerry Stokes*, London seamstress who helps Alan); George Sanders (*Major Quive-Smith*, Gestapo officer who tracks Alan); John Carradine (Nazi agent killed by Alan); Lucien Prival (Nazi Henchman); Frederick Worlock (*Lord Gerald Risborough*, Alan's brother); Heather Thatcher (*Lady Alice*, Gerald's wife); Herbert Evans (*Reeves*, Gerald's butler); Roddy McDowall (*Vaner*, Cabin boy who hides Alan); Roger Imhoff (*Jensen*, Ship's captain); Sven Hugo Borg (Ship's mate); Holmes Herbert (*Saul Farnsworthy*, Alan's solicitor); Olaf Hytten (*Peale*, Saul's clerk); Frederick Vogeding (German ambassador); Ludwig Stossel (Doctor at Berchtesgaden); Keith Hitchcock (London Bobby); Egon Brecher (Shopkeeper who sells the hatpin); Eily Malyon (Postmistress at Lyme Regis); Virginia McDowall (*Mary*, Daughter of the postmistress).

APPRAISAL AND SYNOPSIS: Fritz Lang (1890–1976) was the foremost German director during the 1920s and early 1930s. Hitler deeply admired his work, particularly the two part *Die Nibelungen* (1924) consisting of *Siegfried* and *Kriemhild's Revenge*. *Die Frau im Mond* (1929) was credited for sparking Hitler's interest in missile technology. When the Nazis came to power, Goebbels banned Lang's most recent film, *The Testa-*

ment of Dr. Mabuse (1933), but he did offer him the chance to literally head up the German film industry. According to Lang, he fled Germany by train that very evening and later established himself as a leading Hollywood director. When hostilities broke out in Europe, Lang chose to make a series of anti–Nazi films, beginning with *Man Hunt*, a thriller involving the attempted assassination of the Führer and based on an amazingly popular serial story by Geoffrey Household that appeared in *Atlantic Monthly*. Working closely with Land, screenwriter Dudley Nichols fleshed out the story as a screen thriller, principally by adding a leading role for Joan Bennett (but then killing her off, a daring and unconventional choice). Walter Pidgeon was ideally cast as the somewhat arrogant lead, and smug George Sanders as the heavy, a Gestapo officer who can be accepted as an Englishman, making good use of the actor's fluency in German. Lang crafted the film with his usual dedication, producing one of the most sensational of the early films to deal with Nazi terror.

The action of the story opens on July 29, 1939, the date when Captain Alan Thorndike sneaks up on a ridge opposite the patio of the Führer's home at Berchtesgaden. Lying flat on the ground, Thorndike sets the sights on his rifle to 550 feet, and aims at Hitler as he emerges from the French doors onto the patio. The gun clicks when Thorndike pulls the trigger, but the weapon is unloaded. Thorndike smiles and flicks a dismissive wave in the direction of Hitler. Hesitating, Thorndike decides to put a bullet in the chamber. He aims again, but a German guard sees Thorndike and jumps on him. The rifle goes off in the struggle, and Thorndike is captured.

An unnamed Gestapo official questions Thorndike after he is arrested and detained at Hitler's house. The hunter claims that he was engaged in a "sporting stalk" to see if he could possibly get close enough to the most heavily guarded man in Europe. After much banter, the Gestapo agent offers to release Thorndike if he would sign a statement saying that he attempted to kill Hitler on orders from the British government. When Thorndike refuses, he is told he will be killed, his death arranged to resemble an accident. Thorndike is taken to a high ledge and thrown off. Injured, but still alive, Thorndike manages to crawl away before the Germans return hours later to "accidentally" discover his corpse. The Gestapo agent is stunned that the Englishman not only survived but was able to escape.

Thorndike makes his way to a German port and climbs aboard a freighter. A British cabin boy befriends him and agrees to hide him during their passage to England. Meanwhile, a mysterious man played by John Carradine, books passage on the ship using Thorndike's own passport, which the Nazis confiscated when he was arrested. Once the ship docks in London, Thorndike sneaks off into the evening fog and finds himself stalked by a group of thugs headed by the mysterious man. Thorndike takes refuge in a hallway, forcing a woman, Jerry Stokes (Joan Bennett), to hide him in her apartment. As they chat, they become friends. She takes him by cab to the mansion of his brother, Lord Risborough, with whom he discusses the political complications of his predicament. Thorndike decides to go into hiding. The next day, after buying an arrow hatpin for Jerry, Thorndike visits his solicitor. He also arranges a cash gratuity for Jerry, but learns that the Nazi agents have tracked his movements. He escapes into the subway, but the mysterious man follows him onto the tracks. They struggle, and the Nazi agent is electrocuted. Thorndike flees back to Jerry's apartment. When the police find the body in the subway, it had been hit by a train. They identify the victim as Alan Thorndike based on the passport found on the body. Thorndike gives Jerry the address of Lyme Regis, a rural post office, asking her to inform his brother that he is alive and asking him to write to the address in three weeks. A master sportsman, Thorndike plans to camp out in the woods. Jerry never gets to deliver the message, however, since the Nazis ambush her in her apartment. The Gestapo official from Berchtesgaden, now posing as an Englishman named Major Quive-Smith, undertakes her questioning. She refuses to talk, but he finds the address left by Thorndike.

Three weeks pass. Having grown a beard, Thorndike goes to Lyme Regis, but is suspicious when the postmistress reacts strangely when he asks for his mail. He grabs the letter and rushes back to his hideout, a cave in the wilderness. The letter is from his Gestapo adversary, saying that he was waiting for him to call for his mail, and that this is not a sporting stalk. As he reads the note, Quive-Smith calls out his name, saying that he has blocked the entrance to his cave, trapping him. They speak through a small air vent. Using a stick, Quive-Smith pushes Jerry's hat through the vent, as a token of his seriousness. He also boasts that Germany invaded Poland that very morning. When the Nazi admits he killed the girl, Thorndike becomes enraged, saying that he should have killed Hitler. Perhaps he would have if he hadn't been stopped. Quive-Smith again demands that he sign the confession, passing the document through on a stick. Instead, Thorndike takes the arrow hatpin and creates a makeshift bow and arrow. He tells the Nazi that he will sign. After Quive-Smith removes the blockade, Thorndike shoots the Nazi through the vent. When he crawls out of the cave, he is struck by a bullet fired by Quive-Smith, who then collapses and dies. After recuperating at a hospital, Thorndike decides to resume his stalk of the Führer. He arranges to parachute into Germany, intending to track down and kill the Führer.

Lang's film is an excellent thriller, but numerous plot weaknesses become apparent when reconsidering the story. The time frame is one. Considering the German invasion of Poland occurs on September 1st, only thirty-three days pass in the story from Thorndike's original stalk. Considering the slow pace of Thorndike's escape from Germany as well as his three week hiatus in his cave, there is simply not enough time to ac-

commodate the events of the plot. In addition, there is the inability of the British government to aid Thorndike, as outlined by Lord Risborough, who believes the authorities would meekly hand over his brother to the Germans. Nazi agents roam and operate as easily on the streets of London as if it were Munich, which also seems a stretch. The large number of unlikely events is somewhat hard to swallow, but the other elements of the picture, the editing, music, cinematography, direction are first rate. Joan Bennett is not really convincing as a Cockney, but she does play well opposite Walter Pidgeon. George Sanders is well cast as the villain, repulsive and arrogant, the epitome of many Nazi antagonists that would follow on the screen for the next decade.

HITLER PORTRAYAL: There are only three quick shots of Adolf Hitler in *Man Hunt*, all occurring within the first two minutes of the film, and all featuring Hitler being seen through the crosshairs of the telescopic lens of a rifle. Carl Ekberg effectively portrays the cameo, appearing on the patio of the Berghof at Berchtesgaden, strutting in a characteristic Hitler pose. and it is interesting to note that his final film appearance, again as Hitler, occurred twenty five years later, in *What Did You Do in the War, Daddy* (1966).

REPRESENTATIVE QUOTES

• We Nazis are finding a new life, a new vitality for our people by returning to the primitive virtues... We do not hesitate to destroy in order to create a new world. *(Quive-Smith, boastfully, to Thorndike)*

• Don't forget their Reichstag fire trial. You know their genius for producing witnesses and documents to prove their enemies guilty of what they intend to do. *(Lord Risborough to his brother)*

• You believe that the death of our sacred Führer would be no great loss to the world, didn't you? Surely then the death of a girl like that would be no loss at all. *(Quive-Smith to Thorndike after trapping him in his cave)*

• He's guilty, guilty against me and

against humanity, against every decent peaceful person in the world. He is guilty of hatred, intolerance and murder. *(Thorndike, denouncing Hitler and finally admitting that he actually intended to kill him)*

59. *The Miracle of Morgan's Creek* (1944)

Bobby Watson as Adolf Hitler (cameo)
Comedy

Paramount. Written by Preston Sturges; Photographed by John F. Seitz; Edited by Stuart Gilmore; Music by Charles Bradshaw & Leo Shuken; Produced & directed by Preston Sturges. B & W 99 minutes

CAST LIST: Eddie Bracken (*Norval Jones*); Betty Hutton (*Trudy Kockenlocker*); William Demarest (*Constable Kockenlocker*); Diana Lynn (*Emily Kockenlocker*); Brian Donlevy (*Governor Dan McGinty*); Akim Tamiroff (The Boss); Byron Foulger (McGinty's secretary); Porter Hall (Justice of the Peace); Almira Sessions (Justice's wife*);* Jimmy Conlin (Mayor); Emory Parnell (*Tuerck*); Alan Bridge (*Johnson*); Julius Tannen (*Rafferty*); Victor Potel (Newspaper editor); Chester Conklin (*Pete*); Joe Devlin (*Benito Mussolini*).

COMMENTARY: *The Miracle of Morgan's Creek* was one of the cleverest comedies of the 1940s, a genuine American screen classic. The plot revolves around Norval Jones, a 4-F American everyman whose girlfriend, Trudy Kockenlocker, is wild over men in uniforms. After a wild party with departing GIs, Trudy awakes with groggy memories of a wedding ceremony. She later discovers she is pregnant, and Norval marries her to protect her honor. When Trudy gives birth to sextuplets, Trudy and Norval become worldwide celebrities. In particular, Hitler is outraged that a Nazi woman didn't make the same accomplishment. Of course, the humor of *The Miracle of Morgan's Creek* is considerably risqué given the subject matter, which is handled in a hilarious, satirical fashion. Paramount held up release of the film, which was actually filmed during the winter of 1942/43, until 1944 because they were nervous about the social satire and subject matter. Sturgess, however, correctly judged the American sense of humor and the film clicked with audiences, and its reputation has grown with the passing years. The brief Hitler cameo occurs toward the end of the film, when news of the multiple birth causes a worldwide sensation. The Führer receives the news at a staff meeting. Bobby Watson is seated at a table. He stands, and the general next to him also stands. Seated, they were the same height, but the general towers over Watson as he gets up, making Hitler look ridiculous. Watson sputters and screams in German, and the scene dissolves into a newspaper headline proclaiming, "Hitler Demands Recount!" It is a short bit, lasting approximately ten seconds. It is hilarious, even if the sight gag is not related to the rest of the film.

60. *Molokh* (1999)

Leonid Mozgovoy as Adolf Hitler
Drama

Lenfilm/Zero Film. Written by Juri Arabov & Marina Korenova; Photographed by Aleksei Fyodorov & Anatoli Rodionov; Edited by Leda Semyonova; Produced by Thomas Kufus & Victor Sergeev; Directed by Aleksandr Sokurov. Color 102 minutes

CAST LIST: Elena Rufanova (*Eva Braun*); Leonid Sokol (*Dr. Joseph Goebbels*); Yelena Spiridonova (*Magda Goebbels*); Vladimir Bogdanev (*Martin Bormann*); Anatoli Shvedersky (The Priest).

COMMENTARY: *Molokh* is a genuine curiosity, an experimental Russian-made film shot in German. The setting is the Berghof during a late spring or early summer day in 1942. The main figure of the story is Eva Braun, somewhat bored by the splendid isolation and troubled about her relationship with "Adi" who she fears is really a monster. On this day, there is some company, Joseph and Magda Goebbels, as well as the omnipresent Martin Bormann. The Führer has forbidden all talk about the war, so the characters engage in a series of rather oblique conversations, with Eva being the only one who dares to contradict Hitler, interspersed with walks through the beautiful Alpine countryside. The film could well be described as a cross between *Waiting for Godot*, *Hitler's Table Talk* and Eva's famous home movies. The film won a prize for best screenplay at the 1999 Cannes Film Festival, but a number of noted critics loathed it and wrote hostile reviews that panned the film, criticizing the incredibly slow pace. Distribution has been erratic since then, although versions have been prepared with French, Italian, English and Russian subtitles.

61. *The Moon Is Down* (1943)

Ludwig Donath as Adolf Hitler (cameo)
Drama

20th Century–Fox. Written by Nunnally Johnson based on the novel by John Steinbeck; Photographed by Arthur C. Miller; Edited by Louis R. Loeffler; Music by Alfred Newman; Produced by Nunnally Johnson; Directed by Irving Pichel. B & W 90 minutes

CAST LIST: Cedric Hardwicke (*Colonel Lanser*); Henry Travers (*Mayor Orden*); Margaret Wycherly (*His wife*); Lee J. Cobb (*Dr. Albert Winter*); Dorris Bowden (*Molly Morden*); William Post, Jr. (*Alex Morden*); Peter van Eyck (*Lieutenant Tonder*); E.J. Ballentine (*George Corell*); Henry Rowland (*Captain Loft*); Irving Pichel (*Peder*); Violette Watson (*His wife*); Hans Schumm (*Captain Bentick*); John Banner (*Lieutenant Prackle*); John Mylong (Staff officer); Jeff Corey (*Albert*); Ernst Deutsch (*Major Hunter*); Louis V. Arco (*Schumann*); Charles McGraw (*Ole*); Helen Thimig (*Annie*); Ian Wolfe (*Joseph*); Natalie Wood (*Carrie*).

COMMENTARY: *The Moon is Down* is based on John Steinbeck's novel about the impact of the Nazi occupation of Norway as represented by a typical community. The Hitler cameo occurs during the credits, in which a map of Norway is shown on the screen. A hand then appears, and grasps at the country on the map, finally turning into a fist and pounding it. Almost instantly, the audience realizes the hand is that of Adolf Hitler, who continues to shout and blather in German as the credits continue. Even though the sequence is brief, and we never see Ludwig Donath's face, it is a very powerful introduction to the film.

62. *Mussolini and I* (AKA *Mussolini: The Decline and Fall of Il Duce*) (1985)

Kurt Raab as Adolf Hitler
Historical drama

Filmalpha/HBO. Written by Nicola Badalucco, Alberto Negrin & Kenneth Taylor; Photographed by Alberto Nannuzzi & Daniele Nannuzzi; Edited by Robert Perpignani & Peter Taylor; Music by Egissto Macchi; Produced by Mario Gallo; Directed by Alberto Negrin. Color Original version 192 minutes; revised version 146 minutes

ANNOTATED CAST LIST: Bob Hoskins (*Benito Mussolini*, Dictator of Italy known as The Duce); Susan Sarandon (*Edda Mussolini Ciano*, Mussolini's daughter); Anthony Hopkins (*Count Galeazzo Ciano*, Her husband & Foreign Minister of Italy); Annie Giradot (*Rachele Mussolini*, The Duce's wife); Barbara DeRossi (*Claretta Petacci*, The Duce's mistress); Massimo Dapporto (*Vittorio Mussolini*, The Duce's eldest son); Dietlinde Turban (*Felicitas Beetz*, German countess who spies on Ciano); Marne Maitland (*Victor Emmanuel III*, King of Italy); Antonella Angelucci (*Princess Mafalda*, The king's daughter); Alex Serra (*General Paolo Puntoni*, Military aide to the king); Hans Dieter Asner (*Joachim von Ribbentrop*, Nazi Foreign Minister); Harald Dietl (*Otto Skorzeny*, SS officer who rescues Mussolini); Karl-Heinz Heitman (*General Karl Wolff*, Chief SS officer in occupied Italy); Micaela Giustiniani (*Carolina Ciano*, Ciano's mother); Vittorio Mezzogiorno (*Sandro Pavolini*, Minister of Culture & Ciano's friend); Stefano DeSandro (*Count Dino Grandi*, Fascist

Council member who leads revolt against Mussolini); Leslie Thomas (*Emilio de Bono*, Fascist Council member); Franco Meroni (*Giuseppe Bottai*, Minister of Education & Fascist Council member); Pietro Palermini (*Roberto Farrinachi*, Fascist Council member); Franco Mazzieri (*Giovanni Marinelli*, Fascist Council member); Mario Ingrassia (*Luciano Gottardi*, Fascist Council member); Luciano Baglioni (*Carlo Scorza*, Fascist party secretary & Mussolini loyalist); Franco Fabrizi (*Navarra*, Mussolini's servant & doorkeeper); Carolyn Rusoff de Fonseca (*Giuseppina Petacci*, Claretta's mother); Ted Rusoff (*Francesco Petacci*, Claretta's brother); David George Brown (*Aldo Castellani*, The Duce's diagnostician); Pier Paolo Capponi (*Don Chiot*, Priest at the execution of Ciano); Olliver Dominick (*Deilman*, SS Colonel); Fabio Testa (*Lorenzo*, Edda's lover); Marino Mase (*Don Pancino*, Priest who meets with Edda); Dieter Schidor (*Major Franz Spögler*, German bodyguard of Claretta Petacci); Ulrich Ernst (*Major Otto*, German officer who tricks the Cianos into flying to Munich); Guido Mariotti (Carabinieri captain); Diego Verdegiglio (Carabinieri officer); Matthias Peterson (*Birzer*, Nazi officer who tries to smuggle Mussolini past the partisans); Sergio Gibello (*Furlotti*); Eric Valsecchi (*Romano*, The Duce's youngest son); Manuela Mortera (*Anna Maria*, The Duce's daughter); Julian Jenkins (Judge who condemns Ciano); Luca Orlandini (*Fabrizio*, Ciano's younger son); Gian Paolo Vetturini (*Marzio*, Ciano's elder son); Francesca Rinaldi (*Dindina*, Ciano's daughter).

APPRAISAL AND SYNOPSIS: *Mussolini and I* is the first of two impressive miniseries that played in 1985. Originally shown in two parts on HBO as *Mussolini: The Decline and Fall of Il Duce*, the production was reedited into a feature film called *Mussolini and I*, which was widely syndicated on television, as well as video. It was also shown theatrically in foreign markets, so that *Mussolini and I* has come to be regarded as the standard version of the production. The "I" in the title refers to Edda Mussolini Ciano, her father's favorite, who found herself torn when her husband was dismissed as Foreign Minister by the Duce after he argued for withdrawal from the war. In many ways, Count Galeazzo Ciano, brilliantly played by Anthony Hopkins, is the central focus of the film rather than Benito Mussolini. Ciano is a complex and compelling figure, at times ambitious and scheming, then groveling and accommodating, but at other times principled, self-sacrificing and a genuine statesman. Mussolini, on the other hand, is a figure in decline, worn-out and easily manipulated. The contrast between these two figures is the main impetus of this film, leading some to believe that the "I" in the title should be interpreted as being Ciano, since his perceptive and controversial diaries exposed the rotten core of Fascist Italy and the Axis leaders as clearly as Albert Speer did with the Nazi hierarchy in his book *Inside the Third Reich*. The film also concentrates on Mussolini's complicated family relationships. He remains close to his son, Vittorio, and other family members, but they worry about the influence of Claretta Petacci, Benito's mistress. The Duce's wife, Rachele, tries to pretend that Claretta doesn't exist, and Edda fears that Claretta is primarily interested in accumulating power for the Petacchi family. She is also aware that Claretta is attempting to discredit Ciano. These family battles play out against the broader picture of the country at war, and rather than distract, these events tend to intensify the overall scenario.

The picture opens in 1930, at the wedding of Count Ciano and Edda Mussolini, the Duce's favorite of his five children (Edda, Anna Maria, Vittorio, Romano and Bruno). With a narrator filling the gaps, we follow the progress of Ciano as he becomes the Foreign Minister of Italy, capably managing a complicated range of issues. At first, Ciano works to establish the alliance with Nazi Germany, and to support Franco's fascist insurrection in Spain. But by the summer of 1939, Ciano has started to have serious doubts about Hitler, whose bellicose policies he believes will lead to a bloody and futile war. At an elegant banquet, Joachim von Ribbentrop tries to convince Ciano that England and France will not interfere with the Führer's planned invasion of Poland. Ciano proposes to wager a Renaissance painting that Ribbentrop is wrong. Hitler finally concedes that Italy need not enter the war and abruptly declares that the dinner is over.

By the end of 1942, Ciano is convinced that the Axis cause is lost. He tries to convince the Duce that the only way to save Italy is to seek a separate peace with the Allies. Mussolini refuses his advice, calling it defeatist talk. Later, Hitler sends the Duce a critical report about Ciano. Meanwhile, Ciano records his observations and the intimate details of statecraft in his diaries. Finally, the Duce dismisses Ciano as Foreign minister. On July 10, 1943, the Allies invade Sicily. Mussolini is forced to convene the Fascist Grand Council, and a vote is taken to transfer military power to the king. Ciano votes with the majority against the Duce. The next day, Mussolini is summoned by King Victor Emmanuel III, who forces him to resign. He is then detained and placed under protective custody. Edda fears that her husband will be arrested, so she makes a deal with the Germans, trading the hidden location of the Duce for passage of her entire family to Spain. The Germans double cross her and transport them to Munich instead. Mussolini is freed from detention in an SS raid. Brought to Germany, Mussolini is informed by Hitler that he will be set up as the ruler of a new Italian government, but the Duce realizes he will be a mere puppet leader. The Führer instructs Mussolini to dispose of members of the Fascist Council who voted against him, especially Count Ciano.

Edda implores her father to spare Ciano. He pretends to forgive his son-in-law, but then he is arrested. All those who voted against the Duce are sentenced to death. Edda denounces her father and flees to Switzerland, where she turns over Ciano's secret diary to the Americans. As the Axis forces collapse, Mussolini decides to flee to Switzerland. He is escorted by German forces, but they are trapped by Italian partisans. Mussolini poses as a German soldier, but the partisans spot him and arrest him. The credits roll over a freeze frame of Mussolini as he is arrested, and a radio bulletin announce the execution of the Duce and his mistress, Claretta Petacci.

Mussolini and I is a class production on all fronts. The settings are magnificent and well captured by the first rate photography. The music is superb, with echoes of Richard Strauss. The acting is exceptional. Susan Sarandon has seldom been better. Dietlinde Turban is brilliant as Felicitas, the German spy whose sympathy for Count Ciano yields to genuine compassion. Bob Hoskins' performance is very subtle, and cannot be fully appreciated in one viewing. His Mussolini is very human, almost frail but not sympathetic. The lion reduced to a mouse, Hoskins' Duce is shadowy and remote, filled with self-pity, continually lamenting, "I never had a friend," yet offering friendship to no one in return. He seems incapable of the challenges before him, and merely takes the path of least resistance, even at the cost of the love of his daughter and wife. One major flaw is that the script and editing are occasionally erratic and sloppy. For example, in one scene, a radio bulletin proclaims, "Today, September 23rd, 1943, in the 21st year of the Fascist era, the Duce has constituted his new government." Simultaneously, a lower screen title card reads: "Salo—Villa Feltrinelli, October 1943." It is a startling gaffe that demonstrates the chaos that can result when the sound editor and the film editor fail to work together. On the other hand, the sequence of the Duce's rescue by glider is quite brilliant and masterful. Filled with both creative highs and lows, *Mussolini and I* is definitely a worthy and respectable effort

HITLER PORTRAYAL: Kurt Raab presents a rather different interpretation of Hitler, unctuous and manipulative, bullying Mussolini yet using a velvet touch because he has a sincere reservoir of genuine affection for his fellow dictator and one time role model. Hitler is a man who stifles his anger in front of the Duce, if not his disappointment. In Raab's approach, Hitler is highly focused, yet casual, disciplined and in total control, a side of Hitler seldom portrayed on film. Of course, the Hitler/Mussolini relationship has been largely unexamined in the cinema. In this portrayal, Hitler is like a mesmerist who weaves a spell over the Duce with equal parts of charm and guile. At the same time, the German dictator has a brooding dislike for Count Ciano, because the Führer senses that he is immune to his influence and genuinely puts Italy first. Raab's most interesting moment as Hitler is in his last telephone call to Mussolini, in which he says goodbye to the Duce. The scene is very well played by Raab and Bob Hoskins. Raab was a veteran Czech character actor of exceptional range. The colorful actor passed away from AIDS several years after his riveting performance in *Mussolini and I.*

REPRESENTATIVE QUOTES

• I have been meaning to tell you, Count Ciano, that Italy needn't bother to participate in this war, and even if she did, I don't think it would make any difference. *(Hitler to Ciano during a summer 1939 banquet)*

• Now, now, you must enjoy your life. It is all a joke, all a dream. *(Ciano, playing the piano, to his party guests during an air raid)*

• What is this fascism that just melts like snow in the sun? *(Hitler to Mussolini after his rescue)*

• Do you know what Hitler said about you? *(Mussolini to Ciano)* No, but I can imagine. *(Ciano)* No, you can't imagine. Do you know what he said—"Galeazzo Ciano is four times a traitor. He betrayed his country, betrayed fascism, the alliance with Germany and his own family. Count Ciano must die four times." *(Mussolini)*

• Duce, I don't know if we shall ever have another opportunity to meet or speak again, but let me say to you, Heil the Duce! *(Hitler to Mussolini on the telephone)* Heil the

Führer. *(Mussolini's reply as he hangs up the phone)*

63. *Mussolini: The Untold Story* (1985)

Gunnar Möller as Adolf Hitler
Historical drama

NBC. Written by Stirling Silliphant; Photographed by Robert Steadman; Edited by Ronald J. Fagin, Rod Stephens & Noelle Imparto; Music by Laurence Rosenthal; Produced by Stirling Silliphant; Directed by William A. Graham. Color 3 episodes, approximately 290 minutes

ANNOTATED CAST LIST: George C. Scott (*Benito Mussolini*, Dictator of Italy known as the Duce); Lee Grant (*Rachele Mussolini, The Duce's wife*); Gabriel Byrne (*Vittorio Mussolini*, The Duce's eldest son); Mary Elizabeth Mastrantonio (*Edda Mussolini Ciano*, The Duce's daughter); Raul Julia (*Count Galeazzo Ciano*, Her husband, who serves as Foreign Minister); Virginia Madsen (*Claretta Petacci*, The Duce's mistress); Robert Downey, Jr. (*Bruno Mussolini*, The Duce's son, killed in a plane crash); Stephen Marshall (*Romano Mussolini*, The Duce's youngest son); Kenneth Colley (*Victor Emmanuel III*, King of Italy); Richard Kane (*Joachim von Ribbentrop*, Nazi Foreign Minister); Wolf Kahler (*Otto Skorzeny*, SS officer who rescues Mussolini); David Suchet (*Dino Grandi*, Fascist Council member who leads revolt against Mussolini); George Coulouris (*Emilio de Bono*, Fascist Council member); Annabel Leventon (*Giuseppina Petacci*, Claretta's mother); Tracey Ward (*Maria Ciano*, Galeazzo's sister); Vernon Dobtcheff (*Oswaldo Sebastiani*, The Duce's private secretary); Anna Louise Lambert (*Orsola*, Vittorio's wife); Gina Bellman (*Gena*, Bruno's wife); Michael Aldridge (*Giocomo Matteotti*, Deputy critical of Mussolini who is slain by Fascists); Godfrey James (*Marshal Pietro Badoglio*, Military leader appointed by the King to replace Mussolini in 1943); Paul Herzberg (*Major Franz Spögler*, German bodyguard of Claretta Petacchi); Michael

Forest (Prison Commandant); David Poulan (German officer at prison); Milton Johns (*Prince Bismarck*, German ambassador); Constantine Gregory (*Baron Domenico Russo*, Fascist leader); Michael MacKenzie (*Amalfi*); Robert Gwilyn (Partisan leader); Spencer Chandler (*Young Vittorio*); Paul Kehagias (*Young Bruno*).

APPRAISAL AND SYNOPSIS: *Mussolini: The Untold Story* appeared several months after the Bob Hoskins/HBO version, playing on NBC from November 24 through 26, 1985. The miniseries received major publicity, including George C. Scott as Mussolini on the cover of *TV Guide*, and generally positive reviews. Unlike *Mussolini and I*, however, it received no follow up broadcasts and was not issued on video. The contrasts with *Mussolini and I* are fascinating, since both are quality productions. The George C. Scott version is painted on a broader canvas, covering the Duce's career from his assumption of power and heyday to his decline, whereas the Hoskins production focuses principally on the Italian dictator's downfall. Both versions give heavy emphasis to the Duce's personal life. The Scott version, based largely on Vittorio Mussolini's memoirs, casts a more critical eye on Count Galeazzo Ciano, portrayed as somewhat mercurial and irresponsible. The Hoskins version, based upon Edda Mussolini Ciano's viewpoint, is far more sympathetic to Mussolini's son-in-law. *Mussolini and I* seems to stick closer to actual historic detail. Ciano's dismissal from his post as Foreign Minister, for example, is omitted in the Scott miniseries, which makes his controversial vote of July 24, 1943, against the Duce seem like a betrayal out of the blue. In fact, *Mussolini: The Untold Story* changes the nature of this vote of the Fascist Grand Council from the transfer of full command of the armed forces to the king (which it actually was) into a motion for the dismissal of Mussolini himself as Prime Minister (which it was not). The Scott miniseries changes history by altering the death of Bruno Mussolini in a plane crash from the summer of 1941 to the summer of 1938,

prior to the Munich conference. The purpose of this alteration is to provide a tragic conclusion to the opening episode of the miniseries. The Scott version casts Claretta Petacci, the Duce's mistress, in a completely favorable light as a pure hearted, unselfish woman devoted only to the Duce. The production also portrays her as a blonde. The competing version views her in a more accurate light, with suspicion, especially given her manipulative and profiteering family. The Hoskins version seems more international in tone even though it was filmed on location in Italy. However it is the Scott version, shot in Yugoslavia, which stresses the Italian characteristics of the Duce. At times, the production seems far too heavily influenced by *The Godfather* (1972) with Scott assuming the counterpart of the Marlon Brando role. The excellent music score by Laurence Rosenthal is also highly reminiscent of *The Godfather*.

Another problem with *Mussolini: The Untold Story* is the lead, George C. Scott, a legendary performer of exceptional ability, but he did not fill the role of Benito Mussolini with any conviction as he did, for example, the role of George Patton. Physically, he wasn't right for the part, appearing like an over-the-hill professional wrestler with his shaven head. All actors have a bag of thespian tricks that they rely on, such as Scott's half smile that he assumes at key moments in his performance. For some reason, these characteristic gestures seemed unsuited to the Duce, and when Scott assumed some of Mussolini's traditional gestures, they seemed artificial. At one point, for the Munich conference, the miniseries switches to using actual historical clips of Chamberlain, Hitler and Mussolini. The brief shot of the real Duce signing the accord seemed to confirm that Scott was not right for the part. The rest of the cast of the miniseries is excellent. Robert Downey, Jr., is superb as Bruno Mussolini, and Lee Grant portrays the Duce's long suffering wife with a bittersweet edge. Kenneth Colley, Admiral Piett from the *Star Wars* cycle, makes an excellent King

Victor Emmanuel. Gabriel Byrne is memorable as Vittorio. Raul Julia is a bit hard to take as Count Ciano, as he lays on the playboy characteristics a bit thick, but it is still a valid interpretation, although not in the same league as that of Anthony Hopkins as Ciano. Mary Elizabeth Mastrantonio is magnificent as Edda, as rich as Susan Sarandon's reading in *Mussolini and I*, but of an entirely different slant. David Suchet and screen veteran George Coulouris are exceptional in the key roles as Mussolini's opponents on the Fascist Grand Council. But the lion's share of screen time is accorded to Scott, who largely dominates *Mussolini: The Untold Story*. In comparison, Bob Hoskins provided more of an ensemble reading, more human, more complicated and in the long run, one of greater depth. This is not to suggest that Scott's performance is not skillful and entertaining. It just doesn't click with the same intensity as so many other of his masterful interpretations.

The screenplay to *Mussolini: The Untold Story* is strongest in the first episode, but becomes far less interesting in the second chapter and the first half of the third before recovering with a solid finish. The script makes some odd and puzzling choices. For instance, the dramatic confrontation in which King Victor Emmanuel asks for the Duce's resignation, one of the highlights of *Mussolini and I*, is strangely absent in the Scott version. This key event happens off-screen. Scott's rescue scene is also a disappointment, and is halfheartedly staged compared with the Hoskins film. However, it makes up for these dramatic gaps with an excellent recreation of Mussolini's final hours, ending with the abuse of his corpse when it is hung upside down in Milan. The Hoskins version, on the other hand, ends at the moment of Mussolini's capture by the partisans. Other major depictions of Mussolini include Rod Steiger's exceptional performance in *The Last Tyrant* AKA *The Last Days of Mussolini* (1974), Antonio Banderas in the rarely seen and poorly distributed *Mussolini* (1993) and Nehemiah Persoff in a

brilliant *Playhouse 90* episode from the late 1950s entitled "Killers of Mussolini." Hitler is not portrayed in these productions, appearing only in historic newsreel clips.

HITLER PORTRAYAL: Gunnar Möller is unimpressive as Hitler, largely due to the script which allows him few decent scenes. But when he does have an opportunity, he merely squanders it. Möller neither looks like Hitler (his makeup is mediocre and his mustache is far too large) nor can he successfully mimic any of Hitler's gestures. He gives a superficial, matter-of-fact and empty reading. He does nothing to suggest Hitler's evil, his passion or even his madness. He is simply an unimpressive stock figure. His scenes with George C. Scott, in particular, lack any flair or tension. Their scenes, which should be among the most interesting in the film, instead are stiff and disappointing, making it seem like the actors failed to connect on a creative level. Scott, as Mussolini, simply seems to dwarf Möller. As the script unfolds, Hitler is relegated to the background, even as all the characters remark how Mussolini is increasingly dominated by him. At their last conversation, when Hitler telephones to bid his comrade farewell, we neither see him on the telephone nor hear his voice. Instead, Scott vacantly listens as he holds the receiver and blandly whispers, "Auf Wiedersehn." Compare this to the scene that serves as its counterpart in *Mussolini and I*, in which Bob Hoskins and Kurt Raab endow the scene with a magnificent tension that brings it to life.

REPRESENTATIVE QUOTES

• At first sight, I don't like him. *(Mussolini to Ciano, as he sees Hitler for the first time at the airport in Venice, June 1934)* Genghis Khan in a raincoat. *(Edda Mussolini's appraisal)*

• Führer, we are on the march. Victorious Italian troops crossed the Greco-Albanian border at dawn today. *(Mussolini to Hitler when the Führer arrives for a conference in Florence on October 28, 1940)* How can you do such a thing? It's madness. You will get nowhere against the Greeks in autumn rain, in winter snow. The whole outcome will be a military catastrophe. *(Hitler's dismissive response)*

• I suggest you make a radio announcement to the Italian people immediately. Tell them the monarchy in Italy is now abolished. Tell them a new Italian Fascist state with power centered in you has taken its place. In this way you guarantee that the world knows our alliance is still strong and valid. *(Hitler to Mussolini)* I will need a few days to consider the implications. *(Mussolini)* I have already considered them. *(Hitler)*

• If Hitler can face the Russians in Berlin, can I do less against our enemies closing on Milan? *(Mussolini to his wife)*

64. *The Night Train to Munich* (AKA *Gestapo*) (1940)

Bill Russell as Adolf Hitler (cameo)
Thriller

Gaumont British Studios. Written by Sydney Gilliat & Frank Lounder based on a story by Gordon Wellesley; Photographed by Otto Kanturek; Edited by R.E. Dearing; Music by Louis Levy; Produced by Edward Black; Directed by Carol Reed. B & W 93 minutes

ANNOTATED CAST LIST: Rex Harrison (*Richard Randall*, British intelligence agent who poses as street singer Gus Bennett & German officer Major Ulrich Herzog); James Harcourt (*Axel Bomasch*, Czech scientist who flees the Nazis); Margaret Lockwood (*Anna Bomasch*, His daughter, captured by the Nazis); Paul Henreid (*Karl Marsen*, Nazi undercover agent who arranges Anna's escape); Basil Radford (*Charters*, English businessman on the night train to Munich); Naunton Wayne (*Caldicott*, His companion); Felix Aylmer (*Dr. John Fredericks*, British eye doctor & secret Nazi agent); Wyndham Goldie (*Charles Dryton*, British Intelligence official); Roland Culver (*Roberts*); Raymond Huntley (*Kampenfeldt*, Superintendent of Berlin Documents Bureau);

Eliot Makehsam (*Schwab*, Records employee detained due to a critical comment); Austin Trevor (*Prada*, Commander of Constructions Department); Kenneth Kent (*Wingarten*, Head Controller); C.V. France (*Hassinger*, German admiral); Fritz Valk (Gestapo officer at Munich RR station); Morland Graham (Teleferic attendant); Ian Fleming (British official at Home Office); Torin Thatcher.

APPRAISAL AND SYNOPSIS: *Night Train to Munich* was written in the fall of 1939, filmed during the winter and released in the spring before the Nazi blitzkrieg swept across the Benelux countries and France. The picture is an unofficial sequel to Alfred Hitchcock's *The Lady Vanishes* (1938), using two of the same characters from the earlier film, eccentric and stuffy British businessmen played by Basil Radford and Naunton Wayne. Although not the equal of the Hitchcock masterpiece, the film is nevertheless an excellent one with a taut script and an exciting, if implausible, cable car conclusion. The lead performers, Rex Harrison, Margaret Lockwood and Paul Henreid (billed as Paul von Henreid) deliver splendid readings, and the director, Sir Carol Reed, brings many clever and interesting touches to the film.

The opening sequences cover the German absorption of the remainder of Czechoslovakia in March 1939, a mere six months after they were ceded the Sudetenland as a result of the Munich conference. Axel Bomasch, a Czech inventor working on an advanced type of armor plating, flees to England, but his daughter, Anna, is trapped and detained by the Nazis. She escapes from a concentration camp with the help of Karl Marsen, a Czech teacher imprisoned by the Nazis. They make their way to England, where the audience learns that Marsen is really a Nazi agent attempting to locate the inventor. Anna receives a secret message leading her to Gus Bennett, a down-on-his-luck singer, who actually is Richard Randall, a British intelligence officer. He helps to reunite her with her father, now working for the British government. However, she and her father are kidnapped by German agents led by Marsen and brought to Berlin. Embarrassed, Randall proposes to his superiors that he go to Germany and try to arrange their escape. In Berlin, he poses as Major Ulrich Herzog, an army engineer and expert on fortifications. He bluffs his way in to see Anna, who is outraged that she was deceived by Karl Marsen. Randall tells her to pretend that Major Herzog is an old flame, one who might convert her and her father to work for the Nazis. Meanwhile, Hitler has invaded Poland, and the German military is on edge waiting to see how the British and French will respond.

When Bomasch and his daughter are ordered by the Führer to be sent to Munich for interrogation, Randall/Herzog insists on accompanying them, much to the displeasure of Marsen. With several guards, the group takes the night train to Munich. Also on this train are two British businessmen, Charters and Caldicott, who have not yet learned that Britain declared war against Germany. Caldicott recognizes Randall as an old school chum and is puzzled by his masquerade as a Nazi. When the train is delayed at a remote station, Caldicott overhears a phone call to Berlin by Marsen indicating that the Germans are aware that Herzog is an impostor. Back on the train, Caldicott slips a note to Randall/Herzog telling him that the jig is up. Randall explains that he is on a secret mission, and Charters and Caldicott agree to help him. By the time the train reaches Munich, they overpower the Nazi guards and take their uniforms. Marsen is also tied up, and Randall assumes his identity. SS troops meets them at the station and provides them with a car to bring Bomasch to his interrogation. Instead, the auto heads off on a mad dash to the Swiss border. When Marsen is untied, he sets off with the SS in pursuit. Randall takes a back road to a remote mountain pass where a cable car, called the teleferic, is used to cross the German-Swiss border. Marsen's car is delayed by a flat, and Randall bullies the operator to start the ma-

chinery to operate the cable car. When Marsen arrives, Randall locks up the operator and sends Charters, Caldicott and the Bomaschs across to Switzerland, holding the Nazis back with gunfire, killing several of them. When he attempts to cross in the next car, Marsen breaks into the station and reverses the direction of the car. Randall climbs out of the car and manages to wound Marsen. Randall then leaps onto a second car heading to Switzerland. Marsen looks on in frustration as the British agent escapes.

HITLER PORTRAYAL: The Hitler sequence occurs immediately after the credits, and involves a rather neat editing job, intercutting clips of the genuine Hitler with those of Bill Russell mimicking the Führer. The opening shot is the exterior of Hitler's summer home, the Berghof, in Berchtesgaden. The camera pulls toward the large picture window, into the interior where Hitler (Russell) is pacing furiously, screaming in German, threatening an individual cowering in a chair, presumably Dr. Kurt von Schuschnigg, the Austrian Chancellor. There is a closeup of the Führer's desk, and Hitler starts pounding his fist on the map of Austria, which dissolves into footage of storm troopers marching in the streets of Vienna and Hitler (genuine) addressing a mass rally. The montage continues as Hitler (Russell) is back at his desk pounding the map of Sudetenland in Czechoslovakia, which similarly dissolves as storm troopers march again and Hitler (genuine) crosses the Czech border to inspect the new territory annexed by the Third Reich. Finally, Hitler is heard bellowing in his office as German officers pace outside. Inside, Hitler (Russell) is thumping his fist against Prague on his map. We never get a clear image of Russell, but the montage is quite well done and makes an excellent curtain raiser for this espionage thriller, one of the first British films of World War II.

REPRESENTATIVE QUOTES

• Germany is as much your country as it is ours now. We don't hate the Czechs. We only wish to protect them. *(Marsen to Anna)*

As you're protecting the people of Poland? *(Anna's reply)* You've been in Britain too long... I was doing my duty as a citizen of the Reich and a subject of the Führer, for whose sacred mission no sacrifice is too great. *(Marsen)*

• I bought a copy of *Mein Kampf*. Occurred to me it might shed some light on all this howdy-doo. Ever read it? *(Charters to Caldicott)* Never had the time. *(Caldicott)* I understand they give a copy to all the bridal couples over here. *(Charters)* I don't think it's *that* sort of book, old man. *(Caldicott)*

65.   *On the Double* (1961)

Bobby Watson as Adolf Hitler (cameo)
Danny Kaye as a caricature of Adolf Hitler
Comedy

Paramount. Written by Jack Rose & Melville Shavelson; Photographed by Harry Stradling, Sr., & Geoffrey Unsworth; Edited by Frank Bracht; Music by Leith Stevens & Sylvia Fine (Songs); Produced & directed by Melville Shavelson. Color 92 minutes

ANNOTATED CAST LIST: Danny Kaye (*General Sir Lawrence Mackenzie-Smith*, Leading British military strategist & *PFC Ernie Williams*, an American soldier who is his double); Dana Winter (*Lady Margaret Mackenzie-Smith*, The General's wife); Wilfred Hyde-White (*Colonel Somerset*, British officer & narrator); Margaret Rutherford (*Lady Vivian*, Mackenzie-Smith's aunt); Diana Dors (*Sergeant Bridget Stanhope*, Mackenzie-Smith's chauffeur & mistress); Jesse White (*Corporal Joe Praeger*, Ernie's army buddy); Gregory Walcott (*Major Rock Houston*, American officer); Terrance De Marney (*Colin Twickenham*, Mackenzie-Smith's batman); Alan Cuthbertson (*Captain Patterson*, British traitor working with the Nazis); Rex Evans (*General Carleton Brown Wiffingham*, British officer nicknamed Puffy); Pamela Licht (*Penelope*, Puffy's wife); Rudolf Anders (German High Command officer); Edgar Barrier (*Blankmeister*, Gestapo officer); Ben Astar (*General Gregor Zlinkov*, Russian officer).

APPRAISAL AND SYNOPSIS: *On the Double* is an amusing Danny Kaye vehicle from the high point of his cinema career, the remarkable series of films starting with *The Court Jester* (1956) and concluding with *The Man from the Diner's Club* (1963). Kaye's talents are particularly showcased in the film, which seems ideally tailored for him, including slapstick, mimicry (from Churchill to Marlene Dietrich), musical numbers, word play and double talk. In fact, the title *On the Double* is a pun, referring not only to the military phrase to hustle but a reference to Kaye playing a double role.

The picture starts as Wilfred Hyde-White narrates a whimsical opening, at one point hurrying the credits to finish, remarking, "Never heard of any of those chaps, have you?" General Sir Lawrence Mackenzie-Smith is introduced as the leading Allied strategist planning D-Day. Hitler has ordered his underground operatives in England to assassinate this key leader. In response, the Allied intelligence division, led by Colonel Somerset, plans an elaborate ruse. They recruit an American soldier, Ernie Williams, who is the spitting image of the general to pose as Mackenzie-Smith. The real Mackenzie-Smith heads off on a secret mission. Ernie is paraded around in public as bait for the assassins. The general's batman is poisoned after he drinks from the general's flask. Ernie is shot at when he addresses the troops at a rally. When Lady Margaret, the general's wife, returns home from a war bond tour in Canada, she immediately detects the impostor, but she agrees to cooperate. When she learns that Ernie is merely a sitting target, she warns him of his predicament. Lady Margaret has begun to feel great affection for her husband's double. News arrives that the real general has been killed in an airplane crash however, and Ernie agrees to continue to pose as Mackenzie-Smith in the interests of the war effort.

Mackenzie-Smith's chauffeur, a shapely blonde, is actually a Nazi agent. She is also the general's mistress and continues to be fooled by Ernie's masquerade. She lures him into a trap, and Ernie is kidnapped and brought to Berlin where he confounds his captors with gibberish about the Allied plans for D-Day. Ernie feigns depression after he delivers his information, and the German commandant offers him a gun for suicide. Instead, Ernie shoots the Nazi and escapes, ducking into the opera house. When German troops pursue him, Ernie tries various disguises to elude them, finally posing as Hitler. At first, his deception is successful, but then he encounters the real Hitler coming down the opera house staircase. The Führer, totally astonished, throws a fit and Ernie escapes in the confusion. He slips into a cabaret, and his new disguise gets him mistaken for the chanteuse. The wily American finally poses as a drunken German airman, and departs with a crew heading off to their airbase. Mistaking Ernie for one of their comrades, the air crew take Ernie on their bombing mission to England. When his true identity is finally uncovered, Ernie parachutes out and is captured by the British, who take him to the nearest military base. At first, Ernie is relieved when he recognizes the commander as General Wiffingham, a friend of Mackenzie-Smith. His relief is short lived when he realizes that Wiffingham is actually the leading Nazi agent in Great Britain. Ernie is ordered to be shot, but he is saved at the last minute by Colonel Somerset and his men. Ernie plans one final deception to learn if Lady Margaret actually loves him. She does, and the camera pans off to watch a military parade as they embrace.

Although rather late as a World War II comedy, *On the Double* manages to be a consistently amusing and rather innocent comedy, never hinting at the real horrors of war or the intensity of the military situation in undertaking the Normandy invasion. The Nazis are strictly comic foils who maintain the light-hearted nature of the film. Ernie Williams is the pure, good-hearted American, although a total hypochondriac and a misfit. His natural charm wins over Lady Margaret, who had grown hard after years of marriage to the stuffy, pompous rascal, Lawrence Mackenzie-Smith. When captured by the Nazis, Ernie's motivation for action is not really to win the war, but to save Lady Margaret, after he learns that she is in danger because she thinks the man who serves as the head Nazi agent in England is actually her friend. Unlike other wartime comedies, this film has no real depth or dark underside. It is simply an undiluted humorous escapade, and a damned funny one at that.

HITLER PORTRAYAL: This was Bobby Watson's swan song, his final screen appearance as Adolf Hitler. The remarkable resemblance to the real Hitler was beginning to be a stretch, as Watson was now in his seventies, and his physical features betray his actual age, particularly his flabby jowls. He only appears on screen briefly, coming down the stairs as Danny Kaye, in Hitler disguise, marches up the same staircase. His wide-eyed double-take is priceless, however, then he pivots to pursue Kaye, shouting in guttural tones. It is a brief but appropriate final bow for Watson as one of the most memorable screen Hitlers. One should also mention Danny Kaye, who impersonates Hitler three times in the film. The first time, Ernie is in the mess hall, casually entertaining the British soldiers with his impersonations of Winston Churchill and Louis Armstrong. As Hitler, he merely slaps a phony square mustache on his upper lip, and he launches into Germanic doubletalk which sounds remarkably similar to Chaplin's hilarious spiel in *The Great Dictator*. By the end of his rant, Ernie lapses into English, but when his moustache falls off his lip, the routine ends. The second Hitler take-off occurs in the military headquarters in Berlin with the Nazi interrogators. At this point, Ernie is trying to convince them that he is not Mackenzie-Smith, merely a talented mimic. He again slaps on the moustache, and the German officers instinctively snap to attention and give him the Nazi salute. They quickly come to their senses, and start to pound on Ernie in slapstick fashion to show their displeasure at his attempts to imitate the Führer. At this point, Ernie mutters that nobody seems to like that particular impersonation. His final Hitler masquerade is the only one not played for laughs by Ernie. Trapped in the opera house, he decides that his appearance as Hitler might give him an opportunity to escape. He is at first accepted as Hitler, but then he has the misfortune to bump into the genuine Führer on the stairs. Of course, Kaye's impersonation of Hitler is totally incongruous, but it nonetheless is quite amusing.

The rest of the cast are quite good in their supporting roles. Diana Dors is sassy as the general's mistress. Gregory Walcott is best remembered for his role as Trent, the pilot in *Plan Nine from Outer Space* (1956/59), the memorable Ed Wood classic bad film. In *On the Double*, his role as Major Houston is rather similar. Rudolph Anders plays his part with typical zest. Jesse White and Wilfred Hyde-White also excel in their brief turns. Dana Wynter is the only performer who lacks credibility, simply because her role isn't humorous. As written, it is nearly impossible to pull off the heroine's part successfully, but at least she makes a sincere effort.

REPRESENTATIVE QUOTES

• Berlin, 1944—A secret radio message from Adolf Hitler personally to his spies in Great Britain: "Kill General Mackenzie-Smith! *Please!*" Hitler wasn't himself that day—those terrible headaches you know. *(Opening narration)*

• There will always be an England, but they will be driving Volkswagons! We will have… *(Ernie, imitating Hitler in the mess hall).* Ernie, your mustache fell in the mashed potatoes. It looks right at home. *(His pal Joe, interrupting him)*

• This will please the Führer immensely. *(Nazi officer, believing he has broken Mackenzie-Smith)* I presume, gentlemen, he will go into his dance again. *(Ernie, disguised as the general)*

66. *Once Upon a Honeymoon* (1942)

Carl Ekberg as Adolf Hitler (cameo)
Comedy

RKO. Written by Sheridan Gibney based on a story by Sheridan Gibney & Leo McCarey; Photographed by George Barnes; Edited by Theron Worth; Music by Robert Emmett Dolan; Produced & directed by Leo McCarey. B & W 117 minutes

ANNOTATED CAST LIST: Cary Grant (*Pat O'Toole*, American reporter in Europe); Ginger Rogers (*Baroness Katie von Luber*, American burlesque star who marries an Austrian nobleman); Walter Slezak (*Baron Franz von Luber*, Her husband, a secret Nazi provocateur); Albert Dekker (*Gaston LeBlanc*, American agent posing as a French photographer); Harry Shannon (*Ed Cumberland*, Manager of European News Service); Hans Conreid (*Schneider*, Viennese clothes fitter); Ferike Boros (*Elsa*, Viennese maid); Albert Bassermann (*General Borelski*, Polish military leader); John Banner (*Captain von Kleinoch*, German attaché in Poland who is assassinated with Borelski); Felix Basch (*Nicolaus von Kelman*, German Ambassador to Poland); George Irving (American Consul in Poland); Natasha Lytess (*Anna*, Jewish cleaning woman to whom Katie gives her passport); Alex Melesh (Waiter in Warsaw); Dorothy Vaughan (*Mrs. O'Hara*, Katie's mother); Fred Niblo (Ocean liner captain); Jack Gardner (*Vidkun Quisling*, Norwegian politician who collaborates with the Nazis); Fred Aldrich, Johnny Dime, Hans Fuerberg, Henry Guttman, Bob Stevenson, Henry Victor (Nazi storm troopers); Walter Bond, Gordon Clark, Arno Frey, Manart Kippen, Bill Martin, Jack Martin, George Sorel, Hans Heinrich von Twadowski (German officers).

APPRAISAL AND SYNOPSIS: *Once Upon a Honeymoon* was a pet project of filmmaker Leo McCarey, who not only produced and directed but concocted the original story. Therefore, he deserves the lion's share of the blame that the film fails to hold together, seems like a stitched together series of disjointed fragments. Several scenes are very impressive, particularly when McCarey deals with previously taboo issues such as the persecution of the Jews and even enforced sterilization. Yet these dark moments are awkwardly grafted onto the general story in which the humor seems forced unlike *To Be or Not to Be*, released the same year. Another reason the picture doesn't gel is that the storyline keeps stopping and starting. Some sequences seem unresolved, while others stretch on for far too long. Nevertheless, McCarey had far greater success with his next project, *Going My Way* (1944), for which he won the Academy Award.

The picture opens with a most impressive prop, a large clock with a rotating swastika in the center of the dial, labeled the timetable of Adolf Hitler. This image is followed by the map of Austria in 1938 at the time of the Anschluss. In Vienna, brash American reporter Pat O'Toole starts to investigate Baron Franz von Luber, suspected of being a secret Nazi operative. The baron is about to be married to an American, a upper class lady known as Katherine Butt-Smith, who is actually former Burlesque dancer Katie O'Hara. Initially posing as a clothes fitter, Pat tries to interview her, and he becomes infatuated with her. He tries to inform her that the baron is a Nazi agent, but the apolitical woman dismisses the idea, saying her fiancé hates Hitler. When Baron von Luber shows up, he pretends to be upset by Hitler's arrival in Vienna, and he takes Katie to Czechoslovakia to get married. Coincidentally, Czechoslovakia is the next country absorbed by the Third Reich, and the von Lubers move to Poland. O'Toole also shifts his operations to Warsaw, warning military leader General Borelski that von Luber is not to be trusted. Shortly afterward, the general is assassinated, together with the genial German military attaché who befriended Katie. The Nazis invade Poland. Katie now believes that Pat was right about her husband. Ed Cumberland, a news service operator and Pat's boss, helps get her name listed

as a war casualty, and she and Pat leave Warsaw. For a brief time, they are detained by Nazi authorities, who mistakenly believe they are Jews. Fortunately, they are handed over to the American Consul. They head to France, passing through Norway, Holland and Belgium. Nazi aggression seems to follow in their wake. The exploits of Baron von Luber are also traced, including his negotiations with the Nazi collaborator Quisling in Norway.

In Paris, Katie and Pat prepare to leave for American when they encounter photographer Gaston LeBlanc. He reveals himself to Katie as an American secret agent who is pretending to work for the Gestapo. He implores Katie to return to Baron von Luber in order to spy on him and learn the plans of the Nazis. Pat is crushed when she returns to the baron. Only after the Nazis take over Paris does he learn that she is working as a spy. He meets von Luber, who persuades him to make a propaganda broadcast to America praising the Nazis.

Katie photographs all of the baron's papers, including the secret code of Hitler's cabinet. LeBlanc's role as a double agent is discovered. When he is killed by the Gestapo, Katie is also detained, but manages to escape to the radio station, where Pat is delivering his broadcast, double crossing the Nazis and proclaiming von Luber as a potential rival to the Führer. At that precise moment, the baron is hosting a reception for high Nazi officials, including Hitler, who summons him to a secret meeting.

Katie and Pat escape to a ocean liner heading for America, unaware that the baron is also aboard. That evening, he confronts Katie on deck. He explains that the Führer had granted him a divorce and accepted his explanation that the broadcast was a stunt to blacken his reputation. He boasts that Hitler is sending him on a new mission to America. Offscreen, Katie pushes the baron into the ocean. She tells Pat, but they hem and haw telling the ship's captain. He turns the ship around, but when Katie explains the baron couldn't swim, the last shot of the film is the ship turning back to its original course.

Once Upon a Honeymoon falls flat on many levels. Neither Cary Grant nor Ginger Rogers seem comfortable in their roles, and their comic timing seems off. Walter Slezak appears somewhat disengaged, only shining in his scene when he hears Pat's radio broadcast which gets him in hot water. The most exceptional performance in the cast is delivered by Albert Dekker. His highlight is his telling of his life story to Katie, adapting regional accents of the places he had lived in America. Natasha Lytess is convincing as Anna, the Polish cleaning lady who reveals her fears of the Nazis because she is Jewish. Katie doctors her own passport to give to Anna, so she and her two children can leave the country. Later, Anna repays her gratitude to Katie in Paris, posing as a decoy so Katie is able to escape her guards. Another interesting scene features John Banner as the German military attaché in Warsaw. Many viewers will not recognize the slimmer, younger Banner, who is best remembered as the heavy-set POW camp guard Sergeant Schultz in *Hogan's Heroes*. Banner chats amiably with Ginger Rogers, but in his next scene he is assassinated with the Polish general played by Albert Bassermann. The Nazis considered the affable attaché expendable in their ruthless plans.

HITLER PORTRAYAL: Carl Ekberg's cameo as Adolf Hitler is one of the briefest screen appearances, as he passes by a doorway and gives a Nazi salute to Walter Slezak standing just inside the room. Earlier, a newsreel clipping of the actual Hitler at the Eiffel Tower is inserted in a montage representing the Nazi occupation of Paris. After Cary Grant's that promotes the baron as a rival to Hitler, the Führer summons Slezak to a meeting, but this confrontation occurs entirely offscreen. We only learn the details later when he encounters Ginger Rogers on the ocean liner and boasts that the Führer gave him a new mission. Like many aspects of this film, the underuse of Hitler as a comic foil is disappointing.

REPRESENTATIVE QUOTES

• Hey, Hitler is here. *(Pat, while knocking on Katie's bedroom door after spotting Hitler's motorcade from the hotel window)* Well, I can't see him now, I'm dressing. *(Her reply, as if the Führer was in her suite)*

• Do you mean it is up to Hitler who can have babies and who can't? *(Katie to Pat, after learning of the sterilization program)* Yes, it used to be the will of God. Hitler doesn't like that. Too many people might be born who wouldn't agree with him. *(Pat's response)*

• As I have said, the baron doesn't know the meaning of the word fear. He doesn't ever fear the Führer. There are even rumors of a second party movement, headed by this modest man who heretofore, had written all of the Führer's speeches and has been content to remain in the background. *(Pat's broadcast, intended to embarrass von Luber)*

• Well, I thought the Führer had purged you by now. *(Katie to von Luber, after seeing him on the ship)*

67.   *Order of the Black Eagle* (1986)

Tony Ellwood as Adolf Hitler (cameo)
Fantasy/Adventure

Polo Players Ltd. Written by Phil Behrens; Photographed by Irl Dixon & Dan Kneece; Edited by Mathew Mallinson; Music by Dee Barton; Produced by Robert P. Eaton & Betty J. Stephens; Directed by Worth Keeter. Color 93 minutes

ANNOTATED CAST LIST: Ian Hunter *(Duncan Jax,* Secret agent); Charles K. Bibby *(Star,* Head of spy agency); William Hicks *(Baron Ernst von Tepisch,* Leader of a Neo-Nazi group); Anna Rapagna *(Maxie Ryder,* Female soldier of fortune and special agent); Jill Donnellan *(Tiffany Youngblood,* Interpol agent); Shangtai Tuan *(Sato,* Agency gadget inventor); Stephen Krayn *(Dr. George Brinkman,* Scientist kidnapped by Nazis); Gene Scherer *(Dr. Kurtz,* Nazi scientist); Wolfgang Linkman *(Colonel Wilhelm Stryker,* Nazi security chief); Joe Coltrane (*Willie Brown, Jr.*, Mercenary nick-named Hammer); James Eric (*Juice*, Hard-drinking mercenary); Bill Gribble (*John Thaddeus Stevens*, cowboy mercenary); Flo Hyman (*Spike*, Female warrior mercenary); Terry Loughlin (*S.D.*, Bespectacled demolition expert); Dean Whitworth (*Bolt*, Bearded mercenary resembling Chuck Norris); Ed Thorgersen (Newsreel commentator); Typhoon (*Boon*, Simon's baboon pet).

APPRAISAL AND SYNOPSIS: *Order of the Black Eagle* is a strange concoction, a ripoff of James Bond that mixes some high quality production values with sophomoric acting. The cinematography, sets, costumes, special effects, make up and stuntwork are actually superb. The editing, music and direction, on the other hand, are simply amateurish. Worst of all is the script, a bumbling effort that keeps getting bogged down, and seems uncertain exactly which targets the film is targeting for satire. The production was largely financed by the Polo Club of Hilton Head, South Carolina. yet most of the cast seem like Australian or British cast-offs. The only decent performance in the entire cast is by William Hicks as the villainous Baron von Tepisch, a former member of the Hitler Youth who resembles a mad cross between Sebastian Cabot and Sidney Greenstreet, with a touch of Gorilla Monsoon. With his eye patch and gray beard, he seems like a demented, overweight Wotan, yet he plays the role with such loony zest that he makes a splendid send up of a typical James Bond villain. Unfortunately, the rest of the cast lacks any focus. Worst of all, the mercenary group seems like rejected counterfeits from other action films. There is a cowboy who gives a miserable impression of Clint Eastwood from his spaghetti Western period. There is also a Chuck Norris wannabe, a Terry O'Quinn double, a Grace Jones replica and a Mister T clone. This group of misfits, perhaps based on the *A-Team*, bumble and mug their way through the last half of the film making it tedious and maddening. Add to the mixture a tank-driving baboon who spends most of the film making

obscene gestures, and the picture comes close to being impossible to watch. Ian Hunter plays Simon Jax, a James Bond stand-in with zero charisma. His female associates on the mission, Jill Donnellan and Anna Rapagna, are pretty to look at, but both are rather hopeless in the acting department. Needless to say, this film was quickly consigned as a bargain basement video release that was among the first targets for discard whenever a store weeded its collection. Yet in overall quality, it is probably as good or better than many low budget rivals.

Order of the Black Eagle opens with a Movietone newsreel proclaiming, "World Criminal Adolf Hitler Dead as Berlin Falls." The story includes shots of Ernst Röhm, Joseph Goebbels and Hermann Göring, with Benito Mussolini thrown in for good measure. It briefly traces the Führer's career, ending with the collapse of Nazi Germany. The scene then shifts forty years, using the title card, "They said it couldn't happen again," alerting the audience to the basic plot. A scientific conference at Geneva, Switzerland, is unexpectedly besieged by hooded terrorists who kidnap Dr. George Brinkman, the world's leading expert on laser technology. Duncan Jax, a top secret agent, is called into the case by Star, the head of a covert American spy agency, to investigate the Order of the Black Eagle, a neo–Nazi group suspected of the abduction. Oddly, Jax brings Boon, his pet baboon, to his briefing with Star. By coincidence, Jax is the exact double of Conrad Blayden, the head of the American branch of the Order. Blayden's assistant, Marta, is actually Interpol agent Tiffany Youngblood, and she assists in the detention of the real Blayden and the substitution of Jax in his place. They head to a meeting in the jungles of South America where the head of the Order, Baron Ernst von Tepisch, has called a meeting of all the leading members of the terrorist group. The Order's stronghold is a renovated Mayan temple, and Jax is readily accepted when he arrives at the headquarters, which is guarded by an army of storm troopers dressed in beige uniforms and wearing baseball caps with swastikas.

Baron von Tepisch announces his ambitious plans of world conquest at the meeting. The group has developed a new super weapon called the proton beam, a laser of incredible strength. He demonstrates the power of the weapon by demolishing a communications satellite in space. He then reveals the Order's greatest secret. The leader of the Third Reich, Adolf Hitler still lives, his body preserved by "cryotherapy." He will be awakened from his suspended animation as soon as the proton beam is perfected, which was the reason behind the kidnapping of Dr. Brinkman. The leaders of the Order gather around the silver tube containing Hitler's body and toast him with their champagne glasses.

That evening, Jax and Youngblood sneak out of their quarters and attempt to rescue Dr. Brinkman. Apparently, Baron von Tepisch had penetrated Jax's impersonation and set a trap with Colonel Stryker, the Order's Head of Security. The agents are captured, and the Baron attempts to drown Jax by placing him in the large cooling tank of his nuclear reactor. But Jax escapes when it is flooded, breathing with a special gadget developed by Sato, the agency's weaponry expert. Uncovering a drainage pipe, Jax swims off to a nearby river in the jungle. He meets up with Maxie Ryder, a soldier of fortune hired by Star to recruit mercenaries to attack the headquarters of the Order. Star himself arrives at the jungle town of El Gato Grande ("Fat Cat") to oversee the assault. Their troops, however, appear more like rejects from *The Dirty Dozen* (1967). Each of them is based on film action hero such as Grace Jones' dynamic warrior known as May Day in *A View to a Kill* (1985), Roger Moore's final James Bond film. The remainder of the film is a series of action sequences dealing with their struggle to breach the Nazi compound. The boat skirmishes on the river are expertly handled, but the ground scenes are repetitious and awkwardly staged, particularly the moments with the cowboy mercenary and the baboon operating a small tank. Once they break into the Nazi/Mayan temple, Maxie frees Tiffany from her prison cell. Jax confronts the Baron, learning that the proton beam is programmed to be unleashed in fifteen minutes. Holding a gun on Jax, the Baron boasts that the only way to stop the attack would be by the simultaneous application of his fingerprint with that of Dr. Kurtz on the control panel. Jax kills the Baron with a spear and cuts off his index finger. He next destroys Hitler's body, breaking into his capsule and taking his personal iron cross insignia. Finally, he rescues Dr. Brinkman, forcing Dr. Kurtz to disable the weapon using his own finger with the snipped digit of the Baron.

Victorious, Star and the mercenaries set off down the river in their boat. Jax is divided over which girl to romance, Tiffany or Maxie. He settles on Tiffany, and they leave the ship with one of Sato's gadgets, a hot air balloon. Jax's pet baboon salutes his owner with an obscene gesture and the film ends.

HITLER PORTRAYAL: At the end of the film, the cast list coyly includes the entry "Adolf Hitler ... Himself." Of course, this is true considering the opening newsreel. Also, when Baron von Tepisch brings his followers into the laboratory with Hitler's body, the Führer's face is visible inside the capsule. Clips of the real Hitler are superimposed over this image. When Jax breaks into the capsule at the end of the film, Hitler's visage cracks and decomposes with the inrush of air. Stripped of his skin, the raw, bloody face of Hitler screams as he dies. This image of the screaming Hitler is supposedly rendered by Tony Ellwood, who served as principal make-up man on the shoot. This Hitler appearance is brief, but is probably the most striking image of the entire film. Cryogenics usually refers to a body that is completely frozen (and therefore dead), but the Hitler in this film is actually alive but preserved by being maintained at low temperature. Yet Hitler's face appears to be solidly frozen, with an unfrozen, semi-conscious Hitler under the skin. This confusing contradiction is never clarified in the story, but with the large number of unresolved plot points, such as the target of the proton beam, an additional inconsistency doesn't matter.

REPRESENTATIVE QUOTES

• Tonight, we have gathered to celebrate the birthday of our beloved Führer. Also, to celebrate the culmination of forty years of work and dedication, work and dedication to the building of a new world, a new order. *(Von Tepisch to his followers at dinner)*
• Chief, the Baron makes Quaddafy look like a pussy cat. He plans to destroy the world's major communications satellites tomorrow night. We have to move fast to stop it, and I don't think our allies are going to help us. *(Maxie Ryder to Star via long range broadcast)* The world is threatened and they always turn to the United States for leadership. *(His reply)*
• There's one more bit of news, Star. Adolf Hitler, he's alive, cryogenically preserved *(Jax to his boss on the bus ride through the jungle)*
• There can only be one master, one leader, who can rise like the phoenix out of the ashes. *(Von Tepisch to Jax during their final confrontation)*

68. *Osvobozhdeniye*
(AKA *Liberation*) (1967-71)
Fritz Diez as Adolf Hitler
Historical drama

Mosfilm. Written by Yuri Bondarev, Oskar Kurganov & Yuri Ozerov; Photographed by Igor Slabnevich; Edited by Y. Karpova; Music by Yuri Levitin; Produced by Yuri Ozerov & Dino De Laurentiis; Directed by Yuri Ozerov. Color 470 minutes

CAST LIST: Mikhail Ulyanov; Vasili Shukshin; Nikolai Olyalin; Hardy Kruger; Laris Golubkina; Mikhail Nozhkin; Nikolai Kokshenov; Angelika Waller; Valeri Vinogradov; Klyon Protasov; Ignacy Machowski; Andre Petrov; Yuri Leghov; Alfred Struwe;

Igor Ozerov; Vlad Davydov; Willi Schrade; Hannjo Hasse; Vladimir Nosik; Gerd Michael Henneberg; Siegfried Weiss; Boris Zaydenberg.

COMMENTARY: *Osvobozhdeniye* is an epic Russian cycle of five films dealing almost exclusively with the German/Soviet front from the Nazi invasion in June 1941 through the fall of Berlin. Made between 1967 and 1971, the series is noted for an enormous cast of thousands, and it contains some of the most elaborate battle sequences ever filmed, in particular, the huge tank encounter known as the Battle of Kurst. On the whole, the series deals with the war in a more realistic fashion than the earlier Stalinist screen depictions. The generals of the Soviet military, who were belittled in the earlier films, are now provided with their proper share of credit. Hitler is portrayed by Fritz Diez, Eastern Europe's equivalent to Bobby Watson in terms of the frequency of his Hitler appearances. Although he is present in all five films, he has the most screen footage in one of the central titles, *Napravleniye Glavnogo Udana*, or loosely translated as *The Direction of the Main Blow*. This entry, at 140 minutes, is the lengthiest of the series, and supposedly the most popular segment. It concentrates on the Soviet counterattack during the summer of 1944. Diez is featured in the extensive sequence dealing with the Rastenburg assassination attempt. In particular, this episode gives a clear indication that the German people were also victims of the Nazi regime. The Polish and East German film industries participated in the making of this series, as well as Italian film mogul Dino De Laurentiis. The theatrical films were later recut in the 1970s as a television miniseries which was principally distributed in Eastern Europe and Finland. It also became a tradition for Soviet television to broadcast the entire cycle each year in early May between May Day and Victory Day (May 9th).

69. *Our Hitler*
(AKA *Hitler, Eine Film aus Deutschland*) (1978)

Heinz Schubert & others as Adolf Hitler
Surreal Fantasy

WDR/TMS/Solaris/Zoetrope. Written by Hans-Jürgen Syberberg; Photographed by Dietrich Lohmann; Edited by Jutta Brandstädter; Music by Richard Wagner, Ludwig van Beethoven, Franz Lehar, Gustav Mahler, Johann Strauss, Franz Josef Haydn & Wolfgang Amadeus Mozart; Produced by Bernd Eichinger; Directed by Hans-Jürgen Syberberg. B & W/Color 407 minutes

ANNOTATED CAST LIST: (Note—each actor appears in multiple roles, with major ones listed.) Heinz Schubert (Circus barker; *Heinrich Himmler*); Peter Kern (Murderer from Fritz Lang's *M*; *Hermann Göring* puppeteer; 4th SS man; Director of tourism at Berchtesgaden); Hellmut Lange (Joseph Goebbels puppeteer; *Karl-Wilhelm Krause*, Hitler's valet; 1st SS man); Rainer von Artenfels (Clown imitating Hitler; Magician; *Charlie Chaplin* as he appeared in *The Great Dictator*; *Joseph Goebbels* as he appeared in 1923; 2nd SS man); Martin Sperr (*Felix Kersten*, Himmler's masseur; Mayor of Berchtesgaden); Peter Moland (Albert Speer puppeteer; *Ferdinand Marian*, Actor who played the lead in *Jew Süss*; Astrologer; 3rd SS man); Johannes Buzalski (Eva Braun puppeteer; Socialite; Concentration camp guard); Alfred Edel (Man of Destiny; Street haranguer); Harry Baer (King Ludwig II puppeteer; *Fritz Ellerkamp*, Hitler's projectionist; Hitler puppeteer; Man with long cloak); Peter Lühr (Cosmologist; *Dr. Ko*, Tibetan teacher); Amelie Syberberg (Young girl carrying a cloth dog with Hitler's face); Andre Heller (Commentator; Lecturer).

APPRAISAL AND SYNOPSIS: When Orson Welles completed *F for Fake* (1974), he referred to it as a cinematic essay. In essence, Hans-Jürgen Syberberg's *Our Hitler* is also a cinematic essay, a surreal four-part meditation on Adolf Hitler and his Faustian hold on not only the German soul, but that of mankind as a whole. It is also a treatise on film itself, the art form of the Twentieth century. *Our Hitler* can be considered part of a loose film trilogy, an informal companion piece to the director's *Ludwig* (1972) and *Karl May* (1974). The film has provoked controversy, hostility, condemnation as well as considerable adulation, everything but indifference, since its debut in 1977. Susan Sontag enumerated it among the greatest films ever made. To appreciate *Our Hitler*, the viewer must be knowledgeable not only about the Weimar Republic and Nazi Germany, but about cinema history in general. There are countless references to the characters from the noted films of the German Expressionist movement, to Thomas Edison as well as Orson Welles. The film also requires tremendous concentration, as it blends numerous historical and cultural references presented in many different guises, including radio excerpts, a puppet extravaganza, a slide show, an art exhibit, a travelogue and a circus sideshow.

Our Hitler is the title of the English subtitled version of the film. Syberberg's working title for the project was *The Grail*, and, indeed, the words "Der Gral" still appear at the start and end of the production, appearing from a background of stars, accompanied by the strains of the Prelude to *Parsifal*, Wagner's grail opera. Syberberg's film is divided into four parts, a tetralogy inspired, no doubt, by Richard Wagner's operatic cycle *Der Ring des Nibelungen*. Each of these four movements opens and closes with the appearance of a young girl, played by Amelie, Syberberg's daughter. The first section is called *Hitler, a Film from Germany*, which is also the alternative title for the entire work. In this section, a young girl enters a fog enshrouded set, placing a cloth dog with Hitler's face into a cradle surrounded by images from *The Cabinet of Dr. Caligari* (1919). The devil also investigates the contents of this cradle. Finally, a carnival barker appears and announces that, since there is no caged Hitler to place on display, everyone

Heinz Schubert as Hitler in the Wagner's grave sequence from *Our Hitler*.

should conjure up the image of Hitler in himself. As if presenting a series of sideshow acts, each member of the cast enacts a rendition of Hitler, culminating in the murderer from Fritz Lang's classic, *M* (1931), who was originally played by Peter Lorre. This is followed by a series of presentations of the Nazi elite in puppet form, with different cast members operating the puppets and speaking their lines. There is a mock book burning, then a series of references to film figures such as Erich von Stro-

heim and Gloria Swanson. The purveyors of Nazi culture are then analyzed on blackboards, before ending with a roll-call of intellectuals who became victims of this philosophy. Part Two, *A German Dream*, is basically built around two long monologues, the first by Hitler's projectionist, Fritz Ellerkamp, a fictionalized character who is actually a composite of a number of individuals and Karl-Wilhelm Krause, who served as Hitler's valet between 1934 and 1939. Krause's long narration concentrates on the minutia of Hitler's daily routine and wardrobe is principally drawn from the book *I Was Hitler's Valet*, a mundane account which Krause penned after the war. Between these two long accounts which stress the ordinariness of Hitler, is a rather grotesque appearance by the Führer himself as a living corpse who emerges from Wagner's grave to deliver a number of repellent comments. Part Three, *The End of a Winter's Dream*, centers on Heinrich Himmler, as he converses with his masseur as he receives a rubdown. A number of SS men appear to declaim authentic reports that Himmler had received, leading up to the collapse of the Nazi regime. The fate of the victims of the SS is examined, finally leading Himmler to dismiss the fate of the Jews, comparing them to the Indian tribes which were wiped out by the Americans. Himmler next meets with his astrologer. Attention then shifts to a post-war tour of the Berghof is conducted by Ellerkamp. The act closes as a ventriloquist's dummy of Hitler provides an analysis of the post-war world, denoting how many leaders have taken pages from his book with their actions, and ending with a dark prediction of the future. Part Four, *We the Children of Hell*, features an extraordinarily lengthy presentation by Andre Heller sitting at a desk with a landscape by Caspar David Friedrich projected behind him. Heller later introduces a series of genuine Hitler film clips, and relates numerous anecdotes, including the story of the occasion when the sixteen-year-old daughter of his photographer, Heinrich Hoffmann, directly reproached the Führer for his persecution of the Jews. In response, Hitler simply tells her that she needed to learn to hate. After Heller's discourse concludes, the scene shifts to Berchtesgaden where the mayor and director of tourism present a modern day Hitler museum, filled with historical objects. This leads to a celebration of the collapse of the Reich. Heller returns and chastises the Hitler dummy, sitting mute and lifeless at the edge of a table. Heller disappears into a small glass globe (Syberberg's "Rosebud"),

with a model of Thomas Edison's original film studio. This model also serves as a visual leitmotif in the film. Finally the little girl returns with the same cloth dog with Hitler's face, and the picture ends, or literally dissolves, into a series of mystic images.

Naturally, the reaction to *Our Hitler* is a highly personal one, as it contains an incredible number of images and ideas for the viewer to process and analyze. As a film essay, *Our Hitler* is incomparable, but it is also confusing, self-indulgent and repetitive, and while many passages are moving, intriguing and stimulating, much of it is also redundant, filled with overkill, so that so that a portion of the film's brilliance is awash with tripe as well. Nevertheless, *Our Hitler* is a unique and almost overwhelming entry in the *Hitler Filmography*.

HITLER PORTRAYAL: Images and representations of Hitler haunt almost every frame of the film, including puppets, statues, dolls, posters, dummies and recorded speeches by the authentic Hitler. Each of the cast members assumes some aspect of Hitler in the course of the film. In Part One, for example, the circus barker presents a series of acts in which the cast members impersonate Hitler in various guises, as a house painter, a madman, the Frankenstein monster, Charlie Chaplin as Hynkel in *The Great Dictator* and "the greatest fart of all times." It is Heinz Schubert, however, who comes closest to a portraying an unadulterated Hitler, which occurs in Part Two, when he emerges from the grave of Richard Wagner as if he were a demon from hell. In fact, the staging of this scene was inspired by a Gustave Doré print of Dante and Virgil passing a figure in an open grave from *The Inferno*. Schubert's depiction is the longest lasting of the Hitler images in the film. He wears a Roman toga, and music from Wagner's *Rienzi* accompanies his lengthy address, providing his assessment of his place in German history. He also speaks of his artistic temperament, fueled by Wagner's music as inspiration and anti–Semitism as his motivation. He eventually compares himself to

Leonardo da Vinci, Michelangelo and Beethoven as a monumental genius. Toward the end of his address, he turns to his critics and ironically paraphrases Shylock, the Jewish moneylender from Shakespeare's *Merchant of Venice*, declaring, "When you prick me, do I not bleed?"

The longest Hitler monologue occurs at the end of Part Three, when actor Harry Baer holds a Charlie McCarthy-style Hitler dummy on his lap while it rambles through a long assessment of a list of various heirs on the political scene, from Stalin, Mao and Castro to Pol Pot. The capitalists of the world are included as well in the puppet's tabulations. Music from *Götterdämmerung* accompanies this passage. At first Baer engages the dummy in conversation, but then the puppet drones on by itself, as Baer keeps changing the clothing of the figure. The puppet cynically predicts that mankind will eventually self-destruct. The Hitler puppet reappears in Part Four, as Andre Heller berates the Führer and his influence. "You are the executor of Western Civilization ... the plague of our century, the wretched artist as a hangman, degenerating into a politician." The very last appearance of Hitler is the same as the first, a cloth dog with the Führer's face, carried by a child, accompanied by Beethoven's music from the *Finale* of the *Ninth Symphony* and *Fidelio*. The message at this point, after six and three-quarter hours, is that Hitler and his dark influence may be inescapable.

REPRESENTATIVE QUOTES

• Anyone who wants to see Stalingrad again, or the 20th of July plot, or the lone wolf's last day in the bunker or Riefenstahl's Nuremberg will be disappointed. We are not showing the unrepeatable reality. *(Circus barker)*

• His most secret desires, his dreams, the things he wanted beyond the real world: 2 or 3 movies every day. *Broadway Melody* with Fred Astaire, Walt Disney's *Snow White*.... And I saw him watching John Ford's big movies about settlers, the Westerns with so many graves and fights with the Indians. The great operettas of life. How he loved John Wayne. And I saw him struggling for Greta Garbo and trying to get Marlene Dietrich to come back to Germany. He watched the movies over and over again, six or seven times in a row, focusing on image after image, shot after shot. *(Ellerkamp)*

• Hitler is not dead. He is in the cosmos. When he was born, he was a cosmic baby placed on Earth as a foundling. His parents took him in and baptized him Adolf. *(Socialite)*

• I know I will be elected the greatest man of all time or perish, cursed and damned by all, for all time. *(Hitler, speaking from Wagner's grave)*

• With his stockings, he always had something to complain about, for they were usually too short, so that they supposedly slid down his calves. He would then exclaim, "Isn't it possible for the Führer of the German people to get a pair of decent socks?" *(Krause)*

• Certainly the Jews will suffer a great deal. But what did the Americans do? The Indians wanted to go on living on their hereditary soil, and the Americans exterminated them in the most dreadful way. *(Himmler)*

• I praise Idi Amin, Africa's spokesman and my venerator. He was received by the Pope, isn't that something? And in front of the UN, Arafat, the Arab, with his gun in his pocket, at the same UN in which 110 of the 159 states violate human rights, 110 out of 159 torture and murder, which is why, at every vote, they vote for inhumanity by majority, very democratic. *(Hitler puppet)*

70. *Pétain* (1992)

Ludwig Haas as Adolf Hitler
Historical drama

Gala Films. Written by Jean-Pierre Marchand, Alain Riou & Jean Marboeuf based on *Pétain* by Marc Ferro; Photographed by Dominique Bouilleret; Edited by Anne-France Lebrun; Music by Georges Garvarentz; Produced by Jacques Kirsner; Directed by Jean Marboeuf. Color 129 minutes

ANNOTATED CAST LIST: Jacques Dufilho (*Marshal Philippe Pétain*, Elderly war hero & Premier of the Vichy government); Jean Yanne (*Pierre Laval*, Vice Premier & leading French collaborationist); Jean-Pierre Cassel (*Hans Roberto*, Bandleader at the Hotel du Parc); Catherine d'At (*Judith*, Jewish musician in Roberto's band); Antoinette Moya (*Eugenie Pétain*, The Premier's wife); Laurence Ligneres (Laval's wife); Julie Marboeuf (*Colette*, Maid at Hotel du Parc); Clovis Cornillac (*François*, Colette's husband, a waiter); Pierre Cognon (*Bergaugnon*, François' friend); Violette Ferrer (Bergaugnon's mother); Jean-Claude Dreyfus (*Dumoulin*, Pétain's advisor); Jean-François Perrier (*Gillouin*); Roger Dumas (*Colonel Bonhomme*, Pétain's aide-de-camp); Christian Charmetant (*Bernard Menetrel*, Pétain's doctor & advisor); André Penvern (*Raphael Alibert*, Vichy Justice Minister); Eric Prat (*Jacques Doriot*, Head of fascist youth movement); Max Morel (*Joseph Darnand*, Head of Vichy secret police); Götz Burger (*Otto Abetz*, German ambassador); Ruger Vonmeurs (American ambassador); Denis Manuel (*Paul Reynaud*, French Premier at the time of the Nazi blitzkrieg); Frederique Timont (*Helene de Portes*, Reynaud's mistress); François Aragon (Priest who preaches after Pétain is voted full power); Noel Simsolo (*Fernand de Brinon*, Vichy official); Michel Modo (*Pierre Pucheu*, Vichy Minister of Industry); Jacques Bourgaux (*Paul Baudouin*, Vichy Secretary of State for foreign affairs); Jacques Mignot (*Marcel Peyrouton*, Vichy Secretary of State for internal affairs); Max Desrau (*General Charles Huntzinger*, Vichy Secretary of War); Philippe Brigaud (*General Laurie*, Vichy Secretary-General); André Thorent (*General Maxime Weygand*, Former head of French army); Nicolas Donato (*Camille Chautemps*, Politician who urged Pétain to seek an armistice); Vincent Grass (*Georges Mandel*, Politician opposing the armistice); Pierre Soulard (*Bousquet*, a policeman); Pierre Court (*Charles Roux*);

Georges Montant (*Léon Blum*, Socialist Party leader); Jean-Luc Guitton (*Michel Grenier*, Mayor of St. Lazarre); Daniel Léger (*Cocurat*); Vincent Gauthier (*Rene Bousquet*); Severine Vincent (*Lisette*); Rene Bourdet (*Desfourneaux*); Pierre Aussedat (*Herve*); Christian Auger (*Jean Giraudoux*, a writer); Francois Sayan (*Jean François Darlan*, French admiral who replaces Laval in 1941); Jean-Pierre Hutinet (*Marcel Déat*, Journalist & Laval supporter); Jacques Chailleux (*Boudot*, Laval's driver); Jean-Louis Perrier (Radio announcer at Laval assassination attempt).

APPRAISAL AND SYNOPSIS: *Pétain* is an intense examination of one of the most divisive issues of French history, the question of collaboration during World War II. In fact, the film can be easily compared to any great screen epic such as *Doctor Zhivago* (1965) or *Khartoum* (1966), especially when one considers its scope and use of fictional characters. The film concentrates almost equally on three individuals. The first is Marshal Philippe Pétain, the aged and vainglorious hero of Verdun during World War I, who decides to accept the leadership of the rump French state known as Vichy France, created in 1940 by the armistice with Germany. The second is Pierre Laval, the leading French proponent of collaboration with the Germans. The third is Colette, a fictitious maid at the Hotel du Parc in Vichy, who serves as a personification of the French nation, much as the character of "Marianne" stood for Revolutionary France. The first two choices are historical and obvious, whereas the third character, Colette, is purely symbolic. When Pétain arrives in Vichy, Colette has just been married, and the Marshal embraces and kisses the young woman. When her friend Judith is about to be exiled from Vichy because she is Jewish, Colette intercedes with Pétain's wife to get her a dispensation. Later, when she waits upon Pétain in his room, he speaks with her, suggesting that she become a mother since France needs a new generation. Then, she typifies the shifting public sentiment when

Jacques Dufilho as Marshal Pétain greets Ludwig Haas as Hitler. Jean Yanne, bareheaded in center, looks on approvingly in the role of Pierre Laval.

she and her husband abandon their jobs to join the French resistance. Marching triumphant in the streets as American forces approach, Colette is finally shot when she opposes a brigade of French fascists.

Pétain starts with the collapse of the French army before the German invaders in 1940. Refugees fleeing from the front are bombed as they try to cross a bridge. Marshal Pétain, touring the scene moments later, decides the carnage must come to an end. The government has already abandoned Paris, and while attending a fly-by-night meeting, Pétain declares that he will not leave French soil. He agrees to head up a new government that will seek an armistice with the Germans. Many politicians vie for positions in the regime, among them Pierre Laval, a controversial figure who urges for collaboration. Laval becomes Vice Premier and Foreign Minister, believing that he will be able to easily manipulate the eighty-four-year-old Pétain.

A peace accord is signed with Hitler in the identical railroad car in which the Treaty of Versailles was signed. Pétain does not at-tend, hearing the terms from General Huntzinger, his War Minister. The Nazis will occupy the northern provinces and the Atlantic coastal regions. The rest of the country, a little over one third of the original nation, will be managed by self-rule under Pétain. Vichy is selected as the seat of the new government with the Hotel du Parc as headquarters. Pétain is voted full dictatorial powers by the legislature, which disbands itself. Laval arranges a conference between the Führer and the Marshal.

Laval finds that Pétain is resistant to his influence. The Marshal resents his minister's arrogant manner. Laval arranges a big ceremonial event with Hitler in Paris, bringing the ashes of Napoleon's son for internment in Napoleon's tomb. Pétain uses the opportunity to sack Laval, and Otto Abetz, the German ambassador, reports Hitler's displeasure to the Marshal. As time passes, Pétain begins to promote a series of fascist decrees, including persecution of the Jews. An assassin shoots Laval, who wins unexpected public sympathy as he recovers. Eventually, Pétain brings him back into power. When Allied forces invade North Africa in November 1942, the French colonies rally to the American side. After this, German troops occupy Vichy France, and Pétain's government becomes almost irrelevant, a mere shadow regime. Using increasingly harsh and brutal measures, the Vichy government loses all credibility. Jews are rounded up for extermination, and Frenchmen are deported to Germany to become forced laborers. The French Resistance starts to thrive, growing stronger every day. In the months after D-Day, Pétain and Laval are escorted under Nazi protective custody to a castle in Germany. Laval realizes he is doomed, and the Germans provide him with cyanide capsules to use when necessary. Meanwhile Pétain, increasingly self-absorbed, writes a new constitution for France. When Laval pays him a final visit, they go for a short walk and review their past actions. As they part, a closing narration discusses their fate. Laval would be executed, and Pétain would be condemned to death. His sentence, however, would be commuted by Charles De Gaulle. Pétain passed his last few years in exile on the Isle d'Yeu off the French coast, where he died in 1951 The final message of the film appears in a title card, saying that "Pétainism, unfortunately, had never been put on trial."

Pétain clearly presents the moral dilemma surrounding the chieftains of the Vichy government, whose original good intentions are unalterably corrupted by their accommodation to the will of the Nazis. The film is spellbinding as it portrays this step by step process away from compassion and patriotism into collaboration and evil. Veteran actor Jacques Dufilho is brilliant as Pétain. One can find an extraordinary range of nuances in his performance. Three scenes in particular stand out: the first is near the beginning when he salutes a mortally wounded soldier of the retreating, disintegrating French army; the second is when he courageously decides to write to Hitler to offer himself as the sole hostage when the German occupation forces start rounding up

captives, only to change his mind a few moments later; the third, near the end, is the most ironical and the most moving, as Pétain leaves his French headquarters to relocate in Germany and French officers softly sing *La Marseillaise* as he departs. Alternately a misguided autocrat, a crafty scoundrel or a befuddled weathervane, Pétain remains a cipher, a complex and ultimately tragic figure, who never comprehends what he has become. Dufilho is no stranger to historical drama, having worked in the genre many times, such as his role as Jean-Paul Marat in *Marie Antoinette* (1955). Jean Yanne, on the other hand, earns little sympathy for his chain-smoking and corrupt Laval, who seems quite aware of where he is going with his pro–German policies which he saw as necessary. Yanne is totally convincing in the role. Jean-Pierre Cassel is also memorable as the bandleader who is convinced that his music could shelter or possibly deliver people from the nightmare world around them, much as the famous conductor Wilhelm Furtwängler believed in Germany. *Pétain* is a rich film worthy of multiple showings, since many fresh and different aspects only become apparent upon a second or third viewing. *Pétain* is unique because it legitimately tries to challenge its audience intellectually, a most rare and stimulating quality.

HITLER PORTRAYAL: Ludwig Haas plays a poker-faced Hitler in *Pétain*, the evil yet impassive spider at the web of the malevolent network of Vichy France. He first appears as he arrives for the signing of the peace treaty at Compiegne. Unlike the beaming triumphant Hitler of history, Haas makes the Führer appear cautious and vigilant. He assumes the same watchful expression as he is seated in the historic railroad car, as if he doesn't quite believe the victory he has achieved. The second appearance is at train station at Montoire, in the recreation of the meeting of Hitler and Pétain on October 24, 1940. Comparing this scene with the famous photograph of the meeting, the only difference is that Haas is far taller than the actual Führer, but is otherwise a fairly close match. At this point, Hitler has his only line of dialogue in the picture. Even though his physical presence is limited, the shadow of Hitler seems to dominate the entire scenario, as the images of Vichy France become closer and closer to those of Nazi Germany, until near the end they seem indistinguishable.

REPRESENTATIVE QUOTES

• The Lebruns, Pétains, Chamberlains and Hitlers will pass. Music shall remain. Songs speak louder than war. *(Hans Roberto to the members of his band)*
• I greet the Frenchman not responsible for this war. *(Hitler to Pétain upon their meeting)*
• Hitler is a little nothing! And I feel that the French did not appreciate that meeting. *(Pétain to his Ministers while complaining about the activities of Laval)*
• Laval has earned the Chancellor's friendship and the Führer is tempted to take your action as a personal insult. *(Otto Abetz to Pétain, after the Marshal dismisses Laval)*

71. *The Plot to Kill Hitler* (1990)

Mike Gwilym as Adolf Hitler
Historical drama

Warner Brothers. Written by Steven Elkins; Photographed by Freddie Francis; Edited by Bernard Gribble; Music by Laurence Rosenthal; Produced by Alfred R. Kelman & David L. Wolper (executive); Directed by Lawrence Schiller. Color 94 minutes

ANNOTATED CAST LIST: Brad Davis (*Count Claus von Stauffenberg*, Colonel who plants a bomb to kill Hitler); Madolyn Smith (*Countess Nina von Stauffenberg*, His wife); Helmuth Lohner (*General Friedrich Fromm*, Home Army commander who straddles the fence over his support of the conspiracy); Michael Byrne (*General Friedrich Olbricht*, Chief of General Army office in Berlin & anti–Hitler conspirator); Jona-

than Hyde (*Dr. Joseph Goebbels*, Propaganda Minister); Timothy Watson (*Otto Remar*, Officer who arrests Goebbels and receives a counterorder from Hitler on the telephone); Kenneth Colley (*Wilhelm Keitel*, Field Marshal & Chief of the High Command); Michael Fitzgerald (*Major Ernst von Freyend*, Keitel's aide); Ian Richardson (*Ludwig von Beck*, Retired general & leader of anti–Hitler group); Helmut Griem (*Erwin Rommel*, Field Marshal & leader of *Afrika Korps* who later conspires against Hitler); Jack Hedley (*Werner von Haeften*, Stauffenberg's aide); John McEnery (*General Adolf Heusinger*, Officer injured in bomb blast); Vernon Dobtcheff (*General Erich Fellgiebel*, Officer in charge of disrupting communications from Rastenburg); Rupert Graves (*Major Axel von dem Büssche-Streithorst*, Officer who turns against Hitler after witnessing the mass shooting of Jews); Christopher Einhorn (*General Helmuth Steiff*, Anti-Hitler conspirator); Burkhard Heyl (*Colonel Albrecht Mertz von Quirnheim*, Stauffenberg's friend and fellow conspirator); Paul Herzberg (*Constantin von Dietz*, Professor opposed to Hitler); Heather Chasen (Nina's mother); Bradley Kleyne (*Berthold*, Stauffenberg's eldest son); Nirit Einik (*Valerie*, Stauffenberg's daughter); Eliak Einik (*Franz*, Stauffenberg's youngest child).

APPRAISAL AND SYNOPSIS: *The Plot to Kill Hitler*, unlike *Jackboot Mutiny*, the other major film on the Rastenburg assassination attempt, presents a rather different focus, concentrating primarily on the character, motivation and background of Count Claus von Stauffenberg. The 1990 telefilm, in fact, would have more appropriately been called *Stauffenberg*, except that title would lack any recognition value for the average television audience. *The Plot to Kill Hitler* compliments rather than supplants *Jackboot Mutiny*, adding additional detail and a human drama at the heart of the story. Perhaps some of the poignancy of the film is due to the exceptional portrayal of Stauffenberg by Brad Davis, who was seriously ill with AIDS while the picture was being filmed. Davis died later that the same year. The film was principally shot in Yugoslavia, and the locations add an authentic feel to the production. The only serious miscalculation is the luxurious setting of the living quarters at Wolf's Lair in Rastenburg, featuring marble floors and a huge dinning hall with columns. In truth, the Wolf's Lair headquarters was rather simple and rustic. Another improvement compared to the other bomb plot films is that the role of Hitler is far better integrated into the overall storyline. Kenneth Colley, Admiral Piett from the *Star Wars* trilogy, is excellent as General Keitel, and so is Ian Richardson as General von Beck. But too many of the other supporting actors deliver static readings that weaken the plot at key moments. Then there are other flaws, such as the pacing of the film which is uneven, and the numerous scenes which seem pedestrian and dry, lacking any spark whatsoever. The technical support is solid, and the musical score by Laurence Rosenthal is quite good.

The film opens as Stauffenberg is winged by a bullet as forces loyal to Hitler storm Army Headquarters in Berlin after the revolt collapses on the evening of July 20, 1944. A flashback takes us to Africa in April 1943, at a meeting in which Stauffenberg and Field Marshal Rommel exchange treasonous opinions about the mental fitness of Adolf Hitler. This sequence helps to establish the fact that Stauffenberg's opposition to Hitler was not due in any fashion to his wartime injuries.

After he is seriously wounded by an exploding shell, Stauffenberg faces a long, slow recovery, gradually learning to function with the loss of his right hand, left eye and two fingers from his left hand. His wife and children offer him total support as he mends. His wife also approves his decision to return to active duty. Stauffenberg consults with General von Beck, the former head of the army who resigned in protest to Hitler and his policies. Beck confesses that he has been behind numerous attempts on Hitler's life, all of which had failed, and time is running

out. The count agrees to dedicate his efforts to the overthrow of the Nazi regime.

As a military analyst, Stauffenberg's talents are put to immediate use at Berlin Army Headquarters. He also makes contact with a network of officers who are members of the German resistance, including General Olbricht. The count proposes a framework for emergency military actions on the home front, known as the Walküre alert, to be used in case of revolt. Hitler is delighted when he hears these ideas, and he summons the count to Berchtesgaden together with General Fromm, head of the home army.

Receiving the Führer's personal approval for his plans, Stauffenberg actually intends to use the Walküre alert to overthrow Nazi officials and seize control of the government. The assassination of Hitler is the key event, setting the revolt in motion. The plan calls for the liberation of the concentration camps, the cessation of the slaughter of the Jews and other persecuted people, and the opening of immediate peace negotiations with the Allies. He sounds out a number of the military commanders in the field, such as Rommel. In this second scene with Rommel, another key point is stressed. The crucial decision to dispose of Hitler would still be essential if Germany had been winning the war, due to the inhuman and shameful issue of the death camps. General Fromm catches wind of the conspiracy, and he tells the count that he will not openly support it, but he wants a position in the new government if their plans are successful. Stauffenberg sounds out individuals who could carry out the assassination of Hitler, and comes to the conclusion that only he himself of all the conspirators had regular access to the Führer, who wanted regular briefings from him on the home army.

The second half of the film covers the events of July 20th, which closely resemble the sequence of events as portrayed in *Jackboot Mutiny*, eliminating the need to repeat any additional synopsis of the action. The major difference is that *The Plot to Kill Hitler* also covers the viewpoints of Countess

Stauffenberg, as well as the Führer himself, after the bomb blast. The film ends as Countess Stauffenberg holds Berthold, her eldest son, while listening to Hitler's speech announcing the crushing of the revolt. A closing narration speaks of the victims of the Führer's revenge, but ends on the positive note that after the end of the war, Countess Stauffenberg was released from prison and reunited with her children, and that Count Stauffenberg is honored as a true patriot and hero after the war.

HITLER PORTRAYAL: Mike Gwilym is a noted Shakespearean performer best known for his many BBC appearances in the Bard's plays such as *Coriolanus*, *Love's Labors Lost*, *Comedy of Errors*, and, most importantly, the title role in *Pericles, Prince of Tyre*. Gwilym has craggy features and a block-like forehead that at first glance seem unsuited to the role, but his acting skills quickly overcome the physical differences to render a rather cogent Hitler portrayal. He attempts to bring a variety of shadings to the role which makes his conception far better than average. For example, he keeps Hitler's volcanic rages to a minimum. He avoids any accent in his dialogue for the most part, keeping his voice in the lower register for the most part and making effective use of the whisper. Gwilym is aided by a decent use of makeup, particularly in his disheveled appearance after the bomb blast. He doesn't rant or rave but is generally matter-of-fact, but with a smoldering intensity just below the surface. When he vows to obliterate the conspirators, he doesn't need to shout it, since he knows as a certainty that his wishes will come to pass. Gwilym is also aided by a script which incorporates as many authentic Hitler utterances as possible. His speech which concludes the film is, in fact, a verbatim translation of the actual broadcast delivered by Hitler without any embellishment. The only disappointment is that the Führer's meeting with Mussolini after the blast is not included.

REPRESENTATIVE QUOTES

• You are a realist. *(Stauffenberg to Rommel, in Africa, 1943)* And the Führer? *(Rommel)* Mad, I'm afraid. *(Stauffenberg)* Dangerous words, Count Stauffenberg. *(Rommel)* Dangerous times, Marshal Rommel. *(Stauffenberg)*

• Of all the animals on the face of the earth, which do you think is the strongest. *(Hitler to Fromm, during dinner at Berchtesgaden)* Wouldn't that be the elephant? *(Fromm)* That is correct. The elephant indeed is the strongest animal, and he also cannot stand meat! *(Hitler)*

• How do you like my new trousers? ... I'm receiving Il Duce this afternoon. Il Duce deserves my new trousers, don't you think? *(Hitler to his aide as he heads to the General staff meeting)*

• They can't kill me. Don't they know that by now? ... I'm the child of fate. Providence has spared me to complete my mission. My destiny will be fulfilled. *(Hitler to himself, after Keitel informs him that the bomb had been planted by Stauffenberg)*

72. *The Producers* (AKA *Springtime for Hitler*) (1968)

Dick Shawn as a caricature of Adolf Hitler
Comedy

Embassy. Written by Mel Brooks; Photographed by Joseph Coffey; Edited by Ralph Rosenbloom; Music by John Morris & Mel Brooks; Produced by Joseph E. Levine; Directed by Mel Brooks. Color 88 minutes

ANNOTATED CAST LIST: Zero Mostel (*Max Bialystock*, Theatrical producer fallen on hard times); Gene Wilder (*Leo Bloom*, Timid accountant who becomes Max's partner); Dick Shawn (*Lorenzo St. DuBois*, Hippie actor who stars as Hitler); Christopher Hewitt (*Roger DeBris*, Extravagant play director); Andreas Voutsinas (*Carmen Giya*, DeBris' private secretary); Kenneth Mars (*Franz Liebkind*, Author of *Springtime for Hitler*); Madlyn Cates (Liebkind's concierge); Lee Meredith (*Ulla*, Max's new secretary); John Zoller (*New York Times* drama critic); Shimen Ruskin (Max's landlord); Brutus Peck (Hot dog vendor); Josip Elie (Restaurant violinist); Frank Campanella (Bartender); William Hickey (Man in bar); Bill Macy (Jury Foreman); Old lady show investors: Estelle Winwood ("Hold me, Touch me"); Anne Ives (Leaving office); Amelie Barleon (On coach); Lisa Kirk (On motorcycle); Nell Harrison (With hearing aid); Mary Love (In restaurant); Cast call Hitlers: Arthur Rubin (*Arthur Picard*, "A Wandering Minstrel I"); Zale Kessler (*Jason Green*, "Have you ever heard ze German band"); Bernie Allen ("The Little Wooden Boy"); Rusty Blitz ("Beautiful dreamer"); Anthony Gardella (Cowboy Hitler); Springtime for Hitler cast: Renee Taylor (*Eva Braun*); Barney Martin (*Hermann Göring*); David Patch (*Joseph Goebbels*); David Evans (*Rolf*); Tucker Smith (Lead dancer); Michael Davis (Lead tenor); Mel Brooks (Bit singer).

APPRAISAL AND SYNOPSIS: Mel Brooks' first comedy film, *The Producers*, was a blockbuster for which he won the Academy Award for best original screenplay. It also resurrected the career of Zero Mostel and made a star out of Gene Wilder. Wacky and irreverent, it also began a trademark of Brooks to use Hitler as a target of ridicule in his work. With his approach, Brooks makes a statement as profound as any by the historians, philosophers and theologians whose positions have been examined in Ron Rosenbaum's brilliant *Explaining Hitler*. By turning Hitler from a figure of evil and loathsomeness into a mere buffoon, Brooks demonstrates the life-affirming fortitude and spirit of not only the Jewish people, but of humanity as a whole.

The basic storyline of *The Producers* is relatively simple. Max Bialystock, once a Broadway producer of stature, is reduced to developing shoestring shows using funds that he raises by courting wealthy widows. When his accountant, Leo Bloom, comments that it is possible to make more money by putting on a flop, Max seizes upon the idea. He makes Leo his partner and seeks out the worst play imaginable. He finds it in *Springtime for Hitler*, a musical that is virtually "a love letter to Hitler" written by a former Nazi living in Manhattan. They meet Franz Liebkind, the strange author, and convince him that they wish to bring his vision of "Hitler with a song in his heart" to the Broadway stage. Max next secures the services of Roger DeBris, a crossdressing director totally lacking in talent. Max then goes on a fund raising campaign among the old lady investors, raising a thousand times the amount needed to finance the show. An open casting call is launched to find the worse possible performer to play Hitler. Max decides on Lorenzo St. DuBois, an almost incoherent hippie who prefers being called "L.S.D."

When the show opens, Max tries to insure its failure by attempting to bribe the drama critic of the *New York Times*. From the back of the theater, Max and Leo watch the opening number of the show, an absurd Busby Berkeley inspired number including showgirls dressed as Valkyries in costumes decorated with eagles, beer steins, pretzels and Nazi medals. A tenor sings the title song with lyrics such as, "We're marching to a faster pace. Look out, here comes the master race! Springtime for Hitler and Germany, winter for Poland and France. Springtime for Hitler and Germany, come on Germans, go into your dance." The tap routine that follows includes goose steps and swastika formations. The audience is numbed into silence by this extravagant display of bad taste. Max and Leo leave the theater, convinced the show will be a colossal flop. However, once L.S.D. appears as Hitler, the audience starts to roar, thinking the show to be a hip satire. Waiting in a local bar, Max and Leo are shocked when intermission comes and the bar fills up with theater goers buzzing with excitement over the show. They watch the second act, utterly baffled by the audience reaction. The following day, Max is depressed by the

Dick Shawn and Renee Taylor as comic Adolf and Eva in *The Producers*.

glowing reviews. Leo threatens to surrender to the police and confess their scheme. Franz Liebkind shows up and threatens to shoot them since the show was an insult to Hitler. Max convinces him to blow up the theater instead. However, they use the wrong fuse and get trapped in the explosion. At their trial, Leo speaks up for Max, saying that he was the only person ever to make him happy. When Max, Leo and Liebkind get sentenced to prison, they hit upon a new scheme, and put on a show with the convicts called *Prisoners of Love*. They also begin to oversell the show with backers including the warden and other prisoners.

The Producers is a unique, madcap production, unlike anything seen since the original *Hellzapoppin'* or the early Marx Brothers films. Brooks' direction, script and pacing are excellent. The cast is magnificent. The satirical staging of the opening number is one of the most unforgettable scenes in motion picture history. The humor is sometimes risqué and vulgar, but it succeeds time and again in reducing audiences to convulsive, side-splitting laughter. There is also a subtle level to much of the proceedings. Consider the names of the characters, almost all of which have unusual references. Bialystock comes from the city of Bialystok in Poland, under Soviet control in 1941 and one of the first to fall in the Nazi invasion of Russia. Leo Bloom is an allusion to the leading character of James Joyce's *Ulysses*. The Nazi author's name, Liebkind, literally means "Love child" in German, or, in other words, a bastard. The name of Roger DeBris sounds like a synonym for rubbish. Carmen Giya is based on Karmann Ghia, a model of the Volkswagon (which also is linked to

Hitler, since he sketched the original Volkswagon design). So there are level upon level with some of the jokes.

In 2001, Mel Brooks revamped *The Producers* as a Broadway musical, adding a batch of clever new songs. Starring Nathan Lane as Max and Matthew Broderick as Leo, this show became a megahit. It is interesting to note that he eliminated the character of L.S.D. and had Roger DeBris take over the part of the Führer in *Springtime for Hitler*. The show, an unqualified success, is expected to run for years.

HITLER PORTRAYAL: An entire stageful of Hitlers is featured in the casting scene of *Springtime for Hitler*. Very few of them resemble Hitler, which is what makes the scene so hilarious. There is a fat one who resembles Oliver Hardy, a hunk in a bathing suit, Hitlers in various different uniforms, Hitlers in business suits, tall Hitlers, bald Hitlers, Prussian Hitlers, even a Hitler dressed as a cowboy. Remarkably, there is one dead ringer for Hitler, played by Bernie Allen, who also looks remarkably like Bobby Watson. He is dressed in a tuxedo, but Max dismisses him before he can sing a note, judging, no doubt, that the actor's close resemblance would be far too good for *Springtime for Hitler*. Dick Shawn, of course, looks nothing like Hitler. His curly locks not even changed into the traditional Hitler hairstyle. He even wears an earring during the show. His costumes in the show, at least, are sometimes lederhosen, sometimes typical Hitler uniforms. Shawn performs with wacky, surreal zest as a befuddled, stoned hippie. His wild take off is at its finest in his exchanges with Renee Taylor as a daffy Eva Braun and David Patch, who is priceless as a cool Doc Goebbels. Although Shawn sings at his audition, he is not given a song in the show itself, perhaps the only disappointment of his rendition.

REPRESENTATIVE QUOTES

• Let me tell us this, and you are hearing it straight from the horse. Hitler was better looking than Churchill. He was a better dresser than Churchill. He had more hair. He told funnier jokes and he could dance the pants off of Churchill. *(Liebkind to Max and Leo)*

• You know, I never knew the Third Reich meant Germany. I mean it is drenched with historical goodies like that. *(DeBris to Max, discussing Springtime for Hitler)*

• Don't be stupid, be a smarty, come and join the Nazi party. *(Mel Brooks' line in the show's opening song)*

• Baby, baby, why does he say this baby? The Führer has never said baby. *(Liebkind to himself while sitting in the audience)*

• I just laid the morning propaganda progress on the people... I told the people we invaded England *(Goebbels in show to Hitler)* That's a groove, daddy. How did we come out? *(Hitler)* We beat 'em, baby. *(Goebbels)* Groovy, that's my Joe. That's my Little Joe. I love my Little Joe. *(Hitler)*

73. *Ring of Passion* (AKA *Countdown to the Big One*) (1978)

Barry Dennen as Adolf Hitler
Historical drama

20th Century–Fox. Written by Larry Forrester; Photographed by Jules Brenner; Edited by Sidney Katz; Music by Bill Conti; Produced by Lou Moreheim; Directed by Robert Michael Lewis. Color 97 minutes

ANNOTATED CAST LIST: Bernie Casey *(Joe Louis)*; Stephen Macht *(Max Schmeling)*; Britt Ekland *(Anny Ondra Schmeling)*; Allen Garfield *(Damon Runyan)*; Percy Rodriguez *(John Roxborough)*; Joseph Campanella *(Paul Gallico)*; Norman Alden *(Max Machon)*; Julius Harris *(Chappie Blackburn)*; Mordecai Lawner *(Joe Jacobs)*; Al Lewis *(Mike Jacobs)*; Shaka Cumbuka *(Honey Bear)*; Mel Stewart *(Julian Black)*; Denise Nichols *(Marva Trotter Louis)*; Beah Richards *(Lily Brooks)*; Wonderful Smith (Minister); Geo Latka *(Referee Donovan)*; Stephen Roberts *(Franklin D. Roosevelt)*; Johnny Heymer (Nazi official); Clement St. George (German commentator).

COMMENTARY: *Ring of Passion* was broadcast February 4, 1978, on NBC, received indifferent reviews, and quietly disappeared from the scene, receiving few if any local station rebroadcasts. Boxing fans were most critical, decrying the unconvincing and relatively brief ring sequences and objecting to the soap opera character of the family lives of the two boxers, Max Schmeling and Joe Louis. Schmeling was a former heavyweight boxing champion who lost the title in a controversial split decision, prompting his American manager, Joe Jacobs, to issue the famous comment, "We wuz robbed!" The two Louis-Schmeling matches occurred in June 1936 and June 1938. At the time, Schmeling was considered past his prime and overmatched. However, Schmeling unexpectedly tagged the undefeated Louis, knocking him out in the 12th round of their first match. Two years later, having won the world championship, Joe Louis again fought Schmeling, and their rematch evolved into a propaganda war, with both fighters (particularly Schmeling) becoming unwilling symbols of their nation's political ideologies. Louis was at the top of his game in this ballyhooed second match, decisively knocking out Schmeling in the first round. In real life, Schmeling was quite different than the idealized German superman portrayed by the Nazi propagandists. For example, his manager, Joe Jacobs, was Jewish, and Schmeling refused to dump him despite pressure from the Nazis. During the war, Schmeling became a paratrooper and war hero, but he also rescued two Jewish boys from Nazi persecution and helped smuggle them to America. After the war, Schmeling made a brief attempt at a comeback. He later succeeded in business, landing a soft drink distributorship and becoming wealthy. Schmeling is still alive at the time of this writing, and he is perhaps the only individual surviving until the 21st century who had known and spoken with both Hitler and Roosevelt. In the film, Hitler was played by Barry Dennen, and his performance was considered brusque and unconvincing by one commentator, but adequate by several others. Dennen was Barbara Steisand's first boyfriend. As an actor, he is best remembered as Pontius Pilate in both the Broadway and film versions of *Jesus Christ Superstar*. Of the other actors, Bernie Casey and Stephen Macht received lukewarm notices, with only Britt Ekland, as Schmeling's actress wife Anny Ondra (the star of two early Hitchcock films) and Julian Harris getting rave notices.

74. *Rogue Male* (1976)
Michael Sheard as Adolf Hitler
Thriller

BBC. Written by Frederic Raphael based on the novel by Geoffrey Household; Photographed by Brian Tufano; Edited by Dan Rae; Music by Chris Gunning; Produced by Mark Shivas; Directed by Clive Donner. Color 100 minutes

ANNOTATED CAST LIST: Peter O'Toole (*Sir Robert*, British sportsman who stalks Hitler); Alastair Sim (The Earl, Sir Robert's uncle); Michael Byrne (Gestapo interrogator); John Standing (*Major Quive-Smith*, Nazi agent in England); Harold Pinter (*Saul Abrahams*, Sir Robert's solicitor); Hugh Manning (*Peale*, Saul's clerk); Robert Lang (*Jessel*, Sir Robert's valet); Ian East (*Muller*, Quive-Smith's henchman); Dennis Chinnery (Nazi agent killed in the subway); Cyd Hayman (*Rebecca*, Robert's beloved killed by the Nazis); Ray Smith (German fisherman who helps Sir Robert); Mark McManus (*Vaner*, First mate who hides Sir Robert aboard ship); George Seeway (*Jensen*, Ship's captain); Declan Mulholland (Ship's cook); Philip Jackson, Nicholas Ball (Seamen in beer garden); Ray Mort (*Gerald*, Man who sells his bike to Sir Robert); Maureen Lipman (*Freda*, Gerald's girlfriend); Ivor Roberts (*Drake*, Farmer who rents a room to Quive-Smith); Jean Rimmer (Postmistress at Lyme Regis); Julia Chambers (*Mary*, Daughter of the postmistress); Shirley Dynevor (*Eva Braun*, Hitler's mistress).

APPRAISAL AND SYNOPSIS: *Rogue Male* is a fascinating film which stands up quite well in comparison to Fritz Lang's version, *Man Hunt*. Both productions, in fact, are rather fine adaptations of the original novel by Geoffrey Household. In fact, portions of Frederic Raphael's screenplay are taken from the Lang film as well as the novel. The plot itself is virtually identical, as synopsized in the entry on *Man Hunt*, although with a handful of details jumbled around. A brief comparison is in order, since it does credit to both productions. In the novel, the protagonist is unnamed. The Lang film dubs him Captain Alan Thorndike. The same character is now called Sir Robert, with no last name ever mentioned. In *Man Hunt*, Thorndike is the brother of an important politician, Lord Risborough. In the BBC version, he is the nephew of an important Earl, again not identified by name. In the original novel, no such character existed. The seamstress character, the love interest, is also original with the Lang film, but dropped from *Rogue Male*. The Lang film merges the Gestapo interrogator with Major Quive-Smith, whereas the later film keeps their identities separate, as in the novel. Vaner is a cabin boy in the first film, and the first mate in the remake and the book. *Rogue Male* wisely includes an encounter with a German sportsman fishing in the river. Sir Robert drops any pretense, and openly tells the man his situation. The man asks him if he is being pursued because he is Jewish. Sir Robert says he is not, but admits the matter is political. The fisherman agrees to help him, casting a glance in the direction of Berchtesgaden and pronouncing the Nazis to be nothing but "scum." This encounter is extraordinarily moving and well played, one of the picture's highlights. All things considered, *Rogue Male* is closer to the original text, but it has a few innovations of its own. Sir Robert is given motivation for his hatred of Hitler by memories of a lost love, Rebecca, who was killed by the Nazis. Whereas the original film had many lighter touches, the remake is deadly serious, except for some very British witticisms quipped by the Earl, who calls his nephew "Bobbity," such as equating Saskatchewan with hell. Major Quive-Smith, in this version a genuine Englishman as in the novel, lays on the British upper crust bit somewhat too thick. In the first film, our hero kills him with an arrow-shaped hatpin. In the latter, he is killed by the fountain pen he provides to Sir Robert. The time frame is more nebulous in the remake, and at times the process by which Quive-Smith tracks down Sir Robert (using a hunting tactics book written by Sir Robert) is far too smug. The music in these pastoral scenes sounds very reminiscent of that of Ralph Vaughan-Williams. At times, the different mood makes it feel that a sequence from a different movie had been edited in by error. The scene of Sir Robert trapped in his cave also goes on a bit two long. Quive-Smith even takes time to leave and return to the site three times, leaving a henchman on guard while he is gone.

The acting and directing are strong trump cards in both films. Peter O'Toole is particularly intense, recalling his impassioned portrayal of Lawrence of Arabia. Harold Pinter, best known as a writer, gives a rare and exceptional performance as Sir Robert's solicitor. Note how his expression changes as he repeats the name "Adolf" three times after Sir Robert states that he tried to "pop off" the Führer. Clive Donner's direction is taut and sparkling, and the editing and cinematography are first rate. A final comparison centers on the hero's inner convictions. In the Lang film, one believes that Thorndike was actually on a sporting stalk, the same feeling isn't true about Sir Robert. His mention of it during his interrogation sounds hollow, a weak excuse tossed off. This, of course, weakens the finale in the remake. In *Man Hunt*, Thorndike has a sudden realization that he was an unconscious assassin, a brilliant moment which the remake is unable to match. Instead, after killing Quive-Smith and warding off his henchman, Sir Robert visits his uncle again, who suggests that he visit "Winston" at the Admiralty to see if he can use him. Instead, he decides to resume his stalk of Hitler, as in the novel and the Lang picture.

HITLER PORTRAYAL: Michael Sheard's appearance as Hitler is rather expanded compared to Carl Ekberg's cameo in *Man Hunt*, where the Führer only appears in Alan Thorndike's gunsights. The home movies of Eva Braun shot at the Berghof were no doubt studied in preparing the sequence. Two servants are first shown bringing platters of refreshments out onto the patio. Then Eva Braun is seen as she pours tea while seated at a table. Someone snaps a picture of her as she hands a cup to her companion. Playfully, she pulls the cup away as the Führer's hands appear, and he wags his finger at her. Eva hands the cup over, while in the distance, Sir Robert Thorndike prepares his rifle for firing. Next we see the lower half of the Führer's body as he stands upon the stone wall, and he speaks to Eva, sitting below, positioning her for the next snapshot. As she raises her legs, he says, "Ja, gut." Sir Robert aims and the crosshairs of his rifle line up first on Eva, and then shift up to focus on Hitler's face, seen in profile. The Führer turns slightly, and Sir Robert aims at his chest for his target. The photographer takes his snapshot, and the other guests on the patio applaud. Hitler is seen for the third time through the gunsights, and Thorndike loads the rifle. Four additional targeting views are depicted, when a German guard, chasing after a pheasant, sees Sir Robert and jumps him. The screen goes blank as the sound of a shot is heard on the soundtrack. As Sir Robert's interrogation proceeds, the scene shifts back to the patio. Eva places a record on her phonograph and walks back to Hitler's side. They wander to a seat near a flower garden. At this moment, Sir Robert is being tortured as his finger nails are pulled out. We see a two-shot of Eva and Hitler together. The Führer strokes his head with his left hand, then reaches down to touch Eva's hand as they look into each other's eyes. Eva's phonograph drowns out the sounds of Sir Robert's screams. The irony of this cozy interlude between the Führer and his mistress is brilliantly illuminated by the torture going on in the back-

ground. Beneath the surface, the brutal nature of the Nazi regime is clearly revealed.

On the whole, this is the most convincing of Sheard's appearances as Hitler. If a viewer only saw the last clip of Hitler and Eva by itself, he would find it very difficult to distinguish it from a genuine excerpt of Eva's actual Berchtesgaden home movies. Credit must also be given to Shirley Dynevor for her effective and credible performance as Eva Braun. Both she and Michael Sheard make their brief scene seem very natural.

REPRESENTATIVE QUOTES

• Life is not a game of cricket, my friend. *(Gestapo interrogator to Sir Robert, when he mentions the rules of a sporting stalk)* No? Pity. *(Sir Robert's comment)*

• Who did this? *(The Earl to Sir Robert, when he notices his wounded eye)* A follower of your friend Adolf. *(Sir Robert)* The mad Mullah? Well, I know he does employ some very funny folk, but isn't that going a bit far? What did you do? *(The Earl)* Pointed a gun at his master *(Sir Robert)*

• He may look like a middle class denture salesman, but he is, after all, His Majesty's first minister… Neville has this Hitler fellow mesmerized, you wait and see. *(The Earl, commenting on Chamberlain)*

• Whatever use will it be? No one will ever see it. There isn't going to be a war. Your Führer has promised, and we all know that if a man like that gives his promise… *(Sir Robert, referring to his signed confession, to Quive-Smith)* I told you it is a pure formality, unless someone on your side gets up to some nonsense and tries to foment a war against this country's natural allies. *(Quive-Smith)*

75. *Schtonk!* (1992)

Günther Bader as Adolf Hitler (cameo)
Comedy

Bavarian Films. Written by Ulrich Limmer & Helmut Dieti; Photographed by Xaver Schwarzenberger; Edited by Tanja

Schmidbauer; Music by Konstantin Wecker, Franz Liszt & Richard Wagner; Produced by Gunter Rohrbach & Helmut Dieti; Directed by Helmut Dieti. Color 115 minutes

ANNOTATED CAST LIST: Uwe Ochsenknecht (*Fritz Knobel*, Artist & Hitler forger); Götz George (*Hermann Willie*, Unscrupulous reporter); Dagmar Manzel (*Biggi*, Fritz's wife); Veronica Ferres (*Martha*, Model & Fritz's mistress); Christine Hörbiger (*Freya von Hepp*, Göring's niece); Martin Benrath (*Uwe Esser*, Publisher of *HH* magazine); Harald Juhnike (*Kummer*, *HH* editor); Herman Lause (*Kurt Glück*); Rolf Hoppe (*Karl Lentz*, Industrialist fascinated by the Nazis); Rosemarie Fendel (*Mrs. Lentz*, His wife); Ulrich Mühe (*Dr. Lentz*); Karl Schönböck (*Professor Strasser*, Elderly friend of Lentz who had known Hitler); Georg Manschka (*Von Klantz*, Obese Nazi at Lentz's party); Eva Marie Kerkhoff (*Wieland*, Secretary); Thomas Holtzmann (*Cornelius*, Notary); Hark Böhm (Catholic pastor); Thomas Tipton (American GI who buys Hitler's hat); Robert Chaikey (*Fritz Knobel*, Age 9 in post-war Berlin); Peter Roggisch (Nazi officer); Martin Feifel, Thomas Wupper, Michael Kessler, Armin Rohde (SS men); Beate Loibl (*Eva Braun*, Hitler's mistress).

APPRAISAL AND SYNOPSIS: In 1983, the German weekly magazine *Stern* began to publish excerpts attributed to the secret diaries of Hitler. A worldwide bidding war arose for publication rights in various countries. Only after the first excerpt was published in English was the forgery exposed as the work of Konrad Kujau, an artist who had created a number of paintings attributed to Hitler that were sold to private collectors. The German comedy *Schtonk!* weaves the facts of this case into an elaborate farce. The title, incidentally, is a reference to Charlie Chaplin's doubletalk from *The Great Dictator* when he says, "Democratzie schtonk! Liberty schtonk!"

The film opens during the Battle of Berlin. Four SS men carry Hitler's body out of the bunker together with that of Eva Braun. They have difficulty burning the bodies. Soldiers are running around, and the projection speed is subtly increased, making their movements resemble a silent comedy. The shot of the flaming bodies dissolves to that of a young boy, Fritz Knobel, carefully forging Hitler's autograph from a reproduction in a book. Fritz then sells Hitler memorabilia to American soldiers stationed in the war-torn Berlin. One soldier buys a hat from him, believing it belonged to Hitler. The action jumps forward forty years, and Fritz, unhappily married to Biggi, is still working as a forger. He paints a nude, full length portrait of Eva Braun using a farm girl named Martha as his model, and she afterwards becomes his mistress. Attributing the painting to Hitler, he sells it to Karl Lentz, a wealthy tycoon. Meanwhile, Hermann Willie, a tabloid journalist, is working on an article about Hermann Göring. He buys the wreckage of Göring's old yacht, *Carin II*, and makes the acquaintance of Freya von Hepp, the Reich Marshal's beautiful niece. They soon begin an affair. When he tries to sell his story to *HH*, a well-known Hamburg weekly publication, his work is rejected. Kummer, his contact at the magazine, urges him to try to come up with a really big story.

Fritz learns from Professor Strasser, a friend of Lentz, that ten iron boxes containing Hitler's private papers were lost in a plane crash during the final days of the Third Reich. This inspires Fritz to begin to forge one of these lost diaries. Fritz makes a careless mistake, however, putting the letters "FH" instead of "AH" on the cover of one of the volumes, but he lets it go, thinking it could represent the title "Führer Hitler" instead of the initials of his name. (This is a detail from the actual case.) Lentz sponsors a huge party at his castle in honor of Hitler's 100th birthday, including an evening torchlight parade. Willie meets Fritz Knobel at the event, and he is intrigued by the diary, smelling a huge story. Lentz reads reverently from the diary in front of a giant bust of Hitler, and several former Nazi guests,

Strasser and von Klantz pronounce it to be unquestionably authentic.

Willie makes a huge advance deal with *HH* for first publication rights to the Hitler diaries. When Fritz is given his share for the first volume, he promises to "uncover" additional volumes. Writing them proves more difficult, and Fritz begins to use some of his own personal experiences as filler when his imagination begins to falter. But as the volumes are published, Willie and Fritz become rich. Willie restores and refurbishes the elaborate Göring yacht, sparing no expense. Fritz's wife learns of his affair, but accepts it. The Hamburg publisher brings in handwriting experts to verify the authenticity of the diaries, but since they wind up using as their authentic model another forgery previously sold by Fritz, they pronounce the volumes to be completely authentic. (This again is an actual detail that happened in the case.)

Success begins to make Fritz and Willie more reckless, and they begin to work at cross purposes. Fritz tries to market an urn which he claims holds the ashes of Hitler and Eva. Willie, on the other hand, tries to sell an expose that Hitler is still alive. Willie is honored with a special award for journalism. In his mind, he equates the enthusiasm at the presentation with that of the Nazi party rallies. He gets a swelled head and is dumped by Freya. When the Hitler diaries are placed up for bid to secure the international publication rights, the scheme comes crashing down when experts denounce the works as forgeries. Fritz flees with his wife and girlfriend. The police close in on Willie as he speeds off on the Göring yacht.

Schtonk! was a fairly successful comedy, but it received limited distribution outside Germany and Austria. The film has numerous highlights, but few match the clever opening sequence with Hitler's corpse. It is amusing when Fritz uses ashes from his wood stove to pass as those of the Führer. Then there is the wild musical version of "La Poloma" sung on *Carin II* with the lyrics changed to "Hermann Hermann," apparently honoring both Willie and Göring. Uwe Ochsenknecht and Götz George are quite amusing as the two leads. Ochsenknecht seems like a wild cross between Larry Fine and Gene Wilder, and his Hitler obsession is cunningly portrayed. George resembles a tall Terry-Thomas with thick plastic horn-rimmed glasses. While entertaining, the film also has its share of flaws. It is poorly edited and overlong. It could easily be trimmed by one third, cutting out several slow spots. The ending is particularly weak, closing the picture in a disappointing fashion.

HITLER PORTRAYAL: Since Günther Bader plays Hitler as a corpse, there is little one can say except that his resemblance to Hitler is remarkable. A bullet hole is visible on his right temple, with a small trickle of dried blood beneath the wound. As he is placed in a crater with Eva, one of the SS men removes a comb from his pocket and gently combs the Führer's hair into place. He then plucks a stray hair from Hitler's moustache, and carefully positions him besides Eva. After several attempts, he is unable to set Hitler's body on fire, however, and the SS man sheepishly reports back to an officer. They then drench his body with additional gasoline, and this time, when the officer tosses a match, the body erupts like a small bonfire. This entire scene is scored first with a wartime ballad, followed by satirical music, providing the entire proceeding with an unmistakable air of slapstick.

REPRESENTATIVE QUOTES

• He doesn't burn. *(SS man to officer at Hitler's cremation)*

• Forty years dead and still smelling sweaty. *(HH staff member to Willie while sniffing Göring's old robe)*

• The superhuman strain recently causes me gas, and Eva says I have bad breath. *(Entry in Hitler's forged diary read by Willie to HH representatives)* The private Adolf Hitler! *(Older editor, reverently)* A man like you or I. *(Younger editor)*

76. *Sekretnaja Missija* (1950)

V. Savelyev as Adolf Hitler

Thriller

Mosfilm. Written by Konstantin Isayev & M. Maklyarskii; Photographed by Boris Volchek; Edited by E. Ladyzhenskaya; Music by Aram Khachaturian; Produced by V. Viktorov & L. Indenbom; Directed by Mikhail Romm. B & W 91 minutes

CAST LIST: Kalyu Komissarov (*Senator Nicholas*); Yelena Kuzmina (*Marta*); Sergei Vecheslavov (*Garvi*); P. Berezov (*Heinrich Himmler*); V. Belokurov (*Martin Bormann*); M. Perkovsky (*Ernst Kaltenbrunner*); A. Pelevin (*General Schellenberg*); M. Vysockey (*Winston Churchill*); M. Gaideburov *(Rodgers)*; Vladimir Garden (*Dillon*); N. Timofev (American pilot); Vailly Makarov (*Dementyev*); Alexei Gribov (Soviet Intelligence officer); Aleksandr Vhrban (Soviet Intelligence Officer); A. Khokhlov (*Krupp*); L. Fedin (*Lyons*); A. Antonov (*Schitte*).

COMMENTARY: This Russian film, *Sekretnaja Missija*, literally translated as *Secret Mission* is an anti–American propaganda film, in the same spirit as *Fall of Berlin*. In fact, the film uses the same actor, V. Savelyev, who played Hitler in the earlier film, and reportedly his performance here is of the same caliber, bordering on uncontrolled hysteria. The setting of the plot is December 1944 and January 1945, involving an American Senator and a secret agent who try to arrange a separate peace with Nazi Germany, so the Germans could concentrate their forces against the Soviet Union. The scheme falls through, however, thanks to intervention by Russian secret agents working in Germany. The picture ends, however, with warning that American is planning new aggression against the Soviet Union. This film was only moderately successful. It was revived in 1969, and shorted by six minutes, removing a portion of the Stalinst propaganda. The film is only remembered today due to the soundtrack by Aram Khachaturian, which has been arranged into a suite and recorded on a recent CD album of Khachaturian film scores (ASV DCA 966).

77. *Shining Through* (1992)

Ludwig Haas as Adolf Hitler (cameo)

Romance/Adventure

20th Century–Fox. Written by David Seltzer based on the novel by Susan Isaacs; Photographed by Jan de Bont; Edited by Craig McKay; Music by Michael Kamen; Produced by Carol Baum & Howard Rosenman; Directed by David Seltzer. Color 127 minutes

ANNOTATED CAST LIST: Melanie Griffith (*Linda Voss*, Secretary who goes on a spy mission to Berlin posing as a cook named Lena); Michael Douglas (*Colonel Ed Leland*, American Intelligence officer); Liam Neeson (*General Franz-Otto Dietrich*, German officer involved with weapons development); John Gielgud (*Konrad Friedrichs*, German working for Allied Intelligence); Joely Richardson (*Margrete von Eberstein*, German aristocrat who assists Friedrichs); Sheila Allen (*Olga Leiner*, Margrete's mother, a famous concert pianist); Francis Guinan (*Andrew Berringer*, Ed's assistant); Patrick Winczewski (Berlin fishmonger who serves as courier for Allied intelligence); Andrew Walters (*Peter*, Dietrich's son); Victoria Shalet (Dietrich's daughter); Stanley Beard (Linda's father); Sylvia Syms (Linda's mother); Ronald Nitschke (*Horst Drescher*, Nazi official who hires Linda to cook for his banquet); Hansi Jockmann (*Hedda Drescher*, His wife); Peter Fleisher, Alexander Hauff, Claus Plankers (SS men at fish market); Mathieu Carriere (*Captain von Häfler*, Officer at Hero's Day parade); Constanze Engelbrecht (*Stafsan von Neest*, His companion who talks to Dietrich); Wolfgang Hegler (Berlin bus conductor); Wolf Kahler (German border supervisor); Markus Kissling (Swiss border guard); Deirdre Harrison (Singer at dance in Washington); Nigel Whitney (GI at dance); Rob Freeman (GI at dance); Lorinne Vozoff (Personnel director who hires Linda); William Hope (*Ker-*

nohan); Wolfe Morris (Translator who deliberately provides misinformation); Dana Gladstone (New York street agitator); Clement von Franckenstein (BBC interviewer); Janis Martin (Opera singer playing Isolde); Wolfgang Müller (*Herbert von Karajan*, Famous conductor).

APPRAISAL AND SYNOPSIS: *Shining Through* is basically a romance, although one that is exceptionally dark at times. The production is scrupulous in recreating the 1940s, including fashion, hair styles and music. The cinematography is exceptional, and the script deftly combines humor and pathos, while letting strong and well-defined characters propel the story for the most part. The framing device is also interesting, the taping of a segment of a modern day BBC series entitled *Hitler's Germany*. An American, Linda Voss Leland, recounts her memories for an episode entitled "Women and the War." In 1940, Linda is a feisty young secretary who is hired by an exclusive law firm because she is fluent in German due to her Jewish grandmother, an immigrant who never learned English. She is assigned to Ed Leland, a dour executive who incessantly runs through secretaries. A movie addict who always speaks her mind, Linda intrigues Ed, who finds her refreshing. Before long, Linda deduces that her boss is actually a master spy. Ed finds her indispensable, and at one point she subtly catches a German translator who is deliberately providing wrong interpretations. Soon, Ed and Linda begin a romance, but things change after the attack on Pearl Harbor in December 1941. Ed's actual position as a full Colonel with the OSS is revealed, and he heads off on a series of secret missions. Linda is transferred to a Washington secretarial pool with the Intelligence agency. She loses touch with Ed for some time, until he unexpectedly appears at a dance. He transfers her to his office. When evidence is obtained about a new German secret weapon, Linda volunteers to go undercover in Berlin and pose as a cook at the home of Horst Drescher, a key member of the German War Department

who is known to have copies of the latest plans.

Ed and Linda travel to Switzerland, where she is assigned to Konrad Frederichs, an elderly member of the German Foreign office who is an underground Allied spy known as Sunflower. He brings Linda to Berlin where she poses as Lena, a domestic worker from Dusseldorf. Margrete von Eberstein, an aristocratic young woman working with Sunflower, helps her with her impersonation. She brings Linda to a fish market, and points out the worker who is an allied courier. Linda passes a note to the courier, asking if there is any news of her cousins, a Jewish family in hiding. Learning Linda is half-Jewish, Margrete reveals that Hitler himself is a friend of her family, and that he has a crush on her mother, Olga, a concert pianist. She brings Linda to visit her mother, to see if she can fool her. When Horst Drescher plans a dinner party, his chef is involved in an accident, and Linda is installed as a substitute. She botches the meal, serving undercooked doves, and Drescher kicks her out. One of his guests, General Franz Otto Dietrich, offers her a ride. He explains he is a widower with two children who is in need of a nanny. Linda accepts his offer of a job when she notices that he is carrying the secret plans for the new German weapon. However, Linda has no opportunity to inform Friedrichs of her discovery.

Linda spends weeks blending into the Dietrich household, and she notes that among her employer's regular guests are such individuals Reich Marshal Göring, Albert Speer and Count Claus von Stauffenberg. Unfortunately, Linda is unable to find the location where Dietrich stores the secret plans. When Hitler gives a speech on Hero's Day, Linda accompanies Dietrich and his children to view the Führer. A newsreel camera photographs them, and two weeks later, when Ed gets a smuggled copy of the newsreel, he is able to spot Linda in the footage. He now knows she has been installed in the Dietrich household. Meanwhile, Linda brings the children on an excursion to the fish market, and the courier gives her the address where her cousins are hiding. She reveals this news to Margrete.

Ed travels to Berlin to contact Linda. Since his German is very poor, he poses as an officer with a throat wound, unable to speak. Linda tells him that she wants to save her family, and asks Ed for more time in her undercover role. Linda takes the Dietrich children to the zoo, stopping off at the hiding place where she learns that her cousins have just been seized by the Gestapo. The zoo is hit in an Allied bombing raid, and the frightened children tell her that there is a secret room in the cellar of their house. That night, Linda explores the secret room and photographs the critical documents. Dietrich finds out, and suspects that she is a Gestapo agent. Unexpectedly, Dietrich asks her to accompany him to the opera to see Herbert von Karajan conduct Wagner's *Tristan und Isolde*. During the climax aria, "Liebestod," Dietrich holds her hand. Olga, Margrete's mother, spots her in the audience. Dietrich is stunned to learn that Linda is a friend of the famous pianist. Unable to answer his questions, Linda flees the Dietrich house in the middle of the night. She heads to Margrete's house, and discovers that Margrete is not only a double agent working for the Gestapo, but that it was she who had informed on the whereabouts of her cousins. They fight, and Margrete is killed and Linda is shot. The Gestapo ransack the house, but Linda hides in the laundry chute. When the soldiers leave, Ed and Friedrichs search the house and find her, but she has passed out. Ed takes her to the railroad station and books passage to Switzerland. Linda slips in and out of consciousness. At the border, Ed lacks the proper documents, and he is forced to shoot his way into Switzerland. He is seriously wounded, but they manage to reach safety. The Allies obtain the photos of the documents, and they bomb the factory where the German secret weapons are being developed. The BBC interview concludes, and Linda introduces her husband, Ed, and their two children, who are very proud of her wartime exploits.

Shining Through is remarkable in the way it blends together elements of espionage, wartime nostalgia, action, thriller and a love story. It is the human drama that is at the heart of the picture. Even though we only see Linda's cousins through photographs, their betrayal and capture is very moving. The fact that Linda herself leads them to their arrest and eventual destruction is a poignant irony, a tragic event that adds considerable depth to the film. The portrayal of Margrete is also stunning, a piquant and irrepressible soul mate to Linda, whose betrayal is totally unexpected. Joely Richardson is exceptional, as is Liam Neeson as the considerate Fritz Dietrich. Seldom has a German officer been depicted with such compassion. The audience is filled with mixed feelings about this man. Fritz is a loving father, a kind employer and a civilized individual, hostile to the Gestapo. On the one hand, he is a personal friend of Hitler and Eva, yet he is also close to Stauffenberg and others associated with the German resistance. One suspects that his real sympathies are with the latter. Of course, the relationship of Michael Douglas and Melanie Griffith is the central focus of the film, and these actors bring their roles to life with great vitality.

HITLER PORTRAYAL: Ludwig Haas first played Hitler in 1987 on a first season episode of the speculative TV series *Unsolved Mysteries* hosted by Robert Stack. A cross between a legitimate documentary and *Ripley's Believe It or Not*, the show frequently restaged certain events to demonstrate different theories about history. The episode caught the attention of director/writer David Seltzer, who decided to use Haas for the key scene of the Hero's Day Parade as the Führer heads to the Sports Palace for a speech. The actual event this was based on occurred March 21, 1943, one of Hitler's last public speeches. Although Haas is only shown in long shot, he makes a surprisingly convincing Hitler, standing in an open car and responding to the enthusiasm of the crowd. As he is driven by, the Führer holds on to the top of the windshield with his left hand, and he repeatedly salutes with his right. He is loudly cheered, and the crowd waves hundreds of hand-held Nazi flags. The scene is even more effective when it is repeated in black & white as a newsreel reviewed by Ed, who orders freeze frame stills when he identifies Linda among the spectators. It is interesting to note that while Linda raises her arm in salute, she does not look directly at Hitler, nor does she join in the chants of "Sieg Heil."

REPRESENTATIVE QUOTES

• Do you know what Hitler is doing to Jews, even half-Jews? *(Ed to Linda, after her proposal to undertake a spy mission)* Of course I do. I have relatives still hiding there. *(Linda)* I doubt it.... I'm not going to let you commit suicide. *(Ed)* I will quit if you don't let me go. *(Linda)* I'll miss you. *(Ed)*
• Come, meet Hitler's favorite piano player... I want to see her kiss a Jew. *(Margrete to Linda, taking her to meet her mother)*
• His name is Franz Otto Dietrich, right up there in the Wehrmacht, spent last Christmas with Hitler and Eva at Berchtesgaden. Look, they are definitely together. She has got her hand on him. *(Andrew to Ed, after spotting Linda with a German official in a newsreel clip of Hitler in a parade)*

78.   *Snide and Prejudice* (1997)

Angus MacFadden as Adolf Hitler
Psychological drama

VIP. Written by Philippe Mora; Photographed by J. B. Letchinger; Edited by Stephen M. Galvin; Produced & directed by Philippe Mora. Color 119 minutes

CAST LIST: Angus MacFadden (*Michael Davidson/Adolf Hitler*); Rene Auberjonois (*Dr. Sam Cohen/Alois Hitler*); Claudia Christian (*Renata Müller*); T.C. Warner (*Tessa/Eva Braun*); Brion James (*Göring*); Michael Zeiwicker (*Goebbels*); Joseph Bottoms (*Himmler*); Richard Edson (*Hess*); Mena Su-

vari (*Geli Raubal*); Richard Moll (*Ludendorff*); Brian McDermott (*Hindenburg*); Mark Fleetwood (*Picasso*); Jesse Grey Walken (*Jesus Christ*); Sam Bottoms; Jeffrey Combs; Richard Herd; J.P. Johnson.

COMMENTARY: *Snide and Prejudice* is set at the Temporal Displacement Foundation, an exclusive asylum treating patients who believe they are noted historical personages. Dr. Sam Cohen, the brilliant psychiatrist who heads the hospital, concentrates most of his time on Michael Davidson, who believes he is Adolf Hitler. Cohen is fascinated and amazed by Davidson who is incredibly convincing as Hitler. Cohen's treatment consists of reenacting various episodes from Hitler's life, sometimes assuming a role himself, such as Hitler's father, and other times utilizing other patients who believe they are members of the Nazi leadership. He hopes to shock Davidson back to normal, but things go awry when the patient learns that Dr. Cohen is Jewish. *Snide and Prejudice* debuted at the 1997 Cannes Film festival, where it caused a critical furor. Film distribution has been very piecemeal since this auspicious start, however, and until the title is eventually released on cable or video, it will not receive the attention it deserves.

79.   *Stalag Luft* (1994)

Sam Kelly as Adolf Hitler
Comedy

Yorkshire. Written by David Nobbs; Photographed by Peter Jackson; Edited by David Aspinall; Music by Stanley Myers; Produced by David Reynolds; Directed by Adrian Shergold. Color 103 minutes

ANNOTATED CAST LIST: Stephen Fry (*Commander James Forrester*, Senior POW officer); Nicholas Lyndhurst (*Cosgrove*, POW who later becomes acting camp leader); Geoffrey Palmer (*Heinrich Stubenhalle*, Commandant of Stalag Luft); David Bamber (*Professor*, Intellectual POW); Richard Bonneville (*Barton*, POW); Marston Bloom (*Price Eggerton*, POW nicknamed "Einstein"); Todd Boyce (*Morrison*, POW nicknamed "Owly"); Roger Hyams (*Izzy Levinson*, POW who acts as tailor); Wayne Cater (*Shorty Evans*, POW who forges documents); Simon Donald (*Barrington*, POW nicknamed "Haggis"); Benedick Blythe (*Colonel von Steffenberg*, SS Inspector); Tim McMullan (*Donaldson*, POW); Henry Webster (*Holmes*, POW); Stefan Boje (*Smithers*, POW); Robert Packham (Cook); John Duvall (British officer in tank); Pavel Bavolets (*Stefan*, Polish POW); Paul Humpolitz (German trucker); Joerg Stadker (Hitler's attendant); Sarah Buckley (*Eva Braun*, Hitler's mistress).

APPRAISAL AND SYNOPSIS: *Stalag Luft* is a rather surreal comedy set in a British fliers POW camp toward the end of World War II. The screenplay of this eccentric and unconventional British telefilm attempts to startle you by taking the most unexpected plot twists possible. It is almost as if the writer decided, at each critical juncture of the story, to veer off in the least logical direction. This characteristic makes the film almost whimsical, a bizarre mixture of *The Great Escape* (1963) with *Monty Python* and *Hogan's Heroes*.

The credits unfold in unusual fashion, showing the main actors in character as their names appear, except for Sam Kelly as Hitler, who is represented by his photo, seemingly intended to be used as lining for the bottom of a bird cage. Seeing the picture, the parrot chirps, "Heil Hitler!" In the POW camp cooler after failing at his 23rd escape attempt, Wing Commander James Forrester, nicknamed "Big F," conceives a plan for a mass breakout by the entire camp. As senior POW officer, he briefs the other prisoners of his grand scheme. Big F is summoned by Stubenhalle, the camp Commandant, who tries to cozy up to him. Finally, he makes an outlandish request. He knows the British prisoners are planning an escape. If they succeed, the remaining German staff and guards will be shot or sent to the Russian front. Therefore, he asks if the German camp personnel could escape with them. This plea stymies Big F, who is further sur-

prised when his own men decide to go along with the request. Now, they figure, they can just walk out the front gate, but Big F insists that everyone escape through the tunnels, as originally planned.

After the Germans evacuate through the tunnels, some of the POWs get cold feet and tell Big F that they have decided to stay in camp and simply wait out the war. Stunned, Big F exclaims, "What's happened to the Bulldog spirit?" He is outvoted, however, and when the Commandant calls to him from outside the camp gates, Big F sheepishly has to tell him about the change in plans. The Germans, now locked out of camp, decide to hightail it to Switzerland, and pledge to keep silent to protect the POWs. Now without German guards, the POWs post phony guards to accept scheduled deliveries, etc. German-speaking POWs are recruited to act as guards, and others are taught minimal German by Shorty Evans, the most fluent in language of the prisoners. Big F dresses and poses as Stubenhalle. Everything proceeds smoothly until he receives a tip about an SS inspection. Most of the guards pretend to have laryngitis when the inspectors arrive, led by Colonel von Steffenberg, who becomes outraged with camp conditions: the POWs seems happy, the stockade is empty and the prisoner's soup is delicious. The SS Inspector chews out Big F, warning that further unscheduled inspections will be forthcoming, with serious consequences if the lax treatment of the POWs is not corrected. Big F panics, and decides to run the camp along strict guidelines, enforcing harsh conditions, serving swill for soup and punishing even minor infractions. The men, however, are outraged, finding the new regime far worse than the one under the Nazis. When Cosgrove, now acting head of the POWs, tries to stand up to Big F and his reign of terror, the arrogant phony commandant threatens to shoot him. At this precise moment, von Steffenberg pulls his next inspection and is delighted by the harsh new conditions, since the stockade is full and the POWs all seem to be miserable. In fact, he decides to recommend Stubenhalle for the iron cross, since no prisoner has ever escaped from Stalag Luft.

When Big F departs to Berlin to be decorated by the Führer, Cosgrove and all the other men, including those posing as Germans, decide to desert the camp and flee to meet the oncoming Allied forces. As Big F is led to the bunker, the Russian shelling of Berlin has begun. Hitler, however, is completely unconcerned. He is in a dream world, concentrating only on his new modest painting project. Big F is further amazed when Eva Braun lights up a cigarette for the Führer, who puffs on it contentedly, offering one to Big F. After Hitler dismisses him, Big F encounters the genuine Stubenhalle, hiding in the rubble outside the bunker. His escape plans went awry when someone robbed him of his papers. Big F offers him the iron cross he just received, but Stubenhalle turns it down. The two men part, agreeing to meet again at Big F's estate in England after the war.

At Stalag Luft, everyone is walking out of the gates when the British army shows up to liberate them. They explain that the men dressed as German guards are also British POWs. When Big F returns, the British troops capture him. He turns to Cosgrove, Evans and the others, appealing for them to acknowledge that he is a British officer. They refuse to vouch for him, however, and he is led away as a German prisoner as the film ends.

There is much to recommend a viewing of *Stalag Luft*. It has a fresh, irreverent air and unique sense of fun, although some of the humor is geared exclusively toward an English audience, mocking the English class system and with jokes directed at the idiosyncrasies of the Welch, Scottish and New Zealand POWs. A lot of the comedy is rather poker-faced, arising from the absurdities of the situations and characters. It is surprising that the script is able to sustain the plot twists for the entire length of the film. Since language is important to the story, the film scrupulously uses German dialogue with subtitles throughout. Some of the German dialogue is quite whimsical, such that of the character Shorty Evans, who teaches German by use of the song *Cardiff Über Alles*. The editing and pace of the picture are outstanding. Another oddity is that the main character, James "Big F" Forrester is loathsome from his first appearance, whereas the character of the unfortunate German Commandant is rather likable and straightforward. The satirical aspects of the film also require a familiarity with other memorable POW films, such as *Stalag 17* (1953), *Bridge on the River Kwai* (1957) and, of course, *The Great Escape* (1963). Some of the references are subtle. For example, when Big F is in the cooler in an early scene, he plays with a ball exactly like Steve McQueen in *The Great Escape*. It takes several viewings to note the rich and subtle humor of the picture.

HITLER PORTRAYAL: British television veteran Sam Kelly is cast in the role of Hitler, who appears during the last ten minutes of the film. Kelly only marginally resembles Hitler. In fact, he more closely resembles Derek Jacobi playing Hitler than the Führer himself. Kelly performs his scenes entirely in German with meticulous diction. The mellifluous tenor of his voice is atypical, underplaying the traditional guttural bark of other performers. Kelly's Hitler is completely daffy, bored with the trappings of power, ambition and leadership. All he wants to do is paint sweet little pictures with anemic colors like autumn beige, pale paprika and buttermilk. For subject matter, he chooses to portray two men driving a van. Stephen Fry, posing as the Commandant, is utterly amazed at the vapid Hitler he sees, and hardly seems able to contain his urge to break out laughing. As the scene opens, Hitler is draped across his map table in the bunker, receiving a backrub from a lovey-dovey Eva Braun. As Fry is ushered into the room, she shuts off the phonograph playing Wagner, as the Führer nonchalantly searches for an iron cross to place on his visitor. He talks about being let down by most of his followers except Rommel, Göring and Himmler. (Of course, in real life he had Rommel killed for his support of the Rastenburg assassination plot.) The Führer takes no notice of the bombshells that rattle the bunker, talking wistfully about his new art project. He sits Fry down at the table to show him his color scheme. A bomb knocks a water pipe loose over the table, and Hitler calmly places a helmet beneath it to catch the dripping water. He then tests the water with his paint brush, seeing if he can use it to mix his colors. The real capper comes as Eva lights up and hands him a cigarette, which he blissfully puffs. The incongruity of this scene is priceless. Finally, the Führer gets bored with Fry, whom he considers just another "Yes" man, and for a moment, he shows a flash of temper as he snarls for his visitor to go. Then he turns again to Eva to ask for an additional back massage.

Given the plot developments in *Stalag Luft* prior to Hitler's appearance, the offbeat portrayal comes as no surprise, but Kelly still is amazingly uncanny in his mad, dreamlike depiction. Sarah Buckley is also quite good as Eva, reminiscent of Teri Garr in *Young Frankenstein* (1974). Stephen Fry, whose character had become rather wearing in the second half of the film, is delightful in the Hitler scenes. He then goes on to top it in the scene leaving the bunker when he encounters Steubenhalle, the actual Commandant, who is reduced to begging. He offers him the iron cross he has just received, and the Commandant replies, "How much is it worth?" Fry tries to convince him that it is a great honor (!), but the Commandant refuses. Geoffrey Palmer gives a brilliant performance, easily the best one in the film. The give and take between Fry and Palmer as the Commandant is one of the highlights of the picture. It would have been interesting had the script worked Palmer into the Hitler scenes as well as Fry.

REPRESENTATIVE QUOTES

• Heil Hitler! *(Forrester to the Führer)* If anyone had told me I'd ever get tired of that,

I wouldn't have believed them. *(Hitler's reply)*

• I have been let down by useless men. *(Hitler to Forrester)* I'm sorry. *(Forrester)* No, ruling the world doesn't interest me anymore. I started as a painter. Nothing so ambitious this time. I am tired of ambition. No great art. Just two men and a van. I have worked out some color charts ... avocado mist, warm peach, golden apricot. *(Hitler, rambling on)* Most impressive, mein Führer. *(Forrester, completely unimpressed)*

• Oh God, how tired I am of flatterers! *(Hitler, puffing away on a cigarette)*

• I got to go. I've got your camp to run. The irony is, I run a harsher regime than you ever did. *(Forrester to Steubenhalle, dressed as a vagrant outside of the Bunker)*

80. *Stalingrad* (AKA *Stalingradskaya Bitva I* and *II*) (1949/50)

Mikhail Astangov as Adolf Hitler
Historical drama/Propaganda

Mosfilm. Written by N. Virta; Photographed by Yuri Yekelchik; Edited by E. Ladyzhenskaya; Music by Aram Khachaturian; Produced & directed by Vladimir Petrov. Color 220 minutes

CAST LIST: Aleksei Dikij (*Josef Stalin*); Vladimir Gajdarov (*Friedrich von Paulus*); M. Garkavij (*Hermann Göring*); Nikolai Komissarov (*Field Marshal Wilhelm Keitel*); V. Svoboda (*General Alfred Jodl*); Nikolai Cherkasov (*Franklin D. Roosevelt*); K. Mikhajlov (*W. Averill Harriman*); Viktor Stanitsyn (*Winston Churchill*); N. Kolonikov (*General Yeremenko*); Boris Livanov (*General Konstantin Rokossovski*); Vasili Merkuryev (*General Voronov*); Yuri Shumaky (*General Vasilyevsky*); Nikola Siminov (*General Vasili Chuikov*).

COMMENTARY: *Stalingrad* or *The Battle of Stalingrad* was released in two parts, the first in 1949, subtitled *First Front*, the second in 1950, subtitled *The Victors and the Vanquished*. The picture rivals *The Fall of Berlin* in the outright adoration of Soviet dictator Stalin. Since *The Fall of Berlin* featured Stalin's favorite screen representation of himself, Mikhail Gelovani, director Petrov compensated by making the Stalin in his film even more benevolent and godlike, brilliantly managing every aspect of the military campaign. The Soviet generals are portrayed as mere servants of his will, and Russian headquarters is characterized by coolness under fire and serene acceptance of eventual victory under the sure hand of Comrade Stalin. Hitler, on the other hand, is portrayed as excitable and confused, although not quite so off the wall as V. Savelyev in *The Fall of Berlin*. Viktor Stanitsyn as Churchill is the only major performer to play the same role in both pictures, which were filmed simultaneously. The epic battle scenes remain the highlight of the film, rendered with intense drama and almost operatic fervor. Composer Aram Khachaturian wrote of his efforts, "Two hours of battle music alone ... no lyricism, no songs, no digression from the main subject. A high degree of tension was the only thing needed." For most audiences, *Stalingrad* would make almost unbearable viewing today, although some technical experts maintain that the military action sequences are more true to life than the many later portrayals of the lengthy battle that have reached the screen.

81. *Star Spangled Rhythm* (1942)

Tom Dugan as Adolf Hitler (cameo)
Musical

Paramount. Written by Melvin Frank, George S. Kaufman, Norman Panama, Arthur Ross, Fred Saidy & Harry Tugend; Photographed by Theodor Sparkuhl & Leo Tover; Edited by Paul Weatherwax; Music by Harold Arlen & Robert Emmett Dolan; Produced by Joseph Sistrom; Directed by George Marshall. B & W 99 minutes

CAST LIST: Eddie Bracken (*Johnny Webster*); Betty Hutton (*Polly Judson*); Victor Moore (*William Webster*); Walter Abel (*B.G. DeSoto*); MacDonald Carey (*Louie the Lug*);

Richard Loo (*Hirohito*); Paul Porcasi (*Benito Mussolini*); Bob Hope, Bing Crosby, Ray Milland, Veronica Lake, Dorothy Lamour, Susan Hayward, Dick Powell, Mary Martin, Alan Ladd, Paulette Goddard, Franchot Tone, Fred MacMurray, Arthur Treacher, Walter Catlett, Sterling Holloway, Robert Preston, William Bendix, Eddie "Rochester" Anderson, Vera Zorina, Jerry Colonna, Albert Dekker, Eva Gabor, Cecil Kellaway, Cecil B. DeMille, Preston Sturges (Themselves).

COMMENTARY: *Star Spangled Rhythm* is Paramount Studio's all-star cavalcade, similar to *Hollywood Canteen* (1944), *This Is the Army* (1943) and other similar patriotic revues featuring numerous stars appearing as themselves. There is also a slim fictional plot around which the story revolves. The Hitler cameo occurs at the end of a musical stage number introduced by Bob Hope and sung by Paulette Goddard, Dorothy Lamour and Veronica Lake called "A Sweater, a Sarong and a Peek-a-boo Bang" in which the stars mock their trademarks. At one point, the stars pass behind a column, and are replaced by three comics in drag, Arthur Treacher, Walter Catlett and Sterling Holloway, who continue the number. They then pass again behind the column as Goddard, Lamour and Lake emerge again. In the last line of their song, they suggest their trademarks were suggested by other "dress designers." When Goddard calls out, "Mussolini," the Duce appears in a sweater on a balcony in the back of the stage. Lamour calls out, "Hirohitro," and Hirohito, the Emperor of Japan, appears wearing a sarong as he stands next to Mussolini. Finally, Lake says, "And a Peek-a-boo Bang!" Hitler then shows up third in line, his forelock a bit more askew than usual, as he gives a Nazi salute. The curtains then close, and Bob Hope introduces the next skit. Tom Dugan handles the brief sight gag as Hitler quite well.

82.   *The Story of Mankind* (1957)

Bobby Watson as Adolf Hitler (cameo)
Fantasy

Warner Brothers. Written by Irwin Allen & Charles Bennett based on the novel by Hendrik Willem Van Loon; Photographed by Nick Musuraca; Edited by Gene Palmer & Roland Gross; Music by Paul Sawtell; Produced & directed by Irwin Allen. Color 100 minutes

ANNOTATED CAST LIST: Ronald Colman (The Spirit of Mankind); Vincent Price (*Mr. Scratch*, The devil); Nick Cravat (His apprentice); Cedric Hardwicke (Judge of the Heavenly Court); Don Megowan (Primitive man); Burt Nelson (2nd Primitive man); Nancy Miller (Primitive woman); John Carradine (*Khufu*, Egyptian Pharaoh); Marvin Miller (*Armana*, Khufu's advisor); Francis X. Bushman (*Moses*); Dani Crayne (*Helen of Troy*); Charles Coburn (*Hippocrates*, Father of medicine); Virginia Mayo (*Cleopatra*); Bart Mattson (Cleopatra's brother); Reginald Sheffield (*Julius Caesar*); Helmut Dantine (*Mark Antony*); Peter Lorre (*Nero*); Ziva Rodann (Concubine); Cathy O'Donnell (Christian martyr); Melinda Marx (Her child); David Bond (Her male companion); Hedy Lamarr (*Joan of Arc*); Henry Daniell (*Bishop of Beauvais*); Leonard Mudie (Inquisitor); William Schallert (*Earl of Warwick*); Tudor Owen (*Leonardo da Vinci*); Anthony Dexter (*Christopher Columbus*); Chico Marx (Monk who advises Columbus); Agnes Morehead (*Queen Elizabeth I*); Cesar Romero (Spanish Ambassador); Sam Harris (English Nobleman); Reginald Gardiner (*William Shakespeare*); Edward Everett Horton (*Sir Walter Raleigh*); Groucho Marx (*Peter Minuit*); Harry Ruby (Indian); Abraham Sofaer (Chief); Eden Hartford (*Laughing Water*, Chief's daughter); Harpo Marx (*Sir Isaac Newton*); Marie Wilson (*Marie Antoinette*); Franklin Pangborn (*Marquis de Varennes*); Dennis Hopper (*Napoleon Bonaparte*); Marie Windsor (*Josephine de Beauharnais*); Austin Green (*Abraham Lincoln*); Jim Ameche (*Alexander Graham Bell*); George E. Stone, Alexander Lockwood, Richard Cutting, Toni Gerry, Angelo Rossitto.

APPRAISAL AND SYNOPSIS: *The Story of Mankind* is a bona fide clinker, a preposterous and distorted survey of history filled with sweeping generalizations. Hendrik Van Loon's books, such as *The Story of Mankind* and *Van Loon's Lives* offer a similar trivialized and often inaccurate portrait of events. If you regard the picture as an exercise in high camp, it is far easier to swallow, and on those terms it is a laugh riot, with Peter Lorre's cameo as Nero a hilarious high point of parody. Irwin Allen probably would have done better if he did the whole film tongue-in-cheek as with the Marx Brothers' vignettes. Instead, when it tries to be serious, it goes from being just poor to becoming truly awful, especially in the scenes with Cleopatra and Joan of Arc. On the other hand, Agnes Morehead and Cesar Romero bring the right semi-mocking tone to their portrayal of Queen Elizabeth and the Spanish Ambassador. Bobby Watson rendition as Adolf Hitler, however, is the only one that has a truly genuine ring.

The entire film is constructed around outtakes from other pictures, including *The Land of the Pharaohs* (1955), *Serpent of the Nile* (1953) and *Sign of the Pagan* (1954), using clumsily inserted clips of the film's cast. Irwin Allen was so taken with the technique that years later he built a television series, *Time Tunnel*, around the same concept. At times, the script becomes anti–American in tone, with its history reduced to the massacre of Indians and propagation of slavery. France is maligned in a similar fashion, with Napoleon depicted as a conquering madman instead of a codifier of laws and champion of the rights of man. England, however, is given a pass for their national flaws, and one would never guess that the same England portrayed as "heroically" resisting Napoleon at the same time was making war on America, attempting to smother liberty while they burned down the White House.

In a nutshell, this pseudo-saga has a fram-

The Führer (Bobby Watson) speaks.

ing story with heaven deciding to hold a tribunal to decide whether humankind is worth saving and if Earth should be permitted to explode the super-H bomb, a new weapon promulgated by the devil, which would destroy the planet. As spokesman for the human race, one person combining the essence of all mankind is selected to present the case for celestial intervention. Arguing against interference is Satan himself. The celestial high judge, Sir Cedric Hardwicke, who often sports Harry Potter type glasses, permits the litigants to visit any period in history to make their case. Despite having total mastery over time, the court continues to rush the arguments, saying they have a deadline by which they have to make a decision. Similar inconsistencies plague the entire plot. The spirit of Mankind and the devil skip and jump through human history, spending time with such figures as Khufu, Ceasar, Moses, Joan of Arc, Shakespeare, Columbus, Sir Walter Raleigh and Adolf Hitler. Every time the Spirit of Mankind discusses the progress of humans, the devil counters with an equally powerful argument highlighting the evil of man. As a summary, the human advocate presents an infant, the man of tomorrow. Satan notes this final witness is playing with a toy gun and toy sword, but the Spirit of Mankind notes the sword is merely a pencil case. At the conclusion, the celestial court reneges on rendering a decision. This, of course, makes no sense because "at eleven o'clock" mankind was going to detonate the super H bomb and destroy themselves. Therefore it seems there had to be a reprieve after all, to allow the court more time to decide if man is more inclined towards evil or good. At this point, the film abruptly ends leaving everything unsettled, making the purpose of the entire film rather meaningless. The whole thing was just an excise to squeeze in as many two-hour cameos with old stock footage as possible.

HITLER PORTRAYAL: Bobby Watson's scene in *The Story of Mankind* shows the dictator delivering a speech superimposed over actual footage of the crowds from the Nuremberg rallies. His image alternates with newspapers with large type headlines such as, "HITLER INVADES FRANCE" or "HITLER INVADES RUSSIA." A Nazi flag with a large swastika is displayed behind Hitler's right shoulder. Watson's clip is brief, but very effective, and it is without doubt the most successful of the historical celebrity impersonations in the production. Vincent Price is also quite good as Mr. Scratch, the devil, with a suave, almost whimsical approach. Ronald Colman, on the other hand, merely walks through his part.

REPRESENTATIVE QUOTES
• So the world danced on, through the war's end, through the Roaring Twenties and into the Thirties, and nobody cared to notice that one of my most brilliant creations was creeping out of the woodwork. *(The devil as he introduces Hitler)*
• Today, I liberate the Rhineland! This is my last territorial demand. *(Hitler during his speech)*

83. *The Strange Death of Adolf Hitler* (1943)

Ludwig Donath as Adolf Hitler
Thriller

Universal. Written by Fritz Kortner, based on a story by Joe May & Fritz Kortner; Photographed by Jerome Ash; Edited by Milton Carruth; Music by Hans J. Salter & Paul Sawtell; Produced by Ben Pivar; Directed by James P. Hogan. B & W 74 minutes

ANNOTATED CAST LIST: Ludwig Donath (*Franz Huber*, Viennese statistician altered by the Gestapo to become Hitler's double); Gale Sondergaard (*Anna Huber*, His wife); Merrill Rodin (*Hansl*, Their eldest son); Charles Bates (*Viki*, Their youngest son); George Dolenz (*Herman Marbach*, Swiss businessman & friend of the Hubers); Fritz Kortner (*Bauer*, Member of German Resistance & friend of the Hubers); Ludwig Stossel (*Graub*, Huber's assistant who betrays him to the Gestapo); Frederick Giermann (*Heinrich Himmler*, Interior Minister & Head of the SS); Rudolf Anders (*Major Mampe*, SS officer); William Trenk (*Colonel von Zechwitz*, SS officer); Ernst Verebes (*Major Godeck*, SS officer); Lester Sharpe (*Dr. Kaltenbruch*, Plastic surgeon); Ivan Triesault (*Hohenberg*, Hitler's scheduler in Vienna); Joan Blair (*Duchess Eugenie*, Hitler's girlfriend in Vienna); John Mylong (*General Franz Halder*, Chief of the General Staff); Gene Roth (*Alfred Jodl*, General

General staff meeting from *The Strange Death of Adolf Hitler* with Ludwig Donath as the Führer and John Mylong as General Halder standing beside him.

& Chief of Operations); Richard Ryan (*Palzer*, German officer); Hans Schumm (*Profe*, German officer); Kurt Krueger (Nazi Youth leader); Glen Langan (Youth officer who receives the report of the Huber children betraying their mother); Irene Seidner (Petition lady); Trude Berliner (*Frau Reitter*, Anna's neighbor who kills herself after being attacked by a soldier billeted in her home); George Sorel (*Anton Schmidt*, Corporal billeted at Huber home); Hans von Morhart (*Gustav Lotze*, Private billeted at Huber home); Kurt Katch (*Karl Fröbe*, Corporal pushed down stairs by Anna); Wolfgang Zilzer (Anna's lawyer); Hans Heinrich von Twadowski (Judge).

APPRAISAL AND SYNOPSIS: *The Strange Death of Adolf Hitler* is a curious wartime drama penned by Fritz Kortner, the famous German actor whose picture *Danton* (1932) was the first film banned by the Nazis when they came to power. The screenplay has a number of ironic and tragic circumstances. The protagonist of the film, Franz Huber, altered by plastic surgery to resemble Hitler, plans to kill the actual Führer, but is prevented when he is killed by his loving wife. She, on the other hand, tries to shoot Hitler because she mistakenly believes he was responsible for her husband's death, and winds up killing her beloved. Her two young boys, brainwashed by the Hitler Youth movement, turn against their parents, denouncing them and becoming wards of the state, while the generals of the regular army are depicted as conspiring against Hitler. Interestingly, Kortner's script identifies General Franz Halder as a leading opponent of the Führer. Of course the most ironical element is how the picture foreshadows the plot to kill Hitler in July 1944. A number of elements seem strangely similar to the events at Rastenburg and Hitler's survival. Over a year after this film's release, for example, Halder was arrested and sent to Dachau after the Rastenburg assassination attempt. (Halder avoided execution, however, and later worked for the United States Army for fifteen years heading the court martial research staff.) In the film, however, Halder is portrayed as a dangerous individual whose military expertise could have brought victory to Germany if his judgment wasn't overruled by Hitler. The final irony is that Hitler is portrayed as the most preferable German leader due to his military incompetence, an idea later echoed in *The Dirty Dozen: The Next Mission*. In addition to these concepts, *The Strange Death of Adolf Hitler* is packaged to a large degree as a Universal horror film, with dark, mysterious sets and mood music similar to their standard horror pictures. The end title music is lifted from the *Sherlock Holmes* series, the concluding moments during which Holmes usually delivers a homily about the British empire. In this film, Kortner delivers the wrap up speech, stating not only Hitler, but the entire German military establishment "has to go" if there is to be world peace.

The film opens with a bloated rendition of the "Horst Wessel" song. The plot then introduces the Huber family in Vienna, portraying them as closely as possible to an American family. Their house has a white picket fence, and the eldest boy, Hansl, leaves his bike in the walkway. Franz Huber is apolitical and advises his wife, Anna, that it is best to ignore the current political regime. Franz is arrested, however, when Graub, his assistant at work, reports to the Gestapo that his boss likes to imitate the Führer. Taken to SS headquarters in Berlin, Huber explains that he is a talented mimic, and that his impersonation of Hitler was simply accurate, without any exaggeration or mockery. The Gestapo sends off a tele-

gram to Huber's wife, reporting he was executed as a traitor. In reality, they perform plastic surgery on him to render Huber into an exact duplicate of Hitler. They tell Huber that his wife and family will suffer if he does not fully cooperate. Experts are employed to train Huber to act like the Führer down to the most minute detail. Huber requests to observe Hitler at first hand in order to perfect his presentation. The SS leaders arrange for him to have an audience with Hitler in Vienna. Meanwhile, members of the General Staff are starting to clash with Hitler over his war plans, particularly his foolhardy handling of the Stalingrad campaign. General Halder, Chief of Staff, refuses to sign Hitler's orders and insists that Hitler sign the orders himself. After the Führer stomps out of the meeting, Halder suggests that the time is near when they must take a stand against Hitler.

Anna Huber is having a difficult time. All of her friends have abandoned her except Bauer, a member of the German Resistance, and Hermann Marbach, a Swiss businessman. Her children have turned against her, particularly after they join the Hitler Youth. When soldiers are billeted in her home, Anna is accused of pushing one of them down a flight of stairs. Marbach rescues her in court, claiming he is her fiancé. The judge orders that they get married. They secretly plan to emigrate to Switzerland.

When Huber is flown to Vienna, he learns that Hitler's plans have changed. The Führer flies off to a secret conference, and Huber takes over his schedule, appearing in his place to deliver a speech. That evening, Hitler's scheduler makes a mistake by not canceling his engagement with Duchess Eugenie, the Führer's Viennese girlfriend. Huber takes advantage of the situation to order several bottles of "Von Ribbentrop Champagne." He feigns unconsciousness from drink, and sneaks off to visit his home. When he enters Anna's bedroom, he startles her, and she screams, seeing Hitler standing at the foot of her bed. Marbach comes in and comforts her, saying she just had a nightmare. Speaking in the darkness of the living room, Huber confronts Marbach, explaining what the Gestapo had done to him. He asks Marbach to get him gun so he can assassinate the real Hitler. Marbach agrees to help his friend and will smuggle a gun to him the next day. Marbach also agrees not to tell Anna about his predicament.

Meanwhile, the Huber children report to their Nazi youth leader, betraying their mother's plans to take them to Switzerland. The Nazis plan to arrest her. Anna decides to assassinate Hitler, and attends his next speech. She approaches the Führer after his speech, but is unable to shoot when she stares into his eyes. She is startled by the resemblance of his gaze to that of Franz. Hitler/ Huber insists that Anna Huber be brought back to his presence. They bring her to the lobby of his hotel, and she shoots him. He cries, "Anna" as he falls, and the Führer's guards shoot her dead. News of the assassination spreads to the General Staff, who celebrate the death of "Herr Schicklgruber." Halder immediately plans to issue new military orders when Hitler and Himmler storm into the room and place the treacherous generals under arrest. Himmler asks the Führer to step out to the balcony of the hotel and show the people that he is alive.

In the crowd below, Marbach and Bauer discuss the tragic events of Anna's death, having killed her own husband in the belief that he was Hitler. Marbach curses Hitler for his luck in cheating death. Bauer comforts him, saying that the Axis is doomed as long as Hitler holds the reins of power.

HITLER PORTRAYAL: Ludwig Donath does not have a good likeness to Hitler even with a decent makeup job, but his gestures and voice help to create a decent rendition. Donath made his first appearance as Hitler appearance in the credit sequence of *The Moon is Down* (1943), shouting and pounding with his fist on the map of Norway. After *The Strange Death of Adolf Hitler*, Donath undertook another cameo, this time unseen, as the voice of Hitler in the Otto Preminger comedy *Margin for Error* (1943), featuring

At one point an alternate ending was considered for *The Strange Death of Adolf Hitler*, in which Hitler double Franz Huber (Ludwig Donath) is hung for an attempt on the life of the Führer.

Milton Berle as a Jewish cop assigned to protect the German Consul in New York City during the opening days of World War II. During Paramount's serious Hitler study, *The Hitler Gang*, Donath was cast as Gustav von Kahr, Hitler's adversary during the Beer Hall Putsch. Donath had a long, distinguished career, playing a key role as a mad nuclear physicist opposite Paul Newman in Alfred Hitchcock's *Torn Curtain* (1966). Donath's performance as Hitler is bland, straightforward and somewhat lackluster. If Donath is unimpressive as Adolf Hitler, he handles the multi-layered aspects of the role quite well, especially when he slips back and forth from the identity of Franz Huber to that of the Führer. Donath is weakest when he is portraying the genuine Hitler, principally in the scenes with the General Staff. But when he plays Huber in the guise of Hitler, he can be poignant, and the tragic nature of the film is well served by his efforts.

The supporting cast of the film is also particularly strong, including "Spider Woman" Gale Sondergaard in an atypical sympathetic performance. Many of the other players had long careers that included villainous Nazi parts. For instance, Rudolf Anders was the mad Nazi scientist who discovered perpetual energy in the camp classic *She Demons* (1958). Gene Roth, besides playing redneck sheriffs, continued to appear as Nazi heavies as late as 1968 on *Mission: Impossible* as Himmler associate General von Kramm. Ludwig Stossel also played his share of Nazi traitors in such productions as *They Came to Blow Up America* (1944) before becoming the sympathetic "Little Old Winemaker" in television ads during the 1960s. Likewise, similar roles as Nazi villains were often assumed by John Mylong, Frederick Giermann and Kurt Krueger. Fritz Kortner himself was later cast as Nazi bigwig Gregor Strasser in *The Hitler Gang*.

REPRESENTATIVE QUOTES

• More sacrifices must be asked of you. Tighten your belts…. Give your bread, your meat, your warm clothing to your soldiers, who are about to strike the death blow. *(Huber imitating Hitler to Graub, his assistant)*

• Well, perhaps the Führer could be a little bit more cooperative. Couldn't he adopt a few of my mannerisms? *(Huber to Zechwitz)*

• What a relief not to have to discuss strategy with the glorified corporal. Now everything will be done our way, no more stargazing, no more intuitions. Gentlemen, we are going back to military science. *(Halder to the other members of the General Staff after receiving the news of Hitler's assassination)*

• Führer, they want to see you. You must show yourself. *(Softly)* Every precaution has been taken. *(Himmler to Hitler)*

84. *That's Adequate* (1986/90)

Robert Vaughn as Adolf Hitler
Comedy

Adequate Productions. Written by Harry Hurwitz; Photographed by Joao Fernandes; Edited by Sandy Bennet; Music provided by the M.T.O. Music Library & Republic Studios; Produced by Irving Schwartz & Harry Hurwitz; Directed by Harry Hurwitz. B & W/Color 83 minutes

ANNOTATED CAST LIST: Tony Randall (Host/narrator); James Coco (*Max Roebling*, Head of Adequate Studios); Jerry Stiller (*Sid Lane*, His partner); Anne Meara (*Charlotte*, Sid's wife who later marries Max); Ina Balin (*Sr. Mary Enquirer*, Psychic nun); Irwin Corey (*D.W. Gadilla*, Adequate's top director); Dylan Ross (*Wilfred Babcock*, Adequate's suspense director); Susan Dey (Female lead of musical *Slut of the South*); Timothy Agee (Male lead of *Slut of the South*); Robert Downey, Jr. (Star of *Einstein on the Bounty*); Brian Seemann (*Billy Bumpkin*, Adequate's silent comedy star); Richard Lewis (*Pimples Lapedes*, Adequate's sound comedy star); Chuck McCann (*Lowell Westbrook*, Adequate newscaster & impersonator of Stalin, Gandhi & FDR); Louis Tucker (*Bill Washington*, star of *Singing in the Synagogue*); Stuart Pankin (*Freud* in *Sigmund Freud of Sherwood Forest*); Anne Bloom (*Maid Marian* in *Sigmund Freud of Sherwood Forest*); Richard Balin (Sheriff of Nottingham in *Sigmund Freud of Sherwood Forest*); Cameron Lumdon (*Baby Elroy*, as a child); Peter Riegert (*Baby Elroy*, as a grownup); Patrick Mack (Star of *Baby Frankenstein*); Robert Staats (Movie premiere M.C.); Brother Theodore (Children's show host); Maureen McCormick (*Queen Zalia* in *Starwear*); Leland Murray (*Pendar* in *Starwear*); Hank Garrett (Space pilot in *Starwear*); Michael Visconti (*Guido Valentine*, Silent star of *Throbbing Sands*); Jeanne Ford (Female star of *Throbbing Sands*); Ron Jones (*Duke Thorpe*, Adequate's action film star); Judy Brown (*Vanessa White*, TV star eaten by a giant crab); Hazen Gifford (*Frank Dugan*, Private eye hired by Sid); Addington Wise (*Ben Franklin* in *Our Foundling Fathers*); Joel Weiss (*Nathan Hale* in *Our Foundling Fathers*); Harper Roisman (*George Washington* in *Our Foundling Fathers*); Frank D'Amore (Moron No. 1); Jack Banning (Moron No. 2); Jason Christmas (Moron No. 3); Robert Townsend (Blind comic); Andy Abrahams (Star of *Young Adolf*); Arthuro Belsere (Hitler's father in *Young Adolf*); Erma Rossman (Hitler's mother in *Young Adolf*); Marshal Brickman (Himself); Martha Coolidge (Herself); Joe Franklin (Himself); Renee Taylor (Herself); Bruce Willis (Himself); Leo Steiner (Himself); Sinbad (Himself); Rudolf Hess (Himself); Joseph Goebbels (Himself); Hermann Göring (Himself); Heinrich Himmler (Himself).

APPRAISAL AND SYNOPSIS: *That's Adequate* is an amusing pseudo-documentary inspired by *That's Entertainment* (1974) and various film studio histories. It's major influence, however, was *SCTV*, the hilarious series that satirized television. Unfortunately, *That's Adequate* became hung up for years when its star, James Coco, died in 1986 before completing his role. The picture was recut and quietly released in 1990. In almost ironic fashion, one of the funniest gags in *That's Adequate* involves a silent movie in which the star dies before finishing his role in *Throbbing Sands*, Adequate's version of *The Sheik*. The resourceful studio mogul shot a series of close ups of the star in costume at the funeral home, making it appear as though he is riding a horse. The humor in *That's Adequate* ranges from the intellectual to the outright vulgar. Viewers not steeped in the tidbits of Hollywood history might miss some of the more subtle and clever references, but they won't miss the sexual innuendo and scatological humor which is often piled on too thickly. Nevertheless, *That's Adequate* has more than its share of genuine belly laughs, including the Hitler sequence which is the undeniable comic highlight of the picture. The film is organized like a typical Hollywood documentary, with quick cuts shifting between talking head interviews, old publicity stills and selected cuts from old Adequate films, usually in black and white.

Tony Randall serves as host and narrator, telling the story of Adequate Studios and its colorful founder, former circus owner Max Roebling. The studio was always a fly-by-night operation, eking out an existence with ripoffs of well known films. *Birth of a Nation* was transformed into *Slut of the South*, for example, and *The Jazz Singer* became *Singing in the Synagogue*. Adequate also specialized in bad taste and risqué scenarios, yet they managed to stay afloat. They had their own version of the Three Stooges, known as the Three Morons, their own version of John Wayne, of Bill "Bojangles" Robinson, of Alfred Hitchcock, of Woody Allen and even of Lowell Thomas. Adequate always managed to follow a success with a misstep, the most prominent being *Young Adolf*, a warm retelling of the early years of Hitler, drawn from *Mein Kampf* with the Führer's personal blessing. As the 1950s rolled around, Adequate Studios concentrated on television, but soon their unsold pilots began to mount up. In financial trouble, Max Roebling turned to Stan and Charlotte Lane, wealthy clothing manufacturers, who put up the money to star in their own version of *Anna Karenina*. Soon, Adequate began to release a series of classy productions, such as *Hamlet* played by an actress in a Harvey bunny costume, and a feature length animated version of *Macbeth* called *MacBug*, in which all the characters were played by cockroaches. Eventually, Max began to have an affair with Charlotte, and when Stan found out, he fell apart and tried to shoot Max, whose life was saved, however, by a rather thick pastrami sandwich. Later Max himself served a prison stretch when his *Stand Up Comics for the Poor* fundraiser turned out to only benefit Max instead of the poor. After prison, however, Max got back on his feet again, and with Charlotte at his side ended his career with a modicum of dignity, appearing regularly on Joe Franklin's show *Down Memory Lane*. After his death, celebrities who got their start with Max, such as Bruce Willis and Renee Taylor, speak affectionately about the flamboyant showman, all except for the grown Baby Elroy, who had no memory at all of his film career which ended when he was two years old.

Outside of the Hitler sequence, the high points of the comic documentary are the newsreels of Lowell Westbrook, played by Chuck McCann, who doctored footage of disasters and faked interviews with Stalin, Gandhi and FDR, and the television series with Jungle Girl Vanessa White who gets eaten by a giant crab while filming her show on location. Brother Theodore, the eccentric Greenwich Village comic, has a brilliant parody as host of a terrifying children's program. Another outrageous bit is the film clips featuring Abe Lincoln battling alien invaders with the help of a troupe of flying batmen. On the other hand, a number of sequences flop, such as the Czech comedy team based on the Marx Brothers, the inane Albert Einstein on the *H.M.S. Bounty* skit and the semi-nude parody of the raunchy times of the founding fathers. Still, *That's Adequate* is worth a viewing, if only for Robert Vaughn's brilliant parody of the Führer.

HITLER PORTRAYAL: Robert Vaughn is generally not associated with comedy or mimicry, but his spirited and crafty impersonation of Hitler is so hilarious that it rates among the most notable in the book. Vaughn's resemblance to Hitler is not particularly strong, but he crafts his satire very well, and he is magnificently supported by the superlative editing. The sequence opens with the genuine Hitler's entrance to the podium lifted from *Triumph of the Will*. Scenes of Vaughn at the podium are intercut with reaction shots of Hess, Goebbels, Göring and Himmler. As presented in this documentary, this was a rare public address by Hitler in English after his completion of a deal with Adequate Studios to bring his life story to the screen as drawn from *Mein Kampf*. There is a miscue in Tony Randall's narration when he suggests this deal happened after Pearl Harbor, since Hess had flown to England on May 10, 1941, seven full months before America entered the war. Therefore, the setting of this imaginary speech had to be before May 1941. The

Führer enthusiastically praises the films of Adequate Studios as his favorites, and believes that they would be the only film company to portray "a Hitler with a heart, a Hitler with a helping hand." Vaughn exaggerates Hitler's mannerisms quite deftly. Finally, a scene is viewed from the film, entitled *Young Adolf*, in an idealized backwoods Bavarian setting where the seven-year-old Hitler is seen chopping firewood for his family. With Adequate's usual touch of *kitsch*, the soundtrack plays a soupy rendition of "My Old Kentucky Home" in the background. "Keep working hard," his mother advises, "and you may grow up to be a great man." "Perhaps Führer?" young Adolf chirps. When his father later questions the youngster about chopping down a tree he shouldn't have, the youngster blames the deed on the Jews. The film flops when it is released. "Obviously, the American public was not ready for another side to Adolf Hitler," Tony Randall intones as the sequence concludes. Max Roebling then switches gears and grinds out a series of war films, using a John Wayne clone named Duke Thorpe. It should also be noted that Robert Vaughn is the only actor to play both FDR and Hitler in films. He played President Roosevelt in *Murrow* (1986), a telefilm. Other historical characters played by the actor include Woodrow Wilson, General Douglas MacArthur and German Field Marshal Erhard Milch, the Inspector-General of the Luftwaffe.

REPRESENTATIVE QUOTES

• In Berlin, I saw my first Adequate picture, *Slut of the South*, and it changed my life. I was moved by the great struggle of the Aryan race in the American South, and it was then and there that I formulated my racial theories. However, it wasn't until I saw *Singing in the Synagogue* that those theories crystallized, and I knew that Adequate was the only studio to bring the true story of my life, *Mein Kampf* if you will, to the world, to show the man behind the uniform, to reveal the real Hitler, the happy Hitler, the hungry Hitler, the human Hitler. *(Hitler's speech announcing his deal with Adequate Studios)*

• Young Adolf, come here. Someone cut down that linden tree. Do you know how that happened? *(Hitler's father to young Adolf)* Father, I cannot tell a lie. The Jews did it. *(Hitler's reply)*

• The mogul of moguls, the producer of producers! A man whose movies are not just colossal, but they are adequate. *(Joe Franklin, eulogizing Max Roebling at the end of the film)*

85. *They Saved Hitler's Brain* (AKA *Madmen of Mandoras* and *The Return of Mr. H*) (1963/68)

Bill Freed as Adolf Hitler
Horror

Crown. Written by Steve Bennett & Richard Miles; Photographed by Stanley Cortez; Edited by Alan Marks & Leon Selditz; Music by Peter Ziner & Don Hulette; Produced by Steve Bennett, Carl Edwards & Anthony Sanucci; Directed by David Bradley. B & W 73 minutes, original version; 92 minutes, expanded version.

ANNOTATED CAST LIST: John Holland (*Professor John Coleman*, Noted scientist); Walter Stocker (*Phil Day*, CID agent); Audrey Caire (*Kathy "K. C." Day*, His wife & daughter of Professor Coleman); Dani Lynn (*Suzanne Coleman*, Her sister, kidnapped and brought to Mandoras); Carlos Rivas (*Teo Padua*, Agent assassinated in Coleman's car & *Camino Padua*, His brother, another anti-fascist agent); Marshall Reed (*Frank Dvorak*, Coleman's assistant); Scott Peters (*David Garrick*, Suzanne's boyfriend); Keith Dahle (*Tom Sharon*, Texas businessman & David's father); Nestor Piava (*Captain Alaniz*, Mandoran police chief); Pedro Regas (*Juan Padua*, President of Mandoras); Jerry Riggio (Mandoras cafe waiter); Characters played by unidentified actors in expanded footage: *Russ Van Pelt*, CID official; *Victor Gilbert*, CID agent; *Toni Gordon*, CID agent; *Dr. Charles Bernard*, Scientist who is assassinated; Two Nazi hit men wearing dark glasses.

APPRAISAL AND SYNOPSIS: *They Saved Hitler's Brain* is now regarded as a cult film, however a good deal of confusion and misinformation exists about the production. Some sources contend that it was shot in 1958. Other sources claim it was made in the Philippines (or at least the opening footage was shot there.) Fortunately, actor Bill Freed, a year before his death in 1991, provided his recollections about the production with Paul Parla in an unpublished interview, which he has shared with me to help set the record straight concerning *They Saved Hitler's Brain*.

The film was shot under the working title of *The Return of Mr. H* in 1962. The production was beset with financial troubles, and according to Bill Freed, he and a number of others in the cast and crew went unpaid. The picture was released in 1963 under the title *Madmen of Mandoras*. It had a brief run, mainly in drive-ins, and was eventually shelved. In 1968, rights to the picture were obtained by Paragon Films, and they decided to add approximately 18 minutes of additional footage, so the film would exceed 90 minutes and would fetch a higher rental fee when marketed to television in prepackaged lots. This added material, used to open the film, gives it a genuinely surreal air. The actors are not identified, and since they never graduated to legitimate roles, their names are apparently lost to cinema history. Paragon also changed the title to the catchy *They Saved Hitler's Brain*. Freed wondered why they didn't use the more accurate *They Saved Hitler's Head*. Under the new title, the film became a staple of late night television, including weekly shows introduced by horror hosts. The Medved Brothers also skewered it in their *Golden Turkey* books. In this way, the picture gained its reputation as an entertaining "so bad it's good" film. This description is apt, especially when viewed in the extended version, in which the hairstyles and dress lengths clash with the original footage.

Closeup of Bill Freed from *They Saved Hitler's Brain*. Courtesy of Donna Parla.

The expanded cut of *They Saved Hitler's Brain* opens with the new footage. Dr. Charles Bernard leaves his office at the El Camino Chemical Research Lab after placing a call to a man named Van Pelt. Moments later, a shaggy-looking assassin wearing dark glasses receives a call from Van Pelt at a public phone booth. The killer informs him that everything is prepared, and moments later Bernard is blown to smithereens as he starts his car. The scene switches to CID headquarters (the film's equivalent of the CIA), where agent Vic Gilbert is given an assignment by his supervisor, Russ Van Pelt, to investigate the murder of Bernard, who was working on an antidote to nerve gas G. Van Pelt is startled when Vic informs him that another scientist, Professor Coleman, was the original developer of the nerve gas and its antidote. Another agent, Toni Gordon, is also placed on the case. Vic is unaware that Gordon is a female agent until they meet the next day. After some verbal fencing about the value of female agents,

they settle down to investigating the Bernard case. Toni suspects that the case is linked to Mandoras, a South American country where Bernard had spent considerable time. Mandoras is also believed to shelter an enclave of former Nazis. At this point, the film shifts to a lecture by Professor Coleman to some military leaders about the effects of nerve gas G. He shows a film of an elephant succumbing to the gas. After his talk, he introduces his new assistant, Frank Dvorak, to his son-in-law, Phil Day. He then learns from an enigmatic telephone call that his younger daughter, Suzanne, has been kidnapped. He goes to her apartment where he discovers Suzanne's boyfriend David lying unconscious on the floor. When the professor leaves the building he is approached by two men in the shadows. We switch back to the new footage, as Toni Gordon shows up to observe the kidnapping of Coleman. She follows them to a house and overhears one of them telephoning Van Pelt. She is spotted, however, and is shot as she rushes to a phone booth to telephone Vic. By the time he shows up, he walks into a trap set by Van Pelt. The wounded Toni saves Vic, killing Van Pelt just before she herself dies. The two Nazi thugs chase Vic, who crashes his car into an electrical transformer station by the side of the road. This concludes the new footage that padded the start of the picture, except for the lengthy sequence which introduces Professor Coleman, his son-in-law Phil Day, his assistant Frank Dvorak and David Garrick.

The scene now switches to the home of Phil and K. C. Day, as they prepare to head out for a night on the town. As they approach their car, a stranger appears and pulls a gun on them, demanding that they listen to his story. He forces them to drive off with him, explaining that Professor Coleman has been kidnapped and taken to Mandoras. When they stop for a light, a sniper in another car shoots the passenger, and the Days dump the body in a phone booth. They head to the airport and hop on the next flight to Mandoras. The only other passenger on the plane is Tom Sharon, a Texan with a thick drawl, who operates a diamond mine in Mandoras. After they land, Captain Alaniz, the chief of police, meets them at the airport and transports them to the only hotel in the entire country, indicating that the nation is as small as Liechtenstein. That night, a man sneaks into their hotel room, and K. C. knocks out her husband with a vase, confusing him with the intruder. The man tends to the groggy Day, introduces himself as Camino, the twin brother of the man killed in Day's car, the only difference being that the murdered man wore a mustache. He offers to help Day rescue Professor Coleman, held incommunicado by the Nazis. Lighting a cigarette, Camino tells the Days a long story providing the background behind the kidnapping. As he speaks, images of the events he describes are superimposed behind his face on the screen.

Toward the end of the Second World War, German radio broadcast the death of Adolf Hitler, as well as remarks by his successor, Admiral Karl Dönitz. The truth, however, was quite different. Camino's brother, Teo, was a medical technician who participated in a gruesome operation held in Hitler's underground bunker as it was shelled by the Russian forces. The Führer's head was removed from his body and kept alive through special equipment that could extended his life indefinitely. The rest of his body was then burned and left to provide positive proof of the death of the Nazi dictator. Everyone who participated in the experiment was then killed by the Nazis, but Teo was only wounded and he managed to escape. Camino finishes his tale by explaining that Hitler has made Mandoras his headquarters, and he kidnapped Professor Coleman because they have replicated the deadly nerve gas, which Hitler intends to use to gain control of the world. He doesn't want any antidote available to save his enemies.

After Camino leaves, the Days head to the local night club, where they discover Suzanne partying it up. She relates that her captors give her free rein throughout Mandoras, as long as she makes no effort to phone home. The action then stops while a cafe dancer does a Carman Miranda number which ends with mysterious gunfire in the club. When the lights come up, a detective is dead and the dancer is dying. The police chief arrests Phil Day on suspicion in the death of Carlos Vazquez, the police official killed in the gunfire. He protests, and is further alarmed when he discovers that K. C. and Suzanne have disappeared. Instead of the jail, however, Day is brought to the Presidential palace. Day finds his wife and sister-in-law already there, speaking to President Padua, who acts very erratically and suddenly boasts about Mandoras conquering the world. The Texan Tom Sharon is also there. All of them are escorted to a basement cell, where Professor Coleman is being tortured by sonic waves. Frank Dvorak and David Garrick also enter the cell, dressed in Nazi uniforms. Suzanne is stunned by his betrayal. They are next brought into the presence of the head of Adolf Hitler, situated in a glass dome resting upon a box of electronic equipment. Behind the Führer is a giant illuminated swastika, but it is backwards from the traditional Nazi swastika. Hitler blinks at them, the only indication that he is conscious and aware of their presence.

Back in a holding cell, the prisoners are visited by Captain Alaniz and President Padua, who reveal that they are mere puppets of the Nazis whom they intend to fight. Padua explains that Camino and Teo are his sons. The President helps them break out, providing two cars for their escape. An alarm sounds and Nazi troops start to chase them, although K. C. stops to argue about who travels in which car. Padua says that Hitler has been planning his comeback for eighteen years, and intends to launch the nerve gas against the major countries of the world that very night. Reaching town, the car with the Days is pursued by David Garrick, who corners them and prepares to kill Phil when he is shot and killed by Captain Alaniz.

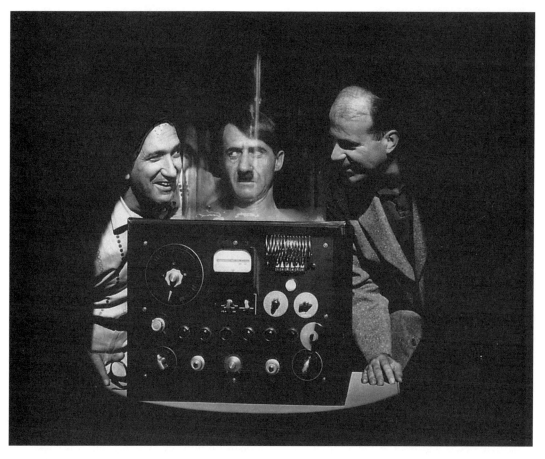

Maurice Seiderman, makeup artist, left, and director David Bradley surround Bill Freed as the Führer in *They Saved Hitler's Brain*.

Meanwhile, the Nazis prepare to release the nerve gas, and they plan to evacuate to some nearby caverns. A planeload of Nazi generals intend to rendezvous with the Führer at that location. Dvorak oversees the transfer of Hitler's head to a car outfitted with special equipment in the back seat. Dvorak drives off with Tom Sharon and a Nazi soldier, stopping at the plaza in town to pick up David Garrick. They find his bullet-ridden body instead, and Tom is shattered. The audience suddenly learns that Tom is David's father. The Texan starts to denounce the Nazis and Dvorak who instantly turns on the Texan and shoots him. The head of Hitler smirks with delight as he watches Tom die.

The opponents of the Nazis, led by Cap-

tain Alaniz, plan a trap for the Nazis outside the caverns. As an airplane lands in a field adjacent to the caverns, the group launch a hand grenade attack against the new arrivals. One of the grenades strikes the car with Hitler's head, and it immediately goes up in flames, killing Dvorak and the Führer. The Nazi threat is then quickly overcome and the world is saved. The following day, President Padua holds a reception to congratulates Coleman, Day and K. C. They receive a call from Suzanne, announcing that she has just eloped with Camino. Suzanne is then shown as she slips into bed with her new husband, and Phil embraces K. C. as the picture fades out.

The numerous plot loopholes contribute to the surreal air of *They Saved Hitler's Brain*.

So many father-and-son relationships turn up unexpectedly in the story, that one almost expects Hitler to claim to be the actual father of Suzanne. The Führer's scheme to take over the world is never really explained, and it almost sounds like the Nazis intend to kill everyone and simply oversee a totally dead world. In addition, the story has numerous dead ends and unexplained developments so that everything seems erratic and offbeat, which is not just due to the padded opening. It is never explained, for instance, why there appears to be smoke in the lower half of the glass case with Hitler's head. Phil Day's connection to the CID, likewise, is never developed. Neither is the sudden and unexpected romance between Suzanne and Camino. Yet, there are a few unanticipated strengths. The dark cinematography by Stanley Cortez is magnificent. The waxen head of Hitler, created by Maurice Seiderman for the scenes in which the head is carried down the corridor is a very decent prop, far more convincing than usual. The closeup shot when it goes up in flames isn't bad either. Some of the sets engender a genuine sense of claustrophobia. The performances, particularly that by Nestor Piava and Carlos Rivas, have flashes of brilliance. The sequence in which Rivas narrates the tale of "Mister H" is an example that combines the superb with the ridiculous. *They Saved Hitler's Brain* will forever remain an inconsistent oddity, never quite attaining the legendary status of the "bad" films of Richard Cunha or Edward D. Wood, Jr., but also one that bogs down too often along the way, causing viewers to frequently check their watches during the tedious passages. Nevertheless, the most entertaining moments of the film are those when the camera is on Hitler.

HITLER PORTRAYAL: Although shorter and slighter of build, Bill Freed's appearance is reasonably close enough to Hitler to suit the role. From the very start, Freed understood that the Hitler part in this film would never be taken seriously, so he took the opportunity to push the envelope and depict the Nazi dictator in as wild and ludicrous a portrayal as possible. When asked if his Jewish background made him feel uncomfortable with the part, Freed replied that he was only too delighted to ridicule Hitler, making him less a figure of menace. In fact, Freed had tremendous fun with the role, and he rants, raves and stalks about, gesticulating wildly in the bunker scenes. He spouted nonsense, Germanic doubletalk, and even Yiddish in these scenes. Freed did this fully aware that his voice would only be heard in the distance, and often drowned out by the narration of Carlos Rivas. In the operation scene, Freed lies dormant as the doctors and technicians buzz around the table. There was some consideration of showing the head in this sequence, but it was decided to delay that shot until later in the film, when Dvorak brings his captors to meet the master. The scene in which all the participants in the operation are killed was more dramatic when originally shot, but it was pared down for the original cut. In his later scenes as the disembodied head, of course, he is more sedate and controlled, but Freed still sneers, smirks and delivers other grotesque facial grimaces that contribute to the camp flavor of the picture. Unfortunately, the actor is underused while playing the head, delivering only a single line of dialogue. Hitler was never known for his restraint, and the film would have been far more entertaining if the Führer had had the opportunity to deliver at least one tirade or bombastic lecture to Coleman and the others. When the automobile with Hitler is set ablaze, the close-up of the head was supposed to be accompanied by Freed's high-pitched screams, but this effect was never edited into the soundtrack. Instead, music cribbed from the soundtrack of *The Creature From the Black Lagoon* (1954) is used during the scene. Freed's last highlight, then, is his leering closeup when Dvorak kills Tom Sharon in the town square.

REPRESENTATIVE QUOTES

• Mr. H was convinced that they could give him perpetual life. *(Camino to the Days)*
• I will show you what you are struggling

against. I will show you the ruler of the world. *(Frank Dvorak to Day, K. C. and Suzanne, as he prepares to lead them to Hitler)*
• Does it give orders, Senior Coleman? Does it really give orders? *(Captain Alaniz to the professor, referring to the head)*
• Mein Führer, everything is as you ordered. The truck with the soldiers has been loaded. The gas is ready in its cylinders. You will see your great victory, mein Führer. That I promise you. *(Dvorak addressing the head)* Mach schnell! Mach Schnell! *(Hitler's response)*

86.   *Thomas er Fredløs* (1967)

Bent Christensen as Adolf Hitler
Fantasy

ASA. Written by Sven Grønlykke; Photographed by Jesper Høm; Edited by Lars Brydesen; Music by Patrick Gowers; Produced by Bent Christensen, Sven Grønlykke & Jens Ravn; Directed by Sven Grønlykke & Lene Grønlykke. Color 62 minutes

CAST LIST: Birger Jensen (Teacher); Povl Dissing (Musician); Peter Belli (Red Indian); Erhard Fisker (Peanut vendor); Jytte Abildstrøm; Jeanette Christensen; Niels Rasmussen.

COMMENTARY: A genuine curiosity, *Thomas er Fredløs*, or *Thomas the Outlaw* has been described as a children's film. It was the first motion picture directed by Sven Grønlykke who had recently purchased the ASA film studio in Denmark. Little other information can be found about the film which did only modest business and disappeared quickly from the scene. The cast list, however, is intriguing, reminiscent of the parody cast lists devised by Peter Schickele for the operas of his fictitious counterpart, P.D.Q. Bach. With the picture unseen for many years, it is hard to imagine exactly how Hitler fits into a children's fantasy. Bent Christensen, who also co-produced, was one of the better known Danish actors and screenwriters of the period.

87.   *To Be or Not to Be* (1942)

Tom Dugan as Adolf Hitler
Comedy

United Artists. Written by Edwin Justus Meyer based on a story by Melchoir Lengyel & Ernst Lubitsch; Photographed by Rudolph Maté; Edited by Dorothy Spencer; Music by Werner Hayman & Frederic Chopin; Produced by Ernst Lubitsch & Alexander Korda; Directed by Ernst Lubitsch. B & W 99 minutes

ANNOTATED CAST LIST: Jack Benny (*Joseph Tura*, Conceited actor); Carole Lombard (*Maria Tura*, His wife, a popular actress); Robert Stack (*Lieutenant Stanislav Sobinski*, Polish bomber pilot); Tom Dugan (*Frederick Bronski*, Second rate repertory actor); Felix Bressart (*Greenberg*, Actor who wants to play Shylock); Lionel Atwill (*Rawitch*, Pompous actor who plays Claudius and General von Seidelmann); Olaf Hytten (Actor who plays Polonius); George Lynn (Actor who plays Seidelmann's adjutant); Charles Halton (*Dobosh*, Theatrical producer); Armand Wright (Theatrical makeup man); Adolf E. Licho (Theatrical prompter); Stanley Ridges (*Professor Alexander Siletsky*, Nazi double agent); Sig Ruman (*Colonel Erhardt*, Gestapo leader in Warsaw); Henry Victor (*Captain Schultz*, Erhardt's adjutant); Rudolf Anders (Desk officer at Hotel Europa); Wolfgang Zilzer (Bookstore clerk); Maude Eburne (*Anna*, Maria's dresser); Halliwell Hobbes (*General Armstrong*, British Intelligence officer); Miles Mander (*Major Cunningham*, British Intelligence officer); Leslie Dennison (Captain); Frank Reicher (Polish officer); Helmut Dantine (Co-pilot); Paul Barrett, James Gillette (Polish RAF flyers); James Finlayson, Alec Craig (Scottish farmers).

APPRAISAL AND SYNOPSIS: Considered a failure when initially released, due in part to the tragic death of star Carole Lombard in a plane crash while on a war bond tour, *To Be or Not to Be* is now considered to be a comedy classic and frequently appears on popular lists of the hundred best films ever made. In many ways, *To Be or Not to Be* is extraordinarily audacious, using comedy as a weapon against the Nazis who were near the peak of their power in mid–1942, and setting their story in Poland, the initial victim of the war. Together with *The Great Dictator*, this film set the satirical model against which all anti–Nazi comedies would be judged.

The film opens with a lavish orchestral arrangement of Chopin's *Military Polonaise*. A narrator sets the scene in Warsaw, August 1939, as citizens stop in amazement as they observe Adolf Hitler walking unaccompanied down the street and looking in store windows. "Is he by any chance interested in Mr. Maslowski's delicatessen?" the film's narrator wonders. "Impossible, he's a vegetarian!" A short flashback clarifies the situation. At a nearby theater, the Tura acting troupe is rehearsing *Gestapo*, an anti–Nazi drama. Bronski appears in the play in the role of Hitler, but when he adds the line "Heil myself" to his dialogue, producer Dobosh stops the rehearsal and criticizes Bronski, claiming that he can't "smell" Hitler in him. The actor becomes upset and stomps out onto the street to prove that everyone would think he is the genuine Hitler. They do, except for one little girl who addresses him as "Mr. Bronski." The Polish authorities ask that *Gestapo* be canceled in order to placate the Nazis, who are currently massing along the border of Poland. Instead, the group returns to the other current play in their repertoire, *Hamlet* by Shakespeare.

The members of the acting company are all eccentric hams, particularly Joseph Tura, their sensitive star. His wife, Maria Tura, is actually more popular, but she manages to placate her narcissistic husband. Although she sincerely loves him, Maria is an irrepressible coquette and enjoys the admiration of her male fans. Her newest admirer is a handsome pilot, Lieutenant Sobinski. She tells him that she can receive him in her dressing room whenever her husband begins his soliloquy "To be or not to be" during their performance of *Hamlet*. However, whenever Sobinski walks out during his so-

liloquy, Tura becomes crushed because a member of the audience has rejected him. Sobinski, however, mistakes Maria's flirting for love and proposes to her. Shortly after, Germany invades Poland and Warsaw is bombed into ruins as the Nazis take over.

Several months pass, and Sobinski, now stationed with the RAF in England, becomes suspicious of Professor Alexander Siletsky, supposedly a Polish patriot who cleverly entices other Polish RAF pilots to hand over the addresses of their loved ones in Warsaw who are members of the Polish resistance. After giving the professor a secret message for Maria ("To be or not to be"), Sobinski is stunned that the professor doesn't know who she is. He reports to British Intelligence officers, who conclude that Siletsky is a double agent. They ask the Polish pilot to parachute into Warsaw to head off and eliminate Siletsky before he can turn over the list of addresses to the Gestapo. Sobinski enlists the aid of the Turas after he reaches Warsaw. Maria is summoned by Siletsky to the Hotel Europe, now run by the Gestapo so he could deliver the "To be or not to be" message. Tura enlists the rest of his theatrical troop to pose as Gestapo agents. He himself will pose as Colonel Erhardt, head of the Gestapo in Warsaw, and get the list of addresses from the professor and then kill him. Some of his actors dressed as Nazis go to the hotel to accompany him to Gestapo headquarters (actually, their well disguised playhouse). The professor is fooled by Tura's impersonation, and hands over the list. Tura slips up, however, when he starts to show jealousy when the conversation turns to Maria Tura. Siletsky is killed while trying to escape, and Tura must now pose as Siletsky to free his wife who is held under German guard at the hotel.

When he reaches the hotel, Tura is picked up by the real Gestapo sent to bring Siletsky to meet Colonel Erhardt. Maria, however, is given clearance to leave the hotel, and she destroys the professor's duplicate copy of the list. Tura bluffs his way through his interview with Erhardt, revealing the names of members of the Polish resistance who have already been captured and executed. Tura learns that Hitler has arrived in Warsaw.

The next day, the body of the real Professor Siletsky is discovered, and Tura is rescued from Gestapo headquarters by his fellow actors posing as Hitler's security detail. Knowing that the Gestapo will soon track them down, the actors cook up a wild scheme to flee from Poland in Hitler's own plane. When their theater is reopened to hold a gala for Hitler, they plan to enact a deception. After the real Hitler is seated in the theater, Bronski will emerge as an impostor Hitler in the corridor and ask to be taken back to his plane. Another actor, Greenberg, poses as a Jewish protester, reciting Shylock's speech from *The Merchant of Venice*. This charade becomes the motivation for the Führer's unexpected early departure. The last part of their plan involves that Maria be picked up at the Tura apartment. Colonel Erhardt, however, has cornered Maria in the apartment. She tells him she is expecting an important visitor. When Bronski shows up as Hitler, Erhardt is stunned and embarrassed. Thinking he has spoiled the Führer's secret tryst, he attempts, and fails, to shoot himself off screen; after the sound of his gunshot, Erhardt cries out in frustration for Schultz, his adjutant.

The acting troupe reaches the plane. After take off, Bronski, still dressed as the Führer, orders the German pilots to jump out of the plane, even though they lack parachutes. Sobinski assumes the controls and heads to England. The plane is shot down over Scotland. Everyone is forced to bail out, and at first the locals think that Hitler himself is defecting. When the Tura troupe is rescued, they explain the entire story to the British authorities. To honor them, the government sponsors them in a special performance of *Hamlet*. When Tura reaches his soliloquy, he is relieved that Sobinski remains in his seat. But then both Tura and Sobinski are startled when another man a few rows back leaves his seat, presumably to have a secret tryst with Maria.

The performances of both Carole Lombard and Jack Benny are incomparable, their best work on film. Benny's timing is superb, and the part of Joseph Tura incorporates the trademark Benny characteristics of vanity, insecurity and overwhelming pride. Even when disguised, Tura fishes for compliments about the "great, great" Polish actor Joseph Tura. Instead, Erhardt tells him, "What he did to Shakespeare, we are now doing to Poland," a tremendous line when coupled with Benny's dazed reaction. Lombard is pure magic as the winsome Maria. As written, her part seems almost impossible, since she is both totally loyal to her husband yet an unabashed flirt. Lombard manages to make her both credible and vibrant. Neither Benny nor Lombard upstages the other, and the entire cast blends together in repertory fashion, sharing the laughs. Lionel Atwill is superb as the pompous Rawitch, and Robert Stack is great as the naive, love-smitten Sobinski. Both Stanley Ridges and Sig Ruman execute the art of being a comic villain to perfection. The legendary "Lubitsch touch" is at its finest here, as every detail of the film seems alive, combining satire with poignant drama. The film seems richer with each viewing. Even the title has various levels. First, there is the Hamlet soliloquy, then the code word for Maria's flirtations More importantly, there is the desperate fate of the actors themselves, once their activities come to the attention of the Gestapo. Finally, there is the fate of Poland itself and of the Jewish people. The inclusion of the Shylock speech has many far reaching implications. Yet all this is rather modestly couched in a deceptively simple comedy.

Benny always regarded *To Be or Not to Be* with fondness, considering it his finest work. Unlike *The Horn Blows at Midnight* (1945), Jack never poked fun at it during his long radio and television career. He did repeat one story, however, concerning his father, whom he persuaded to go and see the film. His father stormed out to the lobby after about five minutes, refusing to go back in. When asked the reason, he railed, "My son in a Nazi uniform. I won't watch that." Only later, after he spoke to Jack on the telephone, did he learn that the film was a comedy in which Jack played a Polish patriot who hoodwinked the Nazis.

HITLER PORTRAYAL: Tom Dugan, who slightly resembles comedian Shemp Howard of the Three Stooges, makes an amusing comedic Hitler. Dugan plays a double role in the film, as the real Hitler and as Frederick Bronski, one of the lower echelon performers of the Tura acting troupe. Bronski's breakthrough part in the company is as Adolf Hitler in the play *Gestapo.* Dugan's appearance as the genuine Hitler is brief, when the Führer steps into the royal box at the theater, and the military audience stands and sings *Deutschland Über Alles.* Seen principally from behind, Hitler gives a limp wrist Nazi salute and surveys the crowd. When Dugan plays Hitler/Bronski, he is cold and stern, such as in the corridor of the theater or in the opening scene on the streets of Warsaw. But then Bronski frequently steps out of character while still dressed as Hitler, to converse with Tura or the others, or when he goes to fetch Maria during the escape. Perhaps the finest moment for Hitler/Bronski is in the airplane. After the Tura troupe takes off in the Führer's plane, Hitler instructs the Nazi pilots to jump out the open door without parachutes. They exclaim "Heil Hitler" and jump without hesitation. Hitler/Bronski exclaims, "Two very obliging fellows," as the Nazis fall to their deaths. This scene is a remarkable visual parable, portraying the illogical fanaticism of Nazis, who will rush headlong into disaster. This metaphor from 1942 surely projected what countless Germans did in 1944 and 1945. The final humorous payoff is when the plane is shot down over Scotland and the Polish patriots are forced to parachute to safety. The camera only follows Hitler/Bronski, who lands in a haystack to the amazement of two Scottish farmers, one of whom is Jimmy Finlayson of Laurel and Hardy fame. Tom Dugan displays terrific comedic timing in all these scenes. He is also particularly

good in his exchanges with Jack Benny. The scene in the car when Dugan questions Benny about his missing moustache is wonderful, eclipsed only by Hitler/Bronski's expression when he crashes in the room with Erhardt and Maria. Quite clearly, many of the major laughs in *To Be or Not to Be* are due to Dugan's exceptional performance.

REPRESENTATIVE QUOTES

• I'm a nobody, and I have to take a lot, but I know I look like Hitler and I'm going to prove it right now. I'm going out on the street and see what happens! *(Bronski to Dobosh, who criticizes his appearance as Hitler)*
• So they call me "Concentration Camp" Erhardt? *(Line repeated several times by Tura, disguised as Erhardt, to Siletsky)*
• A very funny story which is going all over Warsaw, a story about our Führer... They named a brandy after Napoleon. They made a herring out of Bismarck, and the Führer will end up as a piece of cheese. Don't you think it is funny? *(Erhardt to Tura, disguised as Siletsky)* No. Neither would the Führer, and I don't believe he will go down in history as a delicatessen. *(His reply)*
• First it was Hess, now him! *(Scottish farmer to his companion after spotting Hitler parachuting into a haystack)*

88. *To Be or Not to Be* (1983)

Roy Goldman as Adolf Hitler (cameo)
Mel Brooks as a caricature of Adolf Hitler
Comedy

Brooksfilm. Written by Ronny Graham & Thomas Meehan based on a film by Ernst Lubitsch written by Melchoir Lengyel & Edwin Justus Meyer; Photographed by Gerald Hirshfeld; Edited by Alan Balsan; Music by John Morris & Mel Brooks; Produced by Mel Brooks; Directed by Alan Johnson. Color 108 minutes

ANNOTATED CAST LIST: Mel Brooks (*Frederick Bronski,* Vainglorious actor); Anne Bancroft (*Anna Bronski,* His wife, a popular actress); Tim Matheson (*Lieutenant André*

Sobinski, Polish bomber pilot); Ronny Graham (*Sondheim*, Stage manager); Estelle Reiner (*Gruba*, Theater cleaning lady); Zale Kessler (*Bieler*, Bald actor in Bronski's troupe); Lewis J. Stadlen (*Lipinsky*, Actor who wants to play Shylock); George Gaynes (*Ravitch*, Pompous actor who plays Claudius & General von Seidelmann); George Wyner (*Ratkowski*, Actor who plays Polonius & Siedelmann's adjutant); Jack Riley (*Dobish*, Bronski's chauffeur); Earl Boen (*Dr. Boyarski*, Polish Foreign office official who shuts down Bronski's Hitler skit); James Haake (*Sasha*, Anna's dresser); José Ferrer (*Professor Siletsky*, Nazi double agent); Charles Durning (*Colonel Erhardt*, Gestapo leader in Warsaw); Christopher Lloyd (*Captain Schultz*, Erhardt's adjutant); Wolf Musser (Desk officer at Hotel Europa); Henry Brandon (Nazi officer); Lee E. Stevens (2nd Nazi officer); Henry Kaiser (Gestapo officer); George Caldwell (Gestapo guard); Curt Lowens (Airport officer); Robert Goldberg (Hitler's adjutant); Marley Sims (*Rifka*, Jewish lady hiding in theater basement); Larry Rosenberg (Her husband); Max Brooks (Their son); Ivor Barry (*General Hobbes*, British intelligence officer); William Glover (*Major Cunningham*); Ron Diamond (Pub bartender); Gillian Eaton (Barmaid); Paul Ratcliff (British officer who walks out during Bronski's soliloquy); Scott Beach (Narrator).

APPRAISAL AND SYNOPSIS: The Mel Brooks remake of *To Be or Not to Be* retains about fifty percent of the dialogue from the original script, with occasional slight alterations. The script combines the characters of Bronski, the Hitler impersonator and Joseph Tura, the leading actor, giving Brooks the opportunity to spoof Hitler. Instead of presenting straight plays, the Bronski theatrical troupe does a comedy review, *The Bronski Follies of 1939*. This is the only film in which Anne Bancroft stars with her husband, assuming the Carole Lombard role, now named Anna Bronski (an inside joke, since Anna Bronski was a character in Günter Grass' satirical classic *The Tin Drum*). Other

changes include the alteration of her dresser to a homosexual. The remake also has extended stage routines, including their opening "Sweet Georgia Brown" sung in Polish by Brooks and Bancroft, a rather bland number called "Ladies," a clown act and a Nazi skit called *Nasty Nazis*. This is the section of the show the Polish government forces the troupe to delete, and for which Bronski substitutes a serious excerpt he calls *Highlights from Hamlet*. In the original, the theater is forced to close during the occupation, but in the new version they remain open, and in fact, they are asked to perform their comedy review as a command performance for Hitler at the end of the story. This is an interesting wrinkle. because in the original film there is no indication what entertainment had been arranged for the Führer. Another change is the addition of a group of Jewish refugees hiding out in the theater basement, a possible reference to François Truffaut's *The Last Metro* (1980). The rest of the story remains very close to the plot of the original, making any additional synopsis unnecessary.

If one is unfamiliar with the original film, the Mel Brooks version would undoubtedly be regarded as a gem, but watching them side by side, the remake feels forced and somewhat awkward. Brooks and Bancroft cannot compete with Jack Benny and Carole Lombard, and to their credit they do not try, tailoring the role to their own strengths. To this extent, they do a fine job, but if one must compare, they are not in the same league. This is true of the rest of the cast as well. Charles Durning and José Ferrer are magnificent as Colonel Erhardt and Professor Siletsky, but they lack the definitive touches that Sig Ruman and Stanley Ridges brought to the roles. A single exception is Captain Schultz, well played in the original by Henry Victor, but far surpassed in the remake by a wildly entertaining Christopher Lloyd as the straight-laced to the point of absurdity Nazi officer. One of the actors in a minor role, Curt Lowens, is interesting because of his actual role at the end of World

War II. Serving as an young interpreter for the Allies, Lowens was a member of the three man team to whom Admiral Dönitz, Hitler's successor, officially surrendered as head of the Third Reich.

The script of the remake, at least, includes small tributes throughout to the original. The street to which the Bronskis move after the Gestapo requisitions their house is named Kubelsky Street. Jack Benny's real name was Benny Kubelsky. The head of British intelligence is named General Hobbes. In the original film, the character was called General Armstrong, and performed by the eminent character actor Hallowell Hobbes.

Purists will probably dismiss the remake, but it is certainly worth a viewing or two even if it doesn't hold a candle to the Lubitsch film. In one or two instances it even offers an improvement. For example, in the original, Professor Siletsky detects that Erhardt is really a phony because Tura is unable to control his jealousy when the conversation turns to his wife. It is a bit of a stretch that isn't fully successful. In the remake, Siletsky discovers Erhardt is an imposter when Bronski swings around in his swivel chair, and the back of it reads "Property of the Bronski Theater." It is certainly a very clever refinement of the original, and it is these sporadic glimmers of light which elevates this remake from consignment to the video dustbin.

HITLER PORTRAYAL: There are actually three Hitlers in the 1983 version of *To Be or Not to Be*. First there is Roy Goldman as the Führer when he arrives at the theater to watch Bronski's show. Then there is the centerpiece of the film, Mel Brooks' take off as Hitler. However, at the very beginning of the film, the actual voice of Hitler himself can be heard in a radio broadcast listened to by members of Bronski's troupe. One might wonder why Brooks didn't double as the real Hitler as Tom Dugan did in the original. The reason is due to very clever camerawork and actor placement so that the real Hitler and the Bronski Hitler appear in the same shot. Hitler is first seen marching upstairs,

then down a corridor and finally into his box where the theater audience can be observed over his shoulder. Then the camera draws back and the door to the box closes, revealing the Bronski Hitler hiding behind the door. It is a very clever setup, and the expression on Mel's face, half-exhilaration and half-terror, makes the scene work. Goodman is fine in his cameo, although he seems a trifle too short to be the Führer. Goodman's only other major appearance was on the television series *M*A*S*H*, where he was a semi-regular in a handful of episodes. The only disappointment in his use is that the director should have included some reaction shots of Hitler during the clown act. That certainly would have added an extra touch, especially since some of the Jewish refugees are making their escape dressed as clowns in this scene.

Mel Brooks pulls out all the stops in his Hitler routine, performing with real zest. In his initial appearance, he recycles Dugan's "Heil myself" line with spunk. The Nazi office set is filled with clever touches, such as having a sign on the Führer's desk that proclaims, "The mark stops here!" (an anachronistic reference to Harry Truman's trademark). Brooks himself composed the song for the skit, "A Little Piece of Poland, a Little Piece of France," which is very clever, especially when the Polish government official orders the curtain rung down to end the number prematurely. As for Mel's appearance, he looks only superficially like Hitler, but certainly good enough to earn solid laughs. He also acts well in the scene toward the end of the picture when he berates Erhardt for his pickle joke and later barges into the British pub to verify that the troupe reached England.

REPRESENTATIVE QUOTES

• What do they want from me? I'm good natured. I'm good hearted. I'm good looking. Every day, I am out there trying to make the world safe for Germany. *(Bronski as Hitler during his stage skit)*

• I'm sorry to tell you this, Mr. Bronski,

that we cannot allow you to ridicule the leaders of the Third Reich. It is too risky. *(Boyarski to Bronski)*

• That reminds me of a very funny story going around Warsaw, a story about our Führer… They named a brandy after Napoleon. They made a herring out of Bismarck, and Hitler will end up as a pickle. *(Erhardt to Bronski, disguised as Siletsky)* A pickle? *(Bronski)* Yes, because he has such a sour puss. *(Erhardt)* I don't think that is very funny, colonel, and I don't think the Führer will find it funny. Do you think it is funny? *(Bronski)* No, I hate it. *(Erhardt)* [Compare this exchange to the one in the 1942 version]

• Excuse me, is this England? *(Bronski as Hitler, after walking into a British pub)*

89. *The Two-Headed Spy* (AKA *Clock Without a Face*) (1958)

Kenneth Griffith as Adolf Hitler
Thriller

Columbia. Written by James O'Donnell based on a story by J. Alvin Kugelmass; Photographed by Ted Scaife; Edited by Raymond Poulton; Music by Gerard Schurmann & Peter Hart; Produced by Bill Kirby; Directed by Andre de Toth. B & W 94 minutes

ANNOTATED CAST LIST: Jack Hawkins (*General Alexander Schottland*, Nazi officer who is actually a British undercover agent); Gia Scala (*Lily Baroni*, Popular radio singer & secret agent for the Allies); Alexander Knox (*General Heinrich Müller*, Gestapo official); Felix Aylmer (*Anton Cornaz*, Berlin antique clock dealer & Schottland's undercover contact); Erik Schumann (*Captain Reinish*, Schottland's aide & Gestapo agent); Lawrence Naismith (*General Paul Hausser*, Officer who recommends Schottland's promotion); Peter Swanwick (*Quartermaster General Toppe*, Wagner's replacement); Donald Pleasence (*General Hardt*, Nervous officer in bunker); Martin Benson (*Quartermaster General Edward Wagner*, Officer who

conspires against Hitler); Walter Hubb (*Admiral Wilhelm Canaris*, Head of Intelligence for German High Command, executed for his opposition to Hitler); Edward Underdown (*Ernst Kaltenbrunner*, Head of Gestapo); Richard Grey (*Wilhelm Keitel*, Field Marshal & Chief of the High Command); Harriet Johns (*Karen Korschner*, German film star); Deering Wells (*General Merkel*, Supply specialist); Ian Colin (*Colonel Friedrich Heitz*, Officer who conspires against Hitler); Ronald Hines (*Corporal Zutterland*, Soldier shot by Schottland while he attempted to broadcast a secret message); Geoffrey Bayldon (*Dietz*); Victor Woolf (Pawnbroker); Neil Hallett (Hitler's guard); Michael Caine (Gestapo agent who arrests Müller); Bernard Fox (British lieutenant outside London Pub).

APPRAISAL AND SYNOPSIS: *The Two-Headed Spy* is a straightforward espionage film inspired by the wartime exploits of English "sleeper" spy Alexander P. Scotland, who posed as a Nazi officer in the Third Reich. This story, however, is a largely fictional adaptation in which Scotland's character becomes one of Hitler's favorite generals, and whose undercover spying efforts decisively influence the outcome of the Second World War.

The film begins with a scrawl dedicating the picture to the unseen efforts of the officers of the intelligence service, many of whom worked in perilous circumstances for untold years. The action opens at a military briefing where Hitler is overseeing the plans of his invasion of Poland in 1939. Most of the General Staff appear to be lukewarm toward Hitler's demands, saying that it would be impossible to supply the forces that he intends to use. One officer, however, Colonel Alexander Schottland, claims that he has found a way to meet the need. The Führer is pleased, but continues to pound his fist on the table to emphasize that he is not bluffing. Indeed, the invasion occurs on schedule and is a tremendous military success, however it also launches World War II. Schottland is promoted to the rank of general for his contribution. He is assigned a new aide, Lieutenant (soon to be Captain) Reinish, who is also a secret Gestapo informant. Other command officers throw a party in Schottland's honor. When the famous Italian singer Lily Baroni appears at the party, a woman to whom Schottland is very attracted, he asks her to sing her trademark tune, "Ich Liebe Dich" (which bears a curious resemblance to "America the Beautiful"). The general manages to slip away before the song is finished, and visits an antique clock store. The shop is only a front, however, and the proprietor, Anton Cornaz, is an English secret agent. Schottland himself is a "mole," a British operative who has spent the last twenty-five years serving as an officer in the German army. He is frustrated, lonely and isolated, saying he feels like "a clock without a face," a somewhat vague and elusive metaphor that was the original working title for the production. Now that he is a general, Schottland knows he will be under constant surveillance by the Gestapo. Cornaz tries to comfort him, stressing the importance of his work. Schottland's only recreation is his love a clocks, a hobby that he originally undertook to explain his frequent visits to the store. He then returns to the party and to his impersonation of an enthusiastic Nazi. At the conclusion of the party, he invites Lily to his apartment, but he resists her invitation to start a relationship.

Several years pass, as Schottland continues his double life. In 1941, he passes on valuable information when Hitler cancels his planned invasion of England, deciding instead to launch an attack on Russia. Captain Reinish builds a dossier against him, discovering that his parents were English and his birth name was Scott, not Schottland, He brings this information to Admiral Canaris, who dismisses it as part of the known record. In fact, Schottland's mother was German, and he fought gallantly on the German side during the First World War. If he were really a British agent, Canaris maintains, he would have gone home after the war. Gestapo officer Heinrich Müller, how-

ever, shares Reinish's suspicions, and tells him to continue his investigation.

In 1944, Cornaz warns Schottland that his activities have aroused the suspicions of the Gestapo. In case he is arrested, Cornaz provides the general with the means to identify a new contact. He also warns Schottland to protect himself. At the next military staff meeting, Schottland tries to avoid any suspicion by raises the possibility himself that there may be a leak from the General Staff. Kaltenbrunner, head of the Gestapo, questions Schottland and admits that he shares his suspicions.

When the bomb attempt is made against Hitler, Cornaz is arrested. Schottland is summoned by Müller to witness the questioning of the shopkeeper. To protect his friend's cover, Cornaz spits at Schottland and curses at him. Shortly after, Cornaz dies under torture. Müller arrests Schottland as an accomplice, but when Kaltenbrunner hears of this, he orders that the general be immediately released, proclaiming he is the one officer completely in the clear. He also orders Müller to apologize to Schottland.

When the general follows his instructions to meet his new contact by answering an advertisement for rare antique clock known as the "Nuremberg egg," he is surprised to discover that Lily Baroni is an Allied spy. To explain their meetings, they agree to use a love affair as a cover, but soon they also begin a genuine relationship. When Lily's radio program is taken off the air, she thinks that the Gestapo suspects her of sending coded messages to the Allies during her broadcasts. When Hitler plans a counteroffensive on the Western front, Schottland tries to alert the Allies by using a field transmitter during his visit to the front. A German corporal overhears his broadcast attempt, and Schottland is forced to shoot him. Badly wounded, the corporal survives, and when he starts to recover, Müller interrogates him, hoping to expose Schottland as a traitor. Meanwhile, Schottland manages to undermine the Ardennes offensive during a military strategy conference with Hitler.

He decides to undersupply the attack, using the Führer's risky scheme to seize Allied supplies as his operational excuse. These stores fail to materialize, and the Battle of the Bulge fails, largely due to Schottland's efforts.

As the Allies troops continue their advance, Schottland arranges to smuggle Lily across German lines, but Captain Reinish overhears their plans, and he kills Lily when she undertakes her escape. The next day, Reinish pulls a gun on Schottland, but the general battles back and manages to kill the captain. Suspecting the jig is up, he rushes off to see Hitler in the bunker. He plays upon the Führer's paranoia by naming a number of officers as defeatists and traitors, including Heinrich Müller. Hitler orders the arrest of all the men named by Schottland, and also issues a special pass for Schottland allowing him to go through the lines to help organize a new counterattack. From Gestapo Headquarters, Müller orders the arrest of Schottland, but he is shocked when he himself arrested moments later by order of the Führer. Schottland makes his way across the battle lines, grinning broadly as he is captured by British troops. After Germany surrenders, Schottland, now dressed as a British officer, goes to a pub to celebrate. When a lieutenant salutes him, he almost responds with a Nazi salute from force of habit, but then transforms his gesture into a traditional salute as the picture comes to a conclusion.

When released, *The Two-Headed Spy* was poorly distributed and never received the success of similar films such as *Five Fingers* (1952) or *The Man Who Never Was* (1956). A better title would have helped, since *The Two-Headed Spy* conjures up images of a transplant horror film such as *The Manster* (1958) or *The Thing with Two Heads* (1972). The film is of very decent quality, fairly suspenseful and unpredictable. The unexpected death of Lily Baroni underscores the dark and serious nature of the film, which only suffers from lack of comic relief, although the ranting Hitler no doubt provides a few unintended chuckles. *The Two-Headed Spy*, nevertheless, is a worthwhile film deserving rediscovery.

HITLER PORTRAYAL: Kenneth Griffith, screen veteran of many British films dating back to 1941, is an unusual choice to play Hitler. Director Andre de Toth stages the three Hitler sequences in a peculiar fashion so that Hitler is never clearly shown, ironically in similar fashion to Jesus Christ in *Ben-Hur* (1959) or Mohammed in *Messenger of God* (1977). Perhaps, because he is frequently heard, a more apt comparison would be Carl Reiner as Alan Brady during the first two or three seasons of *The Dick Van Dyke Show* or John Forsythe on *Charley's Angels*. Most of the time, the camera is positioned directly behind Hitler's chair, so we see his arms wildly gesticulating and the back of his head bobbing up and down, but without his face ever slipping into camera range. This approach might work if the vocal interpretation is strong, but Griffith's voice is too nasal to be a really effective Hitler. There is also not enough variety in his vocal range, since in every scene he is in the same shrieking mode. The first two Hitler scenes are military conferences, the first dealing with the invasion of Poland in 1939 and the second with the Ardennes offensive in December 1944. Hitler is lambasting his generals in both cases, demanding they find ways to execute his strategy. In both meetings, Schottland butters up the Führer, telling him that his generals will find a way to carry out his wishes. In the final Hitler scene, in the bunker, Schottland has a twofold purpose: first to destroy his major enemy, Gestapo Leader Müller, as well as to throw the German army into chaos by listing a number of key figures as defeatists; and second, to arrange his own escape from Berlin under the pretense of carrying out a mission for the Führer. In this scene, Hitler is like putty in Schottland's hands, as he plays him like a harp to get the results he wants. By comparison, Field Marshal Keitel, also present in this scene, has no influence whatsoever with Hitler. So, the extent of Griffith's interpretation is a Hitler who is stubborn, illogical and a blowhard easily influenced by flatterers.

REPRESENTATIVE QUOTES

• There will be continued negotiations with England and France during the coming week. This will not affect my plans. On the first of September, we will attack! *(Hitler to the General Staff, planning the invasion of Poland)*

• Dual nationalities are common, even among our national leaders. Rudolf Hess was born and raised in Egypt. The Führer himself is an Austrian. *(Admiral Canaris to Reinish)*

• Everyone must serve the Fatherland in his own way, even the occasional half-wit. (Schottland's parting insult to Group Leader Müller, who attempted to arrest him as a bomb plot conspirator)

• Any commander's estimate can be questioned. they always ask for more than they need. We will be able to use captured enemy's stores as we advance. *(Hitler to Toppe and Hardt during the planning session for the Battle of the Bulge)*

• The defeatists! They are the enemy.... Arrest them! *(Hitler, talking to Keitel and Schottland in the bunker)* But if you arrest these officers... *(Keitel)* Ah, nonsense, Keitel. It will reinstall confidence in our loyal officers. Sweep out Hardt and his clique! Schottland has only confirmed my intuition! *(Hitler)*

90. *Under the Rainbow* (1981)

Ted Lehmann as Adolf Hitler (cameo)
Comedy

Orion. Written by Pat McCormick, Harry Hurwitz, Martin Smith, Pat Bradley & Fred Bauer; Photographed by Frank Stanley; Edited by David Blewitt; Music by Joe Renzetti; Produced by Fred Bauer; Directed by Steve Rash. Color 97 minutes

ANNOTATED CAST LIST: Chevy Chase (*Bruce Thorpe*, Secret Service agent); Carrie Fisher (*Annie Clarke*, Special talent coordi-

nator for *The Wizard of Oz*); Joseph Maher (*Duke Ferdinand of Luchow*, Guarded by Thorpe); Eve Arden (*Duchess Susan of Luchow*, His wife); Robert Donner (*DeGaelo*, Assassin after the Duke); Billy Barty (*Otto Kriegling*, Nazi secret agent); Mako (*Nakomura*, Japanese secret agent); Pat McCormick (House detective); Cork Hubbert (*Rollo Sweet*, Midget who befriends Thorpe); Adam Arkin (*Henry Hudson*, Acting manager of the Culver Hotel); Richard Stahl (*Lester Hudson*, Henry's uncle, the regular manager); Jack Kruscher (*Lou*, Studio executive); Peter Isackson (*Homer Engel*, Annie's assistant & Lou's nephew); Anthony Gordon (*Inspector Roy Collins*, British escort assigned to the Duke); Freeman King (*Otis*, Elevator operator); Doodles Weaver (Studio guard); Leonard Barr (*Pops*); Little Pat Bilon (Himself) and scores of extras from Billy Barty's organization, Little People of America.

APPRAISAL AND SYNOPSIS: In the mid-seventies, writer Stuart M. Kaminsky developed a remarkable, charming series of detective stories centered on Toby Peters, a Hollywood gumshoe, whose clients usually are celebrities such as Bela Lugosi (*Never Trust a Vampire*), Peter Lorre (*Think Fast, Mr. Peters*) and W. C. Fields (*The Fatal Glass of Beer*). The second book in Kaminsky's long-running series was *Murder on the Yellow Brick Road*, a delightful and whimsical story that covers the same ground as *Under the Rainbow* in magnificent fashion. This film, however, is the sow's ear compared to Kaminsky's silk purse. It is undoubtedly one of the biggest comic misfires ever produced by a major studio, an embarrassing, demeaning effort devoid of a single unqualified laugh. The most amazing thing is how earnestly Chevy Chase and Carrie Fisher approach their material, trying in vain to make it work. One can tell that their efforts are doomed simply by the soundtrack alone, a juvenile, schlocky score that would be substandard in the most amateurish cartoon. Two examples will suffice to depict the level of the humor in this picture. The first

is a running gag about the Duchess of Luchow's dog, Strudel, which keeps getting
killed. The Duke always replaces the dog
with another, so the Duchess never realizes
the change. That laugh riot is topped by another scene in which an assassin after the
Duke sprays a machine gun burst at the
closed doors of the elevator. House detective
Tiny quips, "I could have held the elevator,
sir!" as he opens the door, revealing a dozen
dead Japanese tourists. The single amusing
sight gag happens near the end of the picture when a gang of midgets interrupts Clark
Gable and Vivian Leigh as they prepare to
shoot a scene for *Gone with the Wind*. It is
just too little. too late.

The plot is launched as Rollo, a midget
and film buff, awaits word from Hollywood
that they will hire him to appear as a
Munchkin in *The Wizard of Oz*. Meantime,
in Berlin, Adolf Hitler hatches a scheme to
supply the Japanese with a secret map he obtained showing the west coast defenses of
the United States. He sends Otto Kriegling,
a midget secret agent, to Los Angeles to deliver this document from a Japanese agent.
Hitler arranges for them to meet at the Culver Hotel. Hitler's proposed rendezvous
backfires, however, when a busload of Japanese shutterbugs breaks down in front of the
Culver at the same time that 150 midgets arrive, the Munchkin pereformers for *The
Wizard of Oz*. In the confusion, Otto gives
the map to the wrong person, who places it
inside the script he was reading of *The Wizard of Oz*. This script is later returned to
Annie Clarke who serves as overseer to the
unruly midgets. The rest of the film involves
the efforts of Otto and Nakomura, the genuine Japanese agent, to recover the document. Also at the Culver is Secret Service
agent Bruce Thorpe, who is serving as bodyguard to the Duke and Duchess of Luchow,
who are pursued by a bumbling assassin
from their homeland. All of these individuals cross paths in madcap fashion. At the
conclusion, the entire escapade is revealed
to have been Rollo's hallucination after he
fell and hit his head while waiting to be

picked up and transported to Hollywood to
become a Munchkin. So, like Dorothy in
The Wizard of Oz, Rollo had merely imag-
ined the entire plot of *Under the Rainbow*.
Although an interesting parallel, this ending
is merely a half hearted and empty gesture,
as if the screenwriters threw up their hands
and simply gave up. Probably only a few
members of the audience, however, stuck
with the picture long enough to reach this
trite finish.

HITLER PORTRAYAL: Not much thought
seems to have gone into the selection of Ted
Lehmann, a minor character actor, to play
Hitler, to whom he bears almost no likeness.
In fact, Lehmann's receding hairline akmost
negates any Hitler resemblance. He delivers
his dialogue in a straightforward fashion,
sprinkled with a few German words, but
with only a trace of an accent. Lehmann is
a rather bland Hitler, whose only purpose is
to introduce Otto and the stolen plans of
America's west coast defenses, into the story.
He sits at a desk positioned in front of a
giant swastika when Otto enters. After giving the midget agent his instructions, Hitler
expresses confidence in his new Japanese allies as a key ingredient in his plans for world
conquest, and he steps in front of his desk
to approach Otto. However, when the
midget gives the traditional Nazi salute, his
arm strikes Hitler in the groin. The Führer
doubles over in pain as the camera cuts to
the bow of the *Queen Mary* docking in Los
Angeles. Among the pitiful sight gags, this
shot ranks as one of the better ones in the
picture.

REPRESENTATIVE QUOTES

• One question, mein Führer ... How
will I know him? *(Otto to Hitler)* He will
greet you with this password, "The pearl is
in the river." *(Hitler's reply)*
• You will look for a Japanese man in a
white suit. *(Hitler to Otto, continuing his instructions)* How will he know me? *(Otto)* He
will look for a man your size. *(Hitler)*

91. *Undercovers Hero* (AKA *Soft Beds, Hard Battles*) (1974)

Peter Sellers as Adolf Hitler
Comedy

Lion International. Written by Leo Marks & Roy Boulting; Photographed by Gilbert Taylor; Edited by Martin Charles; Music by Neil Rhoden; Produced by John Boulting; Directed by Roy Boulting. Color 105 minutes

ANNOTATED CAST LIST: Peter Sellers (*Major Robinson*, British spy in occupied France; *General Latour*, Elderly French officer still fighting World War I; *Schroeder*, Gestapo chief of Paris; *Prince Kyoto*, Japanese general touring France; *Robergé*, French leader who hands out war decorations); Lily Kedrova (*Madame Yvonne Grenier*, Owner of elegant bordello); Curt Jürgens (*General von Grotjahn*, Military governor of Paris); Beatrice Romand (*Marie-Claude Bisset*, Innocent niece of Madame Grenier); Francoise Pascal (*Madeline Vicompté*, Prostitute); Rula Lenska (*Louise Despaire*, Prostitute); Daphne Lawson (*Claudine Dalfonte*, Prostitute); Jenny Hanley (*Michelle Bouché*, Prostitute); Gabriella Licudi (*Simone*, Prostitute); Carolle Rousseau (*Helene*, Prostitute); Hylette Adolphe (*Tom-Tom*, Prostitute); Rex Stallings (*Alan Cassidy*, American Embassy official); Vernon Dobtcheff (*Padre*); Douglas Sheldon (*Captain Kneff*, Officer escorting Kyoto); Philip Madoc (*Field Marshal Weber*, First German killed in the bordello); Thorley Walters (*General Erhardt*, German officer who dies of heart failure); Nicolas Loukes (*Schultz*, Schroeder's assistant); Timothy West (Convent chaplain); Patricia Burke (Mother Superior); Jean Charles Driant (*Jean*); Basil Digman (British Intelligence officer); Nicholas Courtney (French Intelligence officer); Stanley Lebor, Gertan Klauber, Barry J. Gordon (Gestapo agents).

APPRAISAL AND SYNOPSIS: *Undercovers Hero* is a problematic and awkward satire in which the residents of an elegant French whorehouse effect the outcome of the Second World War. Shortly after the occupation of Paris by German forces, the Führer himself visits the establishment with General von Grotjahn, an old client of Madame Grenier, the owner. While making a selection among the beautiful girls, Hitler is upset when he discovers one of them, Tom-Tom, is a Negro, and he storms out. Major Robinson, a member of British Intelligence, is hiding out at the brothel, but fails to recognize Hitler. He later kills one of the clients, Field Marshal Weber. The callgirls ask Alan Cassidy, a client from the American Embassy, to help them dispose of the body. He hides it in the trunk of General Latour, an old, senile French officer who thinks that he is still fighting the First World War. The Germans find the body, however, and the old Frenchman is executed. Escaping back to England, Major Robinson is sent back to Paris to work undercover at the brothel. Working with the local priest, a French Resistance leader, the major recruits Madame Gernier and her girls into working for the French Underground. Madame Grenier's innocent young niece, Marie Claude, also volunteers. But instead of gaining secret intelligence from clients who are German officers (à la Mati Hari), they eliminated them instead, using devices such as trick beds which flip up sending their occupants crashing down an elevator shaft to their deaths. When the Paris Gestapo chief tries to investigate the fate of the missing officers, the brothel is protected by the military governor. Alan goes undercover at the brothel after America joins the conflict.

As the war continues, Hitler invades Russia. As he forces near Moscow, he asks for General von Grotjahn to lead his team of crack officers to help them take the Russian capital. The general treats the men to a farewell visit to Madame Grenier. Marie-Claude slips killer fart pills into their champaigne. The entire company is wiped out, dying from intestinal distress, while on their way to Russia, and Moscow is saved due to this action.

The movie
with the
6 best-Sellers
in one!

LION INTERNATIONAL FILMS present
THE BOULTING BROTHERS' PRODUCTION

PETER SELLERS in

"UNDERCOVERS HERO"

co-starring
LILA KEDROVA · CURT JURGENS · also starring BEATRICE ROMAND

Story and Screenplay by LEO MARKS and ROY BOULTING · Directed by ROY BOULTING · Produced by JOHN BOULTING
A CHARTER FILM Production

R RESTRICTED
UNDER 17 REQUIRES ACCOMPANYING
PARENT OR ADULT GUARDIAN

United Artists

THEATRE

When a new military governor is assigned to Paris, Schroeder moves to investigate the brothel, but finds that Madame Grenier and her callgirls have gone to the countryside on vacation. Schroeder finds the deadly beds that were used to kill the German officers. Meanwhile, the girls hide out at a convent, where Alan sets up a short wave station to contact the Allies. When Prince Kyoto, a Japanese general touring the German defences, has a car breakdown outside the convent, Alan is intstructed by the Allies to make sure he stays the night so they could prepare an ambush for him on the following day. The girls and Alan dress as nuns to blend in with the regular sisters. Marie Claude, dressed as a novice, manages to entice Prince Kyoto to spend the entire night. When the Japanese general and his German escorts leave the next day, Allied fighters blow them to pieces.

When Madame Grenier and the girls return to Paris, they are captured by Schroeder. They manage to overpower their guards. The new military governor decides to refuse to carry out Hitler's orders to destroy Paris. He sends word that he wishes to surrender. Madame Grenier sneaks into German military headquarters and the governor surrenders to her. Meanwhile, Schroeder has been ordered by Hitler to insure his destruct orders are carried out at midnight. Majpr Robinson, Alan and the girls prepare a trap, and they blow up Schroeder while he reports to Hitler on the telephone. After the liberation, Madame Grenier and her callgirls are decorated with medals by a French government official, who enjoys fondling the girls as he decorates them. He ends up kissing Marie Claude. The girls return to work, and a special government plaque is erected on the brothel recognizing their contribution to the war effort.

If this synopsis seems to be an unlikely formula for a comedy, it demonstrates why the film was unsuccessful. It is too much of a patched together effort, lacking the style or wit of a true black comedy. The plot is simply fails to hang together, with too many plot contrivances, such as the convent scene, merely thrown in to allow Sellers a turn in another role. His part as Major Robinson, for example, appears and disappears haphazardly throughout the story without much rhyme or reason. Only the Schroeder scenes sparkle and provoke genuine bellylaughs. Curt Jürgens' role makes little sense, since he is far too charming and sympathetic to be the German military governor. *Undercovers Hero* largely disappeared after its brief theatrical run. There were too many barebreasted scenes in the brothel for the film to be shown on television other than cable. In recent years, a small cult following has developed around the picture, and dedicated Peter Sellers fans might find much to admire in the production. However, much of the humor is too vulgar and juvenile for wider audiences. Watching German officers keeling over and dying from breaking wind, has limited repeat value. Once or twice might seem passably funny, but seeing and hearing it eight or nine times robs it of the slightest pretense of humor. It is simply a clumsy effort that bungles what could have been a very funny film.

HITLER PORTRAYAL: Peter Sellers undertakes six roles in *Undercovers Hero* with various degrees of success. His most hilarious take is that of Schroeder, the Gestapo chief of Paris who seems like a mad cross of Inspector Clousseau and Dr. Strangelove. Wearing a Himmler mustache and walking with an erratic little hop, his colorful caricature deservedly gets the lion's share of screen time. Major Robinson, the "very" British spy, on the other hand, is a mundane character similar to Captain Lionel Mandrake from *Dr. Strangelove* (1964). His Prince Kyoto is very odd, certainly the most bizarre of the characters and although *Undercovers Hero* is a tasteless picture overall,

Opposite: **Newspaper ad for *Undercovers Hero* featuring the six roles played by Peter Sellers in the picture. Hitler is character number three.**

Sellers' role as Major Robinson almost duplicates his role as Captain Mandrake in *Doctor Strangelove.*

his characterizatrion doesn't sink to racial stereotyping. His two French roles are his least successful. General Latour, a doddering satire of Marshal Henri Pétain, is bland and not very amusing. His French official who hands out medals to Madame Grenier and her girls, is a slight improvement, but the comic routine in which he manages to fondle the women is simply clumsy and obvious, providing a stumbling and overlong finale to the farce. The remaining role is Adolf Hitler, and while it is interesting, the satire seems somewhat restrained, as if for some reason Sellers didn't want to pull out all the stops, leaving that to his Schroeder characterization. There are three Hitler sequences. The first appearance is the longest, when the Führer is taken to Madame Grenier's establishment by General von Grotjahn. When introduced to the famous Madame, she curtsies and extends her hand to be kissed. Hitler, however, looks at her with a completely befuddled expression and finally decides to give her a Nazi salute in-

stead. The Madame totters as she raises her extended hand to return his gesture. The Führer looks more appreciative as he is introduced to the scantily dressed women, clasping his hands together at belt level. He smiles, nods and seems on the verge of selecting one when Tom Tom appears. Stunned, Hitler plants his hands on his hips and screams, "Schwarze!" He then gestures to his guards that he is leaving, saying "Come" and he leads them out of the brothel. The second Hitler scene shows him lecturing his military staff, announcing his plans for the invasion of Russia in front of a huge map. When he pokes his finger at Moscow, the staff give out a collective gasp that is quite amusing. The last Hitler bit occurs at the end of the picture while the Führer is on the phone to Schroeder. It is his only closeup in the film. Wearing steel rim glasses, Hitler barks into the phone. As Schroeder answers on the other end of the line, he is cut off in mid-sentence as is blown up. This would have been the perfect opportunity for a reaction shot with the Führer. Instead, the film plunges ahead to the rather disappointing medal scene which ends the picture. Of the six Sellers roles, Hitler is the one that winds up being the most straightforward, and knowing Sellers' talents, it makes his performance as Hitler as somewhat disappointing.

REPRESENTATIVE QUOTES

• Listen, ladies, in this war we Americans are neutral. We don't give a damn who kills Hitler. *(Alan to Simone & Helene)*
• The Führer does not drink. He does not smoke. *(German officer to Madame Grenier)* Then we must find something the Führer does enjoy, mustn't we? *(Her reply)*
• That's a face I have seen before. *(Major Robinson to himself after spotting, but not trecognizing, Hitler in the lobby of the bordello)*
• Is Paris burning? *(Hitler to Schroeder on the telephone)*

92. *War and Remembrance* (1988)

Steven Berkoff as Adolf Hitler
Historical drama

Paramount. Written by Earl W. Wallace, Dan Curtis & Herman Wouk based on his novel *War and Remembrance*; Photographed by Bernie Abrahamson & Dietrich Lohmann; Edited by Peter Zinner & John F. Burnett; Music by Robert Colbert; Produced by Barbara Steele & Dan Curtis (executive); Directed by Dan Curtis. Color 12 episodes, approximately 1,540 minutes

ANNOTATED CAST LIST: Robert Mitchum (*Victor "Pug" Henry*, Career naval officer); Polly Bergen (*Rhoda*, His first wife); Michael Woods (*Warren*, Their eldest son, a carrier pilot killed at Midway); Sharon Stone (*Janice Henry*, Warren's wife); Hart Bochner (*Byron*, Pug's second son, a submarine officer); Jane Seymour (*Natalie Henry*, Byron's wife, trapped in Europe during the war); Brett Bowerbank (*Louis Henry*, Their son, as a baby); Rhett Creighton (*Louis Henry*, as a small child, earlier scenes); Hunter Schlesinger (Louis Henry, as a small child, later scenes); Leslie Hope (*Madeline*, Their daughter, a radio producer); William R. Moses (*Lieutenant Simon Anderson*, Officer who weds Madeleine); John Gielgud (*Aaron Jastrow*, Natalie's uncle, a noted historian); Bill Wallis (*Werner Beck*, Former student of Aaron, a German official); David Dukes (*Leslie Slote*, US diplomat, later killed fighting undercover with the French Resistance); Barry Bostwick (*Carter "Lady" Aster*, Flamboyant naval officer & Byron's friend); Peter Graves (*Palmer "Fred" Kirby*, Scientist in love with Rhoda); Michael Conrad (*Harrison Peters*, Army Colonel who becomes Rhoda's second husband); Jeremy Kemp (*Armin von Roon*, German General hostile to Hitler); Robert Morley (*Alistair Tudsbury*, British journalist); Victoria Tennant (*Pamela Tudsbury*, His daughter, Pug's second wife); Topol (*Berel Jastrow*, Aaron's cousin who escapes from a Nazi work detail); John Rhys-Davies (*Sammy Mutterperl*, Berel's

friend, a Nazi slave laborer who revolts); Sami Frey (*Avram Rabinowitz*, Leader in Jewish escape network); Ian McShane (*Philip Rule*, Cocky British journalist); Michael Elwyn (*Lord Duncan Burne-Wilke*, Pamela's fiance who dies while attempting to recover from a plane crash in India)); Ralph Bellamy (*Franklin D. Roosevelt*, US President); Elizabeth Hoffman (*Eleanor Roosevelt*, His wife); William Schallert (*Harry Hopkins*, Presidential advisor & Secretary of Commerce); Ben Harrigan (*Henry Stimson*, Secretary of War); Leon B. Stevens (*Frank Knox*, Secretary of the Navy); Paul Lambert (*Ross McIntire*, FDR's doctor); Richard Dysart (*Harry Truman*, FDR successor who asks Pug to be his Naval Advisor); Gyl Roland (Truman's secretary); E. G. Marshall (*Dwight D. Eisenhower*, Supreme Allied Commander, European theater); Charles Napier (*Walter Bedell Smith*, General who serves as Ike's Chief of Staff); Jane How (*Kay Summersby*, Ike's chauffeur); Walker Edmiston (*Douglas MacArthur*, Supreme Allied Commander, Southern Pacific theater); William Prince (*Admiral Chester Nimitz*, Supreme Allied Commander, Northern Pacific theater); Robert Hardy (*Winston Churchill*, British Prime Minister); Al Ruscio (*Josef Stalin*, Soviet dictator); Kirstie Pooley (*Eva Braun*, Hitler's mistress); Axel Ganz (*Dr. Theodor Morell*, Hitler's physician); Elizabeth Ofenboch (*Traudl Junge*, Hitler's dictation secretary); Michael Wolff (*Hermann Göring*, Reich Marshal); Ian Gentle (*Dr. Joseph Goebbels*, Propaganda Minister); Erwin Strahl (German broadcaster who introduces Goebbels during Stalingrad speech); Dieter Wagner (*Heinrich Himmler*, Interior Minister & Head of SS); Wolfgang Reichmann (*Martin Bormann*, Hitler's private secretary); Geoffrey Whitehead (*Albert Speer*, Munitions Minister); Wolfgang Preiss (*Walter von Brauchitch*, Head of German Army dismissed by Hitler in 1941); John Malcolm (*Wilhelm Keitel*, Field Marshal & Chief of the High Command); Joachim Hansen (*Alfred Jodl*, General & Chief of Operations);

Anthony Bate (*Gerd von Rundstedt*, Field Marshal & Commander of Western forces); Paul Glowion (*Friedrich von Paulus*, Field Marshal & Commander of 6th Army at Stalingrad); Albert Rueprecht (*Arthur Schmidt*, General & Chief of Staff at Stalingrad); Barry Morse (*Franz Halder*, Chief of the General Staff, later arrested after bomb plot); Peter Vaughan (*Kurt Zeitzler*, General who replaces Halder); Heinz Weiss (*Hans Krebs*, General who replaces Zeitzler); Rainer Penhert (*Erich von Manstein*, Field Marshal & top German strategist); Christian Ebel (*Hans Rattenhuber*, SS Head of Hitler's bodyguards); Justin Berlin (*Ludwig von Beck*, Retired general & leader of anti–Hitler group); Hardy Kruger (*Erwin Rommel*, Field Marshal & leader of *Afrika Korps* who later conspires against Hitler); Andrea Dahmen (*Lucie Rommel*, His wife); Matthias Hinz (*Manfred Rommel*, His son); Reinhard Glemnitz (*Hans Speidel*, Rommel's Chief of Staff); Sky Dumont (*Count Claus von Stauffenberg*, Officer who tries to kill Hitler with a bomb); Rupert Frazer (*Werner von Haeften*, Staufenberg's aide); Eric Caspar (*Adolf Heusinger*, General injured in bomb plot); Carl Duering (*Karl Gördeler*, Former mayor of Leipzig, an anti–Hitler conspirator); Holger Petzold (*Erich Fellgiebel*, General in anti–Hitler plot); Geoffrey Rose (*Dr. Kurt Fredrich*, Nazi official in charge of US detainees at Baden-Baden); Joost Siedhoff (Doctor at Baden-Baden); Milton Johns (*Adolf Eichman*, Officer in charge of the "final solution"); Wolf Kahler (*Anton Burger*, Kommandant of Theresienstadt who kicks and beats Aaron); Robert Stephens (*Karl Rahm*, Burger's replacement as Kommandant); Erhardt Hartmann (Rahm's adjutant); Karl-Otto Alberty (*Rudolf Haindl*, Brutal SS man who threatens Natalie and Louis at Theresienstadt); Uwe Falkenbach (SS man on train to Theresienstadt); Harold Kasket (*Dr. Paul Eppstein*, Head of Council of Elders at Theresienstadt); Michael Mellinger (*Benjamin Murmelstein*, Eppstein's replacement as Head Elder); Eli Danker (*Udam*, Puppeteer at Theresienstadt); Vjen-ceslav Kapural (*Bruckner*, Noted pianist & Theresienstadt prominent); Osman Ragheb (Theresienstadt prominent); Günther Maria Halmer (*Rudolf Höss*, Kommandant of Auschwitz); Immy Schell (*Frau Höss*, His wife); Fritz von Friedl (Höss' adjutant); Derek Newark (*Sergeant Klinger*, Sergeant at Auschwitz); Michael Sarne (*Schwartz*, Captain at Auschwitz); Stelio Candelli (Auschwitz selection officer); Kenneth Colley (*Paul Blobel*, SS Colonel who oversees slave labor taken from Auschwitz); Burkhard Heyle (*Greisler*, SS officer in charge of work detail when Mutterperl revolts); Victor Baring (*Döme Sztojay*, Hungarian premier who visits Hitler on D-Day); Set Sakai (*Admiral Isoruku Yamamoto*, Leading Japanese military strategist); Danny Kamekona (*Vice Admiral Chuichu Nagumo*, Carrier fleet commander at Midway); G. D. Spradlin (*Admiral Raymond A. Spruance*, US Commander at Midway); Michael McGuire (*Miles Browning*, Captain of the *Enterprise*); Earl Hindman (*Lieutenant Commander Wade McClusky*, Head of *Enterprise* air squadrons); Robert S. Woods (*Lieutenant Eugene Lindsey*, Commander of Torpedo Squad Six); Michael Lemon (*Lt. Earl Gallaher*, Commander of Scouting Six); Richard Lineback (*Cornett*, Gunner of Warren's plane); John Sandeford (*Pete Goff*, Warren's bunkmate on the *Enterprise*); Byron Morrow (*Admiral William Lahity*, Head of US Joint Chiefs); Don Collier (*Russell Carton*, FDR's Naval Aide); Jack Rader (Sam Hickman, Captain of *Northampton* relieved by Pug); G.W. Bailey (*Jim Grigg*, *Northampton* Exec); Matt Clark (*Chief Clark*, *Northampton* officer); John Dehner (*Admiral Ernest King*, Chief of US Naval Operations); Christopher Malcolm (*Bunky Thurston*, US Diplomat in Portugal); Howard Duff (*William Tuttle*, US Ambassador in Switzerland); Lee Patterson (*August van Winaker*, Diplomat in Bern who doubts Holocaust); Heinz Bernard (*Dr. Jacob Ascher*, Wealthy Jewish luminary in Bern); Mijou Kovacs (*Selma Ascher*, His daughter, who has a brief romance with Leslie Slote); Aubrey Morris

(*Fr. Martin*, German priest who smuggles documents to Slote in Bern); William Berger (*Jim Gaither*, US Consul in Marseilles); Bertie Cortez (*Itzhak Mendelson*, Plumber in Marseilles who shelters Aaron, Natalie & Louis); Anna Tzelniker (Mendelson's wife); Giancarlo Prete (*Dr. Castelnuovo*, Jewish doctor from Siena who flees Italy with his family); Sarah Franchetti (*Ann Castelnuovo*, His wife); Emanuela Trombetta (*Miriam Castelnuovo*, Their daughter); Remo Remonatti (*Moses Sacerdote*, Cinema chain owner in Italy who helps people in flight); Margherita Horowitz (Sacerdote's wife); Igor Galo (*Frankenthal*, Agent of Rabinowitz who helps people escape from Italy); George Corraface (*Pascal Gaffori*, Corsican fisherman); Martin Cochrane (*Claude Gallfemi*, French resistance member); Michael Anthony (*Dr. Lacroix*, Physician at American Hospital in Paris); Robert Favart (*Comte de Chambrun*, Director of American Hospital); Nina Foch (*Comtesse de Chambrun*, His wife, who looks after Natalie); Vernon Dobtcheff (*Henri Dulle*); Patrick Florsheim (*Leffard*); William Doherty (*Pinkney Tuck*, US chargé d'affaires in Vichy France); Eddie Albert (*Breckinridge Long*, Assistant Secretary of State); H. Richard Greene (*Foxy Davis*, State department director); Bruce French (*Sylvester Aherne*, State Department official); Rod McCary (*Hugh Cleveland*, CBS radio star); Lin McCarthy (*"Blinker" Vance*, Naval attaché & Pug's friend); Leo Gordon (*Omar Bradley*, Commander of 1st Army); Larry Dobkin (*George S. Patton*, Commander of 3rd Army); Norman Burton (*George C. Marshall*, Chief of Army Staff); George Murdock (*Leslie Groves*, US General overseeing A-bomb project); Charles Lane (*Admiral Standley*, US Ambassador to Russia); Geoffrey Toone (British Ambassador to Russia); Brian Blessed (*General Yevlenko*, Russian officer who meets with Pug); R.G. Armstrong (*"Moose" Fitzgerald*, US General who performs Russian dance with Yevlenko); Paul Copley (*Dagget*, Pamela's Moscow chauffeur); Peter Dennis (*Sir Bernard Mont-gomery*, Leading British General); Richard Aylen (*Sir Bertram Ramsey*, British Admiral who plans D-Day invasion); Eric Christmas (*Sir Dudley Pound*, First Sea Lord & Churchill advisor); Alan Brown (*Sir Arthur Tedder*, Chief Air Marshal); Howard Caine (*Lord Maxwell Beaverbrook*, Churchill advisor & Cabinet member); Julio Scala (*General "Hap" Arnold*, Chief of Air Corps); Clifford Rose (*Lieutenant General Henry Kammfer*); Ian Abercrombie (*Vice Admiral Rodney*); Frank Marth (*Admiral Marc Milscher*, Top US carrier commander); Pat Hingle (*Admiral "Bull" Halsey*, Commander of Southern Pacific Force); David Gale (*Admiral Mick Carney*, Halsey's Chief of Staff); J. Kenneth Campbell (*Hoban*, Captain of *Devilfish* who panics); Michael Madsen (*Wilson "Foof" Turkell*, Fire control officer of *Devilfish*); Mills Watson (*Chief Derringer*, Officer on *Devilfish*); Mark Keyloun (*Billy Quayne*, Ensign aboard *Devilfish*); Grainger Hines (*Pete Betmann*, Exec on *Moray*); Ken Shriner (*"Horseshoes" Mullen*, *Moray* crewman killed in strafing attack with Captain Aster); Granville Ames, (*Lieutenant Tom Philby*, *Barracuda* Exec); Jay Avocone (*Maselli*, Quartermaster on *Barracuda*); Robert Ervin (*Jonesy*, *Barracuda* steward); Bata Zivojinovic (Yugoslav partisan leader); Nick Eldredge (Navy Chaplin who marries Pug & Pamela); Ed Van Nuys (*Admiral Lockwood*, Officer who assigns Byron to inspect German U-boats after VE Day); Dorota Puzio (*Katinka*, German woman who propositions Byron); Ann Way (*Gertrude Dana*, Bulldog Bank children's shelter director); Mavis Walker (*Alice Goldberger*, Weir Courtney shelter director who helps Byron find Louis); Addison Powell (*Admiral Harold Stark*, Chief of Naval Operations); Dennis Patrick (*Admiral Tisdale*, Flotilla commander during Battle of Tassaforonga); Barbara Steele (*Elsa MacMahon*, Singapore socialite); William Z. Woodson (Narrator).

APPRAISAL AND SYNOPSIS: The miniseries *War and Remembrance* appeared six years after *The Winds of War*, which led some reviewers to comment that it took longer to

Hitler (Stephen Beroff) enjoys a walk in Berchtesgaden with his dog Blondi in *War and Remembrance*.

film than the actual war it portrayed. At a length of 12 chapters, the miniseries was initially broadcast in two separate runs. Chapters 1 through 7 appeared on ABC in November 1988, and the last five chapters were telecast in May 1989. It can easily be compared to its predecessor, *The Winds of War*, as being twice as long and half as good. But since *The Winds of War* was among the greatest of all miniseries, being half as good

is still a remarkable achievement. Readers should review *The Winds of War* entry before proceeding. One of the relative weaknesses of *War and Remembrance* is due to the basic storyline. It is hard to equal the dramatic impact, for example, of the position of Pug Henry as the American naval attaché in wartime Berlin, confronting Hitler face to face and then serving as FDR's emissary in meetings with Mussolini, Churchill and

Stalin. In *War and Remembrance*, the exploits of Pug pale in comparison, as he is confined to sea duty or retreading his previous assignments in Russia or England. The fact is that Pug Henry is no longer the central focus of the story and is often relegated to the background. In *The Winds of War*, all the major historical figures (except Hitler) were seen through Pug's eyes. In the sequel, this structural arrangement is abandoned, and the historical characters appear helter skelter, in almost random fashion. This may not be readily apparent in a short synopsis.

Pug Henry starts off as Captain of the *Northampton* shortly after the events at Pearl Harbor in December 1941. He participates in the Battle of Midway, a crucial turning point in the war with Japan in which his son, Warren, is killed after distinguishing himself in the sinking of a Japanese aircraft carrier. After the *Northampton* is sunk in a battle, Pug returns to Washington and tries to patch up his marriage with Rhoda, who broke off her relationship with Palmer Kirby only to start another affair with Colonel Hack Peters, a military administrator involved in the Manhattan Project. Pug is sent by the President to Russia, and Rhoda heads to Reno to obtain a divorce. Meanwhile, their daughter Madeline marries Lieutenant Simon Anderson, a brilliant officer also working on the Manhattan Project. Pug is promoted to Admiral and given command of a division of battleships. Rhoda marries Colonel Peters, and Pug romances Pamela Tudsbury, whose fiance, Lord Burne-Wilke dies from complications after an air crash in India. FDR dies, and Truman assumes the Presidency. Pug marries Pamela, and the new President asks him to serve as his naval advisor. Most of the focus of the series, however, is on the career of Byron Henry as he is assigned to a number of submarines, rising in rank and responsibility after his friend, Captain Carter "Lady" Aster, is killed when a Japanese aircraft strafes their ship. Byron is finally given the command of his own ship. Most of his attention, however, is focused on his wife, Natalie, who is detained in Europe with their son Louis and her famous uncle, the writer Aaron Jastrow. They flee from Italy to Corsica and finally Vichy France, where Byron visits her in Marseilles while serving as a military courier. He wants to personally escort her out of danger, but is dissuaded by the U.S consul who urges Natalie to wait until the proper exit papers are processed by the Vichy government. But the Nazis take over Vichy France after the Allies launch an attack in French North Africa. Natalie and Aaron are detained with other Americans first at Lourdes and then at Baden-Baden in Germany. Aaron falls ill and is transferred to the American Hospital in Paris. After he recovers, the three of them are transferred to Theresienstadt, the so called "Paradise Ghetto" in Czechoslovakia where prominent Jews are detained. This model camp is a sham, a publicity stunt, which actually serves as a transition point to the death camps in the east such as Auschwitz. Eichman, the Nazi official in charge of the "Jewish question," oversees the beating of Aaron, forcing him to become an Elder in the camp in charge of cultural affairs. Berel, Aaron's cousin who escaped from a Nazi work crew, now works with the Czech underground, and he slips into Theresienstadt to visit Aaron. He agrees to smuggle Louis to safety. He is unable to save Aaron and Natalie, however, and they are eventually transferred to Auschwitz where Aaron is killed in the gas chambers. Natalie is assigned to forced labor. Auschwitz is abandoned as Russian troops approach, and she is rescued by American forces from a transport train, mostly filled with dead victims. The war in Europe ends. Hitler kills himself in his bunker in Berlin after marrying his mistress, Eva Braun. Byron is transferred to Europe to inspect the captured German U-Boats. Natalie, recovering from typhus and malnutrition, implores her husband to try to find their son, Louis. Avram Rabinowitz, who has been looking after Natalie, suggests that finding him would be a longshot. Byron learns that Berel was killed when the Nazis captured a group of partisan fighters and gunned them down. Byron eventually tracks Louis to a shelter in England where traumatized children are recovering. The war with Japan ends as the A-bomb is dropped. Byron brings Louis back to Natalie, and she is overjoyed as their family is restored. At this point, the series concludes.

There are, of course, numerous other plot lines in the miniseries, such as the attempts of Leslie Slote (David Dukes) to get the State Department to acknowledge and act upon reports of the Nazi Death camps, the travels of Alistair Tudsbury (Robert Morley) and his daughter reporting the news of the war (Alistair is killed in North Africa while en route to interview General Montgomery) and the development of the atomic bomb. These subplots are often given short shrift. Some of them simply peter out, and we never learn the fate of Kommandant Höss or General von Roon, and the death of journalist Philip Rule happens offscreen in a V-2 attack. Some of them are mishandled, such as the death of Slote during a D-Day undercover operation. Most of these plot threads lack cogency and ramble compared to *The Winds of War*, in which all the elements of the screenplay are balanced and fascinating. Only one layer consistently retains the drama and impact of the first miniseries: the tragic plight of Aaron Jastrow, Natalie Henry and Louis, as they are trapped in war-torn Europe, eventually winding up in Auschwitz. The downward spiral of their fate, of course, mirrors the plight of the millions of victims of planned extermination carried out against the Jews, the gypsies and others whom the Nazis wished to eradicate. This powerful depiction of the holocaust is perhaps among the most intense and disturbing images ever committed to film. These sequences are presented methodically, almost in documentary fashion, and are all the more potent because they are not artificially hyped. Some moments of the drama are so devastating that many viewers may simply be overwhelmed. With such a powerful storyline, it is little

wonder that other elements of the plot, such as the affairs of Rhoda Henry or the carousing of Carter "Lady" Aster seem paltry, inconsequential and without interest. There are a few other highlights, principally the battle of Midway and the submarine operations of Byron Henry, but they also lack the overall punch and impact of the collateral plots in *The Winds of War*.

A second handicap to the sequel is the massive reshuffling of the cast. Only about half of the original cast returned in their original roles, principally Robert Mitchum, Polly Bergen, Victoria Tennant, David Dukes, Topol, Jeremy Kemp, Peter Graves and Ralph Bellamy. To render it even more confusing, a number of the secondary performers switched roles. In the original series, for example, Barry Morse played the German banker Wolf Stoller, and Werner Kriendl played General Franz Halder. But in the follow up, Morse is switched to the role of Franz Halder. Others performers are also shuffled around. Sky Dumont, who played Mussolini's Foreign Minister Count Ciano in the original becomes Count Claus von Stauffenberg, the failed assassin of Hitler. On the whole, most of the cast changes are disappointments compared to the original performers. A few are improvements, notably Steven Berkoff as Adolf Hitler, William Schallert as Harry Hopkins, Brian Blessed as General Yevlenko, Sharon Stone as Janice Henry, John Gielgud as Aaron Jastrow and Barry Bostwick as "Lady" Aster. Most of the others, however, seem less suited to their parts, none more obviously than Jane Seymour, who turns in a radically different characterization as Natalie Henry from the portrayal by Ali MacGraw. True, Seymour gives a memorable performance and was nominated for an Emmy, but she never seems like the original character, totally unable to project herself as an American. At one point, when Natalie is in the crowded boxcar heading to Auschwitz, she keeps repeating to herself, "I am an American," yet this also lacks conviction. Ali MacGraw captured this aspect beautifully, making Natalie a unique and unforgettable personality in *The Winds of War*, but Seymour transforms Natalie from her initial appearance into a traditional victim, similar in style to Talia Shire. Imagine how *Gone with the Wind* would suffer if Scarlett O'Hara had a similar transformation in the second half of the novel. Hart Bochner faces a similar problem as Byron Henry, unable to duplicate the fresh vitality of Jan-Michael Vincent in the role. But Bochner wisely patterns his interpretation instead as a younger version of Pug, Robert Mitchum, and he gradually grows into the role and makes it his own by the final chapter. Sami Frey, as Avram Rabinowitz, is somewhat of a cipher, his major purpose being to perk Natalie's interest in relocating to Palestine and to step into Byron's shoes in case the American is killed in action. Frey, however, is so reminiscent of François Truffaut, that Rabinowitz never comes into focus, despite the ample screen time spent on his character. Other cast change letdowns occur in the roles of Madeleine Henry (Leslie Hope), Warren Henry (Michael Woods), Alistair Tudsbury (Robert Morley) and Winston Churchill (Robert Hardy). Hardy formerly played Joachim von Ribbentrop, the Nazi foreign minister, in *The Gathering Storm*. A few of the new characters perform well in their roles, particularly Bill Wallis as Werner Beck, playeded with a nod toward Peter Lorre, and John Rhys-Davies as Sammy Mutterperl. The latter is a particularly important character who represents the countless Jews who fought back against their oppressors while facing hopeless odds. Too often in holocaust dramas, those who resisted the Nazis are seldom portrayed compared to those who seem to just accept their fate. Günther Maria Halmer is brilliant as Rudolf Höss, the Kommandant of Auschwitz, a role he earlier played in *Sophie's Choice* (1982). Milton Johns is terrifying as the icy and fastidious Adolf Eichman, reminisent of the characterization of Peter Cushing as the amoral Baron Frankenstein in numerous films. Hardy Kruger brings

depth and conviction to his interpretation of Erwin Rommel, basically a simple soldier who is upset by the treatment of the Jews and the maniacal policies of the Führer. E. G. Marshall and Richard Dysart are exceptional in their cameos as Eisenhower and Truman. G. D. Spradlin brings stoic dignity to his depiction as Admiral Spruance. On the other hand, Mike Connors, a splendid actor, is given little to do as Colonel Peters, except for one hilarious train scene when he bunks with Pug and pesters him with endless questions about Rhoda. Ian McShane is a washout as the alcoholic British newsman, Philip Rule. Robert Stephens is unconvincing and unbelievable as Rahm, the second Kommandant of Theresienstadt, and he completely ruins the terminal selection scene with his mugging and overacting. Dan Curtis also included two *Dark Shadows* alumni in the cast: Dennis Patrick, best remembered for playing Paul Stoddard, the wayward husband of Collins family matriarch Elizabeth (Joan Bennett) as well as schemer Jason McGuire and Addison Powell, who played Dr. Lang, the resident mad scientist. The producer of *War and Remembrance* was Barbara Steele, veteran of numerous horror films, who appears in a cameo in the opening episode. In 1990, Dan Curtis revived *Dark Shadows* in a prime time version, and he turned again to Barbara Steele to assume the key role of Dr. Julia Hoffman.

War and Remembrance received a considerable number of awards and nominations, but the ratings were significantly lower than *The Winds of War*. Many local stations posted warnings of the graphic nature of some of the death camp sequences, and this no doubt contributed to the lower viewership. A minor controversy was generated by the unfortunate placement of an ad for Tilex shower cleaner directly after a scene depicting in which prisoners were killed in a gas chamber that contained phony shower fixtures. Nonetheless, the production received deserved praise for its frank presentation, which laid out the outrages not only of the plight of the Jews in Nazi Germany, but the deliberate refusal of the US State Department to follow through on reports of these crimes of extermination when they had clear evidence of their occurrence.

HITLER PORTRAYAL: Steven Berkoff is a British-born character actor who has been active in films since the late 1950s, appearing in such varied productions as *I Was Monty's Double* (1958), *Nicholas and Alexandra* (1970) and *A Clockwork Orange* (1971). He began to draw serious attention after his appearance as Lord Ludd in *Barry Lyndon* (1975), eventually becoming the lead villain in the James Bond thriller *Octopussy* (1983) and the Eddie Murphy blockbuster *Beverly Hills Cop* (1984). Berkoff's resemblance to Hitler is only fair to good, except in profile in which case the likeness is remarkable. The wen in the center of Berkoff's forehead is sometimes distracting, however. If the Führer in real life had such a feature, cartoonists would have had a field day drawing it as a "bull's eye" target. Berkoff's interpretation of the role is high-strung and erratic, and the actor manages to capture many of Hitler's gestures quite convincingly. Unfortunately, the role of Hitler is not as well written as in *The Winds of War*, being much narrower in scope and without much variety until the bunker scenes in the last episode. In most of the episodes, the Führer only puts in a token appearance, usually berating one or more of his generals as inadequate, cowardly or stupid. These rants become tiresome and repetitive, but when Berkoff's tantrums get out of control, they are almost amusing, as he sputters, snarls and works himself into a bug-eyed frenzy. Of course, to a certain extent they accurately portray Hitler's activities during the last three years of the war, holed up in his Prussian headquarters at Rastenburg where he micromanaged the army, often undercutting and disregarding practical military tactics. There are several instances which are highlights in Berkoff's depiction of Hitler, the first being his two scenes with Michael Wolff as Göring in which the Führer questions him. After he asks for the Reich Marshal's assurance re-garding the Luftwaffe's capability of supplying the trapped troops in Stalingrad, his face assumes a look of incredible dubiousness. It is the only genuinely satiric moment in Berkoff's reading, and it is priceless. The second instance, however, is chilling, as Hitler screens the footage of the bomb plot conspirators being strung up with piano wire. The Führer roars with laughter at these gruesome clips, and his wholehearted enjoyment is one of the most repellent moments in any Hitler screen portrayal; moreover, it is an event that is historically accurate.

War and Remembrance is divided into twelve chapters, but unlike *The Winds of War*, they are not individually titled. Hitler figures prominently in episodes five, nine, ten and twelve. He appears only briefly in episodes one, two, four, six, seven and eleven, while missing chapters three and eight entirely. Chapter five concentrates on Hitler's response to the Allied invasion of French North Africa in November 1942. Scenes depict Hitler traveling on his special armed train as he learns of the attack. Berkoff delivers his only German language scene in a Munich speech commemorating the Beer Hall Putsch. When he returns to his Prussian headquarters in Rastenburg, Hitler is frustrated to learn of a Soviet counterattack at Stalingrad, and he issues orders to his troops forbidding them to retreat and regroup, but to fight and die where they stand. The results of his foolish orders are depicted in episode six, as the Führer consoles himself over the loss of Stalingrad and his 6th army by playing a recording of Wagner's *Tristan und Isolde* and stroking his pet German Shepherd. In the ninth episode, a number of army officers plan to assassinate Hitler. While at Berchtesgaden, the Führer downplays and totally misreads the impact of the Normandy invasion on D-Day, spending much of his day entertaining the new Prime Minister of Hungary. The tenth chapter features a detailed recreation of the bomb attempt at Rastenburg, one of Berkoff's best scenes. The twelfth chapter contains the most screen time for Hitler, depicting his final days in the bunker, his final tirade and breakdown after he learns that the counter-attack by General Steiner which he ordered was never attempted, and his hasty marriage and suicide plans. In fact, the emphasis on Hitler seems greatest in this chapter, although Berkoff's interpretation of the Führer appears uncertain and somewhat *pro forma* in these last scenes. Berkoff just runs through some of these scenes, excelling only in the one in which he dictates his last will and testament, a passionate liteny of hatred aimed against the Jews. On the whole, Berkoff's performance as Hitler is fairly good, but lacks any real distinction, particularly in the light of other performers who made these scenes unforgettable. Of the other Nazi leaders, Michael Wolff, Ian Jentle and Geoffrey Whitehead are superb as Göring, Goebbels and Speer. Wolfgang Reichmann is only fair as Bormann. The finest depiction is Dieter Wagner as Himmler, a role he also essayed in the first series.

REPRESENTATIVE QUOTES

• Always looking for an easy war, for a simple way while you snicker behind my back at the Bohemian Corporal who knows, from bitter experience, from lying gassed at a field hospital, that war is hard… There will be no withdrawal on the eastern front. Every German soldier will hold or die where he stands. *(Hitler to von Brauchitch & Halder after reading their recommendations for the Russian front during the winter of 1941)*

• Franklin, we shall have that evil man. *(Churchill to FDR, referring to the Führer during their Christmas eve meeting, 1941)* I believe we shall, Winston. Come, you throw the switch and light the tree. *(FDR's reply)*

• Napoleon escaped from Elba. So shall we. *(Aaron to Natalie, en route to the island)*

• Italian intelligence is about as reliable as Italian troops. *(Hitler to General von Roon, on the train to Munich in November 1942)*

• How did he not have the decency to kill himself? Do you know what hurts me the most? That I promoted him to Field Mar-

shal! *(Hitler to his General Staff, raging against Paulus after the fall of Stalingrad in February 1943)*

• Attack? In the East? After Stalingrad? *(Rommel, stunned, to Hitler)* Especially after Stalingrad! They are too cocky now to make a decent separate peace. So, I must tear a great hole in their front. Yes, one good bloody nose, and Stalin and I will be doing business again. *(Hitler's reply)*

• Gentlemen, we face the shakiest coalition of all time, ultra-capitalist states and ultra–Marxist states. *(Hitler, briefing a meeting of military leaders before launching the Battle of the Bulge in December 1944)*

• I should have won this war. I did not make a single mistake. *(Hitler to General von Roon in the bunker on April 29, 1945)*

93.　*What Did You Do in the War, Daddy?* (1966)

Carl Ekberg as Adolf Hitler (cameo)
Comedy

United Artists. Written by William Peter Blatty; Photographed by Philip Lathrop; Edited by Ralph E. Winters; Music by Henry Mancini; Produced & directed by Blake Edwards. Color 119 minutes

ANNOTATED CAST LIST: James Coburn (*Lieutenant Jody Christian*, Company C officer); Dick Shawn (*Captain Lionel Cash*, New commander of Company C); Sergio Fantori (*Captain Fausto Oppo*, Italian commander of Valerno); Jay Novello (*Giuletto Romano*, Mayor of Valerno); Giovanna Ralli (*Gina Romano*, His daughter); Aldo Ray (*Sergeant Rizzo*, Company C translator); Carroll O'Connor (*General Max Bolt*, Regional commander); Harry Morgan (*Major Pott*, Intelligence officer who gets lost in the catacombs); Herb Ellis (*Lumpe*, Cameraman & Pott's driver); Leon Askin (*Colonel Kastorp*, German commander); Henry Rico Cattani (*Benedetto*, Italian thief); Vito Scotti (*Frederico*, His partner); William Bryant (*Corporal Minnow*, Company C radio man); Ken Wales (*PFC Blair*); Art Lewis (*Needleman*); Kurt Kreuger (German Captain);

Robert Carricart (Cook); Ralph Manza (Waiter).

APPRAISAL AND SYNOPSIS: For all intents and purposes, *What Did You Do in the War, Daddy?* seems like a leftover chapter from the last season, 1965-66, of *McHale's Navy*, which was set in Italy. The village of Valerno appears to be the same set as the village of Voltafiore, and the mayor of both towns is played by the same actor, Jay Novello. Vito Scotti, another member of the film cast, also appeared as a guest on the television series. The madcap scenario and flavor of the film is certainly reminiscent of *McHale's Navy* as well. *What Did You Do in the War, Daddy?* also has a number of other television connections. The chief Nazi villain, Leon Askin, played a similar role on *Hogan's Heroes*. In addition, it is reported that Carroll O'Connor's performance as the blustery General Max Bolt helped to win him the part of Archie Bunker in *All in the Family*. Likewise, Harry Morgan's turn as Major Pott helped to inspire his later casting as the similarly named Colonel Sherman Potter in *M*A*S*H*.

What Did You Do in the War, Daddy? is an out and out military farce. Captain Lionel Cash is assigned by General Bolt to take charge of a ragtag, scruffy unit, C Company, and secure the village of Valerno in Sicily in 1943. When they arrive at the remote town, the Italian troops stationed there under the fun-loving Captain Oppo agree to surrender only if they are allowed to celebrate at the town fiesta scheduled for that evening. The by-the-book Cash reluctantly agrees, and almost all the participants get drunk during the festivities. The next morning, Major Pott, an intelligence officer, shows up. Since the American and Italian troops exchanged uniforms during their merrymaking, he is confused as to who's who. Sergeant Rizzo, an American dressed in an Italian army uniform, pretends to arrest Pott, locking him in the local jail. He is freed, however, by two thieves who are trying to tunnel their way into the local bank. Pott escapes, but becomes completely lost in the labyrinth of underground catacombs. Meanwhile, aerial reconnaissance photos, taken during a brief melee, convince the Allies and the Italians that intense, hand-to-hand combat is raging in Valerno. Lieutenant Christian persuades Cash and Oppo to cooperate by staging a mock battle whenever any aircraft passes over the town. Unfortunately, the next plane is German, and the photo of the battle is taken to Hitler himself. He is so impressed by the level of combat that he sends a German division to tip the scales of battle. When this forces arrive, Colonel Kastorp is outraged to find the Italian troops consorting with the enemy. He takes all the Americans and Italians prisoner, bivouacking them in the town square. He issues orders that they all be executed in the morning. That night, a number of the men escape into the catacombs, encountering Pott who is now demented. Meanwhile, Kastorp dies while trying to entertain Gina Romano, the beautiful daughter of the mayor who had previously won the hearts of both Cash and Oppo. The Italians and the Americans cooperate, overwhelming the Nazis one by one and posing in their uniforms. By the following morning, they spring their trap, capturing the entire Nazi division before General Bolt arrives with a relief force. Cash is given a field promotion, and he persuades the general to provide a party for the Italian troops. The picture comes to an end as Gina now entertains General Bolt.

What Did You Do in the War, Daddy? is amusing, but considerably flawed as well. The pacing of the film is poor, and overlong at almost two hours, The story is unfocused and rather confusing at times, particularly since the lengthy dialogue in Italian and German is never translated. It is odd that subtitles were not provided. James Coburn, Aldo Ray and Carroll O'Connor are fine in their parts, but Dick Shawn seems a bit at sea in his role that seems to have been written with Jack Lemmon in mind. The satirical edge of the script by *Exorcist* scribe William Peter Blatty, seems uneven and meandering. There are a few clever touches.

The portrait at the inn, for example, switches from FDR to Hitler depending on who is in charge at the moment, but most of the humor seems forced. There are also too many leftover threads. The episode concerning Major Pott is never resolved, for example, and he is still on the loose as the end credits roll.

HITLER PORTRAYAL: Carl Ekberg made his first appearance as Hitler over twenty-five years earlier, in *Man Hunt*. Due to his age, he is kept in the shadows for most of his brief scene, with the humor coming from his peculiarly phrased hybrid of German and English. He merely watches the projection of the aerial photo over Valerno, issues his order, and steps out onto a balcony to receive a chorus of "Sieg Heil" shouts and cheers. On the whole, this scene seems to have been tossed in as an afterthought. Coincidentally, three actors in the cast had played Hitler in their careers, Ekberg, Shawn and Manza.

REPRESENTATIVE QUOTES

• Three days, three incredible days, and what have we accomplished? I'll tell you. We have misplaced Major Pott. This idiot has made a movie directed by Cecil B. Christian, starring the three knuckleheads and the Italian war hero Kid Guts. The village is in an uproar and I'm queen of the May. In the meantime, there is a war going on, not a documentary, but a war. *(Exasperated Cash to his men and Captain Oppo)*

• Cash, are you out of your mind? What the hell do you mean? Give them a party? *(General Bolt, after hearing the Italian troop's terms for their surrender)*

94. *Which Way to the Front?* (1970)

Sidney Miller as Adolf Hitler
Comedy

Warner Brothers. Written by Dee Caruso, Gerald Gardner & Richard Miller; Photographed by W. Wallace Kelly; Edited by Russell Wiles; Music by Louis Y. Brown, Nikolai Rimsky-Korsakov & others; Produced & directed by Jerry Lewis. Color 96 minutes

ANNOTATED CAST LIST: Jerry Lewis (*Brendan Byers III*, American millionaire & *Field Marshal Eric Kesselring*, Hitler's favorite general); Jan Murray (*Sid Hackle*, Comic in debt to the mob); John Wood (*Finkel*, Tailor who joins Byers' unit); Steve Franken (*Peter Bland*, Milquetoast who wants to escape his wife's control); Bodo Lewis (Bland's wife); Kathleen Freeman (Bland's mother); Dack Rambo (*Terry Love*, Lothario who joins Byers' unit); Willie Davis (*Lincoln*, Chauffeur who joins Byers' unit); Paul Winchell (*Schroeder*, Kesselring's adjutant); Kaye Ballard (Kesselring's Italian mistress); George Takei (*Yamashita*, Combat specialist hired by Byers); Robert Middleton (*Colonico*, Mobster hired by Byers); Harold J. Stone (*General Buck*, American commander at Italian front); Neil Hamilton (U.S. Chief of staff); Joe Besser (Dock master in Naples); Ron Lewis (*Lieutenant Levitch*, Nazi medal winner); Bob Layker (Sergeant); Mike Mazurki (*Rocky*, Thug who hassles Hackle); Martin Kosleck (U-Boat captain); Gary Crosby, Artie Lewis, Mickey Manners (S.S. guards); Danny Dayton, Kenneth MacDonald, Myron Healey, Richard Loo.

APPRAISAL AND SYNOPSIS: Jerry Lewis made at least one film every year from 1949 through 1970, and *Which Way to the Front* was the last effort in this prolific series. Afterwards, his film appearances were sporadic. Toward the end of this string of pictures, Lewis made efforts to choose roles that reflected his actual age, since he had outgrown his "basically a kid" persona. Some of these efforts, such as *Boeing Boeing* (1965) and *Hook, Line and Sinker* (1969) were quite successful, while others were atrocious. *Which Way to the Front?* has been particularly panned by critics, but it was an interesting experiment by Lewis, a broad satire of war films, but one that never completely gels. Some of it is so unfunny that it is almost painful to watch, but there are instances of pure hilarity as well.

The basic plot involves millionaire Bren-

Sidney Miller and Jerry Lewis play the Hitler bomb plot for laughs in *Which Way to the Front?*

dan Byers, a bored industrial magnate who considers it an honor when he receives a draft notice in 1943. After he is classified 4-F (making him inelogible for service), Byers forms his own private army unit to help in the war effort. The title credits appear rather late into the film, using "The Procession of the Nobles" from the opera *Mlada* by Rimsky-Korsakov as the main theme. Byers recruits other army rejects, including Sid Hackle, a stand-up comic in dutch with the mob, Albert Bland, a henpecked husband, and Terry Love, in a pickle for impregnating two different girlfriends. Byers buys uniforms, employs knowledgeable combat instructors and purchases the best military equipment. Finally, together with his small band of men, Byers heads to Italy, where a four month stalemate has bogged down the Allied war effort and cost the lives of countless soldiers. Byers plans to impersonate Field Marshal Kesselring, in command of

the German troops at the front. (In actuality, Field Marshal Kesselring, who was in charge of the Italian campaign at this point, was named Albert, not Eric, and he was the German General most respected by the Allies.) He and his five men slip behind enemy lines and observe Kesselring and his headquarters through binoculars, confirming that the Field Marshal and the American millionaire are indeed doubles. Byers develops a odd scheme to take the place of Kesselring in broad daylight as the Field Marshal walks with his staff.

After the switch, Byers as Kesselring orders the German troops to pull back from their excellent mountain defenses. To his surprise, the Allies do nothing, fearing it is a trap. When they finally advance, Byers attends a meeting of high officers and learns that Kesselring was actually spearheading a plot to assassinate Hitler and end the war. Kesselring had developed the plan to carry and plant the bomb himself at his briefing with the Führer. At the meeting, held in a bunker in a secure location, Hitler greets Byers/Kesselring as if they were long lost lovers. They engage in much byplay, as Hitler invites Kesselring to Berchtesgaden as he complains about the demands placed upon him by Eva Braun. When other officers arrive at the meeting, the briefcase with the bomb gets mixed up with the briefcases of the other officers. Byers flees the scene, and sends the guards into the bunker to report to the Führer. The bomb explodes moments later, and Byers and his men escape, only to be captured by Allied soldiers unaware of their mission. They are soon freed, however, but instead of returning home, Byers and his men head to Japan, where they intend to infiltrate the Japanese High Command and subvert their war effort.

The straight synopsis fails to convey the spirit of this comedy, which is both extravagant and bizarre. The script, although set in 1943, has numerous modern references to such items as dental floss, long playing records and condominium units. The structure is rather free-flowing, with freeze frames used quite frequently to stress the episodic nature of the picture. There are a number of hilarious moments, such as when Lewis learns German by phonograph record, his frantic double talk routine to discover the password from a German sentry and the strange concept of satirizing the Rastenburg assassination attempt as it is depicted in other films. On the other hand, numerous bits fall terribly flat, such as the weak visual gags of the men training, the awkward and unfunny scene between Lewis and Kaye Ballard, Kesselring's mistress, and especially the terrible closing scene at Japanese headquarters, with members of Byers' unit are thinly disguised as Japanese officers, which is not only weak humor but hints of racism as well. The "big band" musical score is inappropriate, and Lewis' sense of timing is rather ham-handed throughout. Too often he steps on his own gags, ruining the humor by over-

doing it. *Which Way to the Front?* can be seen as a rather personal film, which uses a number of Lewis film regulars and family members. He manages to sneak in a reference to his home town, Newark, as well as his actual name, Levitch. On the whole, dedicated fans of Jerry can still find a number of bright moments, but detractors and neutral observers will find it almost unbearable.

HITLER PORTRAYAL: Moon-faced comic Sidney Miller creates a caricature of Hitler straight out of burlesque, brash, silly yet earning a handful of chuckles. Actually, Miller is a screen veteran whose film work dates back to 1931. As a juvenile, he frequently appeared in a number of series such as *Andy Hardy*, *Henry Aldrich* and the *Boys' Town* pictures. In his later years, Miller concentrated on vocal work in cartoons. There is no real visual similarity between Hitler and Miller, but he does a fairly decent lampoon of the Führer. His performance is very physical, employing slapstick and pratfalls. When Hitler greets Byers/Kesselring in his underground bunker, they do a slow motion ballet as the soundtrack plays Tchaikovsky's *Romeo and Juliet*. Then they trade jabs and face pinches, as they go through a number of routines. The horseplay is evenly divided, but the entire sequence is weakened by Lewis' endless shouting which becomes wearisome. Miller, on the other hand, varies his speaking levels, and he is more amusing by far in this extended scene. When the other officers join them, a routine develops about mixing up their briefcases, so the placement of the one with the bomb becomes hopelessly confused. The routine never comes to a proper conclusion as Lewis flees the bunker before the explosion. Lewis based the character of Eric Kesselring on Field Marshal Albert Kesselring, perhaps the most respected of the Nazi generals for his effective defensive campaign in Italy in 1943 and 1944. In real life, Kesselring opened secret negotiations with the Americans to end the war early in 1945, so some of the events of this comedy have an actual historical basis.

Of the other cast members, Paul Winchell and Steve Franken are the most amusing overall and the most successful. Jerry Lewis makes a genuine effort to spread the laughs among the cast, unlike some of his other films where he hogs the limelight. Many bit players, such as Joe Besser, onetime member of the Three Stooges, and screen heavy Mike Mazurki are given an opportunity at center stage. If the overall material in the script weren't so feeble, this ensemble effort might have been more noticeable. As it is, the comic highlight of the film is a co-operative effort. After observing the real Kesselring with binoculars, each member of the unit create his own impression of his walk. This sequence is quite funny, as each character interprets the peculiar walk through his own personality, and Lewis shares and balances equally the humor in this routine.

REPRESENTATIVE QUOTES

• Conrad Veidt would be proud. *(Bland to Byers after his transformation into Kesselring)*

• Ah, Kesselring, do you know everyone? Von Pabst, Von Heineken, Von Busch and Von Schlitz *(The general who introduces Kesselring at the meeting to plan Hitler's assassination)*

• Do you know who that is? *(Hitler, pointing to a photo of a crowd at a party rally)* No, mein Führer. *(Byers as Kesselring)* Max! *(Hitler)* Max who? *(Byers)* Max no difference! *(Hitler)*

• Did you know last year more people died from cigarette smoking than from bombings? *(Hitler)* What will you do about that, Führer? *(Byers as Kesselring)* Increase the bombings! *(Hitler)*

95.   *The Whip Hand*
(AKA *The Man He Found*)
(1951)

Bobby Watson as Adolf Hitler (original version)
Thriller

RKO. Written by Stanley Ruben (original version), George Bricker & Frank L.

Moss (revision); Photographed by Nicholas Musuraca; Edited by Robert Golden; Music by Paul Sawtell; Produced by Lewis J. Rachmil & Howard Hughes (executive in charge); Directed by William Cameron Menzies. B & W 82 minutes

ANNOTATED CAST LIST: Elliott Reid (*Matt Corbin*, Magazine writer on vacation); Carla Balenda (*Janet Keller*, Receptionist who befriends Matt); Edgar Barrier (Dr. Edward Keller, Her brother, the town doctor); Raymond Burr (*Steve Loomis*, Winnoga innkeeper); Lurene Tuttle (*Molly Loomis*, His wife, the Winnoga switchboard operator); Frank Darien (*Luther Adams*, General store owner); Milton Kibbee (Manager of Cash Produce Company in Leonopoc); Bill Nelson (*Ed*, Delivery man for Cash Produce Company); Peter Brocco (*Nate Garr*, Winnoga gas station owner); Michael Steele (*Chick*, Winnoga handyman); Lewis Martin (*Peterson*, Owner of secluded lodge, real name Schwicker); G. Pat Collins (Peterson's armed gate keeper); Robert Foulke, William Challee (Peterson's armed guards); Olive Carey (*Mabel Turner*, Farm woman who drives Matt in her truck); George Chandler (*Jed*, Man tipped off by Turner); Art Dupois (Speedboat pilot); Frank Wilcox (*Bradford*, Editor of *American View* magazine); Jameson Shade (Leonopoc sheriff); Brick Sullivan, Robert Thom (Rangers); Otto Waldis (*Dr. Wilhelm Bucholtz*, Nazi war criminal & germ warfare expert); William Yetter, Sr. (Nazi lieutenant in original version); William Yetter, Jr. (Nazi sergeant in original version).

APPRAISAL AND SYNOPSIS: There were two versions made of *The Whip Hand*. The original film, also known as *The Man He Found*, concerned an American magazine reporter, Matt Corbin, on a fishing vacation who stumbles across an armed, isolated lodge at a remote lake in Winnoga, Wisconsin. Matt learns that the fish in the local lake were wiped out by a virus five years earlier, and that most of the residents moved away after they were bought off by a strange group of newcomers. Investigating further, he makes the shocking discovery that Adolf

Hitler is the resident of the lodge, planning to launch a germ warfare attack against the United States, having poisoned the fish in the lake as an experiment. Trapped in the town run by the Nazis, Matt is able to smuggle a message out to his editor with the assistance of Luther Adams, the elderly general store owner. When the Nazis suspect that Adams is helping the reporter, they kill him with a drug that simulates a heart attack. Matt flees with Janet Keller, the remaining non–Nazi in Winnoga, but they are caught and brought to the lodge where they encounter Hitler face to face. Rangers and State Police units, alerted by Matt's editor, raid the lodge, putting an end to the Nazi menace once and for all.

After the film was completed, Howard Hughes decided to pull it after test marketing. He decided to change the nature of the threat from the Nazis to the Communists. He intended to make the film more topical, inspired by other "Red Scare" films such as *The Red Menace* (1949) and *I Married a Communist* (1950). About 10% of the film was reshot, including a new opening set in Moscow. All scenes with Hitler and references to him were removed. Hitler's germ warfare expert, Dr. Wilhelm Bucholtz, was promoted to the role of chief villain. However, he is depicted as being in the pay of the Communists. Of course, some of the film's elements did not fit smoothly into the new plot slant. For example, the Nazis originally poisoned the lake in late 1945, just before the "newcomers" arrived. This timetable makes sense in regard to a Nazi scheme, but seems premature for a Communist plot hatched in Moscow. Also, according to the old magazine article written by Matt, Dr. Bucholtz didn't defect to the Communist cause until 1946, again causing a contradiction within the timetable of events. A few of the newcomers, such as Chick, distinctly resemble Aryan storm troopers. On the whole, however, the editing of the film smoothly integrates the substitution of the Communists for the Nazis with the exception of the discrepancies already discussed.

While the Communist scenario might have seemed to be more timely, there seems to be little doubt that the Hitler plot would have made a more interesting film, one which would have been worth repeated viewings. *The Whip Hand* largely fizzled at the box office, and it never received much play on television either. The version with Hitler, however, might have become a cult favorite. In any case, it is unlikely that the original version of *The Whip Hand* will ever be seen, unless an enterprising film historian is able to find an original print in an obscure corner of the studio vault or in a private collection. It would probably be successful as a curio in the video marketplace.

HITLER PORTRAYAL: Bobby Watson's lost Hitler performance can be reconstructed from the original script. His first appearance occurs when Matt takes his camera on a hike to the wooded hills overlooking the lodge. He spots the figure of the Führer on the grounds, but is unable to ascertain his actual identity. This does not occur until much later, when Matt and Janet try to sneak onto the grounds of the lodge from a rowboat on the lake. This scene is at night, and they hear a figure conversing loudly in German on the outside balcony of the lodge. He finally steps out into the moonlight, and is revealed as Adolf Hitler. Incidentally, the script makes no mention of how the Führer escaped from Berlin except for a throwaway line referring to a double. In the revised version, Matt spots Dr. Bucholtz instead of the Führer in the first scene and the second scene is eliminated. Reportedly, some of Bucholtz's dialogue at the end of the revised film was spoken by Hitler in the original.

REPRESENTATIVE QUOTES

• First we have interrogation, then fear, a warning shot, now censorship... What are these characters trying to do? Drop an iron curtain around Winnoga? *(Matt to Janet, after she urges him to leave Winnoga)*
• It is uncivilized to let Napoleon brandy go to waste. *(Peterson to Matt)*
• All you Americans are alike, stupid,

guileless. By the time we are finished, American View magazine won't even have any readers. There are enough germs here to destroy the United States, when the word is given. *(Dr. Bucholtz to Matt and Janet)*

96. *The Winds of War* (1983)
Gunter Meisner as Adolf Hitler
Historical drama

Paramount. Written by Herman Wouk based on his novel *The Winds of War*; Photographed by Charles Correll & Stevan Larner; Edited by Bernard Gribble, Jack Tucker, Gary Smith, Peter Zinner, John F. Burnett & Earle Herdan; Music by Robert Colbert; Produced by Dan Curtis & Barbara Steele (associate); Directed by Dan Curtis. Color 7 episodes, approximately 940 minutes

ANNOTATED CAST LIST: Robert Mitchum (*Victor "Pug" Henry*, Career naval officer); Polly Bergen (*Rhoda*, His wife); Ben Murphy (*Warren*, Their eldest son, a carrier pilot); Jan-Michael Vincent (*Byron*, Second son, a submarine officer); Lisa Eilbacher (*Madeline*, Their daughter, a radio network staffer); John Houseman (*Aaron Jastrow*, Historian working in Italy); Ali MacGraw (*Natalie*, His niece, who marries Byron); David Dukes (*Leslie Slote*, American diplomat, in love with Natalie); Peter Graves (*Palmer "Fred" Kirby*, Scientist in love with Rhoda); Jeremy Kemp (*Armin von Roon*, German General who befriends Pug); Michael Logan (*Alistair Tudsbury*, British journalist); Victoria Tennant (*Pamela Tudsbury*, His daughter, who falls in love with Pug); Richard Barnes (*Ted Gallard*, Her fiancee, a RAF pilot lost over English Channel); Topol (*Berel Jastrow*, Aaron's cousin, a Polish Jew); Henryk Raifer (Berel's son, a new bridegroom); Etel Shyc (His bride); Ralph Bellamy (*Franklin D. Roosevelt*, US President); Elizabeth Hoffman (*Eleanor Roosevelt*, His wife); Roy Poole (*Harry Hopkins*, Presidential advisor & Secretary of Commerce); Duncan Ross (*Somerset Maugham*, Author & Roosevelt's dinner

guest); Howard Leng (*Winston Churchill*, British Prime Minister); Jacques Herlin (*Paul Reynaud*, French Prime Minister); Anatoly Chaguinian (*Josef Stalin*, Soviet dictator); Enzo Castellari (*Benito Mussolini*, Italian dictator); Sky Dumont (*Count Galeazzo Ciano*, Italian Foreign Minister); Rene Kolldehoff (*Hermann Göring*, Reich Marshal); Anton Diffring (*Joachim von Ribbentrop*, Nazi Foreign Minister); Reinhard Olemnitz (*Paul Schmidt*, Hitler's interpreter); Dieter Wagner (*Heinrich Himmler*, Interior Minister & Head of SS); Wolfgang Preiss (*Walter von Brauchitch*, Head of German army until 1941); Werner Kriendl (*Franz Halder*, Hitler's Chief of the General Staff); Rainer Penhert (*Erich Raeder*, Head of German navy); Alexander Kirst (*Wilhelm Keitel*, Field Marshal & Chief of the High Command); Joachim Hansen (*Alfred Jodl*, General & Chief of Operations); Peter Bourne (Captain of *Bremen*); Barry Morse (*Wolf Stoller*, German financier allied with Göring); Barbara Steele (Stoller's wife); Stefan Gierasch (Berlin realtor); Ferdy Mayne (*Ludwig Rosenthal*, Jewish industrialist who rents his Berlin home to Pug); Justin Berlin (German businessman at Stoller's party); Karlheinz Heitman (German actor at Stoller's party); James Ray (*Reese Claremont*, American Chargé in Berlin); John Carter (*Bill Forrest*, US army attaché in Berlin); Judith Atwell (*Sally*, His wife & Rhoda's friend); Michael McGuire (*Fred Fearing*, American radio reporter in Berlin); Edmund Purdom (*Luigi Gianelli*, Banker who accompanies Pug to see Hitler); Ben Hammer (*Sumner Wells*, FDR's peace envoy); Peter Brocco (Natalie's father); Belle Ellig (Natalie's mother); Byron Morrow (*Admiral Preble*, Pug's commanding officer); Don Collier (*Russell Carton*, FDR's Navy attaché); Scott Brady (*Red Tully*, Sub school commander); John Dehner (*Admiral Ernest King*, Officer who orders Pug to carry out squadron maneuvers in support of Lend Lease); Jack Ging (Destroyer captain during maneuvers); Albert Rueprecht (Wolf pack commandant); Fritz von Friedl (*Steiner*,

U-boat captain); Reinhold Claszewski (Warsaw doctor); Ivo Jurisa (Swedish ambassador in Poland); Siegfried Rauch (*Ernst Bayer*, German officer who greets Byron after crossing Polish front); Arthur Brauss (SS interrogator who questions American refugees); Osman Ragheb (SS officer who calls off interrogation); Ron Rifkin (*Mark Hartley*, Refugee protected by Leslie); Carolyn Rusoff (*Claire Young*, Woman questioned by SS); Lewis Cianelli (*Tom Stanley*, Man questioned by SS); Paul Karloen (*Rev. Glenville*, Minister who vouches for Hartley); Alberto Morin (Portuguese Admiral); Anton Strunjak (*Manual*, Lisbon marriage bureau official); Demetar Bitnec (German Ambassador in Portugal); Lawrence Pressman (*Bunky Thurston*, US diplomat in Portugal); Ibrica Jusic (Portuguese singer); Karl-Otto Alberty (Gestapo official in Portugal punched by Byron); Stelio Candelli (SS agent with scar); Uwe Falkenbach (Obnoxious Berlin waiter); Deborah Winters (*Janice LaCouture Henry*, Warren's new bride); Logan Ramsey (*Ike LaCouture*, Her father, an isolationist Congressman); Eliose Hardt (Janice's mother); Tom McFadden (*Hugh Cleveland*, CBS radio star); Lin McCarthy (*"Blinker" Vance*, US navy attaché in London); Alan Cuthbertson (*General Tillet*, British officer who serves as Pug's escort in England); Edmund Pegge (*Duncan Burne-Wilke*, British Air Commander to whom Pug delivers the Navy planes); Philip Bowen (*Flight Lt. Killian*, RAF Pilot who flies Pug on a bombing mission over Germany); David Cardy (*Johnson*, Second pilot on bombing mission); Leo Gordon (*"Train" Anderson*, US general at war plans conference with the British); George Murdock (*"Moose" Fitzgerald*, US general at war plans conference); Art Lund (*Admiral Benton*, US representative at war plans conference); Colin Douglas (*Sir John Dill*, British Field Marshal); Guido Wieland (*Dr. Herman Wundt*, Swiss obstetrician); Heinz Weiss (*Heinz Guderian*, Panzer general outside Moscow); Charles Lane (*Admiral Standley*, Officer who accompanies Pug to Stalin ban-

quet); Ben Astar (*Admiral Gorshev*, toaster at Stalin banquet); Venco Kapural (*Gessic*, Soviet Colonel who serves as Pug's Moscow escort); Damir Mejovesk (*Yevlenko*, Russian general at the front); Ben Piazza (*Aloysius Whitman*, State Department official who tries to pressure Pug to write FDR); John Harkins (*August Van Winaker*, US Consul in Rome); Francesco Chianese (*Fr. Enrico Spinelli*, Vatican librarian); William Berger (*Phil Briggs*, NY Times journalist in Rome); Micky Knox (*Herb Rose*, Paramount film executive in Rome); Francesco Carnelutti (*Avram Rabinowitz*, Organizer of boat escape to Palestine); Richard X. Slattery (*Admiral "Bull" Halsey*, Dynamic US naval officer); Andrew Duggan (*Admiral Kimmel*, Fleet commander at Pearl Harbor); Hugh Gillin (*Jacko Larkin*, Head of U.S. Naval Personnel); Jerry Fujikawa (*Yaguchi*, Honolulu greengrocer); Matsie Hoy (*Assa May*, Hawaiian servant); Jack Bernardi (New York newspaper hawker); Dick Armstrong (*Franz*, Pug's butler in Berlin); Felix Nelson (*Fritz*, FDR's valet); Mitch Carter (Warren's flight instructor); Richard Brent (Landing officer on *Enterprise*); Lawrence Haddon (*Miles Browning*, Captain of *Enterprise*); Tommy Lee Holland (*Branch Hoban*, Captain of *Devilfish*); Joseph Hacker (*Lieutenant Carter "Lady" Aster*, Sub officer & Byron's friend); Kirstie Pooley (*Eva Braun*, Hitler's mistress); Chuck Mitchell (Florida boat skipper); John Karlen (*Ed Connelly*, Pilot who flies Pug to Pearl Harbor); William Z. Woodson (Narrator).

APPRAISAL AND SYNOPSIS: *Winds of War* is deservedly ranked among the greatest television miniseries ever made, comfortably sharing the distinction with other entries such as *Roots*, *Shogun*, *The Thorn Birds* and *Marco Polo*. In some ways, it even stands out among this group, since it does an incredible job in recreating the mood, atmosphere and events from early 1939 leading up to America's entry into World War II. The mastermind of the production, Dan Curtis, was previously best remembered for creating the cult horror daytime serial *Dark Shadows*,

The wartime leaders as portrayed in *The Winds of War*. Clockwise from the top, Gunter Meisner as Hitler, Howard Leng as Churchill, Enzo Castellari as Mussolini, Anatoly Chaguinian as Stalin, and Ralph Bellamy as FDR.

which ran from 1967 through 1972. Utilizing Herman Wouk's 1971 novel, *The Winds of War*, Curtis created the seven part series with epic scope and grandeur, filming over thirteen months on locations throughout Europe and the United States, with an unprecedented budget of over $40 million. Author Wouk himself wrote the lengthy screenplay, one of the most literate and impressive scripts ever crafted for television. Robert Mitchum was recruited for the central role, Captain Victor "Pug" Henry, through whose eyes we see the historical events unfold. Subplots involve his wife, Rhoda, and their three grown children, including Warren, training to become a carrier pilot, Byron, doing research with a famous historian working in Italy and Madeline, a college girl with an ambition to break into

radio. Other events in the narrative are centered around Adolf Hitler. Although Churchill, Mussolini, Stalin and Roosevelt are depicted in the series, they are only seen in the presence of Pug. Hitler, however, is portrayed independently, especially during the opening chapters. In fact, the opening teaser for *The Winds of War* begins with Adolf Hitler in April 1939, as he instructs the German High Command to prepare war plans for the invasion of Poland.

After the opening credits, Pug Henry is assigned to serve as naval attaché to the American Embassy in Berlin. He and his wife Rhoda board the German passenger liner *Bremen* in New York, and on the voyage they make the acquaintance of German General Armin von Roon and British journalist Alistair Tudsbury, traveling with his daughter Pamela. At a banquet honoring the Führer's birthday, Pug notices that von Roon puts down his glass when the ship's captain toasts Adolf Hitler. After arriving in Berlin, von Roon arranges for Pug and his wife to attend a state dinner where they meet Hitler face to face. When Rhoda tells the Führer that they are searching for a place to stay, Hitler turns and whispers some instructions to one of his aides. The next day, the Henrys are offered the opportunity to rent a magnificent estate. They learn that the owner of the house, a rich Jewish sugar merchant, is in danger of losing his house due to a new law, unless he rents it to someone with diplomatic immunity. They rent the estate, and Rhoda believes that Hitler was behind the arrangement. Pug writes a report to Washington, predicting that Hitler will form a pact with Russia before he decides to move on Poland. Other specialists, including General von Roon, ridicule his theory, but when the public announcement is made about the agreement, von Roon admits that Pug was the only observer astute enough to forecast the true course of events.

Byron has fallen in love with Natalie Jastrow, the niece of writer Aaron Jastrow. Leslie Slote, an American diplomat who is engaged to Natalie, foresees the upcoming war and urges Aaron to abandon Italy and return to the United States. Aaron, however, is stubborn, and refuses to see any threat to himself, even if he is Jewish. When Slote assumes a diplomatic post in Warsaw, he asks Natalie to visit him. Byron volunteers to be her chaperon, since Hitler has been making war threats against Poland. Shortly after their arrival, the Germans invade, and Byron receives minor injuries when the Luftwaffe strafe civilian cars on the highway. Slote arranges to evacuate American neutrals from Poland during a one hour cease fire at the front. Later the Nazis question Slote, demanding he point out any Jews that are traveling with his party of refuges, but he refuses to comply. When an SS officer questions Natalie, she tells him her name is Mona Lisa. Released from custody, most of the

Americans are given free passage to Stockholm, but Byron goes to Berlin to visit his parents. Later, he travels back to Italy to rejoin Natalie and Aaron, who learns that his American passport has lapsed and he is now unable to leave the country. Natalie tells Byron that she has fallen in love with him.

Pug attends the Reichstag speech by Adolf Hitler, and he is startled by how easily he molds his audience to accept his viewpoint. He is summoned to Washington by President Roosevelt, who is greatly impressed with Pug's report. FDR asks Pug to send him his personal observations on a regular basis. Pug is assigned to accompany an American banker named Gianelli to visit both Mussolini and Hitler to see if a peace accord can be achieved. They are invited to Göring's Christmas party at his estate, where Hitler has agreed to grant them a seven minute audience. Instead, the Führer rants at them for two hours, at which point Pug concludes that future peace with Hitler is impossible. In the spring of 1940, Hitler unleashes a blitzkrieg on Norway, Belgium and France. Winston Churchill becomes Prime Minister and forms a new British government. France surrenders, and Hitler forces them to sign an armistice in the same railway car in which the Germans surrendered at the end of World War I. He next sets his sights on defeating England.

The Henrys return to America to attend the wedding of Warren and his girlfriend, the daughter of an isolationist Congressman. Bryon brings Natalie to the wedding and tells Pug that they have become engaged. Byron also decides to attend the Navy's submarine school. FDR asks Pug to go to England to report on their defense efforts. In London, Pug meets Pamela, who is disconsolate when her fiance, an RAF pilot, is reported missing over the English Channel. When Pug visits Winston Churchill, the Prime Minister challenges him to fly with one of the crews bombing Berlin. Pug accepts, and his plane is almost shot down as it returns to England. Pamela falls in love with him, but Pug resists starting an affair.

The Führer on the march, Gunter Meisner in *The Winds of War*.

He is unaware that Rhoda is being courted by Palmer Kirby, a scientist who is investigating the German plans to build a nuclear bomb.

Hitler calls off his invasion plans for England and informs his generals to prepare for an invasion of the Soviet Union. General von Roon considers this idea to be one that will eventually lead to disaster. When Pug returns to his post as naval attaché in Berlin, he and von Roon meet often to play chess and discuss the course of the war. Von Roon mocks FDR's plans to arm the British under a Lend-Lease agreement, but Pug says that it is just politics. When Pug is recalled by the President, he receives a bribe offer from Göring through his banker, Wolf Stoller, which outrages the American.

Byron is assigned to submarine duty, and when his boat docks in Portugal, he arranges to meet Natalie and they get married. After the wedding, Natalie returns to Italy to try to expedite Aaron's departure. She encounters nothing but red tape from the American Embassy. Pug is assigned to conduct naval exercises in the North Atlantic, but in reality he is on a secret mission to protect the first convoy shipment of Lend-Lease aid to England. A U-boat pack spots the ships, but does not know to respond since neutral American destroyers are protecting them. They radio Berlin for orders, and Hitler responds hours later, ordering them to back down. To honor Pug for his success in this mission, FDR invites him and his family to dinner at the White House. Byron also attends and brings to the President's attention the predicament of Aaron Jastrow, who is unable to leave Italy due to his passport problem. FDR orders the state department to resolve the issue. Back in Italy, Natalie has become pregnant with Byron's child. She learns of her husband's conversation with FDR, and Aaron's passport matter is resolved, but he still has to wait a long time to obtain his exit permit from the Italian government. When Pug is summoned by the State Department, he senses that they have been deliberately dragging their feet in the case of Jewish emigres. He refuses their request to write to FDR and back up the department's lie that they had resolved the issue before the president's inquiry.

In June 1941, Hitler launches his attack on Russia. The German troops make tremendous advances, but their efforts stall outside Moscow when early snows fall in October. Pug is dispatched by FDR to assess the situation. He meets up with Leslie Slote, Pamela and her father. This time he finds it more difficult to resist Pamela's advances. He meets Stalin during a Kremlin banquet and earns his respect after delivering a blunt toast in Russian. Stalin grants him permission to visit the front, where Pug observes that the German troops are totally unprepared for winter combat, lacking even the proper clothing. Across the lines, General von Roon, on a tour of the German forces, also concludes that the winter has completely bogged down the Nazi offensive. Pug receives orders to take over command of the battleship *California* at Pearl Harbor, fulfilling his wish to return to active sea duty. He writes Roosevelt, advising him in his belief that the Russians will withstand the Nazi onslaught. He also tells FDR that the State Department has received documentation of Nazi atrocities upon Jewish citizens in the Eastern lands they have conquered, but they have been ignoring it. He asks the President to personally review this material.

While en route to Pearl Harbor, Pug receives word of the surprise attack by the Japanese on the naval base. Warren, flying a fighter off the carrier *Enterprise*, is shot down over Honolulu, but parachutes safely not far from his home. When Pug arrive in Hawaii, he learns that the battleship he was slated to command is heavily damaged and out of action for at least 18 months. He receives a letter from Rhoda asking for a divorce, and then learns that Byron's sub, *The Devilfish*, is reported sunk off the Philippines.

FDR asks Congress to declare war on Japan. Unexpectedly, Hitler asks for a German declaration of war against the United States, invited the Americans to join the European conflict. In Italy, Natalie has given birth to a son. She and Aaron had booked passage on a liner leaving Italy, but their plans are upset by the entry of America into the war. They go to Rome to hear Mussolini's speech, and when Il Duce also declares war on the United States, they become desperate. Ben Rose, a Paramount Studios executive, helps them obtain passage on a boat that will attempt to illegally smuggle their Jewish passengers to Palestine.

After drinking himself into a stupor while staying at Warren's house, Pug awakes the next day to find things changed. He receives a note from Rhoda asking him to ignore her previous letter, written before the Pearl Harbor attack. Warren's wife receives news that the report of the sinking of the *Devilfish* was false. The Naval Personnel office also leaves word that Pug will be assigned another ship, a heavy cruiser. As Warren sets off again on the *Enterprise*, Pug drive to a hill overlooking the departing carrier, and invokes a prayer that the world will soon rid itself of dictators such as Hitler.

Almost all of the scenes in *Winds of War* are well crafted, and do an excellent job in portraying the historical events. The settings of the film, many reconstructed in Yugoslavia, ring true. Moreover, the performances are magnificent. There is much subtlety and depth in the relationships of the characters. David Dukes brings delicate shading to his role as Leslie Slote. Ali MacGraw brings considerable charm and backbone to the character of Natalie. John Houseman grows wearisome as Aaron, but much of this is the shortsightedness of the character he is portraying. The historical characters come across earnestly and in a convincing manner, particularly Ralph Bellamy as FDR, Howard Lang as Winston Churchill (who duplicates the distinctive voice especially well) and Enzo Castellari as Benito Mussolini. Anatoly Chaguinian is acceptable as Stalin, although he appearance seems too young for the sixty-four year old dictator. Robert Mitchum delivers undoubtedly his finest performance since *Farewell My Lovely* (1975), and in many ways it caps his career. He dominates each scene with quiet authority, but when he does assert himself, as he does in a Berlin restaurant when the fall of Warsaw is announced or in rejecting the bribe offer from Göring, he does it with intense precision. One humorous ploy seems to be his nickname, Pug, which he earned as a boxer in his youth at the naval academy. Each cast member seems to pronounce it differently, so it comes out sounding as Put, Pud, Punt, Dug and other unusual variations. When the show was originally broadcast, it earned terrific ratings for ABC when broadcast during February 1983. Many viewers wondered if he would use any of his *Dark Shadows* cast, and in the last episode, John Karlen, who played Willy Loomis, the servant of vampire Barnabas Collins, made a cameo appearance as the pilot who flies Pug to Pearl Harbor. Composer Robert Colbert is also a *Dark Shadows* alumnus. Associate producer Barbara Steele, a renowned horror star in *The Pit and the Pendulum* (1961), *Black Sunday* (1960) and a string of Italian fright films that have become cult classics. Steele also appears in a small role in the film, and Curtis cast her as Dr. Julia Hoffman in his later prime time revival of *Dark Shadows* in 1991. With the success of *Winds of War*, Curtis undertook a follow-up miniseries based on Herman Wouk's sequel, *War and Remembrance*.

HITLER PORTRAYAL: Gunter Meisner had been excellent as a comic Hitler in *Ace of Aces* and *Inside Out*, but was far less successful playing the Führer straight, and he proved to be one of the few weak links in the cast of *Winds of War*. His performance as Hitler seems forced, unnatural and unconvincing.

Since the part of Hitler was extraordinarily well written by Herman Wouk, this is a genuine disappointment. In close-ups, Meisner's rather horse-like features works against him. He is depicted with a mustache that is too thin and perpendicular than that worn by the real Hitler. Meisner's scenes performed in German are more fluid and impressive, but his English language dialogue sometimes borders on the ridiculous. In his very first appearance, when he states, "I'll cook them a stew they will choke on," it sounds instead like "I'll cock them a stew." He also uses "awoided" instead of "avoided." Incidentally, there appears to be some consistency in the scenes in which Hitler speaks German. If only German characters are in a scene, they speak in English, and we are to assume that they are actually speaking in German. But if a non–German character is in the scene, then Meisner actually speaks in German. For example, Hitler's Reichstag speech after the attack on Poland is delivered in German because Pug is in the audience. In the scene where Pug accompanies Luigi Gianelli in his audience with Hitler, them Führer begins the scene in German and switches to English after a few sentences. Another problem with Meisner's interpretation is his use of gesture. He continually punches his fist into his open hand, a gesture not particularly associated with the Führer. His gesticulation during the Reichstag speech, however, is far more characteristic and effective, and it is one of his best scenes in the film. He is also good in the scenes at Göring's party, especially when he entertains a child. His conference with Pug works rather well, especially since it is set in semi-darkness and the camera frequently focuses on the dictator's eyes. His other exceptional scene is when he has a brief conference with Count Ciano, Mussolini's son-in-law, at Berchtesgaden. Eva Braun is also depicted briefly in this sequence. Structurally, the importance of Hitler to the story declines as the story progresses. In the first episode, *The Winds Rise*, Hitler is featured in seven lengthy sequences. In *The Storm Breaks*, chapter two, there are three appearances, and the middle sequence, a meeting with General von Brauchitsch, who tries to convince the Führer to postpone the invasion of France, is one of the longest and most dramatic in the entire series. In the third episode, *Cataclysm*, there are only two appearances, but the second is the lengthy Christmas party scene and conference with Pug. The fourth chapter, *Defiance*, features only the French surrender ceremony at Compiegne. The Hitler scene in the fifth episode, *Of Love and War*, is one of the weaker ones, in which Hitler gathers his generals and orders them to switch their plans and prepare for an invasion of Russia. Meisner also stumbles in his first sequence of the sixth episode, *Changing of the Guard*, when he rails against Roosevelt after hearing of the destroyers protecting the Lend-Lease convoy. He recovers in the second scene, a 1942 birthday party at Berchtesgaden, when the Führer has a meeting with Himmler to discuss the special operations units that will exterminate the Jews. The final scene, Hitler's last appearance in the series, features the Führer walking with Göring and Blondi, his German Shepherd. The last visuals of Hitler occur as he bends down to pet Blondi, saying "Good dog, good dog." In the final episode, *Into the Maelstrom*, the Führer does not appear, but his voice is heard in one sequence as Aaron listens to a Reichstag speech when Hitler declares war on the United States. Of the other Nazi leaders, Anton Diffring is first rate as von Ribbentrop, the Nazi Foreign Minister disliked by almost everyone but Hitler. Dieter Wagner is most impressive as Himmler. Rene Kolldehoff's Göring, however, is mediocre.

REPRESENTATIVE QUOTES

• It is my belief that if the attack on Poland is started with sudden heavy blows that gain rapid success, general world war will be avoided. But if England and France do march, I'll cook them a stew they will choke on. *(Hitler to his military high com-*

mand in the opening precredit scene of the miniseries)

• Of course, it isn't my choice, but as Sally Forrest says, the Führer's mad about pink. *(Rhoda Henry to Pug, commenting on her attire as they leave to attend a reception with Hitler)*

• The German people understand me. I am Germany! *(Hitler, accompanied by a peal of thunder, to General von Brauchitch after reading his report that the invasion of France be postponed)*

• *Mein Kampf* is just the froth of the cauldron. *(Leslie to Byron at a Berlin cafe)*

• Of course I am giving up my life for the renaissance of my people and I cannot help seeing things from that limited point of view.... I was born to create, not to destroy. I am an artist.... The only road to peace is through German victory, anything else is irrelevant *(Hitler to Pug & Luigi Gianelli in their meeting at Karinhall during Göring's Christmas party, 1939)*

• A very positive report, Himmler! Come to the party. Have a little fun. Relax. You are working too hard, you know. *(Hitler to Himmler during his birthday party in Berchtesgaden, April 20, 1941)*

• Oh, Lord ... maybe the vicious circle will end this time. Maybe not. Maybe it will take Christ's second coming to end. Maybe it will never end. But it is 1941, and I know this: Until the life is beaten out of the monster Hitler, the world cannot move another inch toward a more sane existence. There is nothing to do now but win the war. *(Pug in prayer while watching the Enterprise leave Pearl Harbor)*

97. *Zelig* (1983)

Will Holt as actor playing Adolf Hitler (cameo)
Adolf Hitler as Adolf Hitler
Comedy

Orion/Warner Brothers. Written by Woody Allen; Photographed by Gordon Willis; Edited by Susan E. Morse; Music by Dick Hyman; Produced by Robert Greenhut; Directed by Woody Allen. B & W/ Color 79 minutes

ANNOTATED CAST LIST: Woody Allen (*Leonard Zelig*, The Chameleon Man); Garrett Brown (Actor playing Zelig in *The Changing Man*); Mia Farrow (*Dr. Eudora Fletcher*, Psychiatrist who treats Zelig); Marianne Tatum (Actress playing Eudora in *The Changing Man*); Ellen Garrison (*Dr. Eudora Fletcher*, Interviewed in her old age); Stephanie Farrow (*Meryl Fletcher*, Eudora's sister, a pilot); Elizabeth Rothchild (*Meryl Fletcher*, Interviewed in her old age); John Rothman (*Paul Deghuee*, Eudora's cousin, a cameraman); Sherman Loud (*Paul Deghuee*, Interviewed in his old age); Richard Litt (*Charles Koslow*, Eudora's fiancé, a lawyer); Michael Kell (Actor playing Koslow in *The Changing Man*); Mary Louise Wilson (*Ruth*, Zelig's half-sister); Sol Lomita (*Martin Geist*, Ruth's showman boyfriend); Jean Trowbridge (*Catherine Fletcher*, Eudora's mother); Ken Chapin (Man who interviews Eudora's mother); Jack Cannon (*Mike Giebel*, Reporter for *NY Daily Mirror*); Theodore R. Smits (*Ted Bierbauer*, Reporter for *NY Daily Mirror*); John Buck Walter (*Dr. Alan Sindell*, Manhattan Hospital senior doctor); Charles Denny (Actor playing Dr. Sindell in *The Changing Man*); Paul Nevens (*Dr. Birsky*, Doctor who thinks Zelig has a brain tumor); Deborah Rush (*Lita Fox*, Showgirl who claims that Zelig married her); Jeanine Jackson (*Helen Gray*, Salesgirl who claims Zelig is the father of her twins); Erma Campbell (Black woman who claims Zelig married her); Dimitri Vassillopoulos (*Luis Martinez*, Cowardly bullfighter who romances Ruth); Bernie Herold (*Carter Dean*, Mayor Walker's representative); Kuno Sponholz (*Oswald Pohl*, SS leader in Munich); Dan O'Herlihy, Dwight Weist, Wendy Craig, Gordon Gould, Jurgen Kuehn (Newsreel voices); Patrick Horgan (Narrator); Susan Sontag, Irving Howe, Saul Bellow, Bricktop, Dr. Bruno Bettelheim, John Morton Blum (Celebrity commentators); Josephine Baker, Clara Bow, Fanny Brice, James Cagney, Al Capone, Charles Chaplin, Calvin Coolidge, Marion Davies, Dolores Del Rio, Jack Dempsey, Marie Dressler, F. Scott Fitzgerald, Lou Gehrig, Joseph Goebbels, Red Grange, Hermann Göring, William Randolph Hearst, Rudolf Hess, Herbert Hoover, Charles Lindbergh, Carole Lombard, Adolphe Menjou, Eugene O'Neill, Babe Ruth, Jimmy Walker (Celebrities viewed in archival footage, some interacting with Zelig).

APPRAISAL AND SYNOPSIS: Some readers may be surprised to find *Zelig* in this volume, since the criteria excludes films in which Hitler is depicted through archival footage or in documentaries. *Zelig*, of course, is not a documentary but a satire of the genre, so the latter prohibition does not apply. Moreover, there is a quick shot of an actor, Will Holt, portraying Hitler in a clip from *The Changing Man*, the pseudo film within the film, which qualifies and allows the inclusion of this most singular of all Hitler films.

In essence, Allen's comedy is the story of Leonard Zelig, a bizarre American pop icon who achieves world fame in the late 1920s as the "Chameleon Man," an individual with the remarkable ability to transform himself in order to blend in with the people around him. At first he is confined for observation at the Manhattan Hospital, where a young psychiatrist, Dr. Eudora Fletcher, takes an interest in him. She demonstrates Zelig's ability to the other doctors in a series of tests. When Zelig is placed in the company of two fat men, his body bloats out and he becomes obese as well. If confronted with two Negroes, Zelig transforms himself into a Negro. The same phenomenon occurs whenever Zelig is placed next to any group of people. Apparently, this transformation process is involuntary. While the other doctors theorize that the ability is triggered by some physiological cause, such as a brain tumor, Eudora Fletcher becomes convinced that the root cause is psychological, that Zelig so desperately wants to be accepted, that he takes on the characteristics of the people around him. Before she can treat him, however, Zelig's half-sister removes him from the hospital and begins to exploit his condition with her boyfriend Martin Geist, a carnival promoter. America becomes entranced with Zelig, and a "lizard man" fad sweeps the nation. Zelig is put on display as a sideshow, becoming transformed into an Indian or a Orthodox Rabbi before the eyes of the astonished paying audience. Zelig is taken on a world tour, where celebrities flock to meet the "Chameleon Man." However, Zelig himself is totally devoid of personality, a pitiful individual. In Spain, Ruth has an affair with Luis Martinez, a bullfighter. When Geist catches them in a tryst, he kills them and commits suicide. Zelig vanishes. A massive search takes place, but Zelig is not located until many months later, when he turns up as a phony cleric attending Pope Pius XI.

Zelig is returned to the custody of Dr. Eudora Fletcher, who moves him to a neutral setting and embarks on a lengthy treatment. Her cousin, Paul Deghuee, records the entire process on film. At first, Eudora is unsuccessful because Zelig assumes the character of a psychiatrist when in her presence. She finally makes a breakthrough by telling Zelig that she is only pretending to be a psychiatrist. He becomes disoriented, and she is able to hypnotize him. After this, she is able to cure him, and his own personality emerges. In fact, Eudora falls in love with him. After Zelig's cure is announced, they [plan to marry. Unfortunately, a new wave of publicity uncovers a number of terrible incidents that occurred when Zelig was in his chameleon state. He married several times and fathered numerous children. He committed malpractice while posing as a doctor. Zelig is sued for all these events, and he starts to break down and begins changing again to resemble those around him. He finally vanishes. After a long search, Eudora spots him in a newsreel about Hitler. She goes to Germany, and locates Zelig at a Hitler rally seated with the Nazi bigwigs. Zelig comes to his senses when he sees Eudora, but the distraction ruins Hitler's speech. Fleeing from the SS, Eudora and Zelig escape by plane. Eudora, an amateur pilot, passes out, but Zelig saves the day by transforming himself into a pilot and flying back to America. The amazing feat brings Zelig fresh acclaim, and FDR grants him a full pardon for any offenses committed in his chameleon state. Zelig and Eudora marry, and the closing scrawl says that they spend many happy years together.

The main brilliance of *Zelig* is the clever presentation in documentary style, inspired no doubt by the opening newsreel sequence from *Citizen Kane*. The picture blends new B & W footage intercut with genuine archival footage, and then adds stills, sound bites and recent interviews in color with the now elderly counterparts of the characters in the film. This technique has since been described as a mockumentary. One of the most clever devices is the use of a reported feature film, *The Changing Man*, based on Zelig's life and made by Warner Brothers in 1935. Many jokes and puns are slipped into the footage. In one scene, Zelig is shown literally walking on a wall or with his feet twisted entirely around after an unfortunate encounter with a chiropractor. Through editing and clever vocal inserts, Zelig is shown cavorting with many celebrities, such as Fanny Brice who sings a song mentioning Zelig in the lyrics. Similarly, an Al Jolson rendition of "Sittin' on Top of the World" is heard on the soundtrack with new lyrics mentioning Zelig. Noteworthy individuals, such as Bruno Bettelheim, Saul Bellow and Susan Sontag, are added to the mix to round out the satire. Other humorous tidbits include scenes of Zelig's father playing Puck in an Orthodox version of *A Midsummer Night's Dream*, Zelig on deck as the next batter following Babe Ruth, and the wild dance "The Chameleon," inspired by Zelig. It is rather curious how Zelig is discovered after each of his vanishings. He shows up in the vacinity of the very prominent individuals, so instead of blending in, he instead stands out, first with the Pope and then with the Führer. Yet most critics who analyze the film overlook this point, that there is an exhibitionist side to Zelig. At no point does the film attempt to explain how Zelig is able to transform other than to suggest the power of his will, which ironically echoes the famous Nazi documentary *Triumph of the Will*. Zelig, the shadowy recluse, is able to surpass the Nazis with their self-proclaimed strength. There is also a good deal of black humor, such as when one doctor announces his opinion that Zelig will soon die of a brain tumor, and then the doctor himself dies in that fashion two weeks later. The cowardly bullfighter scenario is another gem. The Hitler scenes, however, provide the genuine climax to the film.

HITLER PORTRAYAL: Will Holt is the name of the stand-in who plays Hitler in *The Changing Man* excerpt of the Munich party rally. He merely stands at the podium in a long shot which is used to show the position of the Zelig character on the stage. This appearance is Holt's only screen credit. Without doubt, the highlight of *Zelig* is the use of the Nazi footage so that Woody Allen is cleverly inserted into the picture, making it appear that Adolf Hitler interacts with him. This clever editing technique paved the way for films such as *Forrest Gump* (1994) in which Tom Hanks was able to interact with John F. Kennedy, Lyndon Johnson and Richard Nixon. The remarkable thing about *Zelig* is the sociological ripples that the scene contains. The standard persona that Woody Allen projects in his films is well known: a witty, highbrow character plagued by self-doubt, obsessed with sex, but mindful of his Jewish heritage. The juxtaposition of Woody with Adolf Hitler, the notorious anti–Semite and anti-intellectual, simultaneously self-confident and sexually repressed, is a pairing of remarkable irony. It is an astonishing concept with many cultural ramifications as well as an incredible surreal moment that provokes gales of laughter.

Let us examine this footage in detail. Hitler first appears in a Universal newsreel shown at a theater attended by Eudora and her sister. The excerpt is entitled "National Socialists on the Rise, Berlin Germany." The Führer is standing on the street surrounded by Nazi party members. Among the brownshirts in the background to his right is Zelig, dressed as a brownshirt follower. A freeze frame zeros in on Zelig, and a circle is drawn around his face. The narrator describes how Eudora travels to Germany to search for him. Additional archival footage shows Nazis on parade. Goebbels is seen reviewing the troops from the sidewalk. The *Horst Wessel* song accompanies this footage. Göring is shown giving a Nazi salute, while Hitler appears over his shoulder standing on a platform saluting in the opposite direction. The narrator mentions how Eudora's hunt has been fruitless, but she decides to attend a huge Nazi rally in Munich as a last resort. The scene switches again, and Hitler is seen entering a large auditorium, followed by Hess and other Nazi officials. The crowd reacts enthusiastically as Hitler begins to speak. He is standing in front of a table with a cluster of microphones placed in front of him. The camera of this historic footage is positioned so that the row of Nazi followers seated to his left are in view. The second figure in the shot is Zelig. The camera intercuts between this viewpoint and the cheering crowd. Eudora herself is not edited into this scene, but the narrator describes how she starts to wave to attract Zelig's attention. Zelig then starts to wave ever more enthusiastically, until Hitler himself swings around, and his movements indicate that he does a double take while staring at Zelig. A clip from *The Changing Man*, is inserted, which shows the reenactment of this scene with actors playing Eudora, Zelig and Hitler, as romantic music fills the soundtrack. Eudora rushes into Zelig's arms and they kiss. An insert of Eudora in her old age is then edited in, and she states, "It was nothing like what happened in the movie." She describes how Zelig came down from the podium to her, and they escaped in the confusion. A modern clip of elderly Nazi Oswald Pohl follows, in which he describes how the incident frazzled the Führer, and how the SS attempted to seize Zelig for this outrage, but he manages to slip through their fingers. (In truth, Oswald Pohl, the SS paymaster, was executed in 1951 as a war criminal). The action then shifts to Eudora and Zelig's escape from Germany in a biplane. A newsreel from UFA records the takeoff, as the German narrator is overheard denouncing the "Schweinhund" Zelig. With this, the Hitler sequence concludes.

REPRESENTATIVE QUOTES

• To the Ku Klux Klan, Zelig, a Jew who was able to transform himself into a Negro or an Indian, was a triple threat. *(Narrator over pictures of a Klan cross burning)*
• What's this? A commotion next to the Papal father? Somebody doesn't belong up there. The guards are summoned amidst chaos as His Holiness, Pope Pius XI, tries to swat the intruder with a sacred decree. *(Newsreel commentator as Zelig is discovered at the Vatican during a Papal ritual)*
• No, I don't agree, I think this guy Mussolini is a loser. *(Recording of Zelig talking to Eudora, and expressing his own opinion for the first time)*
• Although he wanted to be loved, craved to be loved, there was also something in him that desired immersion in the mass and anonymity, and fascism offered Zelig that kind of opportunity. *(Saul Bellow commenting over images of a street scene of Zelig with Hitler)*
• We couldn't believe our eyes. Hitler's speech was ruined. He wanted to make a good joke about Poland, but just then, Zelisch appeared. Hitler was extremely upset. *(Oswald Pohl, SS leader during an interview)*

98. *Zio Adolfo in Arte Führer* (1978)

Giuseppe Diamanti as Adolf Hitler
Comedy

Dania. Written by Franco Castellano & Giuseppe "Pipolo" Moccia; Photographed by Giancarlo Ferrando; Edited by Antonio Siciliano; Music by Carlo Rustichelli; Produced by Luciano Martino; Directed by Franco Castellano & Giuseppe "Pipolo" Moccia. Color 96 minutes

CAST LIST: Adriano Celentano (*Herman & Gustav*); Anna Cardini (*Irma*); Filippo Costanzo (*Hans*); Amanda Lear; Claudio Bigaglia; Paola Orefice; Pietro Ceccarelli; Dana Devin; Bruno DiLuia; Graziella Galvani.

COMMENTARY: *Zio Adolfo in Arte Führer* is an Italian black comedy about two lookalikes, Herman and Gustav. One of them, an amateur magician, becomes a Colonel in the SS. The other, an anarchist, plans to assassinate Hitler. Instead, he gets involved in a series of comic misadventures as both men become confused with one another. This film was released only in Italy and apparently received no distribution. A later critic described the picture as a forerunner of Woody Allen's *Zelig* because of the use of archival footage of Joseph Goebbels, Rudolf Hess and Erwin Rommel. Clips of the actual Hitler also appear in the film in addition to the performance of Giuseppe Diamanti as the Führer. The title can be loosely translated as *Uncle Adolf, the Artistic Führer*.

99. *Zitra Vstanu a Oparim se Cajem* (1977)

Frantisek Vicena as Adolf Hitler
Science Fiction

Filmove Studio Barrandov. Written by Milos Macourek & Jinrich Polak based on a story by Josef Nesvadba; Photographed by Jan Kalis; Music by Karol Svoboda; Produced by Jan Suster; Directed by Jinrich Polak. Color 95 minutes

CAST LIST: Petr Kostka (*Jan & Karel Bures*); Jiri Sovak (*Klaus*); Vladimir Mensik (*Rolf*); Vlastimil Brodsky (*Bauer*); Marie Rosulkova (*Shirley White*); Otto Simanek (*Patrick White*); Valerie Chmelova (*Helena*); Josef Vetrovec (*Kroupa);* Slavka Budinova (*Kroupova*); Zuzana Ondrouchova (*Eva*); Maria Drahokoupilova (*Marketa*); Josef Blaha (*Rousek*); Frantisek Peterka (*Robert*

Nol); Ota Salenka (*Dr. Kryl*); Horst Giese (*Joseph Goebbels*); Jan Sedlisky (*Heinrich Himmler*).

COMMENTARY: This is a Czech science fiction comedy which received little distribution outside of Czechoslovakia. In 1997, however, a video version was issued in the Czech Republic. The story is set in the future in which a company provides recreation time travel tours to the past. A group of neo–Nazi agents hijack one of their planes in an attempt to bring an atomic bomb back to Hitler in 1944, so that Nazi Germany will win the war. They make two attempts, failing both times, with the bomb sinking to the bottom of the same icy pond. Hitler appears in two brief scenes, and is played in a straightforward fashion. The plot is rather complicated with mistaken identities and occasional slapstick. The leading actor, like Michael J. Fox in the *Back to the Future* trilogy, winds up living through the same day a number of times, but he must avoid meeting up with himself to avoid a destructive cosmic paradox. The picture may also bear a passing similarity to *The Philadelphia Experiment II* (1993), in which a time travel experiment leads to an alteration of history in which the Nazis win. Of course, that film provides a far darker vision and it is not a comedy at heart. A loose translation of the original title is *Tomorrow I Will Wake Up and Scald Myself with Tea*.

100. *Der Zwanzigste Juli* (AKA *The Hitler Assassination Plot* and *Der 20. Juli*) (1955)

? as Adolf Hitler (cameo)
Historical drama

CCC Filmkunst. Written by Werner Jörg Lüddecke, Weisenborn & Falk Harnack; Photographed by Karl Löb; Edited by Kurt Zeunert; Music by Herbert Trantow; Produced by Arthur Brauner & Falk Harnack; Directed by Falk Harnack. B & W Original version 100 minutes; revised version 95 minutes

ANNOTATED CAST LIST: Wolfgang Preiss (*Count Claus von Stauffenberg*, Colonel who plants a bomb to kill Hitler); Robert Freytag (*Captain Linder*, German officer and civil engineer who recollects the events of the plot); Annamarie Düringer (*Hildegard Klee*, Tenant of Linder who is the confidential secretary of the Wednesday Society); Maximilian Schell (Civilian conspirator and member of the Wednesday Society); Werner Hinz (*Ludwig von Beck*, Retired general & leader of anti–Hitler group); Wolfgang Büttner (*General Friedrich Olbricht*, Chief of General Army office in Berlin & anti–Hitler conspirator); Paul Bildt (*Carl Gördeler*, Former mayor of Liepzig & anti–Hitler conspirator); Paul Esser (*Erwin von Witzleben*, Field Marshal & anti–Hitler conspirator); Erich Schellow (Protestant minister opposing Hitler); Fritz Tillmann (*General Henning von Tresckow*, Commander of Second Army & anti–Hitler conspirator); Ernst Schroeder (SS officer tracking the conspirators).

APPRAISAL AND SYNOPSIS: This film was the rival production to G.W. Pabst's *Jackboot Mutiny*, beating it to the theaters by one day. While perhaps not as memorable or as artistic as the Pabst film, *Der Zwanzigste Juli* has much to commend it. It was directed and particularly well written by Falk Harnack, who himself was a member of the German resistance, a member of the White Rose movement from Munich University. His film work demonstrates not only passion, but an authentic appreciation of the subject. The basic story is very similar to the historical facts as depicted in *The Plot to Kill Hitler* and *Jackboot Mutiny*. In its original form, the entire story is structured as a flashback, as two fictional characters, Captain Linder, a German officer who was not a conspirator and his tenant, Hildegard Klee, reflect on the events of the Hitler assassination attempt. Years after its release, the film was edited to eliminate this framework, and in this revised version, which is the one usually shown, the story unfolds directly. Hildegard Klee works as confidential secretary for the Wednesday Society, a group of high ranking officers, lawyers, politicians and educators opposed to the Nazi regime. They envision a quick end to the war by killing Hitler and overthrowing the remaining Nazi leaders. The film then depicts one of the earlier assassination attempts, during the Führer's visit to Smolensk on the Russian front on March 13, 1943. A bomb was placed on his plane as he headed back to Wolf's Lair in Rastenburg. By a trixk of fate, the bomb did not detonate. (The failure of this attempt has been blamed on the heater in the plane's cargo hold which malfunctioned. Since the explosive was sensitive to cold, when the detonator went off, the explosive failed to ignite.) After this, the focus of the action shifts to cover the July 20, 1944, plot at Rastenburg. Compared to *Jackboot Mutiny*, the Harnack film is more prosaic and mundane. One exception is the poetic conclusion of *Der Zwanzigste Juli*, which portrays General von Treschow at the front, walking off to blow himself up with a hand grenade when he learns of the collapse of the putsch. The cinematography is very impressive, dark and shadowy. The editing is crisp and the plot proceeds at a swift pace. Although a good deal of screen time is filled with the fictional characters, Klee and Linder, their conversations are most interesting. When they witness the arrest of a Jew, Linder halfheartedly tries to justify the action to Klee but fails, realizing the brutal inhumanity of the Nazi regime. The acting is generally quite good, particularly that of Wolfgang Preiss as Stauffenberg. There is a prominent error in his makeup, however, since he is portrayed with a patch over his right eye. In fact, Stauffenberg's war injury was to his left eye.

HITLER PORTRAYAL: The figure of Adolf Hitler is never clearly seen in this film. The Führer's presence is represented on five occasions. First, his voice is heard over the telephone ordering Field Marshal Kluge to commence a senseless attack on the Russian front. Second, he is seen from behind as he enters army headquarters in Smolensk. Third, his left shoulder and arm are shown during lunch with his General Staff. He is angered when one of the officers suggests leave for some of his battle weary men. Fourth he is seen from behind wearing a trench coat as he boards a plane in which a bomb has been placed. Finally, he is seen from behind sitting at the map table during the military conference at Wolf's Lair. The briefcase with the bomb is shown placed under the table next to Hitler's feet, which are stamping with impatience. The briefcase is then moved away from Hitler and positioned against the outside brace of the table. Probably three different individuals, all unidentified, were used to portray Hitler. The figure entering the headquarters appears to be slightly different from the figure boarding the plane, suggesting that at least two different body models were used. They probably were not actors, but simply stand-ins who were drafted for their brief parts. A third individual, most likely a professional actor, was used as Hitler's speaking voice. His vocal pitch is somewhat lower than Hitler's own voice, but he does a decent enough job in the scant dialogue provided for Hitler in the script. His identity, like that of the others, remains anonymous.

REPRESENTATIVE QUOTES

• I did give you the order, do you understand? *(Hitler to Field Marshal Kluge over the telephone)*

• The fate of the Third Reich is at stake and you talk about leave? *(Hitler to an officer during his luncheon in Smolensk)*

• That guy even has chance on his side. *(General von Tresckow to himself after the bomb in the airplane attempt fails to detonate)*

APPENDIX ONE: MGM'S ABORTED HITLER WESTERN

In 1943, MGM was in the process of developing a major film, an allegorical Hitler Western to be entitled *Storm in the West*. The idea was initially developed in the spring by Dore Schary, who had recently left as head of their low-budget film division to work as a semi-independent producer. His first project became the Hitler Western, a restaging of the events that led up to the Second World War presented as a range feud in the 1870s, with the various major countries represented as local ranches and the major historical personalities recast in the guise of lawmen and outlaws. France, Poland and Germany became ranches known as Franson, Poling and Gorman. Neville Chamberlain was transformed into the elderly sheriff Ned Chambers, Winston Churchill became Wally Chancel, the crusading editor of the town paper and Josef Stalin became Joe Slavin, a crusty rancher who emigrated from Georgia. As the villains, Hermann Göring appears as Gerritt, a tough gunman. Joseph Goebbels appears as Gribble, a wiry scoundrel who limps from an old injury, and Adolf Hitler, the instigator of the troubles, is presented as Arnold Hygatt, a trouble-some cowpoke with a distinctive black forelock and a neatly trimmed short black moustache. Hygatt later forms an alliance with Mullison, an eccentric rancher nicknamed "Bunny" (representing Mussolini) and together they form the Two Axes Mining Company.

To write the screenplay, Schary hired the famous novelist Sinclair Lewis, author of *Babbitt*, *Dodsworth* and *Elmer Gantry*, who quickly became intrigued with the project. By midsummer, Lewis had completed a first draft of the scenario, opening with Hygatt's release from a thirty day stretch in the cooler (corresponding to Hitler's jail term after the Beer Hall Putsch) and ending with a shootout at the roughneck town of Moon Creek, where the bad guys get wiped out. Almost all the events in the story neatly correspond to the European political events of the 1930s, yet anyone who wasn't following European events could follow the story as a typical Western.

By the fall of 1943, costume sketches for the main characters were developed, a slate of possible directors were sounded out including Victor Fleming, William

Stein and Day cover for the published screenplay to *Storm in the West* featuring the illustrations for the cowboy versions of Hitler, Churchill and Stalin.

Wellman and Jules Dassin. Bobby Watson topped the short cast list to play Hygatt. Other actors considered for major parts included Walter Huston as Ned Chambers and Thomas Mitchell as Wally Chancel. However, production ground to a halt in late October when Louis B. Meyer decided to pull the plug, telling Schary that the script was too political. The studio head particularly objected to the brand denoting Slavin's ranch, the hammer and sickle.

Schary was so upset that he decided to leave MGM. Later, Schary tried to revive *Storm in the West* as an RKO project, but MGM refused to relinquish its legal rights to the story, so the Hitler Western remained stillborn as a motion picture. However, the project had a posthumous life when Schary eventually published the screenplay for *Storm in the West* with Stein and Day in 1963.

APPENDIX TWO:
HITLER ON
SERIES TELEVISION

In addition to network telefilms and miniseries, Hitler and the image of Hitler have been represented in a number of episodes from regular television series. This appendix presents several samples from American and British programs in which some of these appearances occurred:

• *Adventures of Fu Manchu* (Adventure series) Glen Gordon starred as the title character in this 1956 syndicated series based on Sax Rohmer's memorable villain. In "The Master Plan of Fu Manchu," the evil Oriental awakens Hitler from suspended animation and provides him with a new face through plastic surgery. They join forces in a new scheme to conquer the world, but are undone by the efforts of Nayland Smith from Scotland Yard. Hitler is played by veteran character actor Steven Geray.

• *Comic Strip Presents* (British anthology series) Thirty humorous episodes were made in the early 1980s by the British comedy troupe known as the Comic Strip Club. Barry Dennen was featured as Hitler in a 1982 episode entitled "Demonella."

• *Highlander* (Fantasy/adventure series) Based on the film *Highlander* (1986) and its sequels, this series concerns a 16th century Scottish clansman who discovers he is an immortal with special powers, who can only be killed by another immortal. Hitler appears in "Valkyrie," an episode which also involves Count von Stauffenberg (played by Martin Evans) and revolves around the Rastenburg assassination plot. Patrick Keating plays Hitler.

• *Hogan's Heroes* (Comedy series) References to Hitler are very frequent in this famous series set in a German POW camp, Stalag 13, which the prisoners actually use as a secret underground base. The Führer himself never shows up, but several impostors do. In "Will the Real Adolf Please Stand Up," regular Larry Hovis (Sergeant Andy Carter) poses as Hitler. In "Heil Klink," regular John Banner (Sergeant Hans Schultz) plays a dual role as a defecting Nazi who is supposed to be Hitler in disguise. In a later episode, "Fat Hermann Go Home," Sergeant Schultz poses as Hermann Göring. In another episode, Colonel Wilhelm Klink (Werner Klemperer) supposedly speaks with Hitler on the telephone.

• *Man from U.N.C.L.E.* (Action/adventure series) The 5th episode of the series, "The Deadly Games Affair" features a dormant Hitler in suspended animation. A Nazi scientist played by Alexander Scourby tries to revive the Führer using secret agent Napoleon Solo (Robert Vaughn), whose blood is compatible with that of the Führer. Hitler awakens and grabs Solo's arm before being pushed into a fire by the secret agent.

• *Masterpiece Theater* (Dramatic anthology series) This is the longest running dramatic anthology series in television history, the centerpiece of public television. Selections with multipart episodes might also be considered as miniseries, but since they appear under the auspices of *Masterpiece Theater*, the entries are here classified as part of series television. In the early 1980s, Hitler appeared in two entries almost back to back. The first was "Private Schulz," a six-part drama by Jack Pullman. Gerhardt Schulz, a petty thief released from prison when war is declared in 1939, finds himself recruited by the SS as a counter-intelligence agent, and he becomes involved in counterfeiting. Hitler is played by Gawn Grainger. The other was an eight chapter drama entitled "Winston Churchill: The Wilderness Years" starring Robert Hardy as the great British statesman for the ten year period from 1929 to 1939, when he was out of power and became the leading English spokesman who warned about the threat of Nazi aggression. Gunter Meisner assumed the role of the Führer.

• *Mission: Impossible* (Action/adventure series) Martin Landau, as impersonator Rollin Hand, undertook a Hitler impersonation in "Echo of Yesterday," a classic second season episode. Industrialist Otto Kelmann (Wilfred Hyde-White) is supporting Marcus von Frank, leader of a Neo-Nazi movement. Assigned to discredit Frank and stop his plans, the Impossible Missions team learns that Kelmann had been a Hitler supporter whose wife might have been killed by the Führer. Kelmann is drugged, and Rollin Hand undertakes a charade as Hitler to reenact this crime as if it were the old man's vision. Later, when Kelmann sees Frank act in a manner reminiscent of Hitler, he shoots him. In another episode, "The Legend," Rollin Hand impersonates Martin Bormann in a similar scheme.

• *Time Tunnel* (Science fiction series) Developed by Irwin Allen, *Time Tunnel* lasted only one season as two scientists, Doug (Robert Colbert) and Tony (James Darren) become lost in time while experimenting with a secret device in an underground government lab. In "The Kidnappers," aliens from the distant future abduct famous people from earth history as their trophies. When Dr. Ann MacGregor (Lee Merriweather) is kidnapped, the time traveling heroes attempt to rescue her. Among the victims of the aliens are Cicero, Erasmus and Adolf Hitler, played by Bob May. The aliens demonstrate their powers by draining all his memories, leaving the Führer as a mindless zombie.

• *Tomorrow People* (British science fiction series) A group of teenagers, known as the "Tomorrow People" have special telepathic abilities which they use to defend mankind against all enemies, including alien invaders from outer space. Hitler, played by Michael Sheard, was featured in a two-part episode entitled "Hitler's Last Secret" Numerous gangs of young Neo-Nazis believe that Hitler is not dead and await his revival. In truth, Hitler is an alien shape-shifter named Neebur. The Tomorrow People expose the Führer's real identity, and the alien loses his hypnotic control over his followers. "Hitler's Last Secret" was made in the early 1970s. A different version of this series was revived in 1992.

• *Twilight Zone* (Fantasy/science fiction anthology series) *The Twilight Zone* ran for five seasons, and Hitler appeared in a number of episodes. The major one was "He Lives," an hour long entry from the fourth season. Dennis Hopper plays a young American fascist and agitator who has not met with much success. Finally, a figure in the shadows starts to advise him, which leads to a modicum of success. When Hopper demands that the man step out of the shadows, he does and is revealed as the spirit of Adolf Hitler (played by Curt Conway). Hopper's career collapses after Hitler persuades him to shoot an elderly Jew, played by Ludwig Donath, another screen veteran who once played Hitler. Oddly enough, the Führer showed up on another hour episode a few weeks later entitled "No Time like the Past," in which Dana Andrews travels back in time in an attempt to kill Hitler in 1939 and prevent the Second World War. Archival footage, however, was used in this entry. The most memorable appearance of Hitler in the half-hour episodes was "Man in the Bottle." Luther Adler plays a timid antique shop owner, who is granted four wishes by a genie in a bottle. Each wish, he is warned, has consequences. Adler asks for power, to become the absolute ruler of a nation who cannot be voted out of office. The genie outwits him, turning him into Adolf Hitler on his last day in the bunker. Adler is forced to use his last wish to be changed back into himself. Of course, Adler is remembered for playing Hitler in two feature films.

• *Wonder Woman* (Fantasy/adventure series) Based on the comic strip series, Wonder Woman is a heroine who is an Amazon warrior with superpowers who poses as Diana Prince. Hitler turns up in "Anchluss '77," an episode in which a former Nazi officer (Mel Ferrer) and a mad scientist named Heinrich von Klemper (Leon Charles) work in a secret underground lab in South America. They manage to resurrect Adolf Hitler (Barry Dennen) through cellular regeneration. When Hitler plans to launch a new drive for world domination, Wonder Woman (Lynda Carter) finds a way to destabilize the regeneration and Hitler fades away into extinction.

APPENDIX THREE: POSSIBLE HITLER FILM PROJECTS

If the last decade of the twentieth century is any indication, interest in films that include Hitler as a character continues to be strong. Since no other historical personage has come as close to being the personification of evil, this is not unusual. There is certainly enough material for countless projects. First, there is the historical record. Although some topics, such as the last days in the bunker and the Rastenburg assassination attempt have probably been milked dry, other events such as Hitler's formative years in Vienna, the Beer Hall Putsch and the Munich Conference have not been fully explored and could serve as the basis for future motion pictures. There is even greater potential in terms of fiction, primarily in the area of alternate history. Several of these titles have already been mentioned in the entry for *Fatherland*, particularly the *Worldwar* series by Harry Turtledove. This appendix will suggest ten novels in alphabetical order that could possibly be developed into successful film projects:

• ***Death of the Führer*** (novel by Roland Puccetti) This tale could be charac-

terized as a hip variation on *They Saved Hitler's Brain*. The Führer's "suicide" is carried out in the bunker after his brain has been extracted and placed in another body. In this new persona, the Führer attempts to revive the Third Reich. A secret agent learns about the operation and tries to hunt Hitler down, unaware that his quarry is now a woman!

• ***The Divide*** (novel by William Overgard) In this alternate history, the Axis powers have won the war and the United States has been partitioned in half between German and Japanese sphere of influence. To celebrate the 30th anniversary of their victory, Hitler and Tojo plan a summit on the "divide," the nickname for the border between the two zones in Victory, Kansas. A group of freedom fighters, long dormant, plan to revive the American resistance movement with a dual assassination. This adventure thriller has many plot twists that make it riveting.

• ***Hitler Has Won*** (novel by Frederic Mullally) Germany wins World War II and conquers Europe after Hitler persuades Japan to attack Russia instead of the United States in 1941. The triumph unravels, however, when an Italian cleric, Cardinal Donati, becomes Hitler's advisor. Feeding the Führer's ego, he persuades him to undertake an outrageous scheme to overthrow the Pope and assume the papacy himself as Pope Adolf I. This mad act leads to a power struggle in the Nazi hierarchy and world outrage leading to the collapse of the Third Reich. Plot is brilliant and subtle and well suited to a cinematic treatment.

• *The Iron Dream* (novel by Norman Spinrad) The plot involves an alternate universe in which Hitler emigrates to America, becoming first a popular magazine illustrator and finally a science fiction writer. His novel *Lord of the Swastika* becomes a cult classic, however, the text wildly parallels the events of Nazi Germany in our universe. *The Iron Dream* would pose a tremendous challenge if adapted to the screen, but a solution could be found, perhaps by mixing live actors with computer animation for scenes from *Lord of the Swastika.*

• *Portage to San Cristobal of A.H.* (novel by George Steiner) Upon first reading, Steiner's wordy, philosophical novel about an aged but mentally alert Hitler who has been tracked down to his hidden lair in the Amazon jungle by Israeli agents would be considered an unlikely candidate for a screen treatment. However, a successful stage adaptation has demonstrated that it could make a similar transference to film. The book is rich in imagery, with more than a hint of Joseph Conrad's *Heart of Darkness*. It concludes with a lengthy self-defense by Hitler which is both frightening and brilliant as he tries to justify that which is unjustifiable.

• *Samuel Hitler* (novel by Sissini) Sissini is the pen name of Dimitris Chorafas, who penned this novel with an intricate premise of an alternate history in which Hitler is Jewish. He nevertheless becomes Chancellor of Germany and provokes a world war leading to nuclear holocaust.

No doubt the screenplay would require a great degree of discretion and tact, but the theme that evil can arise in various guises is both perceptive and relevant.

• *Trial of Adolf Hitler* (novel by Philippe van Rjndt) One of the most exceptional Hitler novels of the past thirty years, van Rjndt's writing style seems ideally suited to the screen. Through a fluke of circumstance, Hitler manages to escape from the bunker, wounded and disfigured but with a fortune in gold. Under the name Werner Busse, he establishes himself as a model citizen and town elder in a small Bavarian community. However, after twenty-five years, he deliberately reveals himself to the world as Hitler, planning his ultimate trial before the United Nations as an opportunity for vindication and martyrdom that will propel the creation of a Fourth Reich. Van Rjndt's Hitler is one of the most convincing portrayals in speculative literature, and Hitler's ultimate failure is masterfully told.

• *Triumph of the Third Reich* (novel by A. Edward Cooper) Crude but nevertheless fascinating alternate history in which the Nazis develop atomic weapons in early 1944 and use them to destroy the Allied forces at D-day and the massive Russian armies. Cooper is very good at entertaining plot twists, including the overthrow of Stalin, the early death of Roosevelt and the presidency of Henry Wallace, FDR's third term Vice President, and his scheming successor, Joseph P. Kennedy. Hitler is assassinated toward the end of the story and Rommel dismantles the Nazi state and restores democracy. This material might not be suited as a feature film, but would make a good miniseries.

• *Who Will Watch the Watchers?* (novel by Edwin Fadiman Jr.) The story is set in the late 1960s, in which CIA agents discover that Hitler is alive in Paraguay. They also encounter a worldwide conspiracy by the world powers, including the Soviet

Union, to keep the information secret to avoid opening old wounds. Thoughtful and provocative, Fadiman's novel nonetheless could be turned into a literate thriller like the Harry Palmer (Michael Caine) spy films.

• *Young Adolf* (novel by Beryl Bainbridge) Historians have been intrigued by the speculation that Hitler might have traveled to England in 1912 to visit his half-brother Alois, living in Liverpool. Bainbridge recreates this possible visit in her sensitive and penetrating novel in which characters and events gain importance because the reader is aware of future events. This treatment could easily be turned into an effective low budget film.

INDEX

References are to entry numbers except PF, *which means Preface,* OV, *Overview, and* A1, A2 *and* A3, *the appendices. Asterisks indicate performers who have played Hitler.* **Boldface** *indicates a photograph.*

Der 20. Juli see *Der Zwanzigiste Juli*
100 Jahre Adolf Hitler—Die Letzte Stunde see *Der Letzte Stunde im Führerbunker*
A-Team (TV series) 57
Aacken, Wilfred von 4
Abbott, Steve 32
Abel, Walter 37, 81
Abercrombie, Ian 92
Abildstrøm, Jytte 86
Abney, William 39
Abrahams, Andy* 84
Abrahamson, Bernie 92
Abramowski, Klaus 18
Ace of Aces (1982 film) PF, 1, 42, 43, 96
Ackland, Joss 39
Adamson, Raymond 12
Adler, Luther* 13, **57**, A2
Adolf Hitler in Prison (theater skit) OV
Adolf Hitler–My Part in His Downfall (1972 film) PF
Adolphe, Hylette 91
Adventure films 1, 15, 28, 36, 42, 43, 50, 58, 64, 67, 74, 77, 88, 95
Adventures of Fu Manchu (TV series) A2
The Adventures of Picasso (1978 film) 2
After Mein Kampf see *Après Mein Kampf Mes Crimes*
Agee, Timothy 84
Agnst, Herta 51

Akdridge, Michael 11
Albee, Edward 12
Albee, Jack 31
Albert, Eddie 92
Alberty, Karl Otto 4, 92, 96
Alden, Norman 73
Aldrich, Fred 66
Aldridge, Michael 63
Alexander, Richard 29
Alfasa, Joe 41
Alfredson, Hans 2
All in the Family (TV series) 93
All Quiet on the Western Front (1929 film) OV
All Quiet on the Western Front (novel) 51
Alland, William 9
Allen, Bernie 72
Allen, Hope 16
Allen, Irwin 82, A2
Allen, Sheila 77
Allen, Steve 16
Allen, Woody 84, 97, 98
Allerson, Alexander 4
'Allo, 'Allo (TV series) 15
Almond, Nina 42
Alternate history films 20, 32, 57, 83, 99
Altsev, L. 22
Amato, Nicholas 3
Ameche, Jim 82
"America the Beautiful" (song) 89
Ames, Granville 92
Amfitheatrof, Daniele 13

Amin, Idi 33, 69
Amir, Gideon 20
"Anchluss '77" (TV episode) A2
Andell, Pavel 20
Anders, Gunther 51
Anders, Rudolf 29, 37, 65, 83, 87
Anderson, Birgitta 2
Anderson, Eddie "Rochester" 81
Anderson, Jurgen 6
Andrews, Dana A2
Andrews, Geno 31
Andrews, Harry 4
Andrews, Jodie 40
Andreyev, Boris 19
Angelucci, Antonella 62
Anna Karenina (novel) 84
Anthony, Michael 92
Antonov, A. 76
Antony, Mark 82
Anwar, Teriq 20
Apollinaire, Guillaume 2
Applegate, Royce D. 34
Après Mein Kampf Mes Crimes (1940 film) 3
Arabov, Juri 60
Arafat, Yassir 69
Aragon, François 70
Archard, Bernard 44
Arco, Louis V. 61
Arden, Eve 90
Arkin, Adam 90
Arlen, Harold 81
Arliss, Leslie 24

267

Armstrong, Dick 96
Armstrong, Louis 65
Armstrong, R. G. 92
Arno, Sig 14
Arnold, Henry 32
Arquette, Lewis 54
Arquette, Patricia 54
Artenfels, Rainer von* 49, 69
Arthur, Bea 34
Arthur, Carol 5
Arthur, Jean 25
Arthur, Johnny 14
Ash, Jerome 83
Ashby, Robert 11
Askin, Leon 49, 93
Asner, Hans Dieter 62
Aspinall, David 79
Astaire, Fred 69
Astangov, Mikhail* 80
Astar, Ben 65, 96
Atlantic Monthly (magazine) 58
Atlee, Clement 27
Attenborough, Richard 8
Attila the Hun 33
Atwell, Judith 96
Atwill, Lionel OV, 87
Auberjonois, Rene 78
Aubert, Georges 28
Auger, Christian 70
Auschwitz (concentration
    camp) 38, 92
Aussedat, Pierre 70
Austin, Robert 7
Avocone, Jay 92
Awdiejew, Aleksy 18
Axmann, Arthur 12
Aykroyd, Dan 8, 55
Aylen, Richard 92
Aylmer, Felix 64, 89

Babbitt (novel) A1
Babes in Toyland (1934 film) 32
Baby Frankenstein (parody film)
    84
Bach, Johann Sebastian 49
Bach, P. D. Q. 86
Back from the Front (1943 short
    subject) OV
Back to the Future (film series)
    99
Backus, Georgia 9
Badalucco, Nicola 62
Bader, Günther* 75
Bader, Matthew 48
Baer, Harry 69
Baglioni, Luciano 62
Bailey, G. W. 92
Bailey, Jack 41
Bailey, Robin 27
Bainbridge, Beryl A3
Baird, Stuart 53
Baker, Carroll 40

Baker, Josephine 97
Balaban, Bob 10
Baldwin, Stanley 27
Balenda, Carla 95
Balin, Ina 84
Balin, Richard 84
Ball, David 31
Ball, Nicholas 74
Ballard, Kaye 94
Ballentine, E. J. 61
Balsan, Alan 88
Balsim, Eric 16
Bamber, David 79
Bambers, Ruth 52
Bancroft, Anne 88
Banderas, Antonio 63
Bang the Drum Slowly (1973
    film) 38
Bannen, Ian* 27
Banner, John 35, 61, 66, A2
Banning, Jacl 84
Bärenklau, Foxi 52
Baring, Victor 92
Barker, Petronella 20
Barleon, Amelie 72
Barnes, George 66
Barnes, Richard 96
Barr, Leonard 90
Barrett, Paul 87
Barrier, Edgar 65, 95
Barron, John 39
Barry, Alan 15
Barry, Ivor 88
Barry, J. J. 34
Barry, John 8
Barry Lyndon (1975 film) 92
Bartok, Bela 30
Barton, Dee 67
Barty, Billy 90
Basch, Felix 36, 66
Basehart, Richard* **35**
Basie, William "Count" 5
Baskomb, John 4
Bassermann, Albert 66
Batc, Anthony 11, 92
Bates, Bert 4
Bates, Charles 83
Bates, Michael 4
Bates, Norman (character) 51
Bathke, Wolfgang 18
Batoris, Caspain 40
Battle of Britain (1969 film) 4
The Battle of Stalingrad see
    Stalingrad
Battle of the Bulge (1965 film) 4
Bauer, Bernhard 43
Bauer, Fred 90
Bauer, Hans 47
Baum, Carol 77
Baur, Remar J. 28
Bavolets, Pavel 79
Bayerett, Christopher 28

Bayldon, Geoffrey 27, 89
Baywatch (TV series) 54
Beach, Scott 88
Beard, Stanley 77
The Beatles 20
Beatty, Robert 27
Beaumont, Victor 28
"Beautiful Dreamer" (song) 72
Bebb, Richard 12
Beck, General Ludwig von 47,
    71, 92, 100
Beckendorff, Ghita 30
Becker, Rolf 48
Beer Hall Putsch 37, 83, 92,
    A3
Beethoven, Ludwig van 3, 15,
    36, 69
Behrens, Phil 67
Belding, William 44
Bell 57
Bell, Alexander Graham 82
Bell, Tobin 55
Bellamy, Ralph 92, **96**
Belli, Peter 86
Bellman, Gina 63
Bellow, Saul 97
Belmondo, Jean-Paul PF, 1, 45
Belokurov, V. 76
Below, Colonel Nicolaus 7, 12,
    39
Belsere, Arthuro 84
Ben-Hur (1959 film) 89
Bendelstein, A. 22
Bendiner, Jessica 48
Bendix, William 81
Benedict, Jay 15
Benfield, John 40
Benford, Gregory 20
Benil, Gul (character) 54
Bennet, Sandy 84
Bennett, Charles 82
Bennett, Joan PF, 58, 92
Bennett, John 39
Bennett, Steve 85
Benny, A. Jonathan 38
Benny, Jack 10, 87, 88
Benoit, Sara 16
Benrath, Martin 75, 89
Berchtesgaden (site of Hitler's
    mountain retreat) 1, 11, 20,
    30, 35, 44, 58, 60, 64, 69, 71,
    74, 77, 92
Berezov, P. 76
Bergen, Polly 92, 96
Berger, Howard 54
Berger, Sarah 20
Berger, William 92, 96
Bergin, Patrick 33
Bergman, Andrew 5
Beria, Lavrenti 19
Berkeley, Busby 34
Berkoff, Steven* **92**

Berle, Milton 83
Berlin, Justin 92, 96
Berlin Olympic Games of 1936 1, 42
Berliner, Trude 83
Berlioz, Hector 53
Bernard, Heinz 92
Bernard, Judd 43
Bernardi, Jack 96
Bernstein, Leonard 31
Berry, Noah, Jr. OV
Bertholf, Sven-Eric 48
Besser, Joe 94
Bettelheim, Dr. Bruno 97
Beverly Hills Cop (1984 film) 92
Beverly Hills Cop II (1987 film) 33
Beyer, Klaus-Peter 10
Bibby, Charles K, 67
Bidlas, Jan 20
Bigaglia, Claudio 98
Bildt, Paul 100
Bilon, Little Pat 90
Bing, Herman 14
Bird, Alistair 38
Biroc, Joseph F. 5, 35
Birth of a Nation (1915 film) 84
Bismarck, Prince Otto von 87, 88
Bitnec, Demetar 96
Black, Edward 24, 64
Black, Jeremy* **6**
The Black Book (1949 film) 35
"Black Market" (song) 25
Black Sunday (1960 film) 96
Blaha, Josef 99
Blair, Isla 4
Blair, Joan 83
Blake, Larry J.* OV
Blakely, Susan 7
Blanc, Georges 3
Blanc, Mel* PF
Blatty, William Peter 93
Blau, Martin Maria 18
Blazhevich, Fydor 19
Blazicek, Jindrich 46
Blazing Saddles (1974 film) 5
Blessed, Brian 92
Blewitt, David 90
Bliesener, Jack* 31
Blitz, Rusty 72
Blondi (Hitler's dog) 7, 12, 19, 20, 39, 45, 96
Blood and Honor: Youth Under Hitler see *Jugend Unter Hitler: Blut und Ehre*
Bloom, Anne 84
Bloom, Marston 79
Blum, John Morton 97
Blume, Renata 28
Blythe, Benedick 79
Blythe, Peter 12

Boa, Bruce 15
Boam, Jeffrey 42
Bochner, Hart 92
Boeing Boeing (1965 film) 41,94
Boen, Earl 88
Bogdanev, Vladimir 60
Bogler, John 55
Bogolyubov, Nikolai 19
Bogoslavia, Agnia 1
La Bohème (opera) 2
Böhm, Hark 75
Böhm, Katharina 10
Böhm, Mark 10
Bohm, Marquand 49
Bohnen, Roman 37
Boje, Stefan 79
Bonanova, Fortunio 9
Bond, David 82
Bond, James (character) 43, 45, 67, 92
Bond, Raymond 25
Bond, Walter 66
Bond, Ward 36
Bondarev, Yuri 68
Bonneville, Richard 79
Bono, Emilio de 62, 63
Bont, Jan de 77
Book burning 42, 51
Boone, Richard 13
Borg, Sven Hugo 58
Borghi, Nino 49
Borgnine, Ernest 15
Bormann, Martin 7, 12, 32, 35, 39, 44, 51, 57, 60, 76, 92, A2
Boros, Ferike 66
Bose, Amit 31
Bostwick, Barry 92
Bottoms, Joseph 78
Bottoms, Sam 78
Bouilleret, Dominique 70
Boulting, John 91
Boulting, Roy 91
Bourdet, Rene 70
Bourgaux, Jacques 70
Bourne, Peter 96
Bow, Clara 97
Bowden, Doris 61
Bowen, Philip 96
Bowerbank, Brett 92
Bowman, Willy 12
Boxing (sport) 1, 73
Boyce, Todd 79
Boyd, Carole 12
Boyd, William 8
Boyer, Charles 45
Boyevoj Kinosbornik 1 see *Fighting Film Album # 1*
Boyevoj Kinosbornik 7 see *Fighting Film Album # 7*
The Boys from Brazil (1978 film) OV, 6
Boys Town (1938 film) 14, 94

Bracht, Frank 65
Bracken, Eddie 59, 81
Brackett, Charles 25
Bradley, David **85**
Bradley, Helen 33
Bradley, General Omar 45, 92
Bradley, Pat 90
Bradshaw, Charles 59
Brady, Alan (character) 89
Brady, Scott 96
Brahms, Johannes 29
Brainville, Yves 7
Brambell, Wilfrid 2
Branch, Tom 42
Brandner, Ernst 48
Brando, Marlon 63
Brandon, David 6
Brandon, Henry 32, 88
Brandstädter, Juitta 69
Brandt, Horst 17
Brandt, Martin 35
Bransford, Bob 32
Braque, Georges 42
Brauchitsch, General Walter von 19, 92, 96
Braun, Eva 1, 7, 12, 16, 19, 25, 26, 31, 32, 35, 39, 44, 51, 55, 57, 60, 69, 72, 74, 75, 78, 79, 92, 94, 96
Braun, Tony 57
Brauner, Arthur 100
Brauss, Arthur 96
Brazil, George 32
Brecher, Egon 37, 58
Breen, Richard 25
Brendl, Willi 17
Brenk, Paul 17
Brenner, Jules 73
Brent, Evelyn 41
Brent, Richard 96
Bressart, Felix 87
Brett, Jeremy 40
Brice, Fanny 97
Bricker, George 95
Brickman, Marshal 84
Bricktop 97
The Bride of Frankenstein (1935 film) 19
Bridge, Alan 59
The Bridge on the River Kwai (1957 film) 79
A Bridge Too Far (1977 film) PF
Bridges, Kenneth 33
Briese, Gerd 47
Brigaud, Philippe 70
Brill, Stephen 54
Brimble, Nick 40
Briskin, Mort 57
British films 4, 11, 12, 16, 27, 39, 64, 74, 79, 89, 91
Briton, Tony 11

Broadway Melody (1929 film) 69

Brocco, Peter 95, 96

Brodal, Sven Erik 30

Broderick, Matthew 72

Brodine, Norbert 13

Brodsky, Vlastimil 99

Bronski Follies of 1939 (stage show) 88

Bronson, Charles 15

Brooke, Paul 40

Brooks, Harry, Jr. 12

Brooks, Max 88

Brooks, Mel* 5, 34, 72, 88

Brother Orchid (1940 film) 36

Brother Theodore 84

Brothers, Dr. Joyce 41

Brown, Alan 12, 92

Brown, Bernard 11

Brown, Colin Eliot 56

Brown, David George 62

Brown, Garrett 97

Brown, Judy 84

Brown, Karl 36

Brown, Louis Y. 94

Brown, Roger 11

Bruhl, Heidi 41

Brunisch, Henrietta 57

Bryan, William Jennings 9

Bryant, William 93

Brydesen, Lars 86

Brynner, Yul 15

Brynych, Zbynek 46

Buchenwald (concentration camp) 17

Buckingham, R, 16

Buckley, Sarah 79

Budanova, Slavka 99

Bülow, Hans von 53

Bunce, Stuart 20

Bunker, Archie (character) 93

The Bunker (1980 film) OV, 7, 15

Bunker films 7, 12, 19, 32, 35, 39, 44, 51, 52, 75, 79, 85, 92

Bupp, Sonny 9

Burgdorf, General Wilhelm 12, 13, 39, 45, 51

Burger, Götz 70

Burke, Patricia 91

Burkhard, Gedeon 48

Burnett, John F 92, 96

Burr, Raymond 95

Burton, Jay 34

Burton, Norman 92

Burton, Richard 17, 27

Bushman, Francis X. 82

Büssche-Streithorst, Baron Axel von dem 47, 71

Büttner, Wolfgang 49, 100

Buttolph, David 37

Buzalski, Johannes 69

"By a Waterfall" (song) 44

Byers, John 33

Byington, Spring OV

Byrne, Gabriel 63

Byrne, Michael 42, 71, 74

Byrne, Patsy 27

Cabaret (1972 film) 16

The Cabinet of Dr. Caligari (1919 film) 51, 69

Cabot, Sebastian 67

Caesar, Julius (Roman states-man) 82

Caesar, Sid 34

Cagney, James 97

Caine, Howard 92

Caine, Michael 4, 15, 48, 89, A3

Caire, Audrey 85

Caldwell, George 88

Caligari, Dr. (character) 51

Caligula, Gaius (emperor of Rome) 17

Callas, Charlie 34

Cameron, Rod 42

Campanella, Frank 72

Campanella, Joseph 73

Campbell, Chellio 56

Campbell, Erma 97

Campbell, J. Kenneth 92

Campbell, Nell 53

Canaris, Admiral Wilhelm 89

Candelli, Stelio 92, 96

Cannes Film Festival 60, 78

Cannon, Jack 97

Caper, John, Jr. 32

Caper films 43

Capone, Al 97

Capponi, Pier Paolo 62

Cardini, Anna 98

Cardy, David 96

Carey, MacDonald 81

Carey, Olive 95

Carey, Ron 34

Carin II (Göring's yacht) 75

Carlin, John 12

Carlton, George 25

Carnelutti, Francesco 96

Caron, Leslie 45

Carradine, John 58, 82

Carricart, Robert 93

Carriere, Mathieu 77

Carroll, Christopher* 54

Carroll, Janice 41

Carroll, Leo G. 13

Carroll, Lewis 19

Carroll, Susette 34

Carroll, Victoria 56

Carruth, Milton 83

Carstensen, Margit 52

Carter, Sergeant Andy (charac-ter) A2

Carter, Jack 34

Carter, John 96

Carter, Lynda A2

Carter, Mitch 96

Cartwright, Lynn 56

Caruso, Dee 94

Carvey, Dana 54

Casey, Bernie 73

Casey, Thomas B. 23

Cash, Tom 32

Caspar, Eric 92

Cassavetes, John 15

Cassel, Jean-Pierre 45, 70

Castell, Rolf 47

Castellano, Franco 98

Castellari, Enzo **96**

Castellucci, Teddy 54

Castro, Fidel 69

Catch the Jews! (board game) 12

Cater, Wayne 79

Cates, Madlyn 72

Cathey, Reg E. 55

Catlett, Walter 81

Cattani, Henry Rico 93

Caunes, Georges de 26

Cavaliere, Salvatore 54

Cavanagh, Paul 13

Cawdron, Robert 12

Ceccarelli, Pietro 98

Cecil, Jonathan 34

Celentano, Adriano 98

Celi, Adolfo 39

Chaguinian, Anatoly **96**

Chailleux, Jacques 70

Chakiris, George 45

Challee, William 95

Chamberlain, Neville 9, 11, 27, 44, 57, 63, 70, A1

Chambers, Julia 74

Champion, Michael 34

Chan, Charlie (character) 42

Chandler, George 95

Chandler, Spencer 63

Chaney, Lon 56

Chang, Gary 20

The Changing Man (parody film) 97

Channon, Dennis 27

Chao, Stephanie 54

Chapin, Ken 97

Chaplin (1992 film) 8

Chaplin, Charlie* OV, 1, 8, **29**, 36, 65, 69 , 75, 97

Chaplin, Geraldine 8

Chaplin, Oona O'Neill 8

Chaplin, Sydney 8

Chapman, Martine 12

Charles, Leon A2

Charles, Martin 91

Charley's Angels (TV series) 89

Charlie Chan at the Olympics (1937) 42
Charlie Chan in City in Darkness (1939 film) PF
Charmetant, Christian 70
Charon (mythological character) 33
Charvat, Karel 46
Chase, Chevy 90
Chasen, Heather 71
Chatel, Peter 49
Chatto, Tom 4
Chaukey, Robert 75
Cheers (TV series) 54
Cheeta (chimpanzee) PF
Cherkasov, Nikolai 80
Chianese, Francesco 96
Chiaureli, Mikhail 19
Chinh, Kiew 56
Chinnery, Dennis 74
Chirkov, Boris 21
Chmelova, Valerie 99
Choltitz, General Dietrich von 45
Chomsky, Marvin 44
Chopin, Frederic 49, 53, 87
Chorafas, Dimitris A3
Christensen, Bent* 86
Christensen, Jeanette 86
Christensen, Jesper 30
Christensen, Per 30
Christian, Claudia 78
Christmas, Eric 92
Christmas, Jason 84
Christmas Story (1983 film) 55
Churchill, Clementine 27
Churchill, Winston 1, 2, 4, 9, 11, 13, 19, 27, 29, 65, 72, 74, 76, 80,s 92, 96, A1, A2
Cianelli, Lewis 96
Ciano, Edda Mussolini 62, 63
Ciano, Count Galeazzo 11, 62, 63, 92, 96
Cicero, Marcus Tullius (Roman statesman) A2
Cilento, Diane 39
Citizen Kane (1941 film) 9, 97
City Lights (1931 film) 29
Clair, Philippe 26
Claire, Imogen 53
Clark, Blake 54
Clark, Bob 55
Clark, Gordon 66
Clark, James B. 13
Clark, Matt 92
Clark, Ron 34
Clarke, Warren 40
Claszewski, Reinhold 96
Clauber, Gertan 91
Claudius, King (character) 87, 88
Clement, René 45

Clements, Celine 16
Cleopatra (queen of Egipt) 33, 82
Clive, E. E. OV
Clock Without a Face see *The Two-Headed Spy*
A Clockwork Orange (1971 film) 92
Cloisters (museum) 42
Clones of Hitler 6, 56
Close Encounters of the Third Kind (1977 film) 10
Clousseau, Inspector Jacques (character) 91
Coates, Anne V. 8
Cobb, Lee J. 61
Coburn, Charles 82
Coburn, James 93
Cochrane, Martin 92
Coco, James 84
Coe, Jennifer 31
Coffey, Joseph 72
Cognon, Pierre 70
Coke, Eddie 9, 36
Colbert, Robert 92, 96, A2
Colbourne, Maurice 40
Cole, Corinne 56
Cole, Stan 55
Colin, Ian 89
Colley, Kenneth 39, 53, 63, 71, 92
Collier, Don 92, 96
Collier, Marian 44
Collins, Barnabus (character) 96
Collins, Elaine 16
Collins, G. Pat 95
Collins, Larry 45
Collins, Ray 9, 37
Collins, Stephen 44
Colman, Ronald 82
Colonna, Jerry 81
Coltrane, Joe 67
Columbus, Christopher 82
Combat (TV series) 15
Combs, Jeffrey 78
Comedy films 1, 2, 5,10, 14, 24, 25, 26, 29, 34, 36, 38, 41, 50, 54, 55, 59, 65, 66, 72, 75, 79, 84, 87, 88, 90, 91, 93, 94, 97, 98
Comedy of Errors (play) 71
Comic Strip Presents (TV series) A2
Comingore, Dorothy 9
Confessions of a Nazi Spy (1939 film) OV, 29, 37
Conklin, Chester 29, 59
Conlin, Jimmy 59
Connery, Sean 42
Connor, Kevin 39
Conrad, Joseph A3

Conrad, Michael 92
Conreid, Hans 66
Conti, Bill 73
Conversation with the Beast (1996 film) OV, 10
Conway, Curt* A2
Cook, Randall William 33
Coolidge, Calvin 97
Coolidge, Martha 84
Cooper, A. Edward A3
Cooper, George Lane 34
Cooper, Rowena 44
Coote, Robert 13
Copley, Paul 92
Coppola, Francis Ford 45
Coquillon, John 43
Corey, Irwin 84
Corey, Jeff 61
Coriolanus (play) 71
Cornillac, Clovis 70
Coronado, Francisco (explorer) 42
Correll, Charles 96
Corrface, George 92
Cortez, Bertie 92
Cortez, Hernando (explorer) 42
Cortez, Stanley 85
Cosma, Vladimir 1
Cossins, James 39
Cossy, Hans 47
Costanzo, Filippo 98
Cotrell, Mike 34
Cottle, Matthew 8
Cotton, Joseph 9
Coulouris, George 9, 63
Countdown to the Big One see *Ring of Passion*
Countdown to War (1989 film) 11
Court, Pierre 70
The Court Jester (1956 film) 65
Courtney, Nicholas 91
Courtney, Weir 92
Covert, Allan 54
Cowardly Lion (character) 55
Cox, Ronny 55
Coy, Jonathan 11
Coyle, James 40
Crabtree, Arthur 24
Crabtree, Paul 32
Craig, Alec 87
Craig, Wendy 97
Cravat. Nick 82
The Crawling Eye (1958 film) 35
Crayne, Dani 82
Craze, Peter 40
Crazy Cats (comedy team) 50
Creature from the Black Lagoon (1954 film) 85
Creighton, Rhett 92
Cremer, Bruno 45

Cribbins, Bernard 2
Cromwell, Richard OV
Cronin, Michael 11
Cronjager, William 41
Crosby, Bing 81
Crosby, Gary 94
Croskin, Philip 40
Crowther, Graeme 42
Cry Wolf (1947 film) 35
Culp, Robert 13, 43
Culver, Michael 7, 11
Culver, Roland 64
Cumbuka, Shaka 73
Cuny, Alain 3
Curcio, E. J. 31
Curran, Tom 9
Currie, Louise 9
Curtis, Billy 41
Curtis, Dan 92, 96
Curtis, Stephen 43
Cushing, Peter 92
Cuthbertson, Alan 65, 96
Cutting, Richard 82
Czech films 46, 99

D-Day invasion 13, 20, 57, 65, 70, 92
Dacae, Henri 6
Dachau 36, 40, 83
Dagover, Lil 49
Dagovitz, Monica 23
Dahle, Keith 85
Dahlin, Isabelle 16
Dahmen, Andrea 92
Daladier, Édouard 11
Dale, Courtney 16
Dali, Salvador 2
Dallas, Lorna 43
Dallimore, Maurice 41
Dalmais 3
Daltry, Roger 53
D'Amore, Frank 84
Dan, Reiko 50
Dance, William 16
Dangerfield, Rodney 54
Daniell, Henry 29, 82
Danielsson, Tage 2
Danish films 30, 86
Danker, Eli 92
Danner, Blythe 44
Dante, Aligheri 9, 33, 51, 69
Dante, Peter 54
Dantine, Helmut 82, 87
Danton (1932 film) 83
Dapporto, Massimo 62
Darien, Frank 95
Dark Shadows (TV series) 92, 96
Darren, James A2
Darvas, Ivan 28
Dassin, Jules A1
D'At, Catherine 70

Dauphin, Claude 45
Davenport, Kolby 16
Davies, Marion 97
Davis, Boyd 25
Davis, Brad 71
Davis, Michael 72
Davis, Willie 94
Davydov, Vlad 68
Day, Diane 34
The Day of Freedom (1935 film) OV
Dayton, Danny 94
"The Deadly Games Affair" (TV episode) A2
Deadrick, Vince, Jr. 42
Dearing, R. E. 24, 64
De'Ath, Charles 20
The Death of Adolf Hitler (1972 film) 12
Death of the Führer (novel) A3
Deckard, Be 33
De Concini, Ennio 39
Deep Space Nine (TV series) 54
DeFarge, Madame (character) 34
Degas, Rupert 20
De Gaulle, Charles 45, 70
De Haven, Carter 29
Dehner, John 6, 92, 96
Deighton, Len 20
Dekker, Albert 37, 66, 81
Delanne, Lena 28
Delano, Lee 34
Dellafemina, Michael 33
Delon, Alain 45
Delpy, Julie 18
Del Rio, Dolores 97
De Luca, Michael 54
DeLuca, Rudy 34
DeLuise, Dom 5, 34, 55
Demarest, William 59
De Marney, Terrance 65
Demerger, Robert 40
DeMille, Cecil B. 81
"Demonella" (TV episode) A2
Dempsey, Jack 97
Demsky, Maurice 32
Dennen, Barry* 73, A2
Dennis, Jack 36
Dennis, Peter 92
Dennison, Leslie 87
Denny, Charles 97
Depot for Catastrophes see *Fighting Film Album # 7*
DeRossi, Barbara 62
DeSandro, Stefano 62
The Desert Fox (1951 film) OV, 13, 57
The Desert Rats (1953 film) 13
Desrau, Max 70
DeStefano, Vincent 31
Destroy All Monsters (1968 film)

50
DeSylvia, B. G. 37
De Toth, Andre 89
Deutsch, Ernst 61
"Deutschland Über Alles" (German anthem) 18, 41, 87
Devereaux, Ed 12
Devil (character) 14, 33, 54, 82
The Devil and Max Devlin (1981 film) 56
The Devil with Hitler (1942/43 film) 14, 36
Devin, Dana 98
Devine, Andy OV
Devlin, Joe **14,** 59
Dexter, Anthony 82
Dey, Susan 84
Diaghilev, Sergei 2
Diamanti, Giuseppe* 98
Diamond, Ron 88
Dick, Phipip K. 20
The Dick Van Dyke Show (TV series) 35, 89
Dicks, John 40
Dickson, Irl 67
Dictionary of the Third Reich (book) PF
Diehl, Karl Ludwig 47
Dieti, Helmut 75
Dietl, Harald 62
Dietrich, Dena 34
Dietrich, Marlene 25, 65, 69
Diez, Fritz* 17, 28, 46, 68
Dietrich, General Sepp 15, 40
Diffring, Anton 96
Digman, Basil 91
Dignam, Mark 28
Dikij, Aleksei 80
DiLuia, Bruno 98
Dime, Johnny 66
DiNys, Crispin 15
Direction of the Main Blow see *Osvobozhdeniye*
The Dirty Dozen (1967 film) 15, 67
The Dirty Dozen: The Deadly Mission (1987 film 15
The Dirty Dozen: The Fatal Mission (1988 film) 15
The Dirty Dozen: Next Mission (1985 film) 15, 83
Dirty Work (1998 film) 54
Disaster at D-Day (anthology) 20
Disney, Walt 2, 32, 69
Dissing, Povl 86
The Divide (novel) A3
The Divine Comedy (epic poem) 9
Dobkin, Larry 92
Dobschutz, Ulrich von 48
Dobson, James 32

Dobtcheff, Vernon 42, 63, 71, 91, 92
Dr. Strangelove (1964 film) 91
Doctor Zhivago (1965 film) 70
Dodsworth (novel) A1
Doherty, William 92
Dokoupil, Tom 52
Dolan, Robert Emmett 66, 81
Dolemz, George 83
Dollfuss, Engelbert 3
Dominick, Oliver 62
Domröse, Angelika 46
Donald, Simon 79
Donald Duck (character) 31
Donath, Ludwig* 37, 61, **83**, A2
Donato, Nicolas 70
Dönitz, Admiral Karl 12, 39, 85, 88
Donlevy, Brian 59
Donnellan, Jill 67
Donner, Clive 74
Donner, Robert 90
Doody, Alison 42
The Doomsday Machine (1967/72 film) 56
Doré, Gustave 69
Doris, Pierre 26
Dors, Diana 65
Doucette, Al 23
Doughty, Chuck 32
Douglas, Buddy 33
Douglas, Colin 96
Douglas, Gordon 14
Douglas, Kirk 45
Douglas, Michael 77
Douglas, Sam 15
Dowding, Hugh C. 4
Down Memory Lane (TV series) 84
Downey, Robert, Jr.* 8, 63, 84
Dracula Sucks (1979 film) PF
Drahokoupilova, Maria 99
Dream in the Hand see *Fighting Film Album # 1*
Dreellen, John van 51
Dressler, Marie 97
Drexler, Anton 37
Dreyfus, Jean-Claude 70
Driant, Jean Charles 91
The Drums of Fu Manchu (1940 serial) 32
Duchovny, David 8
Dudgeon, Neil 20
Duering, Carl 6, 92
Duff, Howard 92
Duffell, Peter 43
Dufilho, Jacques **70**
Dugan, Tom* 81, 87
Duggan, Andrew 96
Dukes, David 92, 96
Dumas, Roger 70

Dumont, Guy 6
Dumont, Sky 44, 92, 96
Duncan, Angus 41
Dunkelmann, Ericka 17
Dunlop, Leslie 27
Dunn, Emma 29
Dunn, Kevin 8
Dunn, Liam 5
Dupois, Art 95
Dur, Poldi 37
Durfee, Ross 56
Düringer, Annamarie 100
Durning, Charles 88
Düsterberg, Theodor 17
Duvall, John 79
Dux, Pierre 45
Dwyer, Kathryn 16
Dynevor, Shirley 74
Dysart, Richard 92
Dyson, Jeremy 38
Dzhugashvili, Yakov (Stalin's son) 18
Dziubinska, Anulka 53

East, Ian 74
Eastwood, Clint 67
Eaton, Gillian 88
Eaton, Robert P. 67
Ebel, Christian 92
Ebel, Ruth 28
Eburne, Maude 87
Eccles, Julie 42
"Echo of Yesterday" (TV episode) A2, 43
Eddison, Robert 42
Edel, Alfred 52, 69
Eden, Anthony 27
Edison, Thomas 69
Edmiston, Walker 92
Edson, Richard 78
Edward VIII (king of England) 27
Edwards, Blake 93
Edwards, Bruce 36
Edwards, Carl 85
Edwards, Darren Mark 33
Eichinger, Bernd 69
Eichman, Adolf 23, 92
Eidsvold, Eindvide 30
Eidsvold, Gard 30
Eig, Taina 48
Eiger, Jacques 3
Eilbacher, Lisa 96
Eilers, Kurt 51
Einhorn, Christopher 71
Einik, Eliak 71
Einik, Nirit 71
Einstein, Albert 84
Einstein on the Bounty (parody film) 84
Eisenhower, General Dwight D. 45, 92

Ekberg, Carl* 58, 66, 74, 93
Ekland, Britt 73
Ekman, Gosta 2
Eldredge, Nick 92
Elfers, Konrad 43
Elie, Josip 72
Elixir of Courage see *Fighting Film Album # 7*
Elizabeth I (queen of England) 82
Elkins, Steven 71
Ellig, Belle 96
Elliott, Denholm 6, 42
Elliott, Peter 12
Elliott, Robert 55
Ellis, Herb 93
Ellwood, Tony* 67
Elmer Gantry (novel) A1
Elmes, Frederick 16
Elmes, John 11
Elphick, Michael 40
Elsom, Jonathan 12
Elvey, Maurice 24
Elwyn, Michael 27, 92
Emberg, Bella 34
Emery, Aquarelle 16
Emery, John OV
Emmett, E. V. H. 24
Emo, Maria 35
The Empire Strikes Back (1980 film) 15, 42
The Empty Mirror (1996 film) OV, 16
The End of a Winter's Dream see *Our Hitler*
Endriss, Elisabeth 48
Engel, Marlies 48
Engelbrecht, Constanze 77
English, David 53
Enquist, Per Olav 30
Epp, Elisabeth 51
Erasmus, Desiderius A2
Erdman, Nikolai 22
Erdody, Leo 36
Erhardt, Hermann 51, 57
Eric, James 67
Erlandsen, Erland 51
Erlich, Ingo 10
Ernst, Ulrich 62
Ernst Thälmann—Führer Seiner Klasse (1955 film) 17
Ernst Thälmann—Sohn Seiner Klasse (1954 film) 17
Ervin, Robert 92
Es Geschah am 20.Juli see *Jackboot Mutiny*
Escapement (1958 film) PF
Esmond, Carl 35
Esser, Paul 100
Ettlinger, Norman 12
Europa see *Zentropa*
Europa, Europa (1991 film) 18

Evans, David 72
Evans, Edward 27
Evans, Herbert 58
Evans, Martin A2
Evans, Rex 14, 65
Exactly at Seven see *Fighting Film Album # 7*
The Exorcist (novel) 93
Explaining Hitler (book) PF, 72
Expressionism 51, 69

F for Fake (1974 film) 69
Faber, Erwin 49
Fabrizi, Franco 62
Fadiman, Edward, Jr. A3
Fagin, Ronald J. 63
Fairbanks, Douglas 8
Falkenbach, Uwe 92, 96
The Fall of Berlin (1949 film) 17, 19, 51, 76, 80
Fall of the House of Usher (1949 film) 56
Fanny Hill (1964 film) 45
Fantasia (1940 film) 2
Fantasy films 16, 33, 42, 53, 54, 67, 69, 82, 86
Fantori, Sergio 93
Farewell My Lovely (1975 film) 96
Farnsworth, Richard 33
Farrow, John 37
Farrow, Mia 97
Farrow, Stephanie 97
"Fat Hermann Go Home" (TV episode) A2
The Fatal Glass of Beer (novel) 90
Fatherland (1994 film) OV, 20, A3
Favart, Robert 92
Faylen, Frank 14
Fazenda, Louise OV
Fearheighly, Don 32
Fedin, L. 76
Fegelein, General Hermann 7, 12, 39, 51
Feifel, Martin 75
Feld, Fritz 34
Fellgiebel, General Erich 47, 71, 92
Fellows, Don 15, 43, 44
Fellows, Jullian 7
Fendel, Rosemarie 75
Fenton, Frank 25
Fernandes, Joao 84
Fernau, Rudolf 49
Ferrache, Rachid 1
Ferrando, Giancarlo 98
Ferrara, Stepane 1
Ferrer, José 40, 88
Ferrer, Mel A2

Ferrer, Violette 70
Ferres, Veronica 75
Ferro, Marc 70
Ferzetti, Gabriele 39
Fest, Joachim C. PF, 47
Fidelio (opera) 69
Fiedel, Brad 7
Fields, Verna 32
Fields, W. C. 90
Fighting Film Album #1 (1941 film) 21
Fighting Film Album #7 (1942 film) 22
Findlay, Frank* **12**
Fine, Larry 75
Fine, Sylvia 65
Finkenzeller, Heli 47
Finlayson, James 87
Finn, Earl 34
Firkin, Rex 12
First Front see *Stalingrad* (1949/50)
Fischer, Adolf 17
Fischerauer, Bernd 48
Fisher, Carrie 90
Fisker, Erhard 86
Fisz, S. Benjamin 4
Fitz, Peter 10
Fitzgerald, F. Scott 97
Fitzgerald, Michael 71
Fitzsimmons, Courtland 14
Five Fingers (1952 film) 89
Five Graves to Cairo (1943 film) 13
Fix, Paul 36
Fleck, John 31
Die Fledermaus (opera) 39
Fleetwood, Mark 78
Fleischer, Rudolph* **20**
Fleisher, Peter 77
Fleming, Ian 64
Fleming, Victor A1
Flemyng, Robert 4
Flesh Feast (1967 film) 23
Fletcher, Lester 35
Florsheim, Patrick 92
Foch, Nina 92
Fogelman, Yuli 21
Folger, Byron 59
Fonseca, Carolyn Rusoff de 62
Footlight Parade (1933 film) 44
For Freedom (1940 film) 24
Forbes, Brian 8
Ford, Glenn 45
Ford, Harrison 42
Ford, Jeanne 84
Ford, John 69
Ford, Lita 33
A Foreign Affair (1948 film) 25
Forest, Delphine 18
Forest, Michael 63
Forrest Gump (1994 film) 97

Forrester, Larry 73
Forsberg, Tony 2
Forsythe, John 89
Forte, Joe 36
Fortress in the Volga (1942 film) 19
Foster, Barry 4
Foster, Doug 23
Foulke, Robert 95
Fowley, Douglas 14
Fox, Bernard 89
Fox, Edward 4
Fox, Julian 12
Fox, Michael J. 99
Foxley, W. G. 4
Frahm, Waldemar 47
France, C. V. 64
Franchetti, Sarah 92
Francis, Clive 27
Francis, Derek 12
Francis, Freddie 71
Franckenstein, Clement von 77
Franco, Francisco 11
Frank, Jeffrey 48
Frank, Melvin 81
Franken, Steve 94
Frankenstein (1931 film) OV
Frankenstein monster (character) 53, 69
Frankenstein, Baron Victor (character) 92
Franklin, Benjamin 84
Franklin, Joe 84
Franz, Eduard 13
Franz, Erich 17
Die Frau im Mond (1929 film) 58
Frauboes, Dietrich 4
Frazee, Terry D. 54
Frazer, Rupert 92
Frederick the Great (king of Prussia) 7, 51
Freed, Bill* **85**
Freeman, Kathleen 94
Freeman, Rob 77
Frelich, Oleg 19
French, Bruce 92
French, Leigh 34
French films 1, 3, 7, 26, 45, 70
Freud, Sigmund 16, 42, 84
Frey, Arno 66
Frey, Erik 47, 51, 57
Frey, Sami 92
Freytag, Robert 100
Frick, Billy* **41**, 45
Friedkin, Gary 31
Friedl, Fritz von 49, 92, 96
Friedrich, Caspar David 69
Friedrich, Hans 47
Friends (TV series) 54
Frizzell, John 16
Fröbe, Gert 45

Fromm, General, Friedrich 47, 71
Fronval, Georges* 3
Frosch, Gerd 1
Fruchtmann, Jakob 48
Fry, Stephen 79
Frye, Dwight OV
Fu Manchu (character) 32, A2
Fuerberg, Hans 66
Le Führer en Folie (1973 film) 26
"Der Führer's Face" (song) 31
Fuijikawa, Jerry 96
Fürst, Christian 52
Furth, George 5
Furtwängler, Wilhelm 70
Furusawa, Kengo 50
Fusco, Maria Pia 39
Fyffe, Will 24
Fyodorov, Aleksei 60

Gable, Clark 90
Gabor, Eva 81
Gaideburov, M. 76
Gajdarov, Vladimir 80
Galabru, Michel 26
Galbraith, Gary 32
Gale, David 92
Gallagher, Bernard 11
Gallico, Paul 73
Gallo, Mario 62
Galloway, Jack 11
Galo, Igor 92
Galvani, Graziella 98
Galvin, Stephen M. 78
Gamlin, Yngve 2
Gandhi, Mahatma 84
Ganibyan, Grigori 22
Gansard, Clara 28
Ganz, Axel 92
Ganz, Bruno 6
Garbo, Greta 25, 69
Gardella, Anthony 72
Garden, Vladimir 76
Gardiner, Reginald 29, 82
Gardner, Gerald 94
Gardner, Jack 36, 66
Garfield, Allen 73
Garin, Ernst 22
Garr, Teri 79
Garrett, Hank 84
Garrison, Ellen 97
Garvarentz, Georges 70
The Gathering Storm (1974 film) 27, 92
Gatliff, Frank 7
Gauthier, Vincent 70
Gavin, John 34
Gavrjusjov, Mischa 30
Gay, Gregory 35
Gay, John 7
Gaynes, George 88

Gearson, Monica 6
Gebhardt, Dr. Karl 12, 39, 44
Gefrorenen Blitze (1967 film) 28
Gehr, A. 21, 22
Gehrig, Lou 97
Gelovani, Mikhail 19, 80
Genghis Khan 63
Geoffroy-Chateau 20
George VI (king of England) 27
George, Götz 75
Georgiou, Penelope 49
Gerasimov, Sergei 21
Geray, Stephen* A2
Gerhardt, Wolfgang (pseudonym of Mengele) 6
A German Dream see *Our Hitler*
German films 10, 17, 28, 30, 47, 48, 49, 51, 52, 60, 69, 75
Gerrhus, Thornton 43
Gerry, Toni 82
Gestapo see *The Night Train to Munich*
Gestapo (play) 87
Geyle, Burkhard 92
Giarraputo, Jack 54
Giatsyntuva, S. 19
Gibello, Sergio 62
Gibney, Sheridan 66
Giddings, Gudrun 16
Gidley, Pamela 33
Gielgud, John 44, 77, 92
Gierasch, Stefan 96
Giermann, Frederick 83
Giermeyer, Frederick 36
Giese, Horst 99
Gifford, Hazen 84
Gilbert, Billy 29
Gilbert, Hershel Burke 57
Gilette, James 87
Gilliam, Burton 5
Gilliat, Sydney 64
Gillin, Hugh 96
Gilmore, Stuart 59
Ging, Jack 96
Ginter, Brad F. 23
Giradot, Annie 62
Gish, Sheila 39
Giustiniani, Micaela 62
Gladstone, Dana 77
Gleizer, Michele 18
Glennitz, Reinhard 92
Glover, Ilsa Blair 42
Glover, Julian 39, 42
Glover, William 88
Glowion, Paul 92
Goddard, Jim 40
Goddard, Paulette 8, 29, 81
The Godfather (1972 film) 63
Godwin, Jeremy 12
Goebbels, Dr. Joseph OV, 7,

10, 11, 12, 14, 16, 17, 19, 25, 32, 35, 37, 39, 42, 44, 47, 51, 58, 60, 67, 69, 71, 72, 77, 84, 92, 97, 98, 99, A1
Goebbels, Magda 7, 12, 39, 44, 51, 60
Goehr, Walter 24
Goff, Rusty 34
Goguel, Constantin de 43
Going My Way (1944 film) 66
Golas, H. G. 31
Gold, Käthe 49
Goldberg, Robert 88
Golden, Robert 95
Golden Turkey Awards (book) 85
Goldfinger (1964 film) 45
Goldie, Wyndham 64
Goldman, Roy* 88
Goldman, William 8
Goldsmith, Jerry 6
Goldsworthy, John 13
Goldwater, Barry 20
Golubkina, Laris 68
Gone with the Wind (1939 film) 90, 92
Good Morning Mr. Hitler (1939 film) OV
The Good Soldier Schwenck in the Concentration Camp see *Fighting Film Album # 7*
Goodliffe, Michael 39
Goodrich, Frances 37
Goodwin, Ron 4
Gorcey, Bernard 29
Gördeler, Carl 92, 100
Gordon, Anthony 90
Gordon, Barry J. 91
Gordon, Gerti 6
Gordon, Glen A2
Gordon, Leo 56, 92, 96
Gordon, Martin 42
Göring, Hermann PF, 4, 7, 9, 11, 12, 14, 15, 16, 17, 19, 35, 37, 39, 42, 44, 51, 57, 67, 69, 72, 75, 77, 78, 79, 80, 84, 92, 96, 97, A1, A2
Goring, Ruth 40
Gorman, Cliff 7
Gotell, Walter 6
Götterdämmerung (opera) 39, 69
Gottfried, Gilbert* 33
Gough, Michael 6, 44
Gould, Gordon 97
Gould, Heywood 6
Gould, Sid 34
Goullet, Arthur 24
Gounod, Charles 49
Gourson, Jeff 54
Gowers, Patrick 86
Graetz, Paul 45

Graf Spee (battleship) 24
Graff, Anton 51
Graham, C. J. 33
Graham, Morland 64
Graham, Ronny 34, 88
Graham, William A. 63
The Grail see *Our Hitler*
Grail lore 42, 69
Grainger, Gawn* A2
Granach, Alexander 37
Grandi, Count Dino 62, 63
Grange, Red 97
Grant, Cary 66
Grant, Lee 63
Grass, Günter 88
Grass, Vincent 70
Graves, Peter 92, 96
Graves, Rupert 71
Gray, Christopher 40
The Great Dictator (1940 film)
  OV, 8, 14, 29, 36, 65, 69, 75,
  87
The Great Escape (1963 film) 79
The Great Gabbo (1929 film) 6
The Great Glow (1938 film) 19
Greatorex, Wilford 4
Green, Austin 82
Green, Ginger 56
Green, Les 44
Greenberg, Martin H. 20
Greene, Danforth 5
Greene, H. Richard 92
Greene, Shecky 34
Greenfield, Ruth K. 82
Greenhut, Robert 97
Greenquist, Brad 55
Greenstreet, Sidney 67
Greg, Bradley 42
Gregory, Constantine 63
Greim, Field Marshal Robert
  Ritter von 12, 39, 51
Greisman, Alan 55
Grey, Joel **16**
Grey, Richard 89
Greyfox 7
Gribble, Bernard 71, 96
Gribble, Bill 67
Gribbon, Eddie 29
Gribov, Alexei 76
Grien, Helmut 71
Grier, David Alan 55
Griffin, David 4
Griffith, Kenneth* 89
Griffith, Melanie 77
Grignon, Marcel 45
Grimm Brothers 19
Grinde, Nick 36
Grønlykke, Lene 86
Grønlykke, Sven 86
Gross, Roland 82
Grossman, Marc 16
Grossman, Victor 28

Growth of the Soil (novel) 30
Guarnieri, Ennio 39
Guderian, General Heinz 7,
  35, 96
Guinan, Francis 77
Guinness, Alec* **39**
Guitton, Jean-Luc 70
Gulag Archipeligo (book) 19
Gunning, Chris 74
Günsche, Colonel Otto 7, 12,
  39, 51
Gurov, P. 19
Guschy, Otto 51
Gutmann, Lieutenant Hugo 1
Gutteridge, Lucy 40
Guttenberg, Steve 6
Guttman, Henry 66
Gwilym, Mike* 71
Gwilyn, Robert 63
Gyillim, Jack 4
Gynt, Greta OV

Haake, James 88
Haas, Ludwig* **70**, 77
Habek, Fritz 51
Hácha, Emil 11
Hacker, Joseph 96
Hackett, Albert 37
Hackman, Gene 55
Haddon, Lawrence 96
Haeften, Werner von 47, 71
Hagen, Uta 6
Hager, Peter 4
Hagiwara, Tetsuaki 50
Hagon, Garrick 20
Haik, Jacques 3
Hailstone, Moe (parody of
  Hitler) OV
Hainisch, Leopold 51
Hajel, Miroslav 46
Halder, General Franz 57, 83,
  92, 96
Hale, Nathan 84
Hall, Kevin Peter 33
Hall, Porter 59
Hallam, John 39
Hallett, Neil 89
Halletz, Erwin 51
Halmer, Gunther Maria 92
Halsey, Admiral William "Bull"
  92, 96
Halton, Charles 87
Hamilton, Guy 4
Hamilton, Neil 94
Hamlet (play) 9, 10, 84, 87
Hammer, Ben 96
Hampton, Richard 12
Hamsun (1996 film) 30
Hamsun, Knut 30
Hana, Hajime 50
Hanack, Sigrid 43
Hancock, Prentis 40

Hand, Rollin (character) A2
Handel, George Frideric 16
Hanfstaengl, Ernst "Putzi" PF,
  44
Hanfstaengl, Helene 37
Hanke, Karl 39, 44
Hanks, Tom 97
Hanley, Jenny 91
Hannemann, Walter 35
Hanno, Eva von 30
Hanoi Hilton (1987 film) 38
Hansen, Joachim 6, 92, 96
Hansen, Thorkill 30
Hanson, Luke 42
Hanussen (1988 film) 30
Harcourt, James 64
Hard Rock Zombies (1984 film)
  31
Hardiman, Terence 7
Harding, Jeff 15
Hardt, Eliose 96
Hardt, Harry 47
Hardwicke, Cedric 13, 61, 82
Hardwicke, Edward 7
Hardy, J. J. 42
Hardy, Lawrence 27
Hardy, Oliver 32, 72, 87
Hardy, Robert 27, 92, A2
Harenstam, Magnus* 2
Harkins, John 96
Harlan, Kenneth 36
Harlem Globetrotters (basket-
  ball team) 54
Harley, Richard 40
Harnack, Falk 47, 100
Harnish, Wolf 4
Harrigan, Ben 92
Harriman, Doug 33
Harris, Julius 73
Harris, Robert 20
Harris, Rosemary 6
Harris, Sam 82
Harrison, Deirdre 77
Harrison, Doane 25
Harrison, Nell 72
Harrison, Rex. 64
Hart, Peter 89
Hartford, Eden 82
Hartford, Kenneth 56
Hartmann, Erhardt 92
Harvey, Richard 11, 15
Harwood, Ronald 11
Haslam, Jonathan 11
Hasse, Hannjo 68
Hasse, Kurt 47
Hasse, Rod 34
Hassencamp, Oliver 47
Hathaway, Henry 13
Hattersley, Stephen 15
Haubold, Gunter 28
Hauck, Gunter 28
Hauer, Jochrn 47

Hauer, Rutger **20**, 44
Hauff, Alexander 77
Hauser, Harald 28
"Have You Ever Heard ze German Band?" (song) 72
Hawkins, Diana 8
Hawkins, Jack 89
Hawthorne, Nigel 34
Hay, Alexandra 41
Hayden, Linda 6
Haydn, Franz Joseph 69
Hayle, Grace 29
Hayman, Cyd 74
Hayman, Werner 87
Hayward, Susan 81
He Lives (1967 film) 32
"He Lives" (TV episode) A2
He Walked by Night (1948 film) 35
Healey, Myron 94
Hearst, William Randolph 8, 9, 97
Heart of Darkness (novel) A3
Heckert, James 44
Hedley, Jack 71
Hedqvist, Staffan 2
Hefner, Hugh 34
Hegewald, Hans-Joachim 28
Hegler, Wolfgang 77
Hehn, Albert 47
"Heil Klink" (TV episode) A2
Heinz, Grainger 92
Heisler, Stuart 35
Heitman, Karl-Heinz 62, 96
Held, Karl 7
Helen of Troy 82
Helgeland, Brian 33
Heller, Andre 49, 69
Heller, Lukas 40
Hellzapoppin' (1941 film) 54, 71
Hemingway, Ernest 2
Hemmerich, Valerie 16
Henderson, Scott* 34
Henker, Paul 17
Henley, Jacques 3
Henneberg, Gerd Michael 28, 68
Henreid, Paul 64
Henry, Mary 12
Herbe, Herbert 51
Herbert, Holmes 58
Herbert, Peet* 32
Herd, Richard 78
Herdan, Earle 96
Here Comes Mr. Jordan (1941 film) 9
Herlihy, Tim 54
Herlin, Jacques 96
Herold, Bernie 97
Herrmann, Bernard 9
Hershey, Barry J. 16
Hershey, Elizabeth 16

Hertzberg, Michael 5
Herzberg, Paul 15, 63, 71
Hess, Rudolf 6, 17, 37, 42, 44, 78, 84, 87, 89, 97, 98
Hessenland, Werner 47
Heuzé, Jean 3
Hewitt, Christopher 72
Hewitt, David L. 56
Heydrich, Reinhard 20, 40
Heyl, Burkhard 71
Heymer, Johnny 73
Hickey, William 72
Hicks, Russell 36
Hicks, William 67
Hidden Faces (musical group) 33
Higgins, Clare 20
Higgs, Stephen 48
Higher Than a Kite (1943 short subject) OV
Highlander (TV series) A2
Highway to Hell (1990 film) 33
Hillerman, John 5, 34
Himmler, Heinrich 7, 12, 14, 15, 16, 20, 28, 35, 37, 39, 40, 42, 44, 51, 57, 69, 76, 78, 79, 83, 84, 91, 92, 96, 99
Hindenburg (zepplin) 42
Hindenburg, Field Marshal Paul von 17, 35, 37, 78
Hindman, Earl 92
Hinds, Samuel S. OV
Hines, Gregory 34
Hines, Ronald 89
Hingle, Pat 92
Hinz, Matthias 92
Hinz, Werner 13, 100
Hippocrates 82
Hirohito (emperor of Japan) 81
Hirose, Kenjuro 50
Hirose, Sholchi 50
Hiroshima (1995 film) 4
Hirshfeld, Gerald 88
Hisler, Tim 42
Historia de "S" (1978 film) PF
Historical dramas 4, 7, 11, 12, 13, 17, 18, 19, 27, 30, 35, 37, 39, 40, 44, 45, 47, 49, 51, 62, 63, 68, 70, 71, 73, 80, 100
History of the World—Part One (1981 film) 34
Hitchcock, Alfred OV, 64, 73, 83, 84
Hitchcock, Keith 58
Hitler (1962 film) 35
Hitler (1977 film) PF
Hitler (Fest biography) PF
Hitler, Alois (Hitler's father) 78, 84
Hitler, Klara (Hitler's mother) 35, 84
Hitler as artist 2, 69, 79, 98

The Hitler Assassination Plot see *Der Zwanzigiste Juli*
Hitler—Beast of Berlin (1939 film) PF
Hitler—Dead or Alive (1943 film) 15, 36
Hitler Diaries (forgery) 75
Hitler, Eine Film aus Deutschland see *Our Hitler*
The Hitler Gang (1944 film) OV, 37, 83
Hitler Has Won (novel) A3
Hitler: The Last Ten Days (1975 film) 39
Hitler Meets Christ (2000 film) OV, 38
Hitler: The Missing Years (book) PF
The Hitler Options (anthology) 20
Hitler Over Germany (1932 film) OV
Hitler Victorious (anthology) 20
Hitler Youth 7, 12, 16, 18, 39, 40, 48, 51, 67, 83
Hitlerjunge Quex (1933 film) 18
Hitlerjunge Solomon see *Europa, Europa*
Hitler's Children (1943 film) PF
Hitler's Daughter (1990 film) PF
Hitler's Germany (TV series) 77
Hitler's Gold see *Inside Out*
"Hitler's Last Secret" (TV episode) A2
Hitler's SS: Portrait in Evil (1985 film) 40
Hitler's Table Talk (book) 60
Hitler's War (book) 11
Hitler's Wild Women see *Lucifer Complex, The*
Hiuju, Erik 30
Hobbes, Halliwell 87
Hochbuchler, Peter (pseudonym of Mengele) 6
Hoff, Anette 30
Hoffa, Jimmy 33
Hoffman, Elizabeth 92, 96
Hoffman, Dr. Julia (character) 92, 96
Hoffmann, Carla 17
Hoffmann, Frank 1
Hoffmann, Heinrich OV
Hofschneider, Marco 18
Hofschneider, Rene 18
Hogan, James P. 83
Hogan's Heroes (TV series) 35, 36, 43, 56, 66, 79, 93, A2
Höger, Karel 46
Holiday, Hope 41
Holland, Agnieszka 18
Holland, John 85

Holland, Tommy Lee 96
Hollander, Frederick 25
Hollmann, Johannes 48
Holloman, Bridget 16
Holloway, Sterling 81
Hollywood Canteen (1944 film) 81
Holm, Ian 44
Holmes, Denis 15
Holmes, Sherlock (character) 40, 83
Holocaust (1978 miniseries) 40
Holt, Will* 97
Holtzmann, Thomas 75
Høm, Jesper 86
Hook, Captain (character) 32
Hook, Line and Sinker (1969 film) 94
Hoover, Herbert 97
Hoover, J. Edgar 8
Hope, Bob 81
Hope, Leslie 92
Hope, William 77
Hopkins, Anthony* **7**, 8, 44, 62, 63
Hopkins, Harry 92, 96
Hoppe, Rolf 75
Hopper, Dennis 82, A2
Hörbiger, Attila 49
Hörbiger, Christine 75
Horgan, Patrick 97
The Horn Blows at Midnight (1945 film) 87
Horowitz, Margherita 92
Horras, Reinhard 4
Horror films 6, 23, 31, 33, 53, 85
Horsfall, Bernard 44
"Horst Wessel Song" 83, 97
Horton, Edward Everett 82
Hoskins, Bob 62, 63
Höss, Kommandant Rudolf 92
Hot to Trot (1983 film) 33
Hotel Berlin (1945 film) 36
Hotten, Walter 47
House of the Seven Gables (novel) 32
House on Telegraph Hill (1951 film) 35
Household, Geoffrey 58, 74
Houseman, John 96
Hoven, Adrian 43
Hovis, Larry* A2
How, Jane 92
How to Seduce a Woman (1974 film) PF, 41, 45
Howard, Clint 54
Howard, John C. 5, 34
Howard, Moe* OV, 9, 14
Howard, Rikki 53
Howard, Shemp 87
Howard, Trevor 4, 44

Howe, Bernhard 18
Howe, Irving 97
Hoy, Matsie 96
Hoyt, John 13
Hubb, Walter 89
Huddleston, David 5
Hughes, Andrew* 50
Hughes, Heather 23
Hughes, Howard OV, 95
Hulette, Don 85
Hulme, Anthony 24
Humes, Margaret 34
Humpoletz, Paul 42, 79
Hungarian Dance No. 5 (Brahms) 29
Hunkel, Holger 18
Hunter, Ian 67
Huntley, Raymond 64
Hurst, David 6
Hurt, John 34
Hurwitz, Harry 84, 90
Huston, Walter A1
Hutchins, Brock 16
Hutchinson, Ron 20
Hutinet, Jean-Pierre 70
Hutton, Betty 59, 81
Hyams, Roger 79
Hyde, Jonathan 71
Hyde-White, Alex 55
Hyde-White, Wilfred A2, 43, 65
Hygatt, Arnold (parody of Hitler) A1
Hyman, Dick 97
Hyman, Flo 67
Hymer, Warren 36
Hynkel, Adenoid (parody of Hitler) 8, 29, 69
Hytten, Olaf 58, 87

I, Claudius (1976 miniseries) 44
I, Justice see *Ja, Spravedlnost*
I Married a Communist (1950 film) 95
I Was Hitler's Valet (book) 69
I Was Monty's Double (1958 film) 92
Iago (character) 12
"Ich Liebe Dich" (song) 89
If the South Won the Civil War (novel) 20
Ifans, Rhys 54
The Ifs of History (book) 20
Ihlow, Klaus-Dieter 28
I'll Never Heil Again (1941 short subject) PF, OV, 9, 14
Imhoff, Roger 58
Imi, Tony 44
Imparto, Noelle 63
Imura, Tadashi 50
Indenbom, L. 76

Indiana Jones and the Last Crusade (1989 film) 42
Inferno (Divine Comedy Part One) 69
Ingalls, Marty 41
Inger, Manfred 57
Ingrassia, Mario 62
Inside Out (1975 film) 43, 96
Inside the Third Reich (1982 miniseries) OV, 44, 62
Inuzuka, Hiroshi 50
The Invisible Man (1933 film) OV
The Iron Dream (novel) A3
Irving, David 11
Irving, George 66
Is Paris Burning? (1966 film) 13, 45
Isaacs, Susan 77
Isackson, Peter 90
Isarov, Boris 44
Isayev, Konstantin 76
Ishibashi, Eitaro 50
The Island (1980 film) 48
Italian films 39, 62, 98
Ito, Emi 50
Ito, Hisaya 50
Ivano, Paul 36
Ives, Anne 72

Ja, Spravedlnost (1967 film) 46
Jackboot Mutiny (1955 film) 47, 51, 71, 100
Jackson, David E. 56
Jackson, Inigo 12
Jackson, Jeanine 97
Jackson, Peter 79
Jackson, Philip 74
Jacob, Peter 45
Jacobi, Derek* OV, 16, 27, **44**, 79
Jacobi, Ernst* 30
Jaeckel, Richard 15
Jaeger, Malte 47
James, Brion 78
James, Godfrey 63
Jane Eyre (1971 film) 27
Janisch, Michael 51
Jansen, Per 30
Japanese films 50
Jarré, Maurice 45
Jarvis, Martin 7
The Jazz Singer (1927 film) 84
Jeavons, Colin* 40
Jefford, Barbara 39
Jeffries, John 48
Jenkins, Clare 12
Jenkins, Julian 62
Jenn, Myvanwy 12
Jennings, Rory 20
Jensen, Birger 86
Jentle, Ian 92

Jesus Christ 34, 38, 39, 78, 89, 96

Jesus Christ Superstar (1973 film) 73

Jew Süss (1940 film) 69

Jewish persecution 1, 16, 18, 20, 29, 37, 40, 44, 69, 70, 71, 77, 92, 96

Jews in Space see *History of the World Part One*

Joan of Arc 82

Jockmann, Hansi 77

Jodl, General Alfred 7, 12, 19, 35, 39, 45, 51, 80, 83, 92, 96

Johns, Harriet 89

Johns, Milton 63, 92

Johns, Stratford 40

Johnson, Alan 88

Johnson, Chic 54

Johnson, David D. 16

Johnson, J. P. 78

Johnson, Lyndon B. 97

Johnson, Nunnally 13, 61

Johnson, Steve 33

Jolson, Al 97

Jonak, Julius 51

Jonathan (1970 film) PF

Joner, Johannes 30

Jones, Gordon 25

Jones, Grace 67

Jones, Indiana (character) 42

Jones, J. Stanley 35

Jones, John Paul 16

Jones, Ron 84

Jones, Spike 31

Jong, Ate de 33

Jordan, Bert 14

Jordan, Richard 7

Joseph, Allen 32

Josephine (empress of France) 82

Jost, Peter 49

Jovovich, Milla 8

Joyce, James 72

Judell, Ben 36

Jugend Unter Hitler: Blut und Ehre (1982 miniseries) 48

Juhnke, Harald 10, 75

Julia, Raul 63

Junge, Traudl (Hitler's secretary) 7, 12, 39, 51, 92

Jungermann, Alf 4

Jupé, Walter 17

Jürgens, Curt 4, 91

Jurgenson, Albert 1

Jurisa, Ivo 96

Jusic, Ibrica 96

Justin, John 53

Kahler, Wolf 6, 15, 63, 77, 92

Kahn, Ilene 20

Kahn, Madeline 5, 34

Kahn, Michael 42

Kahout, Jan 20

Kahr, Gustav von 37, 83

Kalinin, Mikhail 19

Kalipha, Stefan 42

Kalis, Jan 99

Kaltenbrunner, General Ernst 44, 76, 89

Kamekona, Danny 92

Kamen, Michael 77

Kaminsky, Stuart M. 90

Kane, John 27

Kane, Joseph 32

Kane, Richard 63

Kantor, MacKinely 20

Kantsel, Vladimir 21, 22

Kanturek, Otto 64

Kapural, Venco 96

Kapural, Vjenceslav 92

Karajan, Herbert von 77

Karewicz, Emil 28

Karl, Roger 3

Karl May (1974 film) 49, 69

Karlin, Fred 44

Karlin, John 96

Karloen, Paul 96

Karno, Fred 8

Karpova, Y. 68

Karras, Alex 5

Karron, Richard 34

Kasahara, Ryozo 50

Kasket, Harold 92

Kassar, Mario 8

Katch, Kurt 83

Katz, Sidney 73

Kaufman, George S. 81

Kaufmann, Walter 28

Kausch, Brigitte 52

Kauter, Helmut 49

Kaye, Danny* 65

Kayser, Henry 88

Keating, Patrick* A2

Kedrova, Lily 91

Keen, Pat 44

Keeter, Worth 67

Kehagias, Paul 63

Keitel, Harvey 54

Keitel, Field Marshal Wilhelm 7, 13, 19, 35, 39, 47, 51, 71, 80, 89, 92, 96

Keith, Ian 14

Kell, Michael 97

Kellaway, Cecil 81

Kelly, Gene 14, 25

Kelly, Moira 8

Kelly, Sam* 79

Kelly, W. Wallace 94

Kelman, Alfred R. 71

Kemp, Jeremy 92, 96

Kendall, Krista 16

Kenigson, Vladimir 19

Kennaway, James 4

Kennedy, John F. 20, 97

Kennedy, Joseph P. 20

Kennedy, Robert 20

Kennedy, Rose 20

Kennedy, Ted 20

Kennedy-Dohrn, Helga 51

Kenobi, Obi Wan (character) 39

Kent, Kenneth 64

Kent, Suzanne 34

Keown, Brendan 38

Kerkhoff, Eva Marie 75

Kern, Jerome 12

Kern, Peter 49, 69

Kernan, Siegfried 48

Kerry, Otto 51

Kerwin, Harry 23

Kesselring, Field Marshal Albert 4, 94

Kessler, Michael 75

Kessler, Zale 72, 88

Kestleman, Sara 53

Key to Rebecca (1985 film) 13

Keyloun, Mark 92

Keyser, David de 12

Khachaturian, Aram 76, 80

Khartoum (1966 film) 70

Khokhlov, A. 76

Khufu (pharaoh) 82

Kibbee, Milton 9, 95

"The Kidnappers" (TV episode) A2

Kier, Udo* 52

"Killers of Mussolini" (TV episode) 63

King, David 7

King, Freeman 90

King, John OV

King, Jonathan 31

King Kong Escapes (1967 film) 50

Kingsford, Walter 13, 37

Kippen, Manart 66

Kirby, Bill 89

Kircher, Helmet 4

Kirk, Captain James T. (character) 55

Kirk, Lisa 72

Kirsner, Jacques 70

Kirst, Alexander 96

Kissel, Helmut 48

Kissling, Markus 77

Kitchen, Michael 7, 20

Kiwe, Til 47

Klemperer, Werner 36, A2

Klenck, Margaret 55

Kleven. Max 32

Kleyne, Bradley 71

Kline, Kevin 8

Klink, Colonel Wilhelm (character) 36, A2
Kloster, Kristen 16
Kneece, Dan 67
Knight, Castleton 24
Knight, Natasha 44
Knight, Patricia 57
Knight, Ted 35
Knox, Alexander 89
Knox, Micky 96
Kobrinsky, Raul 16
Koch, Leni 37
Koch-Hodge, Wilhelm 17
Koenig, Charles 57
Kohler, Walter 35
Koizumi, Fukuzo 50
Kokoschka, Oskar 42
Kokshenov, Nikolai 68
Kolchak: The Night Stalker (TV series) 32
Kolldehoff, Rene 96
Kolonikov, N. 80
Komissarov, Kalyu 76
Komissarov, Nikolai 80
Königgrätzer March (Piefke) 42
Korda, Alexander 87
Korenova, Marina 60
Korman, Harvey 5, 34
Körner, Dietrich 28
Kortner, Fritz 37, 83
Korvin, Charles 43
Koshiji, Fubuki 50
Kosleck, Martin **35, 37,** 94
Koslo, Paul 55
Kosmatov, Leonid 19
Kostka, Petr 99
Kötteritzsch, Fred 17
Kovacs, Mijou 92
Kovalyova, M. 19
Kowatsch, Klaus 18
Kozlowski, Piotr 18
Kranstal, Erik 30
Kras, Inspector Erich (character) 45
Kraus, Fred 47
Krause, Karl-Wilhelm 69
Krause, Wily 47, **51**
Krauss, Werner 51
Kray, Debora Ann 16
Krayn, Stephen 67
Krebs, General Hans 12, 19, 39, 51, 92
Kreuger, Kurt 93
Kriemhild's Revenge (1924 film) 58
Kriendl, Werner 96
Krjutschkow, Nikolai 17
Kroeger, Berry 35
Krook, Margaretha 2
Krueger, Kurt 83
Kruger, Hardy 68, 92
Krumm, Paul Albert PF

Kruscher, Jack 90
Kryukov, Nikolai 21
Kuecher, Robert Watson See Watson, Bobby
Kuehn, Jurgen 97
Kufus, Thomas 60
Kugelmass, J. Alvin 89
Kuhibrodt, Dietrich 52
Kuhn, Bill 23
Kuhn, Debbie 23
Kühne, Erich 28
Kujai, Konrad 75
Kuklowsky, Val 56
Kunha, Richard 85
Kunkle, Holger 18
Kunstmann, Doris 39, 43
Kunze, Andreas 52
Kureji No Daiboken (1965 film) 50
Kurganov, Oskar 68
Kuroiwa, Yoshitami 50
Kurtzman, Robert 54
Kurzbauer, Inga 51
Kusche, Karen 28
Kuzmina, Yelena 76

Labonarska, Halina 18
Labry, Pierre 3
Labudda, Helga 28
Lacaze, José 3
Lacey, Ronald 42
Ladd, Alan 9, 81
"Ladies" (song) 88
The Lady Vanishes (1938 film) OV, 64
Ladyzhenskaya, E. 76, 80
Laemmle, Carl, Jr. OV
Lake, Veronica 23, 81
Lamarr, Hedy 82
Lambert, Anna Louise 63
Lambert, Paul 92
Lamont, Roger 45
Lamount, Duncan 4
Lamour, Dorothy 81
Lancelot, Jean-Marie 28
Lanchester, Elsa 19
Land of the Pharaohs (1955 film) 82
Landau, Martin* A2, 43
Landham, Sonny 15
Landi, Leonid 21
Landon, Alf 9
Landsberg Prison 35, 37
Lane, Charles 92, 96
Lane, Diane 8
Lane, Nathan 72
Lang, Charles B., Jr. 25
Lang, Dr. Eric (character) 92
Lang, Fritz 45, 58, 69, 74
Lang, Robert 74
Langan, Glen 83
Lange, Hellmut 69

Langhelle, Jorgen 30
Lanje, Rasmus 30
Lanning, William 56
LaPierre, Dominique 45
Larder, Geoffrey 34
Larmore, James 25
Larner, Stevan 96
L'As des As see *The Ace of Aces*
Laser, Dieter 10
Laskin, Boris 21
Lassick, Sidney 34
The Last Act see *The Last Ten Days*
The Last Days of Hitler (book) 39
The Last Days of Mussolini see *The Last Tyrant*
The Last Hour in the Führerbunker see *Der Letzte Stunde im Führerbunker*
The Last Metro (1980 film) 88
The Last Ten Days (1955 film) OV, 39, 47, 51
The Last Tyrant (1974 film) 63
The Last Voyage (1960 film) 50
Laszlo, Ernest 37
Lathrop, Philip 93
Latka, Geo 73
Laurel, Stan 8, 32, 87
Laurenson, James 11
Laurentiis, Dino de 68
Laurie, Piper 7
Lause, Herman 75
Laval, Pierre 70
Law, Phyllida 39
Law and Order (TV series) 38
Lawner, Mordecai 73
Lawrence, Robert 45
Lawrence, T. E. 74
Lawson, Charles 40
Lawson, Daphne 91
Lawson, Sarah 4
Lay, Patrick 11
Layker, Bob 94
Lea, Jennifer 32
Leachman, Chloris 34
Lear, Amanda 98
Leben, Albert 24
Lebor, Stanley 91
Lebrun, Anne-France 70
Leclerc, General Jacques Philippe 45
Lederer, Francis PF, OV, 29
Lee, Christopher 28
Leech, Richard 27
Leeds, Phil 34
Leer, Hunter von 34
Lees, Michael 12
"The Legend" (TV episode) OV, A2
Léger, Daniel 70
Leghov, Yuri 68

Lehar, Franz 69
Lehmann, Ted* 90
Leigh, Vivian 90
Lemken, Carlheinz 48
Lemmon, Jack 93
Lemon, Michael 92
Leng, Howard **96**
Lengyel, Melchoir 87, 88
Lennon, Jarrett 33
Lenska, Rula 91
Leonardo da Vinci 69, 82
Leonov, Leonid 21
Lestrade, Inspector George (character) 40
Letchinger, J. B. 78
Der Letzte Akt see *The Last Ten Days*
Der Letzte Stunde im Führerbunker (1989 film) 52
Levent, Alain 26
Leventon, Annabel 63
Levin, Ira 6
LeVine, Jack 27
Levine, Joseph E. 72
Levinson, Barry 34
Levitin, Yuri 68
Levitus, Christopher 16
Levy, Louis 24, 64
Lewis, Al 73
Lewis, Art 93
Lewis, Artie 94
Lewis, Bodo 94
Lewis, Fiona 53
Lewis, Ira* 55
Lewis, Jerry 30, **94**
Lewis, Richard 84
Lewis, Robert Michael 73
Lewis, Ron 94
Lewis, Sinclair A1
Liberation see *Osvobozhdeniye*
Licho, Adolf E. 87
Licht, Pamela 65
Licuda, Gabriella 91
Liebestod (aria) 77
Lierck, Werner 28
Ligneres, Laurence 70
Likhachyova, Tatyana 19
Lill, Dennis 27
Limmer, Ulrich 75
Lincoln, Abraham 82, 84
Lindberg, Sven 2
Lindbergh, Charles 97
Linder, Christof 1
Lindfors, Vivica 44
Lineback, Richard 92
Linge, Heinz 57
Linkers, Eduard 47
Linkman, Wolfgang 67
Linsted, Alec 40
Lipinski, Eugene 42
Lipman, Maureen 74
Lissek, Leon 44

Lister, Tom "Tiny" Jr, 54
Liszt, Franz 49, 53, 75
Lisztomania (1975 film) 53
Litt, Richard 97
Little, Cleavon 5
Little Nicky (2000 film) 54
Little Old Winemaker (character) 83
Little People of America 90
"A Little Piece of Poland, A Little Piece of France" (song) 88
"The Little Wooden Boy" (song) 72
Litvak, Anatole 29
Livanov, Boris 80
Livingston, Ed 32
Ljungberg, Olle 2
Lloyd, Bernard 40
Lloyd, Christopher 88
Lloyd George, David 27
Löb, Karl 100
Locke, Philip 39
Lockwood, Alexander 82
Lockwood, Margaret 64
Loeffler, Louis R. 61
Loft, Arthur 37
Logan, Michael 96
Lohengrin (opera) 25, 29, 39
Lohmann, Dietrich 49, 69. 92
Lohner, Helmuth 71
Loibl, Beate 75
Lom, Herbert 3
Lombard, Carole 87, 88, 97
Lomita, Sol 97
London Blitz 4, 96
Longdon, Terence 27
The Longest Day (1962 film) 4, 13
Lonsdale, Michael 7, 45
Loo, Richard 81. 94
Looking for Richard (1996 film) 55
Loomis, Willy (character) 96
Loose, William 56
Loose Cannons (1989 film) 55
Lopez, Sylvia 54
Lord of the Swastika (parody novel) A3
Lorente, Isabelle 18
Lorre, Peter 69, 82, 90, 92
Lothario (character) 25, 94
Loud, Sherman 97
Loughlin, Terry 67
Loughran, Jonathan 54
Louis XVI (king of France) 34
Louis, Joe 73
Loukes, Nicolas 91
Lounder, Frank 64
Love, Emily 16
Love, Mary 72
The Love Boat (TV series) 54

Love's Labors Lost (play) 71
Lovitz, John 54
Lovsky, Celia 35
Lowe, Chad 33
Lowens, Curt 88
Lowitz, Siegfried 47
Lubbe, Marius van der 3
Lubitsch, Ernst 10, 87, 88
Lucas, George 42
The Lucifer Complex (1975/78 film) 56
Lucke, Hans 28
Lüddecke, Werner Jörg 100
Ludendorff, General Erich 37, 78
Ludwig (1972 film) 69
Ludwig II (king of Bavaria) 1, 69
Lugosi, Bela 90
Lühr, Peter 69
Lukschy, Wolfgang 43
Lumdon, Cameron 84
Lund, Art 96
Lund, John 25
Luther, Martin 20
Lyndhurst, Nicholas 79
Lynn, Ann 39
Lynn, Dani 85
Lynn, Diana 59
Lynn, George 87
Lytess, Natasha 66
Lyubimov, Viktor 19
Lyueznov, Ivan 22

M (1931 film) 69
MacArthur, General Douglas 84, 92
Macbeth (play) 84
MacBug (parody film) 84
Macchi, Egissto 62
MacDonald, Kenneth 94
MacFadden, Angus* 78
MacGowan, Kenneth 58
MacGraw, Ali 92, 96
Macharty, Gustav 47
Machowski, Ignacy 68
Macht, Stephen 73
Mack, Patrick 84
MacKenzie, Michael 63
MacKey, Paul 33
Macksey, Kenneth 20
MacLeod, Roland 40
Macourek, Milos 46. 99
Macready, George 13
Macy, Bill 72
Mader, Juhus 28
Madmen of Mandoras see *They Saved Hitler's Brain*
Madoc, Philip 91
Madsen, Michael 92
Madsen, Virginia 63
Maetzig, Kurt 17

The Magic Face (1951 film) PF. OV, 13, 57
Magic Fire Music (orchestral piece) 16
Maher, Joseph 90
Mahler, Gustav 49, 53, 69
Maitland, Marne 62
Makarov, Vailly 76
Makehsam, Eliot 64
Maklyarskii, M. 76
Mako 90
Malcolm, Christopher 92
Malcolm, John 15, 92
Malcolm, Robert 25
Malikyan, Kevork 42
Malleson, Miles 24
Mallison, Mathew 67
Malone, Dorothy 50
Malpas, George 42
Malton, Leslie 48
Malyon, Eily 58
Malzacher, Gunther 48
The Man from the Diner's Club (1963 film) 65
The Man from U.N.C.L.E. (TV series) A2
The Man He Found see *The Whip Hand*
Man Hunt (1941 film) 58, 74, 93
The Man I Married (1940 film) PF
"Man in the Bottle" (TV episode) 13, A2
The Man in the High Castle (novel) 20
The Man Who Never Was (1956 film) 89
Mancini, Henry 93
Mander, Miles 87
Manevich, Iosif 22
Mangs, Sune 2
Mankiewicz, Hermann J. 9
Mann, Hank 29
Mann, Sam 31
Mann, Thomas 42
Mann, Yanka 23
Manners, Mickey 94
Manning, Hugh 74
Manschka, Georg 75
Manstein, Field Marshal Erich von 92
The Manster (1958 film) 89
Manuel, Denis 70
Manz, Joe 9
Manz, Mick 31
Manza, Ralph* 5, 93
Manzel, Dagmar 75
Manzialy, Constanza 7, 12, 39
Mao Tse-tung 69
Marat, Jean-Paul 70
Marboeuf, Jean 70

Marboeuf, Julie 70
March to the Führer (1940 film) OV
Marchand, Jean-Pierre 70
Marco Polo (1982 miniseries) 96
Marcuse, Theodore 35
Margin for Error (1943 film) 83
Marian, Ferdinand 69
Marie Antoinette (queen of France) 82
Marie Antoinette (1955 film) 70
Marino, Dan 54
Mariotti, Guido 62
Marischka, Georg 6
Marks, Alan 85
Marks, Callie 16
Marks, Chip 16
Marks, Leo 91
Marmelstein, Linda 48
Marner, Richard 6
Marquis, Peter 40
Marriage of Hitler 7, 10, 12, 19, 35, 39, 44, 51, 92
Marrian, Stephanie 34
Mars, Kenneth 72
"La Marseillaise" (French anthem) 70
Marsh, Jean 20
Marsh, Myra 36
Marshall, E. G. 45, 92
Marshall, Frank 42
Marshall, General George C. 92
Marshall, George 81
Marshall, Sarah 7
Marshall, Stephen 63
Martell, Chris 23
Marth, Frank 92
Martin, Al 14
Martin, Barney 72
Martin, Bill 66
Martin, Charles 41
Martin, Gregory Mars 33
Martin, Jack 66
Martin, Janis 77
Martin, Lewis 95
Martin, Mary 81
Martino, Luciano 98
Martinsen, Sergei* 22
Martov, Iosif 22
Marvin, Lee 15
Marx, Chico 72, 82, 84
Marx, Groucho 72, 82, 84
Marx, Harpo 72, 82, 84
Marx, Karl 42
Marx, Melinda 82
Mase, Marino 62
M*A*S*H* (TV series) 88, 93
The Masked Marvel (1941 serial) 14
Mason, Bob 20
Mason, Jackie 34

Mason, James 6, 13, 43
Mastalerz, Andrzej 18
"Master Plan of Fu Manchu" (TV episode) A2
Masterpiece Theater (TV series) A2
Mastrantonio, Mary Elizabeth 63
Match (magazine) 45
Maté, Rudolph 87
Matheson, Richard 55
Matheson, Richard Christian 55
Mathie, Marion 12
Mati Hari 91
Matisse, Henri 42
Matsumoto, Somesho 50
Mattson, Bart 82
Maugham, Somerset 96
Maxwell, Paul 42
May, Bob* A2
May, Joe 83
May, Karl 49
Mayo, Virginia 82
Mazurki, Mike 94
Mazursky, Paul 34
Mazzieri, Franco 62
McAllister, David 20
McCann, Chuck 84
McCarey, Leo 66
McCarthy, Charlie 69
McCarthy, Joseph OV
McCarthy, Lin 92, 96
McCary, Rod 92
McConnell, Craig 23
McConnell, Judith 41
McCormick, Maureen 84
McCormick, Pat 34, 90
McCoy, Dr. Leonard (character) 55
McDermott, Brian 78
McDermott, Hugh 24
McDowall, Roddy 58
McDowall, Virginia 58
McEnery, John 71
McFadden, Tom 96
McGraw, Charles 61
McGuire, Jason (character) 92
McGuire, Michael 92, 96
McHale's Navy (TV series) 93
McKay, Craig 77
McKay, Michael Reid 33
McKean, Michael 54
McKellan, Ian* 11
McKenna, Virginia 27
McKeon, Doug 16
McLaglen, Andrew V. 15
McManus, Mark 74
McMullan, Tim 79
McNally, Ray 12
McNeil, Allen 58
McQueen, Steve 79

McShane, Ian 4, 92
Meaden, Dan 12
Meara, Anne 6, 33, 84
Medved, Harry 85
Medved, Michael 85
Meehan, Thomas 88
Meeting of Minds (TV series) 16
Meeting with Maxim see *Fighting Film Album # 1*
Megowan, Don 82
Meier, Annie 57
Mein Kampf (book) 3, 16, 35, 37, 64, 84
Mein Kampf–My Crimes see *Après Mein Kampf Mes Crimes*
Meisel, Kurt 47
Meisner, Gunter* 1, 6, 43, 48, **96**, A2
Meissel, Petr 20
Mejovesk, Damir 96
Melesh, Alex 66
Mellinger, Michael 11, 02
Melvin, Murray 53
Memel (Lithuania) annexation 11
Menaul, Christopher 20
Mendelssohn, Felix 19, 53
Mengele, Dr. Josef 6
Menjou, Adolphe 97
Mensik, Vladimir 99
Menzies, William Cameron 95
Merchant of Venice (play) 69, 87
Meredith, Charles 25
Meredith, Jo Anne 41
Meredith, Lee 72
Merkerson, S. Epatha 55
Merkuryev, Vasili 80
Meroni, Franco 62
Merriweather, Lee A2
Messemer, Hannes 45
Messiah (oratorio) 16
Messner, Frank 51
Metrano, Art 34
Metropolitan Museum of Art 42
Meyer, Edwin Justus 87, 88
Meyer, Hans 44
Meyer, Louis B. A1
Meyer, Russ 45
Meyjes, Mary 42
Meyn, Robert 47
Mezzogiorno, Vittorio 62
Michelangelo 69
Middleton, Guy 24
Middleton, Robert 94
A Midsummer Night's Dream (ballet) 19
A Midsummer Night's Dream (play) 97
Midway (1976 film) 4
Mignot, Jacques 70

Mihalesco, Alexandre 3
Mikhajlov, K. 80
Milch, Field Marshal Erhard 4, 44, 84
Miles, Mark 42
Miles, Richard 85
Military Polonaise (piano piece) 87
Milland, Ray 81
Miller, Arthur C. 58, 61
Miller, Ira 34
Miller, Marvin 41, 82
Miller, Michael 34
Miller, Nancy 82
Miller, Penelope Ann 8
Miller, Richard 94
Miller, Sidney* 30, **94**
Milligan, Spike 34
Mills, Royce 34
Milo, Jean-Roger 1
Milovanoff, Sandra 3
Miniseries 44, 48, 62, 63, 69, 92, 96
Minster, Hilary 11
Mints, Klimenti 22
Minuit, Peter 82
The Miracle of Morgan's Creek (1944 film) 37, 59
Miranda, Carmen 85
Missiles from Hell (1958 film) 28
Mission: Impossible (TV series) OV, 32, 43, 83 A2
Mitchell, Chuck 96
Mitchell, Irving 9
Mitchell, Milliard 25
Mitchell, Thomas A1
Mitchum, John 35
Mitchum, Robert 92, 96
Mitterwurzer, Toni 57
Mlada (opera) 94
Moccia, Giuseppe "Pipolo" 98
Modo, Michel 70
Mohnke, General Wilhelm 7
Moland, Peter 49
Moll, Richard 78
Möller, Gunnar* 63
Molokh (1999 film) 60
Molotov, Vyacheslav 11
Monroe, Marilyn 55
Monsieur Verdoux (1947 film) 8
Monsoon, Gorilla 67
Montague, Lee 11
Montand, Yves 45
Montant, Georges 70
Montes, Lola 53
Montgomery, Robert 9
Monty Python (comedy team) 79
Monys, Albert 3
Moog, Heinz 57

The Moon Is Down (1943 film) 61, 83
Moore, Deborah Maria 8
Moore, Mary Tyler 35
Moore, Roger 67
Moore, Stephen 11
Moore, Victor 81
Moore, Wanda 12
Mora, Phillipe 78
Moran, Donald 31
More, Kenneth 4
Morehead, Agnes 9, 82
Moreheim, Lou 73
Morel, Max 70
Morell, Dr. Theodor 7, 12, 35, 51, 92
Morgan, Andrew 27
Morgan, Harry 93
Morgan, Heather Leigh 16
Morgenstern, Janusz 18
Morhart, Hans von 83
Moriarty, Michael* **38**
Morin, Alberto 96
Morishige, Hisaya 50
Morley, Robert 92
Morris, Aubrey 92
Morris, Colin 27
Morris, Howard 25
Morris, John 5, 72, 88
Morris, Reginald H. 55
Morris, Wolfe 77
Morrow, Byron 92, 96
Morse, Barry 93, 96
Morse, John 34
Morse, Susan E. 97
Mort, Ray 74
Mortera, Manuela 62
Mortimer, Caroline **12**
Moses 34, 82
Moses, William R. 92
"Moses Supposes" (song) 14, 25
Moskovich, Maurice 29
Moss, Frank L. 95
Moss, Lisa 12
The Most Dangerous Game (1932 film) 32
The Most Valiant see *Fighting Film Album # 7*
Mostel, Zero 72
Mowbray, Alan 14
Moya, Antoinette 70
Mozart, Wolfgang Amadeus 15, 69
Mozgovoy, Leonid* 60
Mudie, Leonard 82
Mueller-Stahl, Armin* 10
Mues, Joachim Dietmar 10
Mühe, Ulrich 75
Mulholland, Declan 74
Mullally, Frederic A3
Müller, Alfred 28, 40

Muller, Frederick 20
Müller, General Heinrich 40, 89
Muller, Robert 48
Muller, Wolfgang 77
Munich Conference 11, 27, 63, 64, A3
Munster, Hubert 1
Murakmi, Fuyuki 50
Murcell, George 44
Murder on the Yellow Brick Road (novel) 90
Murdoch, George 92, 96
Murphy, Ben 96
Murphy, Bill 25
Murray, Jan 34, 94
Murray, Leland 84
Murrow (1986 film) 84
Musammano, Michael A. 51
Musical films 53, 72, 81
Musser, Wolf 88
Mussolini (1993 film) 63
Mussolini, Benito 11, 14, 16, 27, 29, 36, 43, 47, 57, 59, 62, 63, 67, 71, 81, 92, 96, A1
Mussolini, Bruno 62, 63
Mussolini, Rachele 62, 63
Mussolini, Romano 62, 63
Mussolini, Vittorio 62, 63
Mussolini and I (1985 film), 62, 63
Mussolini: The Decline and Fall of Il Duce (1985 miniseries) 62
Mussolini: The Untold Story (1985 miniseries) 63
Mussorgsky, Modeste 2
Musuraca, Nicholas 82, 95
Mutinov, I. 21
Mutton, Virginia 16
My Autobiography (Chaplin) 8
"My Country 'Tis of Thee" (song) 36
"My Old Kentucky Home" (song) 84
Myers, Stanley 79
Mylong, John 37, 61, **83**

Nadia 31
Nagumo, Vice Admiral Chuichu 92
Naismith, Lawrence 89
Nakamura, Tetsu 50
Nannuzzi, Alberto 62
Nannuzzi, Daniele 62
Napier, Charles 92
Napoleon (emperor of France) 3, 7, 36, 70, 82, 87, 88, 92, 95
Napoleon and the Conquest of the World (novel) 20

Napoloni, Benzino (parody of Mussolini) 29
Napravleniye Glavnogo Udana see *Osvobozhdeniye*
Narenta, Jindrich 28, 46
Narker, Lindsay 12
Nasty Nazis (theater skit) 88
Nato, Dominique 1
Naughton, James 7
Naumov-Straza, Naum 21
Nealon, Kevin 54
Neef, Wilhelm 17
Neeson, Liam 77
Neff, William 25
Negrin, Alberto 62
Nejedla, Eliska 46
Nekrasov, Y. 21
Nelson, Bill 95
Nelson, Burt 82
Nelson, Felix 96
Nelson, Mervyn 6
Nero (emperor of Rome) 34, 82
Nesvadba, Josef 99
Neuber, Rolf* 47
Neuhaus, Paul 4
Neuman, E. Jack 44
Neuman, Sam 35, 36
Neumann, Lena 17
Neuschwanstein castle 1
Nevens, Paul 97
Never Trust a Vampire (novel) 90
New York Daily Mirror (newspaper) 97
New York Times (newspaper) 72
Newark, Derek 40, 44, 92
Newman, Alfred 58, 61
Newman, Paul 83
Newsweek (magazine) 7, 45
Newton, Isaac 82
Die Nibelungen (1924 film) 58
Niblo, Fred 66
Nicholas, Paul 53
Nicholas and Alexandra (1970 film) 92
Nichols, Anthony 4
Nichols, Denise 73
Nichols, Dudley 58
Nico, Willard 29
Niemczck, Leon 28
Niemöller, Martin 37
Night of the Fox (1990 film) 13
The Night of the Generals (1965 film) PF, 13
"Night of the Long Knives" (SA purge) 35, 37, 40
The Night Train to Munich (1940 film) OV, 24, 64
The Nightmare Years (1989 miniseries) 44

Nighy, Bill 40
Nihei, Masanari 50
Nikulin, Lev 22
Nimitz, Admiral Chester 92
Ninetti, Hans-Peter 17
Ninotchka (1939 film) 25
Nitschke, Ronald 77
Nixon, Richard M. 97
No Dough, Boys (1944 short subject) OV
"No Time Like the Past" (TV episode) A2
Nobbs, David 79
Nobel Prize 30, 38
Noble, Thom 43
Noëlle, Jacqueline 1, 3
Noir: Now and Then (book) 9
Norby, Ghita 30
Normand, Mabel 8
Normington, John 40
Noro, Lino 3
Norris, Chuck 67
Norton, Alex 11
Nosik, Vladimir 68
Notter, Fred 47
Novakova, M. 19
Novello, Jay 93
Nowell, Wedgwood 14
Nozhkin, Mikhail 68
Nuremberg Trials 44, 51
Nurney, Fred 37
Nykvist, Sven 8
Nyman, Lena 2
Nyman, Lennart 2

Oakie, Jack 29
O'Brien, Edmond 50
Oceans Eleven (1960 film) 43
Ochsenknech, Uwe 75
O'Connell, Arthur 9
O'Connor, Carroll 93
O'Connor, Donald 14, 25
Octopussy (1983 film) 92
O'Donnell, Cathy 82
O'Donnell, James 7, 89
Oedipus Complex 35
Oertzen, Jasper von 47, 57
Ofenboch, Elizabeth 92
O'Flynn, Damion 25
Ogilvy, Ian 27
The Ogre (1996 film) PF
O'Haco, Jeff 42
O'Hara, David 31
O'Herlihy, Dan 13, 15, 97
Oka, Yutaka 50
Okhlopkev, Mikolai 22
Olbricht, General, Friedrich 47, 71, 100
Olemnitz, Reinhard 96
Olenin, Alexei 21, 22
Olin, Lena 2
Olivier, Laurence 4, **6**, 43

Olsen, Ole 54
Olyalin, Nikolai 68
Olympia (1936 film) OV, 1
Omae, Wataru 50
Omens, Woody 34
On the Double (1961 film) OV,
   65
On Untrodden Paths (book) 30
Once Upon a Honeymoon (1942
   film) 66
Ondra, Anny 73
Ondrouchova, Zuzana 99
"One Hand, One Heart" (song)
   31
O'Neill, Dick 55
O'Neill, Eugene 97
Onyx, Narda 35
Opaterry, Patrick 20
Operation: Walküre (TV series)
   47
O'Quinn, Terry 67
Order of the Black Eagle (1986
   film) 67
Orefice, Paola 98
Organ, Jim 32
Orlandini, Luca 62
Osbourne, Ozzy 54
Oscarson, Per 2
Ostrand, Tracey 54
Osvobozhdeniye (1967-71 film
   cycle) 68
Othello (1965 film) 12
Otomo, Sin 50
O'Toole, Peter 74
O'Toole, Stanley 6
Our Foundling Fathers (parody
   film) 84
Our Hitler (1978 miniseries)
   OV, 69
Oury, Gérard 1
Ousdal, Sverre Anker 30
Overgard, William A3
Owens, Jesse 1
Ozanne, Christine 12
Ozerov, Igor 68
Ozerov, Yuri 68
Ozzle, Admiral (character) 15,
   42

Pabst, G. W. 39, 47, 51, 100
Pace, Enzo 16
Pacino, Al 55
Packham, Robert 79
Padeniye Berlina see *The Fall of
   Berlin*
Page, Mary Anne 33
Page, Wyatt **38**
Pagne, Florent 1
Palermini, Pietro 62
Paley, Peter 42
Paliotti, Michael John 15
Palmer, Gene 82

Palmer, Geoffrey 79
Palmer, Harry (character) A3
Palmer, Lilli 6
Palmer, Maria 33
Panama, Norman 81
Pandora's Box (1929 film) 51
Pangborn, Franklin 82
Pankin, Stuart 84
Papen, Franz von 17, 37
Papineau, Bernard 28
Paris Brûle-t-il? see *Is Paris
   Burning?*
Parla, Paul 85
Parnell, Emory 14, 59
Parry, Ken 53
Parsifal (opera) 42, 69
Parsons, Dete 23
Parsons, Milton 37
Parsons, Nancy 55
Part, Arno 30
Pascal, Francoise 91
Patch, David 72
Patrick, Dennis 92
Patrick, Nigel 4
Patterson, Lee 32, 92
Patton (1970 film) 13
Patton, General George S. 45,
   63, 92
Paul, John 7
Paulus, General Friedrich von
   80, 92
Pavlenko, Pyotr 19
Pearl Harbor (2001 film) 4
Pearl Harbor attack 77, 84, 96
Pearson, Taylor 16
Peck, Brutus 72
Peck, Gregory **6**
Peet, John 28
Peets, Rainer 43
Pegge, Edmund 96
Pelevin, A. 76
Penhert, Rainer 92, 96
Pennell, Nicholas 4
Penry-Jones, Rupert 20
Penvern, André 70
Pera, Lisa 32
Percy, Norma 11
Perel, Solomon 18
Perelshtejn, Rafail 22
Pericles, Prince of Tyre (play) 71
Perkins, Anthony 45
Perkins, Christopher 31
Perkovsky, M. 76
Perpignani, Robert 62
Perrier, Jean-François 70
Perrier, Jean-Louis 70
Perry, Morris 7
Perry Mason (TV series) 32
Perryment, Mandy 12
Persoff, Nehemiah 63
Persson, Jan 2
Perzyk, Adam 28

Pescud, Richard 39
Petacci, Claretta 62, 63
Pétain (1992 film) 70
Pétain, Marshal Philippe 70, 91
Peter Pan (1953 film) 32
Peterka, Frantisek 99
Peters, Josef see Perel,
   Solomon
Peters, Kau 41
Peters, Scott 85
Peters, Toby (character) 90
Peters, Werner 17
Petersen, Marlis 43
Peterson, Mattias 62
Petillo, Maria 8
Petropaviovskaya, Natalya 21
Petrov, Andre 68
Petrov, Vladimir 80
Petrunkin, M. 19
Petrycki, Jacek 18
Petzel, Malte 4
Petzold, Holger 92
Peyer, Karel 46
Phantom of the opera (charac-
   ter) 3
The Philadelphia Experiment II
   (1993 film) 99
Philbin, Phil 23
Philbin, Regis 54
Phillips, John 27
Phillips, Stu 41
Phoenix, River 42
Piava, Nestor 85
Piazza, Ben 96
Picasso, Pablo 2, 42, 78
Picavet, Jean-Louis 7
Piccoli, Michel 17
Pichel, Irving 61
Pickens, Slim 5
Pickford, Mary 8
Pictures at an Exhibition (suite)
   2
Pidgeon, Walter 58
Piefke, Gottfried 42
Pierce, Richard 23
Pierson, Kelly 3
Piett, Admiral (character) 63,
   71
Pignot, Yves 1
Pinter, Harold 74
Pirandello, Luigi 16
Pisier, Marie-France 1
The Pit and the Pendulum (1961
   film) 96
Pitra, Hans 28
Pittack, Robert 14
Pius XI (pope) 97
Pivar, Ben 83
Plan Nine from Outer Space
   (1956/59 film) 65
Plankers, Claus 77
Playhouse 90 (TV series) 63

Pleasence, Angela 39
Pleasence, Donald 39, 89
Plintzner, Karl 17
Plot to Kill Hitler (1990 film) OV, 47, 71, 100
Plotnikov, Nikolai 19
Plotting Hitler's Death (book) 47
Plummer, Christopher 4, 13
Plytas, Steve 27
Pohl, Oswald 97
Pokrovsky, Vladimir 19
Polak, Jinrich 99
Polish films 18, 68
"La Poloma" (song) 75
Polonius (character) 87, 88
Polsterer, Ludwig 51
Pomeshchikov, Yevgeni 22
Pontius Pilate 73
Poole, Roy 96
Pooley, Kirstie 92, 96
Pope, Alexander 37
Porcasi, Paul 81
Portage to San Cristobal of A.H. (novel) A3
Porter, Eric 39
Porter, Jean 14
Post, William, Jr. 61
Pot, Pol PF, 69
Potel, Victor 59
Potter, Harry (character) 82
Potter, Colonel Sherman (character) 93
Poulan, David 63
Poulton, Raymond 89
Powell, Addison 92
Powell, Dick 44, 81
Poyarkov, Anatoly 19
Prack, Rudolf 49
Prager, Stanley 25
Praid, Mark 12
Prat, Eric 70
Preisner, Zbigniew 18
Preiss, Wolfgang 6, 13, 92, 96, 100
Preminger, Otto 83
Preses, Peter 57
Presley, Elvis 55
Press, Wlodzimierz 18
Pressman, Lawrence 96
Preston, Robert 81
Prete, Giancarlo 92
Prevatte, Susan 31
Price, Vincent 82
Prince, Diana (character) A2
Prince, William 92
Prisoners of Love (parody show) 72
Prival, Lucien 58
The Private Life of Adolf Hitler see *Hitler*

"Private Schulz" (TV drama) A2
Processen mod Hamsun (book) 30
Procession of the Nobles (orchestral piece 94
Prockl, Ernst 51
The Producers (Broadway musical) OV, 1, 72
The Producers (1968 film) OV, 72
Propaganda films 17, 19, 76, 80
Prosky, Robert 55
Protasov, Klyon 68
Pryor, Richard 5
Psycho (1959 film) 51
Das Psycho Rangers (motorcycle club) 33
Puccetti, Roland A3
Puccini, Giacomo 2
Puck (character) 97
Pullman, Jack A2
Purdom, Edmund 96
The Pursuit of the Graf Spee (1956 film) 24
Purviance, Edna 8
Putnam, David 53
Puzio, Dorota 92

Q (1982 film) 38
Quaddafy, Muammmar 67
Quaid, Randy 44
Quasimodo (character) 19
Queen Mary (ocean liner) 90
Quilligan, Veronica 53
Quirnheim, Colonel Albert Mertz von 47, 71
Quisling, Vidkun 30, 66

Raab, Kurt* 62
Rachmil, Lewis J 95
Rader, Jack 92
Radford, Basil 64
Radner, Gilda 5
Rae, Dan 74
Raeder, Admiral Erich 96
Raffetto, Michael 25
Ragheb, Osman 92, 96
Rahl, Mady 49
Raid on Rommel (1971 film) 13
Raifer, Henryk 96
Raine, Jack 24
Rains, Claude 9
Raleigh, Sir Walter 82
Ralli, Giovanna 93
Rambo, Dack 94
Ramsay, Todd 33
Ramsey, Logan 96
Ramson, Glenn 56
Randall, Tony 40, 84
Rapagna, Anna 67
Raphael, Frederic 74

Rash, Steve 90
Rashomon (1950 film) 9
Rasmussen, Niels 86
Rastenburg assassination plot 13, 35, 40, 47, 57, 68, 71, 79, 83, 89, 92, 94, 100, A2, A3
Ratcliff, Paul 88
Rattenhuber, Brigadeführer, Hans 7, 57, 92
Rau, Alexander 22
Raubal, Angela (Hitler's half-sister(1, 35, 37
Raubal, Geli (Hitler's niece) 16, 35, 37, 78
Rauch, Siegfried 96
Rautenberg, Kai 10
Ravensbrück (concentration camp) 23
Ravn, Jens 86
Ray, Aldo 43, 56, 93
Ray, Andrew 7
Ray, James 96
Read, Barbara OV
A Real Patriot see *Fighting Film Album # 7*
The Red and the Black (novel) 4
The Red Menace (1949 film) 95
Reddemann, Manfred 4
Redgrave, Michael 4
Reed, Anthony 11
Reed, Carol 64
Reed, Marshall 85
Rees, Angharad 27
Regas, Pedro 85
Regelsberger, Walter 51
Reicher, Frank 37, 87
Reichmann, Wolfgang 92
Reichow, Otto 35
Reichstag fire 3, 17, 35, 37, 58
Reid, Craig 48
Reid, Elliott 95
Reihl, August 47
Reilly, Andrew 53
Reindeer Games (2000 film) 43
Reiner, Carl 89
Reiner, Estelle 88
Reinhardt, Wolfgang 39
Reiss, Hein 4
Reitner, Mimi (Hitler's girl-friend) 35
Reitsch, Hanna 12, 39
Remarque, Erich Maria OV, 42, 51
Remonatti, Remo 92
Renin, V. 19
Rennie, Michael 13, 28
Renzetti, Joe 90
Repnin, Pyotr* 21
Request Concert see *Wunschkonzert*
The Return of Mr. H see *They Saved Hitler's Brain*

The Return of the Magnificent Seven (1966 film) 15
Retzer, Raoul 51
Reynaud, Paul 70, 96
Reynolds, David 79
Reynolds, William 13
Das Rheingold (opera) 51
Rhoden, Neil 91
Rhys, Paul 8
Rhys-Davies, John 42, 92
Ribbentrop, Joachim von 11, 12, 27, 62, 63, 83, 92, 96
Rich, Claude 45
Richard III (1995 film) 11
Richard III (king of England) 11, 55
Richards, Alan 16
Richards, Beah 73
Richards, Martin 6
Richardson, Ian 71
Richardson, Joely 77
Richardson, Miranda 20
Richardson, Ralph 4
Richmond, Fiona 34
Richmond, Michael 12
Richmond, Tom 31
Ridgely, Robert 5
Ridges, Stanley 87
Riefenstahl, Leni OV, 1, 19, 25, 69
Riegert, Peter 84
Riegler, Otto 47
Rienzi (opera) 69
Rifkin, Ron 96
Riggio, Jerry 85
Rigo, Luis 26
Riley, Jack 34, 88
Rimmer, Jean 74
Rimsky-Korsakov, Nikolai 94
Rinaldi, Francesca 62
Der Ring des Nibelungen (opera cycle) 69
Ring of Passion (1978 film) 73
Ringham, John 12
Rintelen, Ernest von 1
Riou, Alain 70
Ripley's Believe It or Not (TV series) 77
Ripperger, Rolf 28
Rippy, Leon 55
Risch, Maurice 26
The Rise and Fall of the Third Reich (book) 16, 20, 44
The Rise and Fall of the Third Reich (1961 film) 35
Ritschel, Jack 8
Rivas, Carlos 85
Rivers, St. John (character) 27
Roach, Hal 14
Roach, M. Jay 16
Roach, Pat 42
The Road Back (1937 film) OV

The Robe (1953 film) 17
Roberts, Ivor 40, 74
Roberts, Stephen 73
Robespierre, Maximilien 35
Robinson, Bill "Bojangles" 84
Robinson, Edward G. 36
Robinson, Jay 17
Rodann, Ziva 82
Roden, K. 19
Rodin, Merrill 83
Rodionov, Anatoli 60
Rodriguez, Percy 73
Rodway, Norman* **16,** 27
Roeves, Maurise 44
Rogers, Bill 23
Rogers, Charles 14
Rogers, Charles R. OV
Rogers, Ginger 66
Rogers, Heather 16
Rogers, Mitzi 12
Roggisch, Peter 75
Rogue Male (1976 film) 74
Rogue Male (novel) 58, 74
The Rogues (TV series) 43
Rohde, Armin 75
Röhm, Ernst PF, 3, 35, 37, 40, 67
Rohmer, Sax A2
Rohrbach, Gunter 75
Roisman, Harper 84
Roland, Gyl 92
Romance films 66, 77
Romand, Beatrice 91
Romeo and Juliet (tone poem) 94
Romero, Cesar 82
Romero, George 31
Romm, Mikhail 76
Rommel, Field Marshal Erwin 13, 35, 57, 71, 79, 92, 98
Roosevelt, Eleanor 92, 96
Roosevelt, Franklin D. 7, 9, 19, 20, 29, 73, 80, 97, 84, 92, 93, 96
Roosevelt, Theodore 9
Roots (1977 miniseries) 96
Rose, Clifford 12, 92
Rose, Geoffrey 92
Rose, Jack 65
Roseanna McCoy (1949 film) 35
Rosenbaum, Ron PF, 72
Rosenberg, Alfred 37
Rosenberg, Brandon 54
Rosenberg, Larry 88
Rosenbloom, Ralph 72
Rosenman, Howard 77
Rosenthal, Laurence 63, 71
Ross, Arthur 81
Ross, Duncan 96
Ross, Dylan 84
Ross, Hector 12
Ross, Joe E. 41

Ross, Merrie Lynn 56
Ross, Ricco 15
Rosseland, Hakon 30
Rossetti, Dante Gabriel 53
Rossini, Gioacchino 53
Rossitto, Angelo 82
Rossman, Erma 84
Rosulkova, Marie 99
Roth, Gene 83
Rothchild, Elizabeth 97
Rothman, John 97
Rousseau, Carolle 91
Rousseau, Henri 2
Rowland, Henry 61
Royal Shakespeare Company 16
Royce, Lionel 37
Rozhikov, Nikolai 22
Ruben, Stanley 95
Rubin, Arthur 72
Rubinstein, John 6
Rubling, Stephen 48
Ruby, Harry 82
Rudnick, Franz 48
Rueprecht, Albert 92, 96
Rufanova, Elena 60
Ruman, Sig 37, 87
Rundstedt, Field Marshal Gerd von 13, 19, 92
Runkehl, Karla 17
Runyan, Damon 73
Ruscio, Al 92
Rush, Deborah 97
Ruskin, Shimen 72
Rusoff, Carolyn 96
Rusoff, Ted 62
Russell, Bill* OV, 24, 64
Russell, Clive 20
Russell, Ken 53
Russian films 19, 21, 22, 60, 68, 76, 80
Russian front 18, 19, 40, 68, 80, 91, 92, 96, 100
Russian Rhapsody (1944 cartoon) PF
Rustichelli, Carlo 98
Ruth, Babe 97
Rutherford, Margaret 65
Rutland, John 27
Rutter, Barrie 11
Ryal, David 20
Ryan, Fran 41
Ryan, Richard 83
Ryder, Alexandre 3
Ryen, Richard 37
Rywin, Lew 18

Sabre (dog) 12
Sabu, Paul 31
Sachs, Andrew 34, 39
Sahl, Mort 44
Saidy, Fred 81

St. Clement, Pamela 7
St. George, Clement 73
Saint-Saëns, Camille 27
Sakai, Set 92
Sakenka, Ota 99
Saki, Eileen 34
Sakurai, Senri 50
Salammbô (opera) 9
Saldanha, Raul Faustino 6
Salter, Hans J. 35, 83
Saltzman, Harry 4
Samuel Hitler (novel) A3
Sand, George 53
Sandeford, John 92
Sander, Otto 10
Sanders, George 50, 58
Sanders, Larry 42
Sanders, Sally 12
Sandler, Adam 2. 54
Sandler, Jana 54
Sandrowiicz, Marta 18
The Sands of Iwo Jima (1949 film) 4
Sanford, Erskine 9
Sanucci, Anthony 85
Saprich, Alice 26
Sarandon, Susan 62, 63
Sargent, William 35
Sarne, Michael 92
Satie, Erik 2
Sauerwein, Ann Maria 47
Savalas, Telly 15, 43
Savelyev, V.* 19, 76, 80
Savident, John 39
Sawai, Keiko 50
Sawtell, Paul 82, 83, 95
Sawyer, William 41
Saxon, Rolf 15
Sayan, François 70
Sayle, Alexei 42
Sazonev, Aleksei 22
Scaife, Ted 89
Scala, Gia 89
Scala, Julio 92
Scales, Prunella 6
Schaeffer, George 7
Schäffer, Hans 17
Schaffner, Franklin J. 6
Schaidler, Karl 47
Schallert, William 82, 92
Schary, Dory A1
Schelcher, Raimund 17
Schell, Immy 92
Schell, Maria 44
Schell, Maximilian 100
Schellow, Erich 100
Scherer, Gene 67
Schickele, Peter 86
Schidor, Dieter 62
Schiel, Hannes 51
Schiller, Lawrence 71
Schiller, Norbert 35

Schilling, Gus 9
Schleicher, Kurt von 3
Schlesinger, Hunter 92
Schlesinger, Otto* 23
Schlesinger, Peter 43
Schlingensief, Christoph 52
Schmeling, Max 73
Schmidbauer, Tanja 75
Schmidt, Annegret 48
Schmidt, Nathalie 18
Schmidtchen, Achim 28
Schmole, Otto 51
Schnablegger, Jake 16
Schnass, Jorg 18
Schneck, Stephen 43
Schön, Horst 28
Schönböch, Karl 75
Schörner, Field Marshal Ferdinand 39
Schrade, Willi 68
Schreiner, Felix 47
Schroeder, David 31
Schroeder, Ernst 100
Schtonk! (1992 film) 75
Schubert, Heinz* **69**
Schühly, Thomas 1
Schultz, Sergeant Hans (character) 35, 66, A2
Schulz, Gerhardt (character) A2
Schumann, Erik 89
Schumm, Hans 61, 83
Schunzel, Reinhold 37
Schurmann, Gerard 89
Schuschnigg, Dr. Kurt von 27, 64
Schwartz, Alan U. 34
Schwartz, Irving 84
Schwartz, Ronald 9
Schwarz, Erich 18
Schwarz, Norbert 18
Schwarzenberger, Xaver 1, 75
Schweitzer, Albert 2
Scibor, Andrzej 4
Science Fiction films 50, 56, 67, 99
Scotland, Alexander P. 89
Scott, George C. 63
Scott, Lori 16
Scott, Nathaniel 34
Scott, Nicola 42
Scotti, Vito 41, 93
Scourby, Alexander A2
SCTV (TV series) 84
The Search for the Evil One see *He Lives*
Seawright, Roy 14
Secret Mission see *Sekretnaga Missija*
Secret Service in Darkest Africa (1943 serial) 42
Sedlisky, Jan 99

Seeman, Brian 84
Seeway, George 74
Seiderman, Maurice **85**
Seidhoff, Joost 92
Seidner, Irene 83
Seifertova, Zdena 20
Seitz, John F. 59
Sekretnaga Missija (1950 film) 76
Selassie, Haile (emperor of Ethiopia) 57
Selditz, Leon 85
Selge, Edgar 30
Sellem, Marie-Lou 52
Sellers, Peter* **91**
Seltzer, David 77
Selwart, Tonio 37
Semler, Peter 1
Semyonova, Leda 60
Seniuk, Anna 18
Sennett, Mack 8
Sergeev, Victor 60
Serpent of the Nile (1953 film) 82
Serra, Alex 62
Sessions, Elmira 59
Sevcik, Otto 46
The Seven Samurai (1954 film) 15
Sex and the Single Girl (1964 film) 41
Seymour, Jane 92
Shade, Jamison 95
Shadix, Glenn 16
Shah, Krishna 31
Shakespeare, William 9, 11, 39, 55, 69, 71, 82, 87
Shalet, Victoria 77
Shannon, Harry 9, 66
Shannon, Michael 20
Sharp, John 7
Sharp, Lester 83
Shavelson, Melville 65
Shaw, Crystal 31
Shaw, Robert 4
Shaw, Warren PF
Shawn, Dick* **72**, 93
Shawyer, David 44
She Demons (1958 film) 83
Shea, John 40
Sheard, Michael* 7, 12, 15, 74, 42, A2
Sheffield, Reginald 82
The Sheik (1921 film) 84
Sheldon, Douglas 91
Sheldon, Louis 42
Shepherd, Morgan 15
Shergold, Adrian 79
Sherlock Holmes (film series) 83
Sherman, Bob 11
Sherman, Harry R. 15
Shiel, Hans 57

Shine (1996 film) 10
Shining Through (1992 film) 77
Shipoff, Emmanuel 31
Shire, Talia 92
Shirer, William F. PF, 4, 20, 44, 57
Shirle, John 40
Shivas, Mark 74
Shogun (1980 miniseries) 96
Shore, Sammy 34
Shostakovich, Dimitri 19
Shoulder Arms (1918 film) 36
Shrapnel, John 20
Shriner, Ken 92
Shuken, Leo 59
Shukshin, Vasili 68
Shumaky, Yuri 80
Shvedersky, Anatoli 60
Shyc, Etel 96
Shylock (character) 69, 87, 88
Siciliano, Antonio 98
Siegfried (1924 film) 58
Siegfried, John 35
Siegfried's Funeral March (or-chestral piece) 39
Sigmund Freud of Sherwood For-est (parody film) 84
Sign of the Pagan (1954 film) 82
Signoret, Simone 45
La Silence de la Mer (1947 film) PF
"Silent Night" (Christmas carol) OV
Silliphant, Stirling 63
Silver, Johnny 34
Sim, Alistair 74
Simacek, Milan 20
Simanek, Otto 99
Siminov, Nikola 80
Simmons, Jean 17
Simms, Michael David 31
Simon, Günther 17
Simons, Robert 54
Simpson, Wallis 27
Sims, Marley 88
Simsolo, Noel 70
Sinbad (comedian) 84
Singin' in the Rain (1952 film) 14, 25
Singing in the Synagogue (parody film) 84
Sink the Bismarck! (1960 film) PF
Sissini see Chorafas, Dimitris
Sistrom, Joseph 81
"Sittin' on Top of the World" (song) 97
Six Characters in Search of an Author (play) 16
Skillicorn, Dale 56
Skorzeny, Otto 62, 63
Skota, Albin* 47, **51**

Slabnevich, Igor 68
Slattery, Richard X 96
Slezak, Walter 66
A Slight Case of Murder (1938 film) 36
Sloane, Everett 9, 13
Slocombe, Douglas 42
Slut of the South (parody film) 84
Smal, Ewa 18
Smart, Pamela 56
Smigel, Robert 54
Smith, Al 9
Smith, Bob 32
Smith, Gary 96
Smith, Madolyn 71
Smith, Martin 90
Smith, Nayland (character) A2
Smith, Ray 74
Smith, Robert 57
Smith, Tucker 72
Smith, Wonderful 73
Smits, Theodore R. 97
"Smoke Gets in Your Eyes" (song) 12
Smolensk assassination plot 92, 100
Snide and Prejudice (1997 film) OV, 78
Snow White (1937 film) 69
Soccer (sport) 26
Söderbaum, Kristina 49
Soderling, Asa 30
Soderström, Elisabeth 2
Soeberg, Camilla 16
Sofaer, Abraham 82
Soft Beds, Hard Battles see *Un-dercovers Hero*
Sokol, Leonid 60
Sokurov, Aleksandr 60
Solo, Napoleon (character) A2
Solzhenitsyn, Aleksander 19
Somers, Russell 15
Sommer, Elke 44
Sondergaard, Gale 83
The Song and Dance Man (1926 film) 14
Sontag, Susan 69, 97
Sophie's Choice (1982 film) 92
Sorel, George 36, 66, 83
Soulard, Pierre 70
The Sound of Music (1965 film) 1
Soutendijk, Renee 44
Sova, Peter 20
Sovak, Jiri 99
Spandau prison 43, 44
Sparkuhl, Theodor 81
Sparrow, Walter 40
Speer, Albert 7, 12, 20, 28, 30, 44, 51, 62, 69, 77, 92
Spelling, Aaron 55

Spengler, Volker 52
Spider Woman (character) 83
Spielberg, Stephen 42
Spinrad, Norman A3
Spiridonova, Yelena, 60
Spoliansky, Mischa 39
Sponholz, Kuno 97
Spradlin, J. D. 92
Springtime for Hitler see *The Producers*
Spruance, Admiral Raymond A. 92
SS-GB (novel) 20
Staats, Robert 84
Stack, Robert 45, 50, 77, 87
Stadden, Gerald 34
Stadker, Joerg 79
Stadlin, Lewis J. 88
Stahl, Richard 90
Stalag Luft (1994 film) OV, 79
Stalag 17 (1953 film) 79
Stalin, Josef PF, OV, 9, 11,16, 18, 19, 20, 29, 69, 80, 84, 92, 96, A1
Stalingrad (1949/50 film) 80
Stalingrad (1993 film) 4
Stalingradskaya Bitva I & II see *Stalingrad* (1949/50 film)
Stallings, Rex 91
Stand Up Comics for the Poor (parody show) 84
Standing, John 74
Stanford, Jim 32
Stanier, John 15
Stanitsyn, Viktor 19, 80
Stanley, Frank 90
Star Spangled Rhythm (1942 film) 81
Star Trek (TV series) 55
Star Wars (1977 film) 15, 34, 39, 63, 71
Starr, Ringo 53
Starrett, Claude Ennis, Jr. 5
Starwear (parody film) 84
Stauffenberg, Count Claus von 13, 29, 35, **47**, 57, 71, 77, 92,100, A2
Steadman, Robert 63
Steck, Jim 34
Steedman, Tony 7, 12
Steele, Barbara 92, 96
Steele, Freddie 25
Steele, Michael 95
Steen, Liv 30
Steffen, Sirry 35
Steiger, Rod 63
Stein, Gertrude 2
Steinbeck, John 61
Steinberg, Norman 5
Steiner, George A3
Steiner, Leo 84
Steiner, Rudolf 10

Stendahl 4
Stepanek, Lilly 51
Stephens, Betty J. 67
Stephens, Robert 8, 92
Stephens, Rod 63
Stephenson, Pamela 34
Stern (magazine) 35, 75
Sterner, Roland 2
Sternwald, Jiri 46
Sterzenbach, Benno 1
Stevens, Lee E. 88
Stevens, Leith 65
Stevens, Leon B. 92
Stevens, Ronnie 11
Stevenson, Bob 66
Stewart, Bill 11
Stewart, Mel 73
Stewart, Patrick 27
Stewart, Paul 9
Stewart-Conner, Kalie 54
Stiekel, Rolf* 4
Stiller, Amy 33
Stiller, Ben 33
Stiller, Jerry 33, 84
Stillwell, Alexandra 16
Stocker, Walter 85
Stoddard, Elizabeth Collins
(character) 92
Stoddard, Paul (character) 92
Stone, Ben (character) 38
Stone, George E. 14, 82
Stone, Harold J. 94
Stone, Philip 39
Stone, Sharon 92
Storm in the West (unfinished
film) A1
The Story of Mankind (1957
film) 82
Stossel, Ludwig 58, 83
Strachan, Alan 15
Stradling, Harry, Sr. 65
Strahl, Erwin 92
*The Strange Death of Adolf
Hitler* (1943 film) 83
Strangelove, Dr. (character) 91
Strasser, Gregor 35, 37, 83
Stratton, John 11
Straus, E. Charles 35
Strauss, Johann, Jr. 30, 34, 39,
69
Strauss, Karl 29
Strauss, Richard 62
Strecke, Hans 1
Streicher, Julius 35, 37
Streisand, Barbra 73
Stroheim, Erich von 6, 13, 69
Stroke, Adam 33
Strunjak, Anton 96
Struwe, Alfred 68
Stuhrmann, Hans 17
Stumpfegger, Dr. Ludwig 12,
39

Sturges, Preston 59, 81
Subbaiah, Muthyala PF
The Submersion of Japan see
Tidal Wave
Subway flooding (Berlin) 19,
39, 51
Suchet, David 63
Suckmann, Erik 51
Suicide of Hitler 7, 12, 39, 51,
52, 55, 75, 92
Sukman 57
Sullivan, Brick 95
Sullivan, Elliott 28
Summerville, Slim OV
Sunday in New York (1963 film)
41
Suschitzky, Peter 53
Susskind, David 7
Suster, Jan 99
Sutherland, Donald 15
Suvari, Mena 78
Svenson, Gunnar 2
Svoboda, Karol 99
Svoboda, V. 80
Swan, Buddy 9
Swanson, Gloria 69
Swanson, Kristy 33
Swanwick, Peter 89
"A Sweater, a Sarong and a
Peek-a-boo Bang" (song) 81
Swedish films 2, 30
"Sweet Georgia Brown" (song)
88
Swift, David 7, 11
Swink, Robert E. 6
Syberberg, Amelie 69
Syberberg, Hans-Jürgen 49, 69
Sydow, Max von 30
Symphony No. 3 "Organ" (Saint-
Saëns) 27
Symphony No. 6 "Pathétique"
(Tchaikovsky) 17
Symphony No. 7 "Leningrad"
(Shostakovich) 19
Symphony No. 9 "Choral"
(Beethoven) 69
Syms, Sylvia 77
Syncopation (1939 film) 14
Szabo, Albert 35

T, Mr. 67
Taffin, Tony 45
Takada, Minoru 50
Takei, George 94
Tamiroff, Akim 59
Tanami, Yasuo 50
Tandy, Jessica 13
Tani, Kei 50
Tannen, Julius 59
Tarantino, Quentin 54
Tarzan Triumphs (1943 film)
PF

Taschner, Herbert 47, 51
Tati, Jacques 2
Tatum, Marianne 97
Taylor, Gilbert 91
Taylor, James PF
Taylor, Kenneth 62
Taylor, Peter 62
Taylor, Renee *72*, 84
Tchaikovsky, Peter Ilyitch 17,
53, 94
Tellefsen, Rut 30
Tellerring, Michael 57
Tempest, Troy 33
Ten Days to Die (book) 51
Tenin, Boris 19
Tennant, Victoria 92, 96
Terboven, Josef 30
Terry, Carol 56
Terry-Thomas 24, 75
Testa, Fabio 62
The Testament of Dr. Mabuse
(1933 film) 58
Testimony (book) 19
Thälmann, Ernst 17
Thanich, Marion 12
That Crazy Adveture see *Kureji
No Daiboken*
That Nazty Nuisance (1943
short subject) 14
Thatcher, Heather 58
Thatcher, Torin 64
That's Adequate (1986/90 film)
84
That's Entertainment (1974 film)
84
Thaw, John 8
Theater of Blood (1973 film) PF
Theodore, Brother see Brother
Theodore
Theresienstadt (concentration
camp) 92
They Came to Blow Up America
(1944 film) 83
They Saved Hitler's Brain
(1963/68 film) OV, 85
Thimig, Helene 37, 61
The Thing with Two Heads
(1972 film) 89
Think Fast, Mr. Peters (novel)
90
13 Demon Street (TV series) 56
This Is the Army (1943 film) 81
Thom, Robert 95
Thomas, Leslie 62
Thomas, Lowell 84
Thomas er Fredløs (1967 film)
86
Thomas the Outlaw see *Thomas
er Fredløs*
Thomass, Eugen 49
Thompson, Daniele 1
Thorent, André 70

Thorgersen, Ed 67
The Thorn Birds (1983 miniseries) 96
Thornton, Randy 33
The Thousand Eyes of Dr. Mabuse (1960 film) 45
Three in a Shell Hole see *Fighting Film Album # 1*
Three Stooges (comedy team) PF, **OV**, 9, 36 14, 84, 87, 94
The Threepenny Opera (1931 film) 51
Throbbing Sands (parody film) 84
Tidal Wave (1975 film) 50
Tillmann, Fritz 100
Tilsey, Vincent 12
Time (magazine) 16
Time Is Terror see *Flesh Feast*
Time Tunnel (TV series) 82, A2
Timofev, N. 76
Timont, Frederique 70
Timoshenko, G. 19
The Tin Drum (novel) 88
Tipton, Thomas 75
Tissot, Henri* 26
To Be or Not to Be (1942 film) 66, 87
To Be or Not to Be (1983 film) 88
Tobisch, Lotte 51
Toklas, Alice B, 2
Toland, Gregg 9
Tolstoy, Leo 4, 9
Tomei, Marisa 8
Tommy (rock opera) 53
Tomorrow I Will Wake Up and Scald Myself with Tea see *Zitra Vstanu a Oparim se Cajem*
Tomorrow People (TV series) 15, A2
Tompkins, Angel 41
Tone, Franchot 81
Toone, Geoffrey 12, 92
Toothman, Lisa 31
Topalofff, Patrick 26
Topol 92, 96
Tora! Tora! Tora! (1970 film) 4
Torn Curtain (1966 film) 83
Torquemada, Tomàs de 34
Totentanz (piano and orchestra piece) 53
Totheroh, Rollie 8, 29
Tover, Leo 81
Townes, Brad 23
Townsend, Robert 84
Trantow, Cordula 35
Trantow, Herbert 100
Trapp Family 1
Traub, Ariane 52

Trauffaut, François 88
Travers, Henry 61
Travis, Nancy 8, 55
Treacher, Arthur 81
Tree, Dorothy 36
Tremblay, Kat 23
Trenk, William 49, 83
Tresckow, General Henning von 100
Trevor, Austin 64
Trevor-Roper, Hugh 39
Trial of Adolf Hitler (novel) A3
Triesault, Ivan 37, 83
Triska, Jan 55
Tristan und Isolde (opera) 77, 92
Triumph of Faith (1933 film) OV
Triumph of the Third Reich (novel) A3
Triumph of the Will (1934 film) OV, 16, 19, 25, 35, 44, 84, 97
Troell, Jan 30
Trombetta, Emanuela 92
Trowbridge, Jean 97
Truffaut, François 10, 92
Truman, Harry S. 88, 92
Tryon, Glenn 14
Tschesno-Hall, Michael 17
Tsouras, Peter 20
Tuan, Shangtai 67
Tucker, Harland 25
Tucker, Jack 96
Tucker, Louis 84
Tudor, Owen 82
Tufano, Brian 74
Tugend, Harry 81
Tüick, Harry 28
Tummler, Manfred 43
Turban, Dietlinde 62
Turner, Michael 12
Turtledove, Harry 20, A3
Tuttle, Frank 57
Tuttle, Lurene 95
TV Guide (magazine) 63
Twadowski, Hans Heinrich von 66, 83
Twilight Zone (TV series) 13, A2
The Two-Headed Spy (1958 film) 89
Typhoon (baboon) 67
Tzelniker, Anna 92

Ueki, Hitoshi 50
Uger, Alan 5
Ulyanin, Mikhail 28, 68
Ulysses (novel) 72
Uncle Adolf, the Artistic Führer see *Zio Adolfo in Arte Führer*
Under the Rainbow (1981 film) 90

Undercovers Hero (1974 film) 91
Underdown, Edward 89
Unger, Beril* 56
Unger, Gustaf* 56
Unsolved Mysteries (TV series) 77
Unsworth, Geoffrey 65
"Unto Us a Son Is Given" (choral selection) 16
Up All Night (TV series) 33
Urasalyev, A. 19
Urquart, Robert 40
Ustinov, Peter 3

Vader, Darth (character) 15, 42
Vale, Eleanor 23
Valk, Fritz 64
"Valkyrie" (TV episode) A2
Valmy, André 3
Valsecchi, Eric 62
Vandenberg, Gerard 10
Van De Sande, Theodore 54
Van Dyke, Dick 35, 89
Vanedi, Pierre 45
Van Eyck, Peter 13, 61
Vanis, Josef 46
Van Loon, Hendrik Willem 82
Van Loon's Lives (book) 82
Van Nuys, Ed 92
Van Rjndt, Philippe A3
Van Rooten, Luis 37
Van Sloan, Edward OV
Van Zandt, Philip 9
Varconi, Victor **37**
Vassillopoulos, Dimitri 97
Vasut, Marek 20
Vaughan, Dorothy 66
Vaughan, Peter 11, 20, 92
Vaughan-Williams, Ralph 74
Vaughn, Robert* 1, A2, 44, 56, 84
Vecheslavov, Sergei 76
Veiczi, Janos 28
Veidt, Conrad 94
Velez, Kimberly 54
Verdegiglio, Diego 62
Verdi, Asia 52
Verebes, Ernst 37, 83
Vetrovec, Josef 99
Vetturini, Gian Paolo 62
Vhrban, Aleksandr 76
Vicena, Frantisek* 99
Vichy France 45, 70, 92
Victor, Henry 14, 66, 87
Victor Emmanuel III (king of Italy) 62, 63
The Victors and the Vanquished see *Stalingrad* (1949/50 film)
Victory in the West (1941 film) OV
Vidal, Gore 45
Vidan, Richard 31

Vidgeon, Robin 33
Vienot, Jainine 3
A View to a Kill (1985 film) 67
Viktorov, V. 76
Vincent, Jan-Michael 92, 96
Vincent, Severine 70
Vincze, Ernest 40
Vinogradov, Valeri 68
Virgil, Publius 69
Virta, N. 80
Visconti, Michael 84
Vitukhnovsky, Mikhail 22
Volpin, Mikhail 22
Vogeding, Frederick 58
Vogler, Karl Michael 13
Volchek, Boris 76
Volkswagon (car designed by
    Hitler) 33, 65, 72
Volpin, Mikhail 22
Vonmeurs, Ruger 70
Voss, Vice Admiral Erich 12,
    39
Voutsinas, Andreas 34, 72
Vozoff, Lorinne 77
Vrstala, Jiri 28, 46
Vutee, Lars-Ake van 2
Vysockey, M. 76

Wagner, Cosima 53
Wagner, Dieter 92, 96
Wagner, Kenneth 48
Wagner, Richard 15, 16, 25,
    29, 30, 35, 39, 42, 51, 53, 69,
    75, 77, 92
Wagner, Walter 7, 12, 39, 51
Wahl, Ken 15
Waiting for Godot (play) 38, 60
Wakeman, Rick 53
Walbrun, Ernst 51
Walcott, Gregory 65
Waldis, Otto 95
Wales, Ken 93
Walken, Jesse Grey 78
Walker, Clint 15
Walker, Fiona 27
Walker, Mayor Jimmy 97
Walker, Mavis 92
Wall, Faye 36
Wallace, Earl W. 92
Wallace, George 54
Waller, Angelika 68
Wallis, Bill 92
Wallner, Martha 51
Walser, Aljoscha 48
Walter, John Buck 97
Walters, Andrew 77
Walters, Thorley 27, 91
Walton, Bill 54
Walton, Sir William 4
Wanamaker, Zoë 44
"A Wandering Minstrel I"
    (song) 72
Wanka, Rolf 57

Wanninger, Ashley 18
Wannsee Conference 20
War and Peace (novel) 4, 9
War and Remembrance (1988
    miniseries) 92, 96
War dramas 3, 13, 15, 19, 45,
    80, 89, 92, 96
Ward, Edward 14
Ward, Simon 39
Ward, Skip 45
Ward, Tracey 63
Warner, David 40
Warner, Richard 43
Warner, T. C. 78
Warren, Eda 37
Warwick, Robert OV
Warwick, Ruth 9
Washington, George 84
Watanabe, Akira 50
The Waterboy (1998 film) 54
Watson, Bobby* PF, OV, **14,**
    19, 25, 36, **37,** 59, 65, 68, 72,
    82, 95, A1
Watson, Bobs 14
Watson, Mills 92
Watson, Timothy 71
Watson, Violette 61
Waxman, Michael 33
Way, Ann 92
Wayne, John 69, 84
Wayne, Naunton 64
We the Children of Hell see *Our
    Hitler*
Weathers, Carl 54
Weatherwax, Paul 81
Weaver, Doodles 90
Webber, Herman 36
Webster, Henry 79
Wecker, Konstantin 75
Wedding March (Mendelssohn)
    19
Wehr, Gerd 17
Wehrl, Hans 17
Weidner, David 48
Weigel, Paul 29
Weisel, Elie 38
Weisenthal, Simon 6
Weisner, Stanley 20
Weiss, Heinz 92, 96
Weiss, Joel 84
Weiss, Siegfried 68
Weissenbach, Johannes 47
Weist, Dwight 97
Weitershausen, Gila von 48
Welles, Orson **9,** 34, 45, 69
Wellesley, Gordon 64
Wellman, William A1
Wells, Deering 89
Wells, Herbert George 42
Wells, Sumner 96
Wells, Ted 31
Wenck, General Walther 29

Wengraf, John 35
Werich, Jan 19
Werner, Oskar 51
Wery, Carl 47
West, Timothy 39, 91
West Side Story (musical) 31
Western films 5, A1
Wetzel, Kurt 17
Weygand, General Maxime 70
Whale, James OV
*What Did You Do in the War,
    Daddy?* (1966 film) 58, 93
"When You're Smiling" (song)
    39
Where the North Wind Blows
    (1975 film) 32
Which Way to the Front? (1970
    film) 30, 94
The Whip Hand (1951 film)
    OV, 95
White, Jesse 65
White, Kiley 16
White, Leo 29
Whitehead, Geoffrey 44, 92
Whitney, Nigel 77
Whitworth, Dean 67
Who Will Watch the Watchers?
    (novel) A3
Who's Afraid of Virginia Woolf?
    (play) 12
Wicki, Bernhard 47
Wieland, Guido 49, 51, 96
Wilcox, Frank 95
Wilcox, Larry 15
Wild Geese II (1985 film) 6, 43
Wilde, Oscar 53
Wilder, Billy 25
Wilder, Gene 5, 72, 75
Wiles, Russell 94
Wilhelm II (kaiser of Germany)
    37
Wilhoute, Dian 23
"Will the Real Adolf Please
    Stand Up?" (TV episode)
    A2
Williams, Brook 27
Williams, John 42
Williams, Pat 24
Williamson, E. Stanley 32
Willis, Bruce 84
Willis, Gordon 97
Willner 57
Wilms, André 18
Wilson, Daniel 48
Wilson, Marie 82
Wilson, Mary Louise 97
Wilson, Meredith 29
Wilson, Paul 34
Wilson, Woodrow 84
Winchell, Paul 94
Winczewski, Patrick 77
Windish, Ilka 57

The Winds of War (1983 mini-series) OV, 1, 40, 43, 92, 96
Windsor, Marie 82
Wings of Victory (1941 film) 19
Winkler, Henry 54
Winston Churchill—The Valiant Years (TV series) 27
"Winston Churchill: The Wilderness Years" (TV drama) A2
Winter, Dana 65
Winters, Deborah 96
Winters, Ralph E. 93
Winwood, Estelle 72
Wirth, Franz Peter 47
Wise, Addington 84
Wise, Herbert 27
Wise, Robert 9
Wisniewska, Ewa 28
Witherspoon, John 54
Witherspoon, Reece 54
Witten, Brian 54
Witzleben, Field Marshal Erwin von 100
The Wizard of Oz (1939 film) 55, 90
Wladon, Jean 4
Wögerer, Otto 51
Wolf, Milicent 24
Wolfe, Ian 61
Wolff, Michael 92
Wolper, David L. 71
The Women of Nazi Germany see *Hitler* (1962)
Wonder Woman (TV series) A2
Wood, Edward D., Jr. 65, 85
Wood, John 94
Wood, Natalie 61
Woodnutt, John 40
Woods, James 8
Woods, Michael 92

Woods, Robert S, 92
Woodson, William Z. 92, 96
Woodvine, John 11, 20
Woodworth, Marjorie 14
Woolf, Victor 89
Wopper, Thomas 75
Worldwar (series of novels) A3, 20
Worlock, Frederick 58
Worth, Theron 66
Wotan (character) 67
Wouk, Herman 92, 96
Wright, Armand 87
Wright, Charles Julian 33
Wunschkonzert (1940 film) OV
Wycherly, Margaret 61
Wymark, Patrick 4
Wynant, H. N. 32
Wyner, George 88
Wynn, Keenan* 56
Wyprachtiger, Hans 1

Yalta Conference 19
Yamamoto, Admiral Isoruku 92
Yandultsky, M. 21
Yanne, Jean **70**
Yasuda, Shin 50
Yekelchik, Yuri 80
Yersini, Marie 45
Yetter, William, Jr. 95
Yetter, William, Sr. 95
York, Susannah 4
You Nazty Spy (1939 short subject) OV, 9, 14
Young, Aida 7, 40
Young, Bert* 9
Young, Carlton 13
Young, Desmond 13
Young, Freddie 4
Young, Richard 42

Young Adolf (novel) A3
Young Adolf (parody film) 84
Young Einstein (1988 film) 2
Young Frankenstein (1974 film) 79
Youngman, Henny 34
Yowell, Shannon 16
Yutkevich, Sergei 22

Zachrisson, Lisbeth 2
Zakon, Paul (character) PF
Zaleski, Jacek 18
Zappy, Robert 34
Zatloka, Stanislaw* 18
Zaydenberg, Boris 68
Zaza, Paul 55
Zeigbergh, Ulf von 2
Zeitzler, Kurt 92
Zeiwicker, Michael 78
Zelig (1983 film) OV, 97, 98
Zentropa (1992 film) 18
Zernick, Peter von 25
Zeunert, Kurt 100
Zhukov, Marshal Georgi 19
Zibaso, Werner P. 47
Zielinski, Randy 16
Zilzer, Wolfgang 83, 87
Ziner, Peter (composer) 85
Zinner, Peter 92, 96
Zio Adolfo in Arte Führer (1978 film) 98
Zischler, Hanns 18
Zitra Vstanu a Oparim se Cajem (1977 film) 99
Zivojinovic, Bata 92
Zohling, Gerd 51
Zola, Emile 42
Zoller, John 72
Zorina, Vera 81
Zwanzigste Juli, Der (1955 film) 47, 100